The Subversive Activities Prevention Law of Japan

Brill's Japanese Studies Library

Edited by

Joshua Mostow (Managing Editor)
Caroline Rose
Kate Wildman Nakai

VOLUME 33

The Subversive Activities Prevention Law of Japan

It's Creation, 1951–52

By

Cecil H. Uyehara

BRILL

LEIDEN • BOSTON
2010

On the cover: The 23rd May Day: May 1, 1952 the conflict between students, labor union members and the police. Copyright The Asahi Shimbun, Tokyo, Japan.

This book is printed on acid-free paper.

Library of Congress Cataloging-in-Publication Data

Uyehara, Cecil H.
The subversive activities prevention law of Japan : its creation, 1951-52 / by Cecil H. Uyehara.
p. cm. — (Brill's Japanese studies library ; v. 33)
Includes bibliographical references and index.
ISBN 978-90-04-18092-5 (hardback : alk. paper) 1. Subversive activities—Japan. 2. Internal security—Japan. I. Title.
KNX2490.U94 2009
345.52'0231—dc22

2009043365

ISSN 0925-6512
ISBN 978 90 04 18092 5

Printed and bound in Great Britain by
CPI Antony Rowe, Chippenham and Eastbourne

CONTENTS

ACKNOWLEDGMENTS

There are many who provided active support, counsel and advice concerning the research for my study of the legislative process in creating the Subversive Activities Prevention Law (SAPL). I met the principal drafter of this law, Seki Itaru, for the first time in 1956, only four years after the enactment of the law. He was then one of the top officials in the Public Security Investigation Agency (Kōan Chōsachō), to carry out the SAPL. I was then residing in Japan to study the Japan Social Democratic Party; since then we met on many occasions whenever I was able to visit Japan over the next almost 50 years, as a visitor, as a consultant and as a researcher. He was the first person with whom I had discussed my hope of writing about the SAPL. He was sympathetic and supportive of my idea to write about how the SAPL came into being; he was patient and tolerant of my queries to him about the drafting process; we met on a bench in front of his nearby railway station, then in the town hall in his residential area; eventually I shared many cups of green tea and cakes in his home talking about this law and his poetry. Over the years, his principal staff assistant, Aoyama Haruki, also supported me in augmenting what Seki had mentioned. I also met with Kimura Tokutarō, then Attorney General overseeing the second and final phase in the drafting process of the law. The Ministry of Justice representatives, Koyama Noriaki and Satō Takafumi, in the Embassy of Japan in Washington, DC, also provided important support to me by obtaining copies of all Supreme Court decisions involving the SAPL.

A number of professors in Japan, also provided support, guidance and insight and interpretations of the law to me: Ōyama Kōsuke of Keio University, Nakamura Akira of Meiji University and Okudaira Yasuhiro of the University of Tokyo and Misawa Shigeo of Saitama University. In the mid-1950s, Professor Misawa was working at the National Diet Library; we were both young men at the time starting out on our respective careers. He most kindly prepared a most useful summary of the developments leading up to the enactment of the SAPL; it was later that he joined the faculty at Saitama University.

In the Library of Congress in Washington DC, Takeo Nishioka of the Law Library was the one person who always provided me with efficient, smooth, unstinting and expert support and personal interest on his part through his knowledge of the contents of the Law Library, especially concerning Japanese law. Through his support, I was introduced to many books and articles, law dictionaries, reference works which otherwise would have required untold hours of my time to find, if at all. I am greatly indebted to his generosity. There were others in LC who also provided support to me: the late Akiba Yōko with whom I enjoyed many hours discussing the various resources available in the Japanese section for my study. Later, I had the special pleasure of working with Eiichi Itō who helped me enormously through his knowledge of the collection and his computer expertise in locating materials. Sayuri Umeda and Edith Palmer of LC's Law Library, both specialists in Japanese and German law, respectively, also periodically gave me important support; the latter in particular helped me understand German legal terms which had been cited in Diet proceedings about the SAPL.

On a number of occasions, I had conversations with Prof John M. Maki, of the University of Washington, on the SAPL. He was, significantly, the first and only one who published an article in English on the SAPL.

There was indeed yet another person, my wife, Allie Marie, who, unlike all the others mentioned above, lived with the ups and downs not merely of the progress of this study over fifty plus years(!) but much more difficult the ups and downs of the enthusiasm and despair of the writer himself.

ABBREVIATIONS

AG	Attorney General
CC	Criminal Code
DG	Director General
EM	Minister of Education
ESS	Economic and Scientific Section (GHQ)
GHQ	General Headquarters under SCAP
GOJ	Government of Japan
GS	Government Section (GHQ)
HofC	House of Councillors
HofR	House of Representatives
JCP	Japanese Communist Party
JSC	Japan Science Council
KK	Kabushiki Kaisha
LM	Minister of Labor
LS	Legal Section (GHQ)
NP	National Police
NPR	National Police Reserve
PM	Prime Minister
PPL	Peace Preservation Law
PRC	People's Republic of China
PSD	Public Security Division (GHQ)
PSEC	Public Security Examination Commission
PSIA	Public Security Investigation Agency
SAPL	Subversive Activities Prevention Law
SCAP	Supreme Commander, Allied Powers
SDP-L	Social Democratic Party, Leftwing
SDP-R	Social Democratic Party, Rightwing
SecGen	Secretary General
SIB	Special Investigation Bureau (Tokubetsu Shinsakyoku)
USJ	United States-Japan

Legend
The Japanese order of family name first followed by a given name is used in this study except when a Japanese name is used in a non-Japanese context, e.g. as author of a book or article in English. Japanese words and phrases, and book titles and names of newspapers will be italicized using the Hepburn system. However, titles of Japanese offices and organizations with English translations will be given in regular font.

INTRODUCTION

This study was "begun" in 1955–56 when I was in Japan on a Ford Foundation grant to study the Japan Social Democratic Party (SDP). When one studied the SDP at that time, inevitably one encountered the role that the SDP played in the struggle against the enactment of the Subversive Activities Prevention Law (SAPL) of 1952, commonly known in Japan as the Habōhō. The strength, determination and drive of this opposition, though ultimately unsuccessful, piqued my intellectual curiosity. The period during which this law was drafted and the ensuing Diet "struggle" to enact this law was somewhat unusual: it occurred during the twilight years of the U.S. Occupation of Japan and the early months after Japan regained its "independence". This period covers only about 18 months but it was a period of great tension, drama, conflict in the Japanese political situation. This period also coincided more or less with another enormous and dramatic conflict which split Japanese society at that time: the negotiations and signing of the Peace Treaty between Japan and most of its former WWII enemies and the attendant U.S.-Japan Mutual Security Treaty—the so-called separate peace treaty arrangement. The peace treaty was opposed by the SDP (and other opposition leftwing groups including the JCP). The treaty was perhaps more crucial in the eyes of some since it resulted in Japan regaining it's "independence" and the SAPL was merely drafting and enacting a new, important and crucial internal security law for post-treaty Japan. The treaty symbolized a new beginning for a NEW Japan; the SAPL would, in the eyes of many other Japanese symbolize a serious retrogressive step, a potential resurrection of the prewar police system epitomized by the Peace Preservation Law (Chian Ijihō) of 1925. It is the story of one of the major events that took place during what might be described as "a transitional period" for postwar Japanese from defeat in 1945 through partial recovery, signing a Peace Treaty and regaining independence in April 1952.[1]

From Prime Minister Yoshida Shigeru's perspective, the enactment of a "permanent law" for internal security was of "parallel importance to the Peace Treaty" (*heiwa jōyaku chōin to heikō-shite jūyō na mondai*). The most important issue facing Japan as it regained independence and assumed responsibility for its own internal security was the lack of a legal footing or basis (*hōritsu-teki ashiba*) for handling the destructive activities (*hakai-teki katsudō*) conducted by the communists. As though to emphasize this point, he devoted a subsection in his memoirs to the enactment of the SAPL.[2] The role envisaged for the SAPL is rather explicitly stated in the "authorized" history of the Yoshida Cabinets:

> the surface or outward legislative reason or rationale (*hyōmen no rippō no riyū*) was to prevent anti-democratic destructive activities whether from the right or the leftwings, but in reality (*jissai wa*) the main objective was to counter the Japan Communist Party and communistic political forces. From the point of view of the Yoshida Cabinet which took a cautious attitude toward the idea of making the JCP illegal, the SAPL was an important lever in managing the Cabinet's anti-Communist measures, and should be regarded as the breakwater against a violent Communist revolution.[3]

In the postwar years under the Occupation, there had been large scale mass movements, most notably the attempted General Strike on February 1, 1947 which was cancelled by the Supreme Commander for the Allied Powers (SCAP). This was a political action organized, in the main, by the Japan Communist Party (JCP) with the active support of the SDP in an attempt to force the then conservative government to control inflation and provide food for a nearly starving population. There had also been numerous somewhat violent labor disputes during this same period. The abortive General Strike of February 1, 1947 was not against a particular proposed law but a mass movement representing

[1] This idea of transition is also the title of a book published in 1997, *Katoki toshite no 1950-nendai*, Tokyo Daigaku Shuppankai. 1997. 259 p. Nakamura Takahide, ed.

[2] *Kaisō Jūnen* 2:290–292.

[3] *Yoshida Naikaku*, Yoshida Naikaku Kankōkai. 1954. p. 484. Sub-sections 1–4 (out of five) in a section 4, Bōei Chian Taisaku (defense and internal security) (pp. 484–494) were devoted to the drafting, Diet considerations and enactment of the SAPL, indeed another indication of how important the enactment of the SAPL was to the Yoshida Cabinet.

broad, deep and frustrated feelings of unhappiness and anger with the existing social, political and economic crisis.

One of the early actions under the Occupation was to abolish all prewar Japanese laws which were regarded as repressive, feudalistic, contrary to democracy. This included those laws and regulations which impinged upon freedoms of speech, press, association, organization. (The Occupation, however, created their own restrictive press code to be followed by the Japanese media). Among those many laws which were abolished was the notorious prewar Peace Preservation Law of 1925. Japanese internal security would be maintained by the Japanese police. In reserve was the implicit and obvious presence of U.S. Army troops stationed in Japan. These U.S. forces fortunately were never used for maintaining internal security in Japan. At the insistence of the Comintern in 1950, the JCP changed its tactics from peaceful to violent, except that these JCP inspired actions did not appear in their form, tactics and strategy to be systematic and determined enough effort to indeed overthrow the government but rather to harass and perhaps hopefully de-stabilize the government. Then there was the outbreak of the Korean War in June 1950 and attendant felt security threats in Japan from the violent JCP actions.

When Japan regained its independence, the Japanese Government would be responsible for maintaining its own internal security without the implied crutch of U.S. forces in Japan. Yoshida's conservative government firmly believed that since the Occupation had nullified the prewar internal law, e.g. the Peace Preservation Law, it would be faced with regaining "independence" without adequate internal security arrangements and laws. There was a firm belief the tempestuous postwar years of labor unrest, political conflict, communist violence, intensification of the Cold and Hot Wars around Japan, would only intensify as Japan regained independence. Indeed without this assurance, this unrest could indeed, and in all probability, would extend into the post-Occupation period of regained independence.

The drafting of the new internal security began about spring 1951. More than 20 versions were considered before it was approved by the Cabinet for submission to the Diet. Numerous foreign internal security laws in the U.S., U.S.S.R., Communist China, Union of South Africa, Portugal, Australia and others were studied in the drafting process. Even before it was presented to the Diet, the SAPL already aroused substantial opposition. As soon as the outline of the proposed bill was revealed, there was a storm of protest. It aroused deep-seated emotional anxieties, antipathies and suspicions long harbored by the political leftwing, the labor unions and a large segment of the academic world, in light of their many personal and organizational experiences in the pre-WWII years in Japan. The opponents to the SAPL naturally compared it to the prewar Peace Preservation Law (PPL). They vowed to prevent enactment of the SAPL almost at any cost. Certain limited concessions were made by the Government during the drafting stage to try to allay opposition fears but with no success. During Diet deliberations a monumental and coordinated opposition movement was organized by the Socialist and Communist parties, labor unions, intellectuals and professors, both in the Diet, in the streets in Tokyo and throughout the country. Every parliamentary tactic and stratagem was used to attack the government's bill, to protract proceedings and delay a vote on the SAPL. The government tried to mollify some conservative labor unions by again making limited word changes, without in any way compromising the basic structure and objectives of the SAPL. Eventually it was enacted and put into effect in July 1952. It was politically significant that the SAPL, an internal security law, would be the first major law to become effective after Japan regained independence. Although the opposition organized the largest and most systematic protestations since 1945 against this law, and it was the only law that was so strongly opposed in a unified manner by labor, political parties, academia, press during this period, surprisingly the process through which this law was created and even the law itself have been ignored in books on postwar Japan; occasionally there was a passing reference to the law in a few books. Despite its potential importance as the internal security law in Japan, its origins, structure and content have not been thoroughly scrutinized in English. Presumably the struggle about the Peace Treaty waged by the same two conflicting groups must have over shadowed the SAPL and it was lost in the shuffle of academic interest.

The purpose of this study is to analyze the interactions between a few occupation officials and a few Japanese government officials concerning a draft SAPL, the Japanese governmental process through which the draft SAPL was created, to describe the various forces in and out of the Cabinet and the internal bureaucratic security apparatus that buffeted this process as the draft evolved, the collision of the political, economic and social forces in and out of the Diet as the Cabinet considered the draft SAPL. It has remained in effect since the law became effective in July 1952 but has been sparingly used by the Japanese Government. To date only eight cases against individuals were tried in court. The Japanese Supreme Court declared selected articles of the SAPL to be constitutional. The SAPL permitted cases to be brought against organizations but since 1952 there have been no successful cases. The government brought a case against the Ōmu Shinrikyō as an organization for its sarin gas attack in 1995 in Tokyo subways but it was rejected by the Public Security Examination Commission.

The bibliography is not a normal straight forward list of books and articles, but is a rather complicated one divided into several sections with an explanation about each group of materials. One other point about the bibliography is the list of books and journal articles on the policymaking process in the Japanese government and case studies written in English and Japanese. The genesis of this list stems from my effort to find such studies that focused on the Occupation period. I found there were only a very small number that might fit this category but in looking for these elusive few I gradually built up quite a list of materials on these topics. Since I had not found such a list in my searches over the years, I decided to include all my findings as part of the bibliography as a reference item for researchers in this field even though these studies do not relate to the SAPL study per se since they are all concerned with a later period, mostly 1950s onwards.

Prior to this study there had been only one journal article and no books in English on the SAPL: John M. Maki, Japan's Subversive Activities Prevention Law, in *The Western Political Quarterly*.[4] It was a pioneering study of the SAPL based on materials available immediately after the enactment of the law in July 1952.

In conclusion, I should note that this study was conducted from the beginning with no financial support from any foundation or government including the U.S. and Japanese governments. All the errors and interpretations are based on my analysis stemming from my study of the process surrounding the creation of the SAPL.

January 2010

[4] *The Western Political Quarterly* 6:3(9/1963):489–511.

CHAPTER ONE

THE CONTEXT

When the Pacific War ended in August 1945, Japan was prostrate, its major cities reduced, to a large extent through aerial bombardment, to a moonscape devastation, its food supply almost completely depleted. The victorious U.S. Forces rode into Tokyo amazingly without incident and their word became momentarily—for a few years—the writ of the land. General MacArthur established his General Headquarters (GHQ) in the Daiichi Building just opposite the Imperial Palace. With the authority of the Potsdam Declaration, U.S. Department of Defense issued instructions on September 6, 1945 to General MacArthur about initial post-surrender policies to be followed (U.S. Initial Post-Surrender Policies toward Japan, SWNNCC 150.4A); GHQ had two major objectives in mind, the military objective of disarming and demobilizing the Japanese armed forces and the "democratization" of Japan. The military objective was understandable, the demobilization of the Japanese Armed Forces so that Japan could never militarily rise again. It was measurable, quantifiable and verifiable. GHQ was sufficiently sensible not to disband the Japanese police. It was the first thin line of defense in maintaining normal public safety in Japan at a time of great anxiety and uncertainty; the U.S. armed forces stationed in Japan would be the final arbiters in maintaining public security or taking action against social disturbances which the Japanese police could not handle. To the best of my knowledge, U.S. Army troops were never used during 1945–1952 in any meaningful manner for this purpose.

The second thrust as a preparatory step to "democratizing Japan" was to eliminate those institutions, people and tendencies in Japanese society which led to creating the milieu and domestic mandate from which to launch its march to create the Empire of Japan. In *Political Reorientation of Japan* the steps to achieve these initial goals were lumped together as part of "The Elimination of Old Order".[1] Soon

[1] *Political Reorientation of Japan: September 1945 to September 1948* was a 2 volume 1300 page report prepared by SCAP Government Section, published by U.S. Government Printing Office.

after arriving in their new quarters in Tokyo, General MacArthur as Supreme Commander of Allied Powers (SCAP) ordered in quick succession (September 1945–March 1946) directives to the Japanese government concerning freedom of speech, removal of restrictions on political, civil and religious liberties, release of all political prisoners, the restoration of voting rights to released political prisoners.[2] Under SCAP's GHQ, Government Section, the first among equals, had the mandate for politically re-guiding, reforming, re-molding, re-creating the Japanese government, the Japanese people and their society politically, spiritually and intellectually—if that could be done. All political prisoners included Communists imprisoned for many years by the "old order" the most famous of which was Tokuda Kyūichi born in Okinawa. In order to set the right example, and in order to avoid a potential confrontation with the Soviet Union then demanding a voice in the Occupation of Japan, communists had to be included in this blanket amnesty. It was a startling move shocking the Japanese "old order". In addition, as part of the democratization and remaking of Japan, over the years, 1945–1948, SCAP with its supra-constitutional authority was also involved in undertaking ambitious measures: reform Japanese education, impose land reform, remold the civil service, deconcentrate economic power, purge "undesirable" ultra-nationalists from public office and dissolve ultra-nationalist organizations and societies. Unfortunately, the dire state of the economy, the livelihood of the people, the non-availability of food stuffs was, in the eyes of GHQ in the beginning, something the Japanese had themselves created, not of concern to the occupying force. The Japanese would have to handle that mess by themselves inexplicably ignoring the close inter-relationship between politics and economics.[3]

---

[2] As MacArthur flew into Japan, he discussed with Maj General Courtney Whitney, one of his trusted aides and later had of GHQ Government Section, the eleven objectives, both liberal and punitive, to be implemented in the early stages of the occupation: 1) destruction of military power, 2) establishment of representative government, 3) women's suffrage, 4) release of political prisoners, 5) liberation of farmers, 6) freedom for the labor movement, 7) encouragement of a free economy, 8) abolition of police oppression, 9) development of a free press, 10) liberalization of education and 11) decentralization of political power. Cited in Hata Ikuhiko, Japan under the Occupation, *Japan Interpreter* 10:3–4 (Winter 1976:367 from Courtney Whitney, MacArthur: His rendevous with history, 1956. p. 213.

[3] The explanation of "the context" in this chapter is not intended to be an analysis of the formal occupation period, 1945–1952, its various reform endeavors concerning education, land reform, etc but rather an analysis of the implications of those actions

When the Japanese government was directed by SCAP in these early months to abolish all laws from before 1945 which restricted civil liberties, the press, speech, thought, it gave the very distinct impression that a new era was born and a new beacon had been lit and was burning brightly.[4] The Japanese government was told to accomplish this task in a week by October 10, 1945. This hopefulness was seemingly encouraged still further with the clear GHQ fostering of the development of labor unions and the union movement. An era of great expectations loomed ahead. While these GHQ directives were welcomed by Japan's moderate conservatives, the liberals, the leftwing and communist movements, there were in and outside of the Japanese government those who did not welcome this wholesale disapproval and even including the dissolution of the internal security structure that had existed from before August 1945. Some even tried to persuade GHQ officials not to order the repeal of certain internal laws, especially such laws as the notorious Peace Preservation Law of 1925. It should be remembered that Yoshida Shigeru, a conservative Prime Minister during most of the 1945–1952 period, was not in favor of dismantling the internal security laws and bureaucratic structure of the "old order". He was not in favor, in contrast, of reviving, re-creating the incipient Japanese military ahead of or even parallel to the great effort for economic recovery; but he did so later at the direct instructions of GHQ in 1950.

As part of the program to eliminate the old order, SCAP issued two directives on 1/4/1946 (SCAPIN-548, 550, Imperial Ordinance #101) to the Japanese government to purge selected categories of Japanese, referred to as "undesirable personnel" from holding public office, to dissolve and dismantle selected ultra-nationalistic organizations. This process, of course, understandably and inevitably, became entangled in Japanese political process and also drew GS/GHQ and other GHQ offices into this maelstrom. The rationale behind this "political purge" was that when the "undesirable" top personnel were removed, this would give a new crop of potential leaders an opportunity to create

surrounding internal security and civil liberties and on the political tinge that evolved during these years.

[4] It was issued on 10/4/1945 as SCAPIN-93 concerning "The Removal of Restrictions on Political, Civil and Religious Liberties". The "IN" of SCAPIN referred to Index. This SCAP directive was a command, a supra-constitutional directive to the GOJ not subject to Diet discussion or enactment and issued by GOJ as an Imperial Ordinance. Significantly, the Prince Higashikuni Cabinet resigned the next day.

a new democratic Japan. Since the next level under those purged had been trained, tutored, indoctrinated by the purgees, it was indeed a great leap of faith that whoever came after the purgees would be committed to the democratic process. The implementation of the purge, often called the "white purge" was completed by spring 1948. About 210,000 persons had been barred from holding public office. It should be understood, however, that 80% were from the Japanese military; of the remaining 20%, 16% came from those who had been leaders in such organizations at the Imperial Rule Assistance Association (Taisei Yokusankai), a government sponsored political organization to spread the word about its objectives, plans and expectations; 1.6% specific individual ultra-nationalists, 1.4% business and the media and a mere 1% from the civilian governmental bureaucracy. These percentages are understandable and the political message was clear, the civilian governmental institutions and the police had been "cleared" although the laws and structures governing the police would be somewhat revised, e.g. attempts would be made to decentralize and democratize the police à la the U.S. system and the creation of an Attorney General's office instead of a Ministry of Justice. The SCAP directive did not give a date when purgees would be allowed to return to the "political world"; presumably it was an indeterminate length of exclusion, "a life sentence".[5]

The Special Investigation Bureau (SIB) was created on December 17, 1946, initially in the former Ministry of Home Affairs and later, after the 1947 Constitution was promulgated, transferred to the Office of the Attorney General to monitor the SCAP purge program, i.e., the activities of the ultra-nationalist purgees and the dissolved ultra-nationalistic organizations to ensure that they were abiding by restrictions imposed on them. The number of SIB personnel was increased several times over the years from a small staff of 150 in the beginning, to 537 May 1950, and to 1,200 in August 1950. Just after the outbreak of the Korean War in June 1950, the SIB structure was revised from a mere four divisions to eight divisions and two departments, pros-

[5] For the purposes of this study, we focused only on the political phase of the purge. There were also three other aspects, the economic, the media and on the Dai-Nippon Butokukai, all described in the afore-mentioned *Political Reorientation of Japan*, pp. 8–118. John Montgomery pointed out in his book, *Forced to be Free: The Artificial Revolution of Germany and Japan* (Chicago, 1957. p. 26), that only 3.2% of the Japanese were screened in contrast to 21.7% in Germany; 0.29% of the Japanese population were barred from public office versus 2.5% in Germany.

ecutors were increased from seven to 25, and personnel in regional bureaus from 20 to 50. Placing the newly created SIB in the office of the AG was supported by the Minister of Labor and former Ministry of Home Affairs personnel against the desires of the National Police.

The economy, on the other hand, which the Japanese government and people were left to figure out, without any help from the victorious Allies, became worse at an exponential rate. Food, clothing and fuel had already became one horrendous issue even in 1944 to 1945 for individuals and families throughout Japan; this crisis became 10 times, 100 times worse after the war ended; scarcity of everything became a crisis. Under these circumstances, inflation became rampant and almost out of control. Freezing bank accounts and allowing one to remove only small amounts each month was merely a momentary band-aid and had, in reality, little impact in controlling inflation. When the war ended, canned goods were given to soldiers and sailors according to rank as they were demobilized; the higher the rank the haul of canned goods would be greater. In addition, there were large amounts of government stored materials, food and clothing. These would be illegally purchased and hoarded to be sold at a higher price at another day. Demands naturally developed for the release of these precious goods to relieve the shortages. Small disturbances occurred, they coalesced into larger demands; frustrations grew with the belief that the government was not demanding the black market hoarders of food, in particular, to release the supplies now instead of at a later date when they could maximize their ill-gotten gains. The government was a conservative cabinet, closely allied with the past old order and seemed unwilling or incapable, probably both, to take drastic measures to provide more food for the people. The more active and more radical political elements mobilized these frustrations into angry demonstrations in many cities and towns in Japan. The less radical socialist/social democrats were less effective in organizing masses of people into direct action; the more radical leftwing, including the Communists, were far more effective and successful. On April 7, 1946, the labor-farmer organizations organized a grand people's rally to overthrow the Shidehara Cabinet and marched on the PM's residence but were turned away by the police. Another mass rally was organized against the formation of the first Yoshida Cabinet to overcome the food crisis. The implication of the gathering momentum of these mass demonstrations was becoming clear, the more radical elements of the leftwing, implicitly the JCP and its supporters had thrown down the gauntlet of challenge to the authority and prestige of SCAP as supreme arbiter in Japan. These implications of the dire situation that was unfolding in Japan was recognized by SCAP in his presentation on May 6, 1946 to the Famine Emergency Committee chaired by Herbert Hoover. He described the food situation as unprecedented in Japanese history for a number of reasons: severe typhoons and floods in mid-September 1945, the 27% reduction of the harvest from 1944 to 1945, breakdown of the wartime collection system, anxiety about the future and sudden growth in population from repatriation of millions of Japanese from various parts of Asia. Since Japan normally imported 15 to 20 percent of its food requirements the daily calory level would be reduced so much that mass starvation would be inevitable during May–September 1946. If adequate food imports are not provided it would be

> impossible to achieve the major objectives of the occupation with a consequent incalculable effect upon the Allies, not only in the Far East but the world over. Particularly is this true since Japan can only be considered a vast concentration camp under the control of the Allies and foreclosed from all avenues of commerce and trade.

As a result food imports did occur; they were not free, for Japan paid for these crucial imports at a later date in millions of dollars. The sometimes violent demonstrations eventually persuaded SCAP to issue another statement on 5/20/1946 this time warning against mob disorder or violence: he cautioned against the "growing tendency toward mass violence and physical processes of intimidation under organized leadership [which present] a grave menace to the future development of Japan.... They constitute a menace not only to orderly government but to the basic purposes and security of the occupation itself". This stance while reasonable and rational under the circumstances, was the first break with the radical leftwing elements opposing the conservative government. At another venue, Ambassador George Atcheson, U.S. Chairman of the Allied Council on Japan, theoretically the overseer of the SCAP dominated occupation, stated in mid-May 1946 that the U.S. would not be in favor of communism in Japan. Thus the tableau in Japan was set for a showdown to occur probably in the near future but it would be a running battle without lethal weapons for several more years.

Notwithstanding these admonitions, the organizers of these demonstrations relentlessly pushed their demands and organized demonstrations against a weak Japanese government which could not in reality effectively respond to the demands of the demonstrators even if it had had the political will to do so. A major labor dispute erupted in the *Yomiuri Shimbun*, exemplifying the blatant Communist attempt to control a major media conglomerate; armed police invaded the Yomiuri Shimbun building to control the situation. Since the internal social situation in Japan did not materially change much in 1946 to 1947, the ruthless organizers, almost all Communists and their union supporters gradually pushed the demands and demonstrations to a steep crescendo, ultimately calling for a General Strike on February 1, 1947—and implicitly a leftwing takeover of the government through the force of this strike, if necessary. The JCP, it must be admitted, came onto the postwar scene untainted, a distinct plus in the postwar chaos; its leaders as mentioned above had been released from Japanese jails based on directives from the Occupation only 15 months earlier. Another Communist leader, Nozaka Sanzō, returned from the Chinese Communist controlled area of China and proclaimed that the JCP would be "a lovable party". This provided an amorphous hope to the disheartened and disillusioned Japanese workers. The Socialist Party and its more conservative labor unions with some tainted background endorsed these demonstrations obviously most reluctantly in a weak kneed fashion but it was always clear that they felt most uncomfortable in this position. The militant attitude of the Communist controlled labor unions mitigated against genuine cooperation with the Socialists. This was a direct and blatant challenge to SCAP from the JCP with implicit and silent Soviet backing only 18 months since the occupation began. The challenge had to be firmly confronted by SCAP. As the clock almost struck midnight, SCAP issued an order to the leaders of the unions which had federated for the purpose of conducting a general strike to desist from the furtherance of such action. He compared the small minority who planned this general strike to the minority which led Japan into a destructive war. He commented dramatically that:

> he [SCAP] could not tolerate the use of so deadly a social weapon in the impoverished and emaciated condition of Japan...I have [intervened] only to forestall the fatal impact upon an already gravely threatened public welfare. Japanese society today operates under the limitations of war, defeat and allied occupation. Its cities are laid waste, its industries are almost at a standstill and the great masses of people are on little more than a starvation diet.

This ordered abortion of the February 1, 1947 general strike was the first major turning point in the relationship between SCAP—and implicitly the supportive Yoshida Cabinet—and the seeming growing influence of the more radical leftwing groups in the political opposition movements in Japan. A large part of the unions behind the General Strike plan had been various unions of government workers from various Ministries; they would be much easier to mobilize as unions and for such a coordinated audacious plan as a General Strike. As confrontation moved forward over the 18 months following September 1945, Japan had adopted a new constitution in early 1947, held a general election resulting in a Socialist-Liberal Conservative coalition government headed by Katayama Tetsu, a Christian from the Socialist Party for a little less than a year, followed by the same coalition but with a different Prime Minister, Ashida Hitoshi, from the alternative conservative party; it lasted but a short time. The Katayama Cabinet was an enthusiastic supporter of the purge concept and most of the proposed reforms; the Ashida Cabinet was less enthusiastic.

But these cabinets were ineffective in economic policy, especially the provision of food (if it was truly available). Yoshida Shigeru was again called upon to form his 2nd cabinet in Fall 1948. Because of his known hostility to many of the political reforms, such as the purge and dismantling of the economic conglomerates (the *zaibatsu*, so-called), his premiership was not welcomed by some in GHQ, especially Government Section. But there was little political alternative to PM Yoshida at the time. While simultaneously, the more mundane aspects of "remaking Japan" in education and land reform, and other fields were slowly and quietly moving forward, a shift in the wind direction beyond the control of Japan was occurring which would lead to the benefit, the authority and influence of PM Yoshida. GHQ-pushed "reforms" of Japanese society also ground to an end, only partially because of his maneuverings, but much more decisively because of the collateral effects stemming from outside influences. In the January 1949 general election, the conservative Liberal Party won a resounding victory in the House of Representatives, and the Socialists and its allies suffered a serious slump in their support but, for the first time, the JCP gained 10% of the votes. The symbolically strong JCP support, an increase from 4 to 35 seats in the Diet, was another shock to the Japanese conservatives, to GHQ and to the USG in Washington. This was but one more incentive for GHQ to work more closely with the conservatives despite their direct lineage to the prewar structure, "the old order", rather than rely on the non-Communist liberals who had not evinced much support at the polls.

The attempted remaking of Japan by a group of dedicated, well-intentioned and enthusiastic non-Japan specialists in GHQ, particularly in Government Section (GS) proceeded merrily along in Japan as though the latter was in a cocoon with seemingly no connection to the outside world. All Japanese were busy bees trying to eke our a living amidst horrendous scarcity and responding disgruntledly, joyfully to SCAP dicta. But outside Japan, a different set of anxieties were slowly leading to a re-appraisal of Germany and Japan's roles in the evolving cold war between the Free World and the Communist sphere. The honeymoon between the victorious allies, the coalition led by the United States in the West and the Soviet Union in the East was soon over. Just listing a number of major events would provide a good impression of a new conflict quickly brewing between the Free World and the Communist Sphere. In October 1945, U.S. Ambassador William Averell Harriman met with Stalin at the Crimean resort city of Sochi where Stalin commented that the wartime partnership was over and the Soviet Union would pursue its own course; Harriman also privately met with the Deputy Foreign Minister in October 1945 and struck a deal: the Soviet Union could control Eastern Europe and Japan would be under sole U.S. control. In February 1946, Stalin gave a campaign speech in Moscow where he declared that the conflict between communism and capitalism was inevitable and re-emphasized that the wartime cooperation was no longer tenable. After the December 1945 Foreign Minister Conference was held in Moscow, George Kennan, then charge d'affaire in the U.S. Embassy in Moscow, despatched his famous Long Telegram to Washington in February 1946 which led to the containment policy by the U.S. against the Soviet Union as enunciated by President Harry Truman in March 1947 and known as the Truman doctrine. Prime Minister Churchill declared in a speech in the U.S. (Fulton, Missouri) in March 1946 that an Iron Curtain had been drawn in Europe. In May 1947 a month before the announcement about the Marshall Plan, Dean Acheson, U.S. Secretary of State asserted that "the greatest threat to peace stemmed from the grim fact of life that the two workshops of Europe and Asia, Germany and Japan, remained idle. World stability required rebuilding the two workshops on which the ultimate recovery of the two continents so largely depended".

On January 6, 1948, Secretary of War Kenneth C. Royale made a speech in San Francisco describing Japan as the bulwark of freedom against totalitarianism in Asia. It is truly ironic that the two defeated countries had become the two pivotal economies that must be rejuvenated, less than three years after being defeated. A Kennan-MacArthur meeting which took place in March 1948 was important in laying the foundation in redirecting the occupation from reform to economic recovery. That Kennan, then only Director of Policy Planning Board in the U.S. Department of State, and known as the creator of the "containment policy" of the Soviet Union, could take on the famed five-star General MacArthur, the *shōgun* of the Occupation of Japan, was indicative that the authority and prestige of the latter had been substantially compromised. Subsequently on October 7, 1948, the U.S. National Security Council approved a policy paper (NSC 13/2) which provided clear and unequivocal "administrative guidance" to SCAP/GHQ to change the occupation emphasis from reform to economic recovery, coinciding with the 2nd Yoshida Cabinet.[6]

The economic aspect of the occupation was initially quite punitive. Naturally Japan's existing external assets were confiscated and Japan's economic recovery was going to be limited to the early1930s and its industrial base, equipment and machinery, would be dismantled and shipped abroad as reparations to such places as the Philippines and China. But by summer of 1947, this approach was revised, the new target was 1935, the apex year for development before 1941. It became clear that the industrial equipment was not being used properly, just lying unused and rusting. The new clarion call was economic recovery and control of the rampant inflation. In December 1948, the U.S. created a set of nine principles of economic stabilization for Japan to follow and; several months later in early 1949 Joseph Dodge, a Detroit banker, was sent to Japan to carry out these nine principles with the necessary drastic measures to change the course of the dangerously sliding Japanese economy. It became known as the Dodge Plan and enforced through draconian budgetary measures using the supra-constitutional authority of the occupation. By the time of the outbreak of the Korean War in 1950 the rampant inflation had been controlled and the foundation to stimulate Japanese trade with the outside world by

[6] The principal points of this policy paper could be summarized as follows: 1) relaxation of SCAP control, 2) development of a self-supporting economy and a halt to reforms, 3) discontinuation of the purge, 4) an end to reparations payments, 5) strengthening and reorganization of the Japanese police and 6) postponement of an early peace treaty (Hata Ikuhiko, Japan under the Occupation, *Japan Interpreter* 10:3–4/Winter 1976:371).

providing credit and raw materials to designated industries had been created. The SCAP Government Section's zeal for political and economic reform, especially in pushing the political purge program was blunted because of opposition from within GHQ itself (e.g. G-2 intelligence) and, of course, the conservative Japanese political leadership which in a number of ways effectively fished in the troubled waters of the occupiers. SCAP quietly ceased to call for the economic deconcentration of Japan, i.e. the dismantling of the *zaibatsu*. When the Chinese Communists took control of China in 1949, this converted Japan into an even more important geopolitical cog for U.S. manipulation in northeast Asia and the results of the 1949 election only heightened anxieties about potential communist activities. The lofty ideals of "the democratization of Japan" had essentially been understandably displaced by the geopolitical imperatives of the U.S. This was the second turning point when the Occupation redirected its efforts to economic recovery, which initially was not a major issue at all, and Japan had become the bulwark in northeast Asia against Communist advances.

Lacking an overall national internal security law and with the continuing occurrence of socio-political disturbances throughout Japan, various cities began enacting their own laws on the maintenance of public security (*kōan jōrei*) for their own protection; this occurred in Fukui city (7/7/1948), Osaka city (7/31/1948) and others in Shizuoka and Niigata prefectures, Utsunmiya and Shimonoseki cities. When GHQ issued a model set of rules for this purpose in April 1949, this spurred even more cities and prefectures to create such laws. These were convenient laws to control demonstrations, marches sponsored by Communist organizations and by organizations advocating various kinds of peace, often a cover for communist front organizations. By July 1952, 22 prefectures, 76 cities, 26 towns and 6 villages had enacted such laws. These local level public security maintenance laws were eventually declared constitutional by the Supreme Court. Labor disputes by government workers continued to erupt, interspersed with admonishing statements from various levels in GHQ. The government telecommunications workers union (Zentei Rōso) carried out a strike in March 1948, in June 1949 the united government workers unions federation (Zen Kankō Rōso) struggled to secure a ¥5200 base salary as the basis for a dispute and won this right in August 1949 and prepared to start a full scale strike (referred to as a general strike). On May 30, 1950, during a demonstration on the People's/Imperial plaza, several

U.S. servicemen were assaulted and injured. In addition, three mysterious unsettling incidents occurred about the time the Japan Railroads were going through a big reduction-in-force and soon after the Korean War began: the President of Japan Railroads suddenly disappeared (7/4/1950), and two unexplained trains wrecks occurred. (7/15/1950 and 8/17/1950).

Slightly earlier on July 22, 1948, SCAP sent a letter to PM Ashida Hitoshi instructing him to issue Cabinet ordinance 201 (based on Imperial Ordinance 542) taking away the right of government workers to strike. The Diet incorporated this major change into the national civil service law effective on December 20, 1948. This later became the core of draft legislation to ban general strikes and strikes in selected main or basic industries (*kikan sangyō*) if the national economy, the livelihood of the people would be compromised; thus, this concept went beyond general strikes to prohibiting strikes in general under a very broad mandate. Nevertheless and despite the overwhelming majority in the House of Representatives held by the Liberal Party from the 1949 election it remained un-enacted. Another purge was initiated against "Communists" and "fellow-travelers" in the public sector toward the end of 1949 remembering that it was this group that had been the spearhead in pushing and pushing the government's and SCAP's patience in arousing passions and planning "destructive activities" unbecoming of legitimate labor union activities. This purge was extended to the private sector shortly after the outbreak of the Korean War in June 1950 beginning with the Japanese media in July 1950. It appears that GHQ was concerned about how the communists in the Japanese media might try to usurp the various means of communications, and developed its own list of communists in the media and sought the cooperation of Asahi, Mainichi, Tokyo, Yomiuri, Nihon Keizai newspapers and the Kyodo and Jiji News services who, under the endorsement (*en'yō*) of the SCAP directive instructing PM Yoshida to purge the JCP leadership, also dismissed communists and their sympathizers on July 28, 1950. The regional and local newspapers followed suit and by the beginning of November 1950 almost 700 people had been dismissed from 47 companies.

This purge in the private sector continued until about November 1950. This "ideological cleansing" became known as the "red purge" and resulted in the dismissal of about 22,000 employees from the two sectors. For their activities, these employees paid a high price because they were probably black balled in seeking employment elsewhere which was difficult at the time to obtain, and being a purgee must have made life absolutely miserable. This purge reminds one of "ethnic cleansing", a term used many years later to describe the slaughter of a certain group of people; in the Japanese case, there was, of course, no physical slaughter of people but from the leftwing and communist point of view it was an attempted "ideological slaughter" carried out by the Japanese government and private enterprise with the implicit support of SCAP under the guise of the occupation directive on removing people who conduct activities inimical to the objectives of the occupation. Probably the Japanese government and private sector could not have succeeded in dismissing so large a number of employees without the known backing of SCAP, otherwise there would undoubtedly have been a major uproar and huge labor unrest. Amazingly there was no resounding outcry or demonstrations against these dismissals as unfair and regrettable. The supra-constitutional authority of SCAP had been effectively used. Nevertheless, these new "purges" were conducted without resort to due process and are a clear example of the collision of civil rights and the ubiquitous maintenance of public welfare (*kōkyō no fukushi*)—discussed at some length in Diet proceedings about the proposed subversive activities prevention law.

The labor unions and much of academia in the social sciences did interpret these purges as a blatant attempt by the arch-conservative government to suppress, if not destroy, labor unions and the labor union movement, using as a cover the presumed communist threat felt by themselves and now with enthusiastic SCAP support. The red purge became a cause celebre as a prime example of how ultimately the U.S. had turned on their own creation. This purge was a natural extension and culmination of SCAP/GHQ's critical attitude toward the increasingly shrill and challenging communist-led activities in labor unions and was particularly solidified with the outbreak of the Korean War. The labor unions vowed to vehemently resist this presumed threat to their very existence in the upcoming new era of independence. Believing it sensed an opening, a momentum to enact restrictive legislation, the Yoshida Cabinet, i.e. the Attorney General began conceptualizing and drafting laws to control mass demonstrations, prohibit general strikes and a new internal security law. These ideas and later drafts came under heavy criticism from the media, academia, political parties and labor unions as will be discussed in later chapters. By unspoken signals only the draft law for a new internal security law was chosen by the conservative government as the path to follow.

In early January 1950, the Cominform, the international communist coordinating body, launched a criticism of the previously "lovable JCP" policy, asserting that to think that Japanese liberation and democratic revolution could be achieved through peaceful means was a mistake, calling for a shift from peaceful revolution to an anti-U.S. militant action in Japan; this was a call tantamount to mounting armed guerilla warfare in Japan. While the JCP leadership initially challenged this approach, in a short while it buckled under Soviet/Chinese pressure and accepted the criticism—resulting in various kinds of attacks attempting presumably to create chaos and uncertainty in Japan. Six months later, almost presciently anticipating the outbreak of the Korean War, SCAP instructed PM Yoshida in a letter to him on June 6, 1950 to purge all 24 members of the JCP central committee and put them under the same prohibitions, restrictions and liabilities under SCAPIN 548 and 550 (Cabinet ordinance 325) which had earlier purged Japanese ultra-nationalists. Another letter the next day, June 7, 1950, purged 17 senior members responsible for the publication of the JCP party organ, *Akahata* (Red Flag). On June 25, 1950, the Korean War began. On July 18, 1950, SCAP also instructed PM Yoshida to "maintain indefinitely the suspensions heretofore imposed upon the publication of *Akahata* and its successors and affiliates employed in the dissemination in Japan of inflammatory Communist propaganda." This series of events resulted in the third major turning point stretching approximately over one year, this time in relation to labor unions, the labor union movement and communist activities. In the eyes of the unions, academics and intellectuals, this was regarded as a betrayal by GHQ after having so strongly encouraged the development of labor unions; this sentiment surfaced strongly, most vociferously when the new internal law, the SAPL was proposed in 1951.

With the outbreak of the Korean War, suddenly the domestic and international context was radically altered. Japan now became the rear-guard support base for U.S./U.N. Forces fighting the North Koreans and later the Chinese Communist armed forces. The Japanese industrial base shattered as it was, was given a totally unanticipated opportunity to provide the U.S. military forces all manner of services, including the repair and maintenance of what was then the latest high technology military vehicles and weapons. Of course, Japanese industry with its skilled workers took full advantage of this economic and technological bonanza for it gave the Japanese economy an enormous boost to the mutual advantage of the U.S. and Japan. It must have saved the U.S.

government hundreds of millions of dollars for not having to ship all this equipment and services back to U.S. territories. (It was called the "special procurement program", *tokuju* in Japanese).

In response to the Korean War, militarily, the USG asked the Yoshida government to create a 75,000 man National Police Reserve (NPR) and add 8,000 more to the Maritime Coastal Service (the incipient Japanese Navy); despite its name, the implication was clear, this "reserve" was the revival and reconstitution of an incipient Japanese Army. It was undoubtedly staffed by younger officers and men of the previous Japanese Imperial Army which was completely dismantled less than five years previously. For Japanese domestic public opinion, for Constitutional and international considerations, it was politic to call it a national police reserve (NPR) with military training and weapons and later "Japanese Self Defense Forces".[7]

With U.S. forces drained out of Japan for the war on the Korean peninsula, the internal security of Japan became a major concern; the newly formed NPR would now be the front line of internal Japanese defense if social stability broke down and social chaos arose beyond the capabilities of a normal police force. The outbreak of armed hostilities with the Communists in Korea just across the straits from Japan was but one more indicator in the eyes of the Japanese conservatives of the communist threat to Japan from the outside. This presumed threat might resonate with dangerous social and political movements in Japan, prompt an escalation of violence that had been initiated by the communists in recent years to disrupt Japanese society and create political uncertainty, agitate the people as a group, and raise doubts in their minds about the stability of Japan under these international clouds. Compared to the presumed intellectual communist threat of the 1920s, this was a "real and tangible threat". The USG now had common ground with the Japanese conservatives, the very group which the USG was avowedly determined to oust from power to give the Japanese people an opportunity for a fresh start with democracy, American style democracy of course.

[7] According to Potsdam Declaration of 7/26/1945, the Allies would (11) permit maintenance of such "as will sustain [Japan's] economy...but not those which would enable her to re-arm for war." The initial planning directive to SCAP under Part III.1 Political, Japan is not have an army, navy, air force, secret police organizations or any civil aviation".

On the domestic side in Japan, in order to strengthen the government's anti-communist stand, the gradual revocation of the initial political purge began to take place in earnest so that those previously purged could return as stalwart members to civil society. This was exemplified by the increasing numbers of ex-purgees in the 3rd through 5th Yoshida cabinets (1949–1954 about 23%), Hatoyama Cabinets (67%), Ishibashi Cabinet (56%), and the Kishi Cabinets (46%). The GOJ began discussing with GHQ in 1951, the possibility of removing members of the dreaded Special Higher Police (*Tokkō*), in a phased manner, from the list of purgees, after all they were dedicated staffers of the old order who eagerly hunted down Communists and fellow travelers. By mid-1951 GHQ had agreed to a phased removal of such personnel from the purgee rolls on a case-by-case basis—a major change in policy for GHQ.

Based on GHQ's initially informal suggestion or what might be regarded as "administrative guidance" the SIB was negotiating with GHQ in early 1949 a revision of Imperial Ordinance 101 (issued in response to SCAPIN 548 of 1/4/1946) when GHQ made an oral demand for this revision. This Ordinance was the vehicle used to purge undesirable persons from holding public office. It was asserted that its purpose must be more clearly clarified (*issō meikaku-narashime*) and its implementation must be more thoroughly and completely executed (*yori kanzen na un'yō*)—Japanese bureaucratic language to rationalize substantive changes. The implication of these "inadequacies, faults" was to provide an acceptable legal foundation to pursue and remove undesirable (*akushitsu*) organizations which, on the surface, advocate democracy and peace; this need was also a reflection of the changing objective circumstances—the evolving perception of the Communist threat. The original objective to purge and dissolve ultra-nationalist organizations had been accomplished but the legal mandate to pursue the above-mentioned undesirable organizations was not clear. It would be the purpose of this revision to clarify these aspects and provide the legal basis to investigate such organizations and, if necessary, take action against them including dissolution. With the revision of the Imperial Ordinance, the SIB would be given the mandate and authority to conduct surveillance of communist party institutions and support organizations and to take legal action against them. It was asserted that by including those organizations which were undemocratic and violent, the ordinance was now "balanced" since both right and left would be treated "equally". The end result was to broaden, re-interpret a previous ordinance, just as was done with the Peace Preservation Law (PPL) of 1925 on several occasions not just revising the basic PPL but to broadening its interpretation in implementation, a major criticism of the PPL. The revised version was issued as Cabinet ordinance #64 on April 4, 1949, known as the Organization Control Ordinance (Dantaitō Kisei-rei).

This was a supra-Constitutional directive not subject to Diet discussion or legislation—thus this directive would expire when the Peace Treaty came into effect. Did the SIB suggest, persuade GHQ to support such a revision or was it the other way around; no one can tell except as reported above. Thus, if ordered by GHQ, the SIB and the government would raise no objection whatsoever for they would be most willing and would take the lead in achieving such a revision to keep track of the communists with a legal mandate. In a book about this ordinance, *Dantaitō Kisei-rei*, items 6 and 10 of the Potsdam Declaration are cited as follows: that irresponsible militarism must be driven from the world and that all obstacles to the revival and strengthening of democratic tendencies among the Japanese people must be removed.[8] This, says the author, was the ultimate imperative or supreme order (*shijō meirei*) to the Japanese people. This is cited as an additional and cogent rationale for potentially taking action against anti-democratic, secretive, violent organizations, i.e. the communist party and its supporting organizations. In order to achieve peace (*heiwa-shugi*), the principal objective of this ordinance was to have complete openness of all political organizations by having them register with the local government where they are located providing the date of creation, address, names of officers and members, the list of principal financial supporters, a list of purposes and objectives. A political organization was defined as one which recommends candidates for public office, which influences the creation of public policy on national, prefectural and local levels and which discusses international relations. The concept of this system of registration was "to assure an openness of the political process". Those organizations which are secretive, militaristic, ultra-nationalistic, or are anti-democratic or advocate violence to achieve political goals shall be banned or ordered dissolved. The AG would designate these organizations and may order their dissolution.

[8] *Dandai tō Kiseirei Kaisetsu*, 1951. 200 p. The author, Yoshihashi Toshio, was a senior officer in SIB.

The SIB/AG lost no time in ordering the dissolution of four organizations of Korean residents in Japan on 9/8/1949, the Tokyo Shinjuku ward JCP Committee, the communists cells in the Dai Nihon Insatsu (the Greater Japan Printing Co.) and at the Tōhō Movie Co., and the labor organization, Zenkoku Rōdō Kumiai Renraku Kyōgikai in July and August 1950, respectively, in addition to the on-going dissolution of ultra-nationalist organizations.

The policy changes outlined above were regarded by some as "reversing the course" of the original lofty objectives of the occupation, a betrayal of the original mandate, promise and social contract seemingly given to or imposed on the Japanese by the victorious Allies, but basically the U.S., to start afresh to create a New Japan. While many remarkable things were achieved, e.g. the educational system was reformed, voting rights were given to Japanese women, the legal foundations for the family system were fundamentally revised. These and other reforms would not have been achieved by the Japanese themselves, only a supra-Constitutional authority such as SCAP could have achieved these changes. But these changes, important as they may have been, were not related to an assessment of Japan (and Germany) as important if not critical geopolitical and politico-military entities or cogs in the evolving conflict, the Cold War, between the Free World under U.S. leadership and the Communist world led by the then Soviet Union. The range of choices in choosing partners in Japan which could revive the economy and provide the political leadership for this purpose was indeed narrow, if there really was a choice at all.

I would suggest there was no choice for the U.S. After an initial flare in the political sky, the Japanese socialists had failed in political leadership, were split into left and right wings as they faced the issue of voting for or against the Peace Treaty. The former did not express a willingness to work with the U.S.; their reliability as a steadfast ally in the Cold War was questionable. The labor union movement was seemingly moderate in the early days after the war ended but soon fell under the dominant influence of the Communists, especially government employee unions and many of the major industrial enterprises. Even the labor federation, Sohyo, "created" by GHQ after the outbreak of the Korean War in June 1950 to counter communist domination, became critical of U.S. policies in Japan. Because of the evolving international relations and confrontation with the Soviet Union, the U.S. relatively soon after the beginning of the Occupation of Japan realized for its own strategic purposes, it must take whatever steps were needed to revive the Japanese economy. The potential politico-military allies in Japan were the relatively still well entrenched second-tier conservatives who had initially survived the white purge and at that time headed by Yoshida Shigeru, who was then PM of his third Cabinet. Despite the seeming anti-U.S. stance and feeling of an influential segment of Japanese society, there was a relatively deep well of goodwill among the people toward the U.S.: it had accepted the imperial institution with Emperor Hirohito as the reigning monarch, the occupation had been relatively benign and beneficent in contrast to how the Soviets had treated Japanese POWs. The Soviets had pillaged the industries in Manchuria while in contrast the U.S. occupation had returned huge quantities of military materiel usable in a civilian economy. The U.S. occupation had achieved a fair number of changes in Japanese society which were accepted, it had provided food at a critical juncture, SCAP had stopped reparations and converted a difficult situation of an occupation into one of cooperation and reconciliation whatever the cynical or sincere reasons.

The Cold War had facilitated and fostered, accelerated and assured the rise of the representatives of "the old order" with U.S. blessing and welcome support. The anxieties of the conservatives had been vindicated: the Japanese ruling groups had been concerned that Japanese society might be insidiously subverted by communist infiltrators in the 1920s when Japan-Soviet relations were normalized. The actual Sorge-Hotsumi communist spy case in the early 1940s brought home the uncomfortable realization that communist spies had penetrated into the upper reaches of the Japanese elite. Prince Konoye, three times PM in the 1930s, penned a Memorial to the Throne soon after Japan capitulated in mid-1945 expressing his great concern about a real communist threat aimed specifically at Japan from the Soviet Union. In the postwar era the superpower Soviet Union loomed just north with a large, formidable and threatening military force, the Chinese Communists had won the Chinese civil war thereby creating a gigantic communist state just across the seas to the west. The Korean War brought a military conflict with the Communists to Japan's backdoor.

Domestically, their anxieties had come true in the form of communist dominated labor unions of government employees and of the private sector, especially in critical industries with the Cominform calling for the JCP to adopt more militant tactics in fighting against the conservative regime in Japan. In the eyes of the survivors from "the old order" as they considered internal security legislation, the communist threat had evolved from an intellectual threat in the 1920 into an imminent threat, a "clear and present danger" to the Japanese state. Since the conservatives were now working hand-in-glove with the U.S. the issue of self-reflection, the issue of war responsibility, the previous role of the Emperor in Japan's path to war and defeat, etc, became non-issues over the next 40–50 years—for Japan to play a significant supportive role in the Cold War was mutually more useful, more beneficial, more imperative and critical for both Japan and the United States. The fourth turning point was the decision by the government and the political opposition to struggle over the enactment of a new internal security law, the Subversive Activities Prevention Law, but this time without supra-constitutional authority to aid and support the cause.

CHAPTER TWO

PHASE I, DRAFTING THE SAPL, 1951 UNDER ATTORNEY GENERAL ŌHASHI

A. *Introduction*

As the task of drafting a new internal security law began, a sense of anxiety, uncertainty and threat to internal stability, almost an air of national emergency pervaded the Japanese government and society due to the outbreak of the Korean War in mid-1950 and the continuing violent tactics of the Japanese Communists in the early 1950s. While the leadership of the JCP had been purged, the JCP as an organization, as a political entity continued to exist. The felt threat by the Japanese, the government and society was not that Japan faced imminent threat of invasion from China or the then Soviet Union, but rather an attempt by the Communists to try to take control of the government and country through subversion, disruptive activities, assassination, etc, or more probably create chaos and uncertainty—the very concerns envisioned by the conservative leadership of Japan at the end of WWII, the summer-fall 1945. Their anxieties of the time appeared to be coming true and staring them in the face in the early 1950s.

While GHQ offices had been deeply involved in day-to-day operations with the Japanese government, these relationships were gradually evolving during the latter half of the Occupation period toward "a more distant intimacy". This evolving relationship is well exemplified in how internal security issues, particularly the creation of the draft SAPL was handled. GHQ's role in many instances had gradually become more advisory, rather than dictatorial, merely counseling toward a smooth transition. Government Section became less important. The State Department was building up its role, replacing military government as an occupying power. Major Jay, the last staff person in GS to work on the SAPL had been informed of this transition when he arrived. When he returned to the U.S. in mid-April 1952, that, he said was "the end of the line, no one came after me."[1]

Based on a study of SCAP documents in the U.S. National Archives, I detected a number of phases in an undulating relationship of ambiguity, clear-cut assertion, seeming indifference, encouragement and tutoring. The role of GHQ will be inserted as subsections as the SAPL story unfolds in order to understand how the GOJ and GHQ interacted with each other in the various stages in the process of drafting a new sensitive internal security law for post-Occupation Japan.[2]

B. *GHQ-I Early Twilight, an ambiguous message*

Shortly before the outbreak of the Korean war in mid-1950, SCAP had ordered the leadership of the Japan Communist Party (JCP) be purged. With the outbreak of this war, using the power of SCAP, to ban, outlaw or dissolve the Japanese Communist Party as an organization would seem to be an attractive solution; it would seemingly be straightforward, simple, and clear cut. While the prewar leadership in the Japanese government had been purged, their successors had been trained with a strong anti-communist ideological tilt and these personnel were now managing the government. In prewar years in Japan, the JCP had been an illegal (*higōhō*) organization. In light of

[1] Based on an interview with Ed Jay on October 14, 1978 in his home in New York state. In this interview, he told me that when he, as a U.S. Army Major (Armor) arrived in Japan, he was en route to Korea but that was suddenly changed to GHQ in Tokyo; fortuitously W.E. Monagan, special assistant to Frank Rizzo, Chief of GS, and who had been covering SAPL developments, was about to leave so Jay was assigned to succeed him in January 1952. Says Jay: constitutional law and the SAPL were the last thing on my mind as an assignment. He received a commendation from SCAP's Chief of Staff for his work on the SAPL. Jay left Tokyo in mid-April 1952, and became a lawyer in New York.

[2] These subsections on GHQ are based primarily on documents found in SCAP records (stored in Washington Records Center, National Archives, Suitland, MD and later in National Archives II in College Park). I studied SCAP documents on numerous occasions between 1978 and 2000 concentrating primarily on Government Section documents, 1945–52. I ploughed through the following boxes under the category RG331: 1447, 1501, 2137, 2142, 2187, 2191, 2193, 2194, 2252, 2253, 2275. I copied about 300 pages of material from boxes 1447, 1501, 2187, 2194. The reproduced pages include memos, reports of meetings between GS officials (mainly Frank Rizzo) and officials of the Japanese Government, and some drafts of the SAPL in English translation (but none in Japanese) and the banning of the JCP.

the provisions in the new postwar Japanese Constitution, banning the JCP would pose rather difficult constitutional problems.

To mark the anniversary of the promulgation of the new Constitution, SCAP issued a statement which apparently led to surmises as to whether SCAP was going to take action against the Communists or "whether it merely gave the Government [GOJ] a green light to proceed on its authority". SCAP did indeed act in the following month June 1950 just before the outbreak of the Korean War to purge the leadership of the JCP. PM Yoshida announced that the GOJ was examining the possibility of dissolving the JCP and had instructed the Attorney General to prepare action under Cabinet Ordinance 64. The Rizzo memo reports that Japanese officials made "repeated inquiries" and were consistently advised that using this Cabinet Ordinance "would be an improper use of that instrument which was designed to safeguard Allied Occupation objectives" and that if it decided to proceed with the banning "as a matter of public policy" it should do so by introducing a law in the Diet to that end.[3]

"Proposals to dissolve the Japan Communist Party had been smoldering for two years" and each time Japanese officials were informed of SCAP's position. The two years goes back to the 1949 elections when the decidedly anti-communist Conservatives won a comfortable majority and undoubtedly would have preferred to wipe the slate clean of such elements as the JCP and supporters. Premier Yoshida first broached this subject in March 1950 in his personal visits with General MacArthur when he "sought advice as to the feasibility of dissolving the party under provisions of the Organizations Control Ordinance" This Ordinance was issued as Cabinet Ordinance 64 implementing SCAPIN 548 and could not be invoked by the GOJ without prior GHQ clearance. This suggestion "was discouraged." If SCAP had accepted this approach the constitutional onus for this action would fall on SCAP and would appear strongly to run counter to the basic principles of the very Constitution that SCAP had persuaded the Japanese

[3] Memo: Background Information on Proposals to Dissolve the Japan Communist Party, 4/25/1951 by Frank Rizzo, Chief, Government Section to the Chief of Staff. 2 p. This memo clearly outlines the back and forth between the GOJ and SCAP about banning the JCP and is used here extensively. The Rizzo memo in para 2 commented parenthetically that "Japanese officials at ministerial level and others who have access to him [PM Yoshida] are convinced that his comprehension of English is rather more faulty that he admits, that he did not always fully understand what General MacArthur told him, and that his memory is not as good as it once was." RG331:2187:1.

to accept. It would have fulfilled the wishes of the anti-communist conservatives.

When it was faced with the notion of outright banning the JCP "as an organization" GHQ decided that action would be better accomplished by the GOJ, if it was to be done at all. In the early years of the Occupation, before the enactment of the New Japanese Constitution, nationalist and ultra-nationalist organizations and leaders had been purged from Japanese political life at the behest of the Occupation. Five years later, GHQ was no longer so eager to issue such orders; the buck was being passed to the GOJ not as an order, but more as a suggestion, an intimation, an expectation; but this time the GOJ was not always so immediately responsive. GHQ wishes were not automatically viewed as "writ". The anticipation was that the route of issuing SCAP ordinances by the GOJ would not be used. Most SCAP-derived Japanese Government Ordinances would cease to be effective when the Peace Treaty became effective. This was symbolic of the changing relationship between the two parties, GHQ and GOJ.

PM Yoshida reshuffled his cabinet in July 1950 immediately after the outbreak of the Korean War. Some time later, the Rizzo memo says that the new AG Ōhashi Takeo was reprimanded by Yoshida for not "prosecuting this project [of banning the JCP] aggressively enough to satisfy the Prime Minister" but was able, on the other hand, to convince the PM that using the Cabinet Ordinance 64 was "not practicable." Some thinking began in the AG's office about how the JCP could be controlled, if not banned.[4]

[4] In order to make the Japanese legal system "more like" the U.S. at least in skeletal structure, at the "suggestion" of GHQ the Hōmuchō (Attorney-General) was created on 2/15/1948 consisting of five Directors General, including two DG's with somewhat similar titles, Bureau of Legal Opinion Research (Hōmu Chōsa Iken-kyoku) and Bureau of Legal Affairs (Hōsei-kyoku, formerly part of the Prime Minister's Office). The latter had been a powerful agency through which proposed legislation was scrutinized before it was sent to the Diet. It had been downgraded and made merely one Bureau under the Attorney General. Under this new arrangement, it still had a similar responsibility to comment on proposed legislation but this was done through and in the name of the Attorney General who had become the highest legal officer in Japan. On 6/1/1949, as part of the attempt to simplify governmental structures, these two Bureaus were combined into one Bureau for Legal Opinions (Hōsei Iken-kyoku) with similar responsibilities and the Japanese name of the AG's Office was upgraded to Hōmufu (the English name remained the same). As part of the re-assessment of Occupation-inspired structural and legal changes, within less than six months after the Peace Treaty became effective on April 28, 1952, this Bureau was transferred back on August 1, 1952 to its original location as part of the Office of the Prime Minister and

Soon after the invasion of South Korea by North Korea in June 1950, the Legal Section in GHQ prepared a long memo (known as "The Oppler Memo") dated August 21, 1950, "Draft for the Essentials of a bill outlawing the Japan Communist Party and other organizations", attempting to justify the banning of the JCP as an organization and creating a draft bill for this purpose.[5] It was prepared "for the record" in response to an assignment given to the Legal Section by the Government Section, to be used as a basis for checking a draft law banning the JCP if such a bill was prepared by the GOJ and submitted to GHQ. It seems not to have been shared with the Office of the Japanese Attorney General (specifically the Special Investigations Bureau, hereafter SIB, the Tokubetsu Shinsakyoku) soon after it had been drafted but at a later date because the Japanese drafter, Seki Itaru, referred to the Oppler memo as having come to his attention in early spring 1951. The aforementioned Rizzo memo also said Government Section had assisted "to the extent of furnishing for his [AG's] information a form of draft bill [to ban the JCP] which might stand the test of a constitutional challenge". GHQ apparently was struggling to find some way to ban the JCP; this message was initially conveyed orally not in a written form to the Japanese. GHQ wanted this action taken under a Japanese law not using a SCAP ordinance, such as the Organizations Control Law (Dantai-tō Kisei-rei) since that legal instrument would automatically cease to exist when the peace treaty went into effect. It suggested that the Japanese law could go as far as the Smith Act in the U.S. which had been declared constitutional by the U.S. Supreme Court. But there was no existing Japanese internal security law under which this could be accomplished; those kinds of laws had been abolished by SCAP order early in the Occupation. The so-called "Oppler memo" was referred to numerous times in my interviews but only in relation to the drafting process in the spring of 1951. This changing relationship was clearly confirmed by the following quotation from section 1 of the Oppler memo:

---

the AG reverted back to being the Ministry of Justice—thus going full circle and so much for the acceptance of the Occupation legacy in this narrow area.

[5] This "memo for the record" (8/21/1950), "Draft for the Essentials of a bill outlawing the Japan Communist Party and other organizations", 11 single-spaced pages and an 11-page draft bill was prepared by Alfred C. Oppler. It was found in the U.S. National Archives RG331-Box 1447. The contents of this memo will be discussed later in this chapter.

> ...the idea...was...to work out the essentials of a draft bill with the purpose of having standards available for comparison and checking in case the Japanese Government submits legislation on this subject [of banning the JCP].

Thus began the thinking in the GOJ about a new law for this purpose or for the broader subject of internal security. Since SCAP/GHQ worked through the Japanese government, legislation banning the JCP would be created in the AG's office. In light of the changing objective conditions, the GHQ-GOJ relationship had somewhat shifted with the result that SCAP/GHQ's wishes were not automatically accepted. But this effort whether to ban the JCP or not was an on-again, off-again type operation in the GOJ. PM Yoshida was not one apparently to give up easily: In January 1951 he again sought SCAP's advice on the timeliness of action. The advice was described as follows in the Rizzo memo:

> the Government [GOJ] might lose more than it gained by such action [as banning the JCP] since the Communists as a party are politically impotent, and so long as they have legal status are likely to stay within the pale of legal activity. Further, their subversive potential in Japan has been effectively minimized through the weeding out of Communists and fellow-travelers from sensitive positions in government, public utilities, information media, and other critical enterprises which took place in 1950.

In March 1951 "a political storm" arose when it was revealed that the Minister of Agriculture and Forestry and former Party Secretary General had met with Tomabechi, chairman of the Peoples Democratic Party to cooperate in banning the JCP. Undoubtedly this was done with the PM support, tacit or otherwise. Then AG Ōhashi, Chief Cabinet Secretary and Liberal Party leaders in addition to Opposition parties all voiced their opposition to this move. Yoshida backed off saying the matter needs to be studied further. This ended the persistent attempts to ban the JCP.

It would seem that PM Yoshida himself was the driving force to ban the JCP, that GHQ played a firm but ambiguous role by definitively denying use of SCAP inspired Ordinances for this purpose but not actively urging the GOJ to ban the JCP, merely providing a draft bill to ban the JCP to the AG "for his information". Yoshida's distaste and abhorrence of the communists was so deeply ingrained in his personality, philosophy and ideological approach that it overcame his own experience of being arrested by the police toward the end of the war under the aegis of the prewar Peace Preservation Law which had been gradually broadened in its interpretation of coverage. This antipathy was so deep that he was willing to ban the JCP as an organization even though the guarantee of various freedoms were clearly and unequivocally enshrined in the Constitution. The Rizzo memo concluded that "while there is a strong desire in influential party circles to outlaw the Communist Party, there is a disinclination to do so by legislative means under the Constitution because any measure to that effect would have difficulty in passing the Diet." Only when, after repeated attempts "to secure SCAP support either in the form of a clearance to use Cabinet Ordinance no. 64 or explicit or implicit approval of Diet legislation which could then be used to overcome political opposition."[6]

By spring 1951 it was decided that legislation would be prepared that could effectively "control" (*kisei*) the destructive activities of the JCP and supporting organizations in addition to banning it, if absolutely necessary. This set in motion a serious effort to draft a law that would fulfill these stringent conditions. It appears the Japanese government felt by spring 1951 it could handle the Communist threat with its ability to use the mobility of the newly formed 75,000-man National Police Reserve; even though the Communists were moving from legal to illegal tactics it was not felt that it would be necessary to ban the JCP at that time. But a legal basis for responding to the destructive tactics was urgently needed.[7] It was hoped that a new internal security law could be prepared in time for submission to the Diet when the peace and security treaties would be discussed in and ratified by the 12th Extraordinary Diet Session convened on October 10, 1951. Three other controversial bills to prohibit general strikes, and to revise the labor laws and to control demonstrations were also placed on the

---

[6] Richard B. Finn in *Winners in Peace: MacArthur, Yoshida and Postwar Japan* (University of California Press, Berkeley. 1992. 413 p.) reports that Yoshida unsuccessfully urged the Occupation not to repeal the notorious Peace Preservation Law of 1925, but to revise it to apply to Communists and terrorist groups (p. 50). Memo (4/25/1951) Rizzo to Chief of Staff, Background Information on Proposals to Dissolve the Japan Communist Party, p. 2 (RG331:2187:1. While Yoshida was described as eager to ban the JCP, in his Japanese memoirs, *Kaisō Jūnen* (v:2:290–292), he says it would be improper to ban *(kin'atsu)* communism as a political belief, and also to ban/prohibit the JCP as an organization would be unconstitutional(*kempō ihan ni dasuru*). The issue of banning, disbanding or declaring the JCP illegal was also discussed in *Red Flag in Japan* (Roger Swearingen and Paul Langer, Harvard University Press, 1952, pp. 245–247).

[7] AG Ohashi interview as reported in *Sankei Shimbun* 1/5/1951.

agenda; all of these bills would be strenuously opposed by the opposition political parties and the labor unions.

Ultimately, the GOJ did not draft a law to ban the JCP; instead, if drafted and enacted a law covering destructive activities either from the left or from the right. The Oppler memo thus was never used by SCAP but did become one of many sources and reference document in the early stages of drafting a new internal security law for post-Treaty Japan. It hovered in the murky background and never came to life. Although Oppler was referring to a slightly later period in the Occupation, his apt description as follows is applicable:

> ...strange days, in a twilight atmosphere. The SCAP headquarters was folding up, the Government Section was no more than a small rump organization, the other Sections were shrinking, the personnel disappearing, and the future development was in a cloud of uncertainty.[8]

C. *Drafts 1 and 2*

The years, 1950–52, were tense times in Japan, and to draft a new internal security law under these conditions raised the anxiety levels of the parties concerned even further. According to Seki Itaru, then the Deputy Director of the Special Investigations Bureau (SIB) in the Attorney General's Office who had been given the task of drafting this new internal security law, and in the memoirs of the AG, Kimura Tokutarō, various meeting places in the Tokyo area were used for security purposes to discuss coordination and the drafts of the SAPL. In order to minimize inadvertent disclosure problems, he worked mostly by himself in doing the necessary research and creating drafts, assisted by one female secretary who probably acted as his typist and scribe, since some drafts were typed and others were hand written. Even his immediate superior, the DG of the SIB, Yoshikawa Mitsusada, acted more as a consultant. For advice on foreign laws on internal security and the constitutionality of his early drafts he called upon a private "brain trust" of University professors. For the inevitable and necessary translation to submit periodic drafts to GS/GHQ he relied on office

---

[8] Alfred C. Oppler. *Legal Reform in Japan: A Participant Looks Back.* Princeton, NJ, Princeton University Press. 1976. p. 291. The use of the Oppler Memo as one of several sources from which ideas were derived in creating the early SAPL drafts will be discussed later.

translators, perhaps the Liaison Offices (i.e. the former Ministry of Foreign Affairs).[9]

After about only two months, the first draft of the SAPL was completed on May 25, 1951; after further discussion with his colleagues in the AG's office, the SIB, the Hōsei-kyoku, a second draft was readied on August 6, 1951; a truncated third draft in early October 1951.[10] The first draft contained 102 articles; the second 174 articles; the third, was incomplete. The second draft was a greatly strengthened version (*yori jūjitsu sareta mono*). They were created, in the first instance basically by adopting and adapting the Organization Control Ordinance issued under the Occupation, the purge ordinance, probably the Oppler memo and draft law banning the JCP into a framework presumably acceptable under the new 1947 Japanese Constitution. It should be remembered that the SAPL was initially drafted in great secrecy and was not vetted through the normal governmental review process for new legislation. This strategy was adhered to because of the sensitivity of the proposed legislation and to try to minimize and control outside reactions; the latter control was particularly unsuccessful. On the GOJ side, PM Yoshida, two AGs (Ōhashi and Kimura), SIB Director Yoshikawa and Seki, and in GHQ, GS Chief Frank Rizzo, staff assistants Robert Monogan, Major Ed Jay in GS and Alfred Oppler in the Legal Section appeared to have been involved in and influential in varying ways at different times about certain parts of the numerous drafts. Those roles and influences can only be surmised through circumstantial evidence. Throughout the drafting process, Seki was always at the actual core of this whole exercise while responding simultaneously to two AGs and other players.[11]

---

[9] Kimura's memoirs, *Sotsu-ō Hyakuwa: Bun to Bu no Ibun* (Tales of a ninety-year old), Tokyo, Shimazu Shobō 1989. 443 p. This is actually a collection of 93 articles originally published monthly in *Budō* (The Way of the Martial Arts), Journal of the Nihon Budōkan (The Japan Martial Arts Academy) from April 1975. Essay 30 (pp. 115–119) mentions meeting in several places for security purposes. The specific places were given to me by Seki in an interview in 1998.

[10] SAPL, the initials for Subversive Activities Prevention Law as enacted in 1952, will be used throughout this study referring to all drafts; referring to different drafts under different names would be confusing and not useful.

[11] Seki said that each draft was translated and sent to GHQ but I was able to find only draft two in translated form, dated August 29, 1951 and the final draft of April 1952 in the archives. Apparently the versions in Japanese were not sent to GHQ, or not requested, or were thrown away by GHQ staffers since they could not read Japanese. The copies of draft 3, dated October 5 (draft 3A) and 10, 1951 (draft 3B) appear to be incomplete. Draft 3A with only 55 articles is missing chapters 5–11; draft

i. *Drafts 1 and 2*

1. *Titles of the Various Draft Proposals.* Before we begin with an analysis of the content of these drafts let us briefly focus on the titles of these drafts. They were called in Japanese, Kōan Hoshō-hō (Law to Assure (*hoshō*) Public Peace, Dantai-tō Kisei-hō (Organizations Control Law), Tokubetsu Hoan-hō (Special Peace Security Law). This is uncomfortably close in image and concept to the terms used for the prewar Peace Preservation Law (*Chian Iji-hō*). It is quite surprising that apparently no known attempt was made to draw a distinct line of demarcation, make a complete break with the past and create a completely new image and concept. This clearly reflects the difficulty of completely breaking with the past starting with the title of a proposed new law on this highly sensitive subject.

2. *Program Outlines (Yōkō).* Program Outlines were prepared by Seki as a reflection of a preliminary agreement, consensus or understanding between himself and the AG and perhaps others on the philosophy and fairly detailed stipulations to be followed in preparing the next draft. They were, in many cases, quite long running as much as 16 pages but they needed to be re-worked into a technically acceptable draft law.[12] In this study, the analysis of each draft will be based, in the first instance, on the specifically dated versions of the draft SAPL;

3B with 90 articles is missing chapters 8–11 on investigations, emergency detention, punishments and supplementary articles. Since the principal changes in these drafts were, I am convinced, concentrated in the first five chapters, these missing articles are not critical to this aspect of the analysis.

Seki's "not normally vetted" comment was made to me on several occasions to emphasize the point. Because of these unusual circumstances, I was unable to find out to what extent it was vetted in the bureaucracy, as distinct from coordination and consultation with the Liberal Party committees. For those who would like to know about the prescribed clearance process in the early 1950s see Satō Tatsuo, Hōritsu ga dekiru made, *Hōritsu Jihō* 25:1(1/1953):45–50. Satō was then DG/Hōseikyoku (Legislative Affairs Bureau).

[12] For example, there was a Program Outline dated June 21, 1951 presumably the basis for drafts 1and 2 although a specific outline for draft 1 was not found in the Ministry of Justice archives. Program outlines dated September 28, 1951 and October 5, 1951 were probably distributed at the time of a press interview and probably became the basis for draft 3. The Yōkō dated December 25, 1951 stemmed from a meeting with Kimura, the new AG, immediately after his appointment as AG in late 1951. Until a draft was finally released or leaked to the press, it is my understanding that critical comments and assessments about the pending draft by the newspapers, academics and commentators relied on these somewhat detailed outlines.

references will be made to these various Program Outlines when necessary.

3. *The Program Outline of June 21, 1951.* It specifically delineated four principles (*hōshin*) for preparing the draft bills for the SAPL, the PSIA, PSEC and a law for the disposition and management of assets of disbanded organization:[13]

a. A law will be created with necessary stipulations and procedures for the maintenance of internal security adopting/adapting ideas from such as the following: a) The stipulations in the Occupation-inspired Organizations Control and the Public Office Purge Ordinances which would be effective for the maintenance of internal security and do not contravene the Constitution; b) similarly, items from directives (*shirei*) and memoranda from SCAP; c) ideas from other sources for this same purpose; d) stipulations including emergency detention.
b. Since the stipulations in this law will affect the human rights of the people, these stipulations must be crafted in such a manner as to be in accordance with various articles of the Constitution, and a path must be created for appeal to the courts for relief and dissent.
c. To carry out this law, a PSIA as an outer bureau of the AG as the implementing agency (*shikkō kikan*) and a PSEC as the deciding agency will be created. For those actions, concerning human rights, the PSEC will make a decision based on a request from DG/PSIA, thereby avoiding a concentration of power and achieving a fair application of the law
d. The staff of the PSIA will be given the necessary compulsory investigative authority (*kōsei chōsaken*).

There was a clear implication that some of the Ordinances stemming from SCAP directives and memoranda were not constitutional. The importance of the need to adhere to and not contravene any of the human rights specified in the 1947 Constitution was made abundantly clear. On the other extreme, the use of emergency detention was elevated from one of many measures to being listed as an objective of the law in extreme cases and lastly that the investigative office would be

[13] In the various drafts there was always an investigative agency and a quasi-judicial agency to make a decision. The names of each changed over time, e.g. Tokubetsu Shinsachō, Kōan Chōsachō, Tokubetsu Shinsa Iinkai. To avoid confusion with acronyms and name changes I will use in this study only two titles with their acronyms, Public Security Investigation Agency (PSIA) and Public Security Examination Commission (PSEC)

given some police powers. These latter points became points of serious bureaucratic contention in the future.

4. *Objectives in Draft 1.* Article 1 defined the objectives of the SAPL as follows:

a. to assure (*hoshō)* the public peace and security (*Kōan*) of the nation (*kokka*) by opening all activities of political organizations to the public and for these activities to be conducted in a public and open manner and
b. to control (*kisei*) organizations and individuals whose activities are secretive, militaristic, extremely [or ultra] nationalistic, violent (*bōryoku*) and undemocratic.

Draft 2 added an important objective:

c. to establish stipulations under which those individuals who disturb the peace (*Kōan o gaisuru mono*) under national emergency conditions may be subjected to emergency detention (*kinkyū kōsoku*).

The addition of this last objective is symbolic of the direction in which these drafts were heading. Putting "emergency detention" as an objective in article 1 is a reflection of the desperate nature of and anxiety about the potential and gathering domestic turmoil in Japan and the growing confrontation with the Communist movement in Japan.[14]

5. *Definitions.* Article 3 (draft 1) on definitions covered an extremely broad range of activities:

Political organizations. They are defined as a political party, association, and other organizations whether as a whole or in part, whether legally constituted (*hōjin*) or not, whose objectives include recommending or supporting candidates for public office, influencing policies of the national or local governmental organizations or which discuss and debate relations between Japan and foreign countries.

All organizations described above will have to register (*todoke'ide*) at the local governmental office where their main offices are located and this governmental office shall, in turn, report to the AG. All the

[14] The "second draft" in the SCAP Archives did not include the third objective included in the Japanese second draft. This is an interesting point to note since GHQ worked only with the translated drafts and the first draft noted as such was not found in the U.S. National Archives.

registered information must be publicly available. The information to be provided in registering was not merely name, address, list of officers but also names, addresses, ages of officers and constituent members, names and addresses of thought organizations of which they have been members in the past, and the names and addresses of principal financial supporters in the past. All organizational journals or newspapers must be submitted, four copies to the local authorities and the AG within 20 days of publication.

Organizational publications. Such publications would be newspapers, journals, annual reports and other documents and printed matter, published regularly or irregularly for the general public concerning its activities.

Public Office (*kōshoku*). Nine categories of positions were specified as public offices:

a. All positions at the national, prefectural (*to, dō, fu, ken*), city, town and village (and special financial districts) level filled in accordance with an election law and all candidates for these positions
b. National government employees specified by the Personnel Authority (Jinji'in)
c. All local government employees designated by the Prime Minister based on the recommendations of consultative councils to the above mentioned local government assemblies and principal officers of these assemblies
d. Positions involved in public business of the national or local governments as designated by the principal officers of these administrative units or by an organization of these administrative units; these positions would be other than those who are national or local government employees
e. All teachers and their supervisors of educational facilities which may be funded wholly or in part by funds from the national or local government treasuries
f. The officers or others who are supervising an appropriate number (*sōtō no*) of employees of enterprises wholly or partially funded by national or local government finances
g. Officers of organizations related to labor
h. Officers and employees of media related enterprises
i. Officers and employees of important industrial organizations (*sangyō dantai*) as designated by the AG.[15]

---

[15] In draft 2 this list was whittled down to a few lines of a generalized statement.

Political Activity. Such activities were broadly defined in eight categories: to form a political organization, joining this organization, directly or indirectly, leading (*shidō*) and influencing these organizations, to publicly announce political opinions to the public orally or through the radio or by other means, to be involved in the editing or publication of a journal of a political organization, to write in support of or to publish or publicly announce written materials, designs or recordings which have a political objective, to make, manufacture and/or distribute flags, badges, or other emblems which have a political objective, to give or receive money or material or other tangible or intangible items, or to give or receive the same items whatever the method used, to persuade persons to become members of specific political organizations, and all actions taken notwithstanding their description or format taken with the objective of evading the limitations stipulated in the previous clauses.

Illegal Activities. Under draft 1, article 1 the second objective was to control those organizations "whose activities are secretive, militaristic, extremely (ultra) nationalistic, violent and undemocratic." Article 3.4 defines ten categories of activities any one of which would permit the AG to declare an organization illegal whether conducted in whole or in part by that organization. For simplification and better understanding, these categories have been grouped together as follows:

a. those organizations which plan, advocate, propagandize,
   - support or justify aggressive military action against foreign countries,
   - the sense of superiority of Japan or the Japanese people in a self-righteous, exclusive, racial, ethnic manner which will adversely affect the trust and cooperation between Japan and foreign nations,
   - in Japan to exclude illegally foreigners from trade, commerce or other activities,
   - actions to oppose appropriate cultural and academic interchange between Japan and other nations,
   - inside Japan except where recognized by treaty or law, urging the execution of military or para-military training, better treatment of former military personnel than the general populace, actions using other methods which may lead to a revival among the populace of a militaristic or pro-war spirit,
   - assassination, violence and other violent plans in order to change policies of the nation or local organization, or actions which tend

to encourage, justify or approve violent activities among the populace,
- those actions which tend to result in violent actions against people,
- or support actions which would overthrow or abolish a legally constitutionally established government through violent action or by communicating with foreign nations, foreigners or foreign organization,

b. those organizations which resist or oppose the armed forces of a foreign country or countries or of the United Nations stationed in Japan according to a treaty, or gather unpublicized secrets of these armed forces and
c. those organizations where more than one-third of its officers and constituent members are officers and constituent members of an organization which is declared to be illegal or has been declared to be illegal.

In the second draft, the types of activities which would be the basis for declaring an organization illegal were defined quite differently under Article 8. The Director-General of the Public Security Agency (Kōanchō) may request reports from an organization in order to understand the prevailing situation (*jittai*) in that organization if he recognizes that there is a possibility or concern (*osore aru ba'ai*) that this organization's objectives or actions may in the future, come under any of the following five categories:

a. if it incites (*aoru*), rationalizes (*seitōka*), plans (*kuwadateru*) or commits acts which contribute to the realization of foreign aggressive military action (*shinryaku-teki taigai buryoku*),
b. if it incites, advocates, plans or commits acts which would contribute to the realization of the overthrow or destruction by force of the Japanese Constitution or a government created under this Constitution.
c. if it incites, advocates, plans or commits acts which would contribute to the illegal overthrow or destruction of the Japanese Constitution or a government established under this Constitution with the guidance and support of foreigners, foreign countries, or organizations in foreign countries,
d. if it incites, advocates, plans, or commits acts which would contribute to or appear to approve plans to change the policies of local autonomous bodies (*chihō kōkyō dantai*) through assassination or violent/subversive plans (*bōryoku shugi-teki kito*) or other actions which would be detrimental (*gai-suru*) to community welfare,
e. if it seeks out and collects information not made public by foreign armed forces or those of the United Nations legitimately stationed in Japan or such information designated by the Japanese Prime Minister

as national secrets with the intention of infringing on Japanese public security.

These stipulations in draft 2 appear to be more strongly stated and more focused on foreign connections, foreign guidance and support. There is also one other important addition: the use of the word "*aoru/aori*". This word, and other words like "*kuwadateru*" are Japanese words in contrast to "*sendō*" or "*kikaku*" which are Chinese compound words and have a more legal sounding ring to them. "*Aoru*" has several meanings in Japanese: to fan a flame, to bolster/boost up, to gulp down and lastly to incite, instigate, inflame. When this kanji is combined with "to move", it becomes "*sendō*", also incite, the term used in later drafts and which became the center of a great controversy about the intent and motivations behind the SAPL. It is particularly significant that this word for incite—aoru—was used so early in the drafting process, in the second draft.[16]

Emergency Detention. The number of articles concerning emergency detention elevated as the third objective in draft 2 concerning people who "disturb the peace" increased from one article to 16 articles. These articles were obviously included to define the conditions under which the Cabinet may instruct the AG to issue a proclamation of national emergency, the designation of SIB personnel to carry out detention measures, the issuance of such orders, the questioning of potential suspects, the creation of detention facilities, the defense of such detainees, the disposition of detainees's objections to such designations and detention, the decision of the Public Security Examination Commission, objections to its decisions, termination and dissolution of detention. It also specified that the Cabinet must report about any emergency proclamation and the actions it had taken in executing this bill to the first Diet summoned after this proclamation had been issued. The drafter's concern with potential abuse of this authority was clear with the various legal and procedural safeguards included in the chapter not only on emergency detention for providing protection of the potential detainees's rights and possibilities of appeal but even specifying that the detention facilities must be such that the detainees's health will not be adversely affected, but also concerning

[16] The controversy surrounding "*sendō*" will be discussed in Chapter 4.

the administration of the PSEC itself. Article 103 of draft 2 stipulated that if and when Japanese territory is attacked (*shinryaku sareta toki*) or when a disturbance (civil unrest, violence, etc.) occurs with assistance (*shinryaku enjo*) from outside Japan, the government may arrest and detain those persons who have carried out any one of the actions specified in draft 2 article 8 described above, or where there may be the possibility that such actions will take place and it recognized that it would be necessary to arrest and detain these persons from the point of view of maintaining public security (*Kōan no hoji*). When such a disturbance occurs the Cabinet may order the AG to issue a proclamation of national emergency; the AG will execute this order through the SIB.[17]

Delegation of Authority to DG/PSIA. Many of the actions to be taken by the AG in the first draft were now given in drafts 2 and 3 to the DG/PSIA for him to make the recommendations for appropriate actions to the PSEC. This would be a bureaucratic elevation, from a Bureau of the AG's office to an Agency under the AG. It would mean higher status and authority for the DG on down, a claim on a much larger organization and greater number of personnel and a claim to a larger budget. This proposed change will become the source of some bureaucratic friction and political rivalry in the future.

Restrictive Administrative Measures. The AG (in draft 1) or the DG/PSIA (in draft 2) may order that the illegal organization:

a. be re-organized to eliminate the illegal aspects
b. expel selected members of that organization
c. be prohibited from conducting certain specific organizational activities
d. be dissolved/disbanded

In draft 2, finer graduations were made adding:

e. be prohibited or restricting its meetings
f. revise its bylaws and charter
g. be prohibited from publishing some or all of its publications

[17] It should be kept in mind that a different kind of "preventive detention" (*yobō kōkin*) was enacted into the 1941 revision of the PPL with its own chapter III, articles 39–65. The PPL system of law is discussed in section Q in this chapter.

Individuals could also be prosecuted and jailed for varying lengths of time; seven articles under a separate chapter on punishments were devoted to these individual punishments.

Investigative Authority of PSIA Officials. The Program Outline of June 21, 1951 stated clearly that PSIA officials would be given necessary compulsory authority to conduct investigations. This authority was described as generally equivalent to that of a tax collector (*shusei kanri*) to 1) request (*motomeru*) reports on specified issues either in writing or orally through a summons, 2) inspect (*rinken*), search (*sōsaku*) and seize (*sashiosae*) with a certificate of permission from a court and 3) with a certificate of permission from a court to have the police arrest a person who is believed to have violated the SAPL.

Draft 1, chapter 6 (articles 75–89) and draft 2, chapter 6 (87–102) were devoted to various aspects of this authority. PSIA officials 1) may request other government agencies to provide reports on selected topics, 2) may request persons or organizations to submit written reports within a specified time or explanations in person, 3) may inspect, search and seize materials and people provided a certificate of permission is first obtained from a court judge and 4) may request the assistance of the police in carrying out the necessary investigations under the SAPL. The request to the judge must be submitted under oath, giving the reasons in writing for this authority; the judge must review this request and issue a certificate specifying the place, person or materials to be inspected, searched and/or seized, the name of the PSIA official, the dates for which this permission is granted and the judge must sign the certificate and affix his seal to it. There must be a witness to this inspection, etc; if the party being so investigated declines, or cannot be present, then a police officer or an official from the local government shall be requested to be a witness. A list of materials seized must be prepared, and a report about this search, etc, must be prepared by the PSIA official and signed by the witness. To arrest a person who is believed to have violated the SAPL, a PSIA official must obtain a certificate of permission as described above and with the police arrest this person.

Because of the power and impact that the PSIA as an outer Bureau (*gaikyoku*) of the AG and because PSEC, as an "independent organization", could potentially have on the political life of Japan, the operations of these two organizations were hemmed in with strict operating procedures. Since some of these procedures later became a major focal point only the principal points will be noted here.

- the investigative authority of the PSIA
- all requests by the PSIA must be in writing in a format specified by the PSEC
- the PSEC may immediately dismiss the request of the PSIA
- a copy of this request must be immediately provided to the affected organization
- the PSEC may request the affected organization to submit a response
- the affected organization must be informed of the date and place where the hearing will be held
- all PSEC proceedings will be held in open session
- at least the chair of the PSEC and two other members must be present at all hearings
- the PSEC may call witnesses, reference persons (*sankō'nin*) and expert witnesses (*kantei'nin*)
- procedures under the civil code (Minji Soshō-hō) will be followed by the PSEC
- a record of the proceedings will be maintained and will be publicly available
- PSEC decisions will be rendered in written form and distributed to all parties concerned, and orders about dissolution of an organization and purging people from public office shall be reported in the Government gazette; the date of effectiveness shall begin on that date.
- the affected organization and persons may appeal their case to the Tokyo Higher Court (Tokyo Kōtō Saibansho) within 30 days from the date of effectiveness.

ii. *Derivations of the Basic Ideas in these Drafts*

1. *Occupation related Ordinances.* The Program Outline of June 21, 1951 stated that the stipulations in the Organizations Control Ordinance (Dantai-tō Kiseirei), commonly known as the Dankihō, Seirei 64, 4/4/1949, Cabinet Ordinance 64*)*, so long as they did not infringe on the new Japanese Constitution and were considered useful for internal security, and other Occupation directives and memoranda which related to the maintenance of internal security and other measures [from other sources, e.g. foreign legislation for example] believed to be useful for this purpose could be used. The two objectives in draft 1 were derived directly from the Dankihō. This was an Occupation-inspired government ordinance to control organizations from Japan's prewar experience. The words were almost identical. The admonition in article

2 that the execution of the draft bill must be conducted within the bounds of the 1947 Japanese Constitution was also extremely similar. The kinds of activities which would lead to dissolution, for example, were also similarly enumerated in the Ordinance, except that references to Occupation Forces were deleted, and so were references to former Japanese military officers. The stipulation that the draft bill would not apply to labor unions and other employee organizations was also borrowed almost verbatim from the Kisei-rei. The Ordinance also included the requirements for political organizations coming under this Ordinance to register with the appropriate governmental level. While these basic concepts for draft 1 were lifted from the Ordinance, drafter Seki included many administrative requirements on the implementing agencies in response to the changed political situation since the enactment of the Constitution in 1947 and the need to pay much greater attention to human and civil rights issues in implementing a highly charged bill to control the political activities of the nation. The concept for registering political organizations and requiring submission of publications was also adopted from the Ordinance. The idea of dissolving organizations as designated by the AG and preventing responsible persons in those organizations from holding other possible public official positions was also described in the Ordinance.

2. *The Oppler Memo of August 21, 1950.* This memo well illustrates the frustrations faced by GHQ in trying to deal with the rising violent challenge to internal order in Japan by the JCP particularly after the outbreak of the Korean War, despite the overwhelming U.S. military forces in Japan to control such direct challenges if necessary and Cominform criticism of JCP strategy and tactics. Japan was the critical area as a rear support base for U.S./U.N. forces fighting in Korea but various justifications for controlling the JCP were always put in the form of safeguarding the new Japanese Constitution, Japanese democracy and human/civil rights. In actuality, the Japanese archipelago was more important in geopolitical terms rather than for philosophical niceties. In part, the difficulty of justifying the banning of the JCP had been created by the Occupation-inspired new Japanese Constitution. Section 1 of this memo also clearly outlines the problems faced in legally trying to ban the JCP.

– *Banning the JCP and prewar Japanese history.* "The particular historical background of Japan in which concepts of thought control have been inherent for centuries made it imperative to avoid legislation against ideas as such solely on the basis of their being erroneous or harmful in the opinion of the groups in power."

– *Banning the JCP and the New 1947 Constitution.* "To reconcile the direct purpose aimed at [i.e. banning the JCP] with the existing limitations in the Japanese Constitution as well as with American legal tradition and with the general objectives of the Occupation appears a task of unprecedented difficulty to the constitutional lawyer....we do not think that this change in the international situation [the Korean War] would justify legislation under Japanese law contrary to the principles of the Constitution. This Constitution provides no possibility for the suspension of civil liberties in case of national emergency as the Constitution of the French Third Republic did by the device of the state of siege and as other basic laws do by different means. "Outlawing a whole Party" under Article 21, the clause which guarantees various rights in the Japanese Constitution presents "similar difficulties as it would under the Constitution of the United States." Even if "the public welfare" factor was used, the memo opined that it remained "doubtful whether the [Japanese] court would give this phrase such an extensive interpretation to permit the outlawing of the Communist Party."[18]

– *A specific law vs general legislation outlawing organizations using violent means to change policies and overthrow government for*

---

[18] To bolster its reasoning, the Oppler memo cites Chief Justice Hughes's opinion as follows quoted in *Freedom of Speech in the U.S.* by Zachariah Chafee.

> "If there was anything against these men as individuals, if they were deemed to be guilty of criminal offenses, they should have been charged accordingly. But I understand that the action is not directed against these five elected members as individuals but that the proceeding is virtually an attempt to indict a political party and to deny it representation in the legislature. This is not, in my judgment, American government.
>
> "Are Socialists, un-convicted of crime, to be denied the ballot. If Socialists are permitted to vote, are they not permitted to vote for their own candidates? If their candidates are elected and are men against whom, as individuals, charges of disqualifying offenses cannot be laid, are they not entitled to their seats?...
>
> "I understand that it is said that the Socialists constitute a combination to overthrow the government. The answer is plain. If public officers or private citizens have any evidence that any individuals, or group of individuals, are plotting revolution and seeking by violent measures to change our government, let the evidence be laid before the proper authorities and swift action be taken for the protection of the community. Let every resource of inquiry, or pursuit, of prosecution be employed to ferret out and punish the guilty according to our laws. But I count it a most serious mistake to proceed, not against individuals charged with violation of law, but against masses of our citizens combined for political action, by denying them the resource of peaceful government; that is, action by the ballot box and through duly elected representatives in legislative bodies."

banning the JCP. The memo then discussed the philosophy and concept of "clear and present danger" citing Justice Brandeis's concurring opinion in Whitney v. California, 274 U.S. 357, 374–77(1927) and declared that this has become "the norm applied by the U.S. Supreme Court" (p. 3).

> But even advocacy of violation [sic for violence?] however reprehensible morally, is not a justification for denying free speech where the advocacy falls short of incitement and there is nothing to indicate that the advocacy would be immediately acted on. The wide difference between advocacy and incitement, between preparation and attempt, between assembling and conspiracy, must be borne in mind. In order to support a finding of clear and present danger, it must be shown either that immediate serious violence was to be expected or was advocated, or that the past conduct furnished reason to believe that such advocacy was then contemplated.... Only an emergency can justify repression. Such must be the rule if authority is to be reconciled with freedom....

If it was decided that a Japanese law would be used it recommended "general legislation outlawing all organizations which aim at the overthrow of the government by violence and constitute a serious danger to the maintenance of the Constitution and the laws" since this approach was used in the Smith Act in the U.S. and used against American Communist leaders. But this generalized approach was not acceptable to General Whitney, then chief of GS. Consequently the proposed law attached to the Oppler memo provided for "the automatic outlawing of the Japan Communist Party" (p. 5) and goes "to the limit of the constitutionally possible." Nevertheless, the draft law while banning the JCP also reflected the initial ideas [put forward by Oppler] that "any other organization which aims at and engages in or incites to violent action as a means to overthrow the government may be individually designated as an unlawful organization. (articles 3.3, 5 and 7.1 of the GHQ draft law banning the JCP). The extension to such organizations appeared imperative, the Oppler memo insisted, "to comply with the principle of equality before the law established by Article 14 of the Constitution of Japan." (p. 5) It was anticipated that the Japanese organizations that would be affected by this extension would be "ultra-rightist, fascists and ultra-nationalists". In article 1, the preamble, the JCP is depicted as "a clear danger to the continued existence of a democratic society" in Japan and also those "at the opposite end of the political spectrum...who in the past brought destruction and despair to the Japanese people, [share] in common with the [Japanese] Communist Party [their] aim to overthrow the government by violence and would once in power deprive the people of their fundamental human rights."

Those who were members of unlawful organizations would be ineligible for public service which were defined as all elective positions in the national, prefectural and municipal/local level, government civil service positions, other appointive positions in government, all teachers and educational supervisors, and others with responsibility and influence in enterprises, organizations, foundations or associations funded in whole or in part by public funds. This array of public service positions is extremely similar in words and concept in the government's first three drafts.

– *The JCP is controllable.* The memo's judgment was that "from a domestic Japanese point of view no such danger [from JCP activities] exists" since the JCP has only a small representation in the Diet (35 out of 456 in the House of Representatives in the 1949 election), has no organized and trained shock troops, and the party has been deprived of its leaders by the GHQ purge and silenced by the ban of their publication organs." Thus the actions "under Occupation law" have already been taken and any further actions "in the interest of the safety of our troops and the suppression of red fifth-columnists in the present serious international conflict could more effectively be enacted by the Occupation which is not bound on constitutional limitations but free to order extraordinary and temporary emergency measures." Japanese legislation for this purpose "is not advisable and might become a dangerous precedent for future repressive measures against legitimate opponents to the government."

3. *Japanese Internal Security Laws.* Several prewar criminal and security laws contained stipulations and concepts that appear in the various SAPL drafts: the Peace Preservation Law (Chian Iji-hō) as amended for example contained the preventive detention clause, Peace Police Law (Chian Keisatsu-hō), the 1940 Draft revision of the Criminal Code making both incitement and instigation independent criminal offenses, the 1943 Special Wartime Criminal Code (Senji Keiji Tokubuetsu-hō). A number of these will be discussed in special subsections in this study.

Under the 1900 Chian Keisatsu-hō, for example, all organizations formed to handle "political matters" (seiji 政事 were required to report this fact to the local police department; the name of its principal officer, its address, bylaws and charter must be reported to the police within three days of formation; three hours before all meetings to discuss political matters are held where the public may attend must be reported to the police; the police may, when necessary to maintain public security, attend these meetings, restrict, prohibit or order the disbandment/dispersal of such outdoor meetings or when such meetings are believed to threaten public security; incitement or instigation of crimes may not be done, pending or actual court cases may not be discussed at these meetings. Some of these stipulations have appeared in SAPL drafts. Initially labor union activities and political activities by women were prohibited.

4. *Security Laws in Other Countries.* In the Oppler memo mention is made of the Australian law of 1950 to ban the Communist Party, and the U.S. Internal Security Act of 1950. There was also a lone newspaper clipping in the SCAP/GHQ archives on the enactment of the Australian law and a complete copy of this law. The following brief description of a few salient points from these laws show the similarities of a number of concepts between the early draft of the SAPL and these laws. Seki had studied the laws of these countries and several others including the then Soviet Union.[19]

a. *Australia. The Communist Party Dissolution Act of 1950.* This law, enacted in October 1950, contained a number of ideas similar to those

[19] Some ideas embodied in Soviet laws were similar to those in these drafts, but, in reality, many ideas that appeared in the early drafts came, instead, from the Oppler memo, the 1950 U.S. Internal Security Act and other foreign countries rather than from the Soviet Union. The SIB compiled a report, *Gaikoku no Han-Kyō Rippō* (Anti-Communist legislation in foreign countries, Tokubetsu Shinsa-kyoku *Chōsa Shiryō*, 8/1/51, 115 p.) which included such legislation in the U.S., Australia, Union of South Africa, Portugal, and Switzerland; in another collection of 30 documents compiled by Seki's office *Hoan Kankei Shiryō*, included internal security laws of the Soviet Union, PRC, and six items from Nazi Germany. I read Germany's High Treason Law, PRC's law on counter-revolutionary activity, the former Soviet Union's law on Crimes against the State. The latter two were aimed at individuals and relatively speaking standard except that the Soviet law was more detailed than others in what constituted a crime against the state. The German law included stipulations about publishing, producing, storing documents, phonographic recordings, photographs, or exhibits for the purpose of disseminating these materials for treasonous purposes, and to take actions to bring to a standstill or to withdraw from their designated purposes a railway, postal service, an enterprise, public transportation, public telecommunication installations, electric, water, heat, light, or other vital necessities, agencies, organization, installation

that appeared in Draft 1. As might be expected, the law was vigorously opposed by Australian labor unions (miners, waterside workers, amalgamated engineers, seamen, ironworkers, sheet metal workers, federated clerks, railway workers, and building industrial workers). Members of the Communist Party according to Article 10.1 in the Australian law stipulated that they

> "shall be incapable of holding office" as an employee of the Commonwealth, or an authority of the Commonwealth, of a body corporate being an authority of the Commonwealth, in specified industrial organizations or in a branch of such an industrial organization and
>
> the same Article (10.3) defined "vital industries" as coal mining, iron and steel, engineering, building, transport and power industries or in any other industry which, in the opinion of the Governor-General, is vital to the security and defense of Australia.

Article 5.3 stipulated that "A body of persons...declared to be an unlawful association may, within 28 days after publication of the declaration in the *Gazette*, apply to the High Court to set aside the declaration."

Once an organization has been declared illegal, persons shall not "become, continue to be, or perform any act as, an officer or member of an unlawful association", "contribute or solicit anything as a subscription or otherwise to be used directly or indirectly for the benefit" of this organization, or "in any way take part in any activity...or carry on in the direct or indirect interest of any unlawful association, any activity in which the unlawful association was engaged, or could have engaged" when it was declared illegal. Positions held by persons who shall be incapable of holding certain positions shall by this Act shall become vacant, or that person shall cease to be so employed. Persons who attended a meeting of an illegal association, a branch or a committee, who spoke publicly in advocacy of that association or its objectives, distributed literature of that organization or in advocacy of its objectives, or wrote, issued or published, or caused to be written, issued or published a document in advocacy of the illegal association

---

or objects for maintenance of order and security. All these illegal acts were aimed at individual actions not organizations as in the draft SAPL. In the German law there was one mention of a Federal Constitutional Court holding a party to be unconstitutional but there was no mention of penalizing a specific organization for its illegal political actions.

or its objects, shall be regarded as a member of the illegal organization.

Since the Australian law was declared unconstitutional by a high court in March 1951, it was, according to Seki, of special interest as a reference point in drafting the SAPL.

b. *Union of South Africa. The Internal Security Law of 1950 of the Union of South Africa.* This law banned the communist party. In describing communism it referred to those who aim to establish a despotic form of government, bringing about political, social or economic change through promotion of disorder, unlawful acts, through directions or under the guidance of or in cooperation with any foreign government or foreign international institution. It prohibits those designated as committing unlawful acts from certain kinds of positions, and prohibiting them from conducting certain kinds of activities, and further activities in the banned organizations.

c. *The United States. The Internal Security Act of 1950* (known as the McCarran Act). It was presented to GOJ as a useful reference law which had incidentally been declared constitutional by the U.S. Supreme Court. The U.S. law was framed completely in the context of the threat from and struggle against the worldwide Communist movement and not from any conceivable threat from the ultra-right since these forces, symbolized in Nazi Germany, Fascist Italy and Imperial Japan had been defeated in WWII. This Act required that the AG create a registry of Communist-action and Communist-front organizations, their officers and members and that this information shall be publicly available with some limiting provisions and the creation of a Subversive Activities Control Board. Ironically the idea of "preventive detention" (or segregation) was Title II, Emergency Detention Act of 1950 of the 1950 U.S. Internal Security Act. The emergency detention concept was created in response to an analysis of the world communist movement that certain persons should be detained where "there is reasonable ground to believe [they will] probably commit or conspire with others to commit espionage or sabotage" and that this detention would be "essential to the common defense and to the safety and security of the territory, the people and the Constitution of the United States" and that this detention shall be executed in such a way "as to prevent any interference with the constitutional rights and privileges of any persons..." (Sec 101.14 and 15). Detailed specifications for detaining such persons, issuance of warrants for detention, holding hearings, reports on such detentions by the U.S. AG, etc were also included in the Act.

The Alien Registration Act of 1940 (known as the Smith Act). Seki told me that he considered this Act more seriously. According to Sections 2 and 3 stipulate that it is unlawful for person 1) knowingly or willfully advocate, aid, advise or teach the duty, necessity, desirability, or propriety of overthrowing or destroying any government in the United States by force or violence, or by the assassination of any officer of any such government; 2) with the intent to cause the overthrow or destruction of any government in the United States, to print, publish, edit, issue, circulate, sell, distribute, or publicly display any written or printed matter advocating, advising, or teaching the duty necessity, desirability or proprietary of overthrowing or destroying any government in the United States by force or violence; 3) to organize or help to organize any society, group, or assembly of persons who teach, advocate or encourage the overthrow or destruction of any government in the United States by or violence, or to be or to become a member of, or affiliate with, any such society, or assembly of persons, knowing the purposes there of. Section 3 stipulates that it would be unlawful for any person to attempt to commit, or to conspire to commit, any of the acts prohibited to commit by the provisions of this title.

After studying the internal security laws, Seki concluded that Japan's legal system, in comparison to other countries, was particularly inadequate for this purpose. The internal security situation in the U.S. and the United Kingdom was light (*keibi na mono*) in comparison to Japan in 1950–1952. In contrast, the security situation in Germany and France was more comparable to that in Japan. The central issue in these Western countries was how to protect one's country from destructive activities while, at the same time, protecting human rights. He concluded that each country was establishing new penalties concerning speech, publication, and assembly, i.e., the tendency was to expand the scope when these freedoms may be limited or prohibited when destructive activities are involved. His second conclusion was that when it was necessary "to prevent" the occurrence of destructive activities, these countries had enacted or were enacting laws allowing administrative actions (*gyōsei sochi*)—note that this was the method to be used by the SAPL in controlling organizations—to be taken against organizations conducting destructive activities by disbanding them, confiscating their properties, limiting or prohibiting their public activities, forced expulsion of those destructive elements, preventing their entry into the country, banning them from holding public offices, and excluding them from specified industries. These conclusions conveniently dovetail with the ideas he had incorporated into the SAPL, but he tried to persuade Diet members in the subsequent interpolations that the proposed SAPL was more generous and less onerous than the internal security laws of other countries.[20]

The above examples refer to specific laws of other countries which were consulted in drafting the SAPL but there is another source that was consulted but not mentioned, not documented, and remains unspoken, that which resides in the mind and memory, i.e., Seki's accumulated experience in prosecuting criminal, civil and "thought" cases, and drafting laws for which he was well known and his scholarly interests in the law. As described in a subsection in Chapter 5, a trilogy of laws were enacted during WWII which were described as having the greatest influence on modern Japanese law up to that time. One of them, the special wartime criminal law was concerned with incitement, instigation, plotting and planning criminal offenses that did throw a shadow over the postwar efforts when drafting the SAPL, but it was never mentioned. When this law was raised at the committee hearings, somehow most conveniently it was ignored and its relationship and impact on drafting the SAPL never pursued nor answered by the government. How did these factors impinge on the crafting of the SAPL is not clear, but they cannot be dismissed.

D. *Seki Itaru, the drafter of the SAPL*

The responsibility for drafting the new internal security law was given to Seki Itaru, then Deputy Director of the Special Investigations Bureau (SIB) under the AG, and assisted by Aoyama Haruki. Seki had graduated from the Law Department of the University of Tokyo in 1932; after passing both the administrative and law exams for the government's elite administrative corps he joined the prewar Ministry of Justice in 1932. He became a prosecutor in the *Keiji-kyoku* (Criminal

[20] These comments were derived from Seki's books on the SAPL published in 1952: *Hakai Katsudō Bōshohō Kaisetsu*: 23–30, *Hakai... to sono un'yō*: 21–24, *Chikujō Hakai... no Kaishaku*: 24–30.

Affairs Bureau) in 1934; he became involved with the implementation of the Peace Preservation Law as a "thought prosecutor" (*shisō kenji*) for two years in the late 1930s–early 1940s handling religious cases under the PPL. He was thus well acquainted with the PPL with which the proposed SAPL would be constantly compared. Being the scholar prosecutor that he was, he was thoroughly knowledgeable about all the "thought control" laws of the prewar years. During WWII he was a prosecutor of economic crimes under Japan's wartime economic controls and became known as an expert crafter of legislation. He was educated during the first major wave of Marxism in Japan and shortly after the enactment of the PPL; later, he became well acquainted with Marxist philosophy, Communist Party operations and tactics in prewar Japan. When the war ended in 1945, he was the Deputy Director of the Personnel Division in the Ministry of Justice and in that capacity he became a focal point in discussions with GHQ concerning abolition of the PPL and other internal security laws, and in developing a list of purgees. In the early postwar years, he drafted the Human Rights Protection Law (Jinken Yōgo Iin-hō) and became the Director of the First Division in the Human Rights Protection Bureau in the Ministry of Justice. The SIB was created in late 1947 and he became Deputy Director in August 1950 when it was expanded for the second time; later he became Director of SIB's General Affairs Department which is normally a powerful position in the Japanese bureaucratic hierarchy. The Ministry of Justice was in disarray (*gata-gata*) with the introduction of U.S. ideas in reorganizing the Japanese system of justice, starting with the name of the Ministry which was changed to Attorney General, an Occupation inspired change to make Japan's system more "similar" to that of the U.S. Under the AG were four Directors-General (Chōkan), probably something akin to the Associate AGs in the USG. Seki was under the Director-General for Judicial Administration (Hōmu Gyōsei Chōkan).

Seki, was a soft-spoken, petite gentleman, an unusual career civil servant who had been given a highly sensitive assignment to create a new law to replace the Organizations Control Ordinance, an ordinance created under the auspices of the Occupation, above the Japanese Constitution in issues of authority and constitutionality since these Ordinances stemmed from Occupation directives. This Ordinance would cease to exist when the Occupation ended and Japan regained its independence. The new law would be immediately compared with the notorious prewar Peace Preservation Law (PPL) and which would arouse fears of a revival of the prewar secret police system (Tokubetsu Kōtō Keisatsu, commonly known as Tokkō) couched in or camouflaged by postwar democratic terminology and jargon. He was assigned to create one of the foundation stones of the new internal security arrangements as Japan signed a Peace Treaty with the U.S. and its other wartime allies (but not the Soviet Union) and regained its independence. He was, of course, highly sensitized to the fact that despite the evolving GHQ-GOJ relationship, GHQ could still exert its influence on Japanese legislation, if it decided to do so but, in this case, chose to play a more passive role of adviser and let the Japanese handle the explosive nature of this kind of internal security legislation on the domestic Japanese political scene.

Long before he was given this daunting assignment, he had created a private study group, the Jinken Shisō Kenkyūkai (Human Rights Philosophy Study Group, 1949–1952), to study human rights declarations broadly interpreted in their various manifestations from AD 1200 onwards, from the Magna Carta to the modern period, and in various countries, U.K., U.S., Italy, Germany, Russia (Tsarist and Communist), Norway, Brazil, Switzerland, France, and others. The study group consisted of a Todai professor, a Waseda professor, Tokyo Prosecutor's Office and Jiyū Jinken Kyōkai ([Japan] Association of Human Rights and Freedom) Their findings were published in 1950–1954 in four volumes. Seki subsequently wrote a separate study on human rights, *Kindai Sekai ni okeru Jinken Sengen no Tenkai to sono Riron* (The development and theory of declarations of human rights in the modern period), submitted it to Nihon University in Tokyo and was given a PhD in 1964 based on this study. In 1949 he drafted a bill protecting human rights (Jinken Yōgo Iinkai-hō). Through these studies, he had become well acquainted with the philosophy behind the desire and the need for creating legislation which would respect human rights, especially in the new Japanese political milieu. This study—before there was any inkling that he would be given the task to draft new internal security legislation—placed him presumably in a good position for this responsibility.[21] His experiences as a thought prosecutor, a drafter of

[21] This five-volume series was known as the *Jinken Shisō Kenkyū Sōsho* (Series on Research of Human Rights Philosophy), published by Ganshōdō, Tokyo. The study group consisted of Professors Kawashima Takenori (Univ of Tokyo), Iizuka Kōji (Univ of Tokyo), Kanō Michitaka (Waseda Univ), Yagi Shinji (Dir First Div, Human Rights Protection Bureau/AG), Fukushima Masao (Dir, Materials Div/AG), Yama-

legislation, his legal publications, his acquaintance and familiarity with the PPL, the 1941–42 Special Wartime Criminal Law, the 1940 abortive revision of the Criminal Code all form part of the unfathomable and unmentioned "roots" of his thinking that evolved into the SAPL.

He also published a number on books on economic labor crimes, human rights and other issues. But perhaps his real joy was to compose Japanese poetry, in the main *tanka* with 31 syllables, more than 30,000 over many decades; he had published one book of his poetry, *Tabiji*.[22] He was indeed a dedicated career civil servant of the old school, a scholar and a poet, an unusual combination indeed.[23]

---

moto Yoshimori (Dir, Second DivAG), Takahashi Tadao (Dir, Third Div, Human Rights Protection Bureau/AG), Inada Shingo (Prosecutor, Tokyo District Procurator's Office), Nishizuka Shizuko (AG, Civil Affairs Bureau), Ōmuro Ryōichi (AG, Dir, Human Rights Protection Bureau), Morikawa Kintō (Jiyū Jinken Kyōkai, Association for Human Rights and Freedom). Vol. 1, U.S., and U.K., 1950, 180 p.; 2, France, Switzerland, 1954, 152 p.; Germany, Soviet Union, Italy, 1952, 238 p.; 4, Collection of human rights declarations, by various countries, international agreements, 1954, 327 p.; 5, Seki's PhD dissertation which was published first in 1960 (560 p.) and later as volume five in 1965 with no changes, 354 p., Keisō Shobō, Tokyo.

[22] Seki Itaru pointed out to me nine *tanka* from his anthology, *Tabiji* (The roads traveled, Nikkan Rōdō Tsūshinsha, 1961, 487 p.), about his travails and joys in working on the creation and enactment of the *Habōhō*. They are:

1. Preoccupied with drafting the Habōhō
   The peace treaty is created
   This day, this hour.

2. Drafting the Habōhō these nine months
   My heart/spirit pummeled
   Long have I traveled.

3. Morning, every morning, alas
   The newspapers voice their
   Opposition to the Haboho

4. Resting my weary self,
   Reflect on the day's
   Diet deliberations.

5. A solitary quiet evening,
   Pondering, devising
   Diet deliberations.

6. The legal affairs committee
   Worked on for a year and a half
   now facing the grand finale.

7. Though hopeful for the Plenary session
   [in the House of Councilors]
   Defeat in Committee
   Loneliness!

8. The bill passed,
   Ah, the heavy weight off my shoulders.

9. A year and a half of repeated difficulties,
   At last a judgment rendered
   Ah, an inexpressible moment.

[23] He was thus described by former Major Ed Jay, GS/GHQ, who was the last Occupation Official to work on the Habōhō, in an interview with me in 1978. Seki's books are as follows: Keizai *Hanzai Gaisetsu* (Outline on Economic Crimes), *Rōdō Keihō Gairon* (Outline on Labor Criminal Law), *Hanzai Sōsa to Jinken Shimpan no Genkai* (The limitations on investigation of criminal acts and human rights), *Jinken Sengen Konjaku Monogatari* (Story about Human Rights, past and present), and several books on the SAPL after it was enacted into law. After the Human Rights Protection Law (Jinken Yōgo Iin-hō) was implemented he wrote a book, *Jinken Yōgo Iin-hō Shakugi*

E. *Evolving Anxieties about Internal Security*

As the attempted Communist disruption to internal stability seemed to the conservative Yoshida government to be on the upswing in 1949–1951, reports of the government's concern began to appear in the newspapers. In the beginning they were relatively low key, precautionary statements but as the months slipped by, the Korean War had begun in mid-1950 with great intensity, and violent activities increased, the tone of precaution began to sound more urgent. For example, a consultative committee of Ministers and government officials concerned with internal security which met on June 11, 1950—just prior to the outbreak of the Korean War—to assess the situation decided that the main emphasis would be placed on maintaining security in the Tokyo area and gradually expand the focus to the local areas, revise the Tokyo-to *Kōan jōrei* and the distribution and allocation of police power in order to cope with a possible national emergency (*hijō jitai*) and strengthen the enforcement and use of existing laws in controlling Communist activities.[24] The Kokkei Headquarters issued a policy of increased preparedness and surveillance to handle "special crimes" (*tokushu hanzai*) to its units throughout the country in light of the worsening labor disputes, increased theft of weapons, attacks against financial institutions where groups (*shūdan jiken*) were involved.[25] The Procurator General (Kenji Sōchō) issued an instruction (*kunji*) asserting that the activities of undesirable elements (*fuon bunshi no an'yaku*) would increase in light of the sudden changes in the Korean War and that the armed Communist struggle against the government (*kenryoku tōsō*) will change from occasional incidents to publicly more

(Legal Treatise on the Human Rights Protection Law) in 1949 (Shin-Keisatsusha, 138 p.). Again, after the enactment of the SAPL in July 1952, he became in succession Director of the SIB General Affairs Bureau, Deputy Director of the SIB, a prosecutor in the Procurator General's office (Saikōken) in 1958, and Department Director (Buchō) of General Affairs in the Procurator General's Office in 1966 and retired that same year. In 1973 he was awarded the 2nd Class of the Order of the Sacred Treasure.In retirement, he led an active life in teaching law at Chūō Gakuin Daigaku and continuing his prolific poetic life. He was born in Nagano Prefecture in 1903, married with two children (son and daughter). He died in 2001 at age 98.

[24] The Ministerial group was called the Chian Kankei Kakuryō Kondankai consisting of Okazaki Katsuo Chief Cabinet Secretary, AG Ueda Shunkichi, LM Suzuki Masafumi, Higai Senzō, Saitō National Police Reserve (Kokkei), Tsuji Chairman National Public Security Examination Commission, Obata Chairman Tokyo-to Public Security Examination Commission, Hara Tokyo Metropolitan Police. 6/11/1950.

[25] *Asahi* 7/8/1950.

violent revolutionary activities.[26] AG Ōhashi during January 1951 made a number of comments about internal security: by about April 1951, the National Police Reserve created in July 1950 would have a strength of about 75,000 and will be sufficiently mobile to respond to incidents anywhere in Japan. Although the JCP was gradually shifting from its passive legal activities to violent illegal activities (armed struggle, *buryoku tōsō*), there were no government plans to declare the JCP illegal but that would remain a topic for future consideration, the forceable return of undesirable Koreans to Korea, revision of the 1947–48 police law should be considered, the most important issue facing Japan as it regains independence was the maintenance of internal security, broad national crimes (*kokka hanzai*) requiring a national police that can effectively respond to widespread coordinated criminal actions, the local police forces of small weak municipalities should be abolished and concomitantly the Kokkei should be increased.[27] The last mentioned almost seemingly incidental references to reorganizing the structure of the police forces in a rather fundamental manner was significant.

F. *GHQ-II: Early Twilight, Modified Controls*

i. *May 1, 1951, General Ridgway's statement on modification of SCAP controls over Japan*

Recognizing that circumstances were changing in Japan's status, SCAP Lt. General Matthew B. Ridgway issued a statement on May 1, 1951 in connection with the observances to be held to mark the fourth anniversary of the New Japanese Constitution on May 3. Quite aside from flourishes about "growing political maturity which should safeguard and nurture the democratic tradition in Japan" and praises of the "purposeful and peaceful reconstruction of Japan under the new Constitution, the essence of his statement was that the Japanese government had been authorized to review the ordinances it issued during the past five years to implement occupation orders and the progressive resumption

[26] *Yūkan Chūgai* 1/19/1951.

[27] *Sankei* 1/5/1951, *Asahi* 1/8/1951 and 1/8/1951, *Jiji* 1/1/0/1951, *Yūkan Chūgai* 1/19/1951.

by Japan of authority to manage her national affairs. It was assumed that "the existing policy of relaxing occupation controls in proportion to the Japanese Government's ability to discharge corresponding responsibilities will be progressively implemented.... Transition to full autonomy will thus be smoothly bridged." The Department of Army in a message (DA-85524 of 10/31/1951) endorsed this change of emphasis from a supervisory to an advisory role. This "review" was understood to include wholesale de-purging of persons—about 182,000—barred from holding public offices since 1946 under early Occupation policy, and many of the laws issued by the GOJ in accordance with SCAP directives. This review would naturally include a review of the internal security apparatus. This new development well describes the evolving ambiguous relationship between the GS/GHQ and the Japanese Government, at least in regard to its role in and impact on the drafting process of "The Subversive Activities Prevention Law".

ii. *GS Rizzo-AG Ōhashi meetings*

The first meeting between GS (Rizzo) and the then Attorney General Ōhashi about the security law was held on June 23, 1951 at the request of the AG. That was just a month after the completion of the first draft (5/25/51) by Seki. A copy of the first SAPL draft either in English or Japanese was not found in the U.S. archives but a copy of draft 2 was found in the Archives. There was no indication that the discussion centered around a particular draft. On the contrary, AG Ōhashi reported that draft legislation—presumably draft 1—had been given to PM Yoshida who wanted time to study the proposal and went on a tour of Kansai. Ōhashi opined that probably Yoshida postponed his decision because he was also concerned with the administrative reorganization of public security agencies—Maritime Safety Board, National Rural Police, National Police Reserve, Fireman's Organizations, and the Special Investigations Bureau(SIB)—possibly under one ministry. There appeared no concern that this first draft had not also been shared with Rizzo, his staff or with GHQ in general. The AG commented that the unification of the SIB and the police would be "identical to the re-creation of the former Tokkō Police [secret police] setup which resulted in evil deeds and atrocities." The AG assured Rizzo in response to the latter's query that the draft would pass the constitutionality test and "encompasses SCAPINS 548 and 550, letters of SCAP, as well as providing for emergency situations and believes that it is comprehensive in nature. Since there was as yet no definite plan, Rizzo gave Ōhashi some "general advice"—also described as basic principles—for future consideration as the drafting process evolved:

a. He likened the unification of security agencies to Gilbert and Sullivan's, *The Mikado* where Chief High Procurator, Chief Justice, and Lord High Executioner were rolled into one person. If these state functions are not kept separate "a police state will have been created in Japan."
b. the AG and the police must be separated.
c. local public entities must be permitted to exercise police functions separate from a centralized authority.
d. the special function of the National Police Reserve must be kept separate and distinct from the ordinary police.

When the AG assured Rizzo that he would do his best but that "he wasn't too strong in his official position", Rizzo somewhat admonished him that "you are the supreme legal advisor to the Prime Minister, the Ministers, the Government and to the Diet. You must dutifully fulfill such duties and others should respect your position as supreme legal adviser established by the Constitution." This apparent lack of confidence in himself is an aspect of AG Ōhashi which was, of course, not reported in the press. It stands in contrast to his later conduct in the train interview and persistent determination to keep involved in the controversy on the future organization of Japan's internal security apparatus in preparation for the post-Occupation, Peace Treaty era; perhaps Rizzo's encouragement gave him strength and the necessary nerve—which later landed him in political trouble.

Two drafts later, Seki, the drafter, reported to GS that a new draft will be available in 2 or 3 days and would contain some changes to "soften up" the law; in reality this must be a reference to the 5th draft of October 20, 1951 which radically changed the legal underpinnings of the SAPL drafts.[28]

G. *Creation of a Cabinet Ordinance Consultative Committee*

Taking the queue from the aforementioned General Ridgway's statement, Prime Minister Yoshida promptly appointed a private informal

[28] Memo (10/11/1951) for Chief, Government Section, Briefing Notes: Public Administration. 1 p.

consultative committee reporting directly to the P.M. on what to do with the "vast array of laws" stemming from the Occupation. This committee had a broad political mandate "to discuss the questions on hand informally and from an absolutely free and untrammeled standpoint" and met for the first time on May 14, 1951; it was an influential extralegal consultative group without even an official name. According to Yoshida's memoirs, it met periodically until Japan regained independence in Spring 1952 and did "much good work in releasing persons who had been purged from public life" and "proved itself of great value in the framing of laws preparatory to the coming into effect of the peace treaty." In the beginning it focused on de-purging wartime leaders, revisions of various laws on economic concentration, the dissolution of the zaibatsu, labor laws and administrative reform. The revision of the Organizations Control Law was one of these laws. This group appears to have supported the concept of appointing a minister to coordinate internal security policies without legal authority to manage directly any of those agencies, i.e., National and Local Police, Maritime Safety Board and over the Attorney General.[29]

H. *The Liberal Party's Self-Defense and Public Security Investigation Committee*

In response to these looming problems, the Liberal Party also created toward the end of June 1951 a policy coordinating group, the Jiei Chian Chōsakai (Self-Defense and Public Security Investigation Committee). It consisted of Diet members and others from outside the party with a mandate to revise the Diet law to create a new standing committee and to carry out the following agenda.[30] In late May the governing

[29] Yoshida Shigeru, *Yoshida Memoirs*, pp. 46–47, Houghton Mifflin Co, 1962. The committee itself did not have a specific name; the media gave it a name: *Seirei Shimon Iinkai* (Cabinet Ordinances Consultative Committee which will be used in this study). It's members were Kimura Tokutarō (former Minister of Justice and AG in late 1951), Nakayama Ichirō (President, Hitotsubashi Univ), Obama Toshie (Adviser, Nihon Keizai Shimbun), Ishizaka Taizō (President, Toshiba Corp), Itakura Takuzō (Media), Hara Yasusaburō (President, Nihon Kayaku/Chemical Company), Tanaka Jirō (Professor, Univ of Tokyo), Ishibashi Tanzan (President, Oriental Economist, Tōyō Keizai Shimpō, joined the Committee July 3, 1951).

[30] *Asahi Shimbun* eve ed (5/27/51), *Tokyo Shimbun* (9/14/51). This Committee was composed of 30 members of the Liberal Party from the House of Representatives and 10 from the House of Councilors. The chairman was Uyehara Etsujirō (House of

Liberal Party had prepared a program outline *(yōkō)* on policies for self-defense and internal security:

a. create a standing committee in the Diet on national security *(kokka anzen)* to oversee the National Police (Kokkei), Local Police (Jikei), the SIB, Maritime Safety Board (Kaijō Hoanchō [coast guard]), immigration office, National Police Reserve
b. appoint a Minister of State who would be responsible for overseeing self-defense and internal security, the same areas as for #1
c. create a national security investigation administration under the Prime Minister headed by the Minister mentioned in #2 above
d. The chairmanship of the National Public Security Commission (kokka kōan iinkai) will be jointly held by the Minister in #2 above
e. The criminal procedure and other laws would be revised, the Organizations Control Law would be abolished and a new national internal security law (Kokka Anzen Hoshō-hō, implying the SAPL) created.

Neither of these committees had a legal status in any governmental structure but played an informal and influential policymaking role. I have found occasional references to them in newspapers briefly reporting on their deliberations. Thus, there were now two committees outside the normal governmental structure, one a private advisory group to the Prime Minister and the other a committee in the governing party structure in the Diet. These two groups significantly influenced in various ways how the SAPL would be structured on some important aspects of defining political organizations, illegal activities and on the limitations and penalties on the affected organizations. So far, I have not found any integrated essay on their roles in the political process.

In contrast, AG Ōhashi had different ideas: to establish a new Ministry of Internal Security would give the impression of re-creating the Keiho-kyoku (Police Bureau) of the defunct Ministry of Home Affairs abolished in Fall 1945; the SIB and the Immigration Administration would be placed under the AG; the Maritime Safety Board would be placed together with the National Police Reserve under one Ministry, Ministry of Defense. He also disclosed that he planned to submit to the Extraordinary Session of the Diet in October 1951 a bill on internal security which had already been cleared with GHQ on August 29, 1951 for the creation of a Public Security Assurance Commission (Kokka

Representatives, Nagano). The vice-chairs were Ikeda Seinosuke, Nishimura Naomi, and Takahashi Shintarō. As per the usual, only about a third of this membership attended committee meetings. Nishimura Naomi was reported to be one of the more active members.

Anzen Hoshō Iinkai) and would be placed under the AG and this Commission's jurisdiction, a press code, an anti-espionage law and a law to prohibit general strikes all of which the AG said were in the process of being drafted and promised to define more clearly what organizations would be banned and under what conditions persons could be purged. He expected to obtain the budget and Diet approval for elevating the SIB to an Agency (PSIA) and increasing SIB personnel from 1200 to 3000, even to as high as 5500 in the immediate future.[31]

I. *Ōhashi Press Interviews, September 1951*

Against this backdrop and as a trial balloon, as a political flanking operation in the intra-governmental debate concerning the future realignment of the internal security laws and governmental security structure including the police, AG Ōhashi held press interviews on September 17 and 28, 1951. He explained that the government was re-organizing the various security laws from the Occupation period into one or more laws, including lessons that could be learned from the internal security laws of several foreign countries. He proposed several laws, a revised Organizations Control Law (including the creation of a Public Security Examination Commission, an enlarged and elevated Special Investigations Agency), a law for the disposition of assets of disbanded organizations and a Press Code. In addition to revising above law, it also became clear about this time, Fall 1951, that the government, i.e., principally the AG under Ōhashi entertained serious thoughts of drafting and submitting several other internal security related laws, a law to control assertive mass movements and demonstrations (Shūdan Ji'i Undō tō no todoke-ide ni kansuru Hōritsuan) and a law to prohibit general strikes (Zenesuto Kinshi Hōan, or Sōgi Kōi no Ran'yō o Bōshi-suru Hōritsuan). It should be pointed out that the drafting process had been basically limited to within the AG's office, specifically the SIB, i.e., it had not been formally vetted, coordinated within the government and there were bureaucratic, functional, political forces and interests that would impinge upon these highly controversial draft

[31] *Mainichi Shimbun* (6/25/51, 9/6/1951), *Asahi Shimbun* (5/27/1951 Eve, 8/30/51), *Shakai Shimbun* (9/5/51), *Tokyo Shimbun* (9/17/51).

ideas. That Ōhashi had chosen "to sound off", so to speak, had repercussions later as the SAPL draft had to be presented to various levels of the government and senior Liberal party leaders and committees for their support and approval.

The SAPL Program Outline dated September 28, 1951, which was used for the second interview, emphasized in the opening paragraph the importance of creating an internal security law which would not contravene Constitutional rights, which must limit any freedom to the least extent possible consistent with the public welfare (*kōkyō no fukushi*) and would create procedures to be followed by government officials in this area which are democratic and would not violate the various rights in the Constitution—the very often repeated mantra in those days of the Occupation but, of course, none of the critics and opposition believed these pious statements of the survivors from the prewar internal security apparatus. It outlined the types of activities which would be illegal and the restrictions of various types including disbandment which could be placed upon the organizations and prohibiting persons violating these stipulations as described above in holding a broad range of public offices, and lastly the emergency segregation (or detention) of those persons who had committed these violations or who might commit these violations during a national emergency declared by the Cabinet. He insisted that public security cannot be maintained if we only wait until certain violations actually take place and emphasized that organizations and persons who had been so restricted may always appeal to the courts up to the Supreme Court.[32] In defining what constitutes anti-democratic activities, Ōhashi referred in his September testimony to article 2 of the 1949 Organizations Control Law specifying that to propagandize and incite (*sendō*) actions to destroy the Constitution, or to search for and collect secret information about foreign military forces legally stationed in Japan or Japanese national secrets would be an illegal activity. Those organizations which committed such acts would be disbanded, and individuals could be banned from holding certain positions and would be held responsible under the criminal code. Ohashi said the system for political organizations to report should be continued.

[32] This is known as the "*sanshin-sei*", the system of three judgments, from District Court, Higher District Court, Supreme Court.

The Press Code. As mentioned above, one of the several pieces forming the mosaic for internal security was the Occupation mandated Press Code. This was a reference to a set of rules, titled "Press Code for Japan" issued on 9/18/1945 in the early days of the Occupation to govern the Japanese media. Japan shall have Freedom of the Press but... understandably criticism of the Occupying Allied Powers, troop movements or any comments that might invite mistrust or resentment of these troops shall be prohibited. Otherwise, the Japanese media shall be free but

- must adhere strictly to the truth
- nothing shall be printed which might, directly or by reference, disturb the public tranquility
- news stories shall not be colored to conform with any propaganda line
- minor details of a news story must not be over emphasized to stress or develop any propaganda line
- no news story shall be distorted by the omission of pertinent facts or details
- in the make-up of the newspaper no news story shall be given undue prominence for shall be given undue prominence for the purposes of establishing or developing any propaganda line.

This, of course, is what is taught in Journalism 101 as cardinal principles of good journalism. But when put into a code and enforced by the government it would rival the prewar control and censorship of the media by the Imperial Government. These rules were issued understandably by the extra-Constitutional authority of SCAP for a military occupation. If literally enforced by the Occupation's censorship staff, it would have created a highly distorted so-called Freedom of the Press. Since the Occupation authorities had now tilted toward supporting the Japanese conservative old-guard for U.S.'s geopolitical purposes, and since the conservative leadership stemmed from the prewar era and it would be convenient and the conservatives would not be averse to having some kind of control over the Press and media, it would be an understandable and a useful ploy to include a Press Code in the internal security "package". Perhaps the idea of a Press Code was put forward seriously, perhaps as a trial balloon, perhaps with the attitude of "At least try it", perhaps because it was acceptable under the Occupation, it could be acceptable in post-treaty Japan. Whatever the motive, it was clearly indicative and symbolic of the thinking, strained expectations of the conservative government leadership. Immediately, the Japanese press opposed this "trial balloon"; when the government suggested that the Japan Newspaper Association itself draft a press code, its overtures were politely but firmly rejected. Nevertheless, the notion of a press code gradually faded away; perhaps, as some feared, attempts would be made to achieve the same objectives through the enforcement of the SAPL.[33]

The Draft Law to Control Mass Demonstrations. The idea behind the proposed law to control mass demonstrations was to unify in a national law the various public security maintenance regulations (*kōan jōrei*) adopted by many towns, cities and prefectures during the heyday of dispersed self-government encouraged by the Occupation, and to codify the 6/10/1951 instruction/directive (*shirei*) issued by the Occupation to the GOJ concerning the control of mass demonstrations. In this case, the conservative Yoshida government and the security apparatus were only too pleased to oblige. A draft law of 11 articles and 4 supplementary articles) was prepared. All organizers of mass demonstrations must report their plans (*todoke-ide*) at least 48 hours before the event to the local Public Security Commission (Kōan Iinkai). The latter may, depending upon traffic considerations, security and danger factors prohibit, revise the routing, time and date of such demonstrations. If the assembly (*shūkai*) violated the legal stipulations, the police may warn, stop or order the dispersal of the assembly and the police may enter (*tachi-iru*) the assembly.

The Conceptual General Strike Prohibition Law. This concept never, it appears, went beyond a program outline (*yōkō*), i.e. the idea did not reach the drafting stage in Fall 1951. It evolved into a proposal to prevent the abuse of dispute actions/strikes (*sōgi kōi*) against key industries (*kikan sangyō*), such as gas, electricity, transportation, communications, water supplies, public hygiene, banks, coal mining, which would affect the everyday life of the people, cause great confusion among the people, adversely affect the economic recovery and cause irreparable damage to the national economy. The PM may, if he believes such a possibility or probability exists, after consulting with

[33] There was one foreign news report on this issue: *New York Times*, 9/18/1951. It was probably the only notice taken by the foreign press about the legislative battle over the enactment of a new internal security law. It reported with substantial and legitimate concern about the AG's idea of a press code. Such a press code "would be a formidable weapon in the hands of any civilian government" and concluded that "It is no secret that the development has left a bitter taste in the mouths of the Japanese who believed that the Yoshida regime would uphold the major liberal measures introduced by the occupation."

a special committee, request the Higher District of Tokyo to order such strikes not be carried our for at least 60 days (reminiscent of the 50-day "cooling off" period under the post-1945 U.S. Taft labor law) if this court agreed there is justification for such preventive action. An appeal to a higher court may be made against this decision but the Higher District Court's decision will stand until the issue is resolved—this concept would later have the same effect when the PSEC under the SAPL made a decision which could be appealed. The legalization of this concept was delayed until later and was incorporated into a revised law in 1953 (#171).

This package of laws triggered clear, forthright, strong and determined criticism and opposition from the media, academia, labor unions and even within the government itself, e.g. the Ministry of Labor was not supporting a general strike prohibition law, corporate management was also lukewarm. While the felt need for preparing new internal security laws to fill the vacuum in the eyes of the government created by the Occupation in 1945 can be appreciated, the totality of these proposed laws was too uncomfortably close to the discredited interlocking prewar structural system of broad social control. This "package" when added to already announced plans to revise labor laws under the Occupation understandably convinced the political opposition that the government was trying to re-create—in the eyes of labor and its political supporters a retrogressive revision to the prewar structure by attempting to push through legislation in time for a new post-Peace Treaty era. It was not a specific item or law but a cumulative effect that galvanized the anger, frustration, anxieties, a sense of betrayal of the opposition and also persuaded the government to focus only on the enactment of the SAPL, the symbol of the new internal security structure.

J. *Draft 3*

i. *Draft 3*

Two somewhat truncated drafts 3 (provisional) and 3, dated October 5 and 10, 1951, respectively, were created. (Hereafter referred to collectively as draft 3 unless there is a reason to make a distinction). Why they were created in the first place is not obvious since draft 5 introduced a totally new approach but draft 3 does reflect some changes which should be noted as part of the evolution of the drafting process.

1. *Objectives.* Under the objectives in draft 3 it was stipulated that emergency "segregation" of those who commit illegal acts under a national emergency will be limited to the smallest number possible. We should note that instead of detention, the word "*kakuri*" was used. In light of how they were proposing to carry out this provision, this word in Japanese probably sounds a little softer, less harsh; *kōsoku* gives the impression of forcible physical restraint or incarceration. While indeed these persons would be legally restrained, government officials are specifically admonished to make sure that the facilities for these persons would be such that they would not be injurious to the detainee's health. Thus, the term "*kakuri*" (segregation) gives a less ominous impression even though the end result may be the same.

A fourth objective was added in draft 3 Article 1: in order to maintain public order and security (*kōan no hoji*) and at the same time allow the people's rights to be advocated, and to create (*seibi-suru*) the means for restitution (*kyūsai no michi*) thereby fostering the healthy development of the desire for peace (*heiwa-shugi*) and democracy, democratic procedures will be stipulated. The use of "segregation" and establishment of democratic procedures to carry out this law were an obvious reflection by the drafter to reactions he probably received from within and without the government, perhaps also from GHQ, in response to anticipated criticisms of the law and to guard against the re-emergence of the legacy from the extremely abusive use of police and administrative authority before 1945.

2. *Definitions.* Under definitions (article 3), draft 3 more broadly defined political activities and organizations as those who support candidates at the national, prefectural, local levels and education committees, a new category who stand for election and/or advocate or oppose various policies, principles, or programs as specified by the DG/PSIA.

3. *Public Office.* In draft 3 this category was more systematically presented and basic industries were separately designated in the draft

but for ease of presentation these have been grouped in the following manner:

> All national and local government employees and teachers
> Officers in political parties, and labor related organizations
> Officers and employees in the mass media and in the following designated basic industries, coal mining, water, electricity, electric power and natural gas supply and transportation.

This exceedingly wide definition of "public office" would probably include a large portion of the Japanese people. This expansion of coverage would be reminiscent of the early postwar purge under the Occupation and the subsequent "red purge". In contrast to this highly broadened range of positions, there was one important deletion: those positions for which a candidate for national and local assemblies must be selected based on a public election law. This broadened definition of "public office" and the deletion of all elective positions probably stemmed, it appears, from a discussion held by the AG and the Cabinet Ordinance Consultative Committee in early September 1951. The AG was called upon to reconsider the employment limitation aspects in the draft along the lines of a strengthened "Red Purge" policy—a measure taken earlier by the government and industry to root out and dismiss communists and incidentally those other elements, e.g. active, boisterous assertive unionists.[34] Again on September 29, 1951, interestingly the day after AG Ōhashi's press interview, this same group and the AG and the Deputy Cabinet Secretary General met again to discuss the three pending internal security laws, the Organization Control bill, bill to prohibit general strikes and control of mass demonstrations. Apparently it was agreed that the AG would revise the drafts accordingly, and report back to the Committee when a final draft of the Organization Control bill had been prepared in order to create a unified governmental position.[35]

4. *Application of the Law.* In the two earlier drafts, the application of this law would be executed in such a manner that it would not infringe on rights guaranteed by the Japanese Constitution. While the intent was the same, the equivalent article 2 in draft 3 the language used is weaker since reference to the Constitution has been left out: the appli-

---

[34] *Asahi* 11/25/51 Eve.
[35] *Sankei* 11/30/51.

cation of law must pay special attention (*ryū'i*) to avoid any improper (*futō ni*) violation of the people's rights, any deviation (*itsudatsu)* from the original objectives of the law, or abusively apply (*ran'yō*) the law for other objectives. The latter reference not to apply this law to other objectives, would seem to reflect the drafter's knowledge about how the application of the prewar PPL was greatly expanded beyond its original relatively narrow set of objectives, one of its well known prewar abuses.

5. *Registration.* In the name of "openness" (*kōkai*) of political organizations, all political parties, and political organizations must register with the local governmental authorities where its headquarters are located.

6. *Political Parties.* The representative or principal officer of a political party which has been newly created and transformed from an existing organization must register within 10 days from its creation providing not only such information as name, objective, address of its main office, date of creation, but also the names and addresses of its principal officers, number of members and name of its journal. If there are any changes in the above, or if the party ceases to be a political party this must be reported within ten days to appropriate local authorities.

7. *Political Organizations.* Likewise, they also must provide the same kind of information and also the beginning date of political activity within ten days, or provide this information if they have been designated as a political organization by the DG/PSIA. Journals published by either of the above will also be submitted to the same local authorities within three days of publication, one copy for the local authority and 4 copies for the PSIA.

The local authorities must submit all of the above information to the PSIA and maintain public availability of this information at all times.

8. *Illegal activities* (3.8) are even more broadly defined in draft 3 in eight categories:

a. raise (*okoshi*) aggressive military action against a foreign country, guide (*yūdō*) or support aggressive military action against Japan
b. destroy by violence (*bōryoku*) a government or local governmental/community organizations (*chihō kōkyō dantai*) established under the Constitution of Japan

c. the use of murder/assassination in order to advance or oppose particular principles (*shugi*), policies, destroy and/or damage the facilities of national or local governmental or comparable organizations and those of basic industries resulting in loss of their functions and stoppage (*teishi*) of these functions
d. with the intention of harming the safety (*anzen*) of Japan, destroy and/or damage facilities provided for military purposes for the use of foreign military forces or those under the United Nations, also inflict damage of military [significance], seek out (*tanchi-suru*) or collect military information which had not been publicly disclosed
e. with the intention of harming the safety of Japan, seek out and collect various categories of national secrets as established by the Prime Minister
f. conspire (*kyōbō*), plan (*kuwadateru*), incite (*aoru*), aid, or instigate (*sosonokasu*) to carry out any actions listed in the previous paragraphs
g. as a general practice, show the power of the masses (*tashō no iryoku o shimeshi*), violent actions (*bōkō*), threats (*kyōhaku*) and other violent actions (*bōryoku-teki kōi*) which would damage the public welfare
h. distribution (*rufu*) of lies (*kyogi no jijitsu*) or committing violent actions with the intention of interfering with execution of treaties which Japan has signed and laws under the Japanese Constitution.

This is a wholesale and extraordinarily broadened definition of "illegal actions" which could be used by any government to stifle an extremely wide range of activities.

9. *Control of Illegal Organizations.* Here again, restrictions were broadened, tightened and made more severe. The DG/PSIA:

a. may "order" (*meirei-suru*) an organization, in writing to its principal representative, to provide a report which would throw light on future policies, plans and actions, if the DG believes that there is a fear/concern (*osore*) that this organization would commit illegal actions.[36]
b. may take the following actions to the extent necessary against organizations whose objectives are to commit or which have committed, illegal actions, if the DG believes that these actions would effectively eliminate the illegal aspects of the organization's activities:

[36] In the slightly earlier version of draft 3, the DG/PSIA could "request" (*seikyū-suru*) instead of "order" the preparation of reports. While there would not be too much difference in actual results, a request is softer, not so severe, could theoretically be refused without a penalty but would probably stiffen the government's resolve to take action against that organization.

- may place conditions on date, time and place of assembly and collective action (*shūdan kōi*), e.g. mass demonstrations, or may prohibit such assembly and collective action for a specified period
- may impose necessary conditions on the contents of or prohibit the publication of an organization's journal and/or other publications
- may order the revision of the organization's program outline (*kōryō*), articles of incorporation, bylaws and regulations
- may order the removal of selected personnel
- may order the closure of selected branches, units or other organs of the organization

These actions must be accomplished in writing and the principal officers of the affected organization must be given an opportunity to explain themselves.

10. *PSIA Authority.* Draft 3 would give the DG/PSIA another authority to control especially those organizations which have violated any of the above orders and which are regarded as likely to commit this violation again: in order to prevent this repeated violation, the printing machines used by this organization could be sealed. Eleven articles, 12–22, were devoted to various aspects of this new restrictive process. Only those machines owned by the organization or by a sympathetic third party would be affected. The DG/PSIA must justify this action to the PSEC, and obtain a permit to do so. That permit must specify the name of the organization, names of involved officers, addresses, location of the printing machines, the period during which these machines would be sealed, etc. The officials to carry out the sealing of the machines must be specified, and they must seal these machines between sunrise and sundown; if the work was begun before sundown then it could continue beyond sundown, if necessary, and the officials must produce ID, if requested by the machine owners. If necessary, police assistance may be requested. The owners of the machines may witness the sealing of these machines. The DG/PSIA may break the seal at any time, if he feels it is no longer necessary; the seals must be revoked after one year has elapsed.

If DG/PSIA believes that the various remedial actions described above would not effectively remove the illegal nature of that organization's actions, he may request the PSEC to disband this organization. If the PSEC so designates an organization, then the latter will cease to conduct activities as that organization. If the parties concerned are dissatisfied with the decision, then, within 30 days, it may request the

PSEC to reconsider its action. The PSEC may revoke its action to disband based on its own authority or based on this request. (Articles 23–27)

Articles 51–55 stipulate that the DG/PSIA may request the PSEC to designate certain individuals from holding public office:

a. those who have committed illegal actions
b. those who held the principal positions in organizations whose activities had been prescribed or ordered to disband (article 23 above), those who knew that the purpose of this organization was to commit illegal actions, had committed such acts, and those who, even though they knew that these acts were being carried out, provided large financial aid to this organization. These individuals must leave "the public office" they held within 30 days from the date of that designation, except those in basic industries, and may not hold another such office and may not provide direction or encouragement to others holding such positions. Such designated persons must, within 10 days, submit a photo of themselves to the local authorities which shall so report to the DG/PSIA. This restriction to hold office shall become null and void if and when the restrictive and/or dissolution orders on that organization are lifted. (Article 56) After five years, the DG/PSIA may petition the PSEC, or the affected persons may petition the SIB to make this petition. (Article 57)

11. *Investigative Authority of PSIA Officials.* Although the details about this authority were not included in the truncated drafts, it can be safely assumed that a similar authority would have been included in draft 3.

ii. *Review of Drafts 1–3*

Under the rubric of assuring that political activities will be conducted in "a public and open manner" and to control selected organizations which had committed or whose members and/or officers had committed or might commit illegal activities these drafts threw a potentially gigantic dragnet across the entire political spectrum. Unlike the internal security laws of Australia and the Union of South Africa, the Japanese draft law did not mention communism, the JCP anywhere in the text except that it was clearly and unmistakably understood that the entire rationale and aim for this drafting exercise was to somehow defang, control, render them politically impotent, if not disband—to ban was not used—the JCP, the Communist movement and it's front organizations. In that process it could sweep up any and all forms of political and advocacy groups, from the extreme left, center, extreme right. It would create a large specialized bureaucracy just to oversee the execution of this draft law.

While the drafts, to be even handed and not to appear to be singling out specific political groups, required the registration of "all political organizations" broadly interpreted, the theoretical underlying and controlling philosophy was to control organizations which were violent, secretive, militaristic and undemocratic by declaring them unlawful, disbanding them, controlling their activities in several ways, purging and prohibiting selected members of these organizations from a wide range of public offices as defined in a specialized manner. The drafts also gave the government added authority under a national emergency to arrest and detain those who might conduct illegal activities, i.e. emergency detention/segregation.

While there was a clear-cut admonition stipulating that the "interpretation and application" of the SAPL "must not deviate from and unlawfully (*futō ni,* other translations could be improperly, unjustly, inappropriately) violate (*shingai*) the freedoms of thought, conscience, beliefs, speech, assembly and organization guaranteed by the Constitution of Japan" in drafts 1 and 2, this was somewhat weakened in draft 3 by eliminating the reference to the Constitution. The drafter was sensitive to the restrictive stipulations in these drafts and their obvious intertwining relationship to the various freedoms clearly enunciated in the new constitution. While this concern was excellent and most appropriate, there was substantial concern about the extent to which this injunction would be compromised by the leeway given the implementing agency created to execute this law. There was a clause that stipulated that a "reference person" may not refuse to make a statement even if that statement may be to his disadvantage or to that of his close relatives but that such statements cannot be used against that person or his close relatives in a future criminal case. These were the minimum restrictions and controls on the government agency which would implement such a law. This proposed bill, if manipulated, would be highly susceptible to considerable abuse and its constitutionality under the 1947 Constitution would be highly questionable even under a conservative Japanese Supreme Court.

The architectural structure of these drafts was adopted, adapted, revised from the 1949 Organizations Control Ordinance, and from the Oppler memo and attached experimental draft law to ban the JCP (and incidentally other similar organizations) and ideas adapted from selected foreign internal security laws.

The concerns in putting together a new internal security law centered in these drafts on trying to define what kinds of activities should be covered and what activities should be defined as illegal and what kinds of controls should be imposed on organizations and individuals who violated this law and what kind of authorities should be given to the PSIA to carry out the law. While the drafter was concerned with procedural safeguards, his critics appear to have been more concerned with the former issues. The drafts were a mosaic; they were stitched together from various sources with other legal requirements for it to constitute a draft law gluing the entire adaptation into an integrated whole. While one ordinance was Occupation inspired, the others were the thoughts of a staff member of the legal section of GHQ which were privately circulated on an FYI basis (*go-sankō no tame ni*), I am sure, to the SIB, and other foreign laws. Seki adamantly maintained, however, in meetings with me over the years, that he was solely responsible for the many drafts. Nevertheless, while the normal bureaucratic procedures were not followed in drafting and clearing a draft law, it does appear that starting in September 1951 high level Liberal Party officials made their ideas known and probably provided "the guidance" that elected officials as a group should not be listed as one of the categories from which violators of the law could be excluded, i.e. a person who violated this law could not be prevented from standing for public election at the national or local levels. This became the first retreat of many in drafting this bill. In these same meetings he also opined that "illegal organizations" could have been so broadly interpreted that the proposed law could even potentially engulf the Japanese social democrats and the ultra-rightwing nationalist groups. The implementation and interpretation of the draft could become more encompassing than the prewar PPL; a fearful law had been proposed (*osoroshii mono*). It was also abundantly clear that the media voiced strong criticisms and anxieties about the proposed law especially in light of the prewar history of the implementation of the PPL. Seki as a former thought prosecutor though only for two years during the Pacific War when national security concerns were at a fever pitch must have been extremely well aware of this history. This rather personal anxiety quietly and silently harbored by Seki as he drafted the new law must have caused him to reflect on an alternative to these drafts especially in light of the various criticisms of the draft as revealed in the Program Outline of September 28, 1951.

K. *Drafts 5 and 6*

Based on the barrage of criticism and skepticism in and out of the government described above, the AG and his staff had to retreat, rethink and revamp the draft bill. The bill was drastically revised by October 20, 1951 (as draft 5) and only a week later on October 27, 1951 (as draft 6)—an incredible speed considering that the basic concept in defining illegal activities under the proposed law had been completely re-oriented in the new drafts. Almost semi-simultaneously, the AG had to respond to interpolations and challenges in the Legal Affairs Committee of the Diet and to the two other committees which had become involved in providing "guidance" as described earlier. A number of relatively important revisions were incorporated into the draft law and resulted in an un-numbered draft of December 22, 1951.

Faced with these difficulties, criticisms and challenges Seki retired to an SIB retreat for some days to completely re-think how the draft bill could be reconfigured.

> I lay on the tatami floor, recounted Seki, and studied the knots in the pine wood ceiling for quite a while and came upon a potential solution on how to define 'illegal activities': reference by inclusion of certain provisions of the Criminal Code and an augmented interpretation (*hosei*) of these clauses.

1. *New Definition of Illegal Activities* (Draft 6. Article 3). A fundamental change took place in draft 5 (and 6) in the basis for defining "illegal activities" from the broad array selected from mainly Occupation-era ordinances to the Criminal Code (CC). It is aimed at individuals; through this revision the Criminal Code by reference would be used for taking action against organizations: a "Dantai Keihō", a Criminal Code for Organizations was thus created. After having achieved this "breakthrough" in stabilizing and clarifying this conceptual framework (*gainen kitei ga meikaku ni natta*) "I was able to relax to some

extent since we had at last conceptualized an acceptable formula", said Seki.[37]

Illegal activities described in Article 3.7 could be presented in the following manner:[38]

a. Actions infringing on specific articles in the Criminal Code: 77 (insurrection), 81 (inducement of foreign aggression, 82 (assisting the enemy), 93 (preparations and plots for private war).
b. Actions taken as a means to push forward (*suishin*), support or oppose political principles, policies and programs (*seiji-jō no shugi mata wa shisaku*) which infringe on articles 106 (riots) and 199 (homicide) or actions which result in damage and destruction of important facilities of national or local or other corresponding governmental facilities and the damage or actions resulting in the damage and destruction of important facilities of designated industries (described later) actions which would infringe on other codes with punishable actions.
c. Actions taken in support of the above articles by plotting, by planning, by plotting and planning to aid, instigate, incite or plan to incite, or advocate the rationality of the actions with the intention of contributing to their realization.
d. Actions which would, as a matter of regular practice, show the force of mass [demonstrations], resulting in homicide (199), violence (208), intimidations (222) or in damaging and destroying objects in general (260, 261).[39]

The above is not merely a substantially enlarged definition of "illegal activities" but also included many kinds and permutations of activities which could lead to insurrection, foreign invasions, riots, etc, etc. PM Yoshida in his memoirs immediately after commenting on the difficul-

[37] Since a "CC for organizations" had been created, I tried in vain to find some journal articles on political crimes committed by organizations; I only found articles on criminal capacity of legal persons (*hōjin*) such as Hōjin no Hanzai Nōryoku to Hōjin Shobatsu, *Jurisuto-Zōkan* 1984:21–22 and Hōjin no Hanzai Nōryoku, *Keihō Sōron* by Nomura Minoru. Seirin Shoin. 1993. 401 p. 60. This is due to the fact that under the SAPL no organization has been successfully charged with a violation of this law, thus no imperative to discuss and analyze the concept of a CC for organizations.

[38] Draft 6 is cited here because it was a later version of draft 5 and presumably reflected further thought on the issue. Art 78 (preparatory planning, insurrection), 79 and 88 (preparatory plotting to induce foreign aggression) were not included in draft 6.

[39] Thomas L. Blakemore's translation of the Japanese Criminal Code have been used in this study, *The Criminal Code of Japan*, as amended in 1947, Tokyo. Nippon Hyōronsha. 1950. 186 p. Translations of articles in this Code cited in this study can be found in Appendix 6.

ties in outlawing the JCP and Communism as a political philosophy states that:

> ...destructive/subversive activities *especially* (*shikamo*) *those taken as a means to achieve political objectives* [emphasis added] must be targeted for control (*torishimari no taishō*). Furthermore, those actions taken to achieve political objectives are not limited to communists but also includes political violence by both extreme leftists and rightists which must, therefore, be the target of control (*Kaisō Jūnen* v.2:291).

With such a wide-ranging authority any particular government's attitude toward the labor movement, labor unions, many labor union activities could easily be construed to infringe on one or a number of combinations of the above, especially when one considers the various types of aiding and abetting phrases.

2. *Controlling Organizations.* Because the method of controlling organizations and individuals was substantially revised in articles 10 and 11, the definition of "public office" (*kōshoku*) was deleted in this draft as a separate category. According to article 11, the PSEC may take any of the following measures against organizations which have as their objectives to conduct illegal activities or which may already have conducted illegal activities:

a. *Against Organizations*

1. May attach necessary conditions on the time and place where assemblies and mass organizational activities (*shūdan kōi*) may be held and may also prohibit such activities for a specified period
2. May impose necessary conditions on their journals and other publications, or prohibit the publication of these materials for a specified period.
3. May order the revision of the program (*kōryō*), bylaws, and regulations of those organizations.
4. May order the removal of specified personnel from a certain range of specified positions.
5. May order the closure (*heisa*) of specified branches and sub-branches and other elements of the organization.

These orders and actions must be taken by the PSEC within its purview of activities and based on a request from the DG/PSIA.

b. *Against Individuals.* Under article 38, the PSEC may take actions to limit the employment of the following categories of persons:

1. Those who have committed illegal activities
2. Those who are the principal officers of organizations so specified in article 11.1 above, who knew that these activities were carried out or were being carried out or those who made substantial financial contributions to these organizations
3. Similarly for persons in organizations which had been ordered disbanded
4. Persons who have been designated as above must vacate their positions within 30 days if those positions are in one of the following categories. However, the PSEC may, if it deems it to be appropriate, exempt those so designated if that person is
   - a public service employee of a national or local governmental organization
   - an officer of a labor union
   - an employee or officer of a designated enterprise described below

This exemption was included in order to avoid unnecessary disruption to economic recovery which was, at that time, a major consideration and this concern does occasionally re-appear in subsequent drafts. Also note that a similar exemption was given to either government employees or to labor union officers. They were more dispensable than those in industrial production. In light of the government's attitude toward these restrictions and exemptions they were well aware of the potential impact these restrictions could have on the labor movement.

c. *Objectives (Art 1).* Emergency detention/segregation included in drafts 1–3 was deleted leaving openness of political organizations, controlling organizations which conduct violent illegal activities—instead of undemocratic illegal activities as in draft 5—and the establishment of democratic procedures to provide for advocacy of the people's rights and to create (*seibi*) the mechanism for relief to achieve these rights.

d. *Designated Industries (Art 3.6).* Earlier this category was called "basic industries" and included only a few industries but had now been renamed and expanded to cover a broad range of industries.

1. Public interest industrial enterprises (*kōeki jigyō dantai*). The following industries were declared vital to the daily livelihood of the people as specified in article 8.1 of the 1946 labor adjustment law (Rōdō Kankei Chōsei-hō): transportation, postal, electrical communications, water, electricity and gas supply, medical services and public health.
2. The second group included newspapers, communications and broadcasting, coal and metal mining, steel manufacturing, shipbuilding,

machine industry, banking, chemicals, automobiles, electrical products and
3. industries specified by the AG (rather than the DG/PSIA) and approved by the Diet.

e. *Investigative Authority.* The same authority as in drafts 2 and 3 to inspect, search and seize provided a court judge's approval was obtained prior to taking these actions.

The Nihon Keieisha Remmei (Association of Japanese Management) met in Osaka on December 1, 1951. The Presidents from Sanki Yawata Steel Manufacturing Co, Chichibu Cement Co, Nisshinbō Textile Co, Azabu Dōkōgyō all from the Tokyo/Kanto area; from Kansai came the Presidents from Kansai Electric Power Co, Kankei Kyōkai, Shimazu Manufacturing, Yuasa Chikudenchi (Battery) Co, a total of about 50. This management group opposed the preparation of a general strike prohibition law for three reasons: labor disputes should be handled within the labor laws and the proposed law, labor relations and public security are two separate issues and to create one law trying to cover both would only blur the meaning and image of the labor laws, and enacting and using the general strike prevention law would only invite the description that this law is a law to suppress labor disputes and invite also considerable misunderstanding in the labor movement. At the November 30, 1951 meeting of the Cabinet Ordinances Consultative Committee, the AG was given the assignment to draft this proposed law but also told that there was no urgency to the draft since many localities had enacted their own public security regulations concerning assembly and demonstrations.

L. *Impact of Cabinet Ordinance Consultative Committee and the Liberal Party's Self-Defense and Public Security Investigation Committee*

According to the known record, these committees met several times with the AG (and his staff) and played an active role in providing him with definite guidance—political administrative guidance in reverse, since it is normally the national bureaucracy that gives this administrative guidance to others, particularly to industry. AG Ōhashi met with the Liberal Party's Self-Defense and Public Security Investigation

Committee on October 13, 1951. The Committee felt that 1) such a law should be kept to a minimum, 2) the military intelligence aspects could be handled under the USJ Mutual Security Treaty, 3) because the enforcement of this law would be closely related to the Constitution, the PSEC should be independent, 4) the restrictions should be on the positions that may be occupied not on restricting the expression of political opinions and 5) reconsider the need for emergency detention/segregation. Newspapers reported that this Committee called for deletion of the inappropriate articles from the draft bill.[40]

In addition to the substantive points in the draft bill, there were issues relating to the position of the AG with the increased power of the DG/PSIA. Apparently, at this level of consideration, the Secretary General (Kanjichō) of the Liberal Party, Masuda Kaneshichi, also became involved together with the aforementioned Committee. When the government was endeavoring to administratively reorganize the government and cut back on personnel, it would be contrary to that policy and inappropriate for the AG to have within its authority an enlarged PSIA with authority to collect all kinds of information which would be concentrating excessive authority in one Ministry and one Minister. It would constitute an excess and a danger to give the PSIA the authority to recommend the disbandment of organizations. It was also excessive for the PSIA staff to have "compulsory investigative authority" (*kyōsei chōsa-ken*) when conducting investigations. It was also reported that SecGen Masuda sent a memo to Prime Minister Yoshida urging that the government move cautiously in the deliberations about the draft SAPL.[41]

There was the amorphous and murky area of the role of interpersonal relations among the high level party officials and government ministers. This appears as the emotional reaction to AG Ōhashi announcing his version of the outline of a draft bill in late September 1951 without having discussed it with his party and cabinet colleagues. This human relationship becomes entangled in the clash between the competing concepts for a revamped internal security structure between the former Ministry of Home Affairs police group (basically Keiho-kyoku) and the Ministry of Justice group (now called the AG under Occupation insistence)—with an overlay of personal feelings about who was

[40] *Asahi Shimbun* 10/13/51, *Mainichi*/Eve 10/13/51. *Yomiuri* (10/14/51).
[41] *Asahi Shimbun* 10/16/51.

more senior than whom in their present positions and what and how they were asserting themselves.

M. *Leakages of Drafts-1 and the AG's Dashed Hopes*

As part of the interpersonal rivalry, someone leaked draft 6 (October 27, 1951) to the *Asahi Shimbun* where it was published in entirety on November 1, 1951 as the lead story on page 1. It reported that the AG had submitted the "finalized" draft to the Liberal Party on October 31, 1951. He hoped that he could win the support of the Party's Sōmukai (Directors Meeting) and the Self-Defense and Public Security Investigations Committee which were meeting on November 1, and then move on to persuade the Cabinet Ordinances Consultative Committee meeting on November 5. Assuming this success, the Cabinet would give its approval, thus a bill would be readied to submit to the Diet.[42] Instead of the anticipated speedy approvals, the AG's draft bill instead ran into an array of troubles and strong opposition described below from within the Party committee, even though numerous revisions had been made in anticipation of and hopefully to counter these objections and from the Cabinet Ordinances Consultative Committee. In anticipation of these meetings, the *Asahi* reported that the Party had at least the following misgivings about the draft:

1. Since the target of the bill would be organizations, it was inappropriate to punish individuals.
2. Strong opposition to the enlargement and elevation of the SIB to PSIA; instead of this, the intelligence gathering capability of the national police should be enhanced.
3. The compulsory investigative authority (*kōsei chōsaken*) for SIB staff was opposed.[43]

At the November 13, 1951 meeting of the Investigations Committee, it was decided that the following six items should be deleted:

1. The newspaper industry from the list of designated industries
2. The requirement for a list of organization members, instead, an annual report on the status of a political organization for national distribution

[42] *Asahi* 11/1/1951.
[43] *Asahi* 11/1/1951.

4. The sealing of all printing machines and other equipment when the publication of a journal is prohibited
5. The confiscation of all properties of an organization which has committed illegal activities, and
6. That courts will be bound by all findings of fact (*jijitsu nintei*) by the PSIA.

In addition, there were three items about which there was only limited agreement: The AG proposed that he could soften the principle of prohibiting certain kinds of employment, but party officials wanted its deletion. The latter also believed that applying this prohibition to publicly elected persons would be inappropriate and probably unconstitutional. The AG agreed to consider the idea of shortening the five year term on prohibition on holding certain positions to three years at which time, it would be possible to petition to have the prohibition lifted. The third issue of contention was the continuing party dissatisfaction with the compulsory investigative authority for the PSIA. It sought for a much more watered down compulsory investigative authority. When this Committee again met on December 13, 1951 their dissatisfactions continued especially over the AG's reluctance—foot dragging—not to delete employment restrictions on government employees and his continued insistence on demanding compulsory investigative authority for the PSIA. Concerning the application of the provision to limit employment only to public service employees, the AG countered that this was already part of the demands of the Cabinet Ordinance Consultative Committee; he would agree with the understanding that if anti-democratic elements could be ousted from the public service then he would agree to the deletion of this clause. But he could not agree to the deletion of compulsory investigative authority since it was crucial and indispensable to carrying out reliable investigations.[44]

On November 5, 1951, the Cabinet Ordinances Consultative Committee took a more drastic stand and opposed the idea of limiting employment only to the principal members of a disbanded organization. If that were the case, it would not be a thorough purge of the "Reds", i.e., left wingers and Communists, and raised the issue as to whether there was a need to limit the types of industries from which certain persons would be barred from employment. This stance

[44] *Asahi* 12/14/1951, *Mainichi* 11/14/1951.

appeared to be at variance with the concerns of the Party Committee.[45] However, at the Cabinet Ordinances Consultative Committee meeting on November 29, 1951 the AG was again pushed to agree to revise still further the SAPL draft as follows:

1. The provision to limit employment will be restricted to public service employees; officers of labor unions and important industries will be deleted from that list of organizations where this limitation may apply
2. The five year term on employment limitation will be reduced to three years
3. The newspapers and publishing industry will be noted as not being included as "political organizations"
4. The sealing of printing machines associated with the prohibition of journals will be deleted
5. Those organizations which might conduct or there is a concern or fear that illegal activities may be conducted will be deleted from the list of organizations against whom actions (*shobun*) may be taken.
6. The draft will be revised so that courts are not bound by findings of fact by the PSIA.[46]

Based on the above description, the powerful and influential government bureaucracy was indeed buffeted between two committees, one a party committee of senior party officials and another the committee which reported directly to the Prime Minister with their repeated objections and demands for revisions. The AG's uncooperative attitude about employment restrictions/limitations and the compulsory investigative authority for the PSIA probably did not sit well with his colleagues but probably reflected the strong insistence of SIB director Yoshikawa who had only less than a decade earlier been the Chief Prosecutor in the famous Sorge Spy Trial in Tokyo. He must have felt that based on this experience anything less than full investigative authority would compromise his position at the SIB and more importantly that of his successors. It should also be observed that while various draft stipulations were whittled away by each committee, seemingly a retreat after retreat, there was no known discussion about the political implications or potential constitutional problems with the definition of illegal activities especially the supplemental, augmented and enlarged interpretation of riots, insurrections, etc. cited from the

[45] *Asahi* 11/8/1951.
[46] *Asahi* 11/30/1951.

Criminal Code. Apparently the assurances from one or two scholars on their constitutionality had disposed of this issue.

It was agreed that meetings would be held later in December for final approval with the anticipation that the bill would be submitted to the next regular Diet session in spring 1952 but the issue of investigative authority was held over to the next phase.

A new program outline reflecting these requested revisions was prepared (12/17/1951) and another draft prepared; the draft was dated December 22, 1951 but un-numbered and was truncated with 59 articles and missing some chapters, e.g. the controversial one of investigative authority. The program outline explained that the "anti-democratic violent and destructive activities" in Japan reflected the world situation and bared the dangerous circumstances then prevailing in Japan. The measures to maintain internal security in Japan largely stemmed from SCAP directives. With the Peace Treaty coming into effect, many aspects of these directives will be abolished, become null and void. Unless alternative legislation was enacted, Japan would, it was asserted, face a dangerous vacuum in this critical area. For the sake of the common welfare (*kōkyō no fukushi no tame ni*), limitations on the right to freedom must be kept to a minimum and avenues of relief [against improper or illegal bureaucratic action] must be adequately assured and maintained. This latter point later becomes a source of contention between the government and the political opposition and labor unions. The program outline stated that the idea of augmenting the various crimes referenced from the Criminal Code with plans to support or encourage incitement and/or instigation, etc as described earlier were adopted from a provisional draft revision of the Criminal Code (No public discussion of this draft could be found; it must have been an in-house exercise which was later abandoned.) Since most violent destructive activities are carried out by organizations, restrictions—restricting publications and certain activities, structural reorganizations of the offending organizations, even disbandment—will be imposed on these organizations. The concept of purges of or employment restrictions on employees in enterprises and in government agencies were abolished. Reflecting the impasse on compulsory investigative authority, this authority was included in the program outline but that this authority must be exercised based on obtaining a written certificate of permission from a judge and that this authority would not extend to the physical restraint of persons (*migara kōsoku*). With this program outline and incomplete revised draft the Ohashi period came to an abrupt end.

Only a few days later, a new phase was begun with the appointment of a new AG, and transfer of AG Ōhashi to another Ministerial position, in the name of strengthening the Yoshida Cabinet to deal with post-Peace Treaty issues.

N. *The Opposition, Fall 1951*

i. *Diet Discussions*

In the Diet, skeptics and the opponents to the idea of an SAPL took every opportunity to pursue the government. Their opposition was accentuated by the fear, anxiety and rumors that there were attempts being made to re-create something like the prewar Ministry of Home Affairs. AG Ōhashi was questioned by a leftwing Social Democrat, Inomata Kōzō, in the Legal Affairs Committee in the House of Representatives on September 18 and October 12, 1951. Ōhashi explained that the proposed SAPL1) must be strictly consistent with the various civil liberties enumerated in the Constitution, 2) may nevertheless unavoidably limit basic rights of speech, assembly and expression, 3) must keep these limitations to an absolute minimum in order to maintain the welfare of the people and to protect democracy, 4) "purge" under the proposed law was different from that under the Occupation, in that it would limit the positions which may be occupied by persons known to destroy democracy, the organs of state and important industries but would not limit their ability to stand for election and express their political opinions, 5) administrative actions permitted in the bill must, in reality, be effective, appropriate and necessary and 6) each and everyone of these administrative steps may be appealed to the courts.[47]

[47] *Asahi Shimbun* 9/19/51, 10/12/51. Ōhashi also commented on the proposed bill to prohibit general strikes. This measure would be applied only when a strike would have a serious deleterious effect on Japan's economic recovery, when there were no other measures that could be effectively taken, or when such a strike would jeopardize an industry which is critical to the national economy. Such a strike would not be prohibited just because it may be political. The law would be applied cautiously based on

ii. *Labor*

The deepening confrontation between the labor unions, labor movement and its political party supporters and the conservative government led by Prime Minister Yoshida was on a continuum of increasing hostility, suspicion, distrust since the conservative Liberal Party secured an absolute majority in the House of Representatives in the 1949 election. Let us begin with developments just before the outbreak of the Korean War in June 1950.

In anticipation of the June 4, 1950 election for the House of Councillors, a mass rally was held on May 30 in the Peoples Plaza/The Imperial Plaza in Tokyo. Unfortunately a small group of eight attacked Allied Forces personnel, i.e., U.S. service personnel, who happened to be on the periphery of this demonstration. The government's response was immediate and drastic: the Tokyo Metropolitan Police forbid another rally about overcoming the industrial crisis facing Japan, and under Municipal regulations on the maintenance of public security (To Jōrei) prohibited demonstrations and assembly. Those who attacked U.S. personnel were tried by a U.S. military court and sentenced to years of hard labor.

Because of the increasing sense of threat from the radical leftwing, i.e. the JCP and its supporters, General MacArthur sent a letter to the Japanese Government on June 6 instructing it to purge 24 members of the JCP Central Committee, and later the editorial leadership of the JCP organ, *Akahata* (Red Flag) were also purged. These leaders naturally went underground and eluded the frantic search for them by the SIB which was later criticized for its apparent incompetence. This effectively deprived the more radical leftwing unions of political leadership. This was followed by police searches of union headquarters offices, arrests were made of union leaders and staff.

Somewhat simultaneously with these developments, were the wholesale dismissal of employees (*jin'in seiri*) by many major corporations, 5,500 at Hitachi, Toyota (2000), Tōhō (1300, Movie Production), Niigata Ironworks (1000), Mitsui Chemical (1600), Kawasaki Railroad Car (800) and many other companies. The unions waged a struggle against these cuts in personnel to little avail. The rationale for these

---

a specially created commission's recommendation to the Prime Minister, approved by the Cabinet, and a request to the courts to impose this prohibition.

cuts had been to increase the health of the company and weed out the inefficient workers. However, after the purge of JCP leadership, Japanese industries began a political purge in July 1950 of JCP members and other boisterous elements in its ranks, about 12,200 people, a purge known as the Red Purge described in the Context Chapter. This new cleansing weakened still more the influence of communist elements at all levels of union activity. Then on August 30, 1950, the SIB invoked the Organization Controls Law in banishing 12 members (which included 8 JCP party members) from holding public office and ordered the disbandment of the Zenrōren, a union federation of almost one million members. Expectedly, constituent unions of this federation denounced these purges and disbandment as fascistic oppression of the labor union movement. Even the more cautious and conservative unions denounced these tactics by the government and warned that such actions would result in the destruction of all popular movements.

At the level of labor federations, a schism had been emerging since the leftwing unions had unsuccessfully opposed the government's attempt to streamline personnel, i.e. decrease personnel. The more conservative labor federation began to re-assert its leadership claims from the left and a preparatory committee to form a new labor federation was created in March 1950. The Sōhyō Labor Federation was created on July 12, 1950 with SCAP/HQ's blessing and with the hope that it, as the pro-democracy, anti-communist labor federation, would be more malleable and supportive of the aims of the Free World. It also joined the Free World trade union movement in opposition to the communist dominated world labor organization. By the end of 1950, numerous other labor unions joined the Sōhyō tent and it swelled to 3.3 million labor union members, establishing itself as the leading non-communist labor federation. It led a vigorous autumn 1950 and spring 1951 spring labor offensive.[48]

After the outbreak of the Korean War in June 1950, the felt need for a Peace Treaty between Japan and the Allied nations gave the discussions toward such a treaty added momentum. As the leading labor

[48] For more information on the formation of Sōhyō, see *Industrial Relations in Postwar Japan* (Urbana, IL. University of Illinois Press. 1958. 200 p.) by S. Levine, Urbana, pp. 74–77.

federation, Sōhyō would need to develop a policy toward a potential peace treaty, international security surrounding Japan and the politico-economic-military regime that would evolve in post-treaty Japan. At its second national convention in March 1951 it adopted its Three Principles of Peace: All around peace including the Soviet Union and PRC, maintenance of neutrality, and against war. Later this slogan was expanded in spring 1951 to four by adding opposition to military bases for foreign forces. Sōhyō had become a center of strenuous opposition to the ideas and policies espoused by the Yoshida Administration, somewhat less than malleable.

Over successive years since the Allied Occupation began in September 1945, the Imperial Plaza, dubbed the People's Plaza (Jimmin Hiroba), was allowed to be used by labor unions to celebrate the almost worldwide international labor day, May Day, on May 1 each year. It was now taken for granted by labor unions that it would continue to be used every year for this purpose, it had become a symbol of the new postwar era for the labor union movement. But to the conservative Yoshida government, for this plaza to be used by such riff-raff as labor union members was total anathema; the Imperial Plaza was tantamount to sacred ground. It should be remembered that on May 30, 1950, a mass rally had resulted in attacks against U.S. Armed Services personnel and the confrontation with the opposition parties and labor unions were gradually intensifying. The Yoshida government decided to reject and prohibit the usual celebration of May Day at the Plaza on May 1, 1951 through a revision of the regulations governing the use of people's parks (Kokumin Kōen Kanri Kisoku). This naturally immediately turned into a full-blown political issue with denunciations from Sōhyō that this was suppression of the freedom of the labor movement; to show its determination, Sōhyō created on April 21 a workers rally to have a May Day Celebration. Initially, GHQ offered no objection on April 24; but on April 25, the Yoshida Cabinet affirmed its decision of no rally. This standoff was resolved when General Ridgway, SCAP, sent a letter on April 27, 1951 siding with the Yoshida government in prohibiting a May Day demonstration on the Plaza. This was symbolically regarded as an act of suppression by the Yoshida Government against the postwar labor union movement—it became one more event that contributed to the ever widening rift between the labor unions and opposition political parties and the Yoshida government. As though to snub the labor movement and political opposition still further, the government held the fourth anniversary celebration of the postwar Japanese Constitution on May 3, 1951 in the same Imperial Plaza. However, about 100 people from Sōhyō-affiliated unions joined the celebrations and sang labor songs. Sōhyō's President Mutō (from Tanrō) and Sōhyō's Secretary General Takano Minoru and 36 senior Sōhyō officials were arrested by the Tokyo Metropolitan Police. While no charges were filed, these "unwarranted" arrests greatly contributed to the anti-government inclinations in the Sōhyō affiliated unions and deepened their suspicions. While Sōhyō dominated the labor union movement at this time—Sōhyō's 3 million vs less than 200,000 of other labor groups (August 1951)—it should not be forgotten that there were some more conservative unions, e.g. seamen's union, who would accept a partial peace treaty just with the Free World countries. Tanrō, the miner's union took a more middle of the road position by suggesting that the issue was not the form of the treaty, whether with all parties, China and the Soviet Union, should or must be included, but the actual content of the peace treaty itself. These differences became somewhat academic as negotiations for the peace treaty progressed and as the conservative Yoshida government made known—rather reiterated—its view about future labor relations.

In light of the known antagonism of the Yoshida Cabinet, since it had assumed power after the 1949 elections, toward the labor movement and labor unions, accentuated even more when they were not properly subservient in Japanese terms and even more when they were led by leftish leaders, it was a logical, inevitable next step for the labor union movement to galvanize itself under Sōhyō initiative into a confrontation with the Yoshida government. With opposition to the "retrogressive revisions" (*kaiaku*) of the labor laws as the central slogan, Sōhyō created on June 19, 1951 a "struggle committee against the retrogressive revision of the labor standard laws" (Rōdō Kijunhō Kaiaku Hantai Tōsō Iinkai); other slogans included the more usual union demands, increasing base pay, summer bonuses, opposition to raising electricity rates, opposition to personnel retrenchment. The committee became known as Rōtō which will be frequently used in this study and it included member unions of Sōhyō and other friendly unions and union federations. Because of political events which followed in Fall 1951, the major preoccupation of Rōtō became staunch and determined, vigorous and organized opposition to the enactment of the SAPL against enormous odds of winning against the Yoshida government; it was thus burdened with a triple front battle, economic demands, opposition to the Peace Treaty and the SAPL.

This prickly relationship was suddenly accelerated still further in summer 1951. As mentioned in this chapter, SCAP, General Ridgway, authorized the Japanese Government to assess various laws enacted under the Occupation in light of the impending return of independence to Japan through the Peace Treaty. PM Yoshida promptly formed a private Cabinet Ordinance Consultative Committee (Seirei Shimon Iinkai) responsible directly to the PM. Only two days after the formation of Rōtō had been announced, the Consultative Committee declared on June 21, 1951 that the three fundamental labor laws enacted under the Occupation would be the targets of substantial revision to be submitted to the Diet as soon as possible. To Japan's labor unions this recommendation to the PM by this private group was tantamount to a government "decision", or green light for the Labor Ministry to begin reconsidering these laws (labor union law, labor adjustment and labor standard laws) in ways disadvantageous to the worker in the new post Occupation era of independence. Gradually the fundamental economic issues of the Autumn Struggle (*shūki tōsō*) became over-shadowed by the political agenda, especially after AG Ohashi announced his outline of a new internal security law at the end of September 1951 and the government's intention to introduce it to the Diet, proposed revisions to the three basic laws and a law to prohibit a general strike. Labor unions expressed their anger by calling for workplace rallies (*shokuba taikai*) on October 25, 1951 to protest these revisions as retrogressive (*kaiaku*), then deciding on 2-hour strikes by union members on November 17, 1951 and registering the strongest protest to the Yoshida Government accusing it of proposing revisions of the labor law which clearly violated and trampled on the spirit of the 1947 Constitution. Labor union coordination and cooperation with opposition political parties and groups in the Diet were intensified.

On November 6, 1951, Mutō Takeo, Sōhyō President, signed a Declaration of Emergency (Hijō Jitai Sengen), which accurately represented the frustration, disappointment, felt threat, and anger about the direction that the Yoshida Government was attempting to take Japan on the eve of re-gaining its independence after almost seven years of Occupation. The presumed dire threat to the labor union movement was described in stark language, severe confrontational terms, drastic for use in a Japanese language statement. It asserted that the very idea of a law to prohibit general strikes and the government's intention of submitting a new internal security law to the Diet [such as that (draft 6) which was leaked to the press in November 1951] were,

> it must be said that this is a manifestation of the politics of terror (*kyōfu seiji*) not even contemplated by the [wartime] Tōjō regime.

While this assertion is somewhat hyperbolic and not quite historically correct in light of the drastic revisions made to the prewar PPL in 1941 it is a good expression of the temper of the times and reflected well the status of the gathering storm over the SAPL and the anticipated revisions of the labor laws and the strength of labor's opposition, distrust and suspicions of the Yoshida government and its determination to confront the Yoshida Government on the street, the workplace and in the Diet.

iii. *Political Party Reactions*

The Liberal Party interestingly gave restrained support, the opposition Parties, the Democratic Party, was critical, and the Democratic Socialist Party was opposed to the potential SAPL.

The Liberal Party, being the conservative government party, through the Secretary General, Masuda Kaneshichi noted that there must be a balance between individual freedom and public welfare in the several laws which would be proposed to the Diet for the maintenance of public security, the Organizations Control Law, the law prohibiting general strikes and other laws are absolutely necessary but we must move cautiously (*shinchō ni zenshoshitai*). This was not exactly a ringing endorsement of the proposed Organizations Control Law by the AG. (*Sankei Shimbun* 10/11/51)

The Democratic Party, a somewhat conservative party which later became the Kaishintō (The Progressive Party), expressed its opinion through the Chairman of the Policy Research Council, Chiba Saburō, that the government should first focus on the fundamental economic policies which would relieve the anxieties of the people and the unemployed; this would then lead to a manageable social stability. (*Sankei Shimbun* 10/11/51)

The Social Democratic Party, through the Chairman of the Party's Political Research Council, Mizutani Chōsaburō and Suzuki Yoshio, members of the Central Executive Committee and Party newspaper, declared that this law and other related proposed legislation could be used by the government to suppress the opposition, not uphold human rights; the government should instead focus on the economic livelihood of the people. There should be no national law for this purpose, instead specialized laws in local areas when and where necessary might be created. The proposed ability to appeal to the courts is a mirage, a camouflage and would take too long to be effective. The law could recreate the prewar regime under the PPL. The Party must oppose this with determination. (*Asahi Shimbun*, 10/3/51, *Shakai Shimbun*, 10/5/51, *Sankei Shimbun* 10/11/51).

iv. *Editorials*

The newspaper editorial reactions were swift and unanimously skeptical, if not antagonistic from the conservative to the liberal newspapers.

The *Asahi Shimbun* (9/30/51). It is recognized that under the Occupation, the freedom of the Japanese people was inevitably somewhat restricted. But in post-Treaty Japan, these freedoms should not be more restricted. Rather, they should be expanded; there is absolutely no need to bring forward the contents of Occupation era Ordinances. Depending on the intentions of existing governments, and how such an internal security law would be implemented, the proposed legislation could create a situation as bad as that which resulted under the prewar military secrets law and national defense law. If, under the name of security *(chian)* freedoms are restricted, a democratic reconstruction of Japan would be in jeopardy.

The *Mainichi Shimbun* (9/30/51). It also recognized that some arrangement needed to be created to control the anti-democratic and violent tactics of both the left and rightwing and especially the international aspects of the communist movement. There is great doubt (*giwaku*) and fear (*fuan*) that this can be accomplished through a rewrite of the Organizations Control Law. The government should focus on improving and stabilizing the economic livelihood instead of trying to strengthen internal security laws.

The *Nihon Keizai Shimbun* (9/30/51). It acknowledged that internal security in post-Peace Treaty Japan was a potentially serious issue but the threat of violence was not merely from the Communists but also from the extreme rightwing organizations and recognized the need for creating a new arrangement for this purpose. The question was how to define "an illegal act" within the context of the Constitution. National secrets must be defined; while certain kinds of written materials maybe regarded as "illegal", the question is how would the government make that decision. Under these uncertainties it would not be impossible to suppress the political, social and labor movements.

The Tokyo Shimbun (10/6/51). The success in maintaining Japanese society rests with the existence of an actual authority in the form of the Occupation forces. It would be impossible to substitute absolute orders (*zettai meirei*) from the state. How to control the left and right wing movements was not merely a matter of police and prosecutor's actions. This is one of the major political problems facing the nation especially since the concept of democracy itself was not unified among the people. There is a danger in trying to control (*rissuru*) political and philosophical issues merely through specific laws.

The *Yomiuri Shimbun* (10/9/51). We cannot easily support this proposed law. Even if it was used with good intentions it is a dangerous law. If it was abusively used with the deliberate intention of oppressing the opposition parties it would fundamentally destroy democracy. In present day Japan, one cannot say that the possibility of this abusive use is not totally absent. While it is the first mission of a government to maintain a state governed by laws, the kinds of activities mentioned in the draft law, are already mentioned in the criminal code, such as insurrection, supporting foreign aggression of Japan; then there are local laws and regulations on public security and to control telecommunications (*dempa*). This is building another structure on a superstructure. This law would be a postwar edition of the prewar Peace Preservation Law; if enacted the political freedom of the people would be seriously jeopardized. While we must reject violence and threats, it is more important to reject the kind of thinking in the government and by bureaucrats that would lead to the loss of the unique rights of the people through just one law.

Based on the above, all the newspapers were skeptical of or opposed to the proposed law, even the government party gave it only lukewarm endorsement. This reaction presaged a stormy welcome for the proposed law. Even before it was presented formally to any approval process, the outline of the draft law was in deep trouble, challenged on constitutional grounds, policy priorities, bureaucratic rivalries, political competition, and distrust of how any such law could and would be implemented in light of prewar Japanese history and the PPL.

v. *The Newspaper and Lawyers Associations*

1. *The Nihon Shimbun Kyōkai* (The Japan Newspaper Association). In its ten-year history (1946–56), the Association described the efforts it had taken to combat the "reactionary" policies of the Government, i.e. the Yoshida Cabinet. It recognized that it had not been entirely successful. When the various SCAP ordinances went out of effect simultaneously with the Peace Treaty, the tendency of the government was to use "maintenance of public welfare" as the cloak to hide behind in its attempts to restrict freedom of speech. While the Occupation itself was restrictive to some extent but with the removal of this protective wall, newspapers will now have to fight for their freedom of speech. The government's attempts to restrict this freedom appeared in the legislation concerning the special criminal law stemming from the Peace Treaty, the proposed SAPL, changes to the Election Law and the proposed law concerning the protection of national secrets. The Association history cited half a dozen instances between late 1952 and 1955 where it believed attempts were made by the government to restrict the press contrary to Article 12 of the Constitution which the Association opposed with limited success.

When the AG announced at a press on September 16, 1951 that the government was hoping to submit to the "Treaty-Ratification Diet" (Hijun Kokkai) four bills concerning internal security, prohibition of general strikes, controlling mass demonstrations, the SAPL and a press code, the executive director of the Association met repeatedly with the Cabinet Secretary General, the Procurator General, and the AG to ascertain their real intentions, to express the Association's concerns for and absolute opposition (*zettai hantai*) to any legislation which would impinge upon the freedom of the press and pressed the government to make public the drafts of any such laws for wide debate in society. Since no bill would be acceptable to the press the AG said it would not be necessary in the future to consult or negotiate with the press in drafting a law for this purpose. Undoubtedly to the surprise of the AG, the *New York Times* on September 19, 1951, the 100th anniversary of the paper, printed an article on page 1 strongly objecting to the AG's concept concerning the freedom of the press. Only ten days later, the AG held a press conference on September 28, 1951 while on a train heading for Kansai to explain the government's plans for a new internal security law.[49]

The Association issued a four point statement on December 15, 1951 strongly condemning the government's draft SAPL as revealed in the leaked draft #6. According to the ten-year history of this association, the proposed law classified newspapers as a "political organization", thereby making it subject to control by that draft law. It protested to the government that by classifying newspapers in this way, there was a danger that a severe restraint could be placed on newspapers. It decided to wage a campaign opposing this draft law through the newspaper pages of its membership. As a result of these protest campaigns against the government, the latter decided in January 1952, according to the Association, not to submit that draft to the Diet. (Actually, the government under a new AG, Kimura Tokutarō, had began a new revision of the SAPL—so-called from scratch, *hakushi ni modoshite*—in late December 1951.)

A select panel consisting principally of university professors drafted a stinging critique of the SAPL draft 6 asserting that it was a most inappropriate/improper law which has the greatest probability of bringing about the interference of the government in national politics. Considering that it was a critical analysis in Japanese, the language used is pointed, sharp and uncompromising. The four points can be summarized as follows:

1. That political parties and political organizations are required to register and report on their activities to the DG/SIB implies that they are being looked upon as "criminal organizations" (*hanzai dantai*); it is a draft law which is insulting to political parties and political organizations (*bujoku-hō*). Why is it necessary to report to, be investigated by and watched over (*kanshi*) by the DG/SIB as the Political Police Officer; this would be a revival of the condemned old feudalistic system. This is hardly an approach to developing a healthy democracy.
2. Depending upon how this law might be implemented, labor unions, social clubs could be labeled as "political organizations". The law would stifle political discussion, hamper the development of democracy, is contrary to the spirit of the Constitution; no amount of explanation

[49] *Nihon Shimbun Kyōkai Jō'nen-shi*. Nihon Shimbun Kyōkai, comp. Tokyo. 1956. 924 p., pp. 393–396.

by the drafters will dispel the anxiety that this draft law will not be abused or implemented beyond its original objectives unless it's structure is fundamentally changed. "It is an unfathomable plan" (*Fukakai na kito de aru*).

3. The coverage of this law is so broad, vague and arbitrary; it covers not merely the act of murder, civil disorder, rioting, but inciting, instigating, assisting or advocating the propriety of such action, or planning to advocate such action. Even actions which were not carried out (*misui no kōi*) are regarded as criminal actions. Depending on implementation by a government official many acts of political participation could be swept under this law. The draft law is thus "an exceedingly fearful political police law (*seiji keisatsu-hō*).
4. The proposed law would create a special investigative commission, a kind of special court and this "court" would sit in judgment of joint responsibility of all constituent members of an organization based on the assertions of the DG/SIB acting as a "virtual prosecutor". While in theory a regular court could revise or overturn the judgment, the damage has been done to the defendant organization since, in the meanwhile, the actions of that organization would have been restricted, prohibited or whatever. "This law reminds one of a revolutionary era law, that of the laws of the Soviet Union."

Even though in subsequent drafts various requirements were deleted from the draft SAPL, such as the need to report the names of the constituent members of an organization, newspapers were not designated as political organizations, the breadth of the restriction on holding public office and compulsory investigative authority were narrowed, the confiscation of properties of illegal organizations were deleted, and changes which appear to be responding to public opinion, they revealed, in reverse, the unconstitutionality of the draft law, the inadequacy of the drafting process and a camouflage in order to assure Diet enactment.[50]

---

[50] The Association was created in 1946 under the friendly guidance of GHQ/CIE. The Shimbun Hōsei Kenkyūkai (The Newspaper Legal Structure Study Group) was created by the Association in May 1950. Anticipating some legal problems about freedom of the press, this group had completed its analysis by September 22, 1951. When new internal security concepts were announced through a summary program at a press interview by AG Ōhashi in Fall 1951 and then draft 6 of the SAPL was leaked to the press in late November, the Study Group was asked by the Association to provide an analysis. For this purpose, the Study Group met three times (10/22/1951, 11/24/1951, 12/17/1951) to assess the contents of the leaked draft SAPL and its implications for the freedom of the press, and drafted the December 14, 1951 statement which was endorsed by the Association and completed its study, *Shimbun no Jiyū* (Freedom of Newspapers), published by the Association in 1952, 217 p.). The membership of the Study Group were as follows: Ono Hideo (Chair and President of

2. *The Tokyo Bengoshikai* (Tokyo Lawyers Association). It issued a statement on November 17, 1951 registering its "absolute opposition" on constitutional grounds to three laws the government said it was drafting: the proposed SAPL, a law banning general strikes (*Zenesuto Kinshi Hōan*) and a law to control mass demonstration (*Shūdan Ji'i Torishimari Hōan*). The longest rebuttal was against the SAPL because draft #6 had been "leaked" to the press. The draft, it pointed out, begins with the most seemingly appropriate phrases to control, through democratic procedures, organizations committing violent destructive activities in order to develop a healthy democracy, while paying special attention to not impinging unnecessarily on the people's fundamental rights and not to abuse the purposes of this law to achieve other objectives. After listing eleven features which it said characterized the

---

the Association), Rōyama Masamichi (Vice-chairman and former Tokyo University professor, active in prewar nationalist think tank activities), Azuma Hidehiko (Professor, Nihon University), Kainō Michitaka (Professor, Waseda University), Tanaka Kazuo (Professor, Hitotsubashi University), Miyazawa Toshiyoshi and Dandō Shigemitsu (both professors, Tokyo University), Kawara Shun'ichirō (Analyst, Supreme Court), Yamane Shinjirō (Lecturer, Senshū University and adviser to the *Tokushima Shimbun*). The Study Group's analysis was approved by the Association's Board of Director's on December 18, 1951, sent by the Association's President to P.M. Yoshida, AG Ōhashi, Chairmen of the Legal Affairs Committees of both Houses of the Diet and distributed widely to government officials, Diet members, political parties and many others. Dandō and Shimane were later invited to testify as expert witnesses opposing the enactment of the SAPL during the hearings on the SAPL in the House of Representatives in April/May 1952.

Earlier on October 1, 1951—just after AG Ōhashi's press interview and revelation about his (in reality Seki's) ideas for a future internal security law—the newspaper group's general meeting was held in Nagoya. Obviously, in reaction to these revelations, it resolved that it will oppose any law which may impinge on the freedom of the press and called upon the government to reconsider very seriously (*mōsei*) any such legislation. This resolution was submitted to the government (presumably the AG) by the President of the general meeting.

While the Association's member newspapers widely publicized this resolution, the Association's own newsletter (*Shimbun Kyōkai-hō*) lamented that only 16 newspapers (members and non-members combined) had editorially commented on the gravity of what was revealed in the AG's press conference on September 28, 1951. Furthermore, instead of writing their own editorials, most of these 16 newspapers just used the news agency reports about the press conference as their "editorial." Even after draft 6 was leaked, this apparent indifference continued. As a result, the government pushed forward with its drafting utilizing, the association claimed, the disorganization of the newspapers in vigorously opposing the draft law.

Nevertheless, the Association's executive director, Tsuda, prepared a lengthy report for the Association on "the influence on newspaper of the draft SAPL". It urged that newspapers prepare editorials opposing this law, otherwise the government will interpret silence to imply acceptance of the government's ideas about a new internal security law. To date a copy of this report has not been found.

leaked draft, it then asserted that these eleven features violated various articles of the Japanese Constitution.

To require political organizations to publicly declare the inner workings of that organization as specified by an administrative agency was a violation of Constitutional articles 21 on the protection of fundamental principles, 41 on the supreme organ, and 73 on the functions of the Cabinet. Requiring the submission of copies of the party organs is a violation of article 21. To delegate the authority to determine what are destructive activities to one administrative agency and for that agency to determine penalties, requiring changes in the parties programs, to determine the existence of these destructive activities and attendant punishments, expropriation of all properties, etc, are contrary to Constitution articles 19, 21, 29, 31, 32, 41 and 73. To limit employment and require reporting of where specified people live is a violation of articles 22, 25, 27 and 28. In appealing a case and requiring the courts to accept only the facts as presented by the administrative agency is contrary to article 76 on the independence of the courts, giving administrative personnel compulsory investigative authority would be a violation of article 33 and 35 on improper arrests and protection of the home. To broaden the definition of what are illegal activities would be a fundamental violation of the criminal code procedures of a nation based on the rule of law, specifically articles 31 and 32. The newly created overly harsh penalties for various new kinds of violations stemming from the SAPL were also in violation of the previously mentioned Constitutional articles.

The association's analysis asserted that the "leaked" draft #6 in reality carried on and unified the "motif" (*moteifu*) of the Organization Control Law (and revised in 1949 as ordinance 64 to broaden the coverage to include left and rightwing extremist and the purge directive of 1947 (Ordinance 1 of 1947) and drastically broadened the dragnet coverage in application and targets. These ordinances were above the Constitution since they emanated from SCAP. However, when the Peace Treaty comes into effect, all laws enacted by the Diet will then have to fall under—not above—the Constitution. But the government is attempting to carry forward and drastically enlarge upon the emergency/special legislation issued under the internationally accepted SCAP's supra-governmental authority, thereby nullifying the political freedoms guaranteed under the Constitution. The government should take as its model the principle of clear and present danger as enunciated by the U.S. Supreme Court to assure the widest possible expression of the people's political freedoms. The objective and enactment of the proposed control law could be accomplished by fully using the existing Criminal Code and associated laws. To attempt to enact the SAPL, implies a conspiracy to resurrect the former police state and limit or take away the rights of the people. The definition and form of illegal activities is so broad and encompassing that it could be administered in any way a particular administration saw fit and could be an even more formidable law than the PPL, the Security Police Law (Chian Keisatsu-hō) and National Defense Security Law (Kokubō Hoan-hō).[51]

O. *The Prewar Peace Preservation Law System*

i. *The Context*

The context of one of the constantly recurring accusations against the SAPL was that it was a "resurrection" of the notorious 1925 Peace

---

[51] Since the details of the other two potential laws prohibiting general strikes and controlling mass demonstrations had not been disclosed, the attacks were not as detailed. The unconstitutionality of the law prohibiting general strikes has a different basis than article 21 which guarantees the basic freedoms of expression; this law runs counter to the rights of the working person to organize and to use this organization for the protection and enhancement of the political, economic, and social position of the working person because he/she is in a weaker and less advantageous position. None of the democratic nations have such a law. A general strike could not be carried out unless it had the general support of the populace. The proposed law would be in violation of Constitutional article 28.

To hold a rally would require an approval from the police which could arbitrarily withhold this approval. Furthermore, the penalties involved would be harsher than under the normal Criminal Code reminding one of the resurrection of the pre-1945 era of the Police Security Law (Chian Keisatsu-hō) and a violation of article 21 of the present Constitution.

The Association believed if such a law as the SAPL were enacted a peaceful and democratic country would not be created; as a result the association's study committee on legal systems decided an opinion would be drafted by the committee chairman and three vice chairmen. It was prepared by November 13, 1951 and approved by the entire committee on November 17 and formally released to the press. It felt that even if the government's draft SAPL was revised partially in response to the constitutional issues raised above, the SAPL would still be an unconstitutional law.

The Lawyers Association's three statements were published in *Sekai* (75:3/1952:118–122).

Preservation Law—in Japanese, *chian Iji-hō no saigen*. This expression of fear, frustration and anger appeared from the moment that an early draft SAPL appeared in the press and continued throughout the Committee hearings in both Houses. They were definitely not saying the SAPL was literally a resurrection of the PPL; their expression meant that they deeply feared that a similar surveillance system and thought control regime created under the PPL would be re-created in the guise of the SAPL. They were both internal security laws, one for the postwar situation and one for the prewar years, in that sense the SAPL is the postwar edition internal security law. This fear lay not with the present AG but with future AG's. The seed would have been planted the opposition feared and a new plant may spring to life in the future (4/26:16). Even a conservative Liberal Party committee member, Taman Hirobumi, expressed his serious anxieties about the SAPL in light of the prewar PPL:

> In article 1, it states that "it is the objective of this [SAPL] law to contribute to the maintenance of public security" but from our point of view, on the contrary, it is a law of great insecurity and this concern stems from the prewar PPL.

In light of the depth of this distrust and fear, it is necessary to provide at this time a description of the PPL, its revisions over 15 years (1925–1940), beginning with the felt need for the PPL, its predecessor law, the PPL law itself. As we will recall from the Introduction, PM Yoshida in his memoirs clearly linked the enactment of the SAPL and ratification of the Peace Treaty as two pillars for post-Occupation Japan. There was a somewhat similar situation in the mid-1920s: under pressure the Diet granted male suffrage but in taking that major step it raised anxieties that the membership of the HofR might become dangerously radicalized as a result of this suffrage—so to counter and probably to balance and control social challenges, the PPL was enacted. This interrelationship will be discussed below under "The PPL and the Universal Manhood Suffrage Act of 1925".

When prewar Diet member Hoshijima Jirō said that if a reactionary government wished to suppress freedom of speech and association, it could with one article in the PPL destroy most associations in Japan. To which then PM Wakatsuki Reijirō assured him that the government had no such intentions, but that there are limits to such freedoms. We cannot maintain public security at the cost of even destroying the national polity in order to maintain freedom of speech. About labor unions he said:

> The public misunderstands that the proposed PPL will result in the prohibition of labor unions. There appears to be labor unions and workers who believe that with the passage of the PPL, they will be restricted in their activities. That is a serious misunderstanding. Not only will it be possible for workers and unions to work for their betterment, furthermore, we in the government have not entertained any such thoughts of imposing restrictions on labor unions and worker. There is, however, a law which will prohibit the advocacy and realization of anarchism. So long as workers and unions do not advocate communism or anarchism, this law will impose no restrictions on them. I wish to make this point most clearly in explaining the draft PPL.[52]

Ogawa Heikichi, then Minister of Justice, stated...incitement is the special characteristic of this law [PPL]. AG Kimura similarly argued that incitement was the "essence" of the SAPL. These terms have basically the same meaning. When one considers these two laws one

---

[52] Murao Shigeo, a member of the HofC and a prewar conservative labor federation official of Sōdōmei, provided this quotation from the past and made additional criticism of the PPL regime as follows: In addition to the PPL, the Dispute mediation law was also passed (*sōgi chōtei-hō*), meaning mainly a forced mediation of labor disputes.. A mediation official was appointed to each prefecture (except 2 to Osaka). They were generally prosecutors from the Naimushō holding this position concurrently. They worked closely with the local police, capitalists/management, and worked with the relevant "dispute team" (*sōgidan*) representing the workers and the labor unions. In those days, these ad hoc dispute teams represented the workers rather the unions. Before the dispute surfaced attempts were made through "forced mediation" (*kyōsei chōtei*). Many disputes were thus settled but the PPL in the background was a high pressure presence and threat. I ask you to remember/recall that by 1935, 1937, the PPL now was used to attack the unions (*osoi kakaru*). At the time there was no anti-strike law but if a strike appeared probable, the leaders of the dispute would be threatened with the PPL, accused of being and labeled "red" and arrested [and probably beaten up by the secret police]. The PPL was a gigantic threat and suppressive to the end of the war in 1945. To those who experienced these years [like me] will never forget these years and this period. Despite the PM's assurances, the PPL was misused and abused in suppressing the union movement....The present postwar labor union movement has a very deep suspicion of the proposed SAPL and we, the movement will have to push forward after the SAPL may be enacted with some grim determination. To which AG Kimura responded candidly: I understand completely the terrible experiences (*nama nama shii*) suffered by the people through the PPL....The PPL went so far as to involve itself into a person's personal thoughts. While Murao did not say so directly to the AG, it was clear that he was expressing an old-timer's frustrations, saying basically what can one expect under the SAPL in light of these historical experiences. (5/31:4–5)

cannot but feel that "the SAPL is an extremely dangerous law and it is doubtful that the SAPL can effectively maintain public security (5/12:8)....There is no other law which is more vague about the target group for punishment (*shobatsu taishō*), it harbors within itself great dangers. Seemingly clearer it is, the color of the law [SAPL] is muddied" (5/12:9). To which the government witnesses tried to point out that the structure of the two laws were totally different, that the SAPL aims only at particularly bad violent destructive activities, a fundamental difference between the two laws.

When the SAPL was being drafted by the government and considered by the Diet, the people involved with the drafting and the early implementation of the SAPL came from the same generation that implemented the prewar PPL, e.g. the drafter of the SAPL, Seki Itaru, was himself a "thought prosecutor" (*shisō kenji*) during the later years of WWII. Many of those opposed to the SAPL had vivid memories of the suffering, physical and psychological, imposed upon them in numerous ways under the implementation of the PPL by this generation. This relationship cannot be minimized one iota. For the first twenty years after 1945, probably the same group of personnel who implemented the PPL in the prewar years, would now implement the SAPL in the postwar years. In the eyes of the opposition, this was a dangerously combustible combination and a combination ne'er to be trusted notwithstanding any assurances to the contrary and any admonition even if inserted into the law. While one could legitimately argue that the social and political milieu had changed drastically in the postwar years, that indeed a fundamental change had actually taken place in Japan since 1945, in the eyes of the opposition this was not convincing. All these intellectual, legal and political niceties could not persuade the political opposition that indeed times had so radically changed that they could rest easy. Considering how often "the PPL system" was invoked by the opponents of the SAPL, it was like a ghostly presence forever present, constantly hovering, never disappearing throughout the whole period that the SAPL was considered in 1951–1952. The government and its supporters were on the defensive, always trying to explain and convince, but always futilely that the SAPL was different, fundamentally different and its implementation would not result in re-creating the past.

After comparing thought control in other countries, Richard Mitchell in his pioneering book, *Thought Control in Prewar Japan*, concluded that

> Thought control in Japan was different; one might even say unique. No mass application of terror, no Japanese executed in Japan under the provisions of the Peace Preservation Law (prior to the single execution in 1944), no deportation or use of forced labor, and no category of non-persons. If executions and prison terms are chosen as the yardstick by which to measure repressiveness, then Japanese thought-control policies appear mild. The reasons for this softer Japanese approach... may be summarized as a feeling that all Japanese were brothers under the emperor, and that no thought offender was beyond salvation. (p. 191)

This assessment may be technically and relatively speaking correct but nevertheless there is an enormous disconnect between how the conduct of Japanese security services and how they treated suspects have been assessed since 1945 in Japan. The depth of the opposition to the SAPL and its anxiety that through the SAPL, the repressive regime of brutal treatment of those arrested, those suspected, the ever present censorship and ever present potential that anyone who was not 110% for the regime might be swept up in the security forces dragnet. The opposition to SAPL was not merely intellectual but was based on a deep seated emotional experience stemming, in many cases, from personal experiences in the prewar years. The PPL was not "a peace law" as some have described it but, in reality, a harsh internal security law; it was envisioned to maintain a peace under the *ancien regime* of Imperial Japan.

For this purpose, I sought, not a post facto post-WWII interpretation, but an explanation of the need for the PPL as put forward before 1945 in the hopes that this could provide a more comparable and useful comparison with what was asserted in 1951–1952 to be the rationale for the SAPL.[53]

---

[53] In writing this subsection, the following materials were consulted:

Griffin's PhD dissertation, chapter VI Passage of the Universal Suffrage Law

Griffin, Edward G. The Universal Suffrage Issue in Japanese Politics, *Journal of Asian Studies* 31:2 (2/1972):275–290.

Ikeda, Katsu. Chian Iji-hō, 1940. *Shin-Hōgaku Zenshū*. Nihon Hyōronsha. 1940. 19:91 p., 1941 ed, supplement, 6, 6 p.

Makino, Eiichi. Chian Iji Hōan, *Hōgaku Shirin* I:27:11 (1925):94–104, II:27:12 (12/1925):107–119.

Makino, Eiichi. Kageki Shakai Undō Torishimari Hōan ni tsuite, *Hōgaku Shirin* I:24:8(8/1922):116–132,II:24:9(9/1922):121-126, III:24:10 (10/1922):113–130.

Makino, Eiichi. Shisō Kokunan-rei Hyōshaku, *Gendaishi Shiryō*. Misuzu Shobō. 1973. 45:186–193.

Mitchell, Richard H. Japan's Peace Preservation Law of 1925: its origins and significance, *Monumenta Nipponica* 28:3 (Autumn 1973): 317–345.

ii. *The Rationale and Felt Need for the PPL*

Since Japan was forced to open itself to the outside world in the mid-19th century, it attempted to control "the modernization process"—the catching-up process—by importing western technology within the context of the Japanese spirit (*wakon yōsai*). In this process, inevitably more than technology crept into Japan; political, social, and economic philosophies, principles, programs emanating from Europe snuck into Japan with varying degrees of success. These ideas were, in the eyes of the ruling elite, distinctly alien to their perception of Japanese modes of thinking and if these ideas became widespread, prevalent even popular, they would, in the eyes of the ruling elite, be a distinctly potential threat to the stability of Japanese society. The first noteworthy incident for this purpose was the famous trial and execution in 1910 of Kōtoku Shūsui, the anarchist. After WWI until the enactment of the PPL in

---

Mitchell, Richard H. *The Peace Preservation Law*, Paper given at the AAS 1994 meeting. 27 p.
Mitchell, Richard H. *Thought Control in Prewar Japan*. Cornell University Press. Ithaca. 1976. 226 p.
Miyake, Shōtarō. Chian Iji-hō, *Gendai Hōgaku Zenshū* 37–38: 85 p. (37:497–542, 38:185–223). Nihon Hyōronsha. 1931.
Naimushō, Keihokyoku. *Dai-55-kai oyobi Dai-56-kai Teikoku Gikai Chian Ijihō ni kansuru sokkiroku*. 541 p.
Okudaira, Yasuhiro. *Chian Iji-hō Shōshi*. Chikuma Shobō. 1977. 272 p.
Okudaira, Yasuhiro. Some Preparatory Notes for the Study of the Peace Preservation Law in Pre-war Japan, *Annals of the Institute of Social Science* 14(1973): 49–61.
Sase, Shōzō. *Seiji Hanzai-ron*. Seikei Shoin. 1936. 407 p.
Shihōshō, Keijikyoku. *Dai-45-kai Teikoku Gikai Kageki Shakai Undō Torishimari Hōan Giji Sokkiroku narabini Iinkai Giji Sokkiroku*. 1933. 360 p. Shisō Kenkyū Shiryō Tokushū Dai-10-gō.
Shinobu, Seizaburō. Chian Ijihō, *Taishō Seijishi*. Keisō Shobō. 1968. 1490 p., pp. 1155–1223.
Steinhoff, Patricia. *Tenkō: Ideology and social integration in prewar Japan*. Garland Publishing. New York, London. 1991. 220 p.

I chose Ikeda Katsu's explanation of the background leading to the felt need to enact the PPL and to revise it culminating in the 1941 revision because of his prominence in the prewar years as a "thought prosecutor" (*shisō kenji*), as a soft-spoken intellectual and scholarly prosecutor who had published books on law and because his presentation, among those I know of from the prewar period, appeared to be more systematic and understandable with some re-arrangement on my part. Ikeda (1893–1977, Todai Law 1917), was one of Ministry of Justice officials involved in the drafting and enforcement of the PPL, the wartime special criminal law and other related internal security laws. He was DG/Criminal Affairs Bureau (Keijikyoku), 1941–1944, involved in the famous Sorge-Ozaki spy case, was purged under the U.S. Occupation but later de-purged, appointed as a judge of the Supreme Court in 1954. He retired in 1963 at age 70.

1925, Japan's bureaucracy and ruling elite became imbued with an ever deepening sense of crisis and threat and which, they feared, was gaining ever more momentum as each year passed. From their standpoint, the influx of these alien ideas must have appeared as a torrent of unwelcome philosophies with practical implications for maintenance of public peace and security. In addition, there was economic unrest and anxiety in Europe, Japan and the rest of the world stemming from an economic depression soon after the end of WWI; in Japan this anxiety was symbolized by the rice riots in 1918 about the soaring rice prices. It was feared that the confrontation between the capitalist class (*shihonka kaikyū*) and the working class would result in a political struggle between them and that the former would appeal to the government for help. The apparently successful Soviet Revolution in Russia and the exportation of Soviet communist ideas around the world, increasing number of labor unions which had been created in Japan, the establishment of labor union federations and thousands of strikes, all accentuated this point. Professor Yoshino Sakuzō of Tokyo Imperial University stirred the pot with the publication of an article in *Chūō Kōron* in January 1916 on constitutional government.[54] As soon as a meeting to create a socialist political organization was held in 1921 it was ordered disbanded by the police. International Communist liaison with Japanese counterparts was detected by the police. The JCP was created secretly in 1922. Ikeda lists many events that occurred in 1922 concerning communist activities, formation of a party, communist guided labor federation, distribution of communist publications, participation of Japanese representatives in Comintern meetings, guidance to the Japanese communists about strategies to be followed

[54] Richard Mitchell writing in the mid-1970s said: Our point of departure on the road leading to enactment of the Peace Preservation is the trial of Morito Tatsuo, a junior professor of economics at Tokyo Imperial University. The precipitating incident was the publication in January 1920 of Morito's article, "Kuropatokin no Shakai Shisō no Kenkyū" (Research on the Social Thought of Kropotkin [the Russian anarchist]) in the first issue of *Keizaigaku Kenkyū*. (1976:39–40). As a result he was forced to retire. In contrast, Ikeda, a highly regarded prosecutor and one of the most knowledgeable experts on thought control issues, writing in 1940 did not mention the Morito trial at all but the far more non-controversial essay by Yoshino as part of the milieu leading to the enactment of the PPL. This contrast is cited here to show how perceptions, rightly or wrongly, of a situation differ between a practicing prosecutor and intellectual interpreting contemporary events and a foreign scholar writing about the 1920s fifty years later. Ikeda—and I am sure his cohorts and colleagues—were unalterably and obsessively focused on the presumed communist ideological threat to and in Japan.

in Japan. The perceived challenge was intensifying and perceived as a crucial threat.

iii. *The Proposed 1922 Law to Control Radical Social Movements*

Three factors led to the drafting of the law to control radical social movements in the summer 1921 and its submission to the House of Peers in February1922. 1) Financial support was being provided to the fledgling Japanese Communist movement for use in Japan. They were not conducting riots or planning and plotting an insurrection. They were planning to disseminate these dangerous thoughts (*kiken naru shugi shisō*) slowing but surely through the populace thereby undermining the state from within. The criminal code was unable to cover these activities. This international connection was particularly galling to the Japanese and to them treacherous and un-Japanese. 2) Through the distribution of printed subversive materials (*fuon naru bunsho*) and the public posting of these materials was again not covered by the publication law. It was urgent to create a law which would pre-empt the distribution and posting of these "subversive" materials. 3) These radical elements would form secret organizations to achieve their purposes. The existing punishment for committing such crimes was not severe enough. The penalties must be made heavier in order to discourage such acts.

The proposed law applied to those 1) who propagandize or who attempt to propagandize communism, anarchism and other philosophies with the purpose of disrupting society (*chōken o binran-suru*) or persuade (*kan'yū*) others and those who respond to this persuasion for this purpose, 2) who create an organization, hold an assembly or conduct mass movements to achieve the above purposes, 3) who propagandize actions to change the fundamental organization of society through riots, violent action, threats and other illegal means and 4) who provide financial resources (*kinpin*) and provide other facilities and those who knowingly accept such resources. The proposed legislation was roundly criticized as a bad law (*akuhō*): the descriptions of the criminal offenses were too vague and unclear, imposition of prison terms to control thought was retrogressive, this vagueness would lead to an abusive implementation of the law. In order to prevent such an abusive implementation, the law was revised to limit it to "only to those items which were the minimum needed for control purposes" (*sono hitsuyō saishō gendo ni seigen shite torishimari-jō no gutaiteki hitsuyō jikō nomi*). The revised law now emphasized liaison with foreigners or those living outside the jurisdiction of this law to propagandize the disruption of society, the creation of an organization, assembly or mass movements for this purpose, to change the fundamental organization of society through illegal means and to provide financial resources or knowingly accept these resources in order to carry out these criminal offenses. The bill passed the House of Peers in this revised form but failed later to pass the House of Representatives. This failure by the House of Representatives must have impressed the government leadership if the universal manhood suffrage movement then in full swing actually did succeed, this House might be even more radical and, in their eyes, irresponsible.

iv. *The 1925 Peace Preservation Law*

During the latter half of 1923, three major events gave those pushing for a tough internal security law an unusual opening and opportunity: on June 5, suspected Japanese and Korean communists were mass arrested and charged under the Security Police Law, the Great Kanto Earthquake occurred on September 1 and on December 27 Namba Daisuke's failed attempted to assassinate the Prince Regent (later Emperor Showa). There was much pillaging, arson, robbery and killings; these were conveniently blamed on Koreans and communists and anarchists. The Ministry of Home Affairs blamed, in particular, the Koreans who then became the targets of Japanese fury. Not wishing to run the risk of another defeat in the Diet, the government issued an Imperial Decree (#403 on 9/7/1923) prohibiting persons from inciting others to injure people's lives, person or property, spreading false words and rumors with the purpose of disturbing the peace. The 45th special session of the Diet approved this decree in December 1923—how could the Diet, under prewar conditions in Japan, do anything other than approve an Imperial Decree.

Communist activities appeared to calm down somewhat after the Great Earthquake; the party even dissolved itself in March 1924. But the international communist movement, in the eyes of the government, still aimed to communize Asia and that would include Japan; for this purpose, financial support from the Comintern was no longer in thousands of yen but was now estimated in tens of thousands of yen, a typical Japanese way of counting, somewhat vague, but indicating a very substantial increase. A new periodical, *Marukusu-shugi* (Marxism) began publishing in May 1925; publications of any sort were believed by Japanese security forces (police and prosecutors) to be a particularly effective tool in instigating, inciting people to action, the most recent example was Namba Daisuke who said he read all kinds of materials on the Kōtoku Shūsui Treason Trial and the Russian revolution and persuaded him of the necessity to take drastic action. Ikeda and his associates were concerned that communist elements would infiltrate the non-communist proletarian leftwing political parties (*musan kaikyū seitō*) which were beginning to be created in the mid-1920s. The signing of a treaty in January 1925 between Japan and the Soviet Union restoring diplomatic relations became another source of substantial anxiety in controlling communist activities in Japan; diplomatic channels could now be used in many ways to guide, organize and finance a Japanese communist movement, thereby intensifying the international personal connections of the Japanese communists. These new developments and anxieties persuaded the government to try yet again to obtain Diet support for a new law to control such perceived threats to the stability of the nation. A new law, the Peace Preservation Law (Chian Iji-hō) was submitted to the 50th Diet on February 19, 1925. Among the assertions made at the time, and echoed in the Diet 27 years later as one of the justifications for the SAPL , was one by the then Minister of Justice on February 26, 1925 who insisted that if the proposed bill did not pass radical, meaning communist radicals, would expand their movements:

> These agitators are people greatly to be feared, since we cannot give them the proper punishment for this terrible crime.... Under present conditions, there is no law to properly punish this kind of dangerous action.[55]

The proposed bill was passed by the House of Representatives on March 7, the House of Peers on March 19 and became effective on May 12, 1925—a super-speedy handling of the bill by the Diet, an indication of how the milieu had changed in the Diet to facilitate such quick enactment of the bill.

The PPL declared in article 1 that it was illegal to form an organization whose objectives were to change the national polity (*kokutai*

[55] Richard H. Mitchell. Japan's Peace Preservation Law of 1925: its origins and significance, *Monumenta Nipponica* 28:3(Autumn 1973:317–345), p. 41 citing pp. 43, 46–48 in the *Dai 50-kai Teikoku Gikai Chian Ijihō ni kansuru Sokkiroku* pp. 43, 46–48.

henkaku) or to deny the system of private property (*shiyū zaisan seido hi'nin*), i.e. the PPL made this purpose an ideological criminal offense; it was a criminal offense to hold and entertain such thoughts. Thus, the mere fact of forming an organization for this purpose now became a criminal offense (*kessha-zai*). Then, carrying out activities to achieve these objectives would be a criminal offense (*mokuteki tsuikō-zai*) notwithstanding how these activities were carried out, whether in a peaceful, democratic manner through the Diet or by using violent methods. It would not matter whether one was a mere member of such an organization or whether one was an officer of that organization. Conferring, consulting, plotting to carry out these activities (*jikkō kyōgi-zai*), to incite others to carry out these illegal and criminal activities (*jikkō sendō-zai, hanzai sendō-zai*), and to receive a benefit for carrying out these activities would become criminal offenses (*hanzai juju-zai*). Of these various offenses, the *mokuteki tsuikō-zai* (activities to achieve these illegal objectives) was the one most often used (*ran'yō sareta*), abused and manipulated to be applied against those arrested and charged under the PPL. The reasoning went something like this: you know of the existence of the JCP, you know that the activities you are conducting will benefit the JCP, thus one is guilty of violating the PPL. Between 1925 and 1945, about 70–80,000 persons were arrested, of those about 5–6,000 were charged with carrying out activities to achieve specific illegal objectives. These were vague concepts subject to broad and abusive interpretations by an existing government. Violations under the PPL included the dissemination of rumors, hearsay, gossip, etc. There were other laws such as the newspaper law, the police peace law (*Chian Keisatsu-hō*) which could also be mobilized to supplement the PPL.

v. *The PPL and Universal Manhood Suffrage Act of 1925*

The PPL was enacted by the Diet on March19, 1925; the Universal Manhood Suffrage Act on 29 March 1925. As a result of this ten day difference, there has been a lingering presumption that the enactment of these two laws was not accidental, especially the PPL to balance the relatively speaking broad enfranchisement of Japanese males in the electoral process. The momentum for both laws had been developing independently for some years and the convergence of their legislative calendars so closely was not originally premeditated to the extent that the enactment dates suggest. It would not be difficult to imagine that, in light of the attitude toward the populace in general, passage of the PPL was a condition for the acceptance of the Suffrage Act. But was that the case?[56]

Quoting a passage from a 1925 Privy Council meeting, Steinhoff said that the Council had "demanded" a law for "the adjustment of education, proper guidance of thought and prevention of extremist speech and action". The government, she reports, responded with the PPL. I read the original Privy Council minutes in Japanese; in typical Japanese indirection the government took their comments as definitive guidance—not specifically a demand but "if you know what's good for you, you'll take my advice"—to propose the PPL which the government had been drafting for several years. Furthermore, she also asserted that "stiff regulation of the limits of acceptable political activity had been the price demanded by both the Justice Ministry and the Diet itself for passage of the suffrage law. (Steinhoff: 30–31). The Privy Council also commented that under the circumstances the Manhood Suffrage Act most probably will be approved by the Diet and there is no alternative but to concur in the Cabinet's decision to submit the suffrage bill to the Diet. The government should definitely take steps to prevent the relatively unprepared populace from being mislead by opportunists and establish facilities for this purpose was most important.[57] Mitchell cites the then Prime Minister, Kato Takaaki's biographer as saying that enactment of the PPL was "the passport for passage of universal suffrage." (Mitchell 1976:58) "A connection existed…but

[56] In analyzing this issue I turned to the following sources:

Griffin, Edward G. The Universal Suffrage Issue in Japanese Politics, 1918–1925, The Journal of Asian Studies 31:2–(2/1972):275–290.

Griffin, Edward G. *The Adoption of Universal Manhood Suffrage in Japan*, p. 176. unpublished PhD dissertation.

Kobayashi, Yukio. Nisso Kihon Jōyaku Dai 5-jō to Chian Iji-hō, *Jimbun Gakuhō.* 10(3/1959):133–164. Kyoto Daigaku Jimbun Kagaku Kenkyūjo.

Mitchell, Richard H. Japan's Peace Preservation Law of 1925: Its Origins and Significance, *Monumenta Japonica* 28:3 28:3(Autumn 1973):317–345.

Mitchell, Richard H. *The Peace Preservation Law.* Unpublished paper presented to the Association for Asian Studies 1974 Meeting. 27 p.

Mitchell, Richard H. *Thought Control in Prewar Japan.* Ithaca. Cornell University Press. 1976. pp. 56–68.

Okudaira, Yasuhiro. *Chian Ijihō. Shōshi.* Chikuma Shobō. 1977. pp. 44–50.

Steinhoff, Patricia G. *Tenkō: Ideology and Social Integration in Prewar Japan.* New York. Garland Publishing. 1991. pp. 30–32.

[57] The Privy Council report is printed in full in a short article by Imai Seiichi, Chian Iji-hō no seiritsu o megutte, *Gendaishi Shiryō Geppō*, a supplementary insert in *Gendaishi Shiryō v.* 45 (8/1973).

one much less direct than critics have charged." (Mitchel 1976:62) Griffin concluded that the sequence of events indicates first of all that "there was not an explicit agreement" between the government and the Privy Council" to exchange one law for the other. (Griffin's PhD dissertation, p. 176)

Another aspect of this balancing act was the Japan-Soviet Union treaty restoring diplomatic relations signed in Beijing (then known as Peking) on February 26, 1925. There was understandably great anxiety in the government and the Privy Council, that radical Soviet communist ideas, programs and propaganda could and would now flow even more freely into Japan through the Soviet Embassy in Tokyo. Japan would now be more exposed to the impact and machinations of the worldwide communist movements under the direction of such an organization as the Cominform. While this treaty was a natural outcome of Japan's diplomacy, it was just another reason that would stimulate the felt need for the immediate and urgent acceptance of the PPL. Kobayashi suggested that this treaty was a direct reason why the government "suddenly submitted [a draft PPL] to the Diet and had it enacted". (Kobayashi:134) This seems to imply that this treaty had an over-riding influence which is difficult to accept because the government had been considering, since almost immediately after WWI in 1918, the kind of internal security law it could persuade the Diet to accept, even resorting to using an Imperial Decree when the Diet was not responsive.

While a so-called "smoking-gun relationship" cannot be pinpointed on this relationship, there is "circumstantial evidence" and accidental historical confluence that these two bills, the PPL and the Manhood Suffrage Act, did share an interdependent relationship. To some extent the validity of this assertion depends on how the comments of Privy Council are to be interpreted. These laws were enacted in 1925. There was anxiety how the newly enfranchised voters would behave and could be influenced, especially on how their presumed ignorance about political issues and how this would impinge on the character and structure of the House of Representatives; in light of how this House had shown its distaste for the proposed internal security laws as proposed by the government, it would be wholly understandable that the conservative political leadership would be most uneasy without a companion security law which may be needed to control, in their eyes, these potentially subversive elements both in and out of the Diet. It was probably an unwritten understanding among the government officials and Diet members that these two bills would be regarded as two sides of the same coin, that, in light of then existing social, economic and political milieu in Japan, an internal security law would be politically necessary if a manhood suffrage law would be passed. Those demanding the suffrage act undoubtedly recognized that acceptance of some kind of internal security law was unavoidable. Although two sets of historical circumstances are never exactly the same, these two laws were inseparable in the minds of the political leadership; similarly, PM Yoshida regarded the Peace and Security Treaties and SAPL as two foundation pillars of the post-treaty era as mentioned elsewhere in this study; the enactment of the SAPL must be secured so that the government has the ability to respond to any threat, in 1951–52 it was the presumed communist threat just as it was in the 1920–30s.

This brief review delineates the obsessive concern by Japan's political elite about the presumed threat from the communist movement, internationally and domestically, the role of international connections in spreading communism, the feared role and impact that the printed word would have in persuading university students, workers, the general populace, especially when intellectuals and professors at the country's most prestigious universities became involved through books and journals of the possible validity of communist theory, programs and principles and in inciting (*sendō*) and instigating (*kyōsa*) the more radical elements to take direct violent action and, of course, concern about the role Koreans might, could and did play in spreading "dangerous subversive thoughts" in Japan. The so-called "leftwing in Japan" (including the rather minuscule Japanese communists even with their Comintern handlers) was fragmented and argumentative among themselves, could not be described as having a viable political organization which could in real terms challenge the power of the state of Japan and internal security agencies. They presented "no real and present danger" to the Japanese state. Since racial equality as a concept was rejected at the 1919 Paris Peace Conference, Japan undoubtedly felt double-crossed by the Western Powers (mainly U.S. and U.K.) and Japan now had to contend with a hostile international environment to its hopes and expectations. Indeed, foreign political ideas had been seeping into Japan since the mid-19th century and particularly after WWI and they appeared to be seeping into the minds of the masses, labor unions, scholars, journalists and others. That very "possibility" constituted a threat to the "presumed" peace and harmony which was assumed unconditionally to be the foundation of Japan. Whether real or not, those who entertained such "foreign ideas" which might intrude upon this peace and harmony as envisioned and assumed by the Japanese power elite were potentially subversive. They were assaulting literally and figuratively—but that was enough—the personality and integrity of the Japanese people and the latter must be saved from this possibility. Many "patriots" felt that Japanese society of the 1920s was becoming unstable (*shisō-teki dōyō, kokujō akka*) because of these foreign connected elements who were betraying the faith of the people. The emphasis in the PPL was on eradicating "wrong thoughts"(*kiken shisō*), direct reflection of the Confucian concept of "correct thoughts". The PPL was a capstone, not a turning point in interwar thought control stemming from Tokugawa practices and Meiji thought control, a direct linear descendant. It was another instance of one concession (manhood suffrage act) and one more counter balancing control (PPL). It was more in line with Japanese history, personality and thinking with the then "Taishō Democracy" of the 1920s being an aberration and deviation from the norm. The PPL was a response to a felt psychological threat to the tranquility of the Japanese state in contrast to the seemingly "physical threat" posed by the scattered violent destructive activities that occurred with increasing crescendo in 1950–52 after WWII.

vi. *The 1928 Imperial Decree Revising the PPL*

After the PPL became effective, the government never seemed to be satisfied with their own control mechanism, harsh as it already was. In the immediate subsequent enforcement of the PPL, the feared minuscule JCP apparatus was demolished. Subsequent developments did show a sort of weak passive opposition harboring "dangerous thoughts" in scattered parts of the country. Perhaps the very nature of this dispersed questioning was disturbing to the government. Perhaps fundamentally they did not quite trust their own people, those newly enfranchised 13–14 million male voters. Perhaps they sought absolute control, absolute obedience and absolute subservience. That was evidently not being realized; so the government called for a tighter and stricter revision of the 1925 PPL only three years later, then again in the mid-1930s, but each time the Diet raised questions and the government was unable to get Diet approval.

What were these "unnerving developments or potential threats" that persuaded the government centering in the Ministry of Justice for these harsh revisions. In January 1926, Kyoto Imperial University students were arrested for their beliefs in Marxism-Communism; they were regarded as the intellectual vanguard to lead the masses and provide the theoretical basis for the movement. That these students all attended a major Imperial University to train future leadership was disturbing itself. In 1927, on the other hand, a group of railroad employees in Asahikawa, Hokkaido, were accused of forming an organization to advance socialization of industry thereby denying the system of private property; this was unsettling since the locale was far removed from the metropole and involved the workers, the proletariat, an indication of widespread dissemination of Communist-Marxist ideas. Earlier the Comintern had called for the re-establishment of the JCP which had dissolved itself in 1923. On March 15, 1928, almost 500 people were arrested as they prepared to re-establish the JCP.

Since the penalties in the original PPL of 1925 appeared not to serve as a deterrent, the proposed revisions submitted to the 55th Diet in April1928 imposed much heavier punishment. It was the issue of heavier punishment that the Diet questioned and resulted in unfinished business (*shingi miryō*). The revisions centered on article 1: it divided the article into two parts and changing the hitherto co-equal status of changing the *kokutai* and denying the system of private property. Those who were organizers, officers, or in other leadership positions of an organization whose objective was to change the national polity could be sentenced to death, life imprisonment or more than five years of imprisonment with or without hard labor; those members of this organization could be similarly imprisoned for a limited term but more than two years; as very significantly, non-members who conduct activities judged to be conduct for the achievement of that organization's activities could now be given prison terms similar to ordinary members of an organization. While the institution of the death penalty was a major change of the first order, the application of the law to non-members drastically broadened the breadth and depth of the dragnet which gave the authorities almost, but not quite, the ability to reach anyone. Those who conduct activities in support of activities of an organization whose objective was to deny the system of private property were now differentiated from that of changing the national polity and their penalties will be the same as the organizers, members of such an organization. This revision for the first time made "changing the national polity" (*kokutai henkaku*) the foremost criminal offense under the revised PPL.

These changes were most aptly characterized by Ikeda in the following manner:

> *Kokutai henkaku* had now become an "ideological insurrection crime" (*shisō-teki nairanzai*), no less important than treason and insurrection under the Criminal Code using violent means for this purpose and
>
> those who conspire with and follow the guidance of organizations outside Japan in support of foreign aggression against Japan and for the overthrow of the Imperial Institution will also be committing an "ideological crime in support of foreign aggression" (*shisō-teki gaikanzai*). (Ikeda pp. 20–21).

Since the Diet would not act positively and cooperatively to the government's urgent conviction about the direct and burgeoning Communist threat to the internal security of Japan, and believing that the Cominform was training Japanese communists to return to Japan to re-build the party structure, the government invoked Article 8 of the Constitution concerning the urgency of maintaining public security and obtained the issuance of an Imperial Decree in June 1928 revising the 1925 PPL; this Decree was subsequently approved by the Diet. (HofR 1/1929, HofPeers 3/1929)

vii. *The Proposed Mid-1930s PPL Revisions*

By the mid-1930s, there were yet other anxieties, international and domestic: the Nazi party had assumed power in Germany and was, among other things, cracking down hard on the Communist Party, the United Front under Communist guidance and influence was spreading in Europe and was also appearing in Japan through various kinds of Communist front organizations. Critical comments about Japan's activities in Manchuria beginning in 1931 were surfacing and advocates of "dangerous ideas" were finding ways to avoid infringing on the PPL. There was also growing concern about what was happening to those offenders who had served their prison terms and had been released, or to those who had recanted (*tenkō*) their communist beliefs and the sincerity of these recantations. According to Mitchell (1976:121–122), a researcher, Sase Shōzō, at the Ministry of Justice stated in his book, *Seiji Hanzairon* (pp. 201–202), that it made him "shiver to think that society has no defense against those who have recanted and left prison." In the postwar years, Sase was elected to the House of Representatives and became the Liberal Party chairman of the House Legal Affairs Committee which managed the SAPL hearings in 1952!

On February 1, 1934, a thoroughly revised PPL was submitted to the 65th Diet. The revisions were a harbinger of what would be proposed in 1941. Because Diet members were taken aback by and raised objections to some of these proposals, especially preventive detention (*yobō kōkin*) and because of other preoccupations of the Diet, again PPL revisions ended up as unfinished business of the 65th session. As an alternative, the government re-submitted a bill for protection and supervision (*hogo kansatsu*) to the 1936 69th Special Diet. The felt need for this "new" program which had already begun was an indication of the success of the thought control program: the authorities had been able "to persuade" communist offenders to recant (*tenkō*) their communist errors creating a flood of people to control. It was a program "to protect", watch over, to supervise and observe those whose prison terms had been delayed (*shikkō yūyo*) or whose indictment had been temporarily postponed to reassure the authorities that their recantations were sincere. Preventive detention was reserved for those who the authorities feared when released after their prison term had been completed would re-commit their thought crimes or for those incorrigibles who, despite their imprisonment, had not, did not and would not recant their misguided communist errors. Furthermore, there was no strong opposition to this program concept. It was enacted into law.

viii. *The Spring 1941 Overall Revision*

In the meantime, the major event was the deepening involvement of Japan in the Chinese quagmire, the outbreak of full-scale war in the summer 1937 and the voices, however weak and subdued, being raised courageously about the wisdom of the attempted military solution to the China problem. However weak the very existence of these voices, their thoughts were unacceptable to the government. Ikeda, writing after the 1941 revisions, noted that since the first application of the PPL against the Kyoto University students, had been enlarged and expanded to the point of diminishing returns and was unable to respond to and control the new situations that were constantly arising. In order to smoothly achieve the objective and mission of the PPL, the latter must be substantively and procedurally revised and strengthened. For this purpose, a special consultative committee chaired by the Cabinet Secretary General was created in 1933 to consider how to respond to thought control issues. These deliberations resulted in a legislative proposal to the 1934 65th Diet but as described above this Diet and again in the 67th Diet both were unobliging. Nevertheless, the urgency of handling thought control issues through a thoroughgoing revision was absolutely necessary. Through the enforcement of the PPL whose main target was communism according to Ikeda, had thoroughly weakened the JCP to the point that it was spreading its word not through an organization (*kessha*) but through study and enlightenment, consulting, propaganda, and incitement utilizing groups (*shūdan, shūkai*). There were also those organizations which had as their objective the debasement of the sanctity of the Imperial Family, in addition to changing the Imperial Institution and also targeted selected religious organizations. The highlights of the revisions of the PPL as approved by the 76th Diet in March 1941 are as follows. PPL which originally was a mere seven article law, now consisted of 65 articles. The crimes have now been more finely divided.

1. Crimes relating to changing the national polity

   a. The original crimes of advocating the changing of the national polity and /or denying the system of private property were now definitively and clearly separated into two distinct crimes with clear and giving unequivocal primacy to national polity. The leaders of organizations committing this crime would be subject to the death penalty, or five years to life imprisonment with hard labor, a major increase in the penalties.
   b. Those who, were officers, or leaders of supporting organizations for crimes in para 1 above would be imprisoned with hard labor from five years to life. This was aimed at communist front organizations who were taking actions to support the commission of such crimes.
   c. Those persons who took preparatory steps to create an organization whose objective was to commit crimes listed in para 1 above would be subject to the same death penalty and imprisonment comparable to para a.
   d. Those who form, lead groups (*shūdan*) to achieve the objectives in paras 1–3 above would be subject to three years to life imprisonment.
   e. Those persons who consult, incite others to take actions to facilitate the achievement of the crimes in para 1–3 above would be subject to punishment of one to ten years of hard labor. The attempt here is aimed at individuals who are also through their own efforts contributing to achieving these objectives.

f. Those who incite others to riot, commit violence, to damage or injure a person or property would be subject to two or more years of hard labor.

2. Crimes debasing the sanctity of the Imperial Family and Shrines

a. Those who create or lead organizations whose objectives are to spread information about crimes denying the national polity, or debase the sanctity of the Imperial Family or related shrines (*jingū*, Shinto shrines) would be subject to more than one year of hard labor.
b. Those who create groups for this purpose will be subject to more than one year of hard labor.
c. Those who provide financial resources to achieve the objectives in paras B.1 and 2 shall be subject to hard labor of less than ten years.

"Denying the national polity" is a passive concept, the premise to changing the national polity which would be taking positive action. Thus "denying the national polity" subsumes changing the national polity. These crimes allowed the government to take action against selected religious organizations, e.g. Ōmotokyō Buddhist organization.

3. Crimes denying the private property system

a. Those who create an organization, knowingly join such an organization, or those who take actions in support this objective will be subject to less than years of hard labor.
b. Those who consult or incite others to achieve these objectives will be subject to less than seven years of imprisonment with or without hard labor.

Throughout Ikeda's analysis of the justification for each version of the proposed internal security laws, there was one constant theme, anxiety about and the political implications for the maintenance of public security and the future stability of Japanese society based on the increasing intensity and influence of the leftwing, particularly and almost exclusively the Japanese communists and the worldwide communist movement and its seeping infiltration into and corrosion of Japan; such other issues as the Namba Daisuke attack on the Imperial person of the Prince Regent though an extremely shocking event in Japanese eyes was not mentioned by Ikeda in his study as part of the imperative rationale for creating the PPL nor was much emphasis placed on the concern about the implications of the rising nationalism among Koreans for this purpose. The Ministry of Home Affairs, however, did not trust Koreans in Japan or in Korea and kept them under strict surveillance.

The enactment of this revision of the PPL on March 10, 1941 was the logical conclusion in the attempt to control "dangerous thoughts" in a more and more detailed fashion even down to individual actions covering an ever broader swath of Japanese society. Many of the 1941 revisions had actually been envisioned and included in proposed legislation starting in 1928. After only three years, the government officials in the Ministries of Justice and Home Affairs had begun building the ground work for what ultimately was enacted by the Diet in spring 1941; they had been frustrated by Diet inaction on several occasions. But by spring1941 Japan was by now bogged down in the Chinese quagmire and the war clouds for a military showdown with the U.S. and Britain was clearly on the horizon. It was clear that there was not unanimity at home for Japan's actions on the China mainland and a potential conflict with the West. This potential dissonance must be controlled to make it impotent or preferably eliminated. Through the 1941 revision, the attempted thought control dragnet was so complete, one might ask what was left that was not outside the reach of the "thought police". Ikeda ended his presentation with the comment that the edifice of a generalized system of law [for thought control] (*sōgō hōten no keisei*) had been created—with the assumption that this web of stipulations, descriptions of "thought crimes", controls, severe punishments, a regime of near total control of the Japanese populace had been achieved. In less than five years hence this system of control was abolished by authority of the Occupation.

Without a great stretch of the imagination, one can fully appreciate the concerns, fears, and determination of the opposition to the SAPL when they assert unequivocally that based on personal experience and knowing that their opponents in the Japanese government's security services were of the same generation of bureaucrats that created this very "edifice of a generalized system of law on thought control". The SAPL in their view was, in light of this history, a gigantic threat to the development of a democratic Japan in the post-peace treaty era.

During 1951–1952, neither the government nor the opposition specifically addressed the meaning and substance of the accusation that the SAPL was a resurrection of the PPL; it was a broad-brush condemnation of the SAPL without any detailed justification—it was, as though to say, so self-evident that the SAPL would lead to a replica of the prewar PPL regime, that it needs no further comment. In the eyes of the political opposition that was to be taken for granted. It is my understanding that the opposition thoroughly understood that the two laws, SAPL and PPL, were two distinct laws each with different structures and objectives and to be implemented in radically different environments. They genuinely feared, however, that the SAPL with its democratic trappings could be manipulated even in seemingly "democratic postwar Japan" to re-install the prewar police system. The presence of the hovering ghost of the PPL was sufficiently bothersome that Seki, the principal drafter of the SAPL, who sincerely went out of his way in the books he wrote after the SAPL was enacted by the Diet to explain the differences between these two laws, the inadequacies of the prewar PPL and how to avoid a repetition of these pitfalls in postwar Japan.

Seki described a number of lessons to be learned from the sad prewar experience:

a. the ambiguity of terms used in prewar internal security laws (such as making it an offense to spread rumors—article 17 of the Genron, Shuppan, Shūkai, Kessha tō rinji torishimari-hō (the temporary law to control speech, publications, meetings and organizations, 12/19/1941, law 97), distributing materials which would confuse people (article 18), publish materials which would impair public morals (*fūzoku*), the newspaper law, articles 23, 24, actions taken to achieve the objectives of the organization (PPL 1–8 and 10)
b. the focus of the security laws, especially the PPL, was on controlling radical ideas, thoughts or philosophies (*kageki shisō*)
c. the overly centralized character of the security agencies, i.e., the police and the prosecutors, which could use a wide array of internal security laws for control purposes. (Under the Yoshida Cabinet, police control was re-centralized to a large extent.)
d. avoid singling out any particular ideology (*kageki shisō*)
e. do not make creating an organization based on a specific ideology a crime
f. do not make activities taken to facilitate the achievement of an organization's objectives a crime.

According to Seki, "a fearful system of abuse which could not be controlled" (*kore o seigen suru yoshi naku, osorubeki ran'yō no kekka o unda wake de aru*) had been created in prewar Japan. It was this "fearful system of abuse" which the opposition to the SAPL feared would be recreated, re-instituted, re-installed through the SAPL with its democratic trappings. The issue, said Seki, in the SAPL was how to learn from these lessons.[58]

We agonized, said Seki, over how not to repeat these errors; we decided we should control *only* [emphasis added] those organizations which have actually committed such criminal activities as objectively violent destructive activities (*kyakkan-teki na bōryoku-shugi-teki na hakai katsudō*) with the intention of achieving specific political objectives. Those criminal acts mentioned in the Criminal Code such as murder, arson, riots, overturning trains and others for a specific political objective had a clear definition and accepted interpretations. Before 1945, the standards concerning actions disturbing social stability, rumors, false information were vague which allowed these standards to be enlarged and expanded to cover almost any action. In contrast to this vagueness, the SAPL will depend on actual specific actions (*gaimen ni arawareta meikaku na katsudō*) not on the specifics of a particular philosophy, political thought AND a judgement about the danger and probability of a given organization (*dantai no kikensei*) repeatedly committing such destructive activities. Through these means the government tried to assure the Diet and the populace that there would not be a repetition and recreation of the repressive prewar prosecutorial and police system.

This review shows the obsessive concern by Japan's political elite about the presumed threat from the communist movement, internationally and domestically, the role of international connections in spreading communism, the feared role and impact that the printed word could have and did have in persuading university students, workers, the general populace, especially when intellectuals and professors at the country's most prestigious universities became involved through books and journals of the possible validity of communist theory, programs and principles and in inciting (*sendō*) and instigating (*kyōsa*) the more radical elements to take direct violent action and, of course, concern about the role of Koreans might, could and did play in spreading "dangerous subversive thoughts" in Japan. In 1951–52,

[58] This analysis was derived from the following:
Seki, Itaru. *Chikujō Hakai Katsudō Bōshi-hō*. Gakuyō Shobō. 1952. 223 p. pp. 9–15.
Seki, Itaru. *Hakai Katsudō Bōshi-hō Kaisetsu*. Shin-Keisatsusha. 1952. 146 p. pp. 30–32.

the Yoshida government was similarly obsessed with the internal and international communist threat in justifying the need for the SAPL.

P. *Phase I Review*

i. *Caught in Many Cross-hairs*

As a result of disarray, distrust, disagreement and delays in coordination in the government and the criticisms from the newspapers, labor unions, and scholars, the promised submission of a new internal security bill to the 12th Extraordinary Session of the Diet convened on October 10, 1951, and even when extended ten days, failed to materialize; this short extension was made in order to approve the peace and security treaties not in order to submit the new internal security law. It became the victim of being caught in too many cross-hairs at one time.

1. *The Diet calendar.* The extraordinary session of the 12th Diet just could not digest all the issues that the government had already piled on its platter. The Peace and Security Treaties were themselves already extremely divisive issues in the country and with the political opposition parties in the Diet. A related controversial issue was the interpretation of Article 9, the "no-war" clause of the Constitution, while the government was calling for increasing the strength and size of the incipient Japanese Armed Forces—euphemistically called Self-Defense Forces—the National Police Reserve, again all vehemently opposed by the social democrats, communists, and equally vociferously by the labor unions and many scholars. The government while pushing for administrative reform could not simultaneously push for substantial increases in internal security personnel, elevating the SIB to Agency status keeping in mind that the PSIA was regarded by many as a cover for re-creating the prewar police system. The government also failed to resolve the lifting of controls on rice production as part of administrative reform. A Diet calendar can handle just so much agenda and thus ultimately ran out of time.

2. *Competing Priorities.* Let us limit the discussion here only to the heatedly controversial several draft laws relating to internal security broadly interpreted. These were the proposals to ban general strikes

pushed by the Labor Ministry, the Organization Control law sponsored by the AG, and the proposal to control mass demonstrations apparently pushed by GHQ. In the super-charged atmosphere of the Diet debate about the Peace and Security Treaty, could the government even with its substantial majority in the Diet seriously entertain the possibility of passing this set of legislation when these bills would arouse extremely bitter and action oriented labor offensives to block the legislation. Because of labor's distrust of the government about the internal security law and the revision of labor relations and other laws, labor made clear that it would weave into their year end (1951) and new year labor offensive their opposition to these laws. In the end, the Government was unable to resolve how this aspect of the legislative agenda would be handled. Note that a major business alliance as mentioned above threw cold water on the need for a general strike prohibition proposal; it was assigned to the AG who was told not to rush it. GHQ's role was ambiguous and it's attention was inevitably focused on the prosecution of the Korean War. Since there was an agreement within the Liberal Party and the government that there was a need for some kind of overall internal security law, a draft SAPL would seem to have the best chance of survival, yet even here the struggling bureaucratic interests would dilute this priority.

3. *The Draft Organizations Control Law.* An ambitious but constitutionally ambiguous draft bill had been prepared by Seki. It was prepared in relative secrecy but was suddenly introduced to the world through, not the details of an actual bill itself, but through a summary outline in late September 1951 by an overly energetic AG. Unfortunately he had not formally coordinated the draft in the government. Even with the summary outline it became the target of a strong wave of criticism not only from labor, media, scholars, but from within the ruling party itself—but each for different reasons for this opposition. While the felt need for such a law was strong in the government and the Liberal Party, it began to focus on the draft in mid-October, after the AG's release of the summary in a train interview. Labor feared that this kind of law however worded would be used against labor unions; others feared that in light of history, the Japanese government would use this law as a thought control weapon as it did with the PPL before 1945. The Liberal Party committees in the vetting process focused on the need and constitutionality of the specifics of the

draft bill. As described above, the AG was forced into one retreat after another as the draft was considered by these committees, but the AG tried to stand his ground on a few items but the direction was clear, the draft was being whittled away, clause by clause, or so it appeared. This assessment process dragged on slowly from mid-October 1951 to about December 22, 1951 and missed the opportunity to be submitted to the Extraordinary Diet Session; now submission to the spring 1952 Diet session was the target. The controversy within the government and Party and the vocal opposition to such a law, probably prompted the Party's SecGen Masuda to suggest to Prime Minister Yoshida that the government should proceed cautiously in handling this draft law.

4. *Bureaucratic rivalries and turf issues, personality clashes.* This is a small but probably a rather important part of the human dimension of the SAPL story. It needs to be constantly kept in mind that 1951 was only six years since the war had ended. Early in the Occupation, many senior officials had been purged by the Occupation from public life, many from the prewar Ministry of Home Affairs, among, of course, many others. As the objective situation surrounding Japan had changed, many once purged personnel were "de-purged" between fall 1951 and spring 1952 and some entered the political arena and were elected to the Diet. AG Ōhashi aroused some considerable resentment when he nonchalantly announced the contents of a highly controversial summary of a new internal security law which also included an elevation of the SIB to Agency, with a much larger proposed budget and a substantially larger number of personnel. It was reported that the discussion/debates within the party committee were quite emotional and heated. These factors brought to the fore the inclination and determination of the former Ministry of Home Affairs faction to prevent such a bureaucratic enhancement, enlargement, elevation of a unit in the AG's office, the successor to the prewar Ministry of Justice and not, it should be emphasized, the Ministry of Home Affairs. The ambitions of the SAPL draft and the conduct of the AG himself re-emphasized the rivalries and turf issues inherited from prewar years. The AG's stance probably exacerbated these tendencies and inclinations although Ōhashi himself had once served in the Ministry of Home Affairs. He had been known in an earlier incarnation as Minister in charge of the National Police in the 2nd Yoshida Cabinet to push in a maximum manner for the revision of the police structure

and then to retreat grudgingly and slowly but always maintaining the core of what he aimed to achieve. He appeared to be following the same tactic in this instance. He is known to have said that pushing a controversial bill is like establishing a beachhead at all costs in front of the enemy; push forward slowly blasting with big cannons, retreat only under pressure always maintaining however the core concept intact until victory is achieved and push for revisions as appropriate in the future.[59]

5. *The Opposition.* Mentioned last, but not last in importance, was the opposition to this proposed law from the press, the opposition political parties, the labor unions and the labor movement, almost all academicians, some lawyer associations. There was a constant reference back to the pre-1945 days of thought police, thought control and prosecutions and the ruthless, continuous and expanded implementation of the prewar PPL by the prewar Imperial Government. After all, it cannot be over-emphasized that while the top leadership of the security agencies had been purged by the Occupation the next lower echelons with similar mind sets—now tempered somewhat by the "new but forced democratic environment" in Japan—were now in charge. Even as the draft bill slowly progressed toward the Diet, the ominous role of the de-purged former senior bureaucrats of the former Ministry of Home Affairs only emphasized the anxieties of the opposition. Although the conservative majority in the Diet had the necessary votes to pass whatever legislation it desired in the lower House, this vociferous opposition must have been a decided nuisance in the eyes of most conservative political leaders in the government and in the Liberal Party; let us say, they were unaccustomed to having to tolerate

[59] For example, this kind of remark was reportedly made by Ōhashi to a fellow Liberal Party member in the Diet members' dining room and overheard by a reporter of the *Chūō Kōron*. This was reported in an expose-type article in the *Chūō Kōron* (66:13:82–96, p. 83, *Chian Kankei Hōan no Uchimaku*) on the background (*uchimaku*) of the security laws proposed by the government. The *Chūō Kōron*, it should be noted was one of several magazines involved in the notorious Yokohama Incident toward the end of the Pacific War. It was forced to cease publication and was reborn after 1945. It would thus be completely antagonistic toward and opposed to such proposed laws. Nevertheless, the comments attributed to AG Ōhashi are quite believable as a governmental and parliamentary tactic; it would dovetail with what happened before 1945 with the PPL. This beach head tactic was also reported in the *Mainichi* on 11/20/1951.

let alone consider such vociferous opposition from such lowly types as union leadership and leftwing and liberal politicians.

As a fore-taste of spring/summer 1952, the labor federation, Sōhyō's 7th councillor's meeting (*Hyōgi'in-kai*) decided on November 6, 1951 as mentioned earlier to declare an emergency in response to the proposed internal security law and to call for a 2-hour strike on November 17, 1951, of about one-million strong against the SAPL draft and the law prohibiting general strikes. This decision by labor backed by the opposition social democrats and communists in the Diet, though in a minority, was nevertheless a serious threat to the government's legislative calendar even though the government with its substantial majority would ultimately win in a final Diet vote. The government's announced determination to counter any such threats implicitly set the stage for a full-scale confrontation when the draft bill was submitted to the Diet. This was a small wave of protest which would gradually gain momentum as the drafting reaches another plateau in 1952.

ii. *Evolution of and Retreats in Drafts 1–6 and the December 22,1951 Draft*

In looking back over the period from spring to late December 1951, one could make the following assessments about the phase I drafting exercise under AG Ōhashi:

1. The 5th draft was an important, critical and fundamental turning point in drafting the SAPL. The application of the Criminal Code by reference in the SAPL to a combination of organizations and persons hereafter became the basis, foundation and core upon which the SAPL would rest.
2. As a result of redrafting, review by the two overview committees various words, phrases, concepts were toned down or deleted.

    a. The first major retreat was in the 5th draft when the emergency detention/segregation objective was deleted from the draft and never appeared again. This deletion was probably due to the unfortunate Japanese experiences under the PPL even though detention was included in the U.S. Internal Security Act of 1950 (including the Detention Act of 1950 which was repealed in the early 1990's but has been resurrected again in the Patriot Act of

2001 for certain categories of people) and was thus seemingly acceptable.

b. Definitions of public offices were deleted because the manner of control of organizations and people were changed radically.
c. Positions subject to local or national elections were eliminated from the list of positions that could be denied to those who had conducted "illegal activities" or who were suspected might conduct such actions. It was probably felt that if challenged in the courts under the 1947 Constitution it would be declared an infringement of a person's civil or human rights under this Constitution.
d. The collection of undisclosed information about armed forces in Japan as an illegal act was deleted. This was regarded as an anti-espionage clause which could be handled separately and more effectively under the USJ mutual security treaty.
e. Teachers as a category subject to PSEC restrictions was deleted.
f. The five year term on employment limitations was reduced to three years.
g. Newspapers and the publishing industry were deleted from a list of political organizations
h. Sealing of printing machines associated with the prohibition of journals was deleted.
i. Organizations which might conduct illegal activities or where there would be a fear that such organizations might carry out such activities were deleted from the list of organizations against whom actions may be taken.
j. the courts will not be bound by findings of fact by the PSIA.

3. Again, because of the prewar Japanese experience and the developing criticism against the SAPL and distrust of the government, there was a gradual tightening of the requirements on how the law would be implemented, e.g. the PSEC must act only upon the request of the DG/PSIA and the DG/PSIA must, in many instances, obtain the permission of the PSEC to take certain actions. Although article 1 paid obeisance to the need for following "democratic procedures", the emphasis of this period was on trying to define "illegal activities" and what kind of corrective and punitive actions could be taken against the offending organizations and selected persons, not on the appropriateness of the implementation procedures. That became a point of major focus in the next phase.

4. Though the word Communist or JCP was not mentioned even once in any draft, it was implicitly clear and obvious that the target of this proposed legislation was to control the activities of the JCP and associated organizations. It was drafted in a politically neutral fashion. Thus, in the future this law could be applied to other kinds of organizations whether on the left or the right, but presumably all politically motivated organizations. Again, in light of Japan's prewar experience with the PPL this would become the source of heated debate because the law was open-ended in how it might be implemented in the future under governments of varying persuasions, ideological inclinations and political motives.
5. A highly important collection of verbs which had been repeatedly used from draft 1 was gradually widened to "cover all bases" so to speak. Significantly, the meanings and implications of these verbs appear not to have been discussed nor analyzed but simply accepted by the reviewing committees in the party. "*Sendō*", for example, will later become the focal point of a fierce parliamentary and public debate. The verbs were:

 to incite (*aoru, sendō*),
 to plan (*kuwadateru*),
 to instigate (*sosonokasu, kyōsa*),
 to advocate (*shuchō*),
 to plot, conspire (*imbō*),
 to advocate the rationality of "illegal activities" (*seitō-ka*),
 to plan to advocate the appropriateness [of illegal activities] with the intention and knowledge of contributing to the realization of these actions,
 to assist in carrying out conspiracies/plots,
 to destroy important facilities in industry or local or national governmental organizations.

Some of the words used were Japanese in contrast to those used later, double kanji words such as "*kyōbō*" which sounded more legalistic and Chinese derived. For example, to instigate later changed from "*sosonokasu*" to "*kyōsa*" and "*aoru*" to "*sendō*".

As Seki commented to me in 1978, he included as much as possible from a variety of sources, particularly Occupation-inspired ordinances, and when criticism occurred and retreat was necessary and inevitable then it was done grudgingly one step at a time. The first drafts threw an extremely ponderous, dangerous and broad dragnet over the political spectrum; even Seki commented to me that an "*osoroshii mono* (a fearful thing) had been drafted. It was fiercely attacked so Seki retreated and pondered the pine knots in the ceiling and arrived at a new solution which did become and remained the legal foundation of the SAPL. The new approach was to include by reference many Criminal Code offenses (insurrection, actions assisting in carrying out and preparations for insurrections, inducement of foreign aggression, assistance to the enemy, preparations and plots leading to private wars, riots, homicide, violence, damage or destruction of structures) as illegal acts under the SAPL, and extremely importantly to augment, supplement these offenses by including other actions as criminal offenses in an extremely broad manner and to apply all these offenses not just to individuals, the traditional target of the CC, but to organizations as well—as mentioned earlier, *a dantai keihō* (a CC for organizations) would thereby be created. The augmenting or supplemental wording (*hosei*) used in article 3.7.4 and 3.7.5 (draft 6) broadened extensively the scope of actions which would become criminal offenses with increased penalties above those prescribed in the CC:

> 3.7.4. Those actions, taken as a means to advance, support or oppose political principles or programs, resulting in violation of articles 106 (riots), 199 (murder) or actions resulting in the damage or destruction of national or local governmental facilities or the equivalent thereof, and damage or destruction of important facilities of designated industries as
> 3.7.5. Plotting, planning, aiding, plotting and planning, instigating, aiding, inciting, or advocating the propriety/justification of the actions mentioned in the previous paragraph with the intention of contributing to their realization, or planning to advocate such actions.

Surrounding the drafting process was a society where the political thermometer was steadily rising and a gathering momentum of confrontation was spiraling with an ever increasing crescendo of shrillness and acrimony, as a result of the continuing Korean War, the expanding violent tactics of the JCP, the political fallout in Japan from the impending conclusion of separate Peace and Security Treaties between Japan and the United States and the latter's wartime allies (except the then Soviet Union and Communist China). The conservative government under Prime Minister Yoshida was expressing its determination to revise basic labor laws (labor unions, labor standards, labor relations). The Socialist opposition party and its labor union allies with equal determination opposed these revisions and the concept of signing a separate treaty. For this purpose, Sōhyō organized an umbrella organization, Rōdō Hōki Kai'aku Tōsō Iinkai (The Committee to Struggle Against the Retrogressive Revision [*Kai'aku*] of the Labor Laws, colloquially known as Rōtō). At its 2nd national convention in March 1951, Sōhyō called for an overall peace treaty and neutrality, against Japanese rearmament and foreign military bases in Japan. This labor movement's determination, including both the conservative and radical labor unions, as a broad front, to oppose the peace treaty merged with and provided an additional momentum for opposing the creation of a new internal security law.

In regaining independence, maintaining internal security was recognized as THE most important issue faced by the government but how this could be accomplished would be the source of a serious philosophical and a deep political chasm in Japan. As mentioned earlier, the government decided not to disband/outlaw the JCP based on a Japanese law, keeping in mind that SCAP/GHQ had used Occupation ordinances (Cabinet Ordinance 325 forbidding criticism of and obstructing the objectives of the Occupation) to purge the JCP leadership and ban the publication of *Akahata*, the JCP organ, before the outbreak of the Korean War in June 1950. Between January and September 1951, AG Ōhashi periodically gave press interviews stressing the increasing gravity of the internal security situation: the need to broaden the authority of the National Police, abolition of police forces of weak cities, and the concomitant increase of National Police, the need for the revision of the criminal procedure law, revision of the system on the appointment of judges, the revitalization of the prosecutorial staff, compulsory repatriation of unsavory (*furyō*) Koreans to Korea, and possibly declaring the JCP illegal (*higōhō-ka*). He looked upon the activities of "the disturbing elements" (*fuon bunshi* in Japanese, troublemakers, conspirators, radicals of all types, disturbers of the peace, those not agreeing with me) as still fermenting trouble in a conspiratorial manner (*an'yaku*) but that they were gradually evolving from periodic struggles against authority to becoming part of public (*kōzen-taru*) revolutionary movements.

Thus, as 1951 drew to a close and a new AG took office in late December 1951, the government had retreated from many positions in drafting the SAPL but its determination to push forward with an internal security law was undiminished despite the barrage of attacks on constitutional grounds by lawyer groups, the political opposition, the Japan Newspaper Association, cultural organizations, academe, labor unions. The array of words and phrases described above that remain throughout the various drafts would appear to constitute the fundamental core from which the government would not withdraw nor compromise, i.e., the "beach head" had been established, and the basic legal framework for the new internal security law created as Phase I of the drafting process ended.

CHAPTER THREE

DRAFTING THE SAPL, PHASE II, 1951–1952, UNDER ATTORNEY GENERAL KIMURA

A. *December 1951 to Initial Cabinet Decision, March 28, 1952*

Though weakened, the draft SAPL survived to see another day. AG Ōhashi's beachhead had been established with some losses. Prime Minister Yoshida reshuffled his Cabinet once again to strengthen his hand in managing the issues stemming from the signing of the Peace and Security Treaties and internal security. AG Ōhashi was shifted to Minister of State for National Police and National Police Reserve, in reality a political demotion at the time; Kimura Tokutarō became the AG. It should be noted that Kimura had been the Minister of Justice in the first Yoshida Cabinet in 1946–47, then politically purged and subsequently de-purged, a prominently lawyer from before the war and a practioner of *kendō*. The first item in his in-box was a resolution of the difficulties surrounding the draft SAPL and create an acceptable alternative draft.

Premier Yoshida called a meeting at the Foreign Minister's Official Residence on December 26, 1951 of AG Kimura, Minister of Construction Noda Uichi, Minister of State for Administrative Management Hashimoto Ryūgo to discuss the governmental structure for maintaining internal security and strengthening the self-defense forces. As a member of the Cabinet Ordinances Consultative Committee, AG Kimura had earlier prepared a private report to PM Yoshida recommending *one* Ministry, Ministry of Public Security (Chianshō), responsible for all security forces, the National Police Reserve (the nascent Japanese Army), the Maritime Safety Board (Kaijō Hoanchō), National Police and the SIB. Now that he had become the AG, Kimura called for the separation of those forces with a defense coloring, the National Police Reserve, and Maritime Safety Board, from those responsible for internal security, the National Police and the SIB. AG Ōhashi had envisioned a parallel system of an enlarged SIB and the National Police and a system to assure their mutual cooperation because he was concerned about the potential resurrection of the old police powers of the prewar Ministry of Home Affairs. Apparently, AG Kimura put greater stress on this cooperation, not much on expanding the SIB. That would suit the National Police in its bureaucratic rivalry with the SIB—this relationship will re-surface a number of times as the drafting process moved forward. Yoshida supported Kimura's concept for internal security arrangements. This gave AG Kimura a relatively freer hand but not a decisive hand to guide the creation of a new draft bill on internal security. This support from the PM would give only a temporary edge and the new and revised draft would still be subject to the prickly and contentious internecine maneuvering by former now de-purged senior officials of the defunct Ministry of Home Affairs. It placed this responsibility into the hands of a conservative nationalist, AG Kimura, who had not been a prewar career official of the government but was himself a de-purgee. His pedigree in that sense was excellent, impeccable and difficult to challenge.[1]

Nevertheless, the proposals concerning the future of the internal security arrangements were complicated by the wholesale de-purging of former government officials in 1950–1951. Those of particular interest in this instance were the groups of officials from the former Ministry of Home Affairs and especially in light of their direct connections to the top levels of the Liberal Party, e.g., Masuda Kaneshichi, Liberal Party's Secretary General and former member of the Police Bureau in that Ministry, Yoshitake Eichi Chairman of the Party's Policy Research Council and later Labor Minister, member of the Social Affairs Bureau, and Ōhashi Takeo, former AG and now Minister for the National Police and the National Police Reserve, formerly with the Home Ministry's National Lands Bureau (Kokudokyoku). The Ministry of Home Affairs (Naimushō) group was disunited in pushing one set of detailed structural concepts except for the re-creation of one centralized influential Ministry of National Affairs (Kokuseishō). If any of these plans were materialized, they might endanger local government embodied in the new Constitution and guide Japan toward a re-emergence of the prewar system of government. These ideas and concepts were being pushed by about 150 de-purgees from the Home Ministry who were reported to have met to try to arrive at a unified plan. Their conflicting plans might be described as centering around the idea to re-centralized police powers pushed by the Police Bureau

[1] *Asahi* 1/11/1952.

de-purgees and a plan for such a Ministry to provide only a coordinating function advocated by the Social Affairs Bureau alumni. These competing groups were reportedly maintaining close contact with their respective former colleagues now senior members of the Liberal Party. GHQ officials expressed their skepticism and displeasure to the Government at these rather blatant maneuvers by de-purgees; apparently GHQ did not have the interest, will, and determination to pursue its displeasure and probably more importantly really no longer had the political authority to do so. No known action was taken by the Yoshida government to curb nor to discourage these former officials and GHQ concerns were ignored.[2]

Since the government had not been able to produce an internally acceptable draft SAPL in time to be submitted to the 12th Extraordinary Session of the Diet, it was determined that under Kimura's drive a bill would be submitted to the 13th Diet Session which had been convened on December 10, 1951. Rather than disperse its efforts to try to submit three bills to the Diet, the government's efforts would now be concentrated on the SAPL draft and temporarily put aside bills to prohibit general strikes and to control mass demonstrations.

i. *GHQ III, Waning Twilight, Courtesy Visits*

As though in a parade, the newly appointed AG, Kimura Tokutarō and Minister in charge for the National Rural Police and National Police Reserve Ōhashi Takeo paid "courtesy calls" on Frank Rizzo, Chief of Government Section/GHQ at 13:30 and 14:30 on December 28, 1951, respectively.

1. *Rizzo-Kimura meeting.* The meeting was generalized, mutually congratulatory, with no specifics about an internal security law being discussed. Kimura expressed his concern for internal security in Japan and asked for Rizzo's "cooperation and advice" for this purpose and was given that assurance that GHQ was "ready and glad to cooperate with the Japanese Government in the preservation of peace and order" and that under AG Kimura "the freedom and peace of the Japanese

---

[2] *Yomiuri* 12/29/1951.

people would be protected from danger coming from underground and outside smugglers."

The more important part of this meeting was focused on rearmament. Kimura asserted that an independent nation should be prepared to defend itself and that the only course for Japan was to cooperate with the U.S. and mentioned that PM Yoshida was considering the issue of rearmament by the creation of an army, unlike the Imperial Army, but a democratic army. Rizzo said in concluding the meeting that it would "take time" for Japan to rearm and that the U.S. had "no intention of forcing rearmament on Japan faster and beyond her capability."[3]

2. *Rizzo-Ōhashi meeting.* Ōhashi thanked Rizzo for his guidance and advice when he was AG and expressed his regret that he was not able to pass the necessary internal security legislation. As the Minister in charge of the National Police Reserve, he said he would strengthen the National Police Reserve by 1) enforcing strict discipline and checking accounts, 2) eliminating the clique and factions formed by the old policemen and former career military men in the Reserve and 3) to cooperate closely with the U.S.

He told Rizzo that he was requested by the Prime Minister to study the Police Law revisions since they would be closely related to administrative reforms of the government and the overall internal security structure. Perhaps more significant from the SAPL point of view were assessments about the intentions of certain ex-purgees in the majority Liberal Party and the Cabinet Ordinance Consultative Committee. He believed that:

a. the ex-purgees now in the Liberal Party and the Cabinet Ordinance Consultative Committee advocated the establishment of the Security Ministry composed of the National Rural Police, the National Police Reserve, the Special Investigation Bureau and the Maritime Safety Board and would, Ōhashi felt, lead to the revival of the Special Higher Police (Tokkō or Tokubetsu Kōtō Keisatsu).
b. on the other hand, the defense related agencies and other security agencies should be placed in different ministries. To avoid duplica-

[3] This was based on a record of a meeting between Rizzo and Kimura, prepared by Raymond Y. Aka found in RG331.2187:4 in the U.S. National Archives II.

tion, subversive activities investigations, now being conducted by the National Rural Police should be done by the SIB. Rizzo appeared to concur that "it would be a fatal mistake to combine the civil police with the National Police Reserve which was military in character. The important thing was to build up public respect for the National Police Reserve, to preserve its integrity and above all to be responsible to the civil authorities."

c. the National Public Safety Commission should be placed under the AG not under the PM's office.[4]

On yet on another occasion, Ōhashi sought Rizzo's support for his reorganization of the internal security structure which he claimed had been submitted to PM Yoshida in late December 1951. He was adamant in trying to avoid the consolidation of security agencies as advocated by the old-line police group in the Liberal Party who, Ōhashi asserted, wanted to re-establish the former notorious Ministry of Home Affairs. But Rizzo begged off supporting Ōhashi's ideas since there were many organizational notions being considered, that GHQ would need to assess whether these suggestions might contravene SCAP's original idea of assuring local autonomy in such police matters.[5]

These meetings were incidentally on an internal security law, with more emphasis on rearmament and the overall structure of the government's security apparatus and Ōhashi's concern as to whether the prewar police state in some form might be revived and the role of ex-purgees in this process which will become evident as the SAPL drama unfolds and Ōhashi's attempts to obtain GHQ approval of his specific reorganization plan.

ii. *December 25, 1951 Program Outline*

The 11-page draft program outline (*yōkō*) of December 25, 1951, resulting from the initial meeting AG Kimura had with his staff and others described a somewhat revised approach to this prickly issue.

[4] This account was derived from December 28, 1951 record of an Ōhashi-Rizzo meeting found in RG331:2187:4 in the U.S. National Archives II.

[5] This was distilled from a memo to Chief Government Section of a meeting between Rizzo and Ōhashi on January 10, 1952, on the latter's plan for a revision of the police law found in RG331:2187:7.

1. *Basic Policy*. The violent illegal tactics in Japan at this time reflected the international situation and when the basis of the internal security laws to control this violence were considered, it was clear that they all relied upon directives issued by SCAP. From the point of view of the contents of these directives there were many that would need to be abolished after the Peace Treaty comes into effect. If we do not take steps to remedy this situation, there will be a vacuum in internal security laws. Japan as an independent country must enact the necessary measures which

a) must be in accordance with and not contrary to the provisions of the Constitution,
b) must be effective in controlling these violent activities,
c) will, from their inherent nature, restrict the various freedoms guaranteed under the Constitution
d) must be kept to the absolute minimum.

2. *Specific Substantive Measures (jittai kitei)*

a. In order to maintain the principle of openness of political organizations and with the need to prevent the development of secret political organizations, the content of the measures for this purpose will be lessened to the extent possible.
b. Since these violent illegal tactics are committed by organizations with an international background, these must be handled effectively and when necessary not merely as individual violations but also as organizational violations. Therefore, measures will have to be taken to restrict, reorganize or disband the publishing and assembly activities of these organizations.

   In light of the spirit of the Constitution, the system of restricting employment of those in general enterprises (*ippan jigyō dantai*) and, of course, public service employees will be abolished and a new system of registering all constituent members of a disbanded organization will be instituted. This was regarded as a retreat from the enforced principle of openness of all political organizations.
c. In order to specify as clearly as possible the legal basis of responding to violent illegal tactics within the narrowest range possible, the provisions of the criminal code concerning civil war, preparations and plots, riots, aiding the enemy and foreign invasion, etc., will be applied together with actions which constitute preparing and plotting, inciting, instigating, advocating and planning to advocate these crimes, aiding such planning, advocating the rationality of these acts knowing that such advocacies will lead to their realization. The articles in the criminal code (CC) involved were 77, 81, 82, 93, 106, 199. AG Kimura

had accepted the use of the CC by reference initiated in draft 5. This program outline also most significantly stated that the 1940 provisional draft revision of the CC (*kaisei keihō kari'an*) would be consulted in drafting the SAPL.

3. *Procedural Stipulations.* In order to avoid excessive authority being vested in the governmental offices to carry out this law which may be abused, the investigative arm must be separated from the agency which will make the quasi-judicial rulings. For this purpose, the Public Security Investigation Agency (PSIA) as an Outer Bureau (*gaikyoku*) under the AG and a separate Public Security Examination Commission (PSEC) will be established. The latter may act only after the former has requested a particular punitive action and that the latter decision may be appealed to a Higher Court.

4. *Control of Organizations.* Political parties will be required to register and provide copies of their published journals to the government. The DG/PSIA will specify what political organizations will have to register except that it shall be clearly stated in the law that those organizations which have been regularly publicly publishing newspapers and magazines and conducting broadcasting will be exempt from the requirement to register as political organizations. Undoubtedly this special treatment stems from the influence of the media representatives on the Cabinet Ordinances Consultative Committee. The AG will be required to report to the Diet once a year.

Based on requests from the DG/PSIA, the PSEC may take various levels of administrative actions against organizations which conducted illegal violent activities: limit time and place of or place conditions on mass actions (*shūdan kōi*), or may prohibit such actions, place similar limitations on that organization's publications including banning their publications, order the revision of the organization's programs, bylaws and regulations, remove specific individuals from a specific range of positions, order the closure of specific organs of an organization, and the disbandment of the organization itself. When an organization has been ordered disbanded, it shall cease operations including rebuilding and reconstructions activities. The properties of these organizations shall be administered by the PSIA and the membership (including address, etc.) of these organizations shall be made public.

5. *Public Security Examination Commission (PSEC).* It shall consist of a chair and four other members. It's quasi-judicial actions shall be taken only after the DG/PSIA has made a request to the PSEC.

6. *Investigations.* The staff of the PSIA may invoke the authority of direct and indirect compulsory investigations (*chokusetsu, kansetsu kōsei chōsaken*) only to the least extent necessary for the investigation of the organization and only after obtaining a court order for obtaining information and the seizure of materials. This authority does not include authorization to take persons into custody. The police may be requested to assist in these investigations.

iii. *Drafts 7–11B*

1. *Draft 7 (1/10/1952).* As he had done in the past, Seki isolated himself for several days, January 3–7, 1952, in the famous hot-spring town of Atami, a little over an hour by express train from Tokyo, to create a new draft embodying the new somewhat modified principles. The 7th draft was completed on January 10, 1952, submitted to the AG and discussed with Liberal Party officials. The salient points in this draft which clarify the above points.

a. *Purposes.* To enhance the open public nature (*kōkai*) of secret political organizations, to prevent the destruction of the social order through illegal destructive activities, to take the necessary control measures following democratic procedures against organizations which carry out illegal activities, thereby maintaining the public welfare. Note that emergency detention is not mentioned and the objective only specifies secret political organizations NOT all political organizations. This was a major change, in the eyes of some, a major retreat.

b. *Exempt Groups.* The law will be executed in such a way as to take only the necessary minimum measures to achieve the aforementioned objectives; however, the law must not be applied (*tekiyō shite wa naranai*) to those organizations which are involved in fair (*kōsei*) announcements concerning issues of thought, religious beliefs (*shinkyō*) and academic studies and those organizations which conduct various normal (*seijōna*) activities in publishing newspapers, telecommunications, broadcasting and labor and those organizations whose conduct are for the purpose of these activities. This is a substantial enlargement of the exempt activities and exempt groups; fair/unbiased studies involving beliefs and genuine academic studies, telecommunications and labor were included for the first time.

c. *The Designated Industries.* They have been expanded to include banking and other enterprises specified by the AG with the approval of the Diet.

d. *Requests for Information.* In order to obtain the openness of secret political organizations, the DG/PSIA may, when he believes it to be necessary for this purpose, with the approval of the PSEC, request these organizations to provide information about their name, purpose, address of their main organization, the date when they became political organizations and the names and addresses of the principal officers of that organization.

e. *Procedures to be followed by the PSEC.* Because of the known criticisms and anxieties about how this law would be implemented by the government, there was an attempt to assure that the concerned or accused organizations and persons involved would be fairly treated. For example, the PSEC cannot take action unless requested by the DG/PSIA and the PSIA must obtain the permission of the PSEC to take certain actions. There was always the theoretical alternative for the accused to appeal to the courts, district, higher district and Supreme Courts.

It is important to note here that the PSEC would be permitted to play an active role in assessing the request by the PSIA. PSEC may

- request the accused party to submit a written response to the PSEC and that party may also make an oral presentation and provide other evidence to the PSEC;
- request other official agencies (*kōmusho*) to provide reports
- obtain the testimony of expert witnesses and reference persons (*sankōnin*)
- request those possessing or managing documents relevant to the case to provide them
- when it deems it necessary, visit and inspect the premises of the parties concerned and when this was done whether by a PSEC member or staff employee the results of these actions must be reported to the PSEC. Recordings of these meetings must be made and they will be publicly available. PSEC hearings must be held in public.

f. *Penalties on Organizations.* The PSEC may impose the following limitations on organizations which have committed illegal violent destructive activities, those which have repeatedly committed such acts and to prevent their recurrence in the future.:

- limit the time, place and other conditions on assembling and mass actions or prohibit them for a specified period.
- similar restrictions on the contents of publications issued by these organizations or prohibit their publication for a specified period.
- order the revision of their program outline, bylaws and regulations.
- order specified staff members of these organizations to be removed from a specified range of positions. In the eyes of some, this would be a dubious process similar to the Occupation's wholesale purging of selected Japanese leaders immediately after the war.
- order the dissolution/disbandment of an organization which has committed illegal acts, or has repeatedly committed such acts and is believed will continue to commit such acts which cannot be effectively prevented.
- based on the dissolution order in "e" above, the principal officers of the affected organization must report the names and addresses of all members of that organization for the past three years and their positions in that organization to the DG/PSIA and that information will be made public.

g. *Compulsory Investigative Authority.* The DG/PSIA may authorize Public Security Officials (*Kōan Chōsakan*) to request the parties concerned to appear in person, question them, request submission of reports and other papers and also to visit the offices of the parties concerned or other places necessary for this investigation and inspect the various papers. But for inspection, search and seizure of materials and persons a court order must be obtained for this purpose from a court judge; a sworn statement delineating the justification for this request must be prepared and submitted to this judge. If the judge believes the request is justified he must issue this certificate of approval. With this authority, the PSIA has the same authority as traditional police agencies—and that, of course, would be the source of future contention. But entering into the premises of the parties concerned must follow strict rules, e.g. not before sunrise, and not after sundown except when the search had begun before sundown and a list of any items removed must be prepared, and a copy given to the parties concerned. If the Judicial Police (shihō keisatsu), in accordance with the Criminal Procedures Law, had commenced a criminal investigation into illegal violent activities, it must immediately report such action to the DG/PSIA.

2. *Party Reactions.* The next day, January 11, 1952, Kimura and Seki held a meeting with the Liberal Party's General Affairs Council (Sōmukai) and the Self-Defense and Public Security Investigation Council to discuss the draft SAPL. Kimura was reported to have asserted that PM Yoshida had agreed to have the local police of the National Police (Kokka Chihō Keisatsu) transferred to the AG, and the internal security aspects of the local police placed under the AG's command. The above joint meeting concluded that

a. the "purge" aspect of the draft SAPL would be deleted (not a surprising demand since some senior leaders had been purged earlier by the U.S. Occupation)
b. since the content of draft bills under AG Ōhashi had been substantially changed, the title of the draft should be appropriately revised
c. the idea of elevating the PSIA to an Agency and increasing personnel would be deleted and abandoned
d. a new standing committee on internal security would be established in the Diet, thus requiring a revision to the Diet law
e. the compulsory investigative authority for the PSIA will be revisited and perhaps in the drafting process revised to concentrate this authority in the National Police—thus revealing the constant struggle about and challenge to giving this critical investigative authority to the PSIA.[6]

[6] *Yomiuri* 1/12/1952, *Asahi* 1//12/1952. I also came across a memo to Chief GS on this same meeting with a slightly different interpretive slant. The Liberal Party was represented by Masutani Shūji (Chairman, Executive Board), Masuda Kaneshichi (Secretary General), Ikeda Shōnosuke (Chairman, Self-Defense and Public Security Investigation Council). According to the memo, the purpose of the meeting was to give a friendly warning to the new AG to consult Liberal Party opinion before making any decisions concerning a new internal security law. There was opposition to expanding the SIB, agreement that a Diet committee on Public Security should be established, that internal security cases should be investigated by the National Rural Police, that a national security investigation agency should be created within the Cabinet with power to control all public security organizations, if the Cabinet was to assume political responsibility. Interestingly, the idea as to whether an existing law could be revised to take account of the provisions in the new draft law was fleetingly considered. Masutani called for an early submission and approval of such a law BEFORE the peace treaty was approved because of the gathering criticisms of such an internal security law. The memo concluded that "An undercurrent throughout the meeting indicated that the Liberal Party desired the abolition of the SIB since this organization was established under SCAP direction and was not 'entirely Japanese.' Memo: Reorganization of National Security Organization. 1/14/1952, RG331:2187:7. 2 p.

Ōhashi may have been shunted to the portfolios of the National Police and National Police Reserve but he adamantly continued to work on his concept of the governmental structure for maintaining internal security. At the end of January 1952, he let it be known that he had created a competitive alternative concept to counter and influence what the AG would be preparing; based on discussions with AG Kimura he hoped to submit a bill to the Diet to revise the police law and to create a Public Security Agency—all this even though clearly Kimura had been given the responsibility for drafting an internal security bill. The general outlines of the Ōhashi concept were as follows. In order to handle "special crimes" (*tokushu hanzai*) the National Police would be divided into two parts: 1) to handle cases concerning internal security, i.e. the special crimes on a nationwide basis, and those concerned with localized police matters; 2) the former would be combined with SIB to form the Investigations Agency (Chōsachō), an Outer Bureau of the AG, with a staff of judicial police with authority to inspect, search and seize; this Agency would also be able to use prosecutors: 3) special crimes would include forgery of currency and securities, bank and financial irregularities, crimes by national civil service employees, resources and facilities owned and managed by the government, civil war/insurrection, foreign invasions, weapons (guns, swords, etc.) and drugs; 4) this Agency could establish branches in Sapporo, Sendai, Tokyo, Nagoya, Osaka, Hiroshima, Fukuoka and Takamatsu; 5) the Scientific Investigation R&D Center, communications and other investigatory facilities now in the National Police would be transferred to this Agency.[7] Ōhashi thus continued to muddy the waters about the ever present debates about the institutional structure concerning internal security.

It is important to note that the concept of using the Criminal Code as the basis for defining illegal activities committed by an organization in the draft SAPL had been accepted by AG Kimura, but the composition, authorities, modes of operation of the PSEC had now become the principal focus of the AG's attention. Even after the comments received on draft 7 had been incorporated into draft 8A the AG still felt the PSEC as proposed could not be carried out and appropriate candidates for the PSEC would not be found—so, on January 29,

[7] *Asahi* 2/1/1952. Probably this report was based not on a detailed draft bill but on a program outline which, if accepted, would form the basis of a full-fledged bill.

1952, he ordered the preparation of drafts with different concepts for the PSEC. Based on these instructions, several drafts were prepared in quick succession from February 3 to 12, 1952: 9A (2/3/1952), 9B (2/3/1952), 10B (2/6/1952), 10C (2/6/1952) and 11B (2/12/1952). In these drafts the role of the PSEC and other aspects were envisioned in the following divergent manner.[8]

3. *Drafts 9A (2/3/1952)—11B (2/12/52)*

a. *Objectives.* Objectives remained the same in the five drafts 9A–11B: They were been changed from attempting to make "secret political organizations" open and to prevent, through democratic procedures, the occurrence of violent destructive activities which would destroy the social order, to controlling those organizations which have conducted violent destructive activities or whose objectives are to conduct such activities and "to supplement" the Criminal Code as a means to control these organizations. This approach would eliminate the need for the PSIA to become involved in the inevitably controversial exercise of designating which organizations were secret political organizations and would also eliminate the need to enforce a registration system.

b. *Proceedings of the PSEC.* The obvious alternatives were presented: two for open session, one closed session and one gave the PSEC authority to the AG and one ambiguous. The PSEC may investigate beyond what PSIA presented to the PSEC; another removed that authority and allowed the PSEC to consider only the facts as presented by the PSIA.

c. *Persons of knowledge and experience.* The number of such persons was increased from three to five—perhaps an influence from Major Jay in GHQ.

d. *Investigative Authority of the PSIA.* The PSEC may conduct investigations as necessary and may order the affected parties, reference persons to provide their opinions or reports, expert witnesses to do the

[8] Draft 7 based on the 12/25/1951 Program Outline was circulated to un-named concerned agencies for comment. A draft 8A was prepared incorporating their comments; but the AG continued to believe that the PSEC as envisioned could not function and appropriate candidates could not be found. Draft 8B was created. According to a list of drafts prepared by the AG's office, draft 8A and 8B are not available, However, it seems that drafts 9A and 9B took their place.

same, those who hold or possess various written and other materials to provide those materials and may keep them and may also visit the premises of the affected parties (Drafts 9A, 9B, 10B, 10C). The PSIA may request compulsory investigations (*kyōsei shobun*) to search, inspect and seize documents and persons by submitting in writing sufficient reasons for this authority to a judge in a district court; in turn, the judge, if he deems there is sufficient reason for this request, must issue a permit for such action but must specify what items and materials (*bukken*) need to be held (*sashiosaeru*), what organizations or persons may be searched and inspected, and where these persons/items are located, the name of the PSIA official, effective dates, and sign and apply his seal to the certificate of permission. However, in executing this certificate it must be issued/given to the judicial police in carrying out this action and the judicial police must hand over to the PSIA official the materials obtained from this action. In draft 11B, there were no requirements to submit a justification to a judge for the issuance of a certificate of permission and no specified requirements to request the judicial police to search, inspect and seize materials on behalf of the PSIA, by implication the PSIA was not given this authority beyond the above-mentioned inspection authority.

Thus, the AG had a pro forma array of possibilities to consider with the PSIA and PSEC functions both under the AG; under draft 9A, the PSEC would conduct its proceedings in the open, 9B would be in camera and would base its decision only on materials submitted to it by the PSIA, 10C would not create a PSEC but give this authority to the AG.[9]

iv. *GHQ-IV, Waning Twilight, Constitutionality-1*

1. *SAPL Constitutionality.* For the first time on February 10, 1952, one finds a detailed description by a GHQ/SCAP official on draft number 10 (B or C not specified) February 6, 1952. In his concluding paragraph, he noted that:

> Upon first consideration, the principal ground of objection would seem to be that the Attorney General is given a broad power of administrative

[9] No record was found that these versions were given to GS/GHQ. The official records in the AG of the various drafts of the proposed SAPL did not include the translated versions, if any; Japanese versions of these drafts were not found in GHQ archives.

> determination; however, this is surrounded by the safeguards of notice and hearings and warrants, and since any administrative action must be reviewed by the courts it is not a final judicial power and, therefore, not unconstitutional.[10]

According to a February 11, 1952 meeting between Rizzo and Yoshikawa, DG/SIB, the SAPL draft was tangled with the reorganization of security agencies in the Japanese Government, the possible amalgamation of the SIB and the District Headquarters of the National Police to form an organization something like the U.S. Federal Bureau of Investigation under the Prime Minister's Office or under the Attorney General. The organizational issue had to be resolved before a definitive SAPL draft could be agree upon.[11] This was followed a few days later by a meeting between AG Kimura and Rizzo. Kimura reported that

> a. There was a need for an inclusive law to curb the increasing threat presented by the Communists and their increasingly destructive activities as manifested in a) the tie-in between the JCP and international communism, b) threat from infiltration into the labor movement to utilize the masses for furtherance of its destructive aims, and c) utilization of the Japan Teachers Union with an annual income of six billion yen and with membership in the Diet.
> b. The SIB, procurator and NPR established during the Occupation should be retained and not combined.

Rizzo expressed "his appreciation for this visit" and commented that "on the whole the law was well drafted because two important ideas had been kept in mind: 1) the object of the government to protect itself against subversive groups who work against the interests of Japan and 2) respecting the basic human rights as required by the [Japanese] Constitution." Rizzo felt there were "a few differences of opinion regarding procedural matters" which should be straightened out in a few days at which time GS clearance could be given. AG Kimura opined that there would difficulties in the Diet with this Bill but Rizzo encouraged him that there was a wide enough area of acceptance by conservative element for its final passage.[12]

---

[10] Memo (2/10/1952) for Chief, GS, by W.E. Monagan, special assistant to GS Chief, Summary of Special Security Act [Tokubetsu Hoanhō] (10th draft).

[11] Memo (2/11/1952) for Chief, GS from S. Hayashi, on SIB and Security Problems [Rizzo-Yoshikawa meeting], 2 p.

[12] Memo (2/16/1952) for Chief, GS from S. Hayashi, Conference with Attorney General Kimura, 3 p.

2. *GS-ESS "Debate" over Clearing Japanese Legislative Proposals.* In January 1952, GS, in line with the above May 1951 policy statement, proposed to the Deputy Chief of Staff on January 16, 1952 a modification of the internal GHQ procedure for clearing Japanese legislative proposals. The Economic and Science Section (ESS) objected, GS countered with a memo stating its disagreements with ESS and recommended that the matter be referred to the Chief of Staff for resolution. Keep in mind that January 1952 was only a few months before GHQ/SCAP would go out of existence. The bureaucratic argument revealed in this memo showed the reluctance of ESS to relinquish its supervisory role over internal Japanese affairs. This bureaucratic debate was quite extraordinary in light of the reality that now pervaded GHQ and the Japanese Government.[13]

v. *Retreating to the Status Quo*

While the AG's office was creating these drafts, the institutional debate about the internal security apparatus intensified several notches from early February to about February 15, 1952. Frequent high level meetings were held with cynical shifting alliances, changing structural proposals and ultimately coming full circle. AG Kimura was summoned by the PM for a meeting on February 7 morning and instructed him to finalize the SAPL draft. This prompted the AG to call a meeting with Minister of Construction Noda and, instead of inviting Minister Ōhashi, the AG summoned the principal career civil service staff from the NPR to hear NPR views, a highly un-bureaucratic and quite contrary to bureaucratic etiquette. This, of course, angered Ōhashi who won sympathy from his colleagues at a subsequent Cabinet meeting the same day. On February 8, AG Kimura (and Noda) met with Party SecGen Masuda and Masutani Director of the Party's Sōmukai and proposed that 1) a Public Security Agency be created as an outer bureau of the AG to handle special crimes, 2) the NPR be integrated into the AG as an outer bureau, 3) the National Public Security Commission (Kokka Kōan Iinkai) be abolished and 4) general police administra-

[13] SCAP's changing role was discussed in a memo to GS Chief by "J.W." of 1/26/1952 concerning clearance of Japanese Legislative Measures. This was in rebuttal to an ESS memo of 1/18/1952 which raised objections to the GS memo of 1/16/1952. Neither of the latter two memos have been located nor whether this bureaucratic issue was indeed referred to the Chief of Staff, GHQ.

tion be transferred to local authorities. But this proposal was strongly criticized as an emerging police state especially when the Public Security Examination Commission and the prosecutorial function would be under the AG and if general police administration was transferred out then national crimes could not be handled effectively. AG Kimura promised to reconsider.[14]

Then on February 11 after "coordinating" with Kimura and Noda, Ōhashi met with Masuda and obtained his informal decision (*naitei*) to put the investigation agency (Chōsachō) as an outer bureau in the PM's office under the Minister for National Police. This Agency would be responsible for most of the work of the SIB, Immigration Agency and the intelligence function of the NP but not prosecutorial and police functions. The NPR and Maritime Safety Board would also be part of the PM's office under a Minister of State. This proposal was a ploy to obtain Masuda's support since it appears he supported this approach; but, of course, this proposed structure would be anathema to the AG.[15]

In order to resolve these differences and paralysis and to push forward with administrative reform PM Yoshida summoned Kimura, Ōhashi and other Ministers concerned with internal security matters to a meeting on February 13 at the Foreign Minister's residence. The Kimura/Noda concept was discussed and accepted as the government's plan: under these uncertain circumstances the consensus was not to change the existing proposed structure! The next day, February 14, final coordination was achieved with a meeting between the AG and the Party's Self-Defense and Internal Security Investigation Committee and a general outline was announced. As a final ironic twist to this saga, responsibility for the NP was transferred to the AG. Ōhashi remained in charge of the NPR. This slight Cabinet re-arrangement, just as the internal security debate had seemingly reach a conclusion, reflected 1) the attempt to avoid the impression of creating a police state by clearly separating military and police functions, 2) the decision to strengthen the self-defense/military forces in future years and 3) after the emotional personal confrontation between Kimura and Ōhashi, the political removal of the latter from future deliberations

[14] *Asahi* 2/9/1952.
[15] *Asahi* 2/12/1952, *Yomiuri* 2/12/1952.

concerning internal security. The decision to retreat to the status quo did not, however, end the continuing wrangle.[16]

The collision of the differing concepts between Kimura and Ōhashi about internal security arrangements as outline above created a near paralysis in the Cabinet. There was a thick overlay of emotional antagonism over this issue between Kimura and Ōhashi about their political primacy. The seeds for this confrontation were probably laid the previous summer in 1951 when Kimura joined the Prime Minister's Consultative Committee on Cabinet Ordinances and made an informal set of recommendations to Yoshida urging the creation of one Ministry of Security including the NPR, NP, Maritime Safety Board and the SIB. At that time, Ōhashi was the AG. When Kimura became AG and Ōhashi was transferred to be Minister in charge of NPR and NP their differing concepts on this issue flared into the open.

Under Occupation guidance and insistence, police powers were dispersed and "democratized a la the U.S. system" and to prevent a recurrence of prewar abuses of police power in Japan. Now as Japan faced the requirements of internal security and the so-called violent challenge from the JCP, it was strongly felt that this diffusion of police power would be ineffective and inefficient and potentially dangerous. This was symbolized in the minds of many by the SIB's inability to track the disappearance of nine JCP leaders who had been purged in 1950. But how to revise and strengthen these security arrangements without possibly recreating the prewar police system and conflicting with SCAP police democratization policies were the thorny issues. AG Ōhashi proposed elevating the SIB to an Agency and substantially increasing its personnel with enhanced authority and bring the NP under the AG. But that was viewed suspiciously by the NP and old line police agencies. As described earlier, Kimura and Ōhashi greatly irritated each other and poisoned the atmosphere by end runs to Yoshida, the Party SecGen, and Ōhashi's sudden switch from advocating the inclusion of the NP and SIB in the AG to placing them in the PM's office, the structure presumably favored by the Party SecGen. While Ōhashi would relentlessly annoyingly pursue his beliefs about internal security arrangements, Kimura arrived as AG and declared that we

[16] *Asahi* 2/15/1952 and 2/15/1952, *Mainichi* 2/13/1952, *Yomiuri* 2/14/1952. However, I have not found any public announcement nor a program outline with that date.

will return to square one (*hakushi ni kaesu*); of course, we really did not but he did call for alternative roles for the PSEC to be considered as described above but did not, it appears, push strongly enough for giving compulsory investigative authority to the SIB—all to the chagrin of his senior career civil service staff, the Bureau Chiefs (Assistant Secretary level in the USG). He also dithered about locating the SIB and NP both in the AG or in the PM's office, thereby appearing not to support his own Ministry.[17]

A member of the PM's Cabinet Ordinances Consultative Committee, Obama Toshie, took his objections to the Ōhashi plan directly to the PM. To add to this surfeit of assertions, Hori, Cabinet Secretary General urged that the line between external defense and internal security should be clearly maintained, thus an influential voice countering Ōhashi and Kimura. PM also intervened by summoning his Ministers to break the impasse.

There was also lurking in the background, the unknown power and influence of public opinion which seemed in the eye of those involved in this process, to be much concerned about the re-creation, intentionally or unintentionally, of prewar police powers. In addition to the amorphous public opinion there was also the threats from the militant labor unions and their political allies in the Diet, the Social Democratic Socialists, and the JCP which would determinedly oppose the proposed bill and the uncertain role of SCAP.

In light of the above, reorganization of self-defense and internal institutional arrangements, the two most important items in the Cabinet's administrative reform program, were buffeted by personality conflicts, factional disagreements, unrequited dreams of prewar Home Ministry purged and de-purged alumni, limited anxiety about the importance about public opinion, the final solution was "to retreat to the status quo" and reduce the scope of the proposed draft SAPL.

[17] It is no wonder that other security agencies were somewhat resentful and jealous of the SIB. When it was formed in 1948 it had only a staff of 150 but because of added responsibilities, it increased in May 1950 to 537, 1200 in August 1950 (prosecutors had increased from 7 to 25). Soon after the enactment of the SAPL, the SIB increased yet again to 1700 in August 1952. *Mainichi Nenkan* 1952:179, John Dower, *Empire and Aftermath*, Rodger Swearingen and Paul Langer, *Red Flag in Japan*, 1952.

vi. *Gaikyoku (Outer Bureau)*

The government insisted that by creating the PSIA and the PSEC as "*gaikyoku*" (outer bureaus) of the Ministry of Justice, it would be independent, removed from political contamination; the PSIA could provide a reasonable, neutral and fair recommendation to the PSEC and the latter could render a fair and neutral decision. The opposition, of course, asserted with similar vehemence quite the opposite especially since a *gaikyoku* would structurally be part of the Ministry of Justice and thus under the Minister of Justice even though the PSEC members would be appointed by the PM with the approval of the Diet.[18] What then was the status and nature of the PSIA and PSEC as "*gaikyoku*"?

The "*gaikyoku*" idea has had a varied, checkered and ambiguous history. Quite aside from the meaning of this term, the use of the term existed from before 1945 by many years, so it is not a term that suddenly appeared after 1945. For example, a cautionary and critical prewar essay by Murakami Kyōichi discussed the structure of the "*gaikyoku*" but it seems that the concept of a *gaikyoku* then was different from what it has evolved into in later postwar years. It noted that 20–30 years previously, between about 1910–20, there were very few such organizations that might be designated as *gaikyoku*. In the late 1930s, each ministry appears to have had two or more such *gaikyoku* and the tendency was for them to gradually increase in number; one might even call it a popular trend. *Gaikyoku* was not yet a term used in laws but a term used colloquially which applied only to the structure of the national government. Without a clear definition of what a *gaikyoku* is, Murakami cited the following examples as *gaikyoku*: under the Cabinet, Legislative Affairs Bureau (Hōsei-kyoku), Ministry of Agriculture Horse Administrative Bureau (Basei-kyoku), Ministry of Commerce Patents Office (Tokkyo-kyoku), Kōsei-shō (Ministry of

[18] This discussion of the position of a "*gaikyoku*" was based on the following references: *A Japanese-English Dictionary of Legal Terms with Supplement* (*Zōho Wa-Ei Hōritsugo Jiten*), Daigaku Shobō, 1972, p. 109; Murakami Kyōichi, Gaikyoku no Kikō ni tsuite, *Jichi Kenkyū* 15:10 (10/1939:45–60; *Roppō Zensho* Iwanami Shoten, 1949 ed., p. 5–6; *Roppō Zensho*, Yūhikaku, 2001 ed., pp. 246–24:7; *Shinpan Hōrei Yōgo no Jōshiki*, (Nihon Hyōronsha, 1964, pp. 155–159; Satō Isao, *Gyōsei Soshiki-hō*, Yūhikaku, 1979, 147–153, 208–214, 251–252, 262–289; *Gendai Hōritsu Hyakka Dai-Jiten*, Gyōsei, 2000, p. 310; *Shin-Hōritsugaku Jiten*, (Yūhikaku, 1988, p. 99; *Hōgaku Jiten*, Nihon Hyōronsha, 1971, p. 71; *Hōritsu Yōgo Jiten*, Yūhikaku, 2000, p. 94. There are many academic studies on *gyōseigaku* (administrative law) in Japanese; I have, however, chosen to rely, in the main, on Satō's book which is regarded as a classic in this field.

Health and Human Welfare) Board of Insurance (Hoken'in) and others; note that they were then, in general, designated as "kyoku". The responsibilities of a Ministry were included in its constituent elements with no theoretical need for an organization handling *gaikyoku*-type matters. Based on this reasoning, *gaikyoku* was an "organizational oddity" (*hentai-teki zonzai*). The organizations under the Office of the Prime Minister (Sōrifu) were by their nature "*gaikyoku*" but he cautioned that as few of them as possible should be created. He cited the "joint" Ministries of Agriculture and War outer bureau as an example of a joint function, the management of horses to assure a necessary national supply for civilian and military purposes, as another kind of *gaikyoku*. Another *gaikyoku* could be designated when there was a national and local component to its responsibilities, such as the Savings Bureau in the Ministry of Communications, the Monopoly Bureau in the Ministry of Finance. Another category would be when a unit had such a large number of employees it would be set aside as a *gaikyoku* with a head who had a higher rank than other heads of Bureaus; this was, he said, the weakest reason for creating a *gaikyoku*. Because these *gaikyoku* "report" to the Minister they are not, says Murakami, part of the top bureaucratic central governmental structure but something less. *Gaikyoku* were, nevertheless, able to make decisions and so announce these decisions publicly but this depends, in each case, on the law or orders defining a *gaikyoku* and the head of a *gaikyoku* should report to the Minister responsible through the Administrative Deputy Minister for this administrative area. A *gaikyoku* is, in reality, not an independent organ but an auxiliary organ (*hojo kikan*); inevitably it may have more independence than other elements in the Ministry but the potential conflict between the head of a *gaikyoku* and the Minister must not be allowed to surface. There is a potentiality that the *gaikyoku* may begin to act as a co-equal in its negotiations with its Ministry and undermine the harmony of a Ministry. Murakami's conclusion, in light of these problems, was to create only the fewest number of *gaikyoku* as necessary.

As part of administrative reform to streamline government operations under wartime conditions, the Kansei Tsūsoku (uniform regulations on government operations, enacted in 1893, abolished 1947) was revised in 1942 (Imperial decree 706); in this reform, the commonly used collective term "*gaikyoku*" was given a formal institutional name, "*shō gaikyoku-bu*" (the *gaikyoku* department in a Ministry). Hitherto, heads of *gaikyoku* reported directly to the Minister not through the

Deputy Minister; under article 16, supervision and control of *gaikyoku* would now be exercised by the Deputy Minister. Perhaps use of the term *gaikyoku* implying a separateness or a distance from the Minister was not entirely correct since the head of a so-called *gaikyoku* had been reporting to the Minister to begin with. Thus the ambiguity of the status and role of the *gaikyoku* was not clarified by this wartime reform, merely carried over without resolution.

In the early postwar period, the Gyōsei Kanchō-hō (law #69/1947:3) stipulated that the *gaikyoku* will be supervised by the Minister "as it had been in the past" and "*gaikyoku*" was used as a legal term (*hōritsu yōgo to shite*) for the first time. In this law, the equivalent of the above mentioned article 16 did not exist; instead article 8 stipulated that unless otherwise stated by law or ordinance (*seirei*) the various kinds of tasks and personnel for these purposes will be placed under the jurisdiction of the Ministry as has been the case in the past.

Later, a new fundamental law governing the structure of the Japanese Government was enacted in 1948, inevitably and obviously under the influence of the then prevailing U.S. Occupation of Japan. Through the adoption of this law, the Kokka Gyōsei Soshikihō (National Administrative Organization Law) a U.S. philosophical approach to the structure of government was used and the prewar German approach seemingly abandoned. One of the obvious examples, among many that could be cited, was the attempt to "reflect" the U.S. image by creating an Attorney-General and abolishing the Minister of Justice and the establishment of independent commissions like the U.S. Federal Trade Commission. Article 3.2 of this law, stipulated that the national administrative organizations (*gyōsei kikan*) would consist of the ministries, commissions and agencies which would be created or abolished according to specific laws. It was hoped that these Commissions would lead to a more democratic government not a bureaucratic government. Some Agencies, like Self-Defense, Economic Planning, are headed by DGs who are also Ministers of State. Then there are such agencies as the Metropolitan Police and the National Public Security Commission which are part of the Prime Minister's Office as *gaikyoku* but not headed by Ministers of State. Yet the next clause, article 3.3, stipulates that ministries would be responsible for their respective areas of responsibilities under the control (tōkatsu) of the Cabinet and that commissions and agencies could be created "as *gaikyoku* in a ministry" (*shō ni gaikyoku toshite okareru*). Note that commissions and agencies were mentioned on par with ministries as basic administrative organizations of the governmental structure of Japan; they appear to be given independent status as a general organization (*dokuritsu-teki na sōgōtai toshite toraeru*). They exist in parallel (*heiritsu*) with the Ministries.

Seven factors could be used, according to Satō (p. 268), to judge a Commission's independence: is under the general supervision of the Prime Minister, the Commission Chair and members can independently wield their authority, their appointments by the PM must be approved by the Diet, both Chair and members have a set term of office, their positions and status are assured, and their salaries are similarly assured, the Commission has a quasi-judicial or quasi-legislative authority. Based on these criteria, the PSEC meets almost all these criteria, except that while the PSEC members are appointed by the PM with the approval of the Diet, the PSEC is not a *gaikyoku* of the PM's office but placed in the Ministry of Justice thereby compromising or complicating its so-called "independent status".

Under Occupation tutelage, independent Commissions proliferated, as many as 23. When the Yoshida Cabinet was given the opportunity to reconsider laws created under the Occupation, it created a special consultative committee, the Seirei Shimon Iinkai, reporting directly to the PM. Its report characterized the "Independent Commission" as a system not friendly: it described them as not in line with Japanese style of governance in contrast to that in the U.S., not responsive to Japanese economic and political requirements, had mushroomed to a large number, lacked clear political authority, were not operating sufficiently efficiently to achieve their administrative responsibilities. It concluded that they should be, in principle, abolished, except where a neutral authority was needed. Thereafter, within a few years, the number of Commissions dwindled from the 23 to about 13.

According to Satō (pp. 208–214), through the Constitution (article 74), the Cabinet Law (article 3) and the Organization Law, all administrative duties and responsibilities for managing the government have been assigned and those for commissions and agencies would derive from those assigned to a Ministry. After internal assignments are made, then assignments for a *gaikyoku* could be given; thus, although commissions and agencies are listed in the law as part of the fundamental structure of the government, their missions are far more specific and narrower than those of Ministries. However, in many cases, commission and agency assignments of duties, responsibilities and authorities are defined in a law enacted by the Diet establishing these organizations not through the inherent authority of a Minister; in that case, the Ministry would merely include these duties, etc., by reference as part of its responsibilities. In contrast to the relationship between a Commission and an Agency with its parent Ministry, the relationship between the office of the Prime Minister and its *gaikyoku* are quite weak and attenuated.

Commissions would be created to handle issues that required special political sensitivity, strict fairness, balance and neutrality detached from the potential hurly-burly political atmosphere in a Ministry, that required a certain distance and independence from the PM's office and its parent Ministry—if indeed such political neutrality and fairness is truly attainable—through a consultative arrangement in arriving at a neutral and fair decision as a commission (*gōgisei kikan*). The underlying legal philosophy in creating such agencies was when the work in a particular Ministry was so large that it would be more appropriate to remove that workload to a specially created agency. The PSIA, however, was proposed for the same reasons used for creating the PSEC, fairness, balance, neutrality, etc., because of the political sensitivities involved. Their decisions were expected to based on thorough research, non-partisan, rational and technically correct policies. They were described as "independent"of, yet part of a Ministry headed by a Minister of State but an agency, based on a reading of the Organization Law (article 7.6) is somewhat more an integral part of the Ministry than a commission; their establishment and areas of responsibility would be specified by Ministry Ordinance (*Shōrei*). Over the years, the DG/PSIA has been appointed on a rotational basis like other DGs in the Ministry from among senior prosecutors, thus outer bureau "independence" was now in name only.

Satō described five kinds of commissions (p. 213): those to maintain administrative neutrality (the National Personnel Office (Jinji'in); to render a fair decision based on specialized knowledge (the Commission to oversee the national lawyers' examination); to render a decision based on a procedure following those of the judiciary to protect individual human rights (the PSEC); to provide a decision stemming from various conflicts of interests (the Central Labor Committee); and lastly to act as a coordinating body when there are many administrative units involved in any particular issue (the Committee to Adjust Opinions concerning Pollution).

What then, as a matter of principle, is the authority of the Minister of Justice (or the Administrative Deputy Minister) in controlling and influencing the PSEC? Or, obversely, what is the degree of independence from, in this case, the Minister of Justice that can be enjoyed and maintained by the PSEC? According to the law establishing the PSEC, it shall carry out its duties "independently" (article 3). This was the nub of the contention between the AG and the political opposition. While a few agencies, like the Bōeichō (the Self-Defense Agency) are headed by Ministers of State, the independence of such an agency as the PSIA, which is more part of a Ministry, cannot be compared to the independence of the PSEC which is psychologically, environmentally and politically more removed from the Ministry. For this purpose, let us review how the Organization Law assigns responsibilities and authorities to these organizations.

Article 7.7. Commissions may establish their own administrative structures including an overall general affairs bureau in accordance with the law creating this Commission.

Article 10. Commissions (and Ministries and Agencies) will control their areas of responsibilities and manage the rules governing their personnel.

Article 12.1. The Minister will issue Ministerial ordinances as an ordinance of the Commission or Agency in executing their areas of responsibilities.

Article 12.2. The head of a *gaikyoku* may request the Minister to issue Ministerial ordinances based on written proposals.

Article 13. The heads of these organizations may issue orders outside of those issued by the Ministry.

Article 14.1. Heads of *gaikyoku* may issue orders and instructions as necessary.

Article 14.2. May issue various instructions (*kokuji*) and regulations governing staff members of these organizations in the execution of their duties.

Article 15. May request another commission or agency involved to provide materials and explanations and voice opinions about the policies pursued by that organization.

Article 18.2. The administrative vice-minister will assist the Minister, supervise and oversee the official business of the Ministry and those of the *kikan* [implicitly including the *gaikyoku* as a *kikan*]. This is in seeming contrast to what was stipulated in article 3 of the Gyōsei Kanchōhō mentioned earlier.

The Kokka Kōmuin-hō (law governing civil service employees) provides the following authority to heads of *gaikyoku*:

Article 55.1. Appointive power over personnel necessary to carry out the assigned tasks.

The government draft of the Organization Law contained a clause *excluding* the supervision of *gaikyoku* areas of responsibilities from those of the Minister but the Diet deleted that phrase; thus, it would be a legitimate interpretation to say that the intent of the Diet was to allow the Minister to supervise and oversee the work of the commissions and agencies. As though to muddy the waters still further, the Organization Law stipulates that the Administrative Deputy Minister (the most senior career official who basically runs the Ministry) assists the Minister, supervises and oversees all aspects of the administration of the various elements and organizations (*kikan*, implying a commission or agency which collectively are referred to as *kikan* but not actually using the term *gaikyoku*) of the Ministry (article 17.2.2).

The issue of the independence of such organizations as the PSEC has also been debated at much length among Japanese scholars of the governmental system (*gyōseigaku*) especially in relation to article 65 of the Constitution which gives all responsibility for the management of the Japanese Government to the Cabinet. Under these conditions, how "independent" can a commission be in strict legal and administrative terms? This factor muddies still further the "theoretical" independence of such commissions as the PSEC.[19]

Satō concluded (p. 265) that it cannot be said that the commissions and agencies will be truly independent from the Minister concerned, a conclusion with which I agree after considering the factors described above. As far as this study is concerned, therefore, both the government and the political opposition could legitimately and simultaneously but ambiguously claim that the PSIA and particularly the PSEC are independent and not independent. The "independence" of these commissions and the agencies, their bureaucratic parity with Minis-

[19] This issue is discussed at some length by Satō in *Gyōsei Soshiki-hō*, pp. 251–289.

ters of State, is almost like a mirage, it is there, yet perhaps it is not there.[20]

vii. *Drafts 12–14 (2/19/1952)*

1. *Draft 12.* Under these circumstances, the AG decided to create draft 12 following along the lines of draft 9B.

a. *Objectives.* To determine the necessary control measures to be taken against organizations which conduct violent destructive activities or whose objectives are to conduct such activities, to augment the punishment stipulations about such violent activities in the criminal code, thereby maintaining public welfare.

b. *Application.* The controls specified in this law would be applied only to the necessary extent, must not deviate from these objects nor infringe on any of the basic freedoms guaranteed in the Constitution (thought, belief, assembly, association, expression and academic freedoms) and the right of workers to organize and to conduct mass meetings and other rights guaranteed in the Constitution.

c. *Definitions.* Violent destructive activities were defined as follows:

a. Article 77 (civil war, insurrection) of the Criminal Code. To conduct civil war, to plot, to plan, to assist, to instigate, to incite, to assist in the planning and plotting, to distribute or to plan to distribute publications which contain material explaining the necessity and appropriateness with the intention of contributing to the realization of such acts.
b. In order to foster (*suishin*), support, or oppose certain political principles (*shugi*) or policies, commit acts stipulated in

[20] Initially, the English translation of "*gaikyoku*" was, it appears, "independent organizations" reflecting U.S. influence and terminology; later they were referred to in English as "external organs" after discussions with Occupation officials who only dealt in English not Japanese terms. This change does imply a weakening of the concept of independence from the mother Ministry; was this the Japanese intent or not, is not clear. To me, "external" gives the impression of not being part of a Ministry. Thus, I prefer the more literal translation of "outer bureau" because in Japanese *gaikyoku* is the apposite of *naikyoku* (although this term is not used in the law). The latter offices are part of the basic structure of the Ministry where, in contrast, the PSIA, the PSEC are supposedly detached but still somehow regarded as a constituent element of the Ministry.

- article 95 (obstructing the execution of public duties) by attacking police or other public employees (national and local) involved in maintaining public peace with dangerous weapons and mass activities (*taishū kyōdō to shite*) or to plot, plan, instigate or incite actions for this purpose.
- articles 106 (riots), 108 (setting fire to dwellings), 109 (Setting fire to structures other than dwellings), 199 (murder), or destroy or damage or cause the dysfunction of the facilities of specified industries (railroads, water, electric power, gas supply, newspaper publication, broadcasting).

The above reflects major changes from the initial drafts which anticipated a far broader dragnet over the entire political spectrum, referenced use of additional articles, 95, 106, 108, 109, 199 from the Criminal Code and deleted others; the mention of attacks against the police reflect the kinds of violent activities happening at about the same time in the drafting process. The admonitions about the application of this law have become highly explicit about not infringing on Constitutional freedoms and exempting organized labor and the media from this law.

d. *The PSEC.* The PSEC shall hear cases only after the PSIA requests the PSEC to take action. The PSEC shall not be limited to PSIA's analysis of the reasoning for the proposed action. The witnesses to the hearings against an organization would be five but only these witnesses shall be permitted to listen to the hearings. Those materials deemed unnecessary by a designated PSEC hearing official need not be investigated any further.

e. *Investigative Authority.* The PSIA's investigative authorities were the same as those stated in draft 9A above.

2. *Draft 13 (2/22/1952).* On February 20, 1952, at an interagency meeting of the National Police, National Police Headquarters (Keishichō) and SIB, the former two demanded that all investigations involving the authority for "compulsory investigations" be delegated to them. In light of "future working relationships" SIB acceded to their demands in the following manner:

a. *Authority of the PSIA Investigating Officer.* In earlier drafts the PSIA Investigating Officer could always request to read and study various materials including evidentiary materials held by the judicial police, prosecutors and the courts necessary for investigations relating to the execution of this law. In draft 13, however, a small change was made: the studying of these requested materials must be made so that the normal work of the agencies holding these materials would not be obstructed. While minor in nature it surely must reveal how the other old-time agencies looked upon the staff of a new upgraded SIB to PSIA as potential nuisances and a potential imposition on their workloads. This was a small slap in the face to the SIB/PSIA through proposed legislation and to the AG.

b. *Compulsory Investigative Authority.* Of the three authorities involving search, inspection and seizure which have been lumped to together in the past appear to have been split in draft 13. The PSIA Investigations Officer may make a written request to a judge in a nearby district court to issue a certificate of permission "to search" the premises, study its financial records and other materials in the premises of the organization under investigation or other related locations provided this is within the necessity and needs of carrying out investigations under this law. This apparently was not regarded as a "compulsory investigation" in the eyes of the police.

When it would be necessary to take action involving "compulsory measures", the PSIA official would request the judicial police to take this action "to search" the premises and then report the circumstances and results (*temmatsu*) of this search. There was no mention of inspection (*rinken*) or seizure (*sashiosaeru*) which had always been mentioned as part of compulsory investigations. The earlier requirement for the police to give the materials from the search, inspection and seizure to the SIB were deleted and perhaps subsumed under "reporting the circumstances and results". Whatever the interpretation may be, this sounded like another major retreat and compromise by the AG to serve bureaucratic turf interests.

3. *Draft 14 (3/3/1952)*

a. *Representatives of the Affected Organization.* Under draft 13, the number was limited to three. Under draft 14, the affected organization may appoint lawyers and others to be their representatives. But at the hearing, they will be limited to five persons including the principal officer and they will be able to make a presentation and give "advantageous evidence" (*yūri na shōko*) to the specified PSIA hearing officer in defense of its actions.

b. *The Witnesses* (Jiken Tachiai-nin) *at the Hearing.* Previously the DG/PSIA was given the authority to choose at least five persons. But in draft 14, the authority to choose was changed from the DG/PSIA to the affected organization and also permitted the representatives of the newspapers, telecommunications and broadcasting industries to attend these hearings. The presiding PSIA Official may declare some evidence submitted to the hearing officer as unnecessary but in so doing he must not abuse his authority and unfairly infringe on a fair and sufficient hearing of the affected organization.

c. *Hearing Report.* The specified PSIA officer must prepare a report of the hearing, read it to the principal officer and representatives of the accused organization and must attach their comments to the report.

d. *The Request to the PSEC.* This request for action to be taken against the affected organization must include the evidence proving the basis of the request and the report mentioned in item 3 above.

e. *PSIA must Justify Requests.* When the affected organization is ordered to appear or to provide various materials, the PSIA must provide a reason explaining the necessity for the order.

f. *Compulsory Investigative Authority.* The revised and limited authority granted to PSIA officials in draft 13 was further limited by deleting their ability to go to a judge to obtain permission for searching the premises of an organization, an almost complete loss of compulsory authority. PSIA officials must rely completely on the cooperation of the judicial police by requesting them to conduct searches, inspections and seizures of materials and people as necessary. The police must report on the results of such actions to the PSIA and, as usual, the PSIA may accompany the police on such actions.

viii. *GHQ-V, Waning Twilight, Constitutionality-2*

Major Jay, special assistant to Frank Rizzo, head of GS, had a difficult role to play in commenting on the drafting of anticipated sensitive legislation in the AG's Office. He needed to be persuasive with the context of an aura of authority of the once all powerful Occupation GHQ. When Jay arrived in late 1951, he was confronted with the 9th and 10th draft versions. According to both Major Jay of GHQ and Seki the principal drafter of the SAPL, they had a cordial working relationship and for many years exchanged Holiday Seasons greetings and they later met in New York. Jay felt that the Director General of SIB was not really interested in the fine points of Anglo-Saxon legal thought but Seki Itaru, SIB Deputy Director, was "a poet and scholar" and interested in understanding these fine points. It is important to note that Jay studied only the English translations of the various SAPL drafts which, he said, were "the governing texts"; the Japanese texts were not given a thought and we paid no attention to them. We approved/disapproved only an English text, not the Japanese original! Since the Japanese Constitution was regarded "as a parallel constitution", on constitutional issues, the U.S. Constitution was the guide. He explained that the biggest problem and greatest difficulty with the Japanese were the concepts of common law and due process of which they have "little understanding". The Japanese side had led the GS officials to believe that the U.S. Smith Act was, in a major way, the model used for the SAPL since this law had been declared constitutional by the U.S. Supreme Court. Apparently Jay was not aware that other internal security laws, e.g., the Soviet law, had been consulted and some ideas had been given serious attention. If I had know that, he said, I would have had a much better understanding of the Japanese drafts and from whence they came and my reactions would have been quite different. These other foreign laws would have been "irrelevant" to us, explained Jay, "the minimum would have been constitutional with the U.S. Constitution". Major Jay said he worked with no one in GHQ except with Frank Rizzo with whom he agreed on fundamental issues, except for one person in the Labor Section in GHQ, whom he said, did not participate even though on the Japanese side, labor unions were vociferous opponents of the SAPL. In theory, GS had the responsibility for formulating a GHQ position and then coordinating that position on Japanese legislative issues with other GHQ sections. By this time, serious coordination did not take place. Jay also said he did not meet with Japanese labor union leaders which spearheaded the opposition to the SAPL and the opposition political parties.[21]

[21] Based on an interview with Ed Jay on October 14, 1978 in his home in New York state. In this interview, he told me that when he, as a U.S. Army Major (Armor) arrived in Japan, he was en route to Korea but that was suddenly changed to GHQ in Tokyo; fortuitously W.E. Monagan, special assistant to Frank Rizzo, Chief of GS, and who had been covering SAPL developments, was about to leave so Jay was assigned to succeed him in January 1952. Says Jay: constitutional law and the SAPL were the last thing on my mind as an assignment. He received a commendation from SCAP's

Draft 13 was translated and given to GHQ (Major Jay and M. Matsukata) and apparently the source of "a great debate" (*iken o tatakawasu*) between Jay and Seki over evidence and investigative authority in the draft bill. GHQ used only the English translation, paying no attention to the original Japanese draft, and Seki naturally had the original Japanese version in mind, and struggling with the English translation; nevertheless, I understand that with Seki's limited knowledge of English, together with some knowledge of German and French he was able to communicate with Major Jay—at least both believed they did adequately well. As a result of this exchange of ideas, draft 14 was created reflecting these discussions. The changes concentrated on providing a fairer opportunity for the accused organization to defend itself, and a more equal balance between the government and that organization and these changes appeared in little ways in several articles. Because of Jay's personal involvement, determination and enthusiasm, the potentially affected organizations under the draft bill would have somewhat better protection from the possible arbitrariness of future government security officials.

Another aspect of draft 13, the chapter on investigations (*chōsa*), articles 23–36, was discussed over two days, February 23 and 24, 1952 between M. Matsukata and SIB Director General Yoshikawa and Seki. The SIB representatives said that the "investigator" (*chōsakan*) in the draft bill would have "less investigatory power" than the existing SIB inspector. This came about when SIB discussed draft 12 with Chiefs of the NP and the Tokyo Metropolitan Police Headquarters. The latter chiefs insisted that the new PSIA must not do investigatory work and not be given the right to issue warrants if they were to support the SAPL draft.

Asked if this draft would "pass the Cabinet", Yoshikawa commented that AG Kimura at first had insisted on "a stronger law", i.e. a law which gave the PSIA regular police powers, but "had changed his mind"—backed down, gave in, surrendered, caved in—when he was confronted with the realities "in the political and governmental fields", meaning, of course, the solidly entrenched bureaucratic strength of the old-line police agencies. He also predicted accurately that the draft will "undergo considerable change before and after it is submitted to the

Chief of Staff for his work on the SAPL. Jay left Tokyo in mid-April 1952 and became a lawyer in New York.

Cabinet." Will this work? To which he gave an equivocal answer: I do not think so.

The memo report on these meetings concluded that "even if this draft is enacted into law in its present form, the enforcement will be ineffective and of little value". Approving or disapproving this draft by GS will be "in effect, shouldering responsibility for such a law.... If and when the ineffectiveness becomes apparent, it will give those forces [in the GOJ] which today desire complete centralization of police powers the strongest argument for such action. Accordingly GS will, in the final analysis, be blamed for having acted in an advisory capacity to the Japanese Government in the accomplishment of this objective."

Matsukata in his report memo recommended that GS inform 1) AG Kimura that GS has faith that he can draft a bill which will be constitutional and that GS "will only advise after a tentative Cabinet approved draft is submitted if he desires and 2) that the draft as presently constituted would be ineffective in enforcement and that "a more complete and effective investigation organization for subversive activities will be necessary to cope with the situation after the effective date of the Peace and Security Treaties and the abolition of Potsdam Ordinances."[22]

Thus, the PSIA was stripped of all semblance of "compulsory investigative authority" and forced merely to request the judicial police to take actions requiring this authority. This was another setback for the AG in creating a draft SAPL. Draft 14 was translated into English and submitted to GHQ (i.e. to Major Jay); GHQ nodded (*ryōshō shita*) its acceptance—keeping in mind that by this time GHQ regarded itself as acting merely as counsel.

ix. *Leakages of Drafts-2*

1. *Draft 13.* Ironically, as this occurred, draft 13—the draft before substantial revisions in favor of the accused organization—was leaked to and was published on February 29, 1952 as the lead story in the

[22] This description was based on a memo (2/25/1952, Special Security Act (13th draft) Investigation (Articles 23–36), for Chief GS by M. Matsukata. What impact did Matsukata have on the GS process? Why was he given this review responsibility and not Major Jay? Who was Matsukata, a Japanese working for GS in a rather sensitive position, or a Nisei U.S. employee? What was his background experience and training? I do not have any answers to any of these questions concerning this intriguing memo.

Mainichi Shimbun; the constitutionality of the bill was challenged by Professor Kaneko Hajime of Tokyo University in an article and in a *Mainichi* editorial the next day on March 1, 1952. He asserted that while various freedoms in the Constitution were guaranteed in article 2 of draft 13, the authorities were empowered to intervene when violent destructive activities were being planned even when there was no known danger, thus placing a large restrictive framework around these freedoms. The authorities may control these persons and organizations when it believed such planning was intended to lead to violent destructive actions. It was the subjectivity of this decision that was of concern. When illegal actions are taken by individuals they should be handled according to the Criminal Code; but to then also administratively disband an entire organization would infringe on the freedom of association. The draft bill puts too great an emphasis on "prevention" which is highly subjective. Professor Kaneko citing the experience under the prewar PPL, the implementation of this or similar laws must be watched most carefully. Ordering third persons who have no direct connection to the issue at hand and threatening punishment if they are not cooperative, is going too far. While there were restrictions on the use of compulsory investigative authority by the PSEC or PSIA personnel, in reality this authority is realized through other personnel. While this authority is appropriate in criminal cases, it is inappropriate in administrative cases. Using the illegal act of a small group of people in an organization which has not gone so far as to deny the Constitution, as the reason to control, restrict even disband that organization is a dangerous trend. Professor Kaneko implied his constitutional concerns but did not actually declare these articles to be unconstitutional. He did emphasize the prewar experiences; thus, again by implication, he expressed his doubts and confidence in a postwar government to implement such a law safely. This prompted a recheck of the constitutionality of the draft with Major Jay at GS/GHQ and with Matsushita Masatoshi, a lawyer, Professors Makino Eiichi and Professor Tanaka Jirō of Tokyo University; they assured Seki verbally with no known written record that the draft would be found constitutional. The major newspapers, *Asahi, Mainichi, Yomiuri* and *Nikkei* and *Sankei Shimbun* gave the government credit for some niggardly "improvements". *Asahi* was somewhat more stringent. Even the conservative *Sankei* warned that if stiff prison terms were not specified for violations of human rights, then the SAPL would not be a bill to protect the people but a threat to the people. None of the newspapers called for the retraction of the proposed SAPL but invoked anxieties from prewar police excesses in implementation.

2. *The Nihon Shimbun Kyōkai (The Japan Newspaper Association).* With the revelations about draft 13, the Association issued its second stringent critique on March 27, 1952, almost a month after it was first published in the *Mainichi Shimbun*. The same basic panel members which prepared the Association's first analysis in Fall 1951 were again asked to render their judgment.[23]

Even though a number of restrictions had been deleted since draft 6 was leaked to the press in the Fall 1951, such as the requirement for political organizations to register with the local government, restriction of organizational activities was now limited to a specified length of time, restrictions on holding positions were relaxed and compulsory investigative authority (*kyōsei chōsakan*) to PSIA staff were now limited. Nevertheless, after an eight-point criticism of draft 13, the panel concluded that it was

> an improper/inappropriate and dangerous law with a very high probability that it will threaten the basic political rights of the people, such as the freedom of speech and organization guaranteed under the Constitution.... It is a great threat not just to members of political organizations but also to the general freedom of speech, broadcasting and publication. The government may say it would not abuse this law but that is no assurance at all in light of past experiences [referring to pre-WWII press censorship and restrictions in Imperial Japan]. This law goes far beyond what is necessary whether one is or is not in favor of an internal security law. Since a net can be thrown over normal and ordinary newspapers and publications, we have no alternative but to conclude that the proposed law is a threat to the freedom of press and speech.

x. *Disruptive Activities in the Drafting Context*

As the drafting process was moving forward slowly toward the adoption of a draft SAPL by the Cabinet, there was a gathering momentum of a confrontation between the ruling conservative government, and the communists on the extreme left and the government's confrontation with students at the University of Tokyo over freedom of speech

[23] The panel now consisted of six members from the Fall study group: Kainō Michitaka, Tanaka Kazuo, Dandō Shigemitsu, Miyazawa Toshiyoshi, Rōyama Masamichi, Yamane Shinjirō.

and expression In the eyes of some, the former "proved" the urgent need for tightened internal security measures and in the eyes of their opposition, the latter "proved" that the government really had not changed its stripes since the war ended and was intent on limiting freedom of speech, assembly, etc.

The JCP had been "ordered" by Moscow to abandon its soft policy of being a "lovable party" and avoiding direct confrontation with the U.S. military occupation and the Japanese government and adopt a direct challenge to them. Momentarily this turnaround was resisted but soon the JCP leadership fell in line and the challenge over the next two years took various forms. This "challenge" evolved into a series of gradually more disruptive violent activities. These tactics involved attacks on government offices, various kinds of demonstrations by Japanese and Koreans. Just taking the first three months of 1952, according to the Japanese press, a number of different kinds of incidents occurred and the breadth, scope and frequency increased in comparison with the past: attacks particularly on police boxes, policemen, police barracks, tear gas attacks by Koreans on SIB offices, tax offices and human excrement thrown into a local governmental office (Yokusuka city). By the end of March 1952, there had been 23 incidents of attacks on tax offices dispersed over eight regional offices (out of 11) in Tokyo, Osaka, Nagoya, Kantō-Shin'etsu, Hiroshima, Fukuoka, Kumamoto and Sapporo. A police division chief (*keibi kachō*) in Sapporo, Hokkaido, was assassinated by a JCP member on February 21, 1952. These attacks from the target agencies and personnel points of view were random, unpredictable, infuriating and created anxiety among the employees; that was probably exactly what the Communists hoped to achieve but to what specific larger achievable overall political objective was not immediately obvious. Some Koreans held 25 demonstrations in many parts of Japan to commemorate the declaration of Korean independence by Korean nationalists on March 1, 1919. Anti-colonial struggle day demonstrations and rallies were held throughout Japan on May 21, 1952. Any involvement of Koreans would loom larger than normal during this period. Then there was the concern that the "illegal" organization of the JCP was preparing for "an armed revolt" and that 70% of its party members (about 80–100,000) and supporters (220–270,000) were underground; 30% were conducting party business openly. The Party was governed by a central bureau, with a military committee. The latter was controlled by a supreme military committee under which were district committees.

Farmers and workers self-defense units were preparing to conduct partisan warfare against Occupation Force facilities, Japanese police units and gather intelligence. The JCP, he claimed, planned to infiltrate mass organizations, large enterprise factories, Sōhyō labor federation, and gather intelligence on Occupation Forces and the Japanese Police. The government raided the JCP journal, *Heiwa to Sekai* (*Peace and the World*), confiscated numerous papers showing its organization, printing arrangements, funding and liaison activities, arrested and indicted numerous people in these offices.[24] On another plane, there was a clash in February 1952 between University of Tokyo students and the police, sparked as usual by clumsy police tactics; while it was settled amicably, it is mentioned here since a number of such confrontations took place a little later.

While these tactics were, in reality, pin prick attacks against Japanese society, they were nevertheless frustrating, did raise the anxiety level among the populace but hardly a substantive threat to the state of Japan. It made those already unfriendly to leftwing causes, to the JCP, to labor unions, even more convinced of and determined to enact a law to control if not eradicate these "nuisances" who were threatening, getting in the way of and compromising Japan's economic recovery. As mention earlier, the Prime Minister himself had made known his long standing distaste for the communists and the leftwing parties. There were many in the government security establishment from before and during the war who also were antagonistic especially to communist causes, programs, principles and policies. The Japanese Government had, however, assured itself and the people that it could handle any attempted Communist "insurrection", even if the JCP attempted an armed insurrection. Based on its incipient army, the NPR, that was probably true; to this would be added the weight of the U.S. Armed Forces stationed in Korea and Japan. It is difficult to imagine that the JCP (or even for that matter Moscow and the Comintern) could seriously entertain the idea of a successful armed insurrection and take over of the Japanese Government. Since a full scale war was raging on the Korean Peninsula at that time, any serious attempted insurrection would cause some chaos and disruption, could potentially somewhat

[24] In order to respond more effectively to maintaining internal security, the Procurator General announced that by the end of March 1952 an additional 80 prosecutors would be assigned to investigate the various kinds of violent activities described above (*Asahi* 3/16/1952).

undermine Japan as a rear echelon support base for the U.N./U.S. fighting forces in Korea and considerably raise a society's sense of anxiety and uncertainty.

It must be assumed these incidents had an impact on the drafter of the SAPL, the AG, the Prime Minister, except that it is nearly impossible to say with certainty how and in what way such tactics affected the actual drafting process. From a personal point of view for family security reasons, however, drafter Seki did temporarily evacuate his family from his home in Den'en Chōfu in suburban Tokyo. It should be kept in mind that while the drafting of a new SAPL was taking place, the attention of the government, including personal absorption of PM Yoshida himself, the political parties, society in general were focused on the long promised peace treaty and accompanying security treaty between the U.S. and Japan and the related administrative agreement. A new era for Japan would evolve after the Peace Treaty went into effect. Disruptive communist activities would be regarded as a blot and potentially a threat to this new milieu and hope and must not be tolerated. The peace treaty naturally would be a major headline issue but the SAPL competed effectively for public attention.

xi. *To the First Cabinet Decision, Drafts 15–20*

After draft 14, from March 3 to March 24, 1952, the SIB reassured by GHQ, their lawyer and academic supporters with a gathering crescendo of activities, meetings during the day and night and after numerous compromises, created another series of drafts: 15 (3/6/1952), 16 (3/15/1952), 17 (3/16/1952), 18 (3/18/1952), 19 (3/19/1952) and the final draft (no. 20) of March 24, 1952 after conferring at various times with the Procurator's Office, the Legal Opinions Bureau (Hōsei Iken-kyoku) in the AG, and, of course, Major Jay in GHQ. Whether "compulsory investigative authority" should or would be given to the PSEC and particularly PSIA personnel continued to be debated. At a Cabinet Members Consultative Meeting (Kakuryō Kondankai) on March 11, 1952 and several subsequent interagency meetings, the pros and con of giving this authority to the PSEC and PSIA were repeatedly debated. At this Kondankai former AG and present Minister in charge of the NPR strongly objected—note, apparently not the AG—to taking away the compulsory investigative authority from the SIB; as a result, AG Kimura was temporarily successful in persuading his Cabinet colleagues to restore this authority to PSIA officials. But no sooner had he instructed his staff than Minister Saitō in charge of NP rushed to AG Kimura strenuously asserting that giving PSIA such authority would be an invasion of traditional police powers. In order to assure a smooth parliamentary process at least in the governing Liberal Party, AG Kimura retreated and gave up the bureaucratic fight for this authority.[25]

Only the major revisions that occurred between drafts 14 and 20, the version that was approved by the Cabinet on March 28, 1952—as it turned out a provisional decision—are described below. Apparently the Labor Minister made a last ditch attempt at this meeting to have the controversial "*sendō*" (incitement) removed from the draft but after being chided by Finance Minister (and future PM) Ikeda Hayato the draft was approved without change by the Cabinet. Immediately thereafter, the draft bill was formally transmitted to GS/GHQ seeking the nod of approval (*ryōshō*) and the draft bill was publicly released.[26]

1. *Illegal Activities.* "Violent destructive activities" were defined as follows:

   a. Those committing acts of insurrection (Art 77 of the Criminal Code), preparations and plots for that purpose (78) and assistance for such

[25] *Asahi* 3/13/1952 and 3/25/1952, *Mainichi* 3/12/1952, *Yomiuri* 3/12/1952 and *Tokyo Times* 4/4/1952. Kimura was reported to have described his position "*Chū naran to hossureba Kō narazu*" (If one were to keep fealty then one would not be filial), i.e. he was between a rock and hard place, a catch-22 situation.

Under GHQ-VI it was noted that because of the fierce opposition from old-line police agencies, PSIA was not given normal police powers. In a SCAP report memo by S. Hayashi of GS, a somewhat different version was provided of a report from DG/SIB Yoshikawa. The latter reported that at a Cabinet meeting on March 11—probably the above-mentioned Kakuryō Kondankai, not a formal Cabinet meeting—which he attended with the AG, the Minister felt that the PSEC ("Security Board" was used in the memo) could not enforce its decisions without judicial police power. Giving the PSEC such power, he told the assembled Ministers "would be contrary to the spirit of the SCAP policy" since such powers are given to the NP/NPR and local autonomous police. The Ministers felt that SCAP policy would not be violated "if an agency similar to the FBI were created and the present police system revised". They were divided over how best to revise the system and instructed AG Kimura to "submit a definite plan to GS on the reorganization of the security agencies for approval and if necessary take it up directly with [SCAP] General Ridgway." (Based on a memo, 3/12/1952, Security discussion at Cabinet meeting, S. Hayashi to Chief, GS.) In a way this was an incredible suggestion and hardly believable since Japan regained full independence in about six weeks after which SCAP policies and positions would be irrelevant: the power of the habit of consulting GHQ/SCAP for 6–7 years lingers on and on!

[26] Actually after the Deputy Minister's Conference had approved draft 19 on March 27, 1952, the Program Outline was released to the press the same day.

acts and those who instigate or incite such acts and those who, with the intention of contributing to the realization of these acts, print, distribute, publicly post, or possess materials with the intention of publicly posting documents or drawings advocating the justification (*seitō-sei*) or necessity for such actions.

b. Any one of the following actions committed in violation of the following laws in order to advance, support or oppose political principles or policies:
   - Criminal Code articles 95 (obstruction of performance of official duties), 106 (riots), 108 (setting fire to dwellings), 109 (setting fire to structures other than dwellings), 117 (destruction by explosives), 125 (endangering traffic), 126.1 and 1 (overturning of trains, etc.), 199 (homicide), 236 (robbery).
   - Regulations concerning the handling of explosive materials (1884 Dajōkan declaration).
   - Any actions which would constitute preparing for, plotting, instigating or inciting any of the actions listed in "a "and "b" above.

2. *Penalties, limitations on Organizational Activities.* If violent destructive activities are committed:

a. during demonstrative mass movements (*shūdan ji'i undō*), mass marches (*shūdan kōshin*), and publicly held assembles, these activities may be limited for not more than six months to a specified area or areas.
b. the publications of that organization, the printing, distribution, or the possession of these publications for the purpose of distribution may be prohibited for not more than six months.
c. By officers and/or constituent members of that organization in support of these activities they may be prohibited from conducting theses activities on behalf of that organization for not more than six months. This is a retreat from a one year prohibition in earlier drafts.

3. *Disbandment of Organizations.* Organizations may be disbanded when they commit activities listed in paras a and b above. Concerning the latter, those organizations which began activities but were unable to complete them, or instigated or incited other organizations and those organizations which continue violent destructive activities even after being penalized as per item 2 above may be disbanded.

4. *Investigative Authority for the PSIA.* As in previous drafts, the PSIA may conduct investigations and issue orders to those affected persons and/or reference persons to appear or produce documents but those orders must give the reasons for these orders. It does not specifically

give the authority to request the judicial police to search, inspect and seize materials but ambiguously allows PSIA officials to be present when they are carried out. While the requirement for the police to report to the PSIA on the circumstances and results (*temmatsu*) of a search, etc., it does allow the PSIA to request various reports relating to the case at hand from the police. Thus with these changes, the substantive authority of the PSIA has implicitly been diminished, another retreat from specificity.

5. *Deletion of Designated Industries.* In draft 7 and others damage to destruction of facilities and their function of selected industries as specified in the 1950 Public Enterprise Ordinance (Kōeki Jigyō-rei, Cabinet Ordinance 343, article 83) and law 132 of 1950 were listed as an illegal activity. Knowing that there would be furious opposition to this bill by the labor unions, and in a faint attempt to mollify this known opposition, this section was omitted in the Cabinet approved draft. This was regarded as quite a concession to labor which seemed to exempt some of their more excessive labor tactics (*yuki-sugi no katsudō*). Since the focus was on "violent destructive activities" by organizations and people, not on the openness of political organizations, there was no longer any need to specifically exempt the newspapers, magazines, and broadcasting as was done in earlier drafts.

xii. *GHQ-VI, Waning Twilight, Constitutionality-3*

1. *Constitutional? But defer to Japanese Judgment.* About a month later, as the need for submission of a security bill to the Diet neared, there were apparently "numerous and extended conferences" between Jay and SIB (Yoshikawa but mostly Seki). In his wrap-up memo on the SAPL, Jay commented that

> On comparing the present and 15th draft [3/6/1952] with the preceding one it is clear beyond question that the representatives of the Attorney General's Office had attempted wherever possible to adopt the suggestions and advice by GS. [The following three points]... represent areas in which the representatives of the Attorney General's Office were bound by instructions from higher authority.

These three areas are "now clearly defined as issues on which there is substantial disagreement" between Seki and Jay. In a memo (3/6/1952) to Frank Rizzo, he maintained that these areas,

> are not matters of routine internal import which should be left to the Japanese Government to decide for themselves since this would regulate political activity. Such regulations must not violate a continuing SCAP responsibility to insure the free exercise of the people's will in determining their form of government.... The determination of the validity of legislation regulating political activity must not rest on the good intentions of the draftsman or the good intentions of the normal executive, but must rest on the meaning of the statute and its various provisions.

2. *The Hearing.* Jay pointed out that the PSEC Commission would reach a decision without a hearing where the accused could make a case for itself. It would make this presentation to a "hearing" officer and also could file a brief to the Commission. The Commission does not hear, see or question witnesses and does not directly hear or see the accused. The Commission's decision would be quasi-judicial and would require a hearing according to "the courts, including the Supreme Court". This would be a summary proceedings which "is not justifiable and constitutes an unwarranted, unlawful infringement of the fundamental right to a full and fair hearing. He recommended GS approval be withheld unless the draft is revised to include in Article 13 the requirement that the accused may "confront, hear and cross-examine the witnesses testifying against them". If that was not acceptable, then the draft should be amended so that before a decision by the Commission against the accused is carried out, the accused shall have the right to a hearing to confront, hear and cross-examine witnesses.

3. *Investigatory Power.* The draft gives the AG broad delegations of authority to create ordinances for the detailed regulations for the enforcement of the SAPL. There is "no standard or yardstick provided by which the AG must measure this ordinance.... This constitutes an excessive and unwarranted delegation of legislative authority to the executive and is therefore unconstitutional by both American and Japanese standards." At this point Jay observed that "whenever Seki agreed to some change in the investigatory powers the succeeding draft included some new unexpected provision which reinstated the unconstitutional investigatory power which has thus appeared in one form or another in each of the drafts." Jay had emphasized this point in the interview with me and noted that this tendency necessitated that one had to reread an entire revised draft, a wearying process. He recommended that the proviso of article 23 (12th draft) be reinstated

in a new article 25 providing that "any enforcement action, unless specifically prescribed by this Act shall not be taken."

4. *Self-Incrimination.* The draft law (article 26) required that a person must appear and produce papers, documents and other things under penalty for failure to comply. This requirement may result in self-incrimination which is prohibited by the Japanese Constitution and this "investigatory power of the executive is one which historically has been most readily abused." Jay recommended that GS approval be withheld unless article 26 (1) [of draft 15] is revised specifying that no persons shall be required to produce documents, papers, or other articles or evidence which may tend to incriminate himself. Or alternately, that immunity from liability in any action in court be spelled out and thirdly, that "the following suggestion" be formally transmitted to the AG: revise article 26 (2) to require identification of the papers, etc. being subpoenaed after "specifying" the words "the documents, papers or other articles to be produced and…"[27]

This assessment well reflects Jay's comments during his interview with me that the American concept of due process under the law was where he had the greatest difficulty in working with his Japanese counterparts and where there was the least understanding. In his interview, Jay said the Japanese had used a shotgun instead of a rifle in drafting the SAPL. This concern with due process as shown in the above was in sharp contrast to those of the Japanese political opposition with "*sendō*," its meaning, how it would be interpreted, applied and enforced by Japanese police, prosecutors, judges and the Commission.

Two days later in a meeting with AG Kimura, Frank Rizzo stated that GS was trying to help develop a draft which would be defensible before the Diet and public opinion, this responsibility lay with the Japanese Government, that "the GHQ role is advisory" that AG staff deserves great credit for drafting a bill which "in the main finds no objections in GS." Rizzo then outlined Jay's three points. The AG explained that these points had been considered and that "modification along the lines of the first and second suggestion would render the law useless to accomplish the desired objectives. Hearings before the

[27] Memo (3/6/1952) for Chief, Government Section, Subversive Activity Prevention Act (15th draft), 4 p.

commission would only lead to demonstrations and pressure against the Commissioners so that the proceedings would be bogged down, the commissioners would be intimidated and it would be hard to get persons to serve on the commission." He felt there were safeguards of constitutional rights and that this law was needed "to protect the state against the subversion and violence which he knows the Communists are planning against the Government in the coming months." Rizzo then stated, clearly reflecting the utterly changed role of GHQ/SCAP:

> ...If the Bill adopted by the Cabinet in its present form and presented to GHQ, it will probably be cleared, since the questions involved are for the Japanese to decide. Nevertheless, if questioned, GS would have to make it plain that the decisions on these points had been Japanese and that at least on the two points under discussion, GS would have preferred different solutions....[28]

AG Kimura pointed out that because it was his aim to assure that public safety was maintained in Japan after the Peace treaty was ratified and gone into effect, that he left his leisurely life as a lawyer to become the AG." He felt confident the SAPL would ultimately be approved by the Diet.[29]

xiii. *GHQ-VII, Waning Twilight, Constitutionality-4*

GS-ESS-LS Disagreement and SAPL Constitutionality. At the last minute, staff meetings and a series of memos flew back and forth inside GHQ between GS and ESS and LS as to whether GHQ should give clearance, or qualified clearance to the draft SAPL for submission to the Diet. GS maintained that the draft SAPL had been given to LS and ESS on March 27 and 28,1952, respectively, that Chief of LS had presented

---

[28] Memo for the (3/8/1952) for Chief, GS, by M. Matsukata on "Attorney General Kimura", 2 p. In his retrospective book, *Legal Reform in Japan*, on his experiences as an Occupationaire in Japan, Oppler provided an interesting anecdote about this decision. He said:

> I met Brigadier General G. Keyser, deputy chief of staff, a very amiable and understanding person, and Rizzo for lunch, and we discussed the matter [of the SAPL] amicably for a long time. The two chiefs were against interference by SCAP at such a late date, but they were not able to convince me, nor did I convince them of the necessity for a veto. Since Carpenter supported me, the dispute had to be settled between the two Section chiefs, and, as was to be expected, the Government Section prevailed, in as much as it had strong diplomatic and security arguments in favor of non-interference. p. 289.

[29] Ibid. The above Matsukata memo.

an analysis of the draft to a staff meeting on March 31 chaired by SCAP (General Ridgway) himself and "had expressed the unequivocal opinion that the proposed legislation was constitutional." At another staff meeting on April 8, 1952 presided over by SCAP, again, "qualified clearance" was still advocated by LS. The choice facing GHQ, said GS, was formally objecting to the bills (the SAPL and two related bills establishing the Agencies concerned) or permitting them to be introduced in the Diet under the 24-hour automatic clearance procedure adopted on March 21, 1952 when the U.S. Senate ratified the Peace Treaty. The Chief of Staff with SCAP concurrence concluded that "as a matter of policy, SCAP should not intervene one way or another at this stage...." On April 9, 1952, the legislation was "routinely cleared" for introduction in the Diet.[30]

On April 8, the day of the meeting with SCAP, ESS prepared a relatively detailed critique of the draft SAPL. It maintained that the draft SAPL and the bills establishing the PSIA and PSEC granted powers to an administrative agency of the executive branch of government.

> which under our [U.S.] concept of democratic constitutional government could be properly exercised only by duly constituted courts of law.

These powers include the authority to prohibit demonstrations, processions, gatherings for a fixed period not exceeding six months, prohibiting and distributing publications, to dissolve an organization, and a number of other powers. It asserted that:

> ...any inference that the Occupation favors or condones summary procedures which could be exercised to abridge the constitutional rights of persons or organizations in Japan could well lead to situations not in the best interest of the United States....It is therefore deemed prudent to make it clear that the introduction into the Diet of the three bills referred to above, and consideration thereof, be entirely free from any implication of Occupation approval or support....The three bills now presented are returned [to the AG] with no Headquarters approval, either expressed or implied....Return of the bill for enactment without qualification may, and probably will, be construed as approval of the full contents thereof. A clear qualification of the Supreme Commander's position strongly supporting protection against subversive activity but not concurring in violations of constitutional rights will serve to relieve

[30] Memo (4/11/1952) for Chief of Staff from GS on "Subversive Activity Prevention Bill and Related Legislation". 1 p.

> the C-in-C and the future U.S. ambassador of *allegation of concurrence by U.S. representatives in the suppression of human freedom* [emphasis added]. It is urgently recommended that the substance of the proposed qualified clearance statement be carefully considered.[31]

Two days later, 4/10/1952, GS rebuts ESS's contentions point-by-point: Investigatory powers [of the PSIA] are non-existent.... none of the three bills [the SAPL, the PSIA and PSEC draft laws] creates any police powers of investigation.... [that the above judgment] is unwarranted at this time." GS reminds ESS that the GOJ could, based on SCAP's statement of May 3, 1950 legislate in this sensitive area, and concluded that the GOJ could legislate in this area.[32]

Yet again, on April 11, 1952, this time LS asserted to GS that the authorities of the PSEC were too broad so that, for example, a labor union conducting a mass demonstration could be dissolved under the bill if one member of the union in the procession had been found with a weapon or resists a policeman. The paramount weakness in the procedure is "the fact that the so-called hearing is on the order of an inquisition, or, at best, a mere taking of testimony as the 'hearing officer' cannot render a decision." It concluded that:

> In general, the constitutionality of the bill may be doubtful from a purely legal point of view. Apart from the constitutional principle that no one may be compelled to incriminate himself, there also arises the question as to whether such fundamental human rights of freedom of association, assembly and speech are violated. How the [Japanese] Supreme Court would decide in an individual case cannot be foreseen with any certainty. It can be said, however, that the weaknesses pointed out in the bill

---

[31] Memo (4/8/1952), ESS to GS, Draft [SAPL] Legislation, 2 p.

[32] Memo (4/10/1952), GS to ESS, Draft [SAPL] Legislation, 3 p. The paragraph cited from the May 3, 1950 Constitution Day statement was as follows:

> The issue is therefore clear and unequivocal—how far may the fundamental human rights be exercised unabridged without becoming the instrument of their own destruction? It is an issue which confronts all peoples, forewarned that others have lost their liberties because, blindly following an ideal, they have failed to see the dangers inherent in reality. While it is the universal desire of all free men to preserve unabridged the exercise of their personal liberties, there is thus an issue projected into every law abiding society which may not be ignored without hazarding the survival of liberty itself. I have utmost faith that should coming events presage the need for definitive action here to preserve the public welfare against the destructive potential of this form of insidious attack, the Japanese people will proceed with wisdom, serenity and justice, without failing the integrity of their Constitution.

would aid an arbitrary administrative interference with freedom of the press and the right to associate and act collectively. *The bill could well be the first step toward revival of the old peace preservation law and be used to suppress criticism and organized activities under the pretext of controlling subversives.* [Emphasis added]. A safer approach to the control of subversive elements would be to make such subversive activities criminal offenses where they are not already covered by the Penal [Criminal] Code and to prosecute the individual offenders in the courts of law.[33]

---

[33] Memo (4/11/1952), LS to GS. No subject. The memos in the above footnotes for GHQ VII were actually part of a series of back and forth memos which had been sent forward to the Chief of Staff as a group all attached to GS's memo of April 11, 1952. The strength of Oppler's conviction about the questionable constitutionality of the draft SAPL, is underscored by what he said in his retrospective book, *Legal Reform in Japan.* While GS consulted with and counseled the Japanese Government, with the Legal Section basically on the sides lines until the last moment, the Legal Section's opinion about the constitutionality of the SAPL should be kept in mind. His chapter, SCAP without MacArthur, in the above book, begins with a rather strong statement on the proposed SAPL.

> While in principle I approved of it [the reduction of supervision and control over Japanese Government actions to a minimum], I clung with a certain inflexibility to the view that, as long as the Occupation lasted, we should not allow any legislation to be passed that would be irreconcilable with what we had tried to achieve. Today [mid-1970s] it may appear almost absurd that a little more than two weeks before the Occupation ended I seriously objected to the controversial Subversive Activities Prevention Bill. Under the disguise of controlling communism, it provided, among other things, for the establishment of a commission with the power to take preventive action against groups suspected of terrorist activities in the future. In a detailed memorandum I expressed doubts about the constitutionality of this legislation, arguing that apart from the principle that no one may be compelled to incriminate himself, such fundamental human rights as freedom of association, assembly, and speech may also be violated. The weaknesses of the bill, I concluded, would aid an arbitrary administrative interference with freedom of the press and the right to associate and act collectively. The bill could well be the first step toward revival of the old Peace Preservation Law, and be used to suppress criticism and organized activities under the pretext of controlling subversives. I suggested that a safer approach to the control of subversive elements would be to make subversive activities criminal offenses and to prosecute the individual offender in the courts of law. (*Legal Reform in Japan*, p. 289).

Oppler pointed out that the Japanese Supreme Court, while giving solemn recognition to the importance of the specific constitutional freedom at issue, would ultimately require that a specific right be allowed only "to the extent that it does not interfere with the public welfare." Because this interpretation could lead to potentially emasculating the guarantees of civil liberties, Oppler pointed out that "critics of the Supreme Court prefer the clear and present danger test in its original Holmes version. The Japanese district courts have used it frequently, for instance in the mass demonstration cases and in acquitting persons charged with violation of the Subversive

On April 11, 1952, GS forwarded the ESS and LS memos and its own rebuttal to the Chief of Staff reminding the C/S that in accordance with the April 8 decision, clearance had been given to the GOJ on April 9, 1952. This "exchange of fire" in GHQ showed that there were strong feelings in some GHQ offices that the constitutionality of the SAPL was distinctly suspect, that as SCAP influence waned GHQ was hardly unified. Faced with the political reality the internal GHQ debate just simply petered out and to the best of my knowledge, this debate did not reach the ears of either the AG or Seki.

xiv. *Editorial Reaction to the Cabinet Decision*

Editorial reactions by the major newspapers, *Asahi, Jiji, Nikkei, Mainichi, Tokyo, Sankei* and *Yomiuri*, were almost immediate but ambiguous. The anxiety about the implementation of the law was an almost unanimous refrain in these editorials, implying a lack of confidence in the police forces to transcend the past and possibly recreate the regime of the PPL—intentionally or unintentionally—was again almost unanimously uppermost in their minds as they pondered the future implementation of this law. Significantly, none of the editorials called for the outright rejection and withdrawal of the proposed bill as had the political opposition in the Diet and the Sōhyō-related unions. A tighter control of the security agencies through legislation and institutional arrangements to prevent the recurrence of this nightmare was called for by both the liberal and conservative press. One can only speculate that the news about and experiences with and observation of the increasingly destructive activities of the JCP and its supporters must have also weighed heavily on the mass media in crafting their reactions and responses to the Government's proposed new internal security arrangements.

xv. *The Political Opposition and Labor Reactions*

The newly formed moderately conservative Kaishintō compared the idea of giving such broad administrative authority to an outer bureau of the AG to the PPL and feared that it could be used capriciously by

Activities Prevention Law to which I raised serious objection before its enactment." (Ibid., pp. 325–326).

the government in power against the opposition and also result in turf wars between the PSIA and the NP.[34]

The SDP-R also compared the law to the prewar PPL, and asserted that the bill, if enacted, would be a violation of all the rights guaranteed in the Constitution and promised to resist and oppose the bill in the Diet.[35] The SDP-L was much more forceful in condemning the proposed bill; it also compared it to the prewar PPL and said it rode rough-shod over the people's rights in the Constitution, that it was an oppressive law, part of the rearmament regime being imposed on Japan.[36]

The Diet Joint Struggle Committee of Sōhyō-Rōtō, SDP-L, SDP-R and Rōnōtō vowed to concentrate their parliamentary efforts on defeating this proposed bill. This bill, it declared, was a political plot (*seiji-teki imbō*) by the government and the Liberal Party to oppress and destroy labor unions and the labor movement, and to recreate a police state, all in the name of anti-communism. The proposed bill would deprive the people of the rights framed in the Constitution. A subcommittee of the Diet Joint Struggle Committee met on April 1 and reiterated its determination to oppose the SAPL bill, would work with and appeal to the Kaishintō in the Lower House. In the Upper House it would work with the Kaishintō and Ryokufūkai to defeat the bill in committee and demand that public hearings be held about the draft bill to expose the bill to public opinion.[37]

On the same day as the Cabinet decision, Sōhyō's Joint Struggle Committee summoned the chairmen of its constituent unions and some neutral unions, about 40 persons in all, to an enlarged strategy meeting. After three days of discussion, it decided on March 31, it would invoke force (*jitsu-ryoku kōshi*) to oppose the SAPL draft bill and to this end would launch the first strike wave on April 12, 1952, followed by a second wave on April 18, 1952. It was estimated that Sōhyō could mobilize about 40+ unions, a total of about 2.5 millions members for this purpose. This would probably be the largest mobilization of labor union members since the abortive February 1, 1947 general strike which was banned by General MacArthur on January

---

34 Kitamura Tokutaro, Policy Committee Chairman, Kaishintō, *Yomiuri* 3/27/1952 (eve).

35 Asanuma Inejirō, SecGen SDP-R, *Yomiuri* 3/27/1952 (eve).

36 Nomizo, Masaru, SecGen, SDP-L, *Yomiuri* 3/27/1952 (eve).

37 *Asahi* 3/30/1952, 4/2/1952.

31, 1947. As this announcement was made, seven major unions with 670,000 members had declared their support for the first 24-hour strike and public employee unions (teachers, national railway, communications and other unions) would hold mass workplace rallies (*shokuba taikai*) and early departure from work (*sōtai*) as an expression of sympathy and support of the strike. These fighting words by the leftwing political parties and the declaration to take "forceful action" by Rōtō, presaged a long and bitter political confrontation in the Diet, in the streets, in the media against the draft bill. The battle lines had now been clearly drawn.[38]

After eleven months and against a somewhat turbulent background, the Cabinet had, at last, been able to approve a bill on March 28, 1952 whose purpose was to control violent destructive activities by organizations and individuals. The Communists or the Communist Party were never once mentioned in any of the drafts but it was clearly understood from the outset that, in light of the domestic and international context that Communists and their organizations were the target of this proposed legislation. But in light of prewar experience with the GOJ, labor unions and labor leadership and all the leftwing parties that depended on how the law would be interpreted and implemented fully understood that this law could be interpreted to apply to them and thus the vehement opposition to the proposed bill.

The PSIA's authority though circumscribed from the beginning was gradually narrowed at almost every turn as the drafts evolved. In the end, it was not given the compulsory investigative authority for search, inspection and seizure and had to rely on the goodwill of other law enforcement agencies.

The first phase (Chapter 2) of the drafting process focused on defining what was illegal; in the second half (Phase II) on "due process and procedural issues" with some input from GHQ and better protection for potential defendants, and whether the PSIA would be given "compulsory investigative authority." At the last minute and momentarily,

[38] *Asahi* 3/31/1952, 3/31/1952 (Eve), *Mainichi* 3/31/1952 (Eve), *Sankei* 3/29/1952, *Yomiuri* 4/1/1952. The struggle tactical conference met on March 29, 1952 with professors specializing in criminal and administrative law and discussed the methodology, form, time and place of the strike. These strikes were called "waves" in Japanese, i.e. *dai-ippa* (first wave), *dai-niha* (Second wave).

the issue of incitement (*sendō*) suddenly began to loom larger on the horizon and a mild disagreement and a somewhat comical momentary distraction in the Cabinet. Yet this one word, *sendō*, will gradually assume a more central role in the fierce dialog to follow. Under normal conditions a Cabinet decision assures the presentation of a draft bill to the Diet. But in this case, it turned out to be merely the beginning of another intense debate in the Cabinet and government and with the vehement opposition.

B. *To the "Final" Cabinet Decision*

An initial Cabinet decision concerning a draft SAPL had been achieved. Now a "final" Cabinet decision must be reached in the near future. Thus, in the next three weeks there would be grand standing, posturing, threats and dire threats and counter threats, apparent but not real negotiations by the government and the political opposition, Sōhyō and its supporters, competing press conferences and the threat of law suits over strike damage and demands for compensation, and even negotiations within the Cabinet as to whether to hold a hard line, revise the draft law or attempt to negotiate with the opposition.

The government was faced with the fact that Japan was on the eve of regaining its independence when the peace and security treaties would go into effect in late April 1952, and with a vacuum in the legal situation concerning maintenance of internal security, a rising number of more violent Periodic destructive activities, presumably by Communists, scattered around the country and a political opposition and formidable array of labor unions determined to fight the enactment of the draft SAPL which was also tied in with its spring labor offensive and its opposition to the peace and security treaties.

- From the government's point of view, how could it neutralize, diminish the labor offensive, and thus sever or diminish that support to the political opposition in the Diet.
- From the labor union's point of view and the political opposition in the Diet, how could they persuade the government to delete certain words and phrases from the draft bill, i.e. somehow induce a fracture in the Cabinet, if not to force it to abandon the proposed bill completely or postpone its submission to the Diet and how to mobilize public opinion to its side notwithstanding the continuing and progressively more violent communist tactics.

i. *The Government*

The government had difficulties in its own rationale for the need for this law. It repeatedly asserted that the two strike waves threatened by the unions were totally and unequivocally illegal and would not have the protection of the labor laws, meaning the unions, their leadership and membership could be prosecuted for the violation of the law. This position was somewhat weakened when it was reported in the press that the Vice Ministers (presumably the administrative vice ministers) of concerned Ministries, DG Yoshikawa of SIB met on April 3 to discuss the legal steps to take if and when these strikes were declared illegal; but the meeting ended without any firm conclusions.[39] Even assuming that these protest demonstrations were indeed illegal, could the government take the political risk of taking the unions to court as the protests evolved and probably inflaming the already touchy situation. Was the government willing to take this risk?

The Government also had the heavy task of trying to persuade the union leadership and the opposition in the Diet that the postwar Japanese government was indeed different from the prewar situation, that the proposed law was aimed at the communist movement in all its ramifications, not the labor unions and the non-communist leftwing. In light of the fact that many of the prewar police and judicial system officials were inevitably still in place and some in influential positions in the government and the Liberal Party and that the prewar law, the PPL, was also enacted to control the communists but gradually broadened and with ever stiffer penalties including the death penalty, it would be too much to expect that labor and the opposition political parties would accept the government's assertions and assurances that this law would not be applied to legitimate labor union activities. The problem here was: who's interpretation of "legitimate" would be used in the application of the law.

The government had to persuade the union rank and file, that the strikes against this controversial bill as proposed by union leadership were not only illegal but contrary to their long term economic interests, and would do much damage to the slowly recovering Japanese economy and that the proposed bill had actually been amended many times to respond to these very anxieties. The government would also

[39] *Sankei* 4/8/1952.

need to prove its credibility, its believeablility when its says that the proposed strike actions were illegal and would be prosecuted. It would need to persuade them why the proposed SAPL was needed when there was adequate coverage under the existing Criminal Code and why it was truly necessary to supplement and broaden the Criminal Code articles on insurrection, riots, assassination, etc with the planning, printing and holding materials, etc which incite and instigate people to commit these crimes under the Criminal Code. Because of the complicated political ideological situation among Sōhyō's constituent unions, perhaps the government could appeal to the more conservative unions, especially the more outspokenly anti-communist unions, not to participate in the protest strikes. Already some unions, such as the Seamen's, Steel Workers, All Textile Workers Alliance (Zensen Dōmei), were wavering since the draft law had been revised and did not specifically include articles to suppress (*yokusei-suru*) labor strikes and did not mention them under the definition of illegal activities.

Since the Cabinet decision of March 28, 1952 on the draft SAPL, LM Yoshitake received a report/recommendations from the labor law consultative council (*shingikai*), visited Nikkeiren (see below), Nakayama Ichirō, chairman of the Central Labor Relations Committee and the Kansai financial leaders to take a reading of their support. Apparently, the financial leaders were initially encouraging about revising the labor laws and the law on general strikes; Nakayama was reportedly skeptical about these changes. Nikkeiren was unenthusiastic about "compulsory arbitration" for inclusion in the labor laws. In light of the known strong opposition from unions and opposition political parties and the skepticism in the Cabinet, LM Yoshitake was forced to back down. However, at the April 1, 1952 Cabinet meeting it was decided that LM Yoshitake would, at some point, meet with Sōhyō, that the AG would prepare an explanatory pamphlet on the draft SAPL and the date of submission of the draft SAPL to the Diet would depend on a reading of public opinion and Sōhyō reactions. This reflected an element of equivocation by the government. Underlying this approach is a Japanese belief that if only the other side, in this case, the unions and political parties—or in other instances, foreign countries in trade negotiations—would "understand" (*rikai*) its position, then those parties would truly understand the situation and their sincerity in making these proposals AND agree with them. There is an assumption among many Japanese that truly understanding the situation as presented would naturally lead to agreement.

In another attempt to sway union sentiment, Hori Shigeru, Cabinet Secretary General said that the general strike and labor law revisions would not be submitted to the Diet and we the government must wait on the verdict of public opinion and not use brute force—this must be a reflection of some anxiety by the Cabinet.[40] Yet again, reflecting on the Cabinet's confidence, just after the second meeting with labor leaders, PM Yoshida summoned Kimura, Yoshitake and Hori on April 10; after an hour of debating, the AG and LM were instructed "to cautiously reconsider" the proposed bill. In subsequent discussions among themselves, the AG and LM re-enacted their strong disagreements particularly about the inclusion of the term "*sendō*" (incitement). At the strong insistence of LM Yoshitake, it was informally agreed the bill would be revised on three counts in order to try to satisfy Rōtō objections and persuade them to call off the strike now only two days away; not withstanding LM's demands eventually the AG and his staff prevailed, "*sendō*" stayed in. This argument about the propriety, need, and definition of "*sendō*" between these two Ministers had been ongoing for some while; it had been a must inclusion item demanded by AG Kimura. Just before the April 11 Cabinet meeting, faced with opposition from the Cabinet SecGen, senior Cabinet members, the AG most reluctantly agreed to some word changes. Note must be taken that notwithstanding the bravado language of the government and its assertions of finality, this limited procrastination was indicative of the Cabinet's concerns about the influence of labor unions and their political allies in the Diet and the amorphous public opinion.

In announcing the following three points to assuage labor's anxieties the Cabinet SecGen made a nationalistic appeal—hopefully a trump card—to the rank and file union member to restrain themselves, i.e. do not strike, for the sake of Japan when it was regaining its independence, to avoid additional hardships on the people of Japan and for the development of a democratic labor movement. Note that the draft law had not been revised but these were "merely promises" to revise the draft bill depending on labor's reaction.

a. A clear statement will be included in the bill that in the enforcement and application of the law there shall be no limit (*seigen*) placed on and no interference in appropriate union activities.

[40] *Asahi* 4/2/1952, 4/3/1952.

b. Consideration will be given to including a provision for relief when an illegal administrative ruling [presumably by the PSEC under the authority of the AG] had been made based on this law.
c. The membership of PSEC would include representatives from labor and from other fields.[41]

Nikkeiren. Nikkeiren, short for Nihon Keieisha Dantai Remmei (Federation of Employers Organizations), is one of the four major business organizations in Japan. It was formed in April 1948 to handle labor relations and its membership is organized by prefectures and by industry. One of its major concerns was to counter the labor union's annual spring struggle for increased pay. The major Japanese business association did not want to worsen labor-management relations, so it downplayed its position that protest strikes on April 12 and 18 would be regarded as illegal and could be subject to civil and criminal prosecution, demands for restitution of business losses, obstruction of business during working hours with the possibility of punishment and firing of employees. Such protests would be regarded as an abuse of union collective action rights. To the best of my knowledge, these threats were not carried out by management so the validity of their assertions were moot. While this threat appeared, the Managing Director (Semmu Riji) of Nikkeiren, Kanai Nobutaka, opined that after the departure of the Occupation such a kind of law as the proposed SAPL would be necessary, lamented that business losses stemmed from a conflict between the government and labor. Businesses would not, of course, pay workers who participated in any protest strike and hoped that differences could be resolved between companies and unions.[42] As the first strike evolved, Nikkeiren took a cautious attitude of trying not to stimulate, irritate the unions in the belief that discussions between the government and labor could come to some understand-

[41] LM Yoshitake and staff made an "unsolicited, unannounced call" at Rizzo's office at 11:40 AM, April 11 to report on these proposed changes. Rizzo's memo to the Chief of Staff mentioned only the first and third of the above proposed revisions and LM Yoshitake's assessment that "the strikes will be called off." Rizzo informed Yoshitake that "GHQ would waive the formal 24-hour waiting period for clearance of the proposed revision, and the Government was free to make it on its own responsibility."

[42] As a cautionary measure just in case management in general or by one or more companies actually became serious about this assertion, such unions as National Railways, Tanrō, chemical workers (Gōsei Kagaku), called for ¥10–15 contribution per member to build up an assistance fund. Sōhyō mobilized 140 lawyers who might defend those who were thus accused by management (*Asahi* 4/6/1952, *Jiji* 4/9/1952, *Yomiuri* 4/8/1952).

ing to prevent the 2nd strike at the last moment. In light of the tense management-labor relations prevailing at the time, and despite the traditionally strong stands normally expressed by Nikkeiren, this was quite a conciliatory approach to an increasingly prickly situation.

ii. *The Labor Front*

The strike dates, wave one of April 12 and wave two on April 18, 1952 were not chosen at random. The Peace and Securities were expected to come into effect about mid-April. This was probably a symbolic gesture to continue expressing labor's displeasure and dissatisfaction with the alliance regime with the U.S. The political party opposition and labor had been unsuccessful in preventing or modifying in any way the creation of this new regime. From labor's point of view, the government with explicit and implied support from GHQ had systematically tried to contain labor's political challenge, especially as it regarded much of labor having been infiltrated by Communist sympathizers and in light of the widespread apparently Communist instigated destructive activities. While in a more private moment, Labor might recognize that there was a "vacuum" in controlling violent political activities, the overall distrust of the government—and by implication management—was much greater and more deeply rooted in their collective consciousness. There was also probably another quite human trait: We have not won a case recently, perhaps it would be possible to win the fight against this draft bill; every effort must be made to do so.

But after having declared a determined opposition to the draft SAPL, and setting the dates for two strikes, could Labor's leadership provide the needed and persuasive rationale to move several million workers and union members to take such drastic action against a specific draft bill before the Diet. These proposed strikes were compared to the February 1, 1947 "general strike" which had been aborted at the command of General MacArthur. The comparison was always in terms of numbers of people involved; the new proposed strikes, if successfully executed, would be the largest since 1947. While this failed "strike" was, in the first instance, an economic strike expressing a grievance in response to the critical lack of food and the essentials of life in immediate postwar Japan with serious political implications, it was master minded by Sambetsu, then the major labor federation and basically under Communist influence—some would say control—and was politically a direct challenge to the U.S. occupation. In the five years that had elapsed, again while the economic situation had improved somewhat, it was not, of course, as desperate as in 1947 and clearly economic rationale was out of the question. The framework for this opposition had now to be far different from that in 1947.

While Sambetsu had directive power in ordering its constituent unions to take strike action in early 1947, Sōhyō had been created in 1950 as a non-Communist alternative to Sambetsu with no directive authority. Because of this important distinction, Sōhyō's leadership had to persuade each one of its constituent unions (*tansan*) of the need and rationale for these strikes. This was especially critical because while the strike action was theoretically part of a larger issue which the union leadership felt they faced—the spring pay offensive, the revision of the labor laws, the peace and security treaties—the focus had been sharpened to the draft SAPL. It was highly ironic, therefore, that this "non-Communist" labor federation was now vehemently determined to take on the government which had a comfortable majority in the House of Representatives. In the eyes of some, particularly the conservative government party and the involved security agencies, this "non-Communist" labor organization must be infiltrated and guided by Communists or their designees for a truly non-Communist organization would surely not take such a drastic position of opposition to a law that aimed at controlling communist organizations.

These historical roots resulted in Sōhyō being burdened with more radical, more conservative and more or less neutral or middle-of-the-road unions, each of whose philosophical approaches would have to be taken into account and somehow reconciled particularly when, as in this instance of opposition to the draft SAPL, if Sōhyō was to take united, coordinated and systematic action. This three way vulnerability—not a split—was a major Sōhyō structural weakness for taking united action and one which could be exploited by those opposed to Sōhyō, e.g. the government. For example, Mutō Takeo, President of Sōhyō, comes from Tanrō, the mining workers union, which conducted some rather pitched contests with mining companies. Takano Minoru, Sōhyō's Secretary, had held many labor union positions since before the war.

Takano was approximately the same generation as his government and Liberal Party counterparts, Mutō a half generation different; nevertheless, they both must have had many prewar experiences in the labor union field and in coal mining which they vividly remember. Their counterparts had graduated from the University Tokyo while they had little formal education. In the Japanese social hierarchy this gap was almost unbridgeable. In prewar days their counterparts would hardly deign to recognize them, let along negotiated with them as equals. The postwar situation had changed radically and they headed large organized influential labor unions. Mutō's and Takano's personal experiences, the pitiful conditions of the coal miners, the prewar suppression of the labor movement for the sake of the Empire must have left an indelible impression and inevitably colored their attitudes toward the SAPL and the potential implementation of that law by the same generation of police officers and internal security agencies from before the war.

That the proposed waves of strikes were of a political nature there could be no argument, but could they be labeled as "political strikes" broadly as a political judgment and assessment or more specifically in legal terms, perhaps contravening labor laws. Were these strike waves, political strikes, thus without the protection of the labor laws and thus presumably illegal. Sōhyō and its constituent unions had to be careful how they were depicted. For example, Tanrō headquarters claimed the strikes were not political but these actions had the protection of Article 28 of the Constitution which guaranteed freedom of organizational activities. And it was asserted that the Constitution was legally above the labor contract. Notwithstanding this ambiguity, Tanrō was in the forefront of the drive against the draft SAPL. Such strikes would be subsumed as one of many labor dispute tactics. The coal mining companies threatened that it would fire the union leadership if the strikes were carried out. Would the workers be more concerned about their jobs than supporting the leadership with this interpretation. It was the hope that such wavering members would not be lost to the cause. Or could the government and management raise enough doubt and anxieties in their minds to neutralize the leadership's attempts to mobilize union members against the draft SAPL. Many unions downplayed the "political" aspect of the strike wave and attempted to roll them into one with other economic disputes in order not to arouse these anxieties among some members.[43]

Takano Minoru, speaking as Sōhyō's SecGen, did not equivocate: these strikes are political, the dates were deliberately chosen to express

[43] Article 28 of the Constitution reads as follows: The right of workers to organize and to bargain and act collectively is guaranteed.

labor's unhappiness with the new peace arrangements. He stressed that unlike the abortive February 1, 1947 strike, this strike though political was not Communist inspired nor controlled by the Communists, and did not aim at a Communist revolution. This strike was wholly within the labors law since it was the government that was disregarding the rights and position of the worker and it was intended to appeal to the government to reflect on its position (*hansei o motomeri*). The purpose of the strikes was not to continue them to the bitter end and create a crisis (*akumade suto o zokkō-shite hakyoku o maneku to iyū mono dewa naku)* but as a protest (*kōgi*) and a warning (*keikoku*).

Sōhyō developed a theory that with the creation of the peace-security arrangements, a new era was dawning which they feared included an agenda to move against labor unions. This is part of the struggle of the unions to survive in this new regime. In any economic struggle there are two parts (as advised by the Sōhyō policy department): one is the economic interest struggle (*rieki tōsō*) and the other is the political struggle (*seiji tōsō*). Thus, this struggle is basic, the very survival and continued existence of unions under the new regime was declared to be at stake. Takano maintained that the strike waves must proceed until the government either withdraws the draft bill or agrees to postpone its submission to the Diet.

By early April 1952, many unions (*tansan*) had agreed to join the April 12 first strike wave but an accurate count was difficult to establish. One report stated that as of April 1, 1952 only about ten industry unions under the Rōtō umbrella had signed on. Looked at another way, Tanrō, Gōsei Kagaku (chemical workers union), electrical workers, mineral workers, metal workers, automobiles, chemical workers alliance (Kagaku Dōmei), Shōwa Denkō, 8 unions with 648,000 members, supported by 1.3 million public employees, almost two million in total. For the second wave on April 18, private railways, steel workers, 226,000 with the support of seaman's union, textiles, Nishi-Nihon Heavy Industry with another 500,000. The unions with a seemingly united front were prepared for the April 12 strike.

iii. *The Political Opposition in the Diet*

At every opportunity, the political opposition in the Diet pursued the government in plenary session and in Committee. Clearly, it was to harass the government and establish a formal record of all the attempts to stop and/or radically revise the draft SAPL, even when that political opportunity in the HofR was close to zero. The AG and Labor Minister replied to interpolations in plenary session in the HoR and in the HofC. At the plenary session on the eve of the 1st strike, Kaishintō and SDP-R Diet members accused the government of themselves creating the situation leading to the proposed strikes. The Kaishintō representative (Moriyama Kinji) reminded the government of the people's experiences with the PPL in prewar years, criticized the SDP-L for its support of mass demonstrations, and the government's intentions about invoking Cabinet Ordinance 325 in controlling general strikes in 1947. SDP-R Representative (Doi Naosaku) was naturally much sharper in asserting that the proposed strikes were not political but stemmed from the draft SAPL itself which proposes to suppress the labor movement, labor is fighting for its life. The SDP-R's position seemed to have hardened during the short period from a somewhat equivocating stance to describing the proposed law as more anti-democratic than the prewar PPL; it was only natural it should be opposed even if it meant an unlimited (*mukigen*) strike, ordered all its prefectural branches to work closely with Rōtō to oppose the law, must not allow the Communists to take over this opposition and the party will strive to fight the law in the Diet and prevent oppression of the unions; this bill was symbolic of the reactionary nature of the government's policies. SDP-R Diet members led by SecGen Asanuma Inejirō met with AG Kimura, LM Yoshitake and Cabinet SecGen Hori on April 4—the day before the meeting with Sōhyō on April 5—to demand the withdrawal of the bill—all to no avail, of course. They knew that would be the outcome but as the SDP-R they were compelled to take a much stronger and unambiguous stand. Even the somewhat conservative Kaishintō stated that even though violent activities must be controlled, there is a danger that basic human rights will be suppressed and the Public Security Examination Commission as a mere Outer Bureau (Gaikyoku) of the AG would be a re-creation of the Tokkō police system of the prewar years.[44] The government had not alternative but to reiterated its assurance like a mantra that the proposed law would not target legitimate labor union activities and the media, except when these movements became large, threatened the general welfare and became a public security issue then there must be rational

[44] *Asahi* 4/2/1952, 4/3/1952, 4/4/1952, 4/4/1952 (eve), 4/5/1952, *Sankei* 4/3/1952, *Yomiuri* 4/7/1952, 4/11/1952.

mechanisms to resolve the problems. Nevertheless, the AG insisted that the idea of a law to control "general strikes" had not reached the preparation stage. The government dangled the probability that it would submit the draft SAPL to the Diet in the next few days—this threat was postponed a couple of times but continued to be used as a threat. On the eve of the first strike LM Yoshitake downgraded the possible size of the strike and its impact by suggesting that only part of Tanrō, metal and auto workers unions would participate. While Japan was "under Occupation" and Cabinet Ordinance was still effective the government did not intend to invoke this Ordinance.[45]

iv. *The Government-Sōhyō Meetings*

The political dance in the two-and-half meetings were not aimed to secure the moral high ground but probably pragmatically to secure the public relations high ground, to appear reasonable, to be willing to meet and "discuss" the core issues—except that these proposals put forward by each side could not be accepted by either side and both sides knew that was the case. At the request of the government, the first meeting took place on April 5, 1952 in the office of LM with the leadership of Sōhyō and its constituent unions. Publicly both sides appeared to be talking but in reality it was a bid for public opinion. Before and after the meeting both Sōhyō and the government issued statements about their expectations which were irreconcilable: labor said the strikes would go ahead unless the government withdrew the draft SAPL; the government would not, of course, entertain such a notion. The AG and LM would repeat their mantra again that the law would be aimed at destructive communist activities not legitimate union activities. The union leaders questioned the Ministers about their intentions and interpretations on various critical phrases and terms. After stating their opposing positions to no avail the meeting was adjourned and a contest of press releases took place.[46]

---

[45] *Asahi* 4/2/1952, 4/11/1952 and *Sankei* 4/3/1952 (reporting on a 3/23/1952 budget hearing). Comment about Cabinet Ordinance were also reported in *Asahi* 4/3/1952 as press interviews with the LM and AG and in response to a direct query from the SDP-R about the nature of the Ordinance (*Asahi* 4/4/1952).

[46] The government's invitation to Sōhyō was conveyed by Kaku Saijirō, DG Labor Administration Bureau (Rōsei-kyoku), Labor Ministry. From the government, the LM, AG, Parliamentary and Administrative Labor Vice Ministers, Yoshikawa DG/SIB, Seki Deputy DG/SIB, and others. From labor, Chairman Mutō, SecGen Takano,

The government still somewhat uncertain adopted a cautious approach by delaying the submission of the bill to the Diet for a short period; in the meantime, watched Sōhyō and union reactions and kept an ear to public reaction to the Government's apparent intent to conduct a dialog with the opposition. If the unions did not heed the government's wishes then the latter would move swiftly to submit the draft to the Diet and enact this legislation and take strong enforcement measures. Sōhyō's Rōtō proclaimed that it was dangerous to give the government such preventive authority through this proposed legislation. While it is now, the government says, aimed at the Communists, tomorrow it may be re-focused on oppressing the union movement which has a constitutional guarantee. The question is how will the term "violent destructive (or subversive) activities" be defined and implemented. If the government persists then Rōtō has no alternative but to conduct its legal protest strike beginning April 12. The *Asahi* aptly reported that the competitive appeal to the populace (*minshū*) might be summed up as "the defense of democratic government" (*minshu seiji*) for the government and for the labor unions a placard (*kamban*) with "defending democracy".[47]

As though to balance the PR tactics of going the extra-half mile, Sōhyō/Rōtō through the good offices of Sasaki Kōzō (SDP-L), requested on April 8 a meeting with PM Yoshida to discuss the SAPL. He could not, despite his distaste for the leftwing political parties and labor unions, appear to be rejecting an overture to discuss the difficult confrontation. The reply from the PM: meet with Hori, Cabinet SecGen on April 9, 1952. Rōtō presented a list of the four demands to the government; tactically they wanted a public rejection of their position by PM's personal representative.

a. The immediate withdrawal of the government's intention to submit the draft SAPL to the Diet.

Rōtō Chairman, and vice chairmen level persons from National Railway, Automobile Workers, Tanrō, Communications, Chemical Workers unions, a total of about 20 at the meeting. *Asahi* 3/31/1952 (eve), 4/1/1952, 4/3/1952, 4/4/1952, 4/5/1952, 4/56/1952, *Mainichi* 4/6/1952, 4/7/1952, *Tokyo* 4/5/1952, 4/7/1952, *Yomiuri* 4/1/1952, 4/5/1952 (eve), 5/5/1952 (eve), 4/7/1952.

[47] *Asahi* 4/6/1952, 4/7/1952, *Yomiuri* 4/5/1952, 4/7/1952. On the same day in the *Tokyo Shimbun*, it was reported the Cabinet SecGen Hori had changed his mind about being conciliatory, that the authority and prestige of the Diet as a legislative body should not be tarnished by delaying consideration of the draft, such delay would create a bad precedent for the post-peace and security situation.

b. There was no reason for the necessity for this special security legislation.
c. The definition of subversive/violent destructive activities is vague and it is clear that any words and actions (*gendō*) critical of the government and labor activities could be suppressed.
d. Instead of relying on this kind of legislation to maintain public security, this should be sought by defending democracy and stabilizing and improving the people's livelihood.

These demands were naturally rejected out of hand by the government. Sōhyō/Rōtō promptly announced that the first strike on April 12 would now proceed as planned. Rōtō and Takano, Sōhyō SecGen, issued a statement reiterating their positions that the government was attempting to clamp down on labor, abridge Constitutional rights, revive the dark days of the Pacific War under Premier Tōjō, that these "protest strikes" not "political strikes" were the culmination of ten months of enlightenment and training of unions to oppose not only the SAPL but also the contemplated disadvantageous revision of the labor laws. On the other hand, the hardline AG's immediate reaction was that the draft bill would be promptly submitted to the Diet. He declared that the bill had been decided by the Cabinet, that it reflected the government's "final position", revision of the approved bill through such activities before submission to the Diet, even withdrawal as demanded would set a bad precedent for future management of the government, and it was now the responsibility of the Diet to debate the merits of the bill. To do otherwise would be a denial of the parliamentary system.[48]

A semi-meeting was requested at the 11th hour (16:30, April 11, 1952) by LM Yoshitake to meet with Sōhyō/Rōtō leaders to discuss the "promissory word changes" mentioned under "The Government" subsection but Sōhyō/Rōtō representatives said word changes were unsatisfactory and the strike would proceed. Again, the government must have known that these promissory word changes would not be acceptable; their moves were aimed at public opinion, that yet again the government was trying to be conciliatory, that the Rōtō and unions were uncooperative, intransigent, and unwilling to be reasonable and

[48] Mutō, Sōhyō President, Sōhyō VP and staff, and representatives from Government Monopoly Workers Union, National Railway Workers Union met with Hori. The AG's office had prepared a pamphlet on the draft SAPL as part of its strategy to try to persuade the unions about the need and merits of the draft SAPL and to dissuade them to strike. I have not been able to locate a copy of this pamphlet.

compromise; they struck a "pose of sincerity" hoping to blame the unions in the eyes of the public opinion as the upcoming strike took place, getting in the last word before the first strike wave.

v. *The First Strike Wave, April 12, 1952*

About 250,000–350,000 participated in various ways in the Sōhyō/Rōtō sponsored strike, some were 24-hour strikes, some 2–4 hour work stoppages, still others were large workplace rallies. This was a far cry, however, from the potential two million plus which was originally forecast. Furthermore, even though April 12 was a Saturday and a workday, the economic damage was regarded as inconsequential. Automobile, metal, chemical and other unions conducted 24 hour strikes or 2–4 hour work stoppages, electrical, surface transportation, seamen, steel, public employee workers unions held workplace rallies but a definite account was difficult to arrive at. However, the last minute change of heart by Tanrō from being an aggressive leader in Rōtō, and Zenkōren (metal workers) deciding not to participate in the first strike wave substantially weakened the impact of this strike. The first strike was not regarded as a success, Rōtō's marching step had slipped somewhat out of sync (*ashinami midaru*). It was nevertheless, the first substantial labor demonstration since the abortive general strike of February 1, 1947.[49]

[49] In the U.S. National Archives, I found several documents in RG331:2187:9 which appear to be G-2 (Intelligence) memos from "R.F.E." to the Chief of Staff on the Sōhyō strikes for April 10, 11, 12 and 13, 1952 and by F. Rizzo, also to the Chief of Staff. Each were a page long. April 10: "G-2 feels that, in themselves, the strikes or possible demonstrations connected therewith are relatively unimportant. The important issue whether or not threats by an organized minority can coerce the *fledgling* [emphasis added] Japanese Government into shelving legislation." Obviously this source has little understanding of the determination of PM Yoshida and AG Kimura to enact some kind of internal security legislation. April 11: "No serious trouble is anticipated by Japanese police who are prepared with any eventuality." April 12: "The dismal failure of the heralded strike action has been a signal victory for the Government and a severe blow to the plans of the leftwing sponsors of the strikes who obviously were exploiting the strike action to strengthen their political future with the labor organizations." April 13: "While Sōhyō headquarters claims that 300,000 workers participated in the 12 April strike... this figure is very misleading and an obvious attempt at face saving.... the greater majority of unions held small workshop meetings which had little or no effect on normal operations or production.... In view of the apparent indifference of the rank and file to the provisions of the Subversive Activities Prevention Bill, prospects for an effective 18 April strike are dim unless labor leaders drum up renewed interest in purely economic aims or protest against the possible revision of

It appears that while Sōhyō/Rōtō focused their attention on the Ministerial level, Kaku DG Labor Administration Bureau in ML played a persuasive role in Tanrō considerations. Chairman Mutō was regarded as a solid personality rather than a fire brand. The last minute Tanrō executive committee meeting voted to delay the strike to April 18 by one vote—including bringing one person in by stretcher to vote! Kaku's persuasiveness and the last minute willingness to suggest word changes described above apparently caused Tanrō not to abandon the strike concept but postpone such action till later and wait and see how the government would act in including the promised word changes. Zenkōren decided in the early hours of April 12 to follow the textile unions (Zensen) and Tanrō. (Zenkōren, a metal mining union, was also part of the same Mitsui *keiretsu* family of companies). Tanrō's last minute about-face caused a strong reaction from around the country against this vote, suggesting that Tanrō would re-join the effort and participate in the second strike. This latent leftwing rightwing cleavage in Sōhyō surfaced with the first strike and perhaps the jockeying among unions in anticipation of the third national Sōhyō convention upcoming in June 1952 played a role in how the first strike evolved.[50]

The government was, of course, rather satisfied with the outcome; LM Yoshitake praised Sōhyō for its restraint and inclinations toward democratic union development, for not using violent tactics and expressed his hope that the second strike could be resolved peacefully. Yoshitake could point with success to the effect of the three point proposed revision of the draft SAPL mentioned previously. While labor

labor laws." Rizzo's report also expected the "size and effects of the strikes will be reduced considerably by the non-participation of important segments controlled by rightwing leaders [in the labor unions]."

There were three levels of protests: 1) 24 hour protest, those participating were Zenkoku Kinzoku (National Metal Workers), Zen-Jidōsha (National Auto Workers); 2) limited protests of 2–4 hours, Showa Denkō, Densan (Electric Power Workers), Kagaku Dōmei, Shin-Sambetsu; workplace rallies, Gōsei Kagaku, Kaiin (Seamens), Tekkō (Steel Workers), Nittsū, Nikkyōso (Teachers Union), National Gas Workers, Kokutetsu (Japan National Railways), Zen-Shinchūgun (Workers for Occupation Forces). In addition, Governmental Workers Unions conducted protest marches.

[50] With the vote 6:6, Chairman Mutō cast the deciding vote to postpone the strike. Tanrō had negotiated a new pay contract but was battling an attempt by the local companies to raise work norms (*rōdō kyōka*) and to raise the consciousness of the rank and file members about such work issues. In an article by Akiyama Shinji in *Sekai* 7/1952, *Rōdō Kōsei* (Labor Offensive) he suggested that ¥30 million had been passed to Tanrō at a private meeting at a Mitsui company hostel just before the strike but there has never been confirmation of this transaction.

had "failed" to maintain a completely united front, Rōtō's determination to fight the draft SAPL had not diminished and their political allies in the Diet reiterated their decision to fight the bill. The legislative battle in and out of the Diet roared on.[51]

vi. *GHQ-VIII, Remaining Twilight, a last courtesy call*

As if to pacify the ego of GHQ/SCAP, and to fulfill formalities, Labor Minister Yoshitake made an "unsolicited, unannounced call" on Rizzo on April 11 to inform him that the SAPL had been amended to "to clarify its non-applicability to legitimate labor activities and that members of organized labor and the press would be included on the Commission." These "concessions" were made by the Cabinet as a "gesture of clarification of sincere intent on the part of the government. In light of the nature of the revisions—to try to ward off protest strikes by labor—Rizzo told Minister Yoshitake that GHQ would waive the formal 24-hour waiting period for clearance and that the government "was free to make it on its own responsibility."[52] What other real political viable alternative did GHQ have at the time? As an organization "virtually in a self-liquidating process" (Oppler's *Legal Reform in Japan*, p. 288), GHQ had little effective political leeway. The dialogue with the Japanese and the afore-mentioned controversy in GHQ revealed clearly the differing concepts of what was probably constitutionally acceptable in Japan and politically and administratively felt to be needed under the prevailing sense of a "Communist threat" in Japan versus what was constitutionally acceptable in the U.S. While the AG was concerned about the effectiveness of the Commission under these threatening conditions with less focus on "due process", the U.S. experts views focused on the constitutional weak-

[51] This subsection was based, in the main, on articles from the following newspapers: *Asahi* 4/10/1952, 4/10/1952 (eve), 4/11/1952. 4/11/1952 (eve), 4/12/1952, 4/12/1952 (eve), 4/13/1952, *Jiji* 4/9/1952, *Mainichi* 4/9/1952, 4/9/1952 (eve), 4/11/1952, 4/12/1952, 4/13/1952, *Sankei* 4/8/1952, *Tokyo* 4/11/1952, *Yomiuri* 4/8/1952, 4/11/1952, 4/11/1952, 4/12/1852, 4/12/1952 (eve), 4/13/1952.

[52] Memo (4/11/1952), Rizzo to Chief of Staff. Report on Subversive Activity Prevention Bill. 1 p. This meeting was also briefly mentioned by *Yomiuri*, 4/11/1952 (eve). Another small point was also mentioned as an "oh by the way" item that GHQ was disinclined to invoke the MacArthur letter of January 31, 1947 canceling the "general strike" for February 1, 1947. Such a small event indicated how insignificant the role of GHQ had become in the scheme of things in internal Japanese affairs. This was to be expected and nothing unusual but this event should be noted.

nesses centering on the dubious lack of attention to "due process in the SAPL and the semi-judicial role of the Commission". Major Jay's and Oppler's memos raised serious questions about the constitutionality of the draft SAPL. It appears that the GOJ/AG-GHQ dialogue was a friendly give and take and did result in nudging the evolution of the drafting a little way in this or that direction but not, it would seem, in any fundamental manner. Notwithstanding GHQ "suggestions" there were no major changes in the government draft about a hearing in the Anglo-Saxon sense, about cross-examination, or about self-incrimination. While Jay felt optimistic that he had had the opportunity of "improving the most outrageous piece of legislation concerning internal security" and recalls he was "shocked by the language of the Act", he nevertheless resignedly commented in his interview that GOJ took what they wanted; we acted merely as counsel. It is of interest that no records were found that the Government Section staff had shown any interest in or attempted to meet with labor leaders to listen to their side of this major political confrontation. Had this contact have occurred it probably would have been interpreted by the GHQ Labor section as an unwelcome intrusion into their turf and unfortunately, no records were found that these two important groups in GHQ consulted horizontally about the SAPL.

vii. *Submission of the Draft SAPL to the Diet, April 17, 1952*

LM Yoshitake could, with some justification, claim that because of his political efforts with the unions using the three points of proposed revisions of the draft SAPL approved by the Cabinet that the first strike wave was "less than successful", had been neutralized and that the labor unions could again be successfully divided and manipulated. Reflecting this "success", he demanded strongly that important revisions be made to the draft in order to persuade the unions not to carry out the second strike on April 18, especially to influence such unions as Tanrō and Zenkōren both of which decided not to participate in the first strike. Yoshitake demanded as he had in the past for the

a. deletion of "*sendō*" (incitement)—as the political opposition was also demanding but that the AG had declared was the essence of the SAPL
b. deletion of Article 27 giving the PSIA indirect compulsory investigative authority
c. insertion of words that appropriate/justifiable (*seitō na*) labor union activities will not be suppressed (*yokusei shinai*)

d. insertion of an article that actions will be taken to recompense persons (*kyūsai sochi*) against illegal administrative actions (*gyōsei shobun*).

The AG and particularly the AG staff strongly opposed these proposed revisions. The ministries were totally unable to agree even working late into the night of April 14, in anticipation of a Cabinet meeting the next morning. AG Kimura, Kiyohara DG Criminal Administration Bureau (Keisei Chōkan), and Seki, the expert drafter of laws, met secretly with LM Yoshitake in the Mikasa Kaikan Building in Ginza but could not budge him from his demands. Each side maintained their positions with great vehemence.

The April 15, 1952 Cabinet meeting decided that the word "*sendō*" remain in the draft supporting the AG. Without that word included the country's internal security forces would be unable to act against those who incite others to insurrection, rioting, assassinations, and other crimes and these crimes are among the most serious crimes in the Criminal Code. An overall slogan "Overthrow the Yoshida Government" advocated by a union would not infringe upon the law but to advocate the assassination of a Minister or incitement to burn down the house of a prosecutor would infringe on this law. This forewarning is critical in maintaining public peace and stability. The deletion of "incitement" would be equivalent to lending one's verandah (*engawa*) to Sōhyō which would then be infiltrated by the Communists and the main house (i.e. Japan) would eventually be taken over. (This is similar to the English expression that if one allows the camel's nose in the ten, then it would take over the tent.)

The second demand to delete indirect partial compulsory investigative authority (Article 27 of the March 28, 1952 Cabinet approved version) was accepted. This article gave the PSIA the authority to order the appearance of selected persons for questioning and to produce documents and other items (*bukken*) but it must provide a reason to those who are ordered to appear and it may request reports from other agencies on the issues at hand. Article 26 stated, however, that the PSIA would conduct the necessary investigations to carry out the law and the articles on cooperating with other security agencies, and having access to their files and being able to call upon their investigative authorities was left untouched. Thus the investigative authority of PSIA may appear to have been diluted and made somewhat ambiguous. Despite potential turf problems, the PSIA could, without doubt, mobilize other security agencies for their investigative support. It is doubtful that this concession was substantive and meaningful in the context of the entire bill and was a concession most grudgingly ceded and could be afforded in order to facilitate the acceptance of the draft.

The third proposed revision was to clearly specify that appropriate, proper, legal labor union activities shall not be the target of this law and that such activities will not be suppressed was inserted as a new subsection (Article 2.2).

The fourth item about relief measures (*kyūsai sochi*) to be taken to compensate persons against whom illegal administrative actions have been imposed. This was not inserted but set aside with the understanding that members of the PSEC would be selected from labor and other fields.

Another set of words and phrases were added to various articles the objective and tone of which was to clarify, to define further—and by implication limit—the objectives of the law and selected actions to be taken under the SAPL. The phrase "as an activity of an organization" was inserted in articles 1, 4 and 6. In article 1 this phrase was inserted to define further the violent destructive organizations to be controlled; in articles 4 and 6 this phrase and "continuously or repeatedly" (*keizoku matawa hampuku-shite*) were added to further define those organizations which the PSEC could take administrative action against or could order disbanded.[53]

Depending upon how cabinet decisions are counted, this latest action to revise the draft SAPL in the above manner was perhaps the third or fourth time that this Cabinet revised its position: March 28, April 8, 11 and 15, 1952. This is highly unusual for a cabinet decision to be revisited that often. The first and fourth times were actual textual revisions. The other cases were probably proposed revisions approved

[53] An additional phrase and "appropriate" (*katsu sōtō na*) was added under article 2 (standards for controlling organizations): only those investigations to achieve the objective of this law which are necessary and "appropriate" was added to further specify the kind of investigation that could be conducted. An organ of a violent organization was defined as a publication published continuously (*keizoku-teki ni*) to advocate, communicate and propagandize the objectives, principles and policies of that organization. In articles 3 (definitions) and 37 (incitement of insurrections) actions which "contribute to" (*shi-suru*) was changed to actions "which make it easier [or facilitate, *yōi narashimeru tame ni*] to commit the crime. The Japanese could be interpreted as a financial contribution; the revision appears to be somewhat broader. A total of ten articles (1, 2, 3, 4, 6, 24, 27, 30, 37 and 43) were revised substantively or technically (*Asahi* 4/16/1952).

by the Cabinet in an attempt to mollify, neutralize and appeal to certain more cautious, more conservative unions not join the two strike waves. The Cabinet decision of April 15, 1952 was seemingly balanced "saving face" for both LM and the AG, but was a decided victory for the AG and his supporters in connection with these narrowly defined specific areas. These revisions were extremely grudgingly accepted by the AG and only because of the insistence of the LM who had appeared to have been "successful " in making the first strike appear unsuccessful. In a press interview after the Cabinet decision, he stressed that there were three main revisions: the insertion of the phrase "as an activity of the organization", the addition of the assurance that legitimate and proper union activities may not be limited nor interfered with and the deletion of Article 27 about the investigative authority of the PSIA. He maintained that only if the destructive violent activities were conducted "as an activity of the organization" may the law be applied. Would these revisions satisfy, mollify, assuage the unions and their political allies in the Diet was not obvious and, in the end, did not. They were peripheral word changes and DID NOT touch upon the core philosophy of the proposed law. That the conservative cabinet felt it necessary to revisit this draft proposal repeatedly, appear to negotiate with the opposition despite the strong avowals to the absolute determination of the Cabinet and that such conduct would set improper and unfortunate precedents for the conduct of government was a clear indication of the split in the government itself, its anxiety about the strength of the unions and even its own concern about the constitutionality of the proposed law although assured by their scholarly allies that it was constitutional. With the final revisions incorporated, the bill was submitted to the Diet on April 17, 1952.[54]

---

[54] The above description was was derived from items in the following newspapers: *Asahi* 4/15/1952, 4/15/1952 (eve), 4/16/1952, *Yomiuri* 4/16/1952. It was reported that the AG was pushed strongly by his staff to stand firm against the LM and that DG/SIB Yoshikawa threatened to resign if the word "*sendō*" was deleted from the draft and when they met secretly with Yoshitake in the Ginza, the AG with this threat in his hip pocket. The cabinet revisions were based on a detailed article and the press interview with the LM both of which appeared in the *Asahi* (4/16/1952). I am unaware of any cabinet decision on a comparably important legislative issue being repeatedly revised. According to Iwamoto Kōichi in *Tokuhon Nihon no Gikai Seiji* (Gyōsei Mondai Kenkyūjo. 1983, 459 p., pp. 272–277 a section on the Cabinet and Prime Minister) the Cabinet has three ways of expressing its "will" (*ishi*): A cabinet decision (*Kakugi kettei*) written and signed by Cabinet members, a cabinet understanding (*kakugi ryōkai*) which may be written or unwritten and a cabinet report (*kakugi hōkoku*).

Foreign Reaction to the Draft SAPL. To the best of my knowledge, no foreign country officially and publicly commented one way or the other to the Japanese Government about the draft SAPL submitted to the Diet except one: Communist China. According to the *Asahi* (4/23/1952), Guo Moruo, Deputy Premier and President of the China Committee for the Protection of Peace, sent a cable to PM Yoshida protesting that this proposed law was intended to make Japan into a military state for aggression in China and contravened the principle of democratizing Japan in accordance with the Potsdam Declaration.

viii. *The Second Strike Wave, April 18, 1952*

The ambiguous first strike took place on April 12, the government argued with itself about potential revisions to the draft SAPL and submitted a bill to the Diet on April 17, 1952. Rōtō, labor's battle command group's response was unambiguous; it vowed a huge more united second strike on April 18, only one day after the Cabinet meeting. Since April 13, Rōtō had been coordinating with its many constituent unions; the number of unions declaring for a strike on April 18 climbed steadily, the numbers grew to well over million members. Tanrō (Shitetsu and Zenkōren) had been willing to sit out the first strike to consider the government's proposed revisions. This willingness to compromise the united front on April 12 exacerbated the tension between the ideologically left and rightwing leaning unions. Sōhyō SecGen Takano criticized Tanrō as having been prey to and duped by government enticements. The government had now spoken. Where is Tanrō's decision? It was well accepted that without Tanrō's participation, the second strike would also be dubbed "a failure." A final decision must be made in 24–36 hours.

Mutō Takeo tantalizingly commented after the cabinet decision that since it had revised the draft again, we must carefully consider their final offer. He claimed he wished to obtain public opinion support for the second strike. On the other hand, even the cautious group (*shinchōron-ha*) in Tanrō tellingly expressed their feelings by noting

---

Although the newspaper reports are not necessarily legally most accurate, LM Yoshitake's approaches to Sōhyō in his attempts to persuade the unions not to conduct the first strike and make selected word changes, was in all probability based on an unwritten cabinet understanding. I have also tried unsuccessfully to find studies about cabinet decisions which have been repeatedly re-visited.

that the government had responded only minimally, like 40% to union demands. Zenkōren and Seamens Union had decided on April 15 to strike on April 18. The latter had switched from a workplace meeting to 8-hour stoppage of ship operations. Even in his own Tanrō, Mutō faced strong criticism from the rank and file members, a possible non-confidence vote at an upcoming Tanrō national convention. There was apparently a strong feeling that LM Yoshitake had not fulfilled "his promise" to obtain revisions to assure labor representation on the PSEC and assurances of relief from illegal and improper administrative actions by either the PSEC or PSIA; the government's refusal to provide this assurance implied that it was willing, even planning, to permit the abuse of authority (*shokken ran'yō*) in implementing this law. Only the assurance that legitimate labor union activities would not be targeted for investigation by the PSIA and subsequent administrative action by the PSEC would be accepted. And even this revision, it observed, was made only as part of the section on standards of control and NOT a substantive article (*jittai kitei*). The Tanrō executive committee met on April 16 and unanimously voted to participate in the April 18 strike and denounced the government as having betrayed the people and workers in their non-response to union requests. Rōtō immediately confirmed the April 18 strike. By this time over a million members had agreed to conduct varying lengths of protests up to one day; another million plus would refuse overtime and conduct workplace rallies, a total of slightly more than 2.34 million people.[55]

The unions were voicing their disapproval of the bill, distrust of the government under conservative control which was decidedly not pro-union but anti-union. It must have been Rōtō's objective to establish its position and role in the new independent Japan under the new peace/security treaty regime. This protest strike was led not by the

[55] Those striking were as follows: Tanrō (270,000, 24 hours), Seamans (130,000, 8), Densan (120,000, 6), Shitetsu (Private Railways, 120,000, 24), Zenkōren (70,000, 24), Tekkō (110,000 4), Zen-Jidōsha (30,000, 1–24), Zenkoku Kinzoku (65,000, 2), Shin-Sambetsu (70,000,2), Zen-Kōwan (Port Workers, 20,000), Nishi-Nihon Jūkō (17,000, 20). Those refusing overtime and held workplace rallies: Zen-Nittsū (110,000), Gōsei Kagaku (60,000), Nikkyōso (450,000), Zen-Nōrin (80,000), Zenkoku Denki (30,000), Zen-Sembai (40,000), Kokutetsu (400,000), Zen-Tei (150,000), Zen-Dentsū (75,000), Kami Parupu (Pulp) Rōren (30,000), Zen-Sen Dōmei (350,000), Zen-Ginren (110,000), Zen-Seiho (13,000), Toshi Kōtsū (40,000), Jichi Rōkyō (180,000), Zen-Shinchūgun Rōso (30,000), Zen-Insatsuchō (8,000), Nichi-Zai (10,000), Jichi Rōren (85,000), Zen-Hyakkan (30,000), Zen-Sekiyu (15,000), Zen-Sonpo (20,000), Zen-Sōko (5,000), Zen-Hoteru (110,000), Zen-Kaiun (3,000), Zenkoku Gasu (10,000), Nichi-Hōrō (7,000).

Japanese Communists as was the case in the abortive February 1, 1947 general strike. It was led by Sōhyō/Rōtō formed in mid-1950 as a counter weight to the Communist-led unions. Although their stand against the peace/security treaty regime was denounced by the government which suspected that communists in disguise must be leading the federation and the protest strike, the leading unions in Sōhyō and Rōtō were generally regarded as "democratic unions". Furthermore, in the second strike, it must be noted that the size and implication of this strike was made that much more impressive with the participation of Tanrō, electric power union, seamen's union, and private railway workers union which were probably participating in conjunction with their negotiations over pay which had broken down just before the strike. Some unions of private railway companies did conclude a new wage contract and withdrew from the second protest strike. These unions had not participated in the April 12 first strike.

It appears the rank and file played an active role in persuading the leaders of some of these unions to participate in the second strike. It was commented that while the government seemed to have succeeded in weakening, neutralizing the first strike, it had earned the disappointment, frustration, even anger of the rank and file that it was manipulating unions, had broken "promises" made about revising the draft SAPL. Instead of cowing the unions, these government manipulations stimulated a new defiance among union members.

Although the second strike was the biggest in Japanese labor history up to 1952, the economic losses from the strike were not regarded as particularly damaging. The private railway unions disrupted the travels of about 13,000,000 people in one day. Losses in yen, about 100,000,000. It was estimated that about 90,000 tons of freight were stalled and about 120,000 tons of coal not produced.

The government's response was significantly low key, not threatening. It left it to industry to take whatever measures it may wish to take in a rational manner and according to the circumstances of each industry and company. Nikkeiren declared that the political protest strike was illegal but cleverly camouflaged. Except for Tanrō, many unions had tied their economic demands with this protest strike. Nikkeiren asserted that strict and strong measures must be taken to pursue those responsible for losses. It should be remembered, however, that in April 1952 between the first and second strikes, the Ube Kōsan union had won a major strike against Ube Industries for unfair dismissal of union members and held a victory march to the company on April 14.

Nikkeiren urged each industry to take appropriate action but urged them to avoid dismissals that would appear to be piggy-backing on this strike, indeed polite guidance to action carefully, if any, discretely, not provocatively, i.e. no action.

In light of the relative success in mobilizing such a potent show of force, Sōhyō SecGen Takano with bravado declared labor's determination to fight this draft bill until it was withdrawn or defeated by resorting to additional "strikes"—even though the probability of such a withdrawal by the government was highly unlikely; on May 8 Rōtō decided to conduct a third strike sometime toward the end of May; this set off alarm bells about the labor union movement's intentions about the conduct of democratic parliamentary government.[56]

Editorial comments followed the same political orientation as before except that *Jiji Shimbun* took their criticism one step further by comparing the strike action to the conduct of the Japanese Army in the so-called attempted military revolts in the 1930s, e.g., the 2–26 (February 26, 1936) Incident. Even the *Nikkei* voiced its concerns about possible suppression of the media. These editorials did express concern about union intentions about future strikes and parliamentary democracy, did continue to express doubts about the government's intentions about how the law would be implemented in light of historical precedent and did call upon the government to yield to the greatest extent possible to obtain a law that has the backing of the people. In addition to editorials, the *Asahi* and *Yomiuri* newspapers published four commentaries on the government's proposal. Three were by university professors (Fujibayashi Keizō/Keio University, Kainō Michitaka/ Waseda University, Ukai Nobushige/ International Christian University), and the fourth by a well known lawyer (Kiyose Ichirō). They were unanimously critical in varying degrees of severity of the government's approach in assessing the urgency of internal security and the proposed law. Most changes they claimed were not substantive, merely changes on the margin. The government will again attempt to control freedom of expression. That *sendō* which was not deleted remains a

[56] The above description was based on reports in the following newspapers: *Asahi* 4/13/1952, 4/15/1952, 4/17/1952, 4/17/1952(eve), 4/18/1952, 4/19/1952. *Jiji* 4/19/1952, *Mainichi* 4/18/1952, 4/19/1952, *Tokyo* 4/17/1952, 4/18/1952, 4/23/1952, *Yomiuri* 4/15/1952, 4/17/1952,4/18/1952. On April 15, Rōtō met with legal scholars to discuss and confirm Rōtō's position that the government revisions were technical and not wholly substantive.

fundamental problem. Japan does need a new internal security law, but not the proposed SAPL. As the proposed SAPL was submitted to the Diet, not only did the Rōtō demonstrate and remonstrate against the bill these four prominent writers expressed little confidence in the government, and also accused the government of drafting a dangerous proposal designed to restrict fundamental rights, demanded that the draft bill should be fundamentally rewritten to excise such terms as "*sendō*" and create a more balanced institutional arrangement to safeguard the rights of the accused.

C. *Concluding with a Cherry Blossom Party*

In the eyes of the conservative government under Prime Minister Yoshida, the emerging political regime under the peace-security treaties, the gathering momentum of the violent and destructive tactics of the Communists in the early 1950s, the imperative of a new internal security law was absolutely necessary and the one point of common agreement. There was another factor common to all participants, a long standing dislike, distaste, distrust, particularly of the Communists and everything that they stood for. They also feared the chaos that they might be able to create just when Japan was regaining its independence and the economy was beginning to move forward. The Communists and their philosophy, tactics, principles were completely contrary to the "new democratic Japan." To emphasize their distaste and distrust were the international strings, especially those with the then Soviet Union. The senior political leadership despite the purges under the occupation and the senior civil servants in the national government had come to adulthood in a Japan which fervently believed in the Russian and Red menace and threat to Japan. Their most recent experiences were the sudden and last minute invasion of Manchuokuo/Manchuria by Soviet forces just before the war ended on August 15, 1945 contrary to the existing Soviet Union-Japan Neutrality Pact and the Communist takeover of many labor unions in the immediate postwar years. To them the Communists and all that they stood for were, as a gut intuitive and deeply felt conviction, "un-Japanese" and a threat to the Japanese way of life—without going into a great controversy, exposition and dialogue as to what that meant. Probably the leftist parties and unions were to be tolerated, held somewhat in contempt but controllable, malleable and manageable—in a similar vein when U.S. writers talk about "managing" the U.S.-Japan relationship, harnessing Japan's power for U.S. purposes.

This task to create a draft law for this purpose was given to Seki, a senior civil servant in the SIB and who began his career in the Ministry of Justice in the early 1930s. Initially he created a mosaic of ideas from Cabinet Ordinances which had been put into effect under the Occupation mandate. It threw a huge net of potential and attempted control over a large portion of Japanese political society. An ambitious AG released a detailed program outline at a premature press conference in Fall 1951. All political organizations would be required to register, the AG or DG/SIB would decide which organizations were political. Violators of the SAPL could be purged from their jobs and a broadly defined set of public offices, organizations disbanded and many other penalties. This unleashed substantial criticism; even the drafter commented we had created a draft law which may been even worse than the prewar PPL!

But after another re-assessment, articles in the Criminal Code on insurrections, riots, assisting the enemy etc., would be made applicable to organizations in addition to individuals. The number of applicable articles in this Code were gradually increased AND more importantly these were "supplemented" and made much more comprehensive in coverage by adding, planning to incite, to instigate, possessing materials which could be regarded as aiding these causes, posting such materials, or committing such acts knowing that such actions would lead to instigation and incitement. This would give the internal security forces an especially broad mandate without specificity; it was the very kind of law that the opposition—from political parties, labor unions, academic, cultural organizations and other political, economic and social groups—most feared; this fear was compounded by the indisputable police record from before the war in implementing the PPL.

Under AG Kimura, there was a renewed determination to create a draft bill which would be the basis for common agreement. Undoubtedly, great expectations were placed on Kimura's determined personality, acumen and stature to control the competing bureaucracies, justice and police. Naturally the drafting agency, the AG, would give itself normal police powers to investigate, search, inspect and seize but this authority was fundamentally challenged from the beginning by the old-line police agencies. This issue of authority was not resolved in the AG's favor despite the PM's support of the AG; it remained a source of unpleasant contention to the last moment. This issue revealed the depth of the feeling about turf control and domination which had nothing whatsoever to do with the substance of the law and its objectives. The turf issue was also complicated by the groups mostly de-purgees who vainly thought of trying to revive a prewar police structure centered around the defunct Ministry of Home Affairs or a new Ministry of Internal Security. This issue was resolved more by a determined stand—a stare or two by senior police officers supported strongly by their political Ministers and not, it appears, brought to the attention of the PM for his decision. Ultimately, AG Kimura was unable to support successfully his own Ministry, his *kendō* stare was less effective than the bureaucratic police stare.

Based on available evidence, the PM played a role of exhortation, called meetings of the concerned Ministers to push forward the sometimes bureaucratically stalled draft. The draft was continually delayed for presentation to the Diet by jealousies and bureaucratic haggling but probably there was a strongly felt need for the enactment of an internal security law soon after the Peace and Security Treaties went into effect on April 28, 1952. The PM would assign the responsibility for the final draft to the AG but even this direct assignment gave him only the lead responsibility to reach a compromise and relatively quickly too.

The two committees, the Cabinet Ordinances Consultative Committee reporting to the PM and the Liberal Party's Self-Defense and Public Security Investigation Committee played an active role mostly in telling the AG to delete fairly numerous provisions in the several drafts, rather than other government agencies normally involved in review of proposed legislation. Again, based on available data, these two committees appeared to have played a rather unusual role in narrowing the application of the law, but because of its membership did seem to support the old-line police agencies in limiting the above-mentioned police powers to them instead of giving such powers to the PSIA.

GHQ officials appeared more concerned about due process. This interest probably resulted in the revision to allow the accused to have more witnesses (*jiken tachiai-nin*), an increase from three to five, for the accused to choose these witnesses and for the press to attend PSEC hearings. But for better or worse, these were not the major concerns of the government nor of the opposition. They were concerned with how the law would be implemented and how this would affect the labor unions. GHQ analysis was not focused on such issues as incitement. There was a clear disconnect between the U.S. style and approach to this and the concerns and anxieties of both the GOJ and its opposition.

In order to avoid further strife with labor and the threatened protest strikes by the labor unions, the Labor Minister insisted on deleting "*sendō*" but at a late night session with the AG and staff lost in a contest of wills. Later he tried to persuade the Cabinet to delete "*sendō*" at the last Cabinet meeting but was cajoled by others ministers and the issue was dropped. Nevertheless, notwithstanding the strong objections of the AG and his reluctant and grudging concurrence, the draft was revised to include a specific assurance that "legitimate" labor union activities would not be the target of this SAPL.

The unions felt they had to take a strong political stand in light of what they fervently believed was a coordinated, planned strategy to weaken, render neutral, perhaps even to destroy the influence of labor unions and their political allies in and out of the Diet. They conducted two protest strikes to make an unalterably clear statement of their intention to play a role in the new regime in the independence era. The Cabinet's concern about the protest strikes, the opposition parties and criticism from many other sources throughout the country probably prompted the Cabinet to revisit its original March 28, 1952 decision several times, a most unusual event in and of itself in the management of Cabinet decisions.

It had taken a little over a year from conception to birth as a bill submitted to the Diet for its consideration. The beach head had been maintained. The broad dragnet concept of the early drafts had been discarded and more narrowly focused. It had survived the twists and turns in the bureaucratic struggle and political demands made by Cabinet members. Numerous substantive, technical and word and phrase changes and retreats were made to respond to Cabinet members, to try to assuage the distrust and suspicions of the labor unions, the political opposition and most other sectors of society. The core concepts underpinning the draft law, articles in the Criminal Code as supplemented and the continued inclusion of *sendō*, were not compromised.

As the second strike proceeded, Prime Minister Yoshida sponsored a Cherry Blossom Viewing Party (*Kan'ō-kai*) for the cabinet.

CHAPTER FOUR

DIET DELIBERATIONS: HOUSE OF REPRESENTATIVES

A. *The Confrontation Intensifies*

A draft for a new internal security law had been created, after much debate inside the government, between the government and senior Liberal Party officials. Even the cabinet had to reconsider its "final" position several times. SCAP/GHQ was dubious about its constitutionality but this was known only to a tiny few in the GHQ offices. In the last days of the Occupation Japanese officials were polite but would not feel obliged to take their "advice" seriously and the Occupation officials did not seriously press their case with the Japanese. Labor unions, the political opposition, media, academia, most cultural figures (so-called *bunka-jin*) were, in most cases, vigorously and determinedly opposed to the enactment of such a law. Labor had launched massive "political" strikes to show their displeasure AND opposition to the draft law. The draft law was inextricably and inevitably linked to the kind of regime, political and legal structure, that was being created for post-peace treaty Japan. The JCP created a military committee and a so-called military apparatus and conducted numerous violent acts of murder, arson, demonstrations. While these were psychologically distressing and created an atmosphere of anxiety, they were never of such dimension that the national government of the state of Japan would be in jeopardy. The Japanese police conducted inappropriate and "illegal" surveillance, raids and intrusions onto university campuses thereby giving credence to the opposition claim that the discredited prewar police system might indeed be in the process of being re-installed. Then there were the expectations, after seven long years of Occupation, of regaining "independence" through the long awaited Peace Treaty, and the possibility of accelerating economic growth in the future.

Now that the SAPL was to be considered by the HofR, the decibel count of the voices of the opposition against the proposed internal security law was indeed raised several notches but against a backdrop of futility, the absolute majority held by the Liberal party. This opposition campaign "had to be continued" despite these odds out of their own self-respect and there was always a chance that a few revisions might be obtained through a constant hammering against the SAPL in House plenary and committee sessions.

Prior to the opening of House Committee hearings, the Nihon Shimbun Kyōkai (Japan Newspaper Association) on April 22, the Nihon Bungeika Kyōkai (Japan Artists Association) on April 23, the Nihon Gakujutsu Kaigi (Japan Science Council) on April 24, 1952 and the Tokyo Bengoshi Kyōkai in Fall 1951 issued statements reiterating their opposition, all before the fateful May 1, 1952 May Day riot in the Imperial/People/s Plaza which dramatically changed the political calculus for the possibility of an SAPL. For example, the Nihon Shimbun Kyōkai had already on two previous occasions, when SAPL drafts were leaked to the press in fall 1951 and spring 1952 (both discussed in chapter 2 and 3, respectively) severely criticized the draft as a threat to the freedom of speech. It issued yet another panel report in a more caustic and more specific manner. Based on available knowledge, the Newspaper Association was the only organization that issued three stringent criticisms of the draft SAPL and waged its campaign of opposition on several levels. The Association felt sufficiently strongly about its opposition to the SAPL, that it even prepared 1,000 copies of a special packet of materials which it distributed to Diet members, senior government officials, and newspaper members of the Association. The packet contained the three sets of criticisms and a second part consisting of an analysis of the U.S. Smith Act of 1940 concerning the registration of foreigners, the McCarran Internal Security Act of 1950 and President Truman's veto of that bill and the opinion of legal scholars on this law, and excerpts (without comment) from the 1925 and 1941 Diet deliberations in both houses concerning the PPL with which the SAPL is frequently compared; for example, the discussion of *sendō* at that time was implicitly compared with a similar discussion in 1952. The Association was vehemently opposed to the use of *sendō* and called for its deletion from the SAPL. It opposed giving an executive agency, the PSEC, quasi-judicial authority on such delicate political matters, felt the definitions of "violent destructive activities" were far to ambiguous, and the penalties to be applied much too broad, and the authorities in the SAPL in articles 3, 4, 6, and others were a clear and distinct threat to the freedoms guaranteed under the Constitution.

All the major national Tokyo daily newspapers voiced varying degrees of opposition (*Yomiuri*) to and praise and support (Jiji Shimbun) of the SAPL. The *Asahi* called for a narrower definition of incitement in light of past history. The conservative business journal, *Nikkei*, appeared to choose freedom of the press to suppressing destructive actions in the first instance. All in all, however, these editorials expressed the same concerns and anxieties as in the past but they were not hard hitting and stringent and concluded in a somewhat ambiguous manner. This ambiguity would give some satisfaction to the government and the Liberal Party as it pondered its Diet strategy, that is, IF such equivocation in the media was of any concern to them since they commanded an absolute majority in the House of Representatives.

The first strike wave by the labor unions on April 12, 1952 had been a semi-success and a semi-failure. Labor let it be known that it would even more strongly oppose any government attempt to further limit workers' right to strike—an even greater opposition than that shown against the SAPL. The government was unable to organize a unified labor policy with management in attempting to limit strikes and create an authority for the PM to order termination of labor disputes, and even went so far as to suggest that such labor law revisions may be temporarily postponed. The second strike on April 18 had been, in contrast, a huge success, the largest labor demonstration in Japanese history, particularly in the context of postwar Japan when a comparison is made with the aborted February 1, 1947 general strike. The potential third strike wave had inherent problems among the unions. There was also a lingering ambiguity between battling against the SAPL and/or energizing the rank and file to vigorously oppose any government attempt to restrict labor union activity and their right to strike. While there was a general fear of the SAPL and how such a law would be implemented by a government so closely associated with prewar governments, the SAPL was also tangled with the internecine leadership struggles in the labor unions, the more radical left versus the conservative right. Sōhyō leadership also felt that the leftwing political parties were not effective in the Diet—by definition they could not be too effective when the governing Liberal Party had a decisive majority in the House of Representatives. Diet deliberations of the SAPL began in this atmosphere of high tension and high expectations immediately after the bill was submitted to the Diet for its consideration and expected approval.

B. *As the Debate Begins, House of Representatives Plenary Session*

As the government must have viewed the parliamentary situation it faced after submitting the draft SAPL to the Diet, the governing Liberal Party had, as a result of the 1949 election, a comfortable majority in the House of Representatives.[1] This majority would provide the necessary assurance that its proposed bill would ultimately be passed by the HofR with the sheer force of numbers.

As the House deliberations opened the positions of the several parties were as follows:

The SDP-L, SDP-R and the JCP demanded withdrawal of the bill. This had been their position from the outset when the bill was being drafted. They knew that a withdrawal of the bill would not happen. In light of the somewhat ambiguous situation in the House of Councillors, these parties were determined to pursue stringent questioning of government witnesses to establish the record of their determined opposition to the draft SAPL and perhaps sway the Upper House to withhold its approval, a not completely impossible goal as deliberations began. A two-thirds approval in the Lower House might not be available to overrule the HofC.

Kaishintō Diet members were philosophically inclined to feel that an internal security law would be needed but hoped to restrict the

[1] The composition of the 13th Diet in the House was as follows: Liberal Party (Jiyūtō, 283), Kokumin Minshutō (64), Nihon Shakaitō (30), Japan Communist Party (15), Kokumin Kyōdōtō (23), Nōmin Kyōdōtō (8), Rōdōsha Nōmintō (4), Daisan Kurabu (6), Independents (3). Total 436. The Kaishintō. When the 13th Diet was convened on December 12, 1951 (and adjourned on July 31, 1952 with the enactment of the SAPL), the Kaishintō did not exist. It was derived indirectly from a number of amalgamations of smaller parties and factions going back to the early postwar years. The Kokumin Kyōdōtō joined with Shinsei Kurabu, Nōmin Kyōdōtō (mentioned above) and the Daiichi Kurabu in the House of Councillors to form the Kaishintō on February 8, 1952. It was this party that played an active—must have been an annoying—role to the Liberal Party during the House hearings on the SAPL. The adviser and President was Kiyose Ichirō (one of the leading Japanese defense lawyers at the so-called Tokyo War Crimes Trial, 1946–1948, and later one of the 18 expert witnesses testifying against the enactment of the SAPL), Standing Adviser Ashida Hitoshi, former PM in 1948–1949, Party Secretary General Miki Takeo, future PM. The Kaishintō stood for modified capitalism and cooperativism and emphasized the rearmament of Japan. The first president of the new Kaishintō was the recently de-purged prewar Foreign Minister, Shigemitsu Mamoru. After October 1952—after the SAPL was enacted—the party tried to form a coalition government with PM Yoshida, then its own cabinet, failing each time. As part of the gradual unification of conservatives, it joined the Nihon Minshutō in November 1954.

meaning and scope of the law, particularly concerning the meaning and scope of *sendō* (incitement). At its Diet Operations Policy Committee meeting on April 23, 1952, eve of the hearings, it developed a four point revision of the SAPL as follows:

1. Recognize the need for a law to control the destructive activities of the extreme right and left organizations.
2. Limit the scope of the SAPL and delete those controls which impinge upon basic human rights, particularly the meaning and scope of "incitement".
3. In order to maintain the separation of the three branches of government, the SAPL would be carried out by the Procurator General (Kensatsukyoku) and the courts; the PSIA and PSEC would not be established.
4. Abolish the Special Investigation Bureau (Tokubetsu Shinsakyoku), streamline and adjust (*seibi-suru*) police responsibilities and structure.

The Diet consideration of a bill, in this case the draft SAPL, begins with separate presentations of the bill at plenary sessions in both Houses of the Diet. Under normal conditions, a bill is remanded to a committee for its consideration with a subsequent vote in the House. Because of the sensitive nature of the of the SAPL (and the National Civil Service Law and the Police Law), it was initially presented at a plenary session on April 17, 1952 by AG Kimura with challenges by representative interpolations by the Kaishintō, Left and Right SDP and the JCP. Nothing particularly new was revealed in these Q&A sessions since both sides had made their positions clear as the draft SAPL was considered by the Cabinet. These plenary sessions were more or less pro forma sparings, a polite prelude to confrontational skirmishes yet to come. It is nevertheless useful to give a presentation of this pro forma initial sparring. The bill was then remanded to the consideration of the Legal Affairs Committee; after general and detailed hearings, the committee sends its report and decision on the draft bill to the full House of Representatives for a final vote.[2]

[2] The following presentation of the Diet deliberations in both Houses are based on several sources: Printed proceedings of the Diet related to consideration of the SAPL, newspaper reports from the *Asahi Shimbun*, *Mainichi Shimbun* and *Yomiuri Shimbun*, journal/magazine articles. Citations will be given only where it is felt to be necessary otherwise the text would be overly crowded with footnotes. Endō Gōsuke, political reporter of the *Asahi Shimbun*, published one of the few useful articles for the purposes of this study on the Diet proceedings on the SAPL, Habōhō no dekiru made, *Sekai* 80(8/1952:162–167). In some instances, references will be made to Diet

At the plenary session, AG Kimura stressed that organized violence using guerilla tactics were being conducted under the auspices of organizations all of which always remained unspecified except that it was commonly understood to mean the JCP and its supporting groups.[3] All democratic nations, he asserted, have adopted measures which permit a nation through its criminal code or administrative action to prohibit the creation of selected organizations, order their dissolution when the actions of these organizations threaten to disrupt the social stability of a nation. Japan's existing criminal code aims to control actions of individuals not organizations. Actions by such organizations would have to be watched from the sidelines (*bōkan-suru*). The purpose of the proposed SAPL was to take administrative measures (*gyōsei sochi*) against organizations which conduct such destructive activities and augment/supplement the penalties in the criminal code which at this time cannot be applied to organizations in connection with planning, preparations to incite and instigate such destructive conduct. Furthermore, to avoid concentration of authority, the agency to investigate such destructive activities by an organization will be separate from the agency which evaluates and make a decision on the penalties to be imposed.

The relatively conservative Kaishintō representative accused the government of attempting to create a police state which will suppress legitimate labor union activities, trample on fundamental human rights and ignore the guarantees in the Constitution. Where are specific stipulations in the draft bill to guard against abuse of the authority by the AG? Contrary to agreement with labor leaders, LM Yoshitake had not secured a revision of the clause specifying incitement and instigations as separate crimes; the LM, of course, denied such an agreement. The SDP-R representatives asserted that the existing criminal and other codes were capable of handling all such violations making the proposed SAPL completely unnecessary. In response to a query by an SDP-L member, the AG said criticism of Allied Forces and the conflict in Korea would not be a violation of the proposed SAPL but if this criticism became violent then government action could be taken

proceedings in the following manner: 5/13:9, May 13 hearings, page 9. The comment about procedure was derived from *Japanese People and Politics*, Chitoshi Yanaga, John Wiley & Sons, 1956. p. 204.

[3] The following presentation on House plenary session debate is based on *Dai-13 kai Kokkai, Shūgiin Kaigiroku Dai-32 gō* (4/17/1952).

under the proposed law. (It should be recalled that the Occupation authorities had prohibited commentary on and any direct, indirect or implied criticism of Allied Forces during the Occupation and violators of this edict were tried in U.S. military courts and given prison sentences which were served in Japanese prisons.)

In anticipation of the opening of the House Legal Affairs Committee hearings to begin on April 24, 1952, the Liberal Party's Diet Operations Policy Committee (Kokkai Taisaku Iinkai) adopted on April 19, a stance of patience and a somewhat conciliatory approach. Since this proposed law was an important element in the government's policy vis-a-vis the JCP after regaining independence, the Liberal Party initially said it would consider revising selected articles in the draft since some articles in the draft might be "misunderstood" by the people. For example, the controls and investigations leading to the imposition of these controls and the standards to be applied for these purposes in article 2 were somewhat vague; there should also be a thorough study, a fundamental and basic discussion about whether preparatory actions, and incitement and instigations should be included in the definition of destructive action under article 3. This seemingly conciliatory approach was probably more cosmetic than real. Since Japan was at last regaining its independence, the ruling party did not wish to give the outside world the wrong impression about the stability of Japan immediately after the Occupation ended. It was also undoubtedly thinking about the impression it may leave with the electorate in the next election. On the eve of the committee hearings, the same committee suggested that it would adjust its position after hearing all opinions at the hearings, even considering a revision of the controversial term, incitement (*sendō*), seeking a compromise which might be acceptable to all parties. It was also trying to soft-pedal the Diet process since it was possible that the Diet would be called upon to enact an even more controversial law banning general strikes.

Ironically, on the same day, the executive committee of the Diet/Rōtō Joint Struggle Committee also adopted a more conciliatory approach. In contrast to the political strike waves it had earlier organized and led, the opposition labor unions and the political opposition in the Diet will, in the future, emphasize the "Diet struggle" and cooperate with the Kaishintō, the Ryokufūkai in the HofC but would continue to try to rouse and rally support to oppose the draft SAPL by holding mass rallies throughout the country.

C. *Legal Affairs Committee Hearings*

Because of the importance and sensitivity of the SAPL, the Legal Affairs Committees of both Houses conducted extensive hearings. The types of questions that would be raised about the SAPL by Committee members of both Houses would inevitably be quite similar. Therefore, rather than repeat the description and analysis of these two sets of hearings, the interpolation parts of these two Committee hearings will be combined under "Topical Analysis" in this section and those issues specifically related to each Committee's jurisdictions will be given under "Overview", Expert Hearings, and internal Committee activities leading to a vote. After reading 1100+ pages of Plenary Sessions and Committee hearings (300+ in the HofR, 700+ in the HofC) on the SAPL one is impressed with the breadth and depth of the questions raised by Committee members and cannot avoid feeling the deep sense of distrust of the government security agencies by the political opposition, a completely understandable sentiment in light of past histories as experienced by both sides, that there will be abuse of authority, that there would be an attempt to expand and enlarge the interpretation and the coverage of the SAPL. This distrust reveals itself in the detailed questions that the government witnesses were peppered with.

i. *Overview*

The HofR Committee was composed of 25 members with the following distribution: Liberal Party 14, Kaishintō 3, SDP-R 1, SDP-L 1, JCP 2, Dai-san Kurabu 1, Shakai Minshutō 1, two vacancies.[4] About twenty

[4] The following presentation on Committee hearings, especially "Topical Analyses", was based in the main on the perusal of the Diet proceedings of: A. House of Representatives
- *Dai-13 kai Kokkai. Hōmu Iinkai Giroku. Dai-41–44, 46–51* (4/24/1952, 4/25/1952, 4/26/1952, 4/28/1952, 5/8/1952, 5/9/1952, 5/10/1952, 5/12/1952, 5/13/1952, 5/15/1952).
- *Dai-13 kai Kokkai. Hōmu Iinkai. Kōchōkai Giroku. Dai-1 gō* (4/30/1952), *Dai-2 go* (5/2/1952).
- *Dai-13 kai. Kokkai. Hōmu Iinkai, Rōdō Iinkai Rengō Shinsakai Giroku. Dai-1 gō* (5/6/1952), *Dai-2 gō* (5/7/1952).

B. House of Councillors Dai 13-kai Kokkai, Sangiin Kaigiroku #29(4/14/1952), #31.2(4/17/1952), #55(6/25/1952), 57(6/28/1952), 58(6/30/1952), 59(7/1/1952), 60 (7/2/1952), 61(7/3/1952). For Committee Hearings: *Dai 13-kai Kokkai, Sangiin Hōmu, Naikaku, Chihō Gyōsei, Rōdō Rengōkai Iinkai Kaigiroku* #1–2(5/10/1952, 5/28/1952), *Dai 13-kai Kokkai, Sangiin, Hōmu Iinkai Kaigiroku* #39–52, 54–60 (5/19/1952–

days were set aside for deliberations concluding with a House vote on the SAPL about May 15. Leaving aside holidays and weekends and public hearings by expert witnesses, committee deliberations would be about ten days, about 58–60 hours. This was a rather unusual, if not unprecedented, approach to conducting hearings. During the House deliberations, 62 petitions and appeals (*chinjō, seigan*) were received. This procedure was a reflection of the majority party's confidence with an absolute majority that it could pass a version of the SAPL it desired, that it could, therefore give an appearance of cooperation and magnanimity and apparent willingness to debate the merits of the draft SAPL, and be generous in allowing the opposition to exceed the number of hours allotted to them for debating the merits and demerits of the SAPL and hold public hearings of experts when they knew there would be more experts by far arrayed against the SAPL than for the bill.

Committee hearings on a proposed bill are, in theory, divided into sessions on generalized questions (*sōkatsu hitsumon*), followed by sessions debating the proposed bill article-by-article (*chikujō shingi*); most of the committee hearings are devoted to the latter category. In reality, however, the SAPL debate swirled around a relatively few controversial articles. Committee members are allowed a certain amount of time for the presentation of their queries, objections, praises, etc. There was a fair amount of repetition in the queries by the committee members; there appeared to be no control over who discussed what issues. These hearings, in order to show the appearance of full and adequate deliberations on a highly controversial bill droned on in a somewhat tedious manner but in a generally civil and polite manner except for occasional voice objections (*yaji*) from some committee members; since they must have appeared interminable to some, especially for the government witnesses whose patience was stretched, after an issue was repeatedly raised by different members through such phrases as "As we have explained previously (or just yesterday, two days ago, etc.)…" Committee members, particularly opposition party members, would seemingly show their frustration by suddenly cutting off the Q&A on

5/24/1952, 5/26/1952–5/27/1952, 5/30/1952–5/31/1952, 6/3/1952–6/6/1952, 6/9/1952–6/10/1952, 6/12/1952–6/14/1952, 6/16/1952–6/19/1952), *Dai 13-kai Kokkai, Sangiin Hōmu Rōdō Rengō Iinkai Kaigiroku* #1–2 (5/30/1952, 5/31/1952). Citations will be made to any of the above materials when it is deemed appropriate and necessary.

In addition, the *Asahi, Mainichi, Yomiuri, Tokyo* and *Jiji* newspapers were consulted.

a particular subject and start on a completely new tack, a new line of questioning.

Because of the sensitivity of the SAPL, members wanted "authoritative" replies to their queries by the AG himself but the AG attended eight sessions out of a total of 14 days of committee hearings. Furthermore, he did not always stay for the complete hearings on a particular day, undoubtedly he had other requirements on his daily calendar. Nevertheless, it remained a source of frustrations to opposition members since they were attempting to build a record on how this bill might be interpreted when implemented. Everyone knew, of course, that the opinion of the AG who was calling for the enactment of the SAPL may or may not be accepted as the future Minister of Justice. The DG/SB Yoshikawa and his deputy and drafter of the SAPL, Seki, on the other hand, as the experts on the details of the draft SAPL, attended every committee session to try to prove the merits of their case. While the AG occasionally played a forceful role in the hearings, government bills were, in the main, explained and defended by career senior civil servants not senior political appointees. (About half century later, the government changed this arrangement to force the political appointees to explain and defend proposed legislation instead of the career senior civil service staff.)

One SDP-L member, Inomata Kōzō, took a somewhat different approach in his persistent pursuit of the government: one he was trying through his questions to establish a basis for when a court case could turn to these hearings for support; secondly, he was the only Diet member who attempted to insert a discussion of the basic legal structure and philosophy underpinning the SAPL by linking it and comparing it to the legal philosophy used by the German Nazis. He made a cogent and important point about the value of obtaining as detailed answers and interpretations from the government witnesses about the SAPL and how it would be implemented. He insistently pursued the government about a bill under consideration based on his prewar experience as a practicing liberal lawyer in prewar Japan. He explained that he was defending a case involving an alleged violation of the prewar Military Secrets Law (Gunji Kimitsu Hogo-hō). When this law was considered by the Diet, Diet members in both House of Representatives and Peers questioned the government witnesses in great depth about the meaning, implications and how the law would or might be implemented. Using these proceedings as THE only reference materials in the court, he asserted, the court declared the accused innocent in both the first and second hearings (*dai-isshin* and *dai-nishin*) against the opposition of Minister of the Army and the Justice Ministry's prosecutors. While the accused was declared innocent the government still held the accused improperly for two years. It is thus eminently important to have the government's interpretation of the law clearly and duly recorded and included in the formal record of the hearings like this about the SAPL. (5/9:10)

He described the SAPL as poorly prepared (*futeisai*) and confused (*ranzatsu*) by trying to include in one law criminal offenses against individuals and administrative action against organizations which when combined create great difficulties and accused the government of a sinister plot, intrigue or intent (*imbō*)—note the use of *imbō* from the Criminal Code. There was confusion as to what actions would lead to administrative actions and what would be causes for criminal action. It was because of these difficulties he said that we have great suspicions about the intentions of the government. If necessary, he suggested, draft a separate law for administrative action, and for the criminal offenses "supplement" and revise the fundamental Criminal Code as needed.

Inomata was obviously convinced of this link since he raised this comparison on more than one occasion during the hearings. He pointed out that under the criminal code when a crime is attempted and does not succeed for whatever reason and the attempt is not regarded as a criminal act (*misuizai*), such as in the case of a riot, then instigation does not become an offense. In the criminal code, attempts to commit crimes under articles 78 (preparation and planning), 79 (assistance to insurrections), 95 (Obstructing Official Duties), 106 (riots), 117 (Destruction by explosives) are not prosecuted as crimes. When one who is instigated but does not go forward to commit the instigated act, then the instigator's act is a "non-accomplished crime" (*funō-han*). To criminalize a "non-accomplished" act implies that "the theory to expand the scope of the kinds of principal crimes" (*kakuchō seihan-ron*) as practiced by the German Nazis was in the background of this criminal approach in the SAPL. Furthermore, in the SAPL the instigator who attempted to instigate someone who did not carry out that act would be charged for instigation as an independent crime. Thus, there is a definite and serious imbalance in handling criminal acts between the SAPL and the criminal code. It has violated the important principle of balance now existing in the Japanese CC. Significantly, Seki agreed that such an imbalance did exist and that the criminal code needed to be reconsidered later from this point of view. But went on to point out that legislation *in the postwar period* all criminalized instigation as an independent crime. Creating this new category, he asserted, was

> ... necessary in light of the danger of such acts as instigation and in order to maintain public security. (5/9:14)

To which Inomata promptly responded, the person who tries to carry out certain crimes but is not successful and thus not prosecuted is far more dangerous than the person who unsuccessfully tried to instigate a person.

Again, in the final summary at the plenary session on May 15, 1952 he asserted that through the legal philosophy underpinning the SAPL and taking administrative action against organizations was a fundamental error and violating several articles of the Constitution. Inomata's sparring with the government about Nazi law was, of course, ignored.[5]

Fourteen days of HofR Committee hearings were held from April 24 to May 15, 1952. During this time, two days were given to hearing 18 "experts" on the issues surrounding the SAPL. Quite by accident, the first day of these hearings was April 30, 1952, followed immediately by the infamous May Day riots which inevitably colored thereafter the probable outcome of the proposed legislation. The second day for the expert witnesses was May 2! The Legal Affairs Committee hearings were again "jolted" but not diverted at all by outside events, this time by serious university student and police clashes on campus.

---

[5] Inomata, Kōzō. *Teikō no Keifu*, Sakai Shoten. 1964. 402 p.; he was perhaps the only one who published his own record of his interpolations about the SAPL in the House of Representatives. I was able to find a brief discussion of Nazi legal theory in two Japanese legal texts, *Keihō Sōron* by Kimura Kameji (Hōritsugaku Zenshū v. 40, Yūhikaku. 1978, p. 72–74, 374–376) and *Keihō Jiten* (edited by Kimura Kameji, Seirin Shoin Shinsha, 1966, p. 32–33).The two Japanese legal terms used were *kakuchō kyōdō seihan-ron* (*Extensiver taterbegriff* in German) and *ishi keihō* (*Willensstrafrecht* or *kiken keihō, Gefährdungsstrafrecht* in German). Based on a reading of these explanations, Inomata was asserting that the SAPL was a reflection of the basic Nazi approach to criminal law: the emphasis was on strengthened state authority concerning the maintenance of public security with more severe sentences at the expense of protecting the rights of the individual which was the basis of the Japanese legal system. In addition, through the concept of *kakuchō seihanron*, the accomplice(s) would also be included in any offense committed by the principal offender. In his final summary speech on the SAPL described at the end of this chapter, he asserted that *ishi keihō* as interpreted by the German Nazis emphasizing the offender's intent, thoughts in framing charges against a person for committing a crime was a basic concept underlying the thinking in creating the SAPL.

These incidents "on the street" so to speak, outside the Committee room provided both sides with persuasive rationales for advocating the urgent need for the SAPL or for being unalterably opposed to the SAPL. For example, at the Committee hearing the day after the May Day Riots the afternoon session began with the Tokyo Metropolitan Police Commissioner, Tanaka Eiichi's explanation of what took place and gave him an opportunity to appeal for the speedy enactment of the SAPL. At the afternoon session on May 10, 1952, the Committee invited President Shimada of Waseda University and senior staff member Takiguchi, and again, Police Chief Tanaka to inform the Committee as to what took place on May 8–9 in the clashes between Waseda University students and the police. These clashes had become instantaneous political issues in the plenary session of the Diet and again raised the questions as to what was the role, duties and responsibilities of the police on university campuses.

Since the labor union movement was so vehemently and determinedly opposed to the SAPL, and believed that the SAPL would be used to suppress the labor movement, as a matter of parliamentary precedent and courtesy, joint Labor-Legal Affairs hearings were held for two days, May 6–7, 1952, another conciliatory gesture by the majority to allow another group of dissenting Diet members a chance to voice their various objections; almost all interpolations were made by members of the SDP, JCP, the Rōdōsha Nōmintō and Minshutō on the Labor Affairs Committee. The AG and associates were queried repetitiously and from every possible angle about the sincerity and true intentions of the government about using the SAPL as a weapon to control and/or suppress the labor union movement; various examples of activities were described to try to elicit from the government a definition of what constituted legal or illegal union activities when committed by an individual or when and how the labor union might be accused by the authorities of violating the SAPL. To which the AG (always supplemented by Yoshikawa and Seki), and on the second day including LM Yoshitake Eiichi, repeatedly with patience tried to reassure the opposition—without success, I am sure—that there never was any intention by the government in the drafting process, nor in their present intentions to accuse labor unions of violating the SAPL so long as unions conducted "legal and legitimate labor unions activities." For example, Maeda Taneo, SDP member and member of both Committees, cited the government's repeated promises in Diet hearings to abide by a law concerning some aspect of the management of

National Railroad system. The government even issued a pamphlet in the name of the Director-General of Labor Affairs in the Ministry of Labor declaring that it would abide by this law and arbitration decisions. The Labor Minister at the time was now the Secretary General of the Liberal Party (Kanjichō). However, when an arbitration decision was handed down later, that same government then declined to accept the decision and refused to honor its promises. The definition of legal and legitimate activities were not satisfactorily clarified by the government. The distrust and lack of confidence in these governmental responses and "promises" were clear. The questioners were survivors from prewar Japanese governmental suppression of the labor union and leftwing political parties. The joint hearings were part of the "grin and bear it" price the government was willing to pay for the appearance of having aired all points of view before a final vote.

On the first day of the hearings, AG Kimura made a generalized statement followed by a more detailed explanation by DG/SIB Yoshikawa who provided reasons for the need for the SAPL and justification of its proposed structure. Most of the remaining sessions were devoted to interpolations by opposition party members. While recognizing that it may be repetitious, it is appropriate to summarize below all these "important issues" outlined by the AG and Yoshikawa to establish a "base line" so to speak for Committee discussions in both Houses.

Behind all destructive activities, the government asserted, lies the systematic distribution of materials as preparatory training and advocacy of the legitimacy of violently overthrowing the government which had been established in accordance with the Constitution, through violent riots and other kinds of destructive activities. All democratic countries, when faced with those who abuse the right of freedom and attempt through an organizational structure to destroy the basic framework of a society, have taken the necessary legal steps or administrative actions to control these particularly obnoxious (*akuhitsu*) and dangerous actions (*kiken na kōi*) by imposing penalties, disbanding and/or prohibiting these organizations. To prevent the danger of destructive activities was in itself a protection of democracy. To take the minimum necessary legal measures for this purpose would be synonymous with the spirit of the Japanese Constitution. The establishment of the PSIA and PSEC as outer bureaus (*gaikyoku*) under the Attorney General (later Ministry of Justice) would provide the necessary detachment and independence for these agencies to operate without political interference.

1. The basic reason and motivation for preparing the SAPL was a) to respond to the present security situation where there is a substantial danger from the destructive activities conducted by organizations about which, if nothing is done, would lead to the destabilization of the social structure and threaten the public welfare and b) when the existing criminal and other laws and penalties cannot effectively respond to or cope with and prevent this serious threat. In the HofC Committee hearings, AG Kimura posed the basic intent a little differently: what kind of Japan do we want in the future to build a democratic, peaceful and independent Japan, the government must assure society against the destructive activities of a few organizations and people. (5/30:19)
2. incitement (*sendō*) as a concept becomes the substance, the essence, the main point of this draft SAPL, it is far more important than merely "instigating" (*kyōsa*) individuals to take certain actions.
3. incitement is already used and accepted in the election law and in a number of other domestic laws.
4. the criminal code does not target organizations, only individuals, yet it is organizations that are carrying out numerous destructive activities, thus it is the objective and emphasis of this law to contribute to the maintenance of the public welfare by defining the necessary controlling actions and supplementing the penalties in the criminal code by controlling those destructive activities carried out as "the activities of an organization". (Article 1, *Dantai no katsudō to shite*). The emphasis here, it should be emphasized, was squarely on the term "the activities of an organization" in contrast to individuals who are the targets of the Criminal Code (CC).
5. Declaring the JCP illegal must be considered extremely carefully since it is a publicly recognized political party in the postwar period and declaring it illegal would have serious international implications; merely carrying around books by Marx and Lenin would not be an infringement of the SAPL but printing, carrying and distributing materials of all sorts "with an intent to incite people to rebellion would be illegal."
6. In preparing the draft SAPL, the following principles were basic: it must be consonant with the intentions of the Japanese Constitution, it must be effective in preventing violent destructive activities and the structure of the law itself must be such that it cannot be abused (*ran'yō*).

7. The underlying assumption of the SAPL was to prevent, through administrative action, an organization from conducting destructive activities; the controls imposed on these organizations through administrative action will be the minimum necessary to achieve the preventive purposes, especially in light of the existing circumstances.
8. "Violent destructive activities" is an administrative concept (*gyōseijō no gainen*) through which control measures (*kisei shobun*) can be taken against an organization. The concept here is to supplement/augment to the least extent necessary the existing criminal actions such as insurrection, assassination/murder, arson included in the criminal code, and the planning, plotting, instigation and incitement thereof.
9. An "organization" which shall be controlled is a group whose many constituent members have formed a body to achieve collectively an objective held by this group including all chapters, branches, sub-branches of this organization.
10. In order for an organization to be the subject of control measures, there must be an objective basis for concluding that there is a great danger that it will continue to conduct or will repeat such violent destructive activities.
11. In order to apply control measures to prohibit or limit the activities of an organization, there must a danger that this organization will conduct such destructive activities. In applying these restrictive control measures they shall be based on rational judgments (*gōri-teki handan sareru*) which shall not exceed normal social concepts (*shakai-teki tsūnen*). These measures shall not go beyond the officers and members of the affected organizations and shall not include their private lives.
12. All facts and evidence forming the basis for control measures shall be presented to the defendants who, in turn, will have an opportunity to defend their actions, provide evidence to their advantage.
13. The PSEC shall consist of persons with knowledge and experience, not government officials, and approved by the Diet. That an administrative agency will decide these control measures is not contrary to the Constitution and such actions concerning security are within the purview of the executive branch. These decisions may be appealed to the courts.
14. Lastly, in order to avoid any possible misunderstanding and danger from the abuse of investigative authority, compulsive investi-

> gatory authority was not given to the PSIA, but only the authority to conduct investigations as needed (*nin'i no chōsa*) and maintain a close cooperative relationship with the police to achieve the objectives of the SAPL.[6]

Following the Kimura-Yoshikawa presentations on the first day, selected members of the majority party, the Liberal Party, were given the opportunity to question the government but their interpolations were polite naturally, not antagonistic, but raised some rather important concerns which gave the government an opportunity to explain, yet again, the intentions and interpretations underlying the SAPL but showing absolutely no budge nor inclination to revise any part of the SAPL. These issues anticipated the expected thrusts of the opposition. Probably they were attempting to establish a legislative record before opposition attacks began. Opposition members, distrustful of how the government might implement such a law, created various kinds of scenarios and asked the government witnesses how the SAPL as proposed might be applied to those scenarios. The interpolations and dialogue were not about the grand theoretical structure about law in Japan, but stemmed from anxieties and mainly prewar but some postwar experiences and encounters with the Japanese security structure, based not on the niceties of legal theory but from unpleasant past experiences.

In explaining the SAPL and responding to challenges, government witnesses repeated to both Legal Affairs Committees almost like a mantra, politically correct references, obeisances, procedures and processes (*minshu-shugi no gensoku*) and with a similar monotony that the procedures implementing the SAPL:

- would follow democratic principles
- would be the minimum necessary
- would abide by Constitutional guarantees of various rights
- would respect human and civil rights and liberties
- would avoid unnecessary and improper actions
- would avoid abuse of authority

[6] These points were summarized from the April 24, 1952 Committee hearings, pp. 9–24. Item 2, *Saikin no Waga Kokunai ni okeru Bōryoku-shugiteki Hakai Katsudō no Jittai no Gaigyō*, in *Hoan Kankei Shiryō*, vol. 1 was undoubtedly the document upon which Yoshikawa's testimony was based; it was dated 4/24/1952.

It was repeatedly stated that the SAPL's target was first to control organizations (*dantai kisei*), and then individuals, that the Criminal Code penalties have been "supplemented" with broader interpretations and the penalties lengthened and made stiffer, to take "preventive action" (*shoyō no yobō sochi*) against activities which threaten the national stability, the governmental structure and to maintain peace and security and which will contribute to strengthening a healthy democratic outlook and education, i.e. take constitutionally acceptable actions to prevent illegal activities creating real damage (*jitsugai*) to society.

Committee members were only partially successful in eliciting satisfactory answers from the government. As these long winded exchanges progressed they became a little snappy and testy based on my reading—not watching—the proceedings. Despite the Chairman's occasional admonition for silence and about exceeding allotted time, the proceedings were conducted with civility and decorum.

ii. *Comparative Rationales for SAPL and other such Laws*

In light of the above elaboration of the rationale for the SAPL, let us re-focus momentarily on the rationales that have been put forward in justifying the need for the SAPL in comparison to prewar internal security laws. While the historical circumstances are always different, it is instructive to assess, on a comparative basis, various reasons for these laws as put forward by the government. The feared undermining of Japanese society by Communist subversion and foreign ideas flowing into (streaming into) Japan since the 19th century and particularly after WWI was, in introspect, merely a theoretical potential threat not a real threat; in comparison, in the early postwar years, 1945–1952, was vastly differently seen by the very same political elites and internal security agencies in the latter years. Even though the postwar years suddenly, for a short period, took on seemingly quite disturbing possibilities of social unrest, the threat was, in reality, only a potentiality but that was used to replay some old rationales.

- *Sendō (Incitement).* When the PPL was first enacted in1925, the then Minister of Justice, Ogawa Heikichi, speaking at a committee hearing on the bill, described *sendō* as a "special characteristic" of the proposed PPL; 27 years later in 1952, AG Kimura described the same term as "the essence" of the proposed SAPL, a term which, under any circumstances, must be included in the SAPL, its inclusion was non-negotiable. Ogawa asserted in 1925 that because those who incite others to action are "most despicable" (*ichiban minikui*), a distinct category was created to distinguish it from the crimes of instigation.

- *Inadequacy of the Criminal Code.* As a result of the evolving nature of criminal acts, the government always insisted that the CC was wholly inadequate to handle these illegal acts; this was mentioned in 1922, 1925, 1941, and the 1943 special wartime criminal law and again in 1952 for the SAPL. Yet outside of the abortive attempt to revise the CC in 1940 to include *sendō,* as a new criminal category there has been no attempt to revise the CC so it could handle these cases. In 1943, a rationale was that the CC enacted in peacetime (1907) was quite inadequate to handle wartime exigencies in WWII, thus these news laws would offset the inadequacies of the CC (*fubi o oginau*). When that possibility was suggested, the government always asserted that one must not tamper flippantly in revising such a fundamental law; by not revising the CC, the government always had a built-in excuse to use to justify another law with yet another type of criminal law.
- *International Connections of the Target Activities.* This referred strictly to international communist connections which influenced and guided domestic destructive activities in Japan. Using this and other reasons (opposition to the Imperial system and the system of private property) the government destroyed the JCP in prewar years. Then and now (1952) the target was the JCP, the communist movement and its front organizations but these words and terms were never mentioned in either pre or postwar internal security legislation, in contrast to such legislation in other countries. Undoubtedly the Yoshida government would have liked to have outlawed the JCP as was done in the prewar years but in the postwar period there was now a Constitutional issue involved which would probably have been insurmountable. This international connection was a convenient and effective rationale to use because it would bring forth the images of potential threat from the Soviet Union to Japan in 1952.

In one of the books on the SAPL which Seki published after the SAPL was enacted, is an interesting chapter on the "objective conditions which necessitated the enactment of the SAPL". These objective conditions consisted basically of three parts: a long analysis of the methods used, weapons used, statistics, places attacked, strategies and tactics used, etc., international connections of these activities and the activities of Koreans living in Japan. I am sure it was not accidental that the only two numbered subsections were the latter two topics. He asserted that there were close connections between the violent activities in Japan and sources outside Japan. These latter sources provide guidance for these activities and criticism of JCP strategies and tactics and are conveyed through radio broadcasts, Cominform statements, Pravda articles on the JCP leader, Nozaka Sanzō, Chinese Communist party organ announcements of a new party program for the JCP and cites eleven examples of such activities, 1950–52. The purpose here was to point out clearly that the Japanese communists were un-Japanese, were beholden to foreign guidance, instructions and finances. This emphasis on sinister foreign orders was a tactic used in the 1920s to justify the PPL. The activities of Koreans was also cited in the 1920s as a factor in justifying the PPL. Seki said 560,000 Koreans were registered as foreigners; there were others in Japan as illegal immigrants and those who have not registered. Their status was vague and their political preferences reflected the north and south divide in Korea. Since the Korean War was raging across the straits in Korea, their potentially subversive activities were of considerable security concern. In the first half of 1952, the North Korean activists were particularly violent: they committed over 80 violent attacks in a two-month period in 1952, 47 attacks against official institutions. They used a number of commemorative days to conduct their attacks using firearms, Molotov cocktails, tear gas, human feces. Perhaps these factors, the international connections and disruptive leftist North Koreans, were the two major objective reasons justifying the enactment of the SAPL.

- *Vagueness of Terms.* After the 1922 draft bill to control radical social movements failed to pass the Diet, and a new law considered, such terms as basic structure of society were too vague for enforcement. This was replaced with opposition to the national polity and the private property system which was then regarded "as specific and clear in concept" in the 1925 PPL. In the 1943 law such old-style Japanese terms as *Chōken binran* (creating chaos against the established government) were used. In 1951–1952, these supposedly "clear concepts" were dismissed as ideological, unclear and subject to severe abuse. Now the SAPL is based on "destructive activities" by an organization for political purposes, presumably infinitely clearer and precise. But the political opposition described such terms as totally vague and equally subject to abuse as had occurred in the past. Now the amorphous "maintenance of the public welfare" (*kōkyō anzen*) would be the new basic criteria.

- *Heavier Penalties.* In every instance, CC prison terms are dismissed as ineffective deterrents; heavier penalties must be imposed for these more vicious, insidious political crimes in order to deter these crimes, e.g. increasing the jail terms from three to five years. Furthermore, the terms used to describe this process in the prewar and postwar fears were not dissimilar at all: in 1941 *bassoku no seibi kyōka* (streamline, straighten out and increase penalties), and augment the in 1952 *bassoku no hosei kyōka* (increase penalties by augmenting, supplementing the CC).

Based on the above, there is an uncomfortably similar set of rationales, excuses, justifications used by the government to justify both pre and postwar internal security legislation, a direct link in phraseology and mode of thinking.[7]

iii. *Topical Analysis*

Analysis will be provided of selected topics organized by article where possible and appropriate that were raised in these hearings from both Houses This analysis is not intended to be a complete exegesis of the SAPL; very far from it. After perusing the verbatim record of these hearings, one is impressed with the constant attempt to try to find out how a particular article, phrase or word is defined, would/could be interpreted and implemented and how it might be interpreted and how it might be narrowed. I discovered an article in *Sekai* on Japanese linguistic consciousness and the law by Kawashima Takeyoshi, Professor Emeritus of Law of Tokyo University.[8] His essay was most illuminating in appreciating questioning tactics at the hearings. He explained that Westerners "unlike Japanese, aspire, due to some postulate or sense of values, to give words clear, limited and fixed meanings.... Japanese

---

[7] The ideas in this subsection were based on excerpts put together by the Nihon Shimbun Kyōkai from the 1925 and 1941 Diet hearings on the PPL as part of its report critical of the SAPL.

[8] Kawashima Takeyoshi. Nihonjin no Gengo Ishiki to Hōritsu, *Sekai* 2/1979:249–262. Also translated in *Japan Echo* 6:3(1979):105–114 as "The Japanese Linguistic Consciousness and the Law"; I have cited the English translated version.

words, by contrast, do not in general have meanings that are clear and limited.... Japanese words do have core meanings but their peripheral meanings are vague and undelimited." He said that Japanese accept "as natural and even desirable" that terms are "unclear, unlimited and unfixed". As a result, "judgments handed down by Japanese courts reflect this national attitude." Kawashima asserted that

> when laws are drafted in Japan, it is taken for granted that the meanings of the words of the provisions will not be clear cut. Once a law is enacted,...no one can foretell how its content will develop.... [Under these circumstances,] Interpretation is used as the almighty key to all legal problems.... Because meanings of laws can be stretched or restricted at will...debate on proposed laws arises in the Diet with regard to how they may be interpreted at some future date.... Once a bill becomes law the meanings of words are altered quite freely...to a degree unthinkable in the West. Nor is strong resistance to changed meanings offered by legal scholars. The prevailing doctrine is that the meaning of a provision should not be restricted to the 'legislators' intent.... Accordingly, no debate in the Diet to clarify the meaning of provisions and no pledges extracted from government leaders are to be relied on...it is inevitable that some degree of uneasiness and mistrust is evoked not only by government pledges but also by the laws themselves.... With statutes whose content is unclear, unlimited, and unfixed, there exists a tendency or potential for disputes to be settled by power rather than rational debate.

Despite this milieu which Kawashima described as "a most deplorable situation" for the people and the government, Diet members pursued the government with fervor and determination trying to pin down the government witnesses, tighten the definitions and interpretations of the law under many different scenarios. In general, the give and take was conducted with civility; I could not detect that voices were raised as I read the verbatim proceedings. But occasionally Committee members, not government witnesses, became impatient with "Don't be insulting, don't be contemptuous, Don't make outrageous statements" (*bōgen*). There was impatience with government evasiveness, some questioning was sharp.

1. *Article 1*

> Article 1. The Objectives of this law
> 1.1. The objective is to contribute to the maintenance of public safety (*kōkyō no anzen no kakuho*) by stipulating the necessary measures to control organizations which conduct violent destructive activities as

actions of an organization (*dantai no katsudō toshite*) and to supplement (*hosei*) the penalty provisions for these destructive activities.

Article 1 states the purpose of the SAPL would be to control destructive organizations and supplement/augment the criminal code, i.e. making penalties heavier, thereby "contributing" (*kiyo-suru*) to the maintenance of public security. The SAPL clearly stipulates in the grammatical structure that the target groups are destructive organizations in the first instance. Individuals/people are not mentioned except by implication by "supplementing/augmenting" the Criminal Code whose target group are individuals who, in this case, have committed crimes as stipulated in the SAPL. The SAPL thus targets two groups:

1. **organizations** which cannot be controlled by CC stipulations but by a separate set of standards described in the SAPL and
2. **individuals** who will be subject to supplemented/augmented articles of the CC included in the SAPL by reference, i.e. increase prison terms

That the primary target of the SAPL was the "violent destructive organization" was repeated over and over again by the government in the Committee hearings, almost as though individual offenses were not too relevant in the internal security equation.

Criminal Code Revision. Ishikawa Kinjirō of the conservative socialist party, SDP-R, insisted that the insurrection clause in the Criminal Code had been substantively revised (*jisshitsu shūsei*) by the supplemental additions in the SAPL; Seki equally insistently maintained that no changes had been made in the CC which probably is technically correct, but "conceded" that this issue will have to be resolved by the courts at a later date. Ishikawa also suggested that instead of including the CC by reference in the SAPL, it would be simpler and more direct, and more understandable to the populace at large if the CC was appropriately revised. To which Seki responded:

> ...The Criminal Code, a permanent fundamental law (*kōkyū-teki kihonhō*), must not be lightly revised. In order to respond to the present objective situation, the offenses stipulated in the Criminal Code have been augmented with supplemental stipulations in the SAPL with the necessary minimum limitations (*hitsuyō saishō gendo*) where there are no appropriate provisions in this Code for actions taken based on 'the fostering of political principles and programs' (*seiji jō no shugi*

> *moshikuwa shisaku o suishin shi*) to conduct violent destructive activities. This was absolutely necessary for the maintenance of the public welfare. (4/28:8)...That approach was the starting point in the drafting the SAPL.... The concept of security of the public welfare is narrower than "public welfare". (4/28:11)

As we know from Chapter 3, the starting point in drafting early versions of the SAPL was not the CC but Occupation-based ordinances, e.g. the Organization Control Cabinet decree; using the CC as the basis of the SAPL was a later insight by Seki.

At the May 13, 2002 hearings, Satake Haruki of the Shakai Kakushintō inquired what other laws "would contribute" together with the SAPL to the maintenance of public security. AG Kimura responded that the Press Code (discussed in Chapter 3), a leftover directive from the Occupation, would not be put forward as legislation. Many prefectures and some large cities had adopted laws for the maintenance of public security (*Kōan Jōrei*) but their form and contents were quite diverse. He would like, therefore, to prepare a draft bill to control mass demonstrations (Shūdan Ji'i Undō Torishimari-hō) which would clarify these laws and reflect the democratic requirements of post-occupation "independent" Japan. Concerning a law to control general strikes, he would prefer to handle such a possibility through the Labor Relations Adjustment Law (Rōdō Kankei Chōsei-hō). This statement by the AG implied that really no new legislation, and highly controversial it would be, would be forthcoming immediately or in the foreseeable future (5/13:9). Thus, by implication the SAPL would become the mainstay internal security law. In the eyes of the DG/Legal Opinions Bureau, Satō Tatsuo, the SAPL was a law to overcome the present situation (*tōmen no jitai o kirinukeru imi* [*no hōritsu*], i.e. by implication a time limited law but without a specified time limit (5/21:5).

"As Actions of an Organization". Toward the end of the drafting process, in order to clarify the target of the SAPL, the short phrase "as actions of an organization" (*dantai no katsudō to shite*) was inserted in Article 1 (and also in article 6.1.1 and 6.1.2), in order to re-emphasize that it was the violent destructive activities (*katsudō*) taken as an organization as distinct from individual actions as an individual (*tandoku no kōi*) that would be the primary target to be controlled under the SAPL. The latter, said DG/SIB Yoshikawa, would never—*zettai ni nai*, rather emphatic language—come under the purview of the SAPL. But individual acts committed by a leader as head of an organization,

or based on the basic program of that organization or to achieve the purposes of that organization, then those actions would be regarded as "actions of an organization". But the SAPL in defining what constitutes a violation of the SAPL, used *kōi* (acts) in article 3, presumably meaning acts carried out by an organization or acts carried out by an individual as an activity of that organization (4/24:23); *kōi* had been defined by the government as an individual act in contrast to an action of an organization. The seeming confusion and possible inconsistency between the AG and his senior staff perhaps was "resolved" when SIB's Yoshikawa responded to Kaji Ryōsaku, by explaining that three conditions need to be met when violent destructive activities are carried out "as part of an organization's activities" (5/12:26). They must be:

1. based on that organization's decision of its intentions (*ishi kettei*).
2. carried out by the officers and members of that organization.
3. carried out in order to achieve that organization's objectives.

As Satake pointed out there appears to be somewhat of a discrepancy between AG Kimura's emphasis in the beginning of these hearings on controlling organizations not individuals; the operating bureaucrats, Seki and Yoshikawa, however made clear that all others who violate the criminal code whether as officers or members of such organizations or not will be prosecuted under the SAPL. Satake pursued the government still further, this time on a grammatical interpretation of Article 1: in addition to controlling organizations, does supplementing the criminal code mean destructive activities committed by, for example, officers and members of the offending organization, or any one individual who has committed such acts. Yoshikawa affirmed that interpretation but Satake reminded him that since the AG had stressed that the law was to be used to control organizations, it had been interpreted that ONLY activities of an organization would be controlled and punished by supplementing the criminal code. Seki tried to explain that

> ...the adjectival phrase 'activities as an organization' refers only to those organizational activities where administrative action has to be taken to control these activities and are not related to 'criminal penalties' (*keibatsu kitei*) [which apply to individuals].... The criminal penalties specified in articles 37–40 will be applied to individuals who committed the violations specified in article 3 whether or not those individuals are members or officers of organizations which have conducted violent destructive activities and regardless of whether those actions were committed as activities of an organization or not. They will be treated

> uniformly in accordance with the criminal code as supplemented by the SAPL. (5/9:17)

Thus, as to whether the SAPL articles concerning illegal acts apply to individuals notwithstanding their affiliation with or lack of affiliation with a destructive organization is somewhat muddy and not quite clear. The two categories, organizations and individuals, are declared to be of co-equal importance yet they are not because of apparent emphasis on violent destructive organizations. Furthermore, individuals will be prosecuted in the courts under the strengthened CC articles with heavier prison sentences, but organizations will be dealt with through "administrative action" as ordered by the Public Security Examination Commission. Probably an individual would be held responsible for politically motivated acts illegal under the SAPL whether committed by an individual as an individual act or as a member of a destructive organization. Would fractional/factional violent destructive activities (*furaku katsudō* in Japanese) carried out by part of an organization be considered "as an organizational activity"? This "factional activity" would have no form, no specific organization, no regulations (*kisoku*), no office; some assert that this is how the May Day Riot of 1952 burst forth. There was interminable, inconclusive, vague, round-and-round Q&A about this possibility. That would be a delicate issue to decide said drafter Seki; we would have to ascertain that it was indeed not an organizational activity through investigation and obtaining "objective facts" showing that the organization's officers and members carried out destructive activities based on an organizational decision. (6/18:11) Itō Osamu of the HofC insisted this was quite unrealistic since most organizations would not formally take actions to incriminate themselves; we are arguing about, said Itō sarcastically, the existence of ghosts (*yūrei*). (6/18:10) Both sides agreed that an"impressionistic decision (*chūshō-teki ishi kettei*) cannot be the basis for controlling an organization. (6/18:13)

What is an organization? An "organization" is defined under article 3 where the main emphasis is on defining illegal activities but since organizations are the main focus of article 1 let us try to find out what is an "Organization". Article 3.2 declares an organization to be an entity in continuous existence (*keizokuteki ketsugōtai*) or an association of such entities (*rengōtai*) consisting of numerous people working to achieve specific common objectives. But when pressed for further clarification, government witnesses ran into difficulty particularly in the HofR Committee. Under questioning by a JCP member, Seki defined "organizations" by excluding three categories for SAPL purposes: 1) blood related familial groupings, 2) organizations under the umbrella of the constitution, e.g. regional and local organizations, including organizations, such as cooperative unions (*kyōdō kumiai*), 3) those organizations created under special laws, e.g., the Bank of Japan Law. Those in category 2 were created by law and involved in the governing structure. To disband them by administrative action would be a legal inconsistency (*hōritsu-teki mujun*). It would be impossible to disband them by administrative action, this could be done only by a law. The mere registration of a foundation (*zaidan hōjin*) would not normally be regarded as an "organization" under the SAPL since it would have been created under a special law for a given group of people to manage a certain amount of financial assets (*zaisan*). However, if it became in reality an organization with a group of people with common political objectives, it could, under certain circumstances, also be regarded as an organization as defined by the SAPL in article 3 (5/12:1, 5/13:5–6). Since an "association" (*kessha*) as used in the PPL is, like an organization, a group which has banded together for a continuing period with common objectives, it is basically the same as an organization in legal terms (5/12:1).

The Threat and Constitutional Freedoms. The term "Organizations that conduct Violent Destructive Activities, just plain Destructive Activities" to achieve political objectives appeared frequently in the hearings, and was used as a major justification for the SAPL. Committee members tried to understand, comprehend and appreciate what these terms meant in reality by prodding the government with various kinds of scenarios. The government insisted that by adding the adjective "violent" it had no other motive than to try to clarify what destructive activities meant—and hopefully help in clarifying article 1.2 of the Labor Union law. (5/8:12) DG/SIB Yoshikawa explained that "not all riots will come under the purview of the SAPL; it was the objective of the SAPL to control organizations which organized riots for a political purpose, and supplemented—[meaning longer prison sentences imposed on individual violators of the SAPL who have violated the SAPL for political purposes]—the penalties in the Criminal Code as stated in the SAPL for this purpose." (5/9:16–17) Thus, there is ample leeway in the phrases and words in the draft SAPL for an expanded interpretation to be made by future prosecutors and court judges to imperil the basic human rights enumerated in the Constitution notwithstanding whatever present officials, including the AG himself, may promise. The definitional debate was, therefore, not an idle discussion since the SAPL says an organization may be controlled if it is determined that organization had made a decision to conduct violent destructive activities—but what organization in reality is going to formally vote to conduct illegal violent destructive activities? But how would it be determined that an organization had made such a decision? The government explained that an organization could follow its internal rules and make a decision or it could choose less transparent more opaque methods of making similar decisions. This, the opposition pointed out, would give the government enormous leeway in enforcing the SAPL (4/28:14–15).

Whose Behind the 1951–52 Violent Destructive Activities. While the words, JCP, Communists, appear no where in the SAPL, then who was behind the "destructive activities" enumerated by the government? According to the AG, the issue was not the JCP per se but the control of organizations conducting such destructive activities whether right or left. While it emphatically denied that the SAPL was drafted with the JCP as its target, the AG did not deny that the JCP could be a target organization under the SAPL after it is enacted but acknowledged that such an action would have serious constitutional issues to ponder. It did state, however, that most of the violent destructive activities were being carried out by JCP members. It placed a strong emphasis in the initial hearings on describing the inter-relationship between violent destructive activities and the JCP military structure. The government was accused by the moderate SDP-R representative, Suzuki Yoshio, for trying to ban the JCP through the back door rather than through the front door [as Australia had done through its 1950 law banning the Communist Party].

Clear and Present Danger. To underscore this judgment that there was a "clear and present danger", DG Yoshikawa of the SIB reported to both committees about numerous violent incidents that had occurred during 1951–52 and the JCP's military structure and preparations of the JCP. He described the attacks 1) against governments offices—tax offices, police stations, prosecutor's offices, employment assistance offices, and the SIB itself, 2) against the railroads and railroad signaling, 3) using various kinds of demonstrations. The methods used were 1) when police alertness were lowest particularly at night, 2) the attackers were not from the area attacked, 3) the attacks were not frontal but to catch the victim off guard, 4) during mass movements avoid direct confrontation with the police, instead use guerilla tactics, 5) in personal attacks, persuade the victim to come out of the house at night, or on the way home in the evening, 6) various kinds of weapons, e.g. pistols or other lethal weapons would be used in addition to arson, extortion, dynamite, tear gas, threats, throwing bottles of human feces into government offices, 163 organized attacks (*shūdanteki shūgeki bōkō jiken*) against police, SIB, tax offices and procurator's offices since December 1951 to March, 1952 were reported. In April 1952 alone there had been 34 such incidents. There were 2,007 various kinds of incidents from November 1951 to March 1952: obstructions on train lines, interference with running trains, and obstructions of train signals. There were also four incidents of overturning trains in January–February 1952. In addition, there were 57 attacks against Employment Offices and other government offices from December 1951 to March 1952. It was anticipated that these destructive activities would continue in the future in an organized and planned manner. Manuals (with a false cover on how to analyze nutrition) were distributed explaining how to make time-controlled bombs, grenades, tear gas, Molotov cocktails. He also mentioned organized attacks by Koreans against government facilities (12 in December 1951, February–March 1952 31 incidents).

To emphasize still further the seriousness of the Communist threat, SIB/DG Yoshikawa provided an analysis of the several JCP conferences where plans for violence were decided upon, the deceptive publications about "nutrition" which actually contained instructions about various kinds of explosives. JCP military preparations and JCP structure for this purpose. He said that the JCP envisioned a three stage revolution: under the direction of the JCP's military committee, central core self-defense units (*chūkaku jiei-tai*) would be organized to mobilize mass resistance against the authorities, with the development of this mass resistance self-defense struggle (*teikō jiei tōsō*) partisans would be used under the direction of the central self-defense units, finally this mobilization would result in the armed revolt of the people and the central units would be transformed into a people's army. It was estimated that there were 121 such lower level units and 21 core self-defense units organized by regions, Kantō, Kinki, Kyūshū, Hokkaidō regions.

Under these so-called threatening circumstances, the AG insisted there was "a clear and present danger" to the stability of the state sufficient to warrant the enactment of the SAPL. SIB's Yoshikawa supplemented the AG's comments by noting that the U.S. Supreme Court declared the Smith Act constitutional and that a government could not stand by and wait for the actual attempt to overthrow the government, rather it must be based on a clear and present danger, take action to prevent an attempt at rioting and insurrection before it actually occurs. Earlier in 1950, the government had asserted that "the Communist threat" could be handled, could be managed implicitly under then existing laws—this was before the SAPL had been drafted, debated and made into a law. The AG asserted that "in the name of public welfare" some limitation on freedom of organization/association cannot be avoided when organizations attempt to disrupt the basic order of society (*kihon-teki chitsujo*). This assertion led to an energetic debate in both Committees about the relationship of "restrictions" in the SAPL and those freedoms guaranteed in the 1947 Constitution.

This interpretation of the threat was, of course, challenged. Even a conservative labor leader, Kikuchi Tadao, expressed his suspicion that the government was propagandizing a false analysis of the Communist threat, as they did in describing the ABCD (America, Britain, China and Dutch) encirclement of Japan as an excuse for greater and greater military budgets in the l930s. He challenged the AG to say whether there was an imminent planned military insurrection by the Communists; he received no answer from the AG on this point. (5/30:1–2) There was a constitutional discussion between Yoshida Hōsei and Nakamura Masao, and the DG on Legal Opinions, Satō Tatsuo: Article 29 of the old Imperial Constitution granted freedoms "within the law" (*hōritsu no han'i nai de*) not guaranteed and could be easily taken away and were through Imperial rescripts, regulations, emergency rescripts, severely restricted during the war, and through various laws, such as the Shuppan-hō, Shimbunshi-hō, Chianiji-hō, Kokubō Hoan-hō, Kokka Sōdōin-hō and the Gunki Hogo-hō, thus, making the executive overwhelmingly superior to the Diet and the Courts. That same generation of senior leaders were trying to maintain this executive superiority. Now, in contrast, freedoms are "guaranteed" by the 1947 Constitution but may be restricted because of public interest (*kōeki*) and for the maintenance of the public welfare and security. The freedoms under the 1947 Constitution cannot be restricted by law, but could be restricted in the name of "public welfare"—sounds very much like the justifications used in the U.S., almost anything becomes acceptable "in the name of national security" even restricting freedoms guaranteed under the U.S. Constitution. Is there much difference between the prewar Imperial and 1947 "democratic" Constitutions in this regard. Were these rights absolute, yes said the opposition but difficult to limit (*seigen shigatai*). Here lies "a great fear, a great danger" said Nakamura. In light of history it is easy to slip backward to prewar laws, Nazi and fascist approaches, said Yoshida. (5/20:4, 5/20:7, 5/23:22, 5/24:15, 5/31:6, 6/6:10–13)

SDP-L's Inomata Kōzō pointed out that in the U.S. the postwar internal security law took two years and eight months to consider in the U.S. Congress, and then President Truman vetoed the bill saying it infringed on the guarantees of freedom and that there must be a "clear and present danger" for this kind of law to be invoked. To which AG Kimura replied that under the present situation there is a clear and present danger there is a movement that is planning "severe internal strife and revolution and rioting" (*sōtō na nairan, sōjō o kitosuru ugoki ga aru*). When asked to name the destructive organizations, Seki responded that the government was still researching this subject, but had names of Korean organizations—data on Koreans were always available—but not on Japanese organizations despite the detailed reports on all the "destructive activities" submitted to Diet members as reference materials. When Inomata demanded the names and organizations which were creating a clear and present danger, Yoshikawa dismissed this demand somewhat arrogantly:

> The government has sufficiently explained the basis of and justification for the SAPL and does not believe, at this time, that there is a need to prove the existence of such organizations, their contents and activities at this time. (4/25:9)
>
> To which Inomata sharply responded:
>
> Your response to my query is an insult to the Diet. Explain the "lack of necessity". (4/25:9)

This was symbolic of the problem with the government. Satake Haruki of the Shakai Kakushintō, pursued still further demanding to know who actually committed the various criminal acts enumerated above. Yoshikawa responded, seemingly over-riding the AG: since we are investigating the suspicions we have about these activities [as possibly riots or insurrections] we have not "reached a decision yet" as to whether these actions constitute a clear and present danger and promised an answer during the phase debating the merits of each article of the SAPL.

Toward the end of the HofR hearings on May 12, Kaji Ryōsaku, a director (*riji*) of the Committee and member of the governing Liberal Party, raised a fundamental issue: if the SAPL was not enacted was the present state of Japan such that there was a genuine fear that the security of public welfare could not be maintained and that Japanese society would be imminently destroyed? This gave Seki the opportunity to restate the government's rationale in stark, dark, threatening and perhaps frightening terms.

> ...the very starting point for creating the SAPL was that if this law was not available public security could not be maintained. As explained earlier by SIB DG Yoshikawa, the pattern of the frequent and widespread violent destructive activities was a phenomenon not seen in the past. The present situation is something that we have not seen since the early years of the Meiji Restoration when there were disturbances somewhat similar to what is seen now.... Behind these activities, unsettling materials (*fuon bunsho*) are being distributed which advocate the propriety and necessity of these activities; they propagandize and incite such activities. They are distributed in a systematic manner.... With existing laws there is no way to combat these activities. If these activities are allowed to continue to advocate, propagandize and incite, the state will come face-to-face with an extremely fearful situation. We cannot tolerate to stand by wringing our hands until these activities result in harmful acts (*jitsugai kōi*) of insurrection, politically motivated riots, even murder. Unless action is taken against those advocating the propriety of these activities which will gather momentum like a snow ball we will be faced with a fearful and dangerous situation.... If one digs down deep, one finds that there is undoubtedly an organizational backing to these activities.... The countries of the world are taking steps to combat these problems by controlling these organizations.... The present Criminal Code is inadequate for responding to this threat. The present legislation was prepared to provide for the minimum necessary supplemental controls within the Constitutional framework of respecting human rights, to maintain the minimum necessary public security from the administrative and judicial standpoints.... We have limited the SAPL to destructive activities with a political objective, and not expanded it to include economic issues (5/12:21–22).

Thus, there was an impasse almost unbridgeable between the opposition which did not believe in such a dire probability and the government which candidly proclaimed that the seemingly uncoordinated violence would coalesce into a real threat against the Japanese ship of state.

2. *Article 2. Standards for Control (as submitted to the Diet on 4/17/1952 and approved by the HofR on 5/15/1952)*

> 2.1. Controls and investigations for these controls to achieve the objectives stipulated in the previous article will be carried out only to the necessary but appropriate extent in order to achieve the objectives stipulated in the previous article and such actions must not in any way improperly (*futō ni*, inappropriately) limit the freedoms of organizations, thought, religious beliefs, assembly and expression, the right of workers to organize and to conduct organizational activities and, freedoms and rights guaranteed by the Constitution.
> 2.2. In conducting investigations or imposing penalties under this law, there must not be to the slightest degree (*iyashikumo*) of any abuse [of this authority], and appropriate (proper, by implication legal) activities of labor unions and other organizations shall not be limited nor shall there be interference in these activities.

Article 2.1 stipulates that controls and investigations must not in any way improperly limit the freedoms of organization, thought, religious beliefs, assembly and expression, the right of workers to organize and to conduct organizational activities, and freedoms and rights guaranteed by the Constitution; appropriate activities of labor unions and other organizations shall not be limited nor shall there be interference in these activities [by the PSIA or any other security agency].

Since in article 3, discussed below, many selected offenses in the Criminal Code are included in the SAPL "by reference", Yoshida Yasugimi of the Kokumin Minshutō suggested that, because of the importance of this protection in the implementation of the SAPL and to emphasize this importance, Article 21 of the Constitution should be included by reference as the CC is included or lists the specific freedoms as they are listed in the Constitution.[9] The draft SAPL, in contrast to the Constitution lumps these together as freedom of "expression". Seki dismissed the query explaining that it was a "drafting convenience" to use "expression" as the overall term for these

[9] Article 21 of the Constitution reads: Every person shall have freedom of assembly and association as well as speech, press and all other forms of expression are guaranteed.

freedoms and was regarded by the government as "sufficient" (*jūbun de aru*) for this purpose—a rather dismissive attitude. (4/28:1) Such a cavalier handling of such an important issue only engendered further suspicions in both Committees. The Japanese term "*jūbun de aru*" was quite frequently used in the hearings by government witnesses, i.e. in our opinion what has been proposed and written is totally acceptable, sounding quite condescending.

The phrases about the "activities of labor unions and other organizations" were made more explicit only under pressure from the Minister of Labor in the drafting process and from labor union demands. They were, nevertheless, regarded by the opposition in Committee hearings not as prohibitions with penalties (commensurate with violations of the SAPL) but merely as admonitions and non-substantive articles included under duress. The government, of course, protested quite the contrary; they were included to prevent the recurrence of the abuses of past history. Indeed, the articles in Japanese speak of "there must not be such actions that would inappropriately limit constitutional rights and limiting or interfering in labor union activities (...*seigen-shi*, or *kainyū-suru yō na koto ga atte wa naranai*). They were merely suggestions to security officials for these abuses not to occur, not to be unpleasant, not to overstep their authority. The Japanese language use of "*no yō na koto*" was indeed an instruction, an admonition, and rather weak. The government claimed otherwise, of course, and refused to consider the insertion of stronger language, such as prohibit (*kinzuru*) during HofR deliberations; the opposition with equal vigor and conviction maintained that such admonitions meant little and had little authority and were inserted without much conviction except to satisfy and mollify labor's demands and to present a face of sincerity for public relations.

Ishikawa of SDP-R declared that by just including the word "appropriate (*seitō na*)" raises deep suspicions because of the need for a judgment as to what is appropriate. In light of past history before 1945, this was a serious issue and a legitimate source of anxiety and distrust. Yet Seki insistently explained ignoring the original reasoning that:

> ...As I have explained previously and as DG Yoshikawa of the SIB has just explained, the intent here was to treat all organizations equally under the law, labor union activities were mentioned only as an example, and to eliminate any anxieties that organizations may be concerned about such abuses. (4/28:12)

Because of past history, distrust of Japanese security agencies, words and phrases were included in several articles beginning with article 2, to allay these anxieties but somehow the style of language was not definitive, e.g. violations of various freedoms must not occur, instead of, as the opposition demanded, violations of various freedoms shall not be violated in the implementation of the SAPL. The government insisted emphatically that some restrictions on these freedoms cannot be avoided, since freedoms are not unlimited. While that is a statement of the obvious and coming from people of the prewar generation of Ministry of Justice staff did not ring true, convincing and reliable. To the query why is it necessary to provide for so many admonitions in the SAPL about respecting human rights, since this should be obvious, Yoshikawa revealingly conceded that the difference between fair administration and abusive implementation of the SAPL is only paper thin. Various scenarios of labor union activities were posed to try to find the limits of "appropriate labor union activities" under SAPL, e.g. studying labor union history including tactics and strategy, Marxism, British socialism and the labor party. All were legitimate so long as they did not result in the advocacy of violent destructive activities which might threaten the state foundations of the country. On the other hand, if, at a union meeting some advocated drastic slow down of and interference with train schedules but lost the vote for adoption of these tactics at the meeting, these advocates probably would be subject to prosecution under the SAPL according to AG Kimura. (5/30:13)

Abuse of Authority. The second part of Article 2 emphasized that in the implementation of the SAPL there must not be any abuse of authority. In light of past history of the police and security forces before 1945, this was probably ONE OF THE issues that caused the greatest anxiety and justifiably so. Did this second part of Article 2 provide a sufficiently strong enough message, a strong enough signal to the police and security services? The government was pursued relentlessly about its genuineness, sincerity, probability, assurances to prevent the abusive use of the SAPL by the government in general but particularly those agencies and personnel involved in enforcing the SAPL. This concern stems not from concerns about "due process" in the Western legal sense, but a step or two before due process would come into play. These anxieties and suspicions stem DIRECTLY from the prewar enforcement of the Peace Preservation Law and other security laws; after all it was only 5–6 years since the end of the war and basically the same security people were still in place with some senior leaders purged temporarily under the Occupation and some now even de-purged and playing an active role in the reconfiguration of the internal security apparatus and the structure of the SAPL and authorities to be given to the PSIA and PSEC. These anxieties and suspicions are not theoretical legal concerns but stem from either personal experiences or having lived through that prewar historical period. Because of how such prewar laws as the PPL, the military secrets protection law (Gunki Hogohō), the national security maintenance law (Kokubō Hoanhō), were enforced, there was no sense that the SAPL could be effectively carried out (*kenzen ni un'yō sareru*) and that the SAPL (together with the Special Criminal Law of 1952, Keiji Tokubetsu-hō) have, according to Suzuki Yoshio (SDP-R, former Minister of Justice in the 1947–48 Katayama Cabinet), a spiritual lineage and connection to these laws, i.e. he was saying that the SAPL was part of a postwar continuum of these laws. Suzuki pointed out that during his prewar legal practice, he was warned by government prosecutors that defending the accused under the PPL could put himself in danger of being accusing of aiding and abetting the defendants! He said he continued defending the accused and was not arrested nor taken to court. In defending the SAPL, AG Kimura admitted that abuse was, from the very beginning, one of his greatest concerns about this law especially by low level staff and that is why certain "safeguards" are included, such as not giving PSIA staff compulsory investigative authority but only limited investigative authority (*nin'i chōsaken*) (6/6:1, 6/14:3), establishing rules of conduct (*shoku kihan*), implementation procedures (*shikō saisoku*), special sensitivity and training courses (*kenshū*), stricter supervision (*kansatsu seido*), and closer liaison with the Human Rights Division.

It will be recalled that the political opposition in the HofR demanded that since political offenses listed in the SAPL were given harsher penalties than those for the same offenses under the CC, correspondingly those who abuse their authority under the SAPL should also face harsher penalties. The CC provides for several categories of government employees with different sets of penalties: for the general civil service employee who abused his authority could be given less than two years of hard labor or imprisonment (CC article 193); special government employees (*tokubetsu kōmuin*), i.e. court judges, prosecutors, and the police who could improperly arrest and detain people and those who assist these categories of personnel, could be given from six months up to ten years of hard labor or imprisonment (CC article 194 and articles 189 and 190 of the criminal procedures law); if this abuse leads to the death of a person, the offender would be given a harsher penalty (article 196); those who insult and bully and violently mistreat (*bōkō*) those arrested and detained shall be punished with sentences of no more than seven years of imprisonment (CC article 195). Mistreatment includes physical and psychological assaults, sexual harassment and rape, depriving one of sleep, food, toilet relief. The government's answer was always somewhat flip by suggesting reference to article 193, rather than the other penalties.

During the Committee hearings, the government refused to impose any harsher penalties on wayward officials than the maximum of two years for national civil service employees, a remarkably one sided and unbalanced arrangement. Since the government described the PSEC as a semi-judicial organization which could make "court-like" decisions governing the life of an organization and its membership this imbalance of penalties was even more obvious. The penalty for abuse of authority in the SAPL as proposed by the Ryokufūkai in the HofC would be limited to no more than three years of hard labor or imprisonment, hardly a major deviation from the original two year prison term, and far from the maximum of ten years specified in CC article 194 for judges, prosecutors and police; it was more a symbolic gesture, a message to the security officials to watch their p's and q's and to satisfy other political demands. It was a small concession that the government had to accept as part of the overall package to obtain the support of the Ryokufūkai in enacting the SAPL.[10]

Downgrading the Human Rights Bureau. This skepticism was reinforced when, in the process of reorganization of the Office of the Attorney General, the Human Rights Bureau was down graded to a mere section (Jinken Yōgoka). In the early postwar years a Human Rights Protection Bureau was created under the AG, undoubtedly with the encouragement of the Occupation authorities. Inomata, SDP-L,

[10] This section was based on material from *Hōritsu Yōgo Jiten*, Yūhikaku. p. 759; *Gendai Hōritsu Hyakka Dai-Jiten*, 2000. pp. 464–465; *Kokumin Hōritsu Hyakka Dai-Jiten*, KK Gyōsei. 1985 pp. 450–452; *Shin-Hōritsugaku Jiten*. Yūhikaku, 1989. p. 763; *Zentei Hōgaku Jiten*. Nihon Hyōronsha. 1971. p. 538. The election law specified up to 4 years imprisonment (art. 226.1).

asserted that this symbolizes the government's attitude toward protection of human rights. The sincerity of the government's assertion about abusive implementation and protection of human rights was challenged by even a Liberal Party member. This institutional down grading and demotion of the Human Rights Bureau under the AG to a mere section in the Civil Affairs Bureau was cited just as an example or symbol of the government's ultimate intentions. Such a demotion would only increase the people's anxieties about this law. Ironically, the SAPL drafter Seki had played a prominent role in the Human Rights Bureau early in the Occupation years; it was a source of some pride on his part. Rather than lessening the role of human rights, we should be increasing its personnel, funding, and status to provide a sense of safety and ease among the people when enacting the SAPL. Since abuses of authority are committed by government officials, it would have to be up to this office, the Human Rights Bureau, not a downgraded section, to prevent, pursue or punish such abuses. But, said the AG, in response, rather than expecting the government to be the defender of human rights, private groups should be the leader in such efforts, a civilian responsibility carried out by private sector funded organizations. He insisted this was not a downgrading since personnel would not be decreased and, in any case, protection of human rights should be mainly a civilian responsibility, such as the lawyer's associations, e.g., the Jiyū Jinken Kyōkai (the Japanese equivalent of the American Civil Liberties Union) and the Dai-ichi Tokyo Bengoshikai of which he was a member, formed its own human rights committee. (6/6:4). But the constant crux is the lack of a budget for such activities in these organizations. The Human Rights Bureau should have been heavily involved in the investigation of the police-student clashes on the Waseda University campus. (5/13:10–11) It was ironic that as the government claimed its avowed commitment to prevent the downgrading of the Human Rights Bureau even as the caseload of human rights violations was increasing: 1948 (49), 1949 (5,000), 1950 (6,000), 1951 (15,000). (Miyagi Tamayo, HofC member, 6/6:4)

While looking to the future one might assume another Hitler or Mussolini would not arise, nevertheless, asserted Diet member Tajima of the governing Liberal Party in the HofR, if such did occur, the SAPL could become an "extremely dangerous law which could be greatly abused". The abuse of the SAPL may not be committed by the present AG, nor his successor and future successors, but the abuses will more likely be committed by officials at the lower levels where they have traditionally occurred.

Writing only five years after the enactment of the SAPL, PM Yoshida devoted a fair amount of space to the SAPL in his ten year memoirs. He commented with some facetiousness and sarcasm when he opens his commentary on the opposition to the SAPL with the sub-title: the tediously constant and unchanging theory or assertion about abusive implementation (*aimo-kawaranu "ran'yō-ron"*). He matter-of-factly asserted that:

> No one objects to making clearly destructive acts as a political means [to achieve a specific objective] (*meihaku na hakai kōi o seiji-teki na shūdan to suru mono*) a criminal offense at the stage of a general outline (*taikō*). But when it comes to details, then objections arise about the suppression of freedom of speech, interference by government officials in people's everyday lives. In reality, over the long period of gestation of the SAPL from spring 1951 to July 1952, the essence of the opposition movement was its assertion that government authority would be inappropriately inserted into [all aspects of life]. In other words, the opposition is centered in the wrongful application (*akuyō*), and abusive implementation (*ran'yō*) of the law. When the SAPL agency is given certain authorities to carry out its duties, these are vehemently criticized in a concentrated manner as a resurrection of the prewar Police Bureau (Keiho-kyoku) and the Tokkō (Special Higher Police). This criticism was not limited to the SAPL but was brought forward without exception concerning all postwar laws which have as their objective some such control (*torishimari*) or restriction (*seigen*) that would limit activities. I believe that any law with a police aspect and not limited to the SAPL would inevitably and naturally limit the freedom of the people in some way or another. If one rejected laws for this reason, then the criminal code and many other laws created to control criminal offenses would be invalid. All such laws have subsequently been carried out peaceably and have contributed to the maintenance of public security. Probably the so-called intellectuals (*iwayuru chishiki'nin*) who opposed and criticized these laws at the time have probably failed or forgotten to conduct their own criticism. (Yoshida Shigeru, *Kaisō Jū'nen* 2:291–292)

This is a sarcastic and not surprising condemnation of the opposition to these laws including the SAPL by PM Yoshida, despite his personal not so pleasant encounter and travails with the enforcement of the PPL by the Special Higher Police toward the end of WWII in 1945. This attempt to caricature and trivialize intellectual commentary on the SAPL was also echoed by Liberal Party members in their comments at the House plenary session just before the House vote on

May 15, 1952. All in all, this dialogue was not regarded by the opposition as particularly reassuring nor enlightening.

Restitution. Since much was made by the government that the SAPL supplemented the Criminal Code, a euphemism for making penalties stiffer for politically motivated destructive activities as crimes under the SAPL, opponents called for similarly stiffer penalties for government security officials in the PSIA who abused their authority in implementing the SAPL and for making wrongful charges and recommendations to PSEC against selected organizations and individuals. Even Liberal Party members, Taman Hirobumi, Kaji Ryōsaku were sharply critical of the draft SAPL which contained no extra penalties against those officials who may have taken or recommended an improper administrative action which resulted in unwarranted infringement of people's constitutional rights. Inomata Kōzō, SDP-L, raised this issue in general interpolations and insistently raised it again toward the end of the hearings in the HofR. Legal action was proposed to be taken against organizations for destructive action, what about collective responsibilities for abuse of authority, citing the use of police at the student-police clash at Waseda University. In Japan there is still the *kanson mimpi* attitude (respect for governmental authority and contempt for the people) well symbolized by the use of police at Waseda University. Instigation and incitement to prepare, plan and conspire to conduct riots and insurrections is all punishable under the SAPL but how does irresponsible police action against the people to be punished on an equal basis as an organization. Present disciplinary action against the police is aimed only at individuals not the organization as a whole or any part of it. What could be the standards for judging organizational police abuse? The government's response was to evade the issue by claiming "we are investigating the circumstances of this clash at this time." (5/13:10–1) Government witnesses listed penalty possibilities in the civil service code which could be pursued by aggrieved parties, the civil procedures law, the national indemnity law (Kokka Baishō-hō). The government response was always the same: we decided that the existing set of laws would be appropriate and sufficient without creating new types of offenses or a special penalty clauses "for this purpose" (5/12:9). It was not necessary from the public service employees point of view to impose yet another layer of disciplinary punishment for a special reason, [e.g. violation of article 2 when laws exist already for this purpose] (5/12:23). If a labor union was improperly treated, activities obstructed and limited and forced to disband, court procedures for restitution would take years making any guarantees in Article 2 meaningless (5/30:5); the government dismissed this concern by merely urging the union to use CC article 193 or the public employees law (Kokka Kōmuin-hō). Thus, a special venue for relief and restitution arising from improper implementation of the SAPL commensurate with its importance, sensitivity and past history was summarily dismissed as unnecessary by the government. Thus, the issue fades away in the HofR until reconsidered by the HofC where penalties were made slightly heavier.

3. *Article 3. Definitions*

3.1. Violent Destructive Activities as stipulated in this law are defined as acts described below:
3.1.1. Acts stipulated under Criminal Code (1907, #45) articles 77 (insurrection/*nairan*), 78 (preparation/*yobi*, planning/*imbō*), 79 (assistance to insurrections/*nairan hōjō*).
[The HofR split the Cabinet draft for article 3.1.1 into two clauses for the sake of clarity and considered by the HofC in this revised form]
3.1.1.2. Instigating and inciting acts described in 3.1.1 above
3.1.1.3. Those who possess materials (*bunsho*) in order to facilitate the realization of the acts described in 3.1.1 above, print, distribute, publicly display materials (*bunsho*) or designs (*zuga*) which advocate the appropriateness/propriety or necessity of realizing such acts, or possess such materials for the purpose of distributing them, publicly displaying them.
3.1.2. Acts committed under any one of the CC articles described below in order to facilitate or push forward, support, or oppose certain political principles (*shugi*) or programs (*shisaku*):
3.1.2.1. Criminal Code (CC) article 106 (riots)
3.1.2.2. CC 108 (arson of inhabited buildings) and 109.1 (arson of uninhabited buildings)
3.1.2.3. CC article 117.1 (first part on explosion of explosives)
3.1.2.4. CC article 125 (danger to the running of locomotive and electric trains)
3.1.2.5. CC article 126.1 and 126.2 (overturning locomotive and electric trains)
3.1.2.6. CC article 199.1 (murder)
3.1.2.7. CC article 236.1 (burglary)
3.1.2.8. Article 1 of Regulations concerning the control of explosives of 1884(#32)
3.1.2.9. CC article 95 (interference with official duties): a large number of people collectively (*tashū kyōdō shite*) with deadly weapons and explosives attempt to interfere with the conduct of prosecutors or police

in carrying out their official duties, those who are assisting them, those who are guarding those in legal custody (*hōrei ni yoru kōkin*), those who are transporting such persons, or those who are conducting investigations under this law [SAPL]
3.1.2.10. Instigation or incitement, planning or preparing for any one of those acts specified in items 1 through 9 above.
3.2. An "organization" is a group of many people (*tasū-nin*) who have formed a group on a continuous basis (*keizoku-teki ketsugōtai*) or a federation of such groups (*rengōtai*) with the purpose of achieving specific common objectives (*tokutei no kyōdō mokuteki*). Any branch, chapter or subsidiary body of such an organization, if it meets the requirements, shall be subject to control under this law.[11] [Article 3.2 was discussed under Article 1 above]

While articles 1 and 2 had their controversial aspects, article 3 which defined what was illegal under the SAPL naturally was regarded as the core of the SAPL and thus the most controversial, subject to the bitterest attacks, subject to the most stringent interpolations. It is this article that prompted Diet members to characterize the entire draft law as overly complex and difficult for the man-on-the-street to appreciate and understand and, in the eyes of the government, to support. It is in this article (together with articles 4–6 on controlling organization, and 37–43 on penalty articles against individuals), where the complexities of administrative actions and prison penalties intersect and mixed in a strained web of inter-relationships. These are articles that prompted a fair number of Diet members to suggest that a special law for controlling organizations and another for violations of the SAPL stipulations by individuals instead of combining them into a difficult law to explain, let alone interpret and implement in the future. It is the spirit and vagueness behind the article which prompted comments that while the SAPL may be unavoidable under the circumstances it was a law that will invoke strong power (*kyōken no hatsudō*) which has unfortunate historical precedents. It is the references to CC articles concerning insurrection which do indeed use "old style" Japanese language, e.g. *chōken binran* which are difficult and vague terms to interpret in modern day more democratic Japan which prompt criticism, not without basis that the SAPL is suffused with the thinking processes underlying the old Imperial Constitution.

[11] There was no translation in *Kenkyūsha's New Japanese-English Dictionary*, 1954 edition for *ketsugōtai* or *rengōtai* nor for *keizoku-teki rengōtai.*

Illegal activities under the proposed SAPL were, in the first instance, initially defined by reference to selected articles in the Criminal Code (CC), then several kinds of activities were added as new categories and certain articles of the Criminal Code were "supplemented" (or augmented) and given a much broader interpretation. It must be re-emphasized that while the objective of the SAPL, beginning with article 1 was to control organizations which conduct violent destructive activities, the latter activities, in reality, were described in this article in terms of *kōi* (individual acts) and penalties for individuals for committing these offenses were stipulated in articles 37–43; "penalties" or "control measures" for organizations are given in quite different terms, e.g. prohibitions of varying lengths for publications, assemblies, rallies, up to disbandment of an organization in articles 4–6.

The first group of articles referenced from the CC, articles 77, 78 and 79, are, relatively speaking, straight forward and have a legal history and are "understood" in a general and vague manner. It is what follows that makes the definition of "illegal activities" so broad and extremely controversial. Article 3 defines three groups of acts that, in an ever broadening circle, define the commitment of illegal acts under selected articles of the Criminal Code included by reference in the SAPL.

Group 1 broadens the definition of what is illegal under the SAPL:

a. acts that incite and instigate people to commit violations of articles 77 (insurrection), 78 (planning and plotting), 79 (assistance to insurrection)
b. possession of materials in order to facilitate the realization of the acts described in these articles
c. printing, distributing, publicly displaying materials or designs which advocate the appropriateness/propriety or necessity of realizing such acts or
d. possessing such materials for the purpose of distributing them, publicly displaying them.

Group 2 covers acts which would facilitate or push forward, support or oppose certain political principles or programs under any one of nine additional articles: CC95 (obstruction of official duties), 106 (riots), 108 (arson of uninhabited buildings), 109 (arson of uninhabited buildings), 117 (explosives), 129 (danger to running trains), 126 (overturning trains), 199 (murder), 236 (burglary), and article one of an explosives law of 1884.

Group 3 broadens yet again acts that instigate, incite, plan, prepare for the illegal acts in the above mentioned nine CC articles.

One might comment after digesting the above expansion of the Criminal Code, what is left out of this dragnet?

The Criminalization of Kyōsa/Sendō as New Categories of Criminal Offenses. Seki asserted that maintenance of public welfare dictates that the government cannot standby, wringing its hands, while a crime was about to be perpetrated. When a crime was being incited, we must take steps to prevent it from happening. For this reason, there is a need to make both instigation and incitement independent crimes according to SIB Yoshikawa (4/28:2). Under the national tax law, it is a criminal offense to incite people not to pay taxes. Using the same reasoning, said the government, under the SAPL two new categories were created as independent crimes (*dokuritsuzai*):

> *Instigation* (*kyōsa*) occurs when *a person* acts to persuade *another person* to make a new decision to commit a particular crime, i.e. that person did not have the intention of committing a particular crime but was persuaded or instigated by another to commit this crime. In this case, the instigator must be aware of the existence of the principal offender. Since "instigation" was created in the SAPL as an independent crime it is not a necessary condition for instigation to have occurred for the other party to make a decision to commit a particular crime or even for that person to carry out that crime. Instigation can be charged as an independent crime against a person whether or not the person who received the instigation (or was instigated) committed the act which was instigated. This is new in the SAPL. (4/26:24 and 5/9:13)
>
> *Incitement* (*sendō*) occurs, in contrast to instigation, when a person creates in an indefinite number or many people the determination to commit a particular crime having lost their reasonable sense of judgment (*chūsei no handan o ushinatte*) or encourages (*jochō-suru*) or stimulates (*shigeki-suru*) an already existing determination to commit a particular crime. Again, for the crime of incitement to have been committed, it is not a necessary condition for these acts to have actually been committed and the person doing the incitement would not be aware of a specific person(s) who might commit the incited crime (4/26:24 and 5/9:13).

Sendō, Its Antecedents. Sendō was emphatically described by the AG as "the essence" (*kosshi*) of the SAPL (4/25:17); he was insisting that *sendō* was the new core concept which must be included in this internal security law. This was non-negotiable. It was further pointed out that *sendō* had been used as an independent crime in several other postwar domestic laws without objections: The National Public Employee Law (Kokka Kōmuin-hō), Local Government Employees Laws (Chihō Kōmuin-hō), Penalty rules concerning the handling of explosives (Bakuhatsubutsu torishimari bassoku), public enterprise labor laws (Kōkyō Kigyōtai Rōdō Kankei-hō) and others each contain incitement and instigation as independent crimes—although in some instances, the Japanese pronunciation, e.g. *sosonokasu*, or *aoru* was sometimes used instead of the compound nouns, *kyōsa, sendō* (5/8:2). While incitement was indeed used in other laws, it was not pointed out that this usage was not in the context of a highly charged political crime as it was used in the SAPL and conveniently did not mention that a major proposed WWII criminal law had called for the criminalization of *kyōsa/sendō.*

1914 and 1949 Court Precedents. Two high court decisions were cited by Seki, in an attempt to bolster his assertions and to clarify the meaning of these controversial and suspected terms, *kyōsa* (incitement) and *sendō* (instigation), one from the Dai-Shin'in (the prewar name of the Supreme Court) on 6/9/1914 and another from the postwar Supreme Court in 1949.

The 1914 case involved a political meeting to denounce and impeach the Cabinet and declare the death penalty for this Cabinet and for this purpose some one should approach the Prime Minister in the Diet and take care of him, but Diet members cannot be relied upon to do this. So some one in the audience was called upon to do this deed. This incitement went beyond merely calling for the change of cabinet but encouraged the bodily harm to an official of the government. This constituted a violation of article 9.2 of the prewar Security Police Law (Chian Keisatsu-hō).

The 1949 case involved the incitement of farmers not to provide (*kyōshitsu*) rice to the government. A meeting of about 250–350 farmers was organized on 11/15/1946 by the Nihon Nōmin Kumiai (Japan Farmers Union) to discuss the system of allocating rice collection targets established by the government. They maintained that the system penalized farmers. The situation has gone beyond petitions and appeals. It was suggested that the farmers demand that the government provide materials for growing rice in exchange for providing rice to the government and the meeting was urged, incited, not to follow the government's rice allocations under the Food Control Law and sell rice to the government. These actions were regarded as an incitement in violation of the law. (4/26:25–26)

Citing these cases did not necessarily improve the governments's case, since it gave the opposition an opportunity to claim that the SAPL was linked to the past, not a new break with the past.

Since the government asserted that *sendō* (incitement) had been accepted in various kinds of legislation in the past, it would be useful to provide a summary of the use of incitement in various laws since the Meiji period.[12]

During the pre-1945 presumably notorious periods of suppression during Meiji, Taisho and Showa-I, a total of 77 years, fifteen laws (including one Imperial decree issued in 1884 before the Constitution created a Diet) were enacted containing *sendō*; in contrast during the post-1945 "democratic" Japan, fourteen laws (including two holdovers from the prewar period and one Cabinet Ordinance) were enacted containing the term, *sendō*.

The pre-August 1945 laws made it a crime to incite others to

- use explosives to disturb public peace (*chian o samatageru*) or to injure a person
- sign a petition to the Emperor
- not pay taxes
- commit the crimes of collecting national secrets for the purpose of revealing them to foreign countries
- reject military service

[12] For this purpose, I consulted a limited number of sources as follows:
Hirano, Ryūichi. Habōhō to Sendō, *Hōritsu no Hiroba* 5:10(10/1952):23–25.
Imoto, Daikichi. Senji Keiji Tokubetsu hōchū Kaisei Hōritsu ni tsuite, *Senji Keiji Tokubetsu Hōchū Kaisei Hōritsu ni kansuru giji sokkiroku narabini iinkai giroku.* 1943 (Reprinted 1978 Tōyō Bunkasha). 2 v. (886 p.). pp. 867–886.
Isobe, Yasushi. Senji Keiji Tokubetsu-hō ni tsuite, *Hōsōkai Zasshi* 12:4(3/1942):111–158.
Makino, Eiichi. Hakai Katsudō Bōshihō no seiritsu: toku ni kyōsa matawa sendō ni tsuite, Keisatsu Kenkyū 23:9(9/1952):3–15.
Miyake, Shōtarō, Sendō, [part of a commentary on Chian Iji-hō], *Hōritsugaku Jiten*, Iwanami Shoten. 1939. III:1842–1845.
Okudaira, Yasuhiro. "Sendō" Kaitai o Kokoromiru Josetsu, *Gendai Rikken-shugi no Tenkai.* Yūhikaku. 1993. 2 v. p. I:609–641.

"*sendō*" in the following law dictionaries:
Hōrei Yōgo Jiten, Gakuyō Shobō, 2001, p. 473.
Keihō Jiten, Seirin Shoin Shinsha, 1966, pp. 301–302.
Shin-Hōritsugaku Jiten, Yūhikaku, 3rd ed., 1989, I:862.

- join or support an organization to commit crimes, reject paying taxes thereby threatening social stability
- organize a group for the purpose of changing the national polity or rejecting the system of private property, or knowingly join an organization with these objectives
- injure others or damage property through riots and violence to achieve the objectives of the previous paragraph
- confer/plot and incite actions for the above purposes

The Meiji Period, 1868–1911. The four laws during the Meiji period were concerned with incitement and the handling of explosives, incitement to tax evasion, newspapers and publication of articles which may incite and threaten social stability and a broader law on internal security. The latter two were liberally used to cajole, persuade and control the press and stifle political opposition in Meiji Japan.

The Taisho Period, 1911–1925. This period, was, for the conservative Japanese governments and the ruling elite, one of fear and anxiety about the very foundations and stability of Japanese society and even their own role as the governing elite resulting from economic unrest after WWI, the introduction of various streams of political ideas from Europe, e.g. philosophies and ideas concerning anarchism, communism, socialism and democracy (fascism, Nazism were yet to arrive) and the rise of leftwing parties and labor unions. Two laws issued by Imperial Decree on the handling of appeals and penalty regulations concerning internal security included articles on incitement. In direct response to the challenging domestic political situation and this unrest, the government proposed a law for the control of radical social movements to the Diet in 1922. The then House of Peers passed a modified bill, but in the House of Representatives it became unfinished business (*shingi miryō*), thus it failed to be accepted by the Diet. The two substantive laws during the late Taisho period were the election law giving Japanese males the right to vote and the notorious Chian Iji-hō (Peace Preservation Law, PPL) both containing "*sendō*". Because of the anxiety and fear of the implications of giving Japanese males the right to vote in those perceived to be treacherous years, the PPL was created to balance any possible threat to the status quo from these newly enfranchised men.

The Showa-I Period, 1926–1945. During these years, there were eight laws (including revisions) which contained "*sendō*" but in reality the first one in 1926 concerned conciliation in labor disputes. A 1940 provisional draft (*kari'an*) revision of the Criminal Code included the addition of *sendō* as a crime; hitherto the CC had not included *sendō* even though it was already included in many laws; this proposed revision was not enacted into law. As discussed in the subsection on the PPL it was drastically revised in 1941. A special wartime criminal law was enacted in 1941 in response to wartime exigencies (but did not include incitement as a crime) This was an obvious stopgap law for it was replaced in 1942 and yet another final revision in 1943 which broadened the dragnet of offenses with substantially heavier penalties. It is highly significant that the 1943 special wartime criminal law:

- was responding to a special set of circumstances, the exigencies of a wartime emergency situation in contrast to 1907 when the CC was enacted under peacetime conditions
- included by reference to a very wide range of criminal offenses under the Criminal Code that would be committed during the war
- made *sendō* into an independent new criminal offense with the same heavy penalty as imposed for the crime of instigation without revising the core Criminal Code
- was based on the asserted inadequacy of the CC to handle crimes committed under stringent wartime conditions
- made the penalties substantially harsher since it was believed that punishments under the CC were not heavy enough, thus not a sufficient deterrent
- substantially elaborated upon and broadened those crimes carried out with the objective of bringing about a change in the national political structure through social disorder, disturbances, rebellion (*kokusei henran*).

The above points are uncomfortably close in their nature, thinking and ideological bent to the several reasons given by the government in justifying the SAPL.[13]

[13] That this law was presumably a temporary law for the duration of the war was made clear by beginning each of the 18 articles in Chapter 1 defining the criminal offenses with "Under wartime circumstances,..." (*Senji ni saishi*) and at the end of the law it specified that when wartime conditions ended, the necessary stipulations for this purpose, i.e. how to end this law, will be handled by Imperial Decree.

The offenses in this chapter were divided into three groups: 1) crimes committed during wartime nation-wide blackout (*tōka kansei*) or when there was a danger of an enemy attack or other conditions which might prompt the feelings of the populace to waiver, e.g. burning cars, trains, buildings, ships, aircraft may result in the death penalty (articles 1–6) and inclusion by reference of numerous crimes listed in the CC); 2) those crimes carried out with the objective of bringing about a change in the national political structure through social disorder, disturbances or rebellion (*kokusei*

There were also laws on the protection of military secrets, punishing those who incited others not to serve in the Imperial Army and Navy. These laws were focused on potential and possible political discontent and their enforcement resulted in severe restrictions on the freedoms of expression, assembly and speech, severe abuses by security personnel, police and the special higher police (Tokkō Keisatsu). In the Showa-I period THE one law which became the focus of the postwar political opposition was the PPL and the ramifications of its revisions (including the death penalty), its expanded interpretations and the brutality of its enforcement. By 1945, *sendō* had become thoroughly embedded in the Japanese criminal justice system.

The Showa Period-II, 1945+. The first thing that should be noted in the postwar period was that all the above laws except two did not survive Occupation scrutiny and the Japanese government was instructed to abolish these laws. The two laws that continued into the postwar periods concerned the 1884 law on explosives and the law on violating tax laws which included the prohibition to incite others not to pay taxes. In addition, the years since 1945, the so-called postwar democratic years, saw a burdgeoning use of *sendō* in a variety of laws in contrast to the prewar period. While, in the prewar years, *sendō* was

henran). *Kokusei* in this case was broadly interpreted to include the national polity (*kokutai*), the established governmental structure and basic national policies, including planning, plotting, consulting, instigation and incitement to commit these crimes; 3) destruction of buildings and facilities or obstruction of services provided by the postal services, electricity, gas, wartime industries, etc.

This law was one of three laws (the other two special laws were concerned with civil affairs and streamlined structure of the courts and the more restrictive and expeditious handling of court cases) which, as a group, were described as the most epoch making legal legislation since the beginning of modern Japan and with a concomitant impact on the legal system and customs. (Isobe 112) The revision of the 1942 law consisted only of four articles, all involved in broadening and strengthening article 7 about activities that could be interpreted to impinge on criticizing the national structure and polity and policies. Both Houses met many times in committee, subcommittee meetings and discussion groups where these revisions were heatedly debated (*hakunetsu-teki ni*) especially those concerning the possible abuse of the authorities given to the security forces through these revisions; depending on how these articles were implemented, Diet members's motives, patriotism, etc might be challenged, if they voiced concerns about the conduct of the war. Or was this law really intended to be a control law against ultra-rightwing organizations which were, of course, denied by the government. PM Tōjō and other Ministers assured them, of course, that there would never be any such abuse of authority and that the judicial police must act under the supervision, orders and direction of a prosecutor who, in turn, must obtain the approval of the actions to be taken up through all levels of prosecutorial responsibility up to and including the Minister of Justice. (Imoto 877–886) aimed, in the main, at *sendō* for political purposes involving social stability, since 1945 *sendō* was used in laws making it a crime to incite others to:

- not sell the required food to the government when food was in drastic short supply during the early postwar years
- violate national civil services regulations
- violate local civil service regulations
- violate prohibitions for labor unions and employees to conduct any actions which would damage the normal operations of businesses
- not pay taxes, not to submit requisite tax papers
- violate the elections law, e.g. extortion, bringing weapons into the polling place, attacking people and facilities involved in elections
- take actions to violate various articles of the CC, e.g. riots, arson, overturning trains, murder, etc.
- gather illegally information concerning national security, releasing it to inappropriate persons in order to harm the nation (This stemmed from the USJ security treaty)
- collect U.S. military secrets and leak them to others in order to harm the interests of the U.S. (This also stems from the USJ security treaty)
- provide education to students in the compulsory education schools by using a particular organization whose members are mainly teachers (meaning the Japan Teachers Union) to support and enhance or oppose a specific political party and its political program
- violate the narcotics control law and publicly incite the abuse of the use of controlled substances and psychotropic drugs.

These laws were enacted by the Diet between 1945 and 1952 under Occupation tutelage (except the school neutrality law was enacted in 1954 and the drug related law in 1991). It is more than a little significant that *sendō* was made a crime in all these laws, but *sendō* was not made a crime under the basic criminal code. When the government was challenged in the Diet that the basic criminal code did not include *sendō* as a crime, the response was always one must not tamper lightly with the basic criminal code just to include *sendō* as a crime—although a proposed but not enacted1940 CC revision did include *sendō*. This dismissal always deepened the suspicions of the political opposition. While I have not studied the legislative history of each and every one of these postwar laws containing sendō, I am unaware of any vigorous political opposition to the inclusion of *sendō* in these postwar laws.[14]

[14] The following laws contain the term "*sendō*":

Meiji period, 1868–1911
1884. Bakuhatsubutsu Torishimari Bassoku (Penalties concerning the handling of explosives), Dajōkan Fukoku Law 32, article 4 (32:4).
1893. Shuppan-hō (Publications Law), 15:16.
1900. Kokuzei Hansoku Torishishimari-hō (Law to control violations of the tax law), 67:27.
1900. Chian Keisatsu-hō (Peace Police Law), 36:9.2.
1909. Shimbunshi-hō (Newspaper Law), 41:21, 37.

Taisho period, 1912–1925
1917. Seigan-rei (Ordinance concerning Appeals), Imperial Decree (Chokurei) 37:17.
1922. Kageki Shakai Undō Torishimari hōan (Draft law for controlling radical social movements, submitted by the government 2/18/1922, no articles on *sendō* included.
1922. Ditto. Passed by House of Peers (3/24/1922) but failed in House of Representatives. No articles on *sendō* included.
1923. Chian Iji no tame ni suru Bassoku ni kansuru ken (Penalties concerning the maintenance of internal security). Imperial Decree 403 (9/9/1923), one article only, *sendō* included. Also known as Chian Iji-rei.
1925. Chian Iji-hō (Peace Preservation Law), 46:3, 4.
1925. Shōgiin Giin Senkyo-hō (Election Law for the House of Representatives), 47:125.

Showa-I period, 1926–1945
1926. Rōdō Sōgi Chōtei-hō (Law for the Conciliation of Labor Disputes), 57:19.
1937. Gunki Hogo-hō (Law to Protect Military Secrets), 72:16.2, 17.
1941. Kokubō Hoan-hō (National Defense Preservation Law), 49:12.2, 12.4.
1940. Keihō Kaisei Kari'an (Draft Revision of the Criminal Code), article 241
1941. Chian Iji-hō (Peace Preservation Law), 54:5, 6, 11, 12.
1941. Senji Hanzai Shobatsu no Tokurei ni kansuru Hōritsu (Law concerning the Punishment of Wartime Crimes), 98.
1942. Senji Keiji Tokubetsu-hō (Special Wartime Criminal Law), 64:7.1.4.
1943. Senji Keiji Tokubetsu-hō (Special Wartime Criminal Law), 58:7.3.

Showa-II period, 1945–1989
1918. Bakuhatsubutsu Torishimari Bassoku, 34:4.
1946. Shokuryō Kinkyū Sochi-rei (Emergency Order concerning Food), Imperial Decree (Chokurei), 86:11.
1947. Kokka Kōmuin-hō (Law concerning National Civil Service Employees), 120:98, 110.1.17.
1947. Kokuzei Hansoku Torishimari-hō (Law concerning the Payment of Taxes), 107:22.
1948. Kōkyō Kigyōtai Rōdō Kankei-hō (Law concerning Labor and Public Enterprises), 257:17–18.
1949. Hikiagesha no Chitsujo Hoji ni kansuru Seirei (Cabinet Ordinance concerning the maintenance of order among repatriates, Cabinet Ordinance 300)
1950. Chihōzei-hō (Local taxes), 226:21.1.
1950. Kōshoku Senkyo-hō (Election Law for Public Office), 100:234.
1950. Chihō Kōmuin-hō (Law concerning local government employees), 61:4.
1952. Keiji Tokubetsu-hō (Special Criminal Law [under U.S-Japan Security Treaty]), 138:7.2.
1952. Hakai Katsudō Bōshi-hō (Subversive Activities Prevention Law), 240:38, 39, 40.
1954. Gimu Kyōiku Sho-Gakkō ni okeru Kyōiku no Seiji-teki Chūritsū no Kakuho ni kansuru Rinji Sochi-hō (A temporary law concerning the maintenance of political neutrality in grade school education), 157:3.

In the originally enacted form, the PPL contained only two references to *sendō*; in the 1941 revision of the PPL, *sendō* was mentioned four times. The Diet admonished the government not to enlarge upon the interpretation of the PPL; this was completely disregarded. Many friends, relatives and associates of the political opposition suffered grievously under the PPL, some suffered themselves. Based on this short history and experience, their determination to oppose the SAPL is wholly understandable; they must take a stand opposing the SAPL as a matter of self-respect. Use of *sendō* had become well established in prewar legislation and deeply embedded in the legal thinking of the prewar Japanese government in the maintenance of public security. Since the people who were well acquainted with this tradition were deeply involved themselves in creating the SAPL, it would be unusual for them not to make *sendō* an absolutely must inclusion in the SAPL. In this sense, the inclusion of *sendō* in SAPL was not a break with the past by any means in postwar "democratic Japan" but merely part of a continuum from prewar Japan.

Scenarios and the SAPL. In a vain attempt to clarify and pinpoint how the SAPL might be implemented, what certain terms and phrases might mean in implementing the SAPL, Committee members spent much time, framing many scenarios for the government witnesses to answer. Whether this sparring was useful or not remains to be seen but it does indicate the polite and seldom emotionally expressed distrust that pervaded among the opposition Committee members. Because of space limitations, only a summary description of these scenarios can be given: opposition to planned road construction, to raising electricity rates, to lifting rice controls, to officially adopted educational policies by a local PTA, against the imposition of a military draft policy, against the Emperor/Tennō system. Whether the SAPL might be invoked was ambiguous and seemed to revolve around the legitimacy of the existing policies, the nature of the protest, individual, organizational, whether it resulted in police intervention and degree

1954. Nichi-Bei Sōgo Bōei Enjo Kyōtei tō ni tomonau Himitsu Hogo-hō (Secrets Protection Law stemming from the U.S.-Japan Security Treaty), 166:5.

Heisei period, 1989–

1991. Mayaku oyobi Kō-Seishinyaku Torishimari tō no tokurei tō ni kansuru Hōritsu (Law for the Control of Narcotics and Psychotropic Drugs and other substances), 94:9.

of scuffling between police and protestors and the legitimacy of the office making the presumed policies. If printed materials advocating resistance to taking of land by eminent domain to enable Japanese military collaboration with the U.S. were distributed, this would probably result in charges of incitement and instigation. Would printing materials merely advocating insurrection and revolution be a violation of the SAPL? No if they remained passively available; yes, if the intent was to facilitate the realization of such a revolution, a find line indeed. Could one be guilty, even though one did not participate in a riot. Yes, if one participated in a vote to conduct a riot which was passed, but did not participate in the riot, one would be guilty of plotting with others to riot. Clashes involving police and union members over labor demonstrations and strikes would not normally come under SAPL but if the clashes involved interference with official police duties then they would. Poles holding placards would not normally be regarded as dangerous weapons but if sharpened and used as spears in clashes with the police then the SAPL would apply. What about so-called "political riots/demonstrations" conducted by labor unions, or federations of labor unions? The government at the national or local level did not move against labor unions during the several strike waves but depending on how narrow or broad a definition were used, unions could be targeted by the SAPL. If a union decided to proceed with a demonstration knowing or expecting that its actions would potentially violate the SAPL it could be charged. A speech to hold a rally at the Plaza to celebrate May would not violate the SAPL, it would not be incitement; but a speech at the rally urging the participants to threaten and riot would be a violation. If the march toward the Plaza went by the Liberal Party headquarters and a fiery speaker denounced the existing government and the marchers physically attacked this building, then that person(s) would be violating the SAPL and would be charged for incitement leading to arson and rioting. But if only a denouncement of the government was voiced without incitement to arson and rioting, such a speech would not constitute incitement. The AG admonishingly and ominously commented that "freedom must not be abused, threatening national stability".

Possession and Role of Written Materials. According to article 3.1.2, the possession of "Written materials and designs" (*bunsho, zuga*) for certain purposes, e.g. with the purpose of facilitating the realization of criminal acts, or possessing them for the purpose of distributing them, publicly displaying them would come under the SAPL. SIB's Yoshikawa regarded the broad distribution of written materials as far more dangerous in committing the crime of incitement than when a person makes a speech inciting the audience to commit a particular criminal act (4/26:27, 5/12:15). If this is so, then why not try to prevent the planning, printing and distribution before the incitement is made. To which both Yoshikawa and Seki explained that

> the government felt it was not necessary and not appropriate to go that far in trying to control such activities.

This response was a back-handed way of implying that taking such action would be uncomfortably close to the re-creation of a prewar type censorship system (4/26:27) and resurrection of an approach used under the PPL system.

Possession of one flyer is not a violation, but two or more could be. A flyer in my pocket to pass around (*kairan-suru*) to my colleagues would not be a violation of distribution (5/10:9).

Ishikawa raised the philosophical issue as to whether if one asserted the "inevitability" of the rise of the proletariat with the use of force to reform the social structure which exploits this group would or would not that action be subject to the SAPL. Seki opined that there was a difference between what is inevitable and advocating the appropriateness of an action, i.e. advocating the inevitability would not violate the SAPL, but advocating the appropriateness of specific presumably violent action(s) could violate the SAPL. While this exchange might appear to be too convoluted, it was a real potential issue in light of how the political philosophy debate by the leftwing was actually conducted in Japan (4/28:12).

An uneasy dialogue took place (5/9) between Yoshikawa and Seki, and Satake about when advocating a revolution was not an incitement. Yoshikawa: If some written materials merely advocated that the realization of revolution in Japan would be appropriate, necessary and inevitable, such materials would not be guilty of violating the SAPL.

Satake: So long as you are DG of the SIB, I would have confidence but you will not always be the DG. In the past, before the war, a professor of the University of Tokyo announced that through the inevitable evolution of mankind, human society will become as one, without the need for government, rulers, thus introducing Kuropotkin's anarchist ideas. But this became a criminal case because it appeared to deny the legitimacy of the existing government, especially the Emperor, its structure and a disturbance to the public peace and he was convicted. This legal precedent is still on the books and legally effective. This clause in article 3 would deny freedom of academic research and provide the basis for a very broad interpretation of Article 3 and would result in the denial of freedom of research and scholarly pursuits. Seki: However, in order for such actions to come under the purview of article 3, they must facilitate the realization of an action, or a person must have had this purpose or determination (*iyoku*) in mind when he had these materials in his possession. It is a necessary condition that these materials must clearly indicate that such a revolution was necessary and appropriate and inevitable. Thus there are two stages to this consideration. SAPL article 3 would not be invoked unless it could be shown that this person had the "intention" (*ito*) to facilitate the occurrence of a revolution in Japan and took action to express this intent or the book discussed, advocated the need for and propriety of an insurrection. (Yoshikawa 6/16:9)

Another related philosophical issue concerned the meaning of "actions to facilitate, support, or oppose political principles and programs" in article 3.1.2. Seki explained that the term, "political principles and programs" was "borrowed" from the Political Funds Control Law. Political principles refers to various "isms", e.g. capitalism, communism, parliamentary government, anarchism, socialism, dictatorship, basic political theories. Political programs refer to price controls, the gold standard, agricultural land reform, termination of interest payments on war bonds, etc. This discussion then involved the definition of "political": decisions made by the state to express its will. Administrative actions would be actions taken by the government to carry out these political decisions. At a later hearing on May 9, 1952, Inomata inquired whether the borrowed phrase from another law which now constituted an element in article 3.2 in framing a potential violation of the SAPL, played a similar role in the Political Funds Control Law. The government admitted that it knew of no such legal cases nor legal theories about the use of this phrase. Inomata sharply criticized the government for claiming that in drafting article 3 of the SAPL in particular, ONLY language from well established legal precedents or legal theories would be used. Therefore, since these precedents and theories do not exist, the government has used extremely new language to describe the constituent elements of an SAPL offense without legal precedent or theoretical legal underpinnings. It is this aspect, the novel use of legal language without precedent that is a cause, one of many, of great anxieties. (5/9:10)[15]

Inomata insistently pursued the government on interpreting "To facilitate, support or oppose political principles and programs..." as stipulated in Article 3 as part of the effort to control organizations and individuals. In the explanatory materials (*kaisetsusho*) provided by the government to committee members, the concept of violent destructive activities would be used for taking administrative action against organizations not criminal action as would be taken against individuals. While Inomata agreed with this interpretation, he pointed out that it was a vague term and phrase and could not be construed to be a viable condition for a criminal offense. Yet when it comes to applying penalties for a criminal offense committed by an individual, he observed that this very phrase was cited in Articles 38 and 39 as the basis for such penalties against individuals:

> This is where the fraud occurs: while this term supposedly applies to administrative action, by the government's own admission, as soon as penalties are to applied to individuals this vague phrase is used and invoked.... Furthermore, the penalties for such political actions are increased substantially from, for example, three years to five years. (5/9:7–8)

To which, Satō Tatsuo, the DG Bureau of Legal Opinions (Hōsei Iken Chōkan under the AG, gave a pained response:

> ...as to legal form, yes, I agree, as a personal opinion, with your observation about the SAPL. In order to make it more understandable all the relevant articles and clauses concerning administrative action and criminal offenses should be clearly enumerated in the SAPL but this may create confusion for the courts as to which clauses to refer to in a particular case. Please accept, tolerate (*gaman shite*) the way the SAPL has been

[15] This law (Seiji Shikin Kisei-hō in Japanese) was promulgated on June 29, 1948 as law 194. It was an attempt to prevent, ameliorate, rampant political corruption in financing political parties and politics in the early chaotic postwar years. Article 3 defined a political party and an association (*kyōkai*) and other organizations or candidates as those which "push forward (*suishin*), support or oppose political principles or programs (*seijijō no shugi moshikuwa shisaku*), basically identical language to that used in the draft SAPL.

> structured by referencing articles in the Criminal Code as somehow or other achieving this objective (*magari narinimo jitsugen shita*). (5/9:8)

Toward the end of the HofR Committee hearings, Inomata again raised the issue of what is a "political program" (*shisaku*). Would opposition to the proposed SAPL and revision of the labor union laws be included under article 3's political programs. Seki: Yes, they would be regarded as a government political program (5/13:5)—by implication depending on the methods used to oppose the SAPL itself could result in being in violation of article 3. The issue of the mere "possession of written materials" became one of the more important issues in the HofC debates to the extent that the government was forced to accept a major revision of this clause in the final HofC draft.

Broad and Ambiguous Scope of Article 3. In an attempt to show how incredibly broad the coverage of Article 3 was in reality, Inomata Kōzō, SDP-L, created the following scenario: A cultural commentator believed that revisions of the Constitution and the SAPL were completely unacceptable. Political forces in the Diet were too weak so he decided that unions should take direct action for this purpose. This commentator came to Inomata with these ideas. Agreeing with his ideas, he (Inomata) decided to discuss these ideas with the leadership (*kambu*) of the unions which, in turn, took these ideas to a meeting of the leaders which decided to hold a general meeting at the People's/Imperial Plaza. There they shouted violently against the police, and some even shouted they should be killed, their facilities burned and it reached a point where peace of the vicinity was now disturbed. What was the responsibility of the parties concerned beginning with the commentator?

Seki politely countered with his somewhat revised scenario that if a cultural commentator came to Inomata and declared that the SAPL was a very terrible law but because of the intransigence of the majority it is passed by the Diet. Now this is going against the grain of civilization, workers rights, labor unions rights will be trampled. Let us go to the Plaza and protest. So they do and those words of opposition and anger were uttered. If the incident ended there, according to Seki, there would be no violations of article 3.1.1 concerning insurrection nor article 3.1.2 concerning rioting (*sōjō*) under the SAPL because the meeting nor shouting did not result in specific action. But if there was an assault or if the threatening words were actually said to the threatened party, then charges of assault and threats would be made against those persons under the SAPL. (5/9:11–12)

After listening to the hearings, even Tajima Yoshifumi of the majority Liberal Party concluded that

> ... incitement and programs (*shisaku*) may perhaps not be vague as legal concepts, but from the general populace's point of view they are vague. This is where the focal point in the debate about the SAPL is to be found (5/12:15).

Seki somewhat candidly confirmed the astonishing breadth of coverage of article 3:

> ... The first phrase in article 3.1.1.2 applies to any kind of instigation or incitement in whatever form, orally or through materials. In this sense it is very broad coverage (5/12:16).

Yoshida Hōsei, SDP-L in the HofC, re-emphasized this point by stating the "... the multiplicity of crimes that could be envisioned under the SAPL through these combinations and permutations is so great that once the PSIA had decided to focus on an organization, it could somehow find the grounds to seek control of this organization through the PSEC. (6/10:1–3) It was repeatedly asserted that the new concepts in the SAPL undermine and destroy the fundamental concepts of the CC. (6/18:23)

A former Justice Minister, Hitotsumatsu Sadakichi, now in the HofC and member of the Committee, emphasized that a law must be understood by the people: in the minds of the people, it is difficult to understand and accept the idea that when a person incites someone or a crowd (an indeterminate group) is incited to commit a crime but no crime is committed, for that person, the inciter, to be punished as proposed in the SAPL. The people would accept and understand if an inciter was successful and crimes committed then he should be punished. Nakayama Fukuzō, who gave the final summary in the HofC, called the SAPL definitions extremely vague. (*aimai moko*) Since the government had made both incitement and instigation both independent crimes, there was much argumentation on how to differentiate these two slippery concepts without much success. For example, Kiyohara Kunikazu, DG/Criminal Affairs Administration, incitement contributes to a gradually eroding proper sense of neutral judgment, and becomes a mass crime (*taishū hanzai*); in incitement an appeal to emotions is made to loosen a moral judgment. "To facilitate the materialization of a political program..." is very vague insisted Hori

Makoto (SDP-L); DG Yoshikawa maintained that such vagueness is inevitable under the circumstances but an indictment must be based "on concrete evidence". (5/31/:16) To make matters a bit more vague, DG Yoshikawa explained that if an inciter "incited a group" but that group did not commit a crime, that person would be charged for incitement and could also be charged for instigation if the inciter/persuader recognized these people. (6/13:13) The tangle in interpreting *kyōsa/sendō* is quite evident.

Let us conclude this subsection on article 3 with Ōnishi Masao's understated comment (Minshutō), that this article provides a loop hole for enormous abuse by security officials who, under their own interpretation of the SAPL could charge a person for violation of article 3; he feared for the future of Japan under these circumstances and maintained that this clause should be carefully considered and cannot be accepted on face value as interpreted (5/8:12–15).

4. *Articles 4 and 6. Control of Destructive Organizations*

> **Article 4**. Limitations on Organizational Activities
> 4.1. The PSEC may impose on organizations, which have conducted violent destructive activities as activities of that organization (*dantai no katsudō toshite*), if there is sufficient reason to recognize that these activities may be continued or repeated or that there is a clear concern (*osore*) that these violent destructive activities will be carried out in the future as activities of that organization, one or more of the following measures; those measures may not exceed that which would be necessary and appropriate to remove that concern.
> 4.1.1. When the said violent destructive activities took place at or during mass demonstrations (*shūdan ji'i undō*), collective marches (*shūdan kōshin*) or at public meetings (*kōkai no shūkai*), the PSEC may impose a prohibition of these activities of up to six months specifying the time and place of this prohibition.
> 4.1.2. When the said violent destructive activities occurred through that organization's organ of publication (which is continuously published by that organization to advocate, inform or propagandize its activities) the PSEC may impose a ban of up to six months to print, distribute, or to possess this publication for the purpose of distribution.
> 4.1.3. The PSEC may impose a prohibition of up to six months on those officers (representatives, leaders/*shukansha* or anyone else who had been involved in the administration of that organization) and members who were involved in these violent destructive activities, any actions which may be taken on behalf of this organization.
> 4.2. After the above measures have taken effect, no person may, as an officer or member of the affected organization, take any actions

mentioned above in article 4.1.3, take any actions which would be against the purpose of the [above-mentioned restrictive] actions. However, this restriction would not apply to those actions which would ordinarily be necessary in preparing a legal appeal of this decision.

Article 6. Designation of Disbandment
6.1. The PSEC may designate organizations described below for disbandment; but this action will be limited to those organizations if there is sufficient reason to recognize that these activities may be continued or repeated or that there is a clear concern (*osore*) that these violent destructive activities will be carried out in the future as activities of that organization, or if it recognized that through the [restrictive] measures mentioned in article 4.1 the concern [about continuing violent destructive activities] cannot be effectively eliminated.
6.1.1. Organizations which have conducted violent destructive activities as activities of that organization as mentioned in article 3.1.1.
6.1.2. Organizations which have conducted violent destructive activities as mentioned in article 3.1.2.1–10, or began undertaking these actions but did not carry them out, or instigated or incited others to commit these actions.
6.1.3. Organizations which conducted violent destructive activities even after restrictive measures mentioned in article 4.1 were imposed on them.

Articles 4 and 6 specify the kinds and gradations of controls, limitations and restrictions that may be imposed by the PSEC on organizations which conduct illegal actions specified in article 3. Such organizations may be banned from holding public meetings, conducting demonstrations, marches, rallies, publishing the organization's journal or its officers may be prohibited from conducting the organization's business up to disbandment of the organization. An organization may be disbanded, IF there is a sufficient reason to believe or there is a concern or fear that this organization will repeat these activities in the future. These limitations will be imposed on these organizations by the PSEC to the extent that the PSEC believes it is appropriate to prevent further recurrence of the specific illegal violent destructive activities. If an organization restricted under article 4.1 continues to conduct violent destructive activities, i.e. it has gone beyond speculation and judgment about future possible action, then it may be ordered disbanded (5/13:2–3).

Actions taken against organizations for violating the articles in the SAPL were not regarded as criminal penalties but administrative actions to control an organization, also called a "security [control] action" (*hoan sochi* by DG Yoshikawa 5/19:16). Drafter Seki commented that the SAPL does not recognize that an organization commits a criminal offense, an individual commits a criminal offense. (5/31:10) It would be possible to take into account violent destructive actions taken by an organization, even before the enactment of the SAPL and those actions could be the first cause (*dai-ichiji no gen'in*) in deciding whether violations of article 3 have been committed by that organization (4/26:27). It would be possible that the first instance of violent destructive activities would not be the target of control but would trigger an investigation with its past actions considered as part of a possible pattern of activity. This rather "flexible attitude" stemmed from Constitutional considerations about an organization's right to association. This approach may appear initially as weak but once an organization had committed such violent activities, then all future administrative actions taken against this organization would take into account this historical record. Subsequently a judgement would have to be made whether this first violent destructive activity might be continued (*keizoku-suru*) and/or will be repeated (*hampuku-suru*) in the future. In making such an assessment, the past activities of the organization before the SAPL became effective would be taken into account. This retroactive practice is in line with existing legal precedents concerning administrative action, and the possibility of continuous or repeated use of such destructive activities would have to occur after the SAPL has come into effect (5/12:3–4). When pressed as to how one would make a judgment about the probability of continuous or repetitive activities, Seki explained that the criteria would be understandable "by the man-on-the-street", a generally understood rational and reasonable, healthy and stable community standard (*gōri-teki na, kenzen na shakai tsūnen*). What then would provide sufficient evidence that there is a clear probability/fear (*osore*) that an organization would repeat its violent destructive activities: it does not change its program, that its new programs even advocate the same or more violent actions. Several laws, such as the Youth Law (Shōnen-hō), fire prevention law, mining safety law, each contain similar provisions like the SAPL that are concerned with administrative actions involving the probabilities of future repetitive actions. In the end, Seki begged off further discussion on the attempt to define the conditions under which continuous and repetitive actions would be applicable because he feared that whatever he might say in a definitive manner (*dantei-teki na go-henji*) might be misunderstood and misconstrued. (5/8:18)[16]

Publication Organ. In article 4, a publication of an organization (*kikan shishi*) is defined as a publication which is continuously (*keizoku-teki*) published by the organization, advocates, informs (*tsūhō*) its readers and propagandizes its policies, objectives, principles and programs. This publication needs to be mechanically reproduced, needs to be published more than once, that it shows it has the intention of being published continuously but it does not need to have been published at a given moment in time for it to be regarded as an organ (5/12:2). An ordinary daily newspaper reporting the news would not be regarded as such a publication but if this newspaper did advocate certain objectives, policies, programs on a continuous basis, it could be regarded as an organ of an organization. Each case must be separately decided. In so far as newspapers editorializing for or against particular political policies they could be regarded as publications under the SAPL but, in reality, it is difficult to imagine that such editorials would advocate violent destructive activities or that such activities would result directly from such opinions; thus, in reality, newspapers would not be looked upon as publications under the SAPL. Ōnishi Masao of the Democratic Party commented:

> that is why there is anxiety among the people about this law because the government cannot categorically say that these daily newspapers would not be the targets of the SAPL (5/12:2).

If political party A decides to create a company to publish a publication which, in essence is an organ of the party, or whether an individual may publish such an organ, then if it has to be banned what is the target which will be the object of this ban, the party, the company or the individual. A determination would have to be made whether the company or organization sponsoring this publication has a sufficiently close enough tie with the party or not, or whether it is of itself independent from the party. If an individual is publishing this publication and that person does not have a direct link to the company or the party, then the activities of this person would probably not be

[16] Article 5 was not discussed because it stipulated the obvious, that officers and members of an organization controlled under article 4 may not take any actions to obviate, evade, or circumvent the restrictions placed on it.

regarded as "organizational activities". The publication of a subsidiary/auxiliary organization (*gaikaku dantai*) would not normally be regarded as the organ of the central organization (5/12:3). Based on the above there appears to be some confusion and lack of clarity in the interpretation of the SAPL.

Disbandment of an Organization (Article 6). The effective date for "disbandment" would be the date of the order issued by the PSEC designating such a dissolution. "In order for an organization of people to be dissolved would, in the final analysis, involve the use of force in a compulsory manner" (*jitsuryoku-teki na kyōsei*). To act in this way, serious constitutional considerations must be taken into account.... From the day of effectiveness, all officers and members of the designated organization may not conduct any business or take any actions on behalf of this organization, except those actions necessary to appeal this decision to the courts and to take steps themselves (*jishu-teki ni*) to dispose of organizational properties.... These limitations were imposed in order that the minimum amount of control will be taken within the spirit of the Constitution.... Some might says these specified steps are somewhat weak and diluted but they were specified in this way to assure the protection of human rights under the Constitution (5/12:14–15).

5. *Articles 37–43 Penalties against Individuals.* SAPL was touted as the law whose primary target were destructive organizations and devoted two articles to various kinds of restrictions that may be imposed on such organizations. In contrast, the penalties to be imposed upon individuals take up several articles. Furthermore, the descriptions of the offenses in these articles use, to a large extent, the words and phrases used in Article 3 delineating illegal acts and also importantly imposed substantially stiffer jail sentences on individuals who violated the SAPL by supplementing/augmenting the CC in the SAPL by adding on several more years for a similar crime under the CC. For example, according to article 39 individuals would be punished for incitement as an independent crime, if they incited people to crimes mentioned in article 106 of the Criminal Code. What if a crime is incited by one person, who instigates another, who instigates another. SIB's Yoshikawa replied that through the accomplice concept (*kyōhan*) under the criminal code would apply in this case (5/13:5).

SDP-L's Inomata Kōzō pointed out that when persons take certain actions "in order to support, advance or oppose political principles or policies" they would receive a heavier sentence, three more years, than those in the criminal code for similar acts. This, he said, was the cause for one of the basic suspicions that the opposition has toward the SAPL, that through such heavier penalties, the "ruling class expects to entrench itself and strengthen its ruling position". To which AG Kimura responded that under a democratic system of government, political activities are a critical element in its success, thus such activities must be carefully controlled from the public security point of view and should be considered quite differently from ordinary criminal acts. The penalties articles in the SAPL most clearly reveal the SAPL was a law attempting to define and control "political crimes".

6. *The Public Security Examination Commission.* The PSEC was probably the second most discussed issue throughout the hearings. This is quite understandable since with its quasi-judicial powers, it would have a potential life and death control over selected political organizations designated as violent destructive organizations. Its authority, degree of independence, composition, appointment of Commissioners, even the fundamental issue of the Constitutionality of PSEC and its decisions were questioned by many Committee members, especially in the HofC committee.

Membership. The government draft bill as originally submitted to the Diet stipulated that the names of PSEC members would be submitted to the Diet by the Attorney General. This drew the ire even of the governing Liberal Party when Tajima Yoshifumi accused the government of demeaning the Diet by not having such personnel recommendations not made in the name of the PM. One of the technical changes made by HofR was to revise this venue to the PM. In contrast, a duly appointed member of PSEC could be removed without the approval of the Diet; thus, in theory a recalcitrant or uncooperative PSEC member could be removed for political reasons. Undoubtedly, there would be a political price to pay in the government's relations with the Diet if such arbitrary actions were taken. The membership was to be balanced: not having a majority from one political party, having a labor representative, and other such factors in order to achieve a balanced decision which will be convincingly acceptable to all concerned.

PSEC As an Outer Bureau. As an Outer Bureau under the AG, it was asserted that the PSEC could hardly be "independent" of the AG. This was emphasized since the PSEC as proposed would be supervised through the office of the AG, specifically the general affairs section of the Minister's Secretariat. The government maintained that—with no intention of revising this arrangement—the PSEC should be under the AG since it would be an extension of the law enforcement responsibilities of the AG and could achieve independence and be removed from political influences even under the proposed arrangement as an Outer Bureau. (5/12:21) In bureaucratic terms, "an Outer Bureau" is, by definition not the mainstream of the AG's office/Ministry of Justice, thus a slightly lower rank as we shall see under implementation in the Conclusion. (For a discussion of the concept of an Outer Bureau see Gaikyoku in Chapter 3)

Constitutionality of PSEC. Article 76 of the 1947 Constitution declares that

1. The whole judiciary power is vested in a Supreme Court and in such inferior courts as established by law
2. No special court (*tokubetsu saibansho*) shall be established, nor shall any organ or agency of the Executive be given final judicial power.
3. All judges shall be independent in the exercise of their conscience and be bound by only by this Constitution and the laws.

Is the PSEC, as described by the AG, Seki and Yoshikawa, a quasi-judicial commission in the executive branch under the jurisdiction of the AG with the power of life and death of an organization a special court as described above? The constitutional dialog on this topic was, in the main, between the opposition members and a senior official of the Supreme Court system—a justice of the Supreme Court could not comment on an hypothetical issue not before the Court. Under prodding from Committee members, Suzuki Chūichi, Actg DG/Supreme Court Administration, explained that

> ...In the past, administrative agencies in the executive branch were in a superior position (*yōi*) and, except in rare cases, administrative actions taken by these agencies could not be challenged. Those rare cases where they were challenged were taken to the administrative court (*gyōsei saibansho*) not to the courts. In the postwar years this principle was changed so that administrative actions could be challenged in the regular courts. This did not mean that the courts could now guide and order (*shiki meirei*) the administrative agencies. The courts would pass

> judgment on whether a particular instance was in accordance with the law. Administrative agencies and actions must, while naturally staying within the law, consider how the public interest (*kōeki*) of the nation may be advanced, how security may be advanced.... An administrative action may be taken against a company but the courts have a role in deciding if a company had been properly ordered to disband. This kind of case is somewhat similar to disbandment as envisioned in the SAPL. Based on history, tradition, legislative policy some cases are assigned to administrative agencies, others are assigned to the courts. Based on this line of thinking, it might be said that the administrative agency [the PSEC] would be making an initial determinations so to speak, a preliminary hearing (*zenshin-teki na*)—earlier the government had already referred to PSEC decisions in this way—then the courts would make a post facto assessment. This arrangement would not result in a reduction, nor detract from the responsibilities and authority of the courts.... *From the point of the Constitution, to create an administrative agency which would make a decision like the [prewar] administrative courts, even though that decision could be regarded only as a preliminary hearing not a final decision (shūshin) it would be contrary to the spirit of the Constitution...to create an organization which would appear to be resurrecting the old administrative court even though it acted merely as a preliminary hearing would appear to be unconstitutional.* (Emphasis added) (5/25:8–10)

The "family court" was challenged as a "special court" under Article 76 of the Constitution asserting thereby that its decisions were invalid but the Supreme Court decided that this court was properly constituted as part of the court system and its decisions valid. Under the 1947 Constitution, the administrative courts permitted under the Meiji Constitution are included as part of the prohibited "special courts" mentioned in Article 76 of the new Constitution and judicial authority if extended to judgements made by administrative agencies. Judicial decisions taken by administrative agencies (*gyōsei kikan ni yoru saiban*) are not being denied or rejected but rather would be regarded as an initial/preliminary hearing (*zenshin*)—except that the Supreme Court decisions concerning the interpretation of article 10 in the Gyōsei Jiken Soshō Tokurei-hō seem to give a much different impression (see later discussion of this subject in this chapter). Only one case in 50+ years was brought by the PSIA to the PSEC for action; the PSEC dismissed the government's case and the government did not appeal this decision to the courts. Thus, the constitutionality of PSEC remains moot. To the best of my knowledge, there has not been any other case that has come before the Supreme Court concerning an administrative agency similar to the PSEC in function and authority. In conclusion, in light of the above dialog, the constitutionality of the PSEC is highly questionable.[17]

PSEC Decisions. The PSEC could order an action to be taken against an organization after the PSIA had first submitted a recommendation to the PSEC; it considered only control actions against organizations; individual violations of the SAPL would be taken to the courts by prosecutors as in a regular criminal case. Initially, the government's thinking was that the PSEC would conduct a paper analysis, evaluation and assessment (*shomen shinsa*) of evidence, statements, analysis, etc as provided by the PSIA to support its recommendations to the PSEC without further investigations by PSEC; this attitude effectively reflects those of the Japanese national bureaucracy that once it had conducted its analysis, investigation, interviewing, gathering of all necessary evidence, how could there be a need for the PSEC (or any other body receiving such reports and recommendations) to conduct its own necessarily smaller and limited additional research, questioning, etc especially after the government had marshaled its entire resources to prepare this definitive report and make its most reasoned recommendations. There is a built-in assumption and presumption well expressed by Satō Tatsuo:

> ...once the state's mind (*kuni no ishi*) has been decided, it shall not be changed or overturned unless circumstances are changed or there is a blemish or fault [in the research, recommendations] and PSEC decision (6/5:10).

If it believes it is necessary, PSEC may request the presence of and seek clarification (*shakumei*) and justification (*benkai*) from PSIA staff, from any of the persons who had been present at or as witnesses (*tachi'ai'nin*) to the hearings for the accused organization and others concerning a given case about any of the documents submitted (the PSIA document requesting PSEC action, the investigative report/*chōsho*, opinion report/*ikensho*). It may seek clarification from these

[17] The following references were used in preparing this subsection:
Higuchi Yōichi, et al., eds. Tokubetsu Saibansho no Kinshi, *Chūshaku Nihonkoku Kempō*. 2:1141–1145.
Mikazuki, Akira. Katei Saibansho e no Jinji Soshō Ikan no Shihō Seisaku-teki Igi, *Katei Saiban Geppō* 56:4 (4/2004):5–11.
Yaguchi, Toshiaki. Tokubetsu Saibansho, *Bessatsu Jurisuto* 131(10/1994):380–381.

persons about the case in point and other issues until it is satisfied that it has a thorough understanding of the issues (Seki: 5/13:1). But committee members remained unconvinced. Can "new evidence" not previously submitted by the accused organization and constituting part of the total package sent to the PSEC for the latter's action, be included in these materials on a "catch-up" basis? These materials may be included with the materials submitted by the hearing officer to the PSEC and their evidential value would be decided by the PSEC at its discretion (*jiyū shinshō*) (5/13:6).

Opponents maintained that such a critical issue as restricting a political organization should be handled through the courts. The government maintained stoutly that maintenance of internal security (*hoan-teki sochi*) was inherently the responsibility of the executive not the courts. If the accused did not accept the PSEC decision, then it could appeal its case to the courts. Seki gave several reasons for handling organization control measures: it was believed that the Cabinet should take full responsibility for the control of organizations as an administrative action; it was, thus, not necessary to use the court system for this purpose *in the first instance*. The initial planned restriction on PSEC's authority to conduct its own investigation was based, somewhat unconvincingly, on the need, the government said, to cut back and simplify administrative structures and limit the number of government officials. Presumably, it would be awkward to create yet another agency while at the same time, attempting to cut back on civil service employees. If the PSEC had authority to question witnesses, the need for the preparation of a report to the PSEC would be obviated and not necessary. Inomata noted that under normal civil and criminal procedures, evidence is submitted to the court and the issue is debated in front of the court. Under the SAPL, in a way, the so-called initial "court debate" takes place as a hearing by the hearing officer, compared to the preliminary hearing (*zenshin*) in the legal system.

The actions taken by the PSEC were described as "Administrative Actions" (*gyōsei sochi*), an action taken by an agency in the name of the government. In general, existing postwar laws specified that the agency which investigates an issue decides on administrative action which will be taken. There are hardly any instances under existing laws where these functions were separated into two parts as was being proposed by the SAPL. Because of the political importance and sensitivity of controlling organizations, it was believed that in order "to follow democratic principles" and avoid the concentration of authority in any one agency, avoid any semblance of unconstitutionality the responsibility for the investigative and requesting (*chōsa seikyū*) function and the responsibility for the decision (*kettei kikan*) as to whether the SAPL had been violated and restrictions and penalties to be imposed should be given to two separate and distinct agencies. These two "scaled-down" (*kansoka sareta*) agencies must conduct their responsibilities in a democratic and fair manner (5/8:3).

What would be the constitutional requirements in order to have an appropriate and fair treatment of such cases? 1) Before a disadvantageous action was taken against an organization, the latter must have had sufficient opportunity to explain and defend its position, and provide evidence on its behalf, 2) that these opinions, defense, and provision and submission must be handled in a fair manner, 3) in order to judge appropriateness or inappropriateness of administrative actions may be appealed to the courts. (5/9:15)

Kojima Yoshihide, a more liberal minded member of the Liberal Party, chided the government witnesses about the structure of the PSEC.

> When I was in involved in the universal suffrage movement [in the 1920s], said Kojima, we were taken by the police more than 60 times. Based on that experience, I know that the police writeup their reports in the way they want, from what they want to hear, what they want to see. They will read what was not even written; if it is disadvantageous to them they will not include it in their report. The DG/SIB will designate a hearing officer, but the investigation will be based on the assumption that the organization has violated the law. Can a fair report be prepared under these conditions? I fear the report will be skewed in favor of the SIB. He will assemble data and materials based on the premise that a request for controlling the organization will be made to the PSEC. Unless the PSEC is given the ability to make its own investigation, a fair report will not be prepared. Inevitably unfairness will creep in. (4/26:31)

Inomata at a hearing on May 9, 1952, called the SAPL approach a "complete fraud" (5/9:15). At the same hearing, Satake of the Shakai Kakushintō asserted that the PSEC was merely a rubber stamp committee, a perfunctory committee for public consumption (5/9:26). Seki countered that the PSIA report will be prepared based on hearings in the presence of the organization's five witnesses, and representatives from radio, TV and telecommunications following numerous stipulations in article 14. But Kojima caustically remarked that allowing witnesses (including lawyers for the organization) to be present at the hearings were merely deceptive stipulations giving the appearance of fairness. (4/26:32) Ōnishi Masao, a moderate conservative of the Minshutō was more caustic about the independence of the PSEC: It can only eat the meal served to it by the PSIA. The investigative agency (PSIA) is separate from the deciding agency (PSEC) but that is in form only; it cannot be expected that real democratic principles will be operational under these circumstances (5/12:7–8).

Seki greatly emphasized that the procedures that must be followed under the SAPL to control an organization up to disbandment are a most stringent set of rules in comparison to other administrative actions that are permitted under other laws. Even under the SAPL, he noted, that this administrative action is taken only after an action recommendation by the PSIA and reviewed and concurred in by the PSEC, quite unprecedented in Japanese law (5/8:24). The rationale for using administrative action against organizations appears to stem from the idea that after having investigated whether an organization may continue or repeat "violent destructive activities",

> the government must take necessary and swift action (*kinkyū yamu o ezaru sochi*) in order to maintain public security. This need stems from the very nature of the action that needs to be taken.... Those actions relating to the fundamentals of maintaining public security cannot be appropriately handled by the courts.... To place these two authorities, administrative action and the courts, in this juxtaposition is completely in line with spirit of the Constitution (5/12:14).

Seki was clearly stating that when a speedy, effective and decisive response was necessary, the most appropriate course was administrative action, not the slower and more deliberate speed of the courts. A further justification was that this approach upheld the basic constitutional principle of the separation of the powers: the maintenance of internal security and public welfare was, in the first instance, the distinct and clear responsibility of the executive branch—subject to subsequent court review if that was needed and appropriate. Because of the under-current of distrust, this approach was never accepted by the political opposition; obviously they felt a greater sense of fairness could be achieved by requiring the courts to be the first venue of action. Unsurprisingly, the government did not point out that this PSEC authority was unusual since the issue to be decided was control over politically motivated violent activities, a rather different kind of concern than just issuing some regulation by one of the executive agencies described below. The government was as emphatically insistent on its approach as was the opposition in its stance. Notwithstanding this haughty attitude, the draft SAPL was modified to allow the PSEC to conduct its own independent research and assessment, etc. as it felt was necessary.

Administrative Action (Gyōsei Shobun). The term "administrative actions" taken by government agencies was dismissed as a scholarly concept (*gakumon-jō no gainen*) to describe collectively the various kinds of governmental acts (*gyōsei kōi*) mentioned below. Such administrative actions could be taken by an agency of the national government and various levels of local governments in accordance with a specific law and the relationship between the two entities would not be equal, the government would be the primary authority; the action would not be a negotiation, not an action between equals, where one party would take the action specified and the government agency would not. Such actions as issuing orders, prohibitions, permits, exemptions, patents and trade marks, approvals would be regarded as administrative actions; government inspection of a company's finances, actions to collect statistical data, routing of roads would not be administrative actions. They must be actions taken in accordance with specific laws to achieve a specific administrative objective. Actions taken by public corporations, for example, would be considered administrative actions, e.g. Japan Tobacco Monopoly Corporation (Nihon Sembai Kōsha) regarding actions about cultivation of tobacco), actions by the Japan Housing Authority (Nihon Jōtaku Kōdan) concerning land use, imposition of fees set by the Shinrin Kaihatsu Kōdan (Forestry Development Public Corp), penalties established by the lawyers's association (Bengoshikai) and the Accountants Association (Benrishikai)—but actions by the PSEC were not cited as examples. It was also explained that some agencies could take administrative action "before the fact" (*jizen ni*) for security reasons: the Keisatsukan tō shokumu shikkō-hō (Police officers official duties act), Shōbō-hō (Fire Prevention act), Kōzan Hoan-hō (Mining safety act), Kangoku-hō (Prison act), Seishin Eisei-hō (Mental health act), Yōsei Hogo-hō (Eugenics protection act).

It should not be forgotten that the government took its prewar case against the leaders of the JCP under the notorious Peace Preservation Law to the courts; at the time, administrative action was not an option for this purpose. The JCP leaders used the platform of the courts to challenge and advocate their case. Although this aspect was not discussed in the Diet, it is hard to believe that this experience did not color drafter Seki's image, remembrances, experiences of this prewar era when he was himself a young prosecutor in the government in the early 1930s, then later as a thought prosecutor (*shisō kenji*) himself during WWII when it came to his turn to draft a new internal security law for post treaty Japan. Administrative action would be more expedient and effective and the verdict would be immediately effective and stay in effect, even during an the appeals process, not subject to a court's injunction or even to a court's decision to modify or reject this action for many years and even longer if the PM chose to intervene. A totally different venue and standard were utilized—the rather mundane "administrative action"—in the postwar period.[18]

PSEC Management. Three assistants, probably lawyers and about ten others as needed would be assigned to the PSEC members to act as the first line of assessment of the documents submitted from the PSIA; other ordinary administrative duties and logistical needs will be handled by the AG/Ministry of Justice secretariat. But the government actually felt that since the PSIA would have conducted a thorough and complete investigation on the possible violation of the SAPL, with all necessary backup documentation including the opinions, explanations, and contrary evidence provided by the accused organization, it would be "unnecessary and improper" (*hitsuyō mo nashi, datō de nai*) for the PSEC itself or a small PSEC subcommittee to conduct yet another investigation. The government continually stressed that this small staff should suffice since the materials submitted to the PSEC have been most thoroughly researched and studied with the authority and complete responsibility of the executive (*zen-sekinin o motte*, 5/31:16) Nevertheless, some members felt that the PSEC had no alternative but to swallow the recommendations of the PSIA; this was "the point of great concern". (Nakamura Masao 5/31:16)

Openness of PSEC Proceedings (Article 14). This article requires, among other factors, that when the accused organization explains (*bemmei*)

[18] Information on "*gyōsei shobun*" was derived from the following Japanese reference documents: *Gyōsei Hyakka Jiten*, KK Gyōsei, 1975, pp. 424–425; *Hōgaku Jiten*, Nihon Hyōronsha, 1971, p. 187; *Hōrei Yōgo Jiten*, Gakuyō Shobō, 1998, pp. 152–153; *Hōritsu Yōgo Jiten, Yūhikaku*, 1994, p. 271; *Kokumin Hōritsu Hyakka Dai-Jiten*, 2:193–194. *Japanese Legal Systems*, University of Tokyo Press, 1976, pp. 380–381 was also consulted.

its position, observers (*tachiainin*) for the accused organization and representatives from the various media may observe the proceedings; note that the general public is not allowed. The government was challenged by Ōnishi Masao when he suggested that the non-open nature of the PSIA/PSEC hearings were unconstitutional. Amazingly, Seki responded as follows:

> The principle of openness (*kōkai no gensoku*) is limited to the courts of law. In regard to administrative action, this must be considered from another aspect.... Based on the reality and content of the deliberations concerning SAPL cases, the proposed arrangement is considered to be completely appropriate in light of fairness (*kōsei*) and speed (*jinsoku*) [needed for handling these cases]. That is why the proposed arrangement was adopted (5/12:7).

Concerning the one sidedness of administrative actions, Yamaguchi Kōichi of the governing Liberal Party raised this issue:

> ...The administrative action to disband an organization, for example, is one-sided and arbitrary. If an error is made in this judgment, it would create an extreme abuse of the SAPL and invite a situation which is to be more feared. Even when all the conditions are taken into consideration, the scope for administrative action is very broad (5/12:15).

To which Seki explained that:

> ...In order to avoid the concentration of power in the PSIA, the PSEC was created and this semi-judicial commission will approve these recommendation. In a way, this can be compared to the judicial three-sided aspects of the court, the plaintiff and defendant. We look upon the PSEC as acting somewhat like a court, an organ making an independent judgement. In contrast to normal administrative actions, we believe that precautions of an unprecedented nature have been established in handling these cases (5/12:15).

After Restrictions Expire. At the request of the PSIA, PSEC may reimpose restrictions, if such actions are justified. If, however, restrictions involved the organ of the involved organization, and the latter had decided to republish its regular journal what then can be permitted, can the same title be used again, what about its editorial policy, can the old editorial staff continue. Can PSIA/PSEC impose an "acceptable policy and story content" as a condition for re-publication? Can the same editorial policy and reporters remain in tact? These immediately become constitutional issues involving censorship, freedom of thought and expression. These issues, while legitimate, were debated in the abstract, and inconclusively.

Restitution. In a much discussed hypothetical case where a court disagreed with PSEC findings and its decision to disband an organization which had to take steps at great expense to disband since PSEC decisions are effective until the restrictions are lifted or the decision nullified by a court, what avenue of restitution would be available to the aggrieved organization? Just apply for relief under the national indemnity law was the flip answer by the government. The government had not considered such needs and ways must be found to remedy such an eventuality (Satō Tatsuo 5/24:26). Basically, too bad. Or it suggested that the political responsibility for such an outcome would lie with PSIA for poor judgment but no meaningful indemnity. Thus, in this manner the human rights of the organization, its officers and members would have been seriously violated, with hardly a reasonable avenue for seeking reasonable compensation.

7. *Appeals to the Courts and Veto Authority of the Prime Minister.* The AG, and Yoshikawa and Seki, made a special point by frequently referring to the ability of the accused in accordance with the SAPL to appeal the decision of the PSEC to the three levels of courts, thereby attempting to show that there is fairness and a genuine venue of appeal. The opposition with equal vigor and constancy insisted that this ability to appeal lacked credibility and was a farce. As to whether the courts could completely review an administrative action taken by the executive branch was a major issue on the first day of the hearings, April 24, 1952, raised with some persistency by Tajima Yoshifumi, a Liberal Party member. If a court was inclined to dismiss the charges against the defendant, the PM could voice his opposition to such action, in accordance with a proviso clause in Article 10.2 of a 1948 law discussed below asserting danger to the maintenance of social welfare and security and prevent the court from taking such action. Since the PSIA and PSEC are both outer bureaus under the AG with some theoretical bureaucratic independence, the PM would naturally be inclined and duty bound bureaucratically to insist on upholding the finding and decision of the PSEC by invoking his authority under this 1948 law.

Yet, the AG himself and other government witnesses vehemently justified this authority to prevent the courts from "invading" (*shimpan*)—becoming involved in, overstepping their judicial authority—

the jurisdiction of the executive. In this way, the government strongly insisted the independence of the three branches of government would be maintained. From the vantage point of the three independent branches of government, it is the responsibility of the executive to take action—administrative action—to control "destructive organizations" and thereby maintain internal security. If the courts were to suddenly (*ikinari*) insert themselves in this process, it would be a clear invasion of and would impinge on the rights and responsibilities of the executive branch of government. Says the AG: "This is a completely appropriate approach. I am completely convinced without a doubt that this is the correct arrangement for Japan as a constitutional state governed by laws (*hōchi kokka toshite*). There are many examples in the law where the executive has disbanded organizations through administrative action. In line with the concept that the executive was responsible for taking administrative action to maintain internal security rather than the courts, the restrictions on organizations and individuals were "simply administrative actions, security measures (*hoan-teki sochi*) and not criminal penalties." (4/25:13) For the courts to make the decision to disband an organization would be excessive. "To seek relief through the courts would be appropriate and in accordance with the concept of the three branches of government... the problem is the provisional disposition (*kari shobun*) by the courts while the appeal proceeds to decide whether the action taken by the executive was appropriate or not." (4/24:22) In response, Tajima continued to assert that if society further deteriorated and a fascistic PM appeared the anxieties of the people would be manifold and the people would have to live under a fascistic style of government as happened previously [before 1945].

A somewhat unusual dialog took place on this sensitive issue between the opposition members and Suzuki Chūichirō, Acting DG of the Supreme Court Administration and Sato Tatsuo:

> [Suzuki]... In prewar years, resort to the courts to appeal an administrative action was not allowed in principle. These appeals were taken to an administrative court, even then only a limited range of issues could be taken. In the postwar period such appeals can be taken to the regular courts but this did not mean that the courts could direct and order (*shiki meirei*) the executive branch. (5/24:8–10)... The two branches will decide what will enhance the public interest (*kōeki*), i.e. what is most convenient and what is legally appropriate.... However, the re-establishment of an administrative court would be against the spirit of the Constitution even as a final assessment (*shūshin*).... The PSEC administrative action is not from a court's point of view a preliminary hearing as in a court

> and it would not be desirable to look upon an administrative action in such a manner. Courts should avoid appearing to take administrative actions.... It is desirable, of course, from the court's point of view for it to be able to stop such an action without the possible objection of the PM.... Article 10.2 proviso is a deviant stipulation inserted under special [U.S. Occupation] circumstances. The courts have to live with it which is undesirable. (6/16:17–20)
>
> [Itō Osamu had earlier called for suspension of the Article 10.2 proviso for SAPL cases; we should have the courage to do so, said he. Satō:...when the courts can issue an injunction against an administrative decision that will create an issue of where to draw the line between the authority of the courts and the executive, creating a constitutional situation. We do not have the courage to do so at this time. [That is the final great danger, said Itō] (5/21:1–2)
>
> The AG: It is conceivable that the PM's objections may not be justified then the courts could put aside the PM's objections. The PM's objections are not absolute.
>
> Sato as though to explain the AG's comments said that 1) if the PM's objections were voiced before a court has issued an injunction to stop an administrative action then the court will be bound by the PM's objections, 2) if the PM's objections came after the court had issued an injunction or restraining order then the court can proceed as it wishes. (5/28:5) This assessment appears to have anticipated the decision of the Supreme Court on article 10.2 proviso.

There have been a number of Supreme Court cases involving the PM's veto authority by voicing his objections. The ability of the PM to object to a potential court decision to set aside an administrative action by putting his objections in writing with reasons based normally on the rationale that if this action were set aside it would have a grave impact on society and the maintenance of public welfare and that his objections are voiced as unavoidable to avert this grave impact—the Japanese magic all-powerful phrase, the equivalent of "for national security" in the U.S. In each case the PM's authority to veto a court action has been upheld as constitutional and appropriate, i.e., in each case the court may not consider the merits of the PM's objections but must meekly reject an appeal, or vacate a court decision if it had taken such action before the PM had voiced his objection. The court's rejection of an appeal cannot be appealed to a higher court. Thus, an organization faced with PSEC imposed restrictions has no real substantive recourse, nor any avenue of effective appeal. The PM's objections cannot be challenged and are not intended to convince a court of the propriety of its actions. On the surface, this would appear to be contrary to Article 76 that the courts will be the final arbiters in legal affairs and that everyone will have their day in court. It would appear that the Supreme Court has given an organization such as the PSEC (with the ultimate backing of the PM with his veto authority) the function of being a final "legal" authority, like a court in an aspect of maintaining public welfare, seemingly contrary to the 1947 Constitution. The Japanese Supreme Court appears to have acquiesced to its own diminution of authority in being the final arbiter at the juncture of the intersection between judicial authority and executive authority. Thus, the PM's veto authority made an appeal almost meaningless and without substance as the opposition had always asserted.[19]

Court Review Time of an Administrative Action. The PSEC may decide to restrict, for example the organ of the accused organization, for three to six months. This restriction is appealed but can the court system adequately handle such cases. The SAPL specifies that a court was to make a decision in 100 days, if possible, but, after questioning, this "requirement" was, in reality not a binding limitation since there was

[19] The following sources were consulted in preparing this section:
Kaneko, Hiroshi. Gyōsei Jiken Soshō Tokurei-hō no Jittai, *Gyōsei Tetsuzuki no Kenkyū*. Yūshindō. 1961. subsection 4 (pp. 306–320). Ed: Ukai Nobushige.
Minami, Hiromasa. *Jōkai Gyōsei Jiken Soshō-hō*. Kōbundō. 1992. pp. 642–652.
Shimada, Shinji. *Gyōsei Jiken Soshōhō Yōsetsu*. Gyōsei. 1992. pp. 270–277.
Sonobe, Itsuo. *Chūkai Gyōsei Jiken Soshō-hō*. Yūhikaku. 1989. pp. 354–357.
Takahashi, Teizō. *Hanrei Gyōsei Jiken Soshō Tokurei-hō*. Hōritsu Bunkasha. 1960. pp. 299–303.

Supreme Court cases: 1/16/1953 and 9/15/1954 appear to be the two cases most cited in the above essays. The former decision was translated and included as an important Supreme Court decision in *Court and Constitution in Japan: selected Supreme Court decisions, 1948–1960.* John M. Maki. (University of Washington Press. 1964. 445 p.) pp. 384–409. The Court was unanimous in rejecting the PMs objection since it was raised after the court had already issued an injunction but it also said that the courts cannot issue an injunction if the PM raised an objection before the court had made a decision. While the Court was unanimous on the narrow subject before the court, some of the supplementary opinions voiced by members of the Court, showed that there was a substantial constitutional issue: for example, Judge Mano Tsuyoshi said that the recourse to the PM's objection would be "an invasion of the judicial field by the Prime Minister, an administrative functionary,…if a governmental power allocated to one organ of government could be invaded at will by another organ of government then it would be easy for one organ improperly and excessively to engross two or more different powers, resulting in autocracy,…I consider this provision concerning objections by the prime minister as unconstitutional and void.… [To do otherwise would be to accept] the view adopted by the administrative courts (essentially not judicial courts but mere administrative agencies) in administrative suits in the days of the old Constitution. This, however, cannot be accepted under the new [1947] Constitution. (pp. 294–400) no absolute requirement that the courts had to reach a decision in 100 days and there was no stipulation as to what would happen if that deadline was not respected; such an appeal does not hold the administrative decision in abeyance, and the courts could not pronounce a temporary injunction against its implementation pending review. In light of the separation of the three branches of government, the 100-day preference in the SAPL becomes only an admonitional article (*kunji-teki kitei*) to the courts without legal force (5/13:5). By the time even the first level of court appeal is completed, it could easily stretch beyond the PSEC imposed restriction period, and the Higher Court and Supreme Court have not gotten anywhere near consideration of the merits of the appeal. Thus, since it takes many years for a case in Japan to go through the three tiered court system, as much as ten years, and since probably the courts may not be able to issue an injunction against the implementation of a PSEC judgment, with a potential PM veto hanging over the courts, this route as a relief or balance is basically without substantive merit and is strongly reinforced with the legal notion and belief that the executive branch can respond more effectively and speedily when necessary to a perceived threat to the social structure and stability in contrast to the more cumbersome court deliberations.[20]

Origins of the PM's Veto Authority. Let us momentarily focus on the unusual nature of the PM's veto authority. The roots of this authority lie in the early years of the U.S. Occupation. When the new Japanese Constitution went into effect in 1947, it was hoped that a number of other subordinate laws would be revised in line with the Constitution; one of them was expected to be the administrative litigation procedure law (gyōsei soshō-hō). Because of the backlog of laws to be revised, the revision of this law was delayed and eventually became entangled with a sensitive political issue. The first PM under the new Constitution was Katayama Tetsu, a Christian and a Social Democrat, who was well received in GHQ and by General MacArthur. However, the Minister of Agriculture, Hirano Rikizō, in his Cabinet (1947–48) was purged

[20] It must be noted that Chairman Sase of the HofR asked the government to provide an analysis of when and how the PM had invoked this veto authority in the past. This would have been a most useful analysis in this context but unfortunately the Committee did not follow up on this request and the government obviously just ignored the request and never provided any data or report.

on January 4, 1948; he appealed to the Tokyo District Court for an injunction against his purge on January 14, 1948; on February 2, 1948 the Court agreed with Hirano. But GHQ on February 5 stated that the PM has the responsibility to execute the instructions of SCAP and instructed the Supreme Court to set aside the District Court decision, i.e. quite aside from the merits of the Hirano purge, GHQ over-rode the Japanese court system in favor of the executive. GHQ said that the court had overstepped its authority by infringing upon the political responsibilities of the PM. The political management of Japan was the responsibility of the PM and not to be interfered with by the courts. This set in motion a series of decisions whose impact is still felt more than half a century later.

By sheer coincidence, the Japanese government team developing the administrative litigation draft law met with GHQ officials (principally Alfred Oppler and Thomas Blakemore, an American highly knowledgeable of Japanese law, both mentioned in Chapter 2). GHQ demanded that the role of the PM in this draft must be strengthened, i.e., stipulate that administrative actions by the executive cannot be reversed especially if the PM raises objections. This PM authority was not in the Japanese draft; despite the tradition of a strong executive in Japan, the government had never arrogated this authority to itself and was not part of the Japanese legal tradition. From before the war, there was a court to hear administrative litigation cases (Gyōsei saibansho). Thus, Japanese legal group opposed this demand as strongly as they could but could not, under the Occupation, prevail. Based on "democratic principles", the Japanese group had envisioned that such administrative cases would be handled by the regular courts. So they tried, obviously as a compromise, to persuade GHQ to accept the court's authority to place an injunction on an administrative action except where this injunction may result in an important impact on public welfare. But GHQ had hardened its position as discussions progressed and demanded that at the very least that if the PM objected to such a court decision, the court would not be able to place an injunction on the government's administrative action and retroactively reverse a court decision if necessary to comply with the PM's objections; this PM authority may be invoked only under extreme circumstances. Thus the Japanese PM was given an authority in the 1948 special law on administrative procedures (Gyōsei Jiken Soshō Tokurei-hō), an authority that PMs in other countries do not enjoy. It was a postwar authority given to the PM at Occupation insistence since it was using the Japanese government to carry out SCAP directives and reforms.

Under the 1948 law, the PM invoked this authority 18 times mostly on behalf of local governmental jurisdictions after the court decision had been made; this was regarded as an abuse of this authority. When the 1948 law was abolished and incorporated into the 1962 Gyōsei Jiken Soshō-hō, the continued inclusion of this authority as article 27 became highly controversial: it could be used politically and its constitutionality was questioned despite Supreme Court decisions since the PM could over-ride a court decision, perhaps thereby compromising the authorities of the three branches of government. Since the birth of this authority lay in unusual circumstances during the Occupation years, there was serious question as to whether it should be continued when the 1962 law was considered. In order to prevent an abuse of this authority, it was required that it could be invoked only under extreme circumstances as a last resort and the PM must report to the next regular Diet when he used this authority. Since 1962, this authority has been much more sparingly invoked by the PM in connection with mass demonstrations (*shūdan ji'i undō*), another to vacate the prohibition of a demonstration based on the Hiroshima prefectural security regulations (*hoan jōrei*) when the Emperor and Empress visited Hiroshima. This was a significant change in the reasons used for invoking this unusual authority by the PM and the kind of use that the opponents of the SAPL envisioned when they asserted that appealing to the courts was rather meaningless. It would appear that the political opposition to the SAPL were on firm ground when they asserted that the appeal venue to and through the courts was theoretical and ultimately unreliable and basically non-existent because even though the PM had not used it in this manner over the past decades, it is a legal tool that will hang ominously over any and all appeals to the courts stemming from PSEC decisions. Ironically, it was the U.S. Occupation that insisted on giving this extraordinary authority to the PM and it was only natural that any executive (the PM in this case) would insist on keeping this powerful authority in any revision of the law.[21]

[21] Those who wish additional details are referred to the only political process study on how this veto authority was created: Satō, Atsushi. Gyōsei Jiken Soshō-hō Tokurei-hō no Rippō Katei, *Gyōsei Tetsuzuki no Kenkyū*. Yūshindō. 1961. pp. 239–266. Ed: Ukai Nobushige.

8. *The Public Security Investigation Agency*

Compulsory Investigative Authority (Kyōsei Chūsaken) and Operations. Under the Dankihō, the SIB was given both direct and indirect compulsory investigative authority but in reality it was seldom invoked. The PSIA under the SAPL, in contrast, was not given this authority and would conduct investigations (chōsa) as necessary with the cooperation of the police as needed, not with criminal investigative authority (*sōsa*). Because in prewar years, it was the low level front line officers who often treated potential suspects with abuse, this delineation was most important to opposition members. They even discussed as to whether PSIA officials would wear uniforms or civilian suits in pursuit of their duties; civvies they were assured would be used! When a search, inspection and seizure of documents was to take place, PSIA officials would merely witness this operation and would take no active part in this procedure. This stipulation (restriction) was created to give the PSIA officials, according to Seki, "a sense of the reality of such a procedure (*kenshō no gemba*) and to contribute to their ability to judge the value of materials obtained in such a manner"; such PSIA officials would have no directive and ordering authority (*shiki meirei*). Yoshida of the Kokumin Minshutō, described this as a "meaningless,

---

Satō's case study was of particular value to me in preparing this summary. His study also "revealed" interesting little facts such as, as the Japanese pondered when or even whether to submit this unwelcome bill to the Diet, GHQ called and instructed the government to submit the bill to the Diet—presumably to keep the Diet busy "legislating" rather than because of the intrinsic importance of the bill itself. Also, rather importantly, the author speculated as to why such a confrontation occurred between GHQ and Japanese government officials over the PM's authority. He noted that in the legal affairs arena, few GHQ officials (except Blakemore who was given high marks) had any knowledge of the Japanese legal system and often resorted, in the end, to "It's an order" to the Japanese officials. On the Japanese side, the early draft emphasized the continuation of the prewar administrative litigation court because of the Japanese drafter's background, but the draft discussed with GHQ emphasized reliance on the courts believing that this was more responsive to the Occupation's objective of democratization. Nevertheless, they both emphasized the authority of the existing governmental bureaucratic structure. Yet it was GHQ which strongly demanded the inclusion of the veto authority of the PM in the bill. Since the Legal Section appeared to be dominated by New Dealers from the Roosevelt era (1932–1944) who were suspicious of the Judicial Branch especially the U.S. Supreme Court in its role of obstructing economic recovery in the 1930s and their belief in the efficacy of a dedicated bureaucratic structure, they moved to increase and entrench Japanese bureaucratic power without a thorough knowledge of the existing power of the Japanese national bureaucracy and unknowingly contributing yet further to this bureaucratic authority in Japan.

empty" structure (*kōbun*); in that case, it would be more meaningful to give this investigative authority completely to the public procurator or the judicial police. When a PSIA official requests another agency for access to certain documents in its possession, the latter is not absolutely bound to produce the materials, it may at its discretion decline to give PSIA even copies of the requested documents. To which Seki replied: the authority of the PSIA officials were severely narrowed and limited in order to maintain a clear distinction between administrative action and criminal proceedings. Administrative action against organizations will be taken invoking the "power and authority of the state (*kokka no kenryoku kengen*)". "From the point of view of the principles of democracy", the authorities that would be invoked in controlling organizations and those of the judicial police (*shihō keisatsu*) should be, from the national standpoint, clearly separated. In addition, in the case of individual criminal actions, there is the strong compulsory investigative authority held by the police, to give yet another agency such powers would only raise fears among the people about such authorities. "We separated the PSIA functions from the police", said Seki, "to prevent a combination of these force which could lead to a revival of the Tokko". (6/16:25) Yet, Yoshikawa, DG/SIB acknowledged that the SIB had paid the police to do certain investigative assignments and insisted that there must be close collaboration between the PSIA and various police forces.

If a PSIA investigator (*chōsakan*) appears on the doorsteps of an organization it is investigating, the latter could refuse to cooperate, not accede to interviews, the officer would not have legal authority to force the issue; if the officer tried to force the issue, a potential case of abuse may arise involving CC article 193 on abuse of authority. Even if he accidentally discovered, uncovered plotting, planning abetting of illegal acts he could not make arrests (6/12:5 and 6/12:8). After the necessary data has been assembled a more senior assessments officer (*shinrikan*) who had not been involved in the first research stage would evaluate the case and make a submission to the DG/PSIA who, if he sees fit, would submit a recommendation "in his personal authority as DG" to the PSEC. In light of these considerations, this "adjustment" or "accommodation" (*chōsei*, a most convenient vague Japanese word for this purpose) was made concerning the allocation of compulsory investigative authority (4/28:4).

PSIA Investigations and Dismissal of Evidence. According to article 26, the PSIA may conduct the necessary investigations for the control of certain organizations, and the procedures for such investigations are specified in articles 27–29. The investigations may be conducted with or without the support of suspect organizations. For example, if a labor union was visited by a PSIA investigative officer for this purpose, it may, according to Seki, rebuff him, summarily without being accused of obstruction of the duties of a public official. (5/9:15–16) The organization being investigated is entitled to a fair hearing (*shinri*) and the hearing officer may not inappropriately limit the rights of this organization. The affected organization may submit evidence to its advantage to the hearing officer who may decide not to consider this evidence according to article 15 if he believed it was not necessary. This authority was thus a sensitive and controversial subject. But his decision must in no way infringe upon the fairness of his investigation. Language in the SAPL on this subject is derived from article 259 of Civil Procedures Code (5/12:11). In order for "evidence" submitted by the accused organization to be rejected/dismissed by the hearing officer, one of the following reasons must be cited according to Seki: 1) if it is completely unclear how and why this evidence (*risshō no shushi*) is being submitted at this time, 2) the submitted evidence has no relationship to the issue at hand and 3) when it is clear that this evidence was being submitted in order to postpone and delay the hearing. If this evidence is rejected, the accused organization may submit an opinion document (*ikensho*) to the PSEC about the rejection of documentary evidence submitted by the accused. (5/9:14, 5/12:27)[22]

9. *The Name of the SAPL.* The name of the bill, *Hakai Katsudō Bōshi Hōan*, in Japanese and the official English title, Subversive Activities Prevention Law, would appear to be of little consequence. A brief comment about the titles of the several draft SAPLs was made in Chapter 2. The titles used though tentative but used officially in press conferences brought back memories of a different era at least to those who opposed the law: "The Organization Control Law" as a title would be reminiscent of Occupation edicts, national security law reminiscent of the prewar police system and its excesses. These titles were indeed

[22] Article 259 reads as follows: Evidence tendered by a party need not be taken if the Court finds it unnecessary to do so.

symbolic of the impression that bureaucratic indifference was creating; this attitude while understandable because of the mind set of the drafters and others as part of a continuum from prewar thinking and predispositions was deplorable especially since a new atmosphere and milieu was supposed hopefully to have been engendered by the Occupation in the postwar period. While it was not a major issue in the interpolations, that it was raised was another concern created by this draft bill.

According to DG/SIB Yoshikawa, the "original idea"—when a formal title had to be chosen when the bill was going to be submitted at last to the Diet—was just "Bōryoku-shugi-teki Hakai Katsudō Bōshi-hō" (Violent Destructive Activities Prevention Law) but that was too long winded. Since the law covered destructive acts by organizations and individuals before they would be committed, the name of the bill was simplified "to reflect reality" and shortened to the present name. He pointed out that it should be kept in mind that the term "*bōryoku-shugiteki*" was used in other existing legislation, e.g. the Occupation era predecessor law to the SAPL, the Organization Control Cabinet Ordinance (5/8:8). The purpose of this Ordinance was to prohibit the formation of "secretive, militaristic, ultra-nationalistic, violent and anti-democratic organizations and persons"; while *bōryoku* (violent) was not linked to violent destructive activities as it was used later, but the implication was clear. PM Yoshida in his memoirs also confirmed this idea for the Japanese title to reflect the target of the law to prevent destructive activities when such activities were used as a means to achieve political objectives. (Yoshida, Shigeru. *Kaisō Jū'nen* 2:290) Presumably it was meant to be a neutral term describing its purpose in a straight forward manner.

However, the English title is not so straight forward. The Japanese word *Hakai* is translated as destruction, demolition, wrecking, breakdown (*Kenkyūsha's New Japanese-English Dictionary* 1954 edition, p. 371) but when made into *hakai-teki* or *hakai kōi katsudō* it becomes destructive, subversive or subversive action/sabotage. By using the word "subversive", I feel that the translation has given such activities a distinctly political tinge and interpretation; the use of "subversive" was borrowed obviously from U.S. legislation around that time on the same subject. In this study, I have used the more neutral "destructive activities" instead of "subversive", more in line with the approach used in selecting a Japanese title.

10. *Duration of the SAPL.* Was the SAPL a temporary law or a permanent one? Since the SAPL as a law has been on the books for over 50 years, it would appear to "a permanent law". Thus, on the surface, it would appear to be a strange notion to even discuss, yet, in reality, early in the hearings, DG/SIB Yoshikawa said the SAPL would be a temporary law, responding to a special situation. It was for this reason that the government asserted that the CC should not be amended. But later in the hearings, AG Kimura however, provided confusing commentary. At one time he emphatically asserted that the proposed SAPL was a permanent law, not temporary at all. Then again, he said: in contrast to the permanent (*kōkyū-sei*) CC, the SAPL is different. The SAPL is to supplement the CC; I believe it could be safely said that in comparison to the CC, the proposed SAPL is a temporary measure (*zantei-teki*). (5/28:18) While it is intended to be responsive to more than one social situation, we hope there will come a time in the not too distant future when it will be unnecessary but we have no outlook when that would be. (5/30:11) Earlier the government had given the distinct impression that the SAPL was drafted to respond to an emergency situation with a temporary law to prevent destructive activities and the government's explanatory materials also gave the "impression" it was a temporary law. (5/9:7) Satō Tatsuo, DG/Legal Opinions Bureau (Hōsei Ikenkyoku) gave yet another strained explanation: from strict interpretation of administrative practices, a temporary law would have a beginning and ending date and titled "...*rinji tokurei-hō*". From a *substantive* (*jisshitsu-teki ni*) point of view, not a *legal point of view,* because it is responding to a particular situation and from the stand point of national interest (*kokka-teki na kankei*), no one seriously thought of this law in the same light as the core CC (6/9:3), i.e. implicitly a temporary law with a specific purpose. While the AG's comment would be authoritative in this strange dialogue there was nevertheless some doubt in the minds of committee members that it was not a permanent law but it did seem to reveal a small divergence among the government staff. This issue again surfaced in the remarks by the Ryokufūkai representative when he presented the Ryokufūkai's proposed revisions of the SAPL to the HofC plenary session on July 1, 1952 where he described the SAPL as a transitional law responding to a special emergency situation in Japan (see concluding section of Chapter 5). However, after the SAPL was enacted this notion of a temporary law faded away and ne'er surfaced again.

11. *Comparison with Foreign Internal Security Laws.* In responding to an inquiry from the HofR committee, Seki explained that:

> The stipulations in similar laws in Britain, the U.S. and other democratic nations against attempts to overthrow the government through riots and insurrections are far more detailed than those in the SAPL. For example, the stipulations concerning instigation, advocacy, organization for this purpose are more detailed. Those stipulations in the [former] Soviet Union are even more severe. When it comes to almost any country, the stipulations in the SAPL are distinctly on the light side (5/10:31)...more lenient and reasonable.... Stipulations in the U.S. Internal Security Law contain the elements of the [prewar] Peace Preservation Law. The strict definition of stipulations enumerated in Article 3 of the SAPL reflects the corrections (*zesei*) made to avoid the legal deficiencies of the PPL. As a result we are not, by any means, following the precedent of the U.S. [Internal Security Law] (5/10:33).

Under the circumstances, this was an obvious response to such a query; based on my reading of internal security laws of other countries, Seki's assessment is probably more or less correct but nevertheless unacceptable from the political opposition in Japan.[23]

[23] The history of past internal security laws in the U.S. has not been particularly glorious; freedom of speech, etc., has been a fragile privilege to uphold and maintain. Under President John Adams (the 2nd President) Alien and Sedition Acts were enacted in 1798 for strictly domestic personal political purposes: to try to prevent the election of Thomas Jefferson as President but the attempt failed. These laws gave the President authority to limit criticism of the government, made it a crime to criticize the government, to banish or imprison foreigners by a simple order if he deemed them "dangerous to the peace"; as a result, and despite the ratification of the first Amendment to the U.S. Constitution only a few years earlier concerning freedom of speech, editors, printers and politicians were convicted under these acts and sent to prison. Adams did not invoke the Alien Acts, but ten journalists supporting Jefferson were arrested for violation of the Sedition Act which prohibited criticism of federal officials made "with the intent to defame". During the Civil War, was a dark period for civil rights with the suspension of habeas corpus and raids on newspapers. But, according to Work "the darkest, most widespread and in some ways least remembered acts of [USG] government repression of dissent occurred in the lifetimes of our grandparents and great-grandparents—before, during and after World War I." What happened in the West was happening in the entire country. The State of Montana enacted the Sedition Act of February 22, 1918 which was followed by a federal Sedition Act of May 16, 1918, about three months later almost word for word the same as the Montana law. During WWI, Germans were the target group. The U.S. Supreme Court unanimously upheld the convictions against German immigrants under the federal Sedition Act. It was felt that speech and writings could lead to violence, thereby developing the "tendency test". Criticism of the government, especially during the war, was criminalized. After WWI, the beatings, lynchings, raids, censorship and jailings did not end

but continued with "a second round of hysteria with the Red Scare of 1919–1920". (Work: 3) A series of bomb blasts occurred in 1919–1920 and raised anxieties about a Red Scare in the U.S. to a frenzied pitch and were compounded by race riots in Washington DC and Chicago. Street mobs attacked so-called leftwing organizations, even dragged a man from jail, hanged him then riddled his body with bullets. The wartime Espionage Act of 1917 and the Sedition Act were invoked by Attorney General A. Mitchell Palmer which permitted the government to deport without trial or hearing any non-citizen who had ever belonged to a group deemed subversive. This resulted in many thousands being rounded up, put on ships bound for the new Soviet Union—these came to be known as the Palmer Raids. Gradually during the late 1920s, the Supreme Court began to reconsider these excesses and adopted a more moderate stance based on the idea of a narrowly defined "clear and present danger" doctrine. This was called by Work "The Dawn of Free Speech". During WWII, however, there was the forced internment of Japanese-Americans after Pearl Harbor was attacked in December 1941. Then another round of communist hysteria swept over the U.S. in the late 1940–1950s leading to the Internal Security Act of 1950. The latest wave of hysteria and anxiety came after the 9/11/2001 bombing and collapse of the Twin Towers in New York city and the aerial attack on the Pentagon and the enactment of the Patriot Act soon thereafter, the greatest threat to Constitutionally "guaranteed" freedoms in the U.S. in modern times. This Act allows the government to imprison citizens and non-citizens indefinitely without trial or hearings in the name of national security and to protect "us" from terrorists and terrorism. The FBI's spying powers over all those living in the U.S. has been vastly expanded to include obtaining materials about a person without their knowledge, without the need to show probable cause including activities based on one's First Amendment activities, one's financial records, one's reading habits at the public library, and there shall be a permanent gag order on anyone who knows this investigation is taking place, e.g. librarians and supervisors at one's workplace. Again, as happened in prewar Japan, the FBI has liberally enlarged and expanded the interpretation of the Patriot Act to obtain financial information, e.g., on local politicians, the largest strip-club baron in Las Vegas, Nebraska which have no connection to fighting terrorism. "In effect the Patriot Act allows the Feds to search every financial institution in the country for the records of anybody they have suspicions about—the very definition of a fishing expedition. Under present conditions in Japan, this intrusion would be inconceivable under the existing *modus operandi* of the SAPL. Compared with laws enacted in a state of frenzy and fear in "democratic" U.S., so-called democratic model to the world, one is forced to admit that the SAPL is, on the surface, not as draconian as these laws.

The U.S. also has a more moderate and generous side. The infamous Ober Act of the State of Maryland, the thirty year old anti-subversive law, was repealed by Maryland's State Assembly without objection in June 1978. It had been enacted in the latter 1940s during the height of anti-Communist phobia. It had provided for a 20-year jail term for advocating revolution, barred "subversive persons" from government jobs, required dissolution of "subversive organizations" and confiscation of their funds, records, books and property, established a system of loyalty investigations and oaths aimed at teachers and created a pile of dossiers which still exist on political activists. A U.S. Supreme Court decision in 1967 made the Ober Act null and void but it was still on the books. The attempt to repeal the Ober Act had been tried unsuccessfully in twelve previous State Assembly sessions! After Professor Work's book was published, law students took up the cause, leading to the posthumous pardons in May 2006 by Montana State Governor, Brian Schweitzer, himself a descendant of ethnic Germans, of 78 persons convicted under the Montana Sedition Act. (*U.S. News & World Report* 5/15/2006: 21)

The HofC committee pursued this issue further and Seki graded several countries (UK, France, West Germany, and the then Soviet Union) in their internal security laws. French CC structure was similar to Japan's but its internal security laws were looser and incitement and instigation were independent crimes. However, if those who have been incited or instigated did not commit a crime, then those who did the instigating and inciting would not be guilty. Nevertheless, for "serious crimes" the French CC would be similar to that proposed in the SAPL. "We were surprised to find that in the U.S. and U.K. both the instigators and incitors were regarded as in a similar category as those who had committed the crime and that these democratic countries has such stiff laws concerning incitement and instigation and to our great surprise (*jitsu ni odoroku beki mono ga atta*) found that in the U.S. some persons could be excluded from holding certain positions in selected industries, corporations and that even an oath of office was needed for civil servants". Germany had a relatively strict regime but the U.K. and the U.S. had the greatest restrictions. We in Japan adopted a "middle of the road" approach using the U.K. model as a reference point. (6/14:26–28)

iv. *Materials Prepared in Support of the SAPL*

1. *Documents Submitted to the Diet.* Occasionally references were made in the Committee hearings, almost always by the two government witnesses, Yoshikawa and Seki, both of the SIB, to documents describing the increasing number of attacks against police boxes and stations, tax offices, police officers, other local government offices, etc, by various organizations. These referenced documents were intended to prove the urgent need for the speedy enactment of the SAPL without amendments. Copies of these documents were distributed to Commit-

---

This brief discussion derives from: *The World Book Encyclopedia*, 1964 ed., pp. 1:35 and 1:352; (Clemens P Work. *Darkest before Dawn: sedition and free speech in the American West*. University of New Mexico Press. 2006. p. 3; Crackdown! By Bruce Watson, *Smithsonian* 2/2002:51–53; Resolution of 1798…, Jeff Jacoby, *Boston Globe* 12/30/1998; We've aimed, detained and missed before, David Cole, *Washington Post* 6/8/2003; The Power to Imprison, Philip Heyman, *Washington Post* 7/7/2002; *Unpatriotic Acts*: the FBI's power to rifle through your records and personal belongings without telling you, American Civil Liberties Union, 7/2003:19p; *Newsweek* 12/1/20/2003:36.

tee members in both Houses and they did occasionally refer to these documents in the hearings.

The printed records of hearings in the U.S. Congress include all kinds of materials crammed in at the end of a volume on a particular hearing; these additional materials may have been requested or in many cases instructed by the committee chair or members of the committee for a particular government agency or other participating non-governmental group to supply additional data, supplementary testimony, etc. In many cases, witnesses requested permission to provide extra data for the record to bolster their advocacy. The Japanese Diet record, in contrast, is only the verbatim record of the testimony of those persons participating on any particular day. I have not found any of the referenced materials included in the verbatim record on these hearings on the SAPL although references are occasionally made to them. I was given one overall and 19 supporting documents, a total of about 690 pages, with an overall list of these 19 items and each item had a cover page with an item number corresponding to the list entitled "materials submitted to the Diet". They are not dated but they were prepared for the committee hearings beginning in April 1952. They were mimeographed on rather poor quality paper—paper for whatever purpose was difficult to obtain in those days (1951–52); each printed sheet was 14×10 inches and folded to form a traditional Japanese book sheet. These pages are now changing color around the edges and becoming brittle after 50 years. About 40% of the 19 items were prepared using a cumbersome prewar Japanese typewriter, the other 60% were handwritten on a stencil and then mimeographed—there were no advanced technology printing methods available in those days. The overall document and a summary report on violent destructive activities in Japan in 1951–1952 referred to in DG Yoshikawa's testimony on April 25 and these 19 documents constitute the group of documents submitted to the Diet and given to members of the Legal Affairs Committees of both Houses.

Committee members occasionally tried to extract from the government witnesses what organization was behind these various violent destructive activities elaborated in these 19 items but the witnesses always begged off saying they were still studying the situation although many of the materials in this collection garnered by the SIB clearly stemmed from the Japanese Communists. Many were originally printed with false covers although initially published in JCP secret journals. The first six items concerned communist military tactics, strategy and organization. The purpose of these documents was to prove the dangerous reality of the Communist threat to Japan's society, nation and government and by implication to support the need for the quick enactment of the SAPL.

2. *Background Papers.* I collected 25 items assembled by the SIB, probably by Seki when he was drafting the SAPL; another five items from the National Diet Library. In a way they constitute what might be called background papers used principally by Seki as reference materials in the SAPL drafting process and for possible future reference use at Diet hearings. These documents indicate the thoroughness in Seki's approach in studying other internal security laws and various past uses of controversial legal terms, e.g. *sendō, kyōsa.* These materials included translations of internal security laws of Communist China, the former Soviet Union, Nazi Germany, the U.S. many of which were prepared or translated by the SIB; other items were on incitement in the PPL, pre- and post-publication censorship systems, comparative penalties for instigations not carried out according to several Japanese laws, texts used by DG/SIB Yoshikawa on April 24, 1952 explaining the status of various destructive activities underlying the need for the SAPL, article-by-article explanation of the draft SAPL distributed to Diet House Legal Affairs Committee members, an analysis of the social conditions and commentary at the time of the enactment of the PPL.

3. *Materials Requested by the Committee.* According to the verbatim record of the committee hearings, I counted ten occasions when the Committee Chairman, Sase Shōzō, asked the government witnesses to provide the committee with additional materials. Many of the topics touched on sensitive issues in the debate about the SAPL: for example, a report on the 1943 wartime revision of the 1942 Wartime Special Criminal Law (Senji Keiji Tokubetsu-hō, to be distinguished from the Criminal Code itself) especially concerning the emphasis on incitement (Hearings, 5/15:18), the relationship between violence under the election law and the SAPL (5/9:25), use of administrative action to disband organizations in prewar years and others.

Indeed, it would have been enlightening if the government had provided sufficient, clear and objective research analyses in response to the HofR Committee. Interestingly, I could not find any specific reference by a government witness to the committee that herewith are the requested materials, nor did I find any comment by the committee chairman or any member reminding the government witnesses about the requested materials or any reference in the hearings to the contents of such responses. The requests seem to have faded away into oblivion. Was this amnesia or disinterest on the part of the committee or does this reflect the feeling on the part of the government witnesses not to feel that such requests have to be taken seriously. One might say a few items, for example, those about the definition of an organizations could have been answered because the members queried the government to define its terms quite specifically. I would tend to feel that the committee members were forgetful and the senior bureaucrats were sufficiently cynical and arrogant just to simply ignore the committee's requests. The situation in HofC committee hearings was quite different: the request for information and explanations from Committee members were respected and oral answers were appropriated provided by government witnesses beginning with the Attorney General; the government could not afford to alienate Committee members in the HofC, the vote count was too close to contemptuously ignore.

v. *Public Hearings of Expert Witnesses*

By coincidence, these public hearings by the HofR committee were held one day before (April 30) and one day after (May 2) the notorious Bloody May Day Riot of 1952. By convention, the choice of experts for these hearings was delegated to the chairman; in actuality, he relied on the recommendations from Committee members and the political parties and, in all probability, the SIB provided a list of its preferred witnesses to the committee chairman.[24] Since the Liberal Party did not want to give the impression that it was going to ram the draft SAPL through the parliamentary system, and since it could not enact the law before the peace treaty went into effect based on the Diet calendar and the determined political opposition to the SAPL, it accepted the idea of having most of the expert witnesses from the opposition. Eighteen experts were selected. Since the war had ended somewhat less than

[24] The SIB had prepared a list of potential witnesses dated 4/23/1952 which was divided into several categories: knowledgeable and experienced persons (*gakushiki keikensha*, academics, commentators, cultural organizations and media), lawyers, labor unions, management; several people in each of these categories were invited to comment on the SAPL. It was a list which was not by any means lopsidedly in favor of the SAPL. Ten (Dandō, Ukai, Hirano, Abe, Fushida, Kiyose, Nagano, Ōmori, Yoshida and Hara) of the 18 experts invited were included on this list.

seven years previously, each and every one of the experts who appeared before the committee in both Houses were products of prewar Japan's educational system, had all worked in varying capacities in prewar Imperial Japan, all had experienced the travails of WWII; all had basically established their fame, reputations, notoriety and name recognition before 1945. To the best of my knowledge none can be identified as ultra-rightists, ultra-nationalists nor ultra-leftists. The labor union representative had witnessed and experienced the government's suppression of the labor union movement before the War.

1. *Legal Basis for Expert Hearings.* The legal basis for these hearings lies in article 51 of the Diet Law which stipulates that:

> With respect to matters of importance bearing upon general interest and purpose, Committees may hold public hearings and hear opinions of persons having actual interest in the matter as well as of persons possessed of learning and experience and other persons. (Eibun Hōreisha, Inc. 1993. EHS Law Bulletin Series EHS:1:15)

The concept of holding expert hearings derives from an Occupation initiative to inject the U.S. Congressional experience into the Japanese parliamentary system. Since its introduction in 1947 to June 1952, there had been more 100 expert hearings convened and over 1000 persons had provided their expert opinions on a wide ranging set of issues: police law, commerce law, transaction taxes, civil service employee laws for national and local governments, labor laws, reorganization of the electric power industry, local government law, daylight saving law, abolition of the law concerning adultery, coal production management, religious organizations law. Over the past five years, the sets of expert hearings that have attracted public attention were the October 1947 hearings under the Katayama Cabinet concerning coal production management and the present series of hearings on the SAPL. Concerning coal production, four days of continuous hearings were held with the participation of 60 experts. This was the only expert hearings that involved so many experts representing so many interests, management, labor, and even the general public during this period.

There was a concern that perhaps the "expert hearing system" had been over-worked; many committees felt that they must hold such hearings to maintain their status, keep up with the parliamentary Joneses. Eleven expert hearings were held in connection with laws stemming from the Peace Treaty; that would be one half of the 22 standing committees. Concerning the choice of experts, in many cases, the government gazette announced a call for experts to testify. More than 50 applied to voice their opinions about the SAPL; in the end, however, only those from management, finances, labor, academia and a newspaper were chosen leaving out representatives from the general public. These expert hearings tended to be attended by only a few Committee members; the rationale would be that they already knew the positions of those invited. In order to belittle them, PM Yoshida had dismissed their ideas in a disdainful manner, scorning the academic voices as coming from ivory tower intellectuals who are detached from reality; AG Kimura also contemptuously dismissed "the experts" as only a mere part of the opposition who did not understand the real meaning of the SAPL and had not read or studied each article of the SAPL. (5/30:16) Needless to say, both the Liberal Party and the opposing leftwing parties mobilized "experts" to publicly bolster their political stances and give these Diet members ammunition to pursue and condemn or support the government.[25]

Eighteen experts testified: four in support of the SAPL and 14 in opposition. In light of space limitations, the ideas of one supporter of the SAPL (Matsushita Masatoshi) and two from the opposing group (Dandō Shigemitsu, Ukai Nobushige) will be given below:

2. *Those in Favor of the SAPL.* There were only four, a prominent lawyer, a commentator and two from business. The commentator, Abe Shinnosuke, gave a vague and rambling commentary that certain restrictions must be accepted (*shinobazaru o enai*) so long as the JCP existed but felt the government had not convinced the people about the SAPL and called for a watchful Diet to prevent abuse of authority. **Kawahara Ryōsaburō**, Director, Labor Department, Toshiba Co, thought that since Japan was democratic the probability of abuse was negligent. **Hara Yasusaburō**, President, Nikkakyō (Nihon Kagaku Kōgyō Kyōkai, Japan Chemical Industries Association) supported the SAPL but was apprehensive about the vagueness of some phrases,

[25] Despite the use of "expert hearings" over the years, I was unable to find an academic study on the use and effectiveness of the system of holding expert hearings in the legislative process, except the following three items from journals: Kokkai no "Kōchōkai" o bunseki-suru, *Jurisuto* 31:41/1953:10–12, Seido Shōkai: Kōchōkai, *Jurisuto* 15(4/1/1953:44, Kōchōkai, *Nihon Dai-Hyakka Zensho*, Shōgakkan. 1986. 8:850, Chihō Gikai ni okeru Kōchōkai seido ni tsuite, *Chihō Jichi* 334(9/1975):69–77.

e.g. "possess material for the objective of publicly displaying them", would result in serious conflict during implementation. Some of these phrases he thought might be deleted to avoid this problem but never pushed seriously. Of the control clauses, the most difficult one to contend with would be the authority to disband an organization in light of the Constitution. He reserved his polite yet strongest concern and anxiety about the role of the PSEC, as a second tier (*ni-shin*) court hearing, the first being the PSIA staff investigation which included hearing the defendant's case and third being an appeal to the courts. He described the PSEC's inability to conduct its own investigation as "without arms and legs" as most disturbing (*hanahada moshiroku nai*, perhaps also as "not amusing"). Obviously thinking of the past record, he repeatedly stressed that while the people would have a sense of security with the enactment of the SAPL, if it was abused and incorrectly, improperly implemented it would have the opposite and serious counter-productive effect and this law would itself become a law of violence. Therefore, we must pay special attention to the selection of personnel to carry out the law.

Of those in favor of the SAPL, Matsushita Masatoshi, lawyer, educated at Harvard University, President of Rikkyō (St. Paul's) University, was the first expert to testify and provided the most systematic presentation for supporting the SAPL. He was nationally known for his knowledge and expertise on British and U.S. law. It should recalled that GHQ judged whether the draft SAPL was constitutional by referring to U.S. Constitutional standards, not Japanese constitutional standards. It is, thus, not a coincidence that the first witness was an expert in U.S. law. He was the lawyer who, during the drafting stage of the SAPL was consulted by the government about the constitutionality of the SAPL as drafted. Matsushita explained that the constitutionality issue revolved around three points. 1) Was "incitement" mentioned in article 3 as a criminal act (*tsumi to shite*) in violation of article 21 of the Constitution. Freedom of speech, publication and organization is guaranteed in the Constitution but it is unanimously agreed that this is not absolute and cited three exceptions: a) that exceptions do themselves exist, such as those in the U.S. and British laws and common law about defaming god, contempt of court, libel and slander of individuals, and to incite criminal acts, b) when there is clear and present danger these freedoms may be circumscribed based on legal interpretations in the U.S., such as the Smith Act, and c) whatever speech the Congress declares to be a danger to society (citing the 1924 Gitlow case in the U.S. Supreme Court) cannot be declared not dangerous by the U.S. Supreme Court.[26] 2) Was the administrative authority given to the PSEC to limit or disband organizational activities a violation of articles 11, 13 and 21 of the 1947 Japanese Constitution. These decisions would be constitutional if the standards which the PSEC used for its decision were clear. 3) Would procedures undertaken based on Articles 17–25 of the draft SAPL be a violation of article 13 and others of the Constitution? Constitutionality depends on whether the agency (PSIA) requesting the control measures and the deciding agency (the PSEC) are separate, whether the proceedings are publicly held, not in camera, and whether the PSEC decision can be meaningfully appealed to the courts. In each case, the answer was yes. Thus, Matsushita declared the SAPL constitutional in each of these three points—although GHQ had doubts in the opposite direction about the SAPL—basically by citing U.S. and British legal practices.

3. *Those opposed to the SAPL.* In contrast to the above group of supporters, the opponents came from a variety of fields: writers (3, **Ishikawa Tatsuzō, Masugi Shizue, Funayama Kaoru**), academicians (4, Dando Shigemitsu, Hirano Yoshitarō, Ōmori Shin'ichirō, Ukai Nobushige), labor union leaders (2, Kikugawa Tadao, Yoshida Sukeharu), newspapers(2, Nishijima Yoshiji/*Asahi* Shimbun,Yamane Shinjirō/*Tokushima Shimbun*), lawyers (2, Nagano Kunisuke, Kiyose Ichirō) and women's organizations (1, Kushida Fuki).

[26] In the testimony, a Japanese pronunciation was used, Jitturo. I guessed that it might be Jitrow, Gitrow and found the U.S. Supreme Court case, Gitlow v. The People of the State of New York 268 U.S. 652 (1925). In this case Benjamin Gitlow was convicted and sent to prison for the crime of criminal anarchy (New York Penal Law 160, 161). The Penal Law said it was a felony to advocate "criminal anarchy" "either by word of mouth or writing" for example, his publication of *The Leftwing Manifesto.* There was no evidence of any effect resulting from the publication and circulation of the Manifesto. No mitigating circumstances, such as actual intent, or teaching to one or one thousand people or effectiveness were considered. Just the mere act of writing, publishing, teaching these doctrines was a crime. The [state of New York] legislature has the authority to forbid the advocacy of a doctrine designed and intended to overthrow the government without waiting until there is a present and imminent danger of the success of the plan advocated [this method of reasoning was used by Seki in explaining the need for the SAPL]. It was not necessary, within the meaning of the statute, that the defendant should have advocated 'some definite or immediate act or acts' of force, violence or unlawfulness. Justices Brandeis and Holmes dissented asserting that "there was no present danger of an attempt to overthrow the government by force on the part of the admittedly small minority.... Every idea is an incitement.... But the indictment alleges the publication and nothing more".

The three novelists had one major concern in common: the SAPL created itself an atmosphere of implied censorship, that what they write could be construed as incitement by the whim of a PSIA investigator. Masugi Shizue described the SAPL as a finely honed Japanese sword; depending on who wields it, it cuts effectively to the right or to the left. She derived her beliefs from her prewar experiences as a writer visiting China under the sponsorship of the Japanese Army. Funayama Kaoru said what his group feared most was the possibility, if not probability, of arbitrary and abusive enforcement, particularly by the investigating officer (*chōsakan*). Ishikawa Tatsuzō, novelist and Chairman of the Nihon Bungeika Kyōkai, accused the government of having "impure motives" (*fujun na dōki*) in drafting the SAPL; while it was clear in the government's explanation for the SAPL that it was to control the Communists but communism was not mentioned anywhere in the SAPL. As a result, the scope of the law becomes extremely broad. It must be remembered that during the war [WWII] suppression of speech and the imprisonment of innocent people was also called "preventive" action. The very title of the SAPL contains "Prevention", i.e. detain, arrest, charge a person as a preventive measure. Ishikawa provided some examples:

- The Yokohama Incident where, toward the end of WWII, 34 media people were detained; two died in prison, and one died after his release.[27]
- Ishikawa's friend and commentator went to China and met with some Chinese writers two or three times. When he returned to Japan, he was detained by the police for over ten months, never charged with a crime in a court. Eventually he just came out of the police station and soon after the war died.

Our last line of defense is freedom of speech and the SAPL has the possibility of suppressing this freedom. The wartime patriotic Diet—*yokusan Gikai*—practice of approving without much question whatever the military wanted was a sad record indeed, and no attempt was made to keep alive the right to the freedom of expression. The worsening

[27] Ono Sada, Kiga Sumiko. *Yokohama Jiken: Tsuma to Imōto no shuki* (The Yokohama Incident: Personal notes of a wife and younger sister). Tokyo. Kōbunken. 1987. 219 p.

internal security situation was given as the justification for the SAPL without any reason for the cause of this presumed instability. In the postwar period, we have built an even greater and stronger bureaucratic government (*kanryō kokka*) with a police force with greater powers. Because of the oppression from their own government, the Japanese are a pitiable people (*kawaii sō na kokumin*).

Dandō Shigemitsu, professor of law at the University of Tokyo, raised as one of the most serious objections to the SAPL, the definition of "incitement" as used in articles 3 and 37 of the SAPL. As a base, he cited the prewar Japanese Supreme Court (Dai-Shin'in) decision of 11/4/1930 regarding incitement: an action which leads to a decision/determination in a person or encourages/aids (*jochō-suru*) a person to commit a crime constitutes incitement, however, it would not be necessary for that person to make that decision to commit that crime in order for incitement to have taken place. The definition of incitement is vague here and far too broad and unclear as a definition in the SAPL. To ascribe a crime to the printing, distribution and possession of certain materials would be a great invasion of the freedom of speech. To permit these broad interpretations would extremely widen the net of investigation by the PSIA and will drive the present tendency of the Tokkō-ization of the police. When the Criminal Code already includes the preparation of such crimes as arson, murder, robbery, it is highly questionable whether it is appropriate to so widely broaden the crimes to include plotting, instigation and incitement. He doubts whether there is a legal need to include articles 38 and 39. Under the existing Criminal Code, instigation becomes a crime when it is committed. But in the SAPL, instigation and other acts themselves have been made into independent criminal acts (*dokuritsu-zai*) regardless of whether any acts are committed as a result of the specific instigation or incitement. Aside from the penalties, the constituent elements of the crime are far too broad and unclear and these will result in difficulties (*heigai*) whether decided by a court or investigated by the PSIA. Incitement as a independent criminal act should be deleted from the SAPL. Since the SAPL includes penalties for organizations and individuals, it has, in essence as a special law, revised the basic Criminal Code of the nation, thus it would be preferable to formally revise the CC or treat the SAPL as if we were revising the basic criminal code; the changes are sufficiently important and basic for this action. He asked why there were admonitions about the standards of control but no such admonitions about the investigations. He had a fundamental doubt about the procedures to be followed in deciding on the control of these organizations, i.e., instead of an administrative agency making an administrative decision on the life and death of an organization, that decision should be made through the courts. According to the SAPL, only those documents and materials from among those submitted by the accused as judged by the PSIA investigator will be submitted to the PSEC as the only basis for its decision. As allowed by the SAPL, an appeal to the courts could be made to seek relief and, if the courts decided to dismiss the PSEC decision, this would be "tantamount to nonsense" (*hotondo nunsensu ni chikai*) since the PSEC decision, e.g. disbanding an organization, terminating publications, or prohibiting mass meetings, become effective immediately. Furthermore, the consideration by the court or its decision may be vacated if that court decision would be deemed to have an adverse effect on the public welfare or if the PM objected to the court's actions. Some kind of internal security law was necessary but the legal structure of the proposed SAPL was not acceptable. He explained that the SAPL put the first emphasis on controlling organizations, then on individuals; Dandō recommended that a law should first punish individuals for their actions in the courts, and then, if these individuals had committed these crimes as part of an organization's activities then, as phase two, take administrative actions to control these organizations.

Ukai Nobushige, constitutional law professor at the University of Tokyo (and later after retirement from Tokyo University at the International Christian University in Tokyo), voiced his opposition to the draft SAPL since it was not the correct method to use in responding to the security situation presently facing Japan. He described five points as the basis for his opposition to the SAPL. 1) The use of administrative action for control purposes do not fulfill the conditions necessary for such action and are, as proposed, contrary to the spirit and substance of Article 31 of the Constitution. When a person's life is involved or freedom to be deprived, the defendant must be able to conduct interrogations and have an opportunity to be heard which is not allowed under draft SAPL. 2) Adequate and proper relief from these administrative actions have not been provided under the SAPL. In the first place, the decision of the PSEC becomes effective immediately before relief can be sought in the courts and could be prevented at the request of the PM. He cited the U.S. Internal Security Law of 1950 (the McCarran Act) because it had presumably been used as a model for the SAPL; it requires that while the decision is appealed to the courts, the decision will not be carried out and that it was estimated that such appeals could last 7–8 years. Even then President Truman vetoed the bill fearing it unduly restricted freedom of assembly and speech. 3) While administrative action concerning economic matters may be acceptable in some cases, when it comes to spiritual and philosophical freedoms such administrative actions are unacceptable. Even under the Meiji constitution, prohibition of publication had to be decided by a court. The proposed SAPL under the new Constitution is even more regressive than under the old Meiji Constitution. 4) the controls under the SAPL unduly restrict the freedoms of speech, assembly, belief, and expression and academic freedom. Merely to instigate and to incite without an action arising therefrom has been made into an independent crime in and of itself. It is necessary for these actions to have led to chaos in society for them to be punishable. 5) Notwithstanding how acceptable the SAPL may be, it is subject to serious abuse, that is inevitable. He cited an example which happened on the previous day. Professors on administrative law and the Constitution attended a hearing of the House Legal Affairs Committee as part of the general meeting of the Japan Public Law Association (Nihon Kōhō Gakkai). We were searched upon entering the hearings: a copy of the outline of the Public Elections Law and a small pen knife with a blade less than one inch were taken away. In order to maintain public welfare, the right to private property, to choice of employment and work could be restricted but for other freedoms, this rationale may not be used. Under questioning, he believed that the existing criminal code was adequate for maintaining internal security, the SAPL was not necessary.

The professors of law gave the most detailed legal support and rationale for the SAPL and also the most systematic condemnation of the SAPL; others were more vague in their comments, several provided vivid examples of abuse by the government and from personal experiences. It was pointed out that the PPL did not mention the JCP but the PPL was expanded and then expanded again; similarly the SAPL also does not mention the JCP and could be expanded again as in the prewar legislation. After the initial statements by the experts, various committee members questioned some experts mostly the lawyers in some detail. Even Liberal Party members of the majority often seemed to pursue such issues as potential abuse with seeming sincerity. The two women novelists who themselves gave vague statements of unease with the SAPL were basically ignored by committee members during the Q&A part of the hearings; in contrast, the professors and lawyers were addressed by committee members of all parties with special respect and deference for their scholarly and legal knowledge. It was clear that almost all the expert witnesses distrusted the government centering around how "incitement" would be interpreted and carried out by the PSIA and PSEC, called for radical revisions and many called for outright withdraw which, of course, the government would not accept. The hearings were held with considerable civility except for occasional kibitzing comments, the friendly witnesses and those opposed were treated with equal respect and most polite Japanese language, but it was all undoubtedly done and participated in by both sides with a sense of futility, except to establish a parliamentary record.

D. *Recovery of Independence, the 1952 May Day Riot and Student-Police Clashes*

i. *Recovery of Independence*

On April 28, 1952 the Peace Treaty between Japan and most of the Allied Powers of WWII became effective and Japan regained its "independence". It was a joyous occasion, an occasion which the people obviously had been looking forward to with great expectations, the economy appeared to be gaining momentum and the future was looking brighter, even though a war was raging next door. Japan played no substantive active military role in the Korean War but a passive non-violent supporting role. It was, however, gaining great economic benefit from this conflict. Yet the days and weeks and months leading up to this day must also have been one of simultaneous anxiety, uncertainty and many unpleasantnesses. There were the mass demonstrations against the partial Peace Treaty and bitter wrangling in the Diet which had divided the nation about the merits of a separate or partial peace treaty excluding the Soviet Union and Communist China. There was also the bubbling and occasional eruptions with union strikes against the government's proposed internal security law, the SAPL.

Within three days after the treaty went into effect, several "events" which accentuated the above-mentioned anxiety, uncertainty and unpleasantnesses somewhat over-shadowed the more joyous event.

On April 28, 1952, to emphasize their opposition to the new Peace Treaty without the Soviet Union and Communist China, the Communist dominated Zengakuren student union tried to organize a strike at the University of Tokyo but it was a mere blip on the horizon of more momentous affairs, an annoyance, not a threat.

On May 1, 1952, the *Akahata*, organ of the JCP, which had been ordered to cease publication in mid-1950 by the Government based on a directive from the Occupation, resumed publication. The authority of the directive used for this purpose in 1950 by the Japanese government would ceased to be effective when the peace treaty went into effect. While the conservatives in the government probably would have liked to have continued this prohibition, it would have immediately been challenged in the courts and the probability of success in the courts under the 1947 Constitution would have been extremely small. But it would remind them of the vacuum that did exist in internal security arrangements. Even if the SAPL had already been enacted, the maximum prohibition period would have been six months and the criteria for securing this restriction would have been far stricter and difficult to fulfill than carrying out a mere directive from the erstwhile Occupation authorities. The Japanese authorities were basically powerless to take any sustainable legal action against the JCP and *Akahata*, even if they had wished to do so.

ii. *The Imperial Plaza, The People's Plaza*

The traditional international May Day celebrations had been peacefully celebrated in the spacious grounds in front of the Imperial Palace in Tokyo. To Japanese conservatives, these serene quiet grounds with gnarled pine trees should not be violated by leftist or Communist celebrants, however innocent. But on May 1, 1950 just about the time, the JCP, under pressure from their communist colleagues in the Soviet world, changed their tactics from peaceful to more violent approaches. U.S. soldiers and cars in and around the parade area suddenly found themselves under attack. This changed the nature of these celebrations. Initially, GHQ was willing to allow the May 1951 celebrations to take place as in the past. But the conservative Japanese government appealed successfully to reverse its stand—after all these conservatives were the supporters of U.S. policy and the U.S. also wanted their support for strategic coldwar reasons. On March 13, 1952, the government decided the 1952 May Day rally cannot be held in the Imperial

Plaza but it could be held in Jingō Gaien, near the Meiji Shrine somewhat away from the center of downtown Tokyo particularly away from the Imperial/People's Plaza. The Tokyo District Court decided on April 28, 1952, however, the day when the Peace Treaty came into effect, that it was unconstitutional to prohibit a demonstration on the Imperial Plaza. Suddenly the legal situation became ambiguous. Sōhyō and its affiliates decided to proceed with celebrations as worked out with the government to be held Jingō Gairen, near the Meiji Shrine but away from the center of Tokyo. The event took place as planned in a quiet and orderly manner. But as the event came to a close, a small group shouted onward to the People's/Imperial Plaza. It had been planned that five columns would march through various parts of Tokyo but toward the Plaza. As one column neared the Plaza, it erupted into a violent melee between protesters and the riot police, a bloody riot of smoke, overturned cars, teargas, pistol firing, fighting with staffs without the use of heavy weapons, artillery, and aircraft; over 1000 demonstrators and police were injured but amazingly only two deaths at the time (some later from injuries). The riots subsided around 6:30 PM, a politically decisive confrontation lasting only a few hours. To the conservatives in general and to those then in power, these riots were unforgivable, blasphemous and a desecration of Imperial Grounds, especially since they were literally in front of the Imperial Palace where His Majesty the Emperor resides. Demonstrations were never held again on these grounds; they have returned to their original serene atmosphere where many lovers now gather at various times of the day under the enticing gnarled pines. This violent clash was the worst riot in the postwar history of Japan except for the subsequent 1960 anti-Security Treaty demonstrations eight years later which ultimately persuaded President Eisenhower not to go to Japan on a state visit. The 1960 demonstrations were massive and threatening yet not destructively violent (even though one death occurred); the 1952 riots were challengingly massive and deliberately violent. It is difficult to imagine, why, if the JCP was genuinely opposed to the proposed SAPL, it would organize such violent mass demonstrations on the Imperial Plaza, the Jimmin Hiroba, for it must have known that this would radically change the tone of the dialogue and debate about the merits and need for an SAPL. Probably the violent May Day riots were a natural extension of the pin-pricking violent attacks mainly against government facilities as mandated by the International Comintern in 1950; it was a momentum that either the JCP could not, would not or did not want to stop, even to derail the SAPL. Perhaps and probably, they felt that the enactment of the SAPL could not be prevented and thus let the momentum continue unabated, even if the ultimate target, revolution as described above, was unattainable. A last desperate burst of violence.

In one fell swoop, the May Day Riots had completely compromised Sōhyō-Rōtō's struggle against the SAPL. Sōhyō, the principal organizer of the May Day Celebrations; promptly on May 2 it denounced these violent tactics as the work of radical elements in the JCP, disclaimed any relationship with these rioters, asserted that such acts would only lead to the rise of reactionary fascism, injure the development of democracy in Japan and a betrayal of the working class. It pointed out that the government will be handling the rioters under the riot provisions of the CC, thereby proving the lack of a need for the SAPL and will use this incident as an excuse to retrogressively revise the labor laws and push for the enactment of the SAPL and trample on the rights of workers. On the other hand, at House Committee hearings on May 2, the Commissioner of Police, the AG and LM took great pains to point out that detailed arrangements and agreements had been concluded between the authorities and several national labor organizations about how and where the May Day celebrations would be held and the five routes that would be used for the demonstration marches, and that Sōhyō and Sōdōmei affiliated labor unions had conducted the celebrations peacefully, smoothly and with solemnity, and in accordance with the agreements and disbanded at the agreed points in Tokyo—although, of course, the Ministers had earlier denounced their strike tactics opposing the SAPL as illegal. They drew a clear distinction between the activities of the regular unions and the "violent destructive activities" of some union members, about 5000 Zengakuren student radicals and about 2500 Koreans (mostly north Koreans of course) who broke ranks and swarmed from Hibiya Park onto the People's Plaza. The Police Commissioner described these rioters in unusually strong Japanese for presumably sedate public hearings—*kichiku*, the devil, symbolic of darkness and destruction—reserved for those for whom one has great distaste, dislike, contempt. He reported that 68 police were critically wounded, light injuries 672 and that 143 had been arrested; some were indicted but years later the indictments were rejected by the courts.[28]

Meeting on May 3 in response to the May Day Riots, the Yoshida Cabinet was enormously concerned with the foreign reaction to these riots and the worldwide image this would leave about post-treaty Japan; in addition, it decided to recommend that the Metropolitan Police Commissioner will, in the future, appoint the members of the National Public Security Commission (Kokka Kōan Iinkai), that it will submit as early as possible to the Diet revisions of the basic labor laws, and enact the SAPL without changes. As Committee hearings were concluding the AG made a rather revealing comment about the May Day riots and the security apparatus:

> ...Tokyo is designated as a special area and has its own Public Security Examination Commission. The national government does not have the authority to intervene in this area. In regards to the May Day riots, the government had no way of intervening and taking any action. The Public Security Examination Commission for the Tokyo special area is solely responsible for the management of the security for this area. Since Tokyo is the political and economic center of the country, and where foreign envoys are all located, and from the overall responsibilities of the national government, this inability of the government to intervene in police matters is totally unacceptable. We must consider ways to be able to intervene into police matters for the special Tokyo area. But this issue must be handled in a democratic manner by a democratic country. For the national government to issue instructions to the Tokyo special area must be most carefully considered before decisive action is taken. It is from this point of view that the government hopes to revise the Police Law [without giving any details since they had not been worked out at that time] for this purpose (5/13:10).[29]

---

[28] As a result of police investigations, 1137 were arrested, 261 were indicted for rioting and violent activities under the Criminal Code in mid-July 1952. The SAPL, though enacted by the Diet in early July did not become effective until after this indictment. A large amount of the evidence provided by the prosecution was not accepted by the court in April 1964. The indictments were ultimately rejected in 1966, 14 years after May Day 1952. (*Sengo Nijūnen*-shi, 3:421–425). In the HofC Committee hearings, Baba Yoshitsugu, a government prosecutor, reported that as of 6/16/1952, of the 180 indicted to date, three were under 16 years, ten under 19 years (6/17:7).

[29] Reflecting the anxieties of the government stemming from the May Day Riots, it decided to push forward for an early submission to the Diet of a revised police law. It should be recalled the restructuring of the internal security apparatus was a major concern of the government parallel to drafting the SAPL. A few days later on May 7, 1952, the Cabinet decided to give the PM broad new powers: 1) because the security

iii. *Student-Police Clashes on University Campuses*

There is a long history of police-university student confrontation and conflict going back to the 1930s. The autonomy and freedom of the academy and the clash with what the police presume to be their responsibilities. While universities naturally did not enjoy extraterritoriality the balance between self-governance and police intrusion was in delicate balance even before 1945. In the postwar period, the student movement symbolized by the extremist Zengakuren had been radicalized unfortunately, especially under Communist influence. Because of the government's determination to enact a new internal security law and because of the well known past history of such laws in Japan, it was only natural and to be expected that the more active student leaders would attempt to mobilize university students in opposition to such laws. The police gave the students opportunities for creating, agitating for and provoking incidents on campuses by sending in plainclothes policemen surreptitiously to interrogate students and university officials, to photograph bulletin boards, surreptitiously enter student meetings, theatrical presentations and other events. These indeed were reminiscent of prewar Japanese police tactics. To continue these tactics while the controversial law was being considered would appear to be quite unnecessary, seemingly quite provocative and counter-productive whatever rationale the police may have had for such intrusions. In testifying to the Diet about the Kyoto University clash, President Ushioda of Keio University speculated that perhaps students had "an instinctual dislike" of police officers, suggesting something fatalistic and inevitable about these clashes (*Asahi* 5/10/1952) and I would add, a dislike of university students as a privileged bunch and especially if the police thought they were politically radical students. From January to early May 1952, there were at least eight major clashes between university students, a rowdy and boisterous minority of students and the police:

---

of the capital, Tokyo, was fundamental to national security, the Prime Minister would appoint the Tokyo Commissioner of Police and part of the Tokyo police budget would be provided from the national treasury, 2) the Minister in Charge of the Police (*Kokkei*) would also be appointed by the PM, and 3) if the PM believes it was necessary from the standpoint of maintaining public security, he may provide the necessary instructions for this purpose, to the national Public Security Examination Commission or to the head of the police forces.

University of Tokyo, 2/20/1952 on campus and about the same time, police units dispersed General Education students of Todai demonstrating against rearmament of Japan in front of Shibuya station.
University of Hokkaido, 3/18/1952
University of Tokyo second clash, 4/20/1952
Kyoto University, 4/23/1952
University of Tokyo third clash, 4/30/1952
University of Tokyo General Education students, 5/2/1952
Aichi University, 5/7/1952
Waseda University, 5/8/1952

During the Committee hearings, two clashes between students and police occurred, one at Aichi University in Aichi Prefecture midway between Tokyo and Osaka, on May 7 and at Waseda University which began on May 8 and continued into the early morning hours of May 9, 1952.[30] Coming as they did just after the May Day riot and during Committee hearings, they struck a raw nerve on both sides. A student group found a plainclothes officer clandestinely taking notes at a theatrical meeting (the first mistake by the police at this sensitive time). The students angrily surrounded him, detained him, took away his police notebook, questioned him, without informing the university authorities (the first mistake by the student group). Eventually this resulted in discussions between university officials and the police which dragged on and on into the night. Then in a provocative move, several hundred heavily armed National Police Reserve (NPR, the incipient Japanese Army) were stationed outside the University gate in a highly threatening posture. While there are many details that could be narrated, the end result was that while negotiations were still on-going, the NPR troops stormed the University and beat the sitting, unarmed, unprepared and un-resisting students resulting in many injuries; as many students as possible fled. Even a senior university official who was trying to mediate was beaten and trampled without mercy by the NPR. At a Committee hearing the Minister of Education stated that the students were restrained, he accepted (*ryōshō*) the statement by

[30] This account is derived from newspapers and the testimony to the House Legal Affairs committee in the afternoon session on May 10 (pp. 12–22) by Waseda Univeristy president Shimada Kōichi, Takiguchi Hiroshi, Director, Student Welfare Department (Gakusei Kōseibu Buchō), and Tanaka Eiichi, Chief of the Tokyo Metropolitan Police. Their respective reports do not completely dovetail each other and do differ in some of the details.

the President of Waseda University asserting that we must decisively (*danko*) fight/resist/struggle against the police to defend the freedom of the academy (*gakuen no jiyū*), that while universities do not have extraterritoriality, under present social conditions, controls must be used carefully and with proper preparation. (The opposition clapped in his support while the Liberal Party shouted [Minister of Education] "Amano resign"!). The DG of the University Affairs Bureau (Daigaku Gakujutsukyoku) passed judgment on the conduct of both the students and the Police: student actions when too far (*yuki sugi*) when they directly interrogated a police officer without first consulting with university authorities and the actions by the Police, judging by the results, while discussions and negotiations were in progress, were most regrettable. At a later HofC committee hearing, AG Kimura made a similar comment that while the May Day Riot was planned and premeditated, the police-student clash at Waseda University was most regrettable (*hijō ni ikan de atta*) (5/19:14) and stated that force must be used to the least extent necessary to carry out police responsibilities based on the judgment of the officer-in-charge on the scene. Based on reports received so far, it was regrettable that judgment and liaison by the police were inadequate. Depending on one's predisposition, such clashes vividly "proved" the need for the SAPL and conversely the imperative to reject the SAPL as a resurrection of the prewar PPL.

E. *House Approval*

Because of the May Riots, the Liberal Party's General Affairs Committee (*Sōmukai*) decided that the government's draft SAPL would be passed expeditiously without revisions by the House in plenary session. The initial attitude to make some accommodations was discarded. This decision was brought to the attention of the hearings of the experts and resulted in a rather emotional confrontation with those opposing the law and heckling by Liberal Party members. Nevertheless, several Liberal Party members of the Committee (Chairman Sase Shōzō, Kaji Ryōsaku, Tajima Yoshifumi) appear to have been genuinely interested in working with the Kaishintō in revising the draft SAPL in a few places in a substantive manner. It was felt that this cooperative effort might lesson the confrontation and facilitate passage of the bill in the House of Councillors, and be responsive to public opinion.[31] Those points were to create a stipulation about penalties against officials who abuse their authority and more narrowly define what destructive violent activities would be under the term "incite". But the Liberal Party members in the Upper House let it be known that such revisions were not welcome and the senior leadership (*kambu*) of the Liberal Party also decided to call for a Committee vote without revisions of the draft SAPL.

Committee hearings ended on May 13. The Legal Affairs Committee convened on the morning of May 15 to hear final arguments, an explanation of two sets of proposed revisions and vote on these proposals and finally the complete bill; since the Liberal Party's Diet Operations Committee had decided that a final House vote would be taken on May 15 on the SAPL, the last few days reached a new crescendo of frenzied activity.

The majority Liberal Party members on the House Legal Affairs Committee decided, with persuasive pressure from Party leadership that "incitement" (*sendō*) and other controversial terms would remain in the SAPL and did propose some important revisions which, while not challenging the core philosophy of the SAPL, were relatively significant. The interplay of party discipline, demands of the Party leadership for a vote on the SAPL without changes, the drumbeat impact of the hearings, the relative validity of the many issues raised continuously at these hearings, undoubtedly had a cumulative impact on the ideological propensities of even some conservative Liberal Party members of the Committee, and did have some impact on the outcome. The Legal Affairs Committee chairman, Sase Shōzō, pressed for revisions described below which he hoped would be acceptable to the Kaishintō, persuade them not to submit an alternative legislative

[31] *Yomiuri Shimbun* (5/9/1952) reported that based on letters to the editor (*tōkō*) those opposed to the SAPL were slightly higher than those in favor. Though not "scientific" it was a measure of the public's reaction to the draft SAPL. Those opposed felt that the enactment of the SAPL would result in destroying the freedom of labor unions, ignoring human rights, and a revival of police politics (84), strengthen the existing criminal code and police powers, and consider other measures to control JCP violent activities (34). Those in favor of the SAPL felt it was only natural to have an internal security law after achieving independence and in light of the violent group activities (68), avoid abuse of authority by carrying out this law fairly and accurately (40). There were also those in the "middle" who wished to let the Diet deliberations make the decision, assuring the democratic management of the PSEC, the protection of human rights and freedom (58). The younger generation generally were opposed to the SAPL, the older generation in favor of the SAPL.

plan. He hoped for Kaishintō cooperation in passing upcoming legislation on police laws, labor laws, prohibition of general strikes and emergency situation legislation and apparently these revisions would also help incidentally to persuade the Ryokufūkai in the HofC, which would be a pivotal force in that House in securing the passage of the SAPL. Reluctantly the Liberal Party managers allowed him to try.

Liberal Party member, Tajima Yoshifumi's explanation of the proposed revisions especially his parallel sentence structure to drive home his points could hardly have pleased the party leadership and the government witnesses. He stated that even those who favored the SAPL expressed concern that:

> ...was there not a fear (*osore*) that in implementing this law, there would be an infringement on human rights, was there not a fear that there could be abusive implementation, and was there not a fear that the SAPL would provide the basis/foundation for the bureaucratic authorities to move in the same direction as happened under the prewar PPL?
> The PSEC would be faced with making a decision about the life or death of an organization based on the unilateral investigation by the PSIA without any ability on its part to make its own investigation. If that is the case, then it would be necessary to remove these fears and present to the people a better law.... We have concluded that because investigations could be without limit (*museigen*)—open ended in colloquial English—there is a fear that this could lead to the 'abuse of authority' and proposed the following changes:

1. In article 3.1.1.2 a grammatical clarification was proposed by making 3.1.1.2 into two subsections as follows: a new 3.1.1.2 would now read simply, to instigate and incite those actions mentioned in 3.1.1.1 and the remainder of 3.1.1.2 beginning with "those who possess materials would be made into a new 3.1.1.3.
2. Article 15. Materials submitted by the defendant organization may be deemed "unnecessary" and the reference to the Hearing officer would be deleted.
3. Article 21. The PSEC would be given its own authority to investigate a case presented to it by the DG/PSIA. This would balance the potentially one sided nature of the PSIA investigation responding partially to concerns expressed by several of the expert witnesses and in reality would somewhat down grade the potential authority of the PSIA report since it could be challenged more directly. The PSEC would remain an outer bureau of the AG but seemingly more independent from the AG.
4. PSEC Establishment Law. Article 5 will stipulate that the members of the PSEC will be nominated to the Diet by the PM instead of the AG as in the original draft submitted to the Diet.

5. PSEC Establishment Law. Article 14 would give the PSEC its own secretariat to manage its affairs, not the secretariat under the AG or later under the Minister of Justice (5/15:1–2).

These and other lesser revisions were intended to clarify, avoid misunderstandings but not to change the proposed law in any fundamental manner. Minor clarifying textual revisions were made to articles 1, 3, 4, 6, 37, and supplementary articles. These revisions would establish more clearly that the independent character of the crime to incite and instigate and would contribute to dispelling an ambiguity and differentiate between these offenses and others.

Sase appealed to the Kaishintō for its support but failed. Instead, the Kaishintō's Diet Operations and Policy committees decided it would present its own motion of five points to revise the draft SAPL to the Legal Affairs Committee and the House plenary session and would not support the Liberal Party unless it accepted these fundamental revisions—which it must have realized would be rejected by the Liberal Party. The Kaishintō's position, it must be emphasized, was based on the recognition of the need for some kind of internal security law was unfortunately necessary in light of the present international position of Japan and in order to guard against violent destructive activities by both the extreme left and extreme rightwing. In explaining his party's revisions, Nakamura Mataichi described the SAPL as the most unpopular bill he had seen so far in his parliamentary experience; this unpopularity stemmed from the fact that the SAPL does not provide assurances that it would provide the most effective method in controlling destructive activities without infringing inappropriately on human rights. He described the SIB as a relic from the Occupation which was used as a springboard for creating the SAPL, expanding the SIB under a new name, quite a severe and strong critique of the Occupation security structure which was being proposed by the conservative Yoshida government to be extended into the post-independence period. The Party felt sufficiently strongly enough that national resources could be more efficiently used if the prosecutorial and police functions and organizational structure were strengthened and made more effective rather than creating a separate bureaucracy for this purpose.

1. Legislation to create the PSIA and PSEC would be withdrawn
2. An SAPL would be created but a) a District Court would be substituted for the PSEC and prosecutors (*kensatsukan*) for the PSIA, and a system to handle appeals would be created, b) detailed regulations

to be followed by the District Court concerning its structure and procedures for handling administrative actions would be decided by the Supreme Court.
3. The SIB under the AG would be abolished.
4. In response to the above changes, the Procurator's office and the police will be strengthened.
5. If the control functions are sufficient (*jūjitsu sureba*), then the clauses concerning "incitement" and the "possession" of written materials (*bunsho no shoji*) would be unnecessary and would be deleted (5/15:3–5).

There were several supporting and denunciatory statements by members of the Liberal Party and Shin-Liberal Party members of the Committee, supporting statements of the Kaishintō alternative and denunciatory statements of the SAPL by the left and right SDP, the JCP, the Minshutō and the Shakai Kakushintō.[32] Particularly caustic in his denunciations of the SAPL was Inomata Kōzō who compared the SAPL to Nazi German laws and abuse of human rights. In the final vote, the Kaishintō revision was rejected as expected and the revisions sponsored by the Liberal Party's committee majority as described above was passed by that Party's 14 votes and one vote from the Daisan Kurabu, 15 out of 25. Those opposed were SDP-L, SDP-R, JCP, Shakai Minshutō and the Rōnōtō.

Ōnishi Masao of the Kaishintō supported his party's revised SAPL. He characterized the so-called independence of the PSEC as having no content whatsoever. The contents of the SAPL reveals the government's grasp of democracy as weak and shallow. It has tried but has been unable to keep track of the whereabouts of the underground JCP leadership; another law will not improve this situation. The inclusion of "incitement" and the mere possession of certain materials with the presumed intention of displaying them is completely excessive and a fraud which the people will readily recognize (5/15:7–8).

Taman Hirobumi, SDP-R, although of the more conservative group of the SDP, was caustic in his critique and denunciation of the SAPL along following lines: 1) to give such authority to the *wan-man* (one man) arbitrary and authoritarian PM—referring of course to Yoshida Shigeru—to choose members of the PSEC for Diet approval was

[32] Kaji Ryōsaku and Sekō Kōichi (Shin-Liberal Party) made supporting statements for Liberal Party revisions, Ōnishi Masao for the Kaishintō alternative, and the others denounced the SAPL: SDP-R (Taman Hirobumi), SDP-L (Inomata Kōzō), JCP (Tanaka Gyōhei), the Shakai Minshutō (Satake Haruki).

retrogressive and only raises still further the anxieties of the people concerning such a law, 2) the use of collective violence (*shūdan bōryoku*) by the police against, for example, Waseda University students exemplifies the ideology of an authoritarian government to settle such matters through the use of brute police force, 3) the implications of the relevance of the PPL to the present cannot be ignored. Even liberal professor Nitobe Tatsukichi of Tokyo Imperial University was ensnared in its web during the 1930s for his theory that the Emperor was an organ of the state; additionally conservative party leader, Hoshijima Jirō, was against the passage of the PPL. The promises made by the government when the PPL was considered by the Diet were most similar to the assurances being given by government officials in justifying the SAPL; nevertheless the PPL was broadened and penalties raised to the death sentence. 4) Dissolution of an organization by the PSEC under the SAPL is hardly the same as the dissolution of an organization under the commercial, civil and criminal laws; under the former, officers and all constituents members were purged. 5) the present Criminal Code is sufficient to deal with existing security challenges, 6) relief from abuse of authority was dismissed by government witnesses since it could be handled under existing laws, e.g. civil service law, criminal code, national relief act (kokka baishō-hō); if the SAPL is a special law on the sensitive issue of internal security, then an appropriate special section should be included in the SAPL for this purpose, 7) article 13 stipulates advantageous evidence may be submitted by the accused organization, but article 15 stipulates that this evidence may be ignored if it is deemed unnecessary, and 8) since the CC will suffice, instead of spending huge sums of government resources on the PSIA and PSEC, it would be socially more effective in improving the security situation if the government would provide sufficient funds to alleviate the economic problems of the majority of people (5/15:8–10).

Inomata Kōzō, SDP-L, a caustic critic of the SAPL, based on his personal experience with the prewar police and the broad interpretation of the PPL, naturally called futilely for the rejection of the SAPL.

> ...It is a mistaken notion to expect that the social situation will be taken care of with the passage of the SAPL, the underlying social causes must be addressed to achieve social stability. To do otherwise is an ideological expression of power centered authority (*kenryoku chūshin*)...The fundamental reason for opposition to the SAPL lies in the long Japanese tradition of respect for the government and government bureaucrats, despise the people which was well expressed in the PPL and the suppression of

civil and human rights and which ultimately led to the Pacific War... the postwar Japanese police have become more fierce and aggressive than before the war in attacking civilians with their weapons as exemplified in the attacks on unarmed students of Waseda and Tokyo universities [in May 1952].... It is the reality of this attitude that lurks in the shadows of such a law as the SAPL that arouses the greatest concern for this law.... The fundamental fault with the SAPL is in mixing administrative action and supplementing offences and penalties of the Criminal Code in one law, the SAPL.... Article 3 defines what are destructive activities which constitute the conditions for taking administrative action in controlling organizations, which then are rolled over into Chapter 6 as the constituent elements to be used to impose criminal penalties against individuals. This was clearly explained in the government's expository materials given to Diet members. The destructive activities outlined under SAPL Chapter 6 are administrative constructs but not applicable under the CC. While a law to handle administrative actions against organizations should be more appropriate, and a revision of the CC for crimes and penalties against individuals should be pursued, again as separate legislation. Revising the CC in this way, would have high lighted and accentuated the increased heavy penalties, for example from two to five years imprisonment. That would be disadvantageous, creating a stark contrast, thus the rationale for burying it in the SAPL.

May Day Riots are being handled as a crime of rioting under the CC. What then is the need for the SAPL?... Incitement is not mentioned in the CC and instigation is mentioned as an independent crime. The existing Japanese CC is based on liberalism, protection of human rights, penalties are clearly fixed (*hōtei-shugi*) and maintain a balance among public welfare, individual freedom and protection of human rights. In the Japanese CC, the minimum stipulations are defined for actions to counter preparations and plotting/planning, non-accomplished crimes, instigations are not independent crimes, thus they are based on the commitment of certain crimes.

The draft SAPL will violate these fundamental philosophies underlying the Japanese CC by incorporating Nazi legal ideas of expanded joint legal responsibility of more than one principal to a crime (*kakuchō kyōdō seihan-ron*), or the legal theory of using "intent" as a fundamental deciding factor in deciding the guilt of a person (*ishi keihō*). Through this legal theory a lot of people can be charged with involvement in the same crime.... Thus, the SAPL is based on and would realize the fascistic code of 'centralization of authority' (*kenryoku-shugi*), using 'intent' as a major factor in criminal code interpretations, belief in The Leader concept (*shidōsha genri*).... The concept of using administrative action to control organizations infringes on the constitutionality of articles 13, 21, 23 and 28 of the Constitution.... Furthermore, articles 4 and 6 of the SAPL are aimed not at taking actions against acts already committed, but based on a judgment that certain dangerous acts will be committed in the future, overturning the fundamental philosophy of the CC. To

> allow an administrative agency to make such important judgments is a fundamental error.... Furthermore, a judgment against an organization will include officers and its constituent membership regardless of whether some disagreed with that organization's alleged violent activities, thereby introducing a system of collective or joint responsibility, making all members jointly and severally responsible. [This harks back to the *gonin-gumi* system in the Tokugawa era.]...Lastly, the problem of obtaining relief from the abuse of authority. There should be an equivalent article in the SAPL against organizational abuse of authority, as evidenced by violent police action against Waseda University students; there is no such article only articles of admonitions that such conduct must not take place. Cases of abuse of authority would be handled under the civil service law and other applicable laws. There is no balance (5/15:13–15).

Sekō Kōichi, New-Liberal Party, reluctantly supported the SAPL because of the social situation then prevailing in Japan, one of great concern, one which he described as the night before a revolution (*kakumei no zen'ya*). He described the SAPL as hurriedly-created legislation (*niwaka rippō*), thus extremely dissatisfied with the SAPL as it now exists, but supported it because of the existing social situation in Japan and because his hopes that it could lead to a more satisfactory internal security policy in the future. He expressed his concern about the relationship between the SAPL and the potential mobilization of the National Police Reserve (Keisatsu Yobitai). If the Chairman of the National Security Commission (Kokka Kōan Iinkai) requested the PM to declare a national emergency, he would probably agree and would be immediately safely sequested and the National Police Reserve placed on high alert; on the other hand, an imaginative rebel leader could also act quickly and kidnap the PM. He warned that unless the PSIA employs high caliber personnel to implement the SAPL it will become an explosive issue (5/15:15–16).

Satake Haruki, Shakai Minshutō, asserted several cogent points:

1. The government has not proved a clear and present danger. Numerous materials were provided by the government detailing the various violent activities, date, time and place, methodology, implements and weapons used, etc. but did not enlighten the Diet as to what organization was responsible for these activities—the government was always studying the situation and could not provide a definitive answer at this time—and would likely continue these activities continuously or intermittently. It constantly evaded a direct answer in naming an organization(s) behind these violent activities; their vagueness remained subjective throughout.

2. The government insisted that it is incapable of handling the social unrest and violent activities without the SAPL, yet the alleged culprits and perpetrators of the May Day riots were arrested under existing law. If the government wished to control a yet unknown and unspecified organization behind these riots, then indeed the present criminal code can handle such a case, but that could be remedied by revising the CC just for the narrow subject of controlling organizations dedicated to violent activities. But the government had early decided that it wished to have a special law which would supplement the CC. It also subsequently asserted on a post facto basis that it could have used "incitement" article to handle the May Day riots.

3. There was the danger that in defining violent activities, labor union activities, freedom of speech may be curtailed; since the potential government activities are hemmed in with various conditions, the government tried to assure that violations of this trust would not occur. The several admonitions in the SAPL that investigations must not inappropriately infringe upon appropriate labor union activities and freedom of speech, implies the obverse that some restrictions are acceptable; those restrictions would be invoked in maintaining social welfare and security. Probably maintenance of social welfare is symbolized by legislation to protect the privileges of monopoly and financial capitalism sacrificing the freedom of the working masses.

4. The SAPL could be the springboard to re-creating PPL-type repressive legislation. The SAPL presumes certain limitations on the freedom of speech, assembly, organization and place of living. Despite the three co-equal parts of government, it proposes to assert the primacy of the executive branch, to limit the evidence that could be accepted by the courts, drastically revised and expanded the offenses and increased the penalties in the CC, adoption of the feudalistic system of community responsibility (*hōken-teki renzasei*). The proposed name of the SAPL was changed many times. Enacting the SAPL would be phase 1, phase 2 would be to revise the SAPL regressively (*kai'aku*). It was said, "Establish the SAPL beach head", then the revisions of the SAPL would not be so difficult. Indeed the PPL enacted in 1925 was regressively revised in 1928 and again in 1941.

On the same day in the afternoon on May 15, 1952 the House of Representatives passed the SAPL (194 in favor, 103 against) and two associated bills by voice vote establishing the PSIA and PSEC accepting the afore-mentioned revisions passed by the Legal Affairs Committee and sent the revised bills to the House of Councillors for its consideration.

CHAPTER FIVE

PHASE IV, DIET DELIBERATIONS: HOUSE OF COUNCILLORS

A. *The Context with a Challenging Political Array*

While the deliberations in the House of Representatives had an air of finality from the beginning, the government could not completely take the results in the House of Councillors deliberations for granted. In the 1949 elections, the Liberal Party was a given an absolute majority in the House of Representatives. The composition of the House of Councillors as it began deliberations on the SAPL was based on the June 4, 1950 election as shown below where the Liberal Party was given more seats than in the 1947 elections but far from a majority.

Liberal Party (Liberal Party)	80
Nihon Shakaitō (SDP)	61
Ryokufūkai	54
Kokumin Minshutō	28
Dai-Ichi Kurabu	14
Rōdōsha Nomintō	5
Nihon Kyōsantō	3
Unaffiliated	2
Total	250 (3 vacancies)[1]

From the milieu and political atmospherics point of view, it should be kept in mind that the 1950 election of the House of Councillors produced quite a substantive rearrangement of forces: After the 1947 elections, the Ryokufūkai was a large group with 92 members but had slipped to 57 members after the 1950 elections, in contrast the Liberal Party and the SDP both of which had gained substantially from over 40 to 77 and 62, respectively, and became the two largest parties in the House of Councillors. These two parties would now have

[1] *Shiryō: Sengo Nijūnen-shi*. Nihon Hyōronsha, 1966, 1:222.

more influence but would have to court other political groupings to create a majority. Under these circumstances, the opposition to the SAPL felt that they had a precarious chance, nevertheless a chance, to defeat the bill or talk it into oblivion or force substantive revisions; on the other hand, the government party, Liberal Party, had a positive chance of persuading the numerically weakened Ryokufūkai by tempting them with some important but not core revisions to join it and some other non-Liberal Party conservative members to enact the SAPL. The Ryokufūkai probably as a whole tilted toward the government's position concerning the need for an internal security law. For those in the Ryokufūkai who were already inclined to support the government would have had their beliefs strengthened by the Bloody May Day Riots less than a month previously and other violent incidents that had occurred with wide publicity during the past year and, in particular, since the May Diet Riots. Inevitably the Ryokufūkai would be the target of a fierce campaign by the government and opposition forces for its votes; the seriousness of this campaign was accentuated since the Ryokufūkai was not a party where party discipline could be easily enforced. It was a coalition of people with some sense of policy commonalities and if they behaved as a large group could substantially increase their political authority and influence. The Liberal Party would, under these circumstances as the predominant minority party, watch carefully and quietly watch (*seikan-suru*) how the situation might unfold inside the complicated Ryokufūkai and seek an opportunity to strike a deal at the opportune moment.

B. *The Opposition with a Precarious Choice*

With this precarious choice in mind, the various forces opposing the enactment of the SAPL were energized into action in various ways. On the surface, it would appear the opposition reflected the sentiments of a wide spectrum of Japanese society, at least Japanese intellectual life. The true depth and breadth of opposition to or support of the SAPL is difficult to fathom with certainty. Most organizations issued statements of opposition to the SAPL and did not indulge in boisterous street action. The limelight for direct action of varying degrees was reserved for the radicalized university students, and the labor federations. The newspapers dutifully reported on these latter developments on an almost daily basis. In contrast, it was difficult to find any widespread organized movements, and none were found, in support of the SAPL, comparable in size, form, vocality, structure, etc. to the opposition. One could find quite understandably, an occasional article in a police journal in support of the SAPL. Because of space limitations, only a summary of these various kinds of opposition can be provided here.

The cultural groups of writers, novelists, etc., e.g. the Japan Pen Club, the Nihon Bungei-ka Kyōkai and the Japan Science Council strongly reiterated their standing opposition to the SAPL. Though not a major factor, the editorial staff of many well-established publishers, e.g. Iwanami Shoten, Yūhikaku, Sōgensha, for the first time also raised their voices in opposition. The newspaper publishers association, the Nihon Shimbun Kyōkai, continued its opposition but in a rather low key manner to its membership through their association's journal, not a mass appeal to the populace at large. Sōhyō/Rōtō determinedly pushed forward with preparations for the third strike wave although it was somewhat politically weakened and its political punch somewhat deflated when it had to split the third strike into three smaller "strikes" which would appear as a smaller opposition instead of a unified, integrated, and massive opposition as occurred under strike 2. This fragmentation stemmed from the political orientation of the various unions working under the aegis of Sōhyō/Rōtō and the need now to combat both the SAPL and, in the eyes of some labor unions, the highly disadvantageous revisions to the basic labor laws being proposed in the Diet by the government. In addition, notwithstanding the attempts by Sōhyō/Rōtō to differentiate itself from the continuing violent tactics used by the communists involving the radical student group, Zengakuren, various political stripes of Koreans, particularly North Koreans living in Japan and day laborers, its image of rational, systematic and measured opposition probably became blurred in the minds of legislators and the public in general. Its continued use of the extra-parliamentary tactics of the "political strike" as a weapon of opposition—no matter how Sōhyō/Rōtō may explain the legal and rational justification for these strikes—would and did put Sōhyō/Rōtō at a distinct public relations disadvantage. Obviously sensing a possibility of effective opposition, the professorial group became most active in opposing the SAPL, far more vocal and organized than during the House of Representatives discussions. Student activists became more aggressive, even violent, in their opposition bordering on illegality in many instances. Beginning with the violence of the May Day riots, this relatively small group of radical students in cooperation with other groups probably helped solidify any wavering legislators to support some kind of internal security law. The vernacular press editorialized in accordance with their normal political tendencies: none advocated the withdrawal or defeat of the bill probably sensing that this was improbable, instead advocated certain deletions and word/phrase changes to make the SAPL more palatable and reasonable. The strongly partisan press, the *Nikkeiren Taimusu*, for business interests denounced the labor union movement and its use of non-economic political strikes and support for and threatened law suits—but management never took any real substantive legal actions against labor leaders nor against Sōhyō or Rōtō. The government urged firms to take action against labor leaders but industry had had some rather bruising labor disputes which created a climate of disinclination to pursue a campaign of retribution against labor leaders—to begin with labor losses appear not to have been as great as might have been expected from the several "strikes" by Sōhyō/Rōtō. Sōhyō, through its journal *Sōhyō*, carried on a relentless campaign against the SAPL.

What impact did this barrage of articles have on the deliberations in the House of Councillors or even on the final outcome? That would be difficult to assess but one could say that the sheer volume of the debate with a large majority opposing the draft SAPL probably had an unknown effect because of the types of issues presented to the government, e.g. the constitutionality of certain parts of SAPL. Without a doubt one could quite legitimately assert that this torrent of outburst opposing the SAPL did leave behind a record of the anxieties, fears, unhappiness about such a law and did contribute to the creation of an amorphous context in the implementation of the SAPL over the years. The conservatives and the government would and did, of course, dismiss the opposition as leftish, leftwing fuzzy thinkers or even outright Communists, would imply that those labor leaders were re-tainted using extra-parliamentary, illegal tactics to enhance their personal positions and specific political agendas, even implying that they bordered on not being true Japanese patriots, that those wild students (and naturally "those" Koreans) were communist dominated, and would ignore their outcries and demands for the withdrawal of the bill or any radical revision of the proposed law.

C. *Plenary Session-1: A Polite Formalistic Skirmish*

As the deliberations began in the House of Councillors, it was clear that there was a broad swath of Japanese society that was opposed to the SAPL—and the revisions of the basic labor laws—with varying degrees of passion and systematic institutional organization. While there was only a chance for some technical revisions by the House of Representatives, in the House of Councillors there was a chance, though still a long shot, a better chance that the SAPL could be outright defeated, or force the deliberations to a stalemate with no resolution (*shingi miryō*), or obtain substantive revisions of the SAPL. The political composition of this HoC as described earlier gave the opposition this optimism and sense of possibility. The opposition political parties, particularly the SDP-R represented by Itō Osamu, were determined to pursue the government and hopefully to entice the Ryokufūkai or a significant portion of it to its side. In a postwar "democratic society" in Japan, all these oppositional elements must be tolerated in the eyes of the conservative politicians and the security apparatus; nevertheless, the government represented by the elderly but unflappable conservative nationalist lawyer and *kendō* devotee, AG Kimura Tokutarō, took great pains to convince the members of the Committee on Legal Affairs of the House of Councillors about the need for the SAPL.

In accordance with normal parliamentary procedure, the Cabinet proposed SAPL was submitted to the House of Councillors simultaneously with the House of Representatives on April 17, 1952.[2] The AG first gave a brief explanation of the SAPL to the latter followed by a similar address to the former. The SAPL was transmitted to the HofC for its preparatory consideration (*yobi shinsa*) since it would be considering the SAPL after the House of Representatives had acted on the SAPL.

[2] In writing the following account, I read many newspaper articles from the *Asahi, Mainichi, Yomiuri, Tokyo, Jiji* and the following Diet proceedings (over 700 pages). For plenary sessions: *Dai 13-kai Kokkai, Sangiin Kaigiroku* #29(4/14/1952), #31.2(4/17/1952), #55(6/25/1952), 57(6/28/1952), 58(6/30/1952), 59(7/1/1952), 60 (7/2/1952), 61(7/3/1952). For Committee Hearings: *Dai 13-kai Kokkai, Sangiin Hōmu, Naikaku, Chihō Gyōsei, Rōdō Rengōkai Iinkai Kaigiroku* #1–2(5/10/1952, 5/28/1952), *Dai 13-kai Kokkai, Sangiin, Hōmu Iinkai Kaigiroku* #39–52, 54–60 (5/19/1952–5/24/1952, 5/26/1952–5/27/1952, 5/30/1952–5/31/1952, 6/3/1952–6/6/1952, 6/9/1952–6/10/1952, 6/12/1952–6/14/1952, 6/16/1952–6/19/1952), *Dai 13-kai Kokkai, Sangiin Hōmu Rōdō Rengō Iinkai Kaigiroku* #1–2 (5/30/1952, 5/31/1952). Citations will be made to any of the above materials when it is deemed appropriate and necessary.

On April 14, 1952, a few days ahead of the formal submission of the draft SAPL, an "emergency interpolation" (*kinkyū hitsumon*) was requested and granted to Shibaki Shigeo (SDP-R) and Kaneiwa Den'ichi (JCP). They raised three points which had not been mentioned before: 1) when the *Bōryoku Kōi Tō Shobatsu ni kansuru hōritsu* (The law for the punishment of acts of violence) was enacted in 1926, the then government assured the Diet that it would not be used to control the labor and farmers movements nor the Suiheisha (an organization of Japan's so-called untouchables) but to control violent organizations (*bōryokudan*, violent gangs), and there was even "an accessory resolution" (*futai ketsugi*) attached to the passage of this law specifically addressing the issue of expanded interpretation of the law. Notwithstanding these promises and the resolution, citing this law as an example implied that it had been improperly used; evidence to this effect has not been found. While the expanded interpretation was not a new theme, citing this law was new.[3] 2) the *Gyōsei Shikkō-*

[3] This law, consisting only of three articles, was enacted into law on 4/9/1926, revised several times, the latest in 1995, was amazingly not abolished by the Occupation, and is still effective. The rationale for this law arose after WWI when social conditions in Japan became turbulent, at least in the eyes of the political conservatives and the guardians of public order, the Ministries of Justice and Home Affairs security services: "radical" social ideas, philosophies like communism, socialism, anarchism began penetrating society some of which expressed themselves violently, the social disturbances following the great earthquake of 1923, anxiety about influences from the Soviet Union. From the legal structure aspect, this law was intended to augment the inadequacies of the existing CC in order to respond to the fast changing social conditions: the differences between the principal and accomplice were inadequately handled in the CC, the range of criminal activity had widened considerably through the use of organizations, a m ass of or numerous people (*tashū*) with the use of dangerous weapons, the penalties in the CC for assault, threats, etc were too light, the existence of procedural limitations on pursuing these kinds of cases, the lack of criminal stipulations to handle those who used others to commit crimes by providing an incentive and against those who knowingly committed crimes in anticipation of receiving this gain. This example of creating a new law to augment the inadequacies of the CC under evolving social conditions instead of revising the basic Criminal Code was repeated as a part of the rationale for the SAPL; it was not a new approach used in the postwar period.

Article 1stipulated that those persons who, as part of an organization, or a mass of people (*tashū*) show their strength (*iryoku o shimeshi*), or utilizing this strength as though such an organization or mass of people actually existed (*kasō shite iryoku o shimeshi*), or a few people (*sūnin*) in cooperative action commit acts violating CC articles 201.1, 222 and 260 shall be subject to specified fines and imprisonment; article 2 specified that those who obtain improper financial gain (*zaisei-jō fusei no ri'eki*) or those who with the intent of obtaining similar gains demand meetings (*menkai o kyōsei-shi*) or threaten people for such meetings (*kyōdan ihaku*) using methods in article 1.1 shall be subject to specified fines and imprisonment; article 3 stipulated *hō* (the law for the execution of administration) as revised could be used against all kinds of people according to article 1.[4] 3) The Far East Commission (FEC), an organization which theoretically advised General MacArthur in reforming the Japanese Government and society, issued a unanimously approved statement on December 6, 1946 on the 16 "Principles for Japanese Trade Unions". Articles 4 on worker-employer negotiation and need for arbitration machinery, 5 on prohibition of strikes when they would prejudice Occupation objectives and 6 that labor unions may participate in politics and support political candidates. Article 6 later became controversial and resulted in General MacArthur's directive to the Yoshida Government in 1948 to prohibit strikes by government employees thereby fundamentally revising the labor rights of government employees which to this day have not been changed. In addition, article 13 stipulated that the police may not spy on legitimate labor union activities and strikes and may not suppress these activities. Article 28 of the Japanese Constitution gave unions the right to organize, to negotiate and to carry out organizational activities. Why did the Yoshida Cabinet ignore these principles in drafting the SAPL? The government, to the frustration of the interpolators, merely side-stepped these issues by not answering these challenges directly. In the first place, these "principles" were a relic of the Occupation period which the government could now safely disregard especially since the

---

that those who, using the methods described in article 1 above and with the objective of persuading persons to violate CC articles 204, 208.1, 222, 223, 234, 260 or 261, offered financial items (*kimpin*) or other financial gains, or offered a position, requested (*mōshikomi*) or promised such positions or knowingly received such benefits, demand or promise of such benefits shall be subject to specified fines and imprisonment. Also, those who, using methods specified in article 1, attempted to persuade others with the objective of violating CC article 95 shall be subject to specified fines and imprisonment. This law appears to be more concerned with bribery and extortion by individuals and gangs or clusters of people threatening or using the force of an organization, whether real or otherwise.

[4] It was puzzling why this law was cited since it had been abolished on 6/15/1948 except to cite it as yet another example of how the prewar government used various kinds of security laws to control labor and farmers organizations. It has not been possible to ascertain whether this law was used in this way or not. The law was initially enacted in 1900 and consisted of seven articles. The law allowed drunkards, deranged persons who might commit suicide, those with dangerous weapons and those who might struggle (*tōsō*), commit violence and others who might constitute a threat to the public security to be arrested. Other articles focused on how prostitutes would be handled (e.g. compulsory medical exams and treatments) and how these procedures would be paid for.

government itself wished to revise the labor laws and not be reminded of this more idealistic period of the Occupation.[5]

The April 17, 1952 plenary session was a polite preliminary skirmish but a pro forma exercise in parliamentary procedures considering the original draft SAPL as submitted by the Cabinet, not the version later passed by the House of Representatives on May 15, 1952. A representative of each of the principal opposition groups in the House of Councillors—except the Ryokufūkai which could not be described as being in full-fledged opposition to the SAPL and the Liberal Party, the government party—raised various issues and the AG representing the government responded.[6] The kinds of issues raised in this plenary session could not, in the main, be that radically different from those raised in the House of Representatives deliberations; in most cases that was correct. Those issues which were new or were presented in a different manner are presented below. In responding to these interpolations, the AG (and sometimes also the LM) gave standard, routine and formalistic responses, hardly ever really answering the core of the query in a substantive manner:

1. The stipulation in the SAPL that administrative action can be taken swiftly (*jinsoku ni*) and with force (*kyōryoku ni*) and that this action could be taken based on the one-sided opinion (*ippō-teki kenkai*) of the administration then in power would be unconstitutional. It is not at all clear what the legal interests were that were proposed to be protected (*yōgo-subeki hōteki ken'eki*) under the SAPL; what are the circumstances or events that are staring us in the face that so urgently need control under the SAPL. There is thus no assurance that the SAPL would not be abused under these circumstances. A report (probably 1952) issued by the Human Rights Bureau under the AG stated there

[5] The 16 "Principles for Japanese Trade Unions" are included in *Activities of the Far Eastern Commission: 2/26/1946–7/10/1952*, report by the Secretary General, as Appendix 37 (pp. 91–93). A commentary about the discussion in the FEC on these principles is provided in Blakeslee, George Hubbard. *The Far Eastern Commission: a study in international cooperation: 1945–1952*. U.S. Department of State. 1953. pp. 170–171. The Soviet Representative on the FEC strongly objected to this restriction and called for General MacArthur to revoke his instruction but failed to persuade the FEC.

[6] The interpolators were Yamabana Hideo (SDP-L), Itō Osamu (SDP-R), Iwaki Tetsuo (Kaishintō), Hani Gorō (Independent), Hori Makoto (Rōnōtō), Sudō Gorō (JCP).

were 1300 cases where people's human rights were violated, 1050 were committed by public service employees.

2. Because of the fear of punitive administrative action by the government, an implicit censorship system would be created, e.g. reporting the details of a revolution, insurrection in a neighboring country or elsewhere might be interpreted as an incitement for similar action in Japan.

3. In making its decision, the PSEC would be called upon to be, not merely a seer, but something above god, to predict that a particular organization will in the future conduct certain kinds of activities. It will, in essence, step into interpreting the minds of the organization's membership, tens, hundreds, thousands, even tens of thousands, in making this decision. Only those who agree will be able to participate in the national dialogue citing, for the first time in these deliberations, the prewar role of the Imperial Rule Assistance Association (Taisei Yokusankai), the Sangyō Hōkokukai (the Industrial Patriotic Association), and the Dai-Nihon Fujinkai (the National Patriotic Women's Association).

4. A PSEC decision to prohibit publication of a journal for a specified period would be highly similar to the famous case during WWII in Japan where the opinion journal, *Chūō Kōron* was prohibited from publication (*hakkin*) and the staff brutally beaten and mistreated by the Tokkō secret police.

5. Based on past precedent before 1945, the possibility/probability of "an enlarged interpretation" (*kakuchō kaishaku*) of the SAPL must be the item of greatest concern, especially since there are many places in the draft law which are ambiguous and would provide the rationale and excuses for such a broadened interpretation. Yamabana Hideo cited his own case when he was arrested in 1937 for violating the PPL when he opposed the China Incident which began with what happened on July 7, 1937 because this conflict would take Japan down the wrong road; the PPL's original intent was to control/prohibit those organizations which advocated the overthrown of the national polity and the denial of private property, extremely far from and no relation to what Yamabana was asserting concerning Japan's future.

6. The government had insisted from the beginning that it cannot prosecute "organizations" for wrong doings, criminal acts under the Criminal Code which is aimed only at individuals. This was a

fundamental tenet of the CC. Nevertheless, the AG is now without "any sense of shame or conscience" (*ryōshin ni hazuru koto naku*) advocating the abrogation of this fundamental principle underlying the CC. To stress this point, the words of Justice Murphy of the U.S. Supreme Court—at that time, it was useful to cite the decisions of the U.S. Supreme Court for such purposes—in a 1946 decision where he pointed out that criminal acts are "individual and personal" (written in *katakana*). Also cited were the Nurenberg and Tokyo War Crimes Trials where so-called crimes again humanity, crimes against peace, were made against individual leaders of a country, not particular organizations or country. The latter were not charged with certain acts which would result in administrative action, or penalties. If unfortunately Japan under some strange circumstances launched another "war of aggression" one could use the criminal logic now being used in the SAPL to penalize not just the leadership but the entire country of Japan, e.g. declare the disbandment, the dissolution of the state of Japan. What was the legal rationale and absolute urgency to fundamentally change the basis of the Criminal Code. The AG insisted that since democratic countries cannot sit idly by if destructive activities are to take place, countries such as the U.S., UK, South Africa all have the ability to take administrative action, thus Japan's use of administrative action in the SAPL is not unusual and no exception.[7]

D. *Legal Affairs Committee Hearings*

i. *Overview*

The style and speed of the hearings in the two Houses were in stark contrast to each other. Whereas the Legal Affairs Committee under Liberal Party control in the House of Representatives, held eleven days of hearings, about a third of a month, the Legal Affairs Committee in the House of Councillors held 26 days of hearings, more than double the House of Representatives, actually spread out over a month, May

[7] In a computer search of U.S. Supreme Court decisions, I was able to locate the quoted phrase in a 1946 decision but it was by Justice Rutledge writing for the majority, not Justice Murphy. The phrase was, "Guilt with us remains individual and personal, even as respects to conspiracies."

10–June 19, 1952. It was less rigid in the conduct of these hearings, more cautious, individual members were less restricted in the amount of time each member could use interpolating the government. The committee's schedule, furthermore, was generally decided for 2–3 days at a time. Because of the diverse composition of the House of Councillors, the Committee's composition also reflected this diversity and no party had a safe majority, not even an effective plurality: Liberal Party had 4 members on the Committee, Ryokufūkai 3, Kaishintō 2, SDP-R 2, SDP-L 2, Dai-Ichi Kurabu 1, JCP 1, a total of 15. Under these circumstances it was conceivable that the Committee could defeat all proposed bills. Since the Liberal Party had the most members on the Committee, Ono Yoshio of the Liberal Party, was the chairman but he was a chairman who had to take the wishes of his Committee colleagues into serious consideration.

The structure of the Committee hearings followed normal Diet practices of beginning with overall issues (May 19–24, 1952), much longer than the House Committee, two days (May 26–27, 1952) for hearings from a variety of experts. The joint hearings were expanded from two committees (Legal and Labor) to four committees (Legal, Labor, Cabinet, Local Administration on May 28, 30–31), article-by-article interpolations (*chikujō shingi* on June 3–6, 9–14, 16–18, 1952), general discussion and vote on June 19, 1952. There was an unrecorded private meeting of Legal Affairs committee members and 20 representatives from academia and cultural leaders (*bunkajin*) on June 7, 1952 most of whom were against the SAPL. As in the case of the House Committee, the "experts" came from academia, labor, lawyers, media who were against the SAPL, and conservative lawyers, a commentator, industry and a member of the National Security Commission and agriculture were for the bill.

Another indication of how important these Committee hearings were in the eyes of the Government was the attendance of AG Kimura at every Committee hearing except for several short sessions and the two days of "expert" hearings. Seki and Yoshikawa of the SIB attended, of course, every session; there were, in addition, most of the time, the Parliamentary Deputy AG, the Directors General for Legal Opinions, Criminal Affairs Administration and Prosecution and other senior staff of the AG's Office; the AG, Seki and Yoshikawa remained the principal defenders of the SAPL; the other senior officials occasionally testified on highly selective issues.

Since the topics discussed in the Committee hearings of both Houses have been combined and included under "Topical Analysis" in Chapter 4 in order to avoid repetitive analysis in two chapters, the following sections will present a summary of the opinions of the "Experts" and describe and analyze other developments related to the consideration of the SAPL leading to a Committee vote on June 19, 1952.

Immediately after the House of Representatives passed the SAPL on May 15, 1952, the opposition parties and the labor unions vowed to carry on the struggle with even greater determination against the bill in the House of Councillors, and because of the long shot chance of defeating the SAPL or securing substantive revisions to the SAPL to de-fang it to some extent this attack would be more persistent, determined, continuous and thorough. The Liberal Party, on the other hand, hoped that it could, with the support of the Ryokufūkai, ritualistically hold committee hearings as a safety valve, listen politely to the "intellectual experts" criticizing the SAPL, push on to a committee vote and a quick follow-on plenary session to pass the bill about June 6, a mere three weeks of deliberations.

The SDP-R had pushed for the rejection of the SAPL in the House or Representatives. The SDP-R soon realized that a rejection of the SAPL by the House of Councillors was not probable; it was, therefore, willing to accept substantial revisions to the SAPL if those revisions were also acceptable to the labor unions. It thought that perhaps it could persuade the Ryokufūkai to include many of its proposed revisions into its revisions and convince the Kaishintō and others to back this approach in revising the SAPL. It fell to Itō Osamu who was the spear head for the SDP-R in committee interpolations and in attempting to forge a constructive link and dialog with the Ryokufūkai and Kaishintō. With the approval of the SDP-R's Diet Policy Committee (Kokkai Taisaku Iinkai) on June 1, 1952, Itō began floating his set of 17 points to revise the draft SAPL, the principal points of which were:

1. Article 2 on standards for control prohibits the abuse of authority in controlling and investigating organizations, the same standards shall be applied to the investigations concerning individual criminal acts.
2. Delete incitement (*sendō*) from articles 3.1.2, 3.2 and chapter 6 on penalties.

3. Delete "possessing written materials and designs" from article 3.1.3.
4. Add penalties in article 2 and 15 for abuses of authority.
5. Delete hearing officer's authority in article 15 to declare evidence as not necessary to the investigation.
6. In controlling organizations, the PSEC will be the agency to make the substantive decision and the proceedings will be conducted publicly and the PSIA will only conduct the investigation and request the PSEC to make a decision for controlling the organization and shall not itself assess the penalty.
7. Collective obstruction of official duties (*shūden-teki kōmu shikkō bōgai*) in article 3.1.2 will be removed as a destructive activity and the penalty in article 39 shall be revised.
8. Create an article to provide that the PM's veto authority over a court decision shall not apply in SAPL cases.
9. The independence of the PSEC, increase its membership to six persons and strengthen its secretariat and provide the necessary protection for PSEC members.
10. If a PSEC decision is revoked, an article will be included concerning national indemnification.
11. The effective date of the SAPL would be 20 days from when it would be officially made public (*kofu saretaru toki kara*) (*Tokyo Shimbun* 6/1/1952, *Asahi* 6/2/1952).

Just before the House of Representatives cast its vote, AG Kimura met with the leaders (*kambu*) of the Ryokufūkai on May 14, 1952 as a preliminary effort to persuade this large political group though substantially smaller than when it was first organized in 1947 but nevertheless critical in the House of Councillors's vote for the enactment of the SAPL.[8] The Ryokufūkai had tended to operate independently in

[8] The Ryokufūkai was created on May 17, 1947 after the first election for the House of Councillors under the new Japanese Constitution. Its individual members had been elected on their own merits in the 1947 elections. Since individually they would not have much influence in Diet deliberations, a motley group of members formed the Ryokufūkai (literally translated is the Green Breeze Society). The peak strength of the Ryokufūkai was immediately after its formation with 74 members. Under this Constitution, one half of the House of Councillors are elected for six years; in the 1950 election its membership shrank to 57 and gradually became smaller over the years and was eventually dissolved on June 2, 1965. Unfortunately, I have not been able to find any specific study on the history of the Ryokufūkai and its role in Japanese legislation

the HofC without cooperating to any great extent with other groups. However, it made an exception for the SAPL probably because their votes were crucial and their views and demands could perhaps be achieved. While the Ryokufūkai tilted toward accepting the need for such a law as the SAPL, it was not satisfied with the technical revisions made by the Liberal Party and those proposed by the Kaishintō in the House of Representatives and apparently greatly concerned about the long shadow of the prewar administration of such laws in the post-war era—the other opposition parties demanded nothing less than withdrawal of the SAPL. The main points of Ryokufūkai's dissatisfactions centered around the inadequate target definition in citing CC articles, the potential for abuse of authority, the lack of independence of the PSEC, and the feared growing dissatisfaction among the populace about the implications of the SAPL. The Ryokufūkai itself was divided since some members were opposed to the inclusion of *sendō* in the SAPL and those who condemned the Sōhyō strikes as political strikes outside the purview of labor union laws but the depth of that division was unknown. The directors of the Ryokufūkai, and its members on the Legal and Labor Affairs, Cabinet and Local Government committees decided, even before the House of Representatives passed the SAPL, to formulate its own set of revisions to the SAPL and call upon the Liberal Party and the Kaishintō to cooperate with the Ryokufūkai in creating the SAPL. (*Yomiuri* 5/15/1952) In April 1952, it had already rejected cooperating with the left SDP; it was willing to talk with the SDP-R.

Before the Ryokufūkai solidified its proposed revisions to the SAPL, senior SIB staff were invited to one or more private Ryokufūkai discussion sessions. At these meetings they showed Ryokufūkai members documents from the extreme leftwing and explained the difficulties of investigations. A goodly number of Ryokufūkai members who tended toward supporting the House-approved version of the SAPL were more prone to believe the ideas and documents provided in these secret discussions rather the government's public testimony and the opinions of the respected "experts" whose views were given at the Committee hearings on June 26 and 27, 1952. Some members felt that they must not hinder the SIB in its investigations of these radical groups because

---

and politics, 1947–1965, except for the official history of the organization, *Ryokufūkai Jūhachinen-shi* (1971, 535 p.).

of the fear of abuse of authority. They feared that "the remedy (controlling abuse of authority) might be worse than the evil" (the destructive radical groups)—*Tsuno o tamete ushi o korosuna*. This kind of informal persuasion was probably quite instrumental in persuading the majority of Ryokufūkai members to approve the proposed limited revisions to the SAPL on June 5. Obviously persuasion by senior bureaucratic staff from the AG's SIB appears to have been more influential than all the opposition throughout Japanese society and particularly the analyses of the well intentioned professorial intellectuals invited to testify as "experts", such "fuzzy minded leftish—not leftist—intellectual professors" could hardly be regarded as being practical when facing such a "national crisis" created by a small minority conducting sporadic attacks against symbols of public authority. Perhaps rather than being "persuasive", the conservative members of the Ryokufūkai were disinclined from the beginning to give the respected professors much credence in any case, even though they were highly regarded but ubiquitous *bunkajin* (cultural persons).[9] As the Ryokufūkai was gathering its thoughts on the SAPL, labor union groups and cultural organizations camped themselves outside the Ryokufūkai office in the Diet to present their appeals and petitions not to support the SAPL; the SDP-R and the Kaishintō centering around Itō Osamu from SDP-R met with the Chairman of the Ryokufūkai's Policy Research Council and other members of the committee. The impact of the various groups on any decisions is hard to ascertain but the various demonstrations, attacks, etc conducted by the radical leftwing groups only hardened the attitudes of potentially wavering Ryokufūkai members but probably was persuasive in the Ryokufūkai's attempt to define more narrowly the interpretations of such words as *sendō* and in several other ways. (*Mainichi* 7/4/1952)

Thus, a few days after the SDP-R had announced its proposed revisions on June 1, 1952, the Ryokufūkai caucus approved its own 11-point program to revise the draft SAPL. It had been prepared by a subcommittee consisting of officers of the Ryokufūkai's Political Policy

[9] The *Asahi* published an interesting analysis on June 20, 1952, the day after the Committee vote which suggested there were three dates which they called *yama* (mountain) in Japanese, meaning in this case turning points in the Ryokufūkai's process in arriving at a final decision. They have been used here since they do appear to have been a relatively accurate analysis.

Committee and its members on the Labor, Legal, Cabinet and Local Government Affairs Committees.

1. Add "must not in the slightest degree (*iyashikumo*) expand the interpretation of the SAPL" to article 1.2.
2. Add the phrase "must not in the slightest degree deviate from (*itsudatsu-shite*) the authorities provided under the SAPL" after the appropriate investigations in article 2.1.
3. Revise [and strengthen by specificity] article 2.2 by adding at the end of "must not in the slightest degree abuse" the words "authorities provided".
4. Add to article 3.1.1 (definitions), articles 81 (*gaikan yūchi,...*) and 82 (assisting aggression); add to article 3.1.2 "with the objective of realizing" before " the stipulated actions"; revise article 3.1.3 by substituting "with the objective of realizing" instead of "facilitating the realization" and substituting "with the objective of displaying" instead of "for publicly displaying".
5. Add a new article 3.1.4 as follows: In the order to realize the actions specified in article 3.1.1 communications are announced advocating the propriety of realizing such actions or the inevitability of such actions using wireless facilities or communications facilities as specified in the *Dempa-hō* article 100.1.1.
6. Revise article 3.1.2 to read as follows: Acts committed under any of the acts listed below with the objective of pushing forward, supporting or opposing political principles and programs; preparing, plotting, instigating, inciting acts for the objective of realizing any of those acts specified in article 3.1.2.1–9.
7. Add to article 3.2 as a definition of *sendō* the following: In this law, incitement shall be defined as an act through the use of written materials and designs (*zuga*) and through speech and behavior to persuade a person to make a decision to commit a specified act or through a stimulus which would encourage the decision to commit a specified act leading (*yūhatsu*) to a direct action (*chokusetsu kōdō*).
8. Revise article 4.2 concerning controlling organizational activities from "actions contrary to the intentions of the administrative action" to "actions contrary to the prohibitions specified in the previous clause (article 4.1).
9. Revise article 19 to read "all evidence, all reports (*chōsho*)" from just "evidence and reports".

10. For abuse of authority, the penalty will be three years in prison. (*Asahi* 6/6/1952, *Mainichi* 6/8/1952).
11. Delete "Possession of written materials and designs" from article 3. (added 6/18/1952)

Despite their disagreements about whether or not to include incitement in the SAPL and remove the PM's veto authority over a court decision, the SDP-R and the Ryokufūkai did have a number of revisions in common, e.g., removing the clause about possessing written materials, increasing the penalty for abuse of authority, increase the size of the PSEC and its authority to conduct its own investigation.

ii. *Expert Hearings*

Like the House of Representatives, the HofC also held two days (May 26 and 27, 1952) of hearings by "expert witnesses" (*kōjutsunin*).[10] The majority (13) of the twenty experts were, as in the HofR opposed to the SAPL, one wanted revisions, only six were in favor of the bill as passed by the HofR. In the HofR hearings, the Liberal Party "generously" allowed more opponents to testify because the voting outcome was a foregone conclusion. But in the HofC, the Liberal Party did not have a majority and the outcome of the final votes was not a foregone conclusion, thus in the HofC the selection of witnesses was a more sensitive issue. Some witnesses were closely questioned, not in an antagonistic manner but to more thoroughly elucidate that person's interpretations of the SAPL, particularly about the relationship between the SAPL and the Criminal Code; others were invited to make statements, for the record so to speak, with no questioning at all and allowed to leave.

Because of space limitations, we will focus only on three witnesses, one supporting, and two opposing the enactment of the SAPL. Those in favor of the SAPL were Makino Eiichi (see below), Hanai Tadashi (lawyer, professor and member of the National Security Commission), Baba Tsunego (conservative commentator), Utsunomiya Tokuma (Director of Nikkeiren), Harada Kōkichi (a farmer). Those opposed

[10] *Dai 13-kai Kokkai Sangiin Hōmu Iikai Kaigiroku dai 45-gō, 46-gō* contain the record of these two day hearings. References will be made to these hearing when necessary and appropriate in the following manner: 5/26:7 = May 26, p. 7.

to the SAPL were Haseba Gisuke (Sōhyō), Hoshika Kaname (Japan National Railroads), Kainō Michitaka (Professor of law, Waseda University, see below), Ōuchi Hyōe (President, Hōsei University), Shimada Takeo (lawyer, Japan Federation of Lawyers), Shioya Nobuo (Sōhyō), Takikawa Yukitoki (Judge, professor at Kyoto University, see below), Tsukazaki Naoyoshi (lawyer, Supreme Court Judge), Uchida Shigetaka (professor at Waseda University), Unno Shinkichi (lawyer, President, Japan Civil Liberties Union), Ushijima Shinsaku (Kyodo News Service), Wada Haruo (Seamen's Union) and Yoshino Genzaburō (editor, Sekai magazine).

Makino Eiichi (1878–1970). Probably as a mark of respect to his stature as one of Japan's outstanding experts on the criminal code and the PPL though retired, he was invited to be the first witness. He was regarded as one who supported the concept of the SAPL—the SAPL might facilitate "the flow of water" when used in an emergency situation, so a bill like the SAPL would appear to be desirable. He had commented in the early to mid-1920s on the 1925 Peace Preservation Law and the abortive draft law to control radical social movements as a professor of law at Tokyo University;[11] in 1952 he had been retired fifteen years from Todai, a point he stressed a number of times in order to condition his comments and to stress that he was not qualified to testify. This means that he had retired about 1937, four years before the Pacific War started. That the government sought his approval of the constitutionality of the SAPL implied that another professor of criminal law of similar stature in the postwar period was not available. Furthermore, in all probability, Seki had, while attending Todai, studied criminal law under Professor Makino. Nevertheless, Professor Makino did commented critically about a number of rather sensitive and core issues of the SAPL some of which appeared to support the position of the political opposition and some technical legal issues. But he did believe that the proposed draft despite his criticism would be acceptable, would not provide the basis for infringement of rights and abuse as happened under other laws. Nevertheless, the most significant

[11] Makino Eiichi. Kageki Shakai Undō Torishimari Hōan ni tsuite, *Hōgaku Shirin Part* 1) 24:8(8/1/1922):116–132, 2) 24:9(9/1/1922):121–126, 3) 24:10(10/1/1922):113–130. Chian Iji-hōan, *Hōgaku Shirin* Part 1) 27:11(11/1/1925), 2) 27:12(12/1/1925):107–119.

part of his comments concerned his remarks about the controversial use of incitement in this draft bill (5/26:1–7).

1. *Sendō* (incite). "This word is a most awkward and difficult word to handle (*sōtō shimatsu no warui kotoba*). [hardly a complimentary remark]...When this word is used the drafters should be very careful.... It is highly regrettable that *sendō* has created such a sense of unease among the populace; I believe there is leeway to revise it, this should be considered using the art of crafting legislation (*rippō gijutsu*).... *Sendō* in the draft is written as though it is separate from *kyōsa* (instigation) hereby creating some confusion.... In European law (French and German) incitement is regarded as one way of instigating a person, thus part of, not independent of instigation. In the draft SAPL when an instigation occurs it is handled in accordance with the stipulations about instigations, but when an incitement occurs what will happen is not clear.... "Instigation or incitement (*kyōsa matawa sendō*) are used in the draft but from my understanding of criminal law, this does not make sense and needs to be sorted out (*seiri*) and clarified.... From the criminal law point of view there is no need to use *sendō*.... *Kyōsa* is sufficient [this phrase was repeated several times].... If one wishes to corner a person (*totchimeru*) then one could accuse a person of instigation based on incitement and temptations, enticements (*yūwaku*) could be more understandable" By implication, Makino was saying that since incite is merely one way of instigating a person, it does not need to be included; this is quite different from the political opposition's demand that "incitement" be deleted because of its fear that this incitement authority could be but would be abused by the government in light of past historical record of the security agencies in both prewar and postwar Japan.
2. "In light of the suspicion surrounding this law and the somewhat incomplete structure of the proposed law (*yaya fukanzen na...kōsei*) it should be carefully considered whether there is such a necessity to create this law so quickly (*tori isoide hōritsu ni kansuru hitsuyō*) at this time, if the conditions permit.
3. Since it was a worldwide trend to create semi-judicial commissions to handle these cases, the creation of the PSEC would appear not to infringe on the authority of the judiciary.
4. *Yobi, imbō, kyōsa* is mentioned in the draft but from the standpoint of criminal law "does not make sense and I suspect is not acceptable".

5. *Keizoku to hampuku* (continuous and repetitive) as terms also do not make sense and need to be clarified.
6. Organizations are defined as "those with a common objective..." but that definition is "highly suspicious" and inadequate. It is also not clear at all how organizations which have gone underground will be handled.

While he supported the SAPL as a general principle, raising these rather difficult legal, conceptual and definitional issues were not helpful and undoubtedly caused some hesitation in applying the law to destructive criminal activities in the future.[12]

Takikawa Yukitoki, judge, professor of law at prewar Kyoto Imperial University, resigned in 1936 because of disagreement with the government over academic freedom, became a lawyer, was invited back to University in 1946 to chair the Law department and was against the enactment of the SAPL. He commented in a prescient manner that the SAPL, if enacted:

> ...will punish, in the first instance, not organizations which, it is claimed, is the real target of the law, but individuals. Punishment for organiza-

[12] Makino Eiichi published an article in *Keisatsu Kenkyū* soon after his testimony and once again after the SAPL had been enacted: Hakai Katsudō Bōshi Hōan ni tsuite 23:7(7/10/1952):3–16, and Hakai Katsudō Bōshi Hōan no Seiritsu (9/10/1952):3–15. He was seemingly more critical of some parts of the draft SAPL. For example, *sendō* he said was used in a number of prewar laws, but combining "*kyōsa matawa sendō*" (instigation or incitement) was totally new. While there is a Dai-Shin'in high court precedent about the meaning of *sendō* there was no explanation about the difference between incitement and instigation. It is difficult to conceive of the structure of such a concept as "incitement or instigation"; it does not make sense (*igi wo nasanai*). In the second article, Makino stressed the problems about treating several concepts on the same level simultaneously. That incitement and instigation have been combined on the same level in this law gives this law an epoch-making significance (*kakki-teki na igi*). Under the SAPL, an intention to achieve an objective (*mokuteki ishi*) was necessary when considering incitement in connection with destructive activities but under the prewar police and other laws, this intention was completely excluded (*mattaku jogai serareta*), thus under the SAPL there is substantively no difference between incitement and instigation. There are no legal precedents considering these concepts as equals; anxiety about abuse of the SAPL arises when assistance/support (*hōjo*) are combined with these two concepts. That was the reason why *sendō* became such an issue during HofC considerations. There is also considerable logical objection to stipulating *yobi, imbō to kyōsa* together without differentiation (*musabetsu ni*). It is not appropriate nor logical (*datō denai*) to treat/handle (*toriazukau*) these separate concepts simultaneously (*dōretsu ni*). These comments by such a senior criminal law scholar from prewar years must have had an impact on how the SAPL was ultimately implemented in such a limited manner over fifty plus years.

> tions will be concerned, in the main, with dissolution/disbandment and limitation of their activities. Parallel with the shift in industry from individuals to large factory operations, there has also been a shift from prosecuting individuals to punishment of organizations. There should be a law to handle criminal activities of organizations especially when the Criminal Code is inadequate for this purpose.... In order to handle these cases, the government (including the prosecutors, the police and even the courts) indulges in expanding, extrapolating the interpretation of the CC.... It must be recognized that there is a need for handling organizational crimes.... Despite the need for this kind of law, the proposed SAPL violates human rights and a dangerous law as evidenced by the felt need to admonish those who implement the new law not to abuse or enlarge its coverage of activities.... The SAPL would substantially enlarge the interpretation of instigating the preparations and planning/scheming for insurrection as now exists in the CC by making instigation an independent criminal offence.... The definition of *sendō* in other laws is relatively clearly defined, but it is far from clear in the SAPL as proposed. If this law is enacted, the application of "inciting", the preparation and planning for insurrection will be so broad that it will be like a bottomless quagmire.... After the PSEC had rendered its judgment, an appeal would be taken to the court (probably the District Court), for its judgement based on PSIA findings; when an appeal is made to the courts then the effectiveness of the PSEC judgment would be postponed until the court rendered its judgment. (5/26:19–25)

Kainō Michitaka, professor of law at Waseda University, described the SAPL as "a very fearful" law (*taihen osoroshii hōritsu*), a law that implicitly proves that Japan is presently on the brink of a revolutionary insurrection (*kakumei-teki nairan no zen'ya*). He singled out several issues for this judgment: 1) the banning of publications and assemblies in accordance with article 4 of the draft bill is in conflict with article 21.1 of the Constitution. Normally censorship is the reading of materials by an administrative agency before publication. But the SAPL is much broader than that by authorizing the limitation on publication prior to publication "as a preventive measure"; 2) SAPL's ability to interfere with and/or remove officers of an organization not only is more serious than censorship because it impinges on freedom of speech and creates obstacles to lawful disposition of private property and is in conflict with long standing labor practices; 3) the disbandment of an organization as permitted by the SAPL is in conflict with article 21.1 of the Constitution and the sagacity of dissolution of organizations as a socio-political policy is highly questionable; 4) by making a judgment about a given set of facts, the PSEC becomes a special court and would be in violation of article 76 of the Constitution.

There appeared to be an air of non-seriousness in the HofC expert hearings, a sense that certain formalities were being routinely handled with little fervor, or just to hold a series of hearings in parallel to the HofR. There was perhaps a feeling that the "political action" was being decided elsewhere not in listening to the experts in formal hearings. The outcome of the final vote in the Hof R was known, but the in the HofC it was not obvious. In contrast, members of the HofC Legal Affairs Committee held many private "study sessions" (20 or more, *sūjukkai*), with selected experts to discuss the SAPL. That I have not been able to discover how many experts were involved, how often they met, what issues were discussed, how these discussions affected the final legislation, is a reflection of how successfully "private" these sessions were kept. But that they had an impact on the final version in the HofC is a certainty.

iii. *Toward a Committee Vote*

With the proposed revisions put forward by the SDP-R, Ryokufūkai and the SAPL as passed by the House of Representatives, the cards have now been put on the table for a decision by the Legal Affairs Committee to be followed hopefully by a quick vote in the House of Councillors. But could these three versions be reconciled, negotiated, compromised that easily, quickly and expeditiously among the Ryokufūkai, the SDP left and right, and others in order to create an acceptable SAPL for a Committee vote. As in the past, the objections and revisions and persistent debate and disagreement mostly concentrated on articles 1–4. There was one obvious and critical gap among these sets: the Ryokufūkai ideas did not include the deletion of the crucial word, *sendō*. While there were some revisions, e.g. concerning indemnification, penalties on officials for abuse of authority, and others which might be bridged to form a working arrangement between the Ryokufūkai and others, the disagreement about incitement was so critical that ultimately a mode of cooperation could not be sustained.

About half way through the interpolations of the Legal Affairs Committee (described in section C.i and ii above) the government realized that it would have to make some compromises, some revisions of the SAPL but to what extent. The Ryokufūkai's ideas for revising the SAPL were more acceptable to the government and the Liberal Party and could provide the basis for cooperation. Those in the Ryokufūkai who demanded the deletion of *sendō* were insistent but how many were there of this mind. There were also those who wanted a reconsideration of Ryokufūkai revisions and bring them closer to SDP-R's Itō Osamu's proposed revisions. If there were 20 members who would support this approach, the government's bill would be defeated. As the Ryokufūkai held a caucus, the AG and SIB senior staff waited in a nearby room. It was perhaps at this juncture that AG Kimura, according his memoirs where he tells with some relish how he successfully challenged the Ryokufūkai membership with "either you accept *sendō* in the SAPL or I must withdraw"; the Ryokufūkai blinked and accepted the inclusion of *sendō*[13]—perhaps his *kendō* stare had psychologically impressed the Ryokufūkai members. At a Ryokufūkai caucus late June 17, it was revealed that only 3 members wanted *sendō* removed, only 12 wanted "possession of written materials and designs" deleted. This decision led to the rupture of the tenuous dialogue between the Ryokufūkai and the opposition parties. Significantly also, the caucus decided that voting would be left to individual members and their conscience, not enforcing any group discipline. The second turning point had been "successfully" maneuvered. The Ryokufūkai was, of course, condemned as having sold out to the government; after the SAPL was enacted by the Diet, the criticism of the Ryokufūkai became quite harsh, that their proposed revisions were a deception.

As part of the delaying tactics, Itō Osamu demanded the opportunity to speak again which lasted to 8PM on June 18. When the Committee Chair called for a vote to end discussion, it was defeated when one Ryokufūkai member, Miyagi Tamayo, a woman and the leader of the small group demanding the deletion of *sendō* voted with the opposition. That jeopardized an immediate vote and postponed a plenary session to Monday June 23. The opposition demanded that PM Yoshida appear for questioning at the Legal Affairs Committee; through the Cabinet Secretary General Hori, the PM said he could not attend. This became the third important turning point in this wrangling process. A Committee vote on June 19 was accepted provided a plenary session was postponed to June 23, Monday, thereby putting a parliamentary calendar squeeze on the government.

[13] Kimura, Tokutarō. *Sotsuō Hyakuwa*. Shimazu Shobō. 1989. 442 p., pp. 117–118. He did not specify unfortunately when he challenged the Ryokufūkai in the continuum of the legislative process.

In anticipation of a vote sometime on June 19, 1952, the Legal Affairs Committee began its last day of hearings at 4:51 PM. By this time, it had become clear that the opposition's demand for a rejection of the draft SAPL would not succeed but then what would, was the question. Nakayama Fukuzō as representative of the Ryokufūkai read a technical revision article-by-article without commentary of the SAPL as passed by the HofR. Undoubtedly I am sure, the opposition "knew" that this approach would be taken and undoubtedly that this proposed revision, if passed, would form the basis for a final version to be passed by the Diet somewhere down the line. Fukuyama's technical presentation was followed by commentaries by eight Committee members expressing their reasons one final time for support or rejection of the draft bill. They were all innocuous, repetitive, and philosophical summaries obviously being made "for the record". These speeches continued for almost four and a half hours into the night. Eventually as promised, a vote was indeed taken on June 19 and the results were somewhat surprising: the SDP-R proposed revisions, the Ryokufūkai revisions, and the SAPL as passed by the House of Representatives were all voted down.[14] The HofR and Ryokufūkai versions were defeated because Miyagi Tamayo and Kōya Mitsu both of the Ryokufūkai voted against these versions. In their brief statements the two women on the committee claimed, as permitted by the aforementioned Ryokufūkai caucus, they voted according to their consciences, giving as their reasons the need for deleting the controversial term "*sendō*" in light of the historical abuse of the authorities in the PPL and from their viewpoints as mothers; instead they supported the SDP-R proposal. The SDP-R alternative pushed by Itō Osamu was defeated because members of the SDP-L and the Dai-Ichi Kurabu voted against this version. Nevertheless, the Fukuyama revisions presaged many all the important major revisions eventually passed by the Diet. Thus, the plenary session had no recommended committee bill to consider.

[14] The actual vote count was as follows:

	Pro	Con
SDP-R revisions	5	9
Ryokufūkai revisions	6	8
SAPL House version	4	10

According to the Diet proceedings, those who voted against all three proposals were as follows: Ryokufūkai: Miyagi Tamayo, Nakayama Fukuzō, Okabe Tsune, Kōya Mitsu; SDP: Itō Osamu, Matsuura Sadayoshi, Yoshida Hōsei, Uchimura Seiji, Kataoka Fumie; Independent: Hani Gorō.

E. *Plenary Session-II: The Final Confrontation and Ultimate Approval*

i. *Interminable Wrangling and Delay*

Since the committee had rejected all three versions of the SAPL, the opposition felt emboldened that perhaps there was a chance—another long shot—for a number of reasons. Because of majority control by the Liberal Party in the House of Representatives, it was able to pass many bills but again because of the nature of the House of Councillors these bills piled up and a substantial parliamentary log jam developed. Even before the vote on the SAPL in the House of Representatives on May 15, the Diet session had to be extended several times: May 6–June 6 for 30 days, again June 7–20 for another 14 days. The government and PM Yoshida were becoming impatient with the pace of parliamentary action in the HofC and optimistically thought that a few days extension would suffice to push the accumulated bills through the HofC. The few days became another extension of the Diet—the third extension—from June 21–30, 1952 for ten days. Normally, according to articles 11 and 12 of the Diet law these extensions are to be passed by both Houses of the Diet but in this instance, the HofC did not pass this extension. The HofC became consumed with the legality of this extension and parliamentary business was brought to a standpoint for a number of days.

The SDP-R immediately pounced on this discrepancy and declared the extension illegal. This was the first time that this "discrepancy" had occurred between the two Houses since 1947. According to Diet rules, if differing extension dates were adopted by the two Houses, then the House of Representatives version would prevail. This debate dragged on into the night of June 20. The HofR Speaker called for such an extension for ten days. Eventually a vote was taken to extend the session of the Diet (211 vs 77). Temporarily the parliamentary logjam was broken or seemingly so but days had been wasted in this stall and delay—the objective of the opposition—and the HofC had yet to be heard from. Diet operations had been brought to a complete standstill over the "legality" of this extension. The government urged that the Liberal Party, the Ryokufūkai and the Dai-Ichi Kurabu in the House of Councillors combine forces and force the issue, but the latter two politely declined saying that they preferred a more amicable solution to the impasse. The opposition was furious that the Chairman of the

HofC Operations Committee had brought the issue of Diet extension to the fore without the participation of the opposition. They demanded his resignation and a vote on changing the Diet law about extensions if Diet proceedings were going to move forward. The opposition was also threatening to submit a resolution to dissolve the House of Representatives and hold an election; the Liberal Party was inclined to accept this idea. On the other hand, the Liberal Party was seriously considering another extension of this Diet session. With the intercession of the HofC President on June 24, the chairman as demanded resigned, article 13 of the Diet law will be revised in a way to respect the wishes of the HofC and this House would return to normal operations.

The SAPL and the revisions to the Diet law were submitted to the plenary session just before midnight, June 25. This was possible because the opposition SDP-L feared isolation in the parliamentary process, the Kaishintō somewhat weakened and the Minshu Kurabu feared a developing public opinion backlash and the opposition had become somewhat disarrayed. But could the HofC conclude its business in the remaining few days of the parliamentary calendar, by June 30?

On the HofR side, the Liberal Party Diet Operations Committee decided on June 25 to call for a Diet extension to August 20. This date was chosen because according to the Diet law article 59, the House may vote again 60 days later on a bill sent to the HofC; the last bill sent to the HofC was on June 19. This vote would need a two-thirds vote to become a formally adopted law under these special circumstances. Simultaneously, the opposition submitted a no-confidence vote in the Yoshida Government.

While the debate about the legality of the extension rambled on, many other aspects of how to proceed enlivened the debate. The pile of unfinished parliamentary business in the HofC was severe: according to a Liberal Party member, Kuraishi Tadao, in the HofC supporting the controversial third extension, the government had submitted 247 bills, HofR members 75, HofC 20+ bills. (*Asahi* 6/21/1952) The unfinished business consisted of bills on electric power development, local government, labor law revision, demonstrations control law, election law, Japan-India Peace Treaty, U.S.-Canada-Japan Fisheries treaty, police reform and, of course, the SAPL. Because of the political stakes involved by both sides, the government was determined to pass the SAPL and it became the focus and top priority of the seemingly interminable parliamentary wrangle.

Another stalling tactic was the refusal of the committee chairs who were from the opposition to hold meetings to consider legislation. This was possible in the HofC since there was no majority group and chairmanships were given to various political groupings, naturally some went to the political opposition contributing to the stalling tactic and gradually increasing the squeeze on the parliamentary calendar.

Another tactic to stall the proceedings, was to argue over which bill should be brought to a committee and then plenary session votes, always demanding that the SAPL be considered later. Another was to assert that since there was a relationship between the SAPL and the revision of labor laws and administrative reform of the government they should be considered in an inter-related manner.

On June 22, the President of the HofC called the representatives of each political group—Liberal Party, SDP-R, SDP-L, Ryokufūkai, Dai-Ichi Kurabu—to his official residence to find some way to break the impasse but was totally unsuccessful because of the adamancy of each group. Another day lost.

At the Diet Operations Committee (Giji Un'ei Iinkai) meeting on June 23, the opposition demanded that when the Chairman of the Legal Affairs Committee gave the Committee report to the Plenary Session, ten people be allowed one hour each for further interpolations—that would be another day used up. They were also planning to put forward a resolution to remand the SAPL back to the Committee for further consideration since the Committee had not given the Plenary session an integrated proposal to consider—a not totally unreasonable idea except that it would further delay a plenary session vote.

At last on June 25 as mentioned above, the SAPL had been placed on the HofC agenda but that did not provide any assurance of swift consideration, quite the contrary, a whole day was exhausted in wrangling over how to manage the SAPL. The opposition submitted a resolution of non-confidence in the Cabinet on June 25; it was debated and defeated on June 26. The subcommittee of the HofC operations committee could not agree on whether the SAPL or the revision to the Diet Law would be debated first. The HofC President suggested all sides accept his compromise: deliberate on the Diet law first, then the SAPL; if the Diet law revision was defeated, the HofC would go into recess, and the subcommittee would find another solution. This sudden more ameliorated stance had caught the other members of the opposition by surprise and infuriated them, and revealed a chink in their opposition ranks. June 26 was thus another wasted day. For this purpose, the President summoned the plenary session on June 27 based on his authority as President (*Gichō no shokken*). According to the Diet law article 55, he is authorized to summon the Hof C into session when he recognizes this is necessary in an emergency situation (*kinkyū no hitsuyō ga aru to mitometa toki*); he felt justified in this action since the subcommittee of the HofC Operations Committee had been meeting for two days without results. Since 1947 under the postwar Diet law, this emergency authority had been invoked a number of times by the Speaker of the HofR, but only once previously by the President of the HofC. The Rōnōtō, the JCP, and the SDP-L conducted a determined game of parliamentary harassment by submitting resolution after resolution, up to 13 resolutions, at the plenary session on June 27—a record number of such resolutions for any Diet session since 1947; these resolutions required an almost continuous roll-call vote, thereby creating a slowly moving line of Diet members walking up to the center of the HofC to cast their ballots—*dōdō meguri* or *gyōho senjutsu* in Japanese, literally moving slowly like cows, or in English reducing the proceedings to a snail's pace. This forced the plenary session into the night and did not allow for any time to consider the SAPL, the objective of calling for these resolutions. At the 11th hour, a vote was taken on the revision of the Diet law; the proposed amendment was defeated. This so infuriated this group of determined opponents that they confronted the President in his office berating him for not keeping his word to pass the revision of the Diet law.

On June 28, again the HofC President convened another plenary session based on his authority (*shokken ni motozuite*). The Liberal Party demanded that the Chair of the Legal Affairs Committee make his report and the HofC stay in session all night but the Ryokufūkai dissented. When the President said he would call for a vote on the Liberal Party demand to debate the SAPL ahead of all other issues, the determined opposition were provoked to demand that the disciplinary resolution against them should be debated first, in accordance they said with Diet rules. The Liberal Party and government did not have an effective counter-measure to this determined parliamentary disruption. The SDP-R, normally an ally of the SDP-L, was critical of these tactics as excessive but the problem was that there was no appropriate person to act as mediator between these two doggedly determined opponents. On a more comical note, the Hof C had to temporarily stop its proceedings because of a release into the air circulation system of the fowl odors of rotten garbage! When a vote on this demand was attempted the determined opposition tried to stop this roll call by occupying the central rostrum where the ballots would be cast. A photo in the *Asahi Shimbun* (6/28/1952) showed the boisterous, contentious and rowdy conduct of Diet members on June 28, 1952 requiring the intervention of Diet security guards to restore order. Since June 29 was Sunday, a day of rest and recuperation, the Diet took a much needed 24-hour respite.

Since the Diet session was last extended to June 30, now only days away, another extension was necessary, if any of the legislative backlog was to be enacted. A whole week had been spent in bitter parliamentary wrangling and no legislative business had been accomplished. The Diet session was extended on June 28 by the HofR, not for a few days, but for a whole month to July 30, the fourth extension. This Diet session was convened on November 10, 1951; with this extension this wrangling Diet, will have been in session the longest, 224 days in all—a reflection of the depth of the disagreements that were inherent in the legislative program the 13th session of the Diet was called upon to consider. This long extension will probably provide the time to pass most of the proposed legislation, including even the SAPL—at least in the eyes of the government. This lengthy extension was interpreted as a weakness of the government, its inability to control and legislate the necessary program in a timely manner and increased the possibility of another general election.[15]

At last on June 30, it appears Diet members, especially SDP-L and the Liberal Party members had exhausted themselves and other members on this battle over the SAPL, night in and night out, everlastingly. Perhaps the furies of the past week had been spent. The HofC Operations Committee actually was able to agree that the plenary session would be convened on that day and two additional days (July 1

[15] 1. The 19th Diet (11/19/1953–6/15/1954) also made five extensions to its session. As a result, the Diet law was later changed limiting Ordinary Diet (*Tsūjō Kokkai*) sessions to one extension; and two extensions for emergency or special sessions.

2. Partly because of the large number of bills yet to be passed, and partly due to internal disagreement in the government party and also due to varying degrees of opposition, the session was extended by one day to July 31 to wrap up parliamentary business. The Diet passed 236 bills of the 249 submitted by the government, 61 bills submitted by HofR members, 11 of 19 in the HofC, a total of 308 enacted out of 348 proposed bills. The resolution to discipline 17 HofC members did not survive.

and 2) which would be devoted to interpolations on the SAPL with a vote on July 3. After the plenary session was brought to order at 11:10 PM on June 30, it voted to extend the Diet session for ten days, but the SDP-R submitted a motion of no-confidence in the cabinet which was promptly countered by a Liberal Party motion to censure selected opposition members for their obstructionist tactics in stretching out Diet proceedings, listing 17 Diet members from the SDP-L (12 members), Rōnōtō (2), JCP (2), and the SDP-R (1) to be sent to the Disciplinary Committee for action; they had, asserted the Liberal Party, acted in a manner unbecoming of a Diet member by trying to obstruct the orderly conduct of the roll call votes on June 28. The no-confidence motion of course failed.

The turmoil of the past week to ten days can be attributed, in the first place, to the highly controversial nature of THE critical piece of proposed legislation, the SAPL, and the dedicated and determined opposition willing to push to the limits of parliamentary government their opposition to this proposed law. In addition, there was the emotional issue of repeated calls by members, mainly opposition members, for the presence of PM Yoshida at committee hearings; he consistently declined to participate. His studied aloofness merely exacerbated the relationship; in light of his personality and attitudes he would not wish to be interrogated by cheap rabble-rousers such as the labor leaders who happen to have gained a seat in the HofC through their labor union affiliation and backing; they were far beneath his social standing and he probably held them in contempt. The opposition felt they were being snubbed by the PM; they were correct. The atmosphere thus became even more charged than before. Then there was the nature of the Ryokufūkai itself, not a political party but an assemblage of individuals. While their numbers were declining, they had 57 members in this Diet. Together with the Liberal Party and the Minshu Kurabu, these three groups held a majority in the HofC and could take strong united action, but often, again reflecting their institutional nature, the Ryokufūkai would decline to take a certain action, thereby frustrating particularly the Liberal Party. While the Yoshida government had been in power since 1949, its political authority (*seiji ryoku*) was beginning to wane; this slippage appeared in its inability to control the Diet legislative agenda without such turmoil; for example, when the Liberal Party's Diet Operations Committee chair called for strong and decisive actions, he was challenged and could not enforce the dicta of the leadership. The next election of the HofR must be held at the latest in 1953 and depending on the circumstances earlier than that, perhaps even in Fall 1952; members concerns would naturally focus on this election and the focus on the proposed legislative program would be diffused. In the minds of Liberal Party members, passage of the SAPL had been elevated or had been there all the time as a critical post-peace treaty internal security law, second only to the signing and ratifying the Peace Treaty; this immovable stance inevitably would result in a clash with a hardened opposition to the SAPL.[16]

Extension of the Diet Session. This difference between the two Houses in the length of extension of the Diet session was the first such instance since 1947; at issue was the interpretation of articles 11, 12 and 13 of the Diet law. Article 11 stipulates that the Diet session for Emergency (*rinji*) and Special Sessions will be decided by the same resolution by both Houses; article 12 stipulates that a session may be extended by the same resolution passed by both Houses; article 13 stipulated that when both Houses did not arrive at the same resolution, the resolution passed by the House shall prevail. Based on these stipulations, it was generally accepted by scholars and the administrators in the Diet that the HofR decision would take precedence, except that no precedent could be called upon to support this assertion although the language seemed clear enough. Nevertheless, a minority in the opposition camp insisted there was an ambiguity and took this opportunity to utilize this issue for their parliamentary tactical reasons in their campaign to oppose the SAPL.[17]

The HofR members were always sensitive to the possibility of a general election earlier than their four year term of office; in contrast, the HofC members were elected for six years—like the U.S. Senate—and would not face an election in the interim. They could seemingly afford to take a slower and more aloof attitude, they could be more deliberative, their sense of urgency would be different from their colleagues in the HofR; they would enjoy a sense of strength and immunity from elections—for a few years. While the HofR always considered

---

[16] Some ideas for these comments were derived from two articles in the *Asahi*, 6/26/1952, 6/28/1952.

[17] Three years later in 1955 this "ambiguity" was closed through a revision of the Diet law by adding to article 13 the phrase that "when the HofC did not pass a resolution concerning the extension of the Diet session the resolution passed by the HofR will prevail."

the national budget first and sent to the HofC its version of the budget, most of the other bills considered by the Diet were, in reality, also considered by the HofR first and then passed on to the HofC for its consideration. However, the HofR had the parliamentary habit of passing many important bills toward the end of a session. This tended naturally to cause a substantial legislative logjam in the HofC since it would then have a relatively short amount of time to rationally consider these bills. Given these circumstances, the HofC could seemingly not pass certain bills; to avoid such an impasse, the HofR could pass a bill with a two-thirds vote after a bill had been sent to the HofC for its consideration but had not acted on specific legislation or if it had rejected a version passed by the HofR. That arrangement could lead to a constant clash between the two Houses. In setting the length of an extension for the Diet, the wishes and needs of the HofC would need to be kept in mind. The opposition felt that this precedence of the HofR was unfair and should be reconsidered and revised taking into account the needs of and respect for the HofC. To what extent should the HofC be allowed to act somewhat unilaterally, obstruct needed legislation to the annoyance, frustration and anger of the HofR; this touches upon a fundamental relationship of strength between the two Houses. The opposition's demand for a revision of the Diet law was not unfair and not without merit but was this route—as part of a campaign against a particular piece of legislation now facing the HofC—the appropriate approach to remedying this apparent imbalance. The motion to revise the Diet law was defeated. If it had succeeded it might have derailed the SAPL deliberations to some extent though probably not fatally.

Some regarded—obviously mistakenly—the HofC as a successor to the prewar House of Peers; PM Yoshida was known to have sarcastically and with some disdain referred to the members of the HofC as those propertied classes (*yūsan kaikyū*), those intellectuals (*yūshikisha*). Some accuse the HofC of a sense of arrogance in its overly deliberative pace in its consideration of proposed legislation. It was clear that a determined and organized opposition to a particular legislative program could seriously threaten a legislative program or use it as a hostage to wring concessions from the sponsors of a particular program or piece of legislation. This issue was not resolved but activities to push forward with the SAPL proceeded a pace.

The Flamboyant, Determined Minority. The group that was able to tie up the House of Councillors in parliamentary knots for a week or more was centered in the 32 members of the SDP-L, not the JCP, as one might suspect but it, of course supported this strategy.[18] In these tactics, this group pushed with the slogan, "destroy the SAPL and onward toward a general election" while at the same time, they ignored the larger and more moderate SDP-R, whose leader in the anti-SAPL debate in the HofC was Itō Osamu, in pursuing their ruthless tactics. They acted like uncontrolled wild horses determined to use every "legal emergency" parliamentary tactic possible to their advantage. At one time, a strange odor, something like rotten garbage, pervaded the chambers; utilizing this opportunity they put forward a motion to investigate the origins of this obnoxious odor. When roll call votes were taken, they proceeded as in the slow motion style of exit of the traditional Japanese Kabuki, Kyōgen theater, except that the movements would be deliberately slower. The group members were elected, in the main, from the national constituency to the HofC where their constituencies provided a national basis, such as the Japan National Railways (Kikugawa Takao and Uchimura Seiji), Japan Farmers Union (Kōda Saburō and Miwa Teiji) and the Japan Farmers Union (Okada Sōji, leader for the anti-SAPL campaign inside the HofC), Teachers Union (Ogasawara Fumio).[19] They were younger and more energetic than the more sedate, older and quieter members of the Ryokufūkai. When this flamboyant group was gradually gathering criticism for their conduct, their overall leader, Wada Hiroo, formerly with the South Manchurian Railway's Research Division, Minister of Planning in the Katayama Tetsu Cabinet, 1947–48, urged them on by declaring that their actions were correct to destroy the SAPL and push for dissolution of the Diet for a general election, thereby living up to the expectations of the Rōtō. The Rōtō sponsored strikes against the SAPL were led by Sōhyō's SecGen Takano Minoru, a member of the SDP-L. When the third strikes were criticized by the labor federation Mindō rightwing and caused somewhat of a disarray in the labor ranks and these strikes, there was concern that this disarray would result in the loss of leadership in the next Sōhyō national convention. Their insistent and persistent obstreperous tactics in the HofC were

[18] This small "insert" was basically adapted from an article in the *Asahi*, 6/30/1952.

[19] Okada was born in Tokyo in 1902, graduated from Todai Economics, became a writer and commentator, a member of the Central Executive Committee of the Nōmin Kumiai, and elected to the HofC in 1947.

in a way an attempt to prove their bona fides, determination, their steadfastness in the face of poor odds and to assure continued control of Sōhyō leadership, perhaps being able to challenge the Liberal Party and even the SDP-R in the next general election. While the S.P.-L was dismissed as an irrelevant small minority in the HofR by the SDP-R, in the HofC they had 32 members, the largest among the opposition groups and were attempting to prove their relevance in the HofC. The SDP-L Chairman, Suzuki Mosaburō, was often absent in the HofR, but was seen in the spectator's gallery in the HofC cheering on his SDP-L fellow members. When it became evident that the Kaishintō and the SDP-R were willing to accept a revised SAPL, the SDP-L took it upon themselves to submit various motions of non-confidence to the HofC. They thought it would be advantageous in the next election to draw a clear line between themselves and the SDP-R. On June 28, a basket of fruit arrived from Tanrō urging on the SDP-L; similarly a representative of the Teacher's Union was conducting a "hunger strike" just outside the HofC also to encourage the SDP-L in its boisterous tactics inside. After the SDP-L had held a central committee meeting on June 26–27, they pushed their way into the Diet as a show of support to their colleagues and had to be plucked one by one by the Diet police and taken outside.[20]

ii. *The Final Tally*

The vote on July 1 defeating a non-confidence resolution against the HofC President submitted by the SDP-R revealed a split and weakness in the opposition in the voting pattern: SDP-L withdrew, Kaishintō abstained, and the JCP, Dai-Ichi Kurabu, Rōnōtō, and SDP-R voted for the resolution.

Final debate, rather it should be described as a summation (*tōron* as distinct from interpolations, *hitsugi ōtō*) by each political group, on the SAPL actually began in earnest in the afternoon of July 1 and

[20] When I interviewed AG Kimura on April 10, 1978, he told me of his great dissatisfaction with the conduct of the SDP-L et al that he had arranged to have photos taken of their "misconduct" and threatened them with disciplinary action which he claimed "quietened them down". While a disciplinary motion was submitted it was more a political gesture than a real substantive attempt to secure disciplinary action by the HofC.

continued through July 2 and 3. The July 2 session barely proceeded with only the thinnest quorum present. The SDP-R accused the HofC President of deliberately restricting the distribution of gallery tickets. The SDP-R resolution on July 2 to remand the SAPL back to the Legal Affairs Committee was defeated by the combined forces of the Liberal Party, Minshutō and Ryokufūkai, against remanding 124, pro 67, a total of 191 votes cast out of a total of 250.

The Ryokufūkai supported the SAPL and the inclusion of the extremely controversial term "*sendō*", but the revisions it proposed attempted to send an unmistakable message to the enforcement agencies and their staffs that this law must be extremely narrowly interpreted, created a new article for this purpose and to re-emphasize this point increased the criminal penalty for any abuse of authority. In addition, to clarify the application of instigation and incitement they separated them to be grammatically clearer—an issue also raised in the HofR deliberations and did result in a revision but even that revision was further narrowed by the Ryokufūkai—than was in the original government draft passed by the HofR.[21]

Only the Strictest, Narrowest Interpretation of SAPL to be applied. Because of its concern about the precedents from the prewar enforcement of the PPL

a) the phrase "the narrowest possible limits necessary" for the preservation of public safety would replace "necessary and appropriate" in article 2.
b) a new article 3 would be created which would re-emphasize that controls and investigations for the purpose of achieving the objectives as stated in article 1 of the SAPL must be conducted within the "narrowest possible limits" (*hitsuyō na saishō gendo ni oite*), and "must never deviate from the authorized limits of authority (*iyashikumo kengen o itsudatsu shite wa naranu*) by unlawful limitations on the rights and freedom of the people under the Japanese Constitution" and "there shall be no abuses, nor shall there be any interference with or limitations on the legitimate activities of labor unions...." It should be pointed out that use of the term "*iyashikumo*" strongly emphasized

[21] This summary arrangement was created from reading the proceedings of the National Diet (*Sangiin Kaigiroku* #59, 7/1/1952, pp. 1296–1301 where Nakayama Fukuzō of the Ryokufūkai provided its proposal to the Diet), articles in the *Asahi* (7/4/1952), *Mainichi* (7/4/1952), *Yomiuri* (7/3/1952) and from *Ryokufūkai Jūhachinen-shi*.

> the point being made; it is a term which has an older generation ring to it. I would suspect that 21st century Japanese know about it and its message of emphasizing a special point but is not in their style of reading, writing and general conversation.

According to Nakayama Fukuzō, Ryokufūkai's representative making the final summation, it placed the greatest interest and concern (*saidai no kanshin*) on these constitutional issues. (7/1/1952:1299). He reminded the security agencies that these revisions were not hortatory admonitions but that the decisions under this bill could be appealed to the courts and that government security officials could be subject to jail terms for abuse of authority.

Throughout the committee hearings opponents of the SAPL constantly hammered away on the theme that this SAPL will travel the same road as the prewar PPL of abuse and broadened and enlarged interpretation over the years as the SAPL is implemented. Undoubtedly this constant hammering must have played a role in bringing about these particular revisions or had an impact on an audience—some members of the Ryokufūkai—to persuade them to make these much stronger revisions. These revisions were undoubtedly also not welcomed by the security agencies but that was part of the package they had to accept if an SAPL was to be enacted.

Clarification of Instigation and Incitement. In response to the criticism that there was a potential grammatical ambiguity in article 3 of the SAPL version passed by the HofR in defining instigation (*kyōsa*) and incitement (*sendō*), the Ryokufūkai divided the definition process in a new article 4 into several pieces in an attempt to eliminate this possible ambiguity. Violent destructive activities (*bōryoku-shugiteki hakai katsudō*) would be defined as follows:

a. Article 4.1.1.l Those acts committed under CC articles 77 (insurrection), 78 (preparing for and plotting insurrections), 79 (assisting insurrections), 81 (inducement of foreign invasions), 82 (assisting foreign invasions), 87 (unsuccessful attempts to induce invasions and assist invasions) and 88 (preparing and plotting the inducement and assistance of invasions).
b. Article 4.1.1.2. Instigation to commit acts described in the above articles
c. Under article 4.1.2.10, planning, plotting and instigating any acts as stipulated under article 4.1.2.1–9 would be in violation of the SAPL

d. Article 4.2. Incitement (*sendō*) was separately defined as an act

> to create a determination or to further an already existing determination to realize conduct with the object of causing action by strong stimulation (*ikiyoi no aru shigeki*) through speech, conduct, drawings or documents.

The Ryokufūkai speaking through Nakayama felt strongly that through this definition of incitement, and the restrictions stated in Article three above, the abuse of enlarging the interpretation of the SAPL could be avoided, thereby relieving the anxieties of the people in this regard. (7/1/1952:1299)

e. Using the above definition of *sendō*, article 4.1.1.3 would state that those who incite actions to achieve the realization of actions under CC articles 77, 81 and 82 would be in violation of the SAPL.
f. Under article 4.1.2.10, incitement would cover acts which have as their objective the realization of any act to support, promote or oppose any political doctrine or policy under CC articles 95, 106, 108, 117, 125, 126.1 and .2, 199 and 236.1, and para 1 of Penal Regulations Controlling Explosives (Cabinet Ordinance 32/1884). The phrase "which have as their objective the realization of" after acts was to emphasize the subjective desire and determination (*shukan-teki iyoku*) to commit these acts.

Phrases Deleted. a. One of the phrases used to describe incitement and instigation violations under article 3 of the HofR version, "those possessing written papers" (*bunsho shoji*) would be deleted. This phrase had drawn considerable criticism as far too broad and vague a mandate to those who would be implementing the SAPL and easily susceptible to an abuse of authority.

b. Incitement of planning and plotting for insurrection (*nairan*) and foreign invasion (*gaikan*) were deleted from the list of acts which would violate the SAPL under the HofR version (article 3.1.1.2). This deletion was made "in response to the desires of the intellectuals and cultural personages that this was going too far in controlling and maintaining public security" (plenary 7/1/1952:1299) This would indicate that Ryokufūkai was seemingly sensitive to public opinion and comments by the intellectual experts at their hearings discussed earlier—though that cannot be proven conclusively.

Phrases Substituted. Under the HofR approved version article 3.1.2, incitement and instigation to promote or support, oppose political policies or program was revised to include after instigation "with the objective of rather than merely support"...in order to emphasize the subjective nature of this consciousness.

A similar revision was made to article 3.2.10 (article 4.1.2.10 in the HofC version) to revise the phrase "to promote..." to "with the objective of promoting...", again to emphasize the more specific subjective nature of this nature.

Stiffer Penalties for Abuse of Authority. Under article 45, PSIA officials who cause others to commit acts which they do not have to do, or obstruct those acts which they have the right to do, shall be given sentences of hard labor or imprisonment for less than three years, thereby increasing the penalty more than now imposed under CC article 193. The stiffer sentences perhaps stemmed from criticism in the HofR that comments in the draft proposal that the security staff must not abuse its authority were merely toothless meaningless admonitions. The government had rejected all attempts to insert stronger language but reluctantly acceded to this revision by the Ryokufūkai.

Yet Another New Criminal Offense under the SAPL. A new sub-clause, article 4.1.2., was added to the list of criminal offenses under the SAPL: Communications by wired broadcasting or by wireless communication which advocated the necessity or propriety of acts whose objective was to cause the execution of illegal acts stipulated in Articles 81, 82 and 88 of the Criminal Code. It was felt that it would be necessary to take action against those Japanese who collaborate with an enemy to invade Japan.

PSIA Staff Designation. Starting with article 14 in the HofC version, PSIA officials who had been designated as *shinrikan* (literally translated as an official who will assess/examine the situation, in this study the term hearing officer has been used) were re-designated as *jumei shokuin* (literally translated as "as the official who has been so appointed"). The record does not give a reason for this change in contrast to other revisions; one can surmise this sounds less official and officious.

The Public Security Examination Commission. Its membership shall be increased to six members from four. Even the HofR version had given the PSEC an independent authority which provided leeway in how it would assess the PSIA report and backup materials. The Ryokufūkai revisions enlarged upon and spelled out in some detail what the PSEC could do in assessing a request for action by PSIA by adding three new clauses, Article 22.2, 22.3, 22.4 which gave the PSEC substantial new capabilities to carry out their function to make a judgment about the request from the PSIA: it could request the voluntary appearance of individuals concerned or witness and the collection of information or opinion from such persons, request the voluntary presentation of the appropriate materials from the owner or whoever possesses the materials, inspect account books or other business matters, request the presentation of necessary materials or information from any public office or private organization; it could also have PSEC members or staff take the necessary steps to obtain these materials. If requested the PSEC member or staff must present his ID. Keeping in mind that in an earlier draft, the PSEC was allowed only to examine the report submitted to it by the PSIA without being able to make further inquiries as described above, Ryokufūkai's revisions provide the PSEC with substantially expanded authorities.

After completing his explanation of the proposed revisions on July 3, 1952, Nakayama Fukuzō gave a rather interesting and, in a way, unusual summation on the rationale for the SAPL—and to someone acquainted with prewar-style Japanese, the resonance of his speech was somewhat emotional, he even invoked language reminiscent of the Emperor's speech to the Nation on August 15, 1945.[22]

> ...Our people have suffered the baptism of totalitarianism as a result of destructive activities. We must ponder the present situation carefully. *Until the stabilization of our society is reached (kokujō antei ni itaru made)*, let us recognize the need for the Habōhō as a safety valve. Appropriate revisions have been suggested, I strongly urge the passage of this bill. *It is strictly a transitional temporary law. As soon as the present social anxieties are removed this bill should be abolished.* The reason the Ryokufūkai narrowed the definition of *sendō* as proposed by

[22] Nakayama Fukuzō was born in 1887, graduated from Todai Law Department, had been a businessman in the Osaka area, had been elected to the Hof R three times starting in 1932 and elected to the HofC in 1950. Little is known about him but he was definitely a member of the prewar generation in his use of the Japanese language; he was jeered and heckled by some members for his use of such language reminiscent of the past Imperial system.

> the government was because there are radical organizations (*futei no dantai*) in society which are trying to overthrow the present state structure from its foundations. Remembering past experiences where under the prewar PPL and the national mobilization law (*Kokka Sōdōin-hō*) how the authorities conducted themselves, and how constitutional rights of assembly, speech, expression, organization might again be trampled under, *it is truly not without reason* that there is a large movement demanding the withdrawal of this draft law. Fortunately we have Article 11 in the Constitution which guarantees these basic rights. The Diet and State will not stand idly by if authorities over step their bounds. With full and absolute confidence we submit this revised bill in the hope that while we must accept society's criticisms now, bear the unbearable (*shinobi gataki o shinobi*), the day will come that our present position will be praised and accepted. We appeal to you as patriots concerned with the future of our country (*yūkoku no shishi*), that after due consideration will speedily accept this bill [emphasis added]. (Plenary 7/1/1952:1299–1300)

At the July 3 session PM Yoshida provided, on a pro forma basis, the necessary words insisting that the SAPL was not unconstitutional, the people's rights would be respected and not limited, the purpose of the SAPL was not to violate the fundamental human rights of the people but to target those actions which are not controllable under existing laws, that the SAPL is different from the Peace Preservation Law of 1925 and that the SAPL will be administered and implemented in the most appropriate way possible.

A final vote was taken that day supporting the SAPL and the laws establishing the PSEC and the PSIA) as amended by the Ryokufūkai through a combination of votes from the Liberal Party, Ryokufūkai (except for MiyagiTamayo, Yamamoto Yūzō and Oku Mumeo) and the Minshu Kurabu as follows:

> Ryokufūkai amendments pro 132, con 79
> HofR version other than the above amendments pro 133, con 79[23]

The SAPL as amended was immediately sent to the House of Representatives which passed the amended SAPL on July 4, 1952 (228 vs 80). The draft SAPL had been approved by both Houses after 50 days of sometimes quiet, mundane and occasionally insightful committee

[23] The pro votes came from the Liberal Party, the Ryokufūkai, the Minshu Kurabu; the cons votes, from the Ryokufūkai, SDP-R, SDP-L, the Kaishintō, Rōdōsha Nōmintō, JCP and the Dai-ichi Kurabu.

hearings but a tumultuous, rowdy and at times somewhat violent, protracted and bitter wrangling in the plenary session of the HofC over parliamentary procedures to be used in managing the SAPL and 79 days since it was submitted by the Cabinet to the House of Representatives. The SAPL was promulgated as Law 240 on July 21, 1952.[24]

[24] Immediately after this vote, the various political groups issued statements: Liberal Party asserted that it is recognized that to achieve peace and order it is imperative that the destructive activities, riots, and use of brute force (*buryoku tōsō*) of the JCP and Koreans [in Japan] affiliated with North Korea; Ryokufūkai emphasized its main points of concern that in implementation of the SAPL there must be a conciliation of the limitations of human rights and human rights itself and to prevent abuse of authority; Kaishintō recognizes that destructive activities are being carried out but existing laws are adequate to control them and the government's bill and the Ryokufūkai's revised bill are excessive and violate and ignore the principles of democracy; SDP-R asserts that the enacted bill is the first step to destroying democracy and the Ryokufūkai revisions are a fraud and made it more regressive (*kai'aku*); SDP-L said the SAPL that has been approved notwithstanding its determined efforts to stop this legislation is probably unconstitutional and reflects the paucity of policy and the suicidal actions by Diet members.

CHAPTER SIX

CONCLUSION

With the passage and enactment of the SAPL, a beachhead was indeed established after bruising skirmishes, and a battle of attrition which drained the energies of both the supporters and opponents of the bill. It was a desperate battle: the proponents of the SAPL were determined at all costs to secure the passage of the SAPL as a meaningful internal security law and the equally desperate and determined opposition either to defeat the bill, or drag out proceedings beyond the Diet calendar, or weaken or emasculate the draft law through numerous word and phrase changes. It was a contest of wills, not between two different generations, but between two groups of the same generation, both groups surviving from prewar years, both with radically different life experiences and expectations about the emerging Japan after August 1945 and about each other, especially about their respective intentions in the post-peace treaty era. Both groups had been educated, trained and had worked for many years under the discredited ultra-nationalistic *ancien regime*. Members of both groups had held relatively senior positions in their respective careers before the war ended in August 1945. The conservative supporters of the SAPL were the holdover supporters of the *ancien regime*, some reinstated after having been depurged, most held, not the top positions from before and during the war; their formative years in education and work experiences were importantly in the Japan of the 1930s and 1940s. Many of the conservative active supporters who participated in the drafting and legislative process had understandably been in the prewar Ministries of Justice and Home Affairs and the various police agencies. From the point of view of the opposition, they represented and symbolized the oppressive institutions of prewar years and many were themselves actually members of these institutions. These positions were irreconcilable.

Many of those in the then existing postwar security agencies would have, in prewar years, suppressed and silenced some or all of the vocal postwar opposition groups, let alone sit in the Diet with them, sit across the table "negotiating", discussing, debating with them, being harangued in seemingly interminable cross examination in committee hearings by them. The opposing groups came from the prewar labor union movement, prewar leftwing political parties and professorial groups. They had been threatened with suppression, imprisoned for their ideology, in some cases physically mistreated by the prewar police agencies which would be the very agencies and personnel which would implement the SAPL. The conflict was not between two sets of individuals where one group had actually mistreated the others but rather an institutional distrust. In the eyes of the opposition, those who pushed determinedly for the SAPL were attempting to re-institute the prewar police and security agencies with powers to again suppress and oppress the political leftwing parties, organizations, labor unions as they had done since the beginning of the Meiji Restoration in 1868. PM Yoshida's well known disdain and distaste for such a riff-raff opposition and their intellectual supporters well symbolized this attitude. This conviction and belief was re-emphasized when the conservative government attempted to retrogressively revise—*kai'aku* in Japanese—the basic labor laws and the labor standards law when given this opportunity by SCAP to review and reconsider Occupation era edicts and laws. The Occupation had in Fall 1945 ordered the Japanese government to remove all laws which had been used to suppress various freedoms. Successive Japanese administrations had a strongly held felt need, an obsessive compulsion, from at least the 1920s that when granting male suffrage that must be balanced with an internal security law, the 1925 PPL, to counter the potential influences of the rabble, even a possible controlling influence—a ghastly thought—and the potential nightmare of Soviet Russian infiltration especially after diplomatic relations between Japan and the Soviet Union were re-established in the mid-1920s. This concern, anxiety, preoccupation and obsession continued unabated during the pre-1945 years. While it declared in1951 with some confidence that the burgeoning violent Communist activities were manageable, the conservative government, rather inconsistently, must have felt "naked" without an internal security law as a twin pillar with the Peace and Security Treaties as envisioned by PM Yoshida in his memoirs. Other countries had such security laws, especially in light of the U.S. example of the 1950 Subversive Activities Law, why not Japan. It was asserted and assumed by the government that since the U.S. Supreme Court had declared the internal security laws (Smith Mundt and McCarran Acts) to be constitutional these laws were consulted as models thereby implying a seal of approval and reasonableness for a similar Japanese law—less stringent in the eyes of the government. Yet, in reality a much wider range of internal security laws were consulted, including those in Europe, Soviet Union, South Africa, China and Korea. The SAPL became their "traditional security blanket" to fill the presumed internal security "vacuum" whether justified or not.

When the conservative government under PM Yoshida began to draft and attempt to enact an internal security law which though different in format and philosophy from the PPL, the confrontation was merely a continuation of the political battles from the days of the *ancien regime*. The opposition out of sheer self-respect had to determinedly oppose the draft SAPL; the conservative government had obviously under-estimated their doggedness in opposition. Neither side could now backdown. The depth and determination of the opposition to oppose the proposed SAPL must be understood in this prewar/postwar context.

The legal groundwork and political context for the opposition to launch and maintain such a vocal opposition to the SAPL was created by U.S. Occupation fiat in the beginning of the occupation and reinforced by the 1947 new Japanese Constitution. When the dialogue began and evaporated about disbanding and banning the JCP because of its violent activities and accentuated by the outbreak of the Korean War in June 1950, there was still two years to go before the peace treaty would be signed and Japan regained its "independence". But by the time the dialogue began to take place between GHQ Government Section officials about an internal security law in spring 1951, only about a year remained before the peace treaty would come into effect, and an even shorter time until the peace treaty negotiations had been completed. The Occupation period had entered a "twilight period" where GS officials no longer issued the orders, but acted as counselors/advisers to the Japanese drafters of the SAPL. The latter, almost as perforce of habit, duly visited GS officials in GHQ and reported on and discussed various drafts—but it appears not all drafts—of the SAPL. Thus the role of GS officials became ambiguous. Because of the close personal relationship that developed between Major Ed Jay in GS and Seki Itaru, the drafter of the SAPL, GS, it could be said, played a role in persuading Seki to revise the draft so that the accused under a new law would be allowed to have a larger defense team. In the total scheme of the SAPL, this "concession" and improvement accepted willingly by Seki, was a minor issue but one of the few safeguards in the SAPL and symbolized the differing legal philosophies of the two government officials from two different legal systems, cultures and traditions. Ultimately, there was the pro forma role that GHQ played in April 1952 under revised rules of "approving" Japanese government actions. GS made a "political decision" to approve the draft SAPL; politically they could not do otherwise. Disapproval would have meant a public and probably extremely awkward situation for both GHQ and the Yoshida Cabinet and importantly would have given extraordinarily powerful assistance and ammunition to the opposition to the SAPL. There was, however, a last minute constitutional challenge to the validity of the SAPL and opposition to GHQ approval of the draft SAPL by the legal section in GHQ—quite prescient as it turned out. The logic and reasons for this constitutional challenge were similar to those advocated by the Japanese political opposition to the SAPL. Amazingly, this internal GHQ opposition was not leaked "accidentally" to the Japanese opposition; if it had been so leaked, the rationale of this internal GHQ challenge would undoubtedly have had an important effect perhaps to have derailed the SAPL in HofC deliberations.

The target group under the proposed SAPL was described first and foremost as those "organizations conducting violently destructive activities" (*bōryoku-teki hakai katsudō dantai*); although the word "Communist" was not mentioned once in the SAPL, it was implied and understood clearly that the SAPL was aimed at the violent activities then sponsored by the Communists whether inner-directed or due to "guidance" from foreign sources, Soviet or Chinese. That THE emphasis of the SAPL was on the control of such destructive violent organizational activities was stressed, asserted and explained in the strongest and clearest terms possible by the government witnesses, with monotonous repetition throughout committee hearings in both Houses of the Diet cannot be ignored. Actions against these organizations were to be recommended by the PSIA to the quasi-judicial PSEC which, in turn, would make legally binding decisions on these recommendations. Of course, individual violators of SAPL provisions would also be prosecuted under the referenced articles of the Criminal Code strengthened and expanded under the SAPL. It was made utterly clear time and time and time again in the Committee hearings that the thrust of the SAPL was focused on controlling these violently destructive organizations and not individuals, the latter being secondary. It is in this context and emphasis that we should recall that in 1950 much thought was expended on how the JCP could be disbanded under the new 1947 Japanese Constitution. (See chapter 2) It could be done by fiat by the U.S. Occupation, but that would not set a good example and an unfortunate precedent for follow-on Japanese government actions and legitimate any action against the Communists they might take with great delight. Thus, the basic approach to control organizations which have committed violent, destructive activities or might commit in the future could be a convenient Constitutional approach to disband, dissolve, ban the JCP. Indeed, the unspoken indirect objective of the SAPL was "to get at" the Communists through the clause "violent destructive activities as the actions of an organization". The violent activities described earlier were, it was believed, carried out with the approval, encouragement, funding, training and direction by the JCP and gave the government what it believed to be a built-in rationale and seemingly Constitutional sanction in the name of maintaining public welfare and security.

The so-called threat in the 1920s was not a clear and present physical threat to the Japanese nation state but a perceived psycho-emotional spiritual and ideological threat and challenge to the psyche of the nervous Japanese political elite. In contrast, in 1950–1952 the Communists launched a series of assassinations, burglaries, fire-bomb attacks, etc, which did cause annoyance, frustration, anger and successfully aroused the anxiety and fear levels of these same kinds of political elites and reinforced the long held felt needs to fill the potential vacuum in internal security laws that it saw developing with the signing of the Peace Treaty. But even this so-called threat level was declared manageable, i.e., not a physical threat to the Japanese nation state. Nevertheless, there was a strong conviction that a law was needed that will nip any such "destructive activities" from happening. It was only natural (*tōzen*) in the name of maintaining public security and welfare (*kōkyō anzen hoji*) to control such organizations which conduct such activities; even those who opposed such actions by their organizations would be penalized (Seki, HofC 6/18:9), i.e. the SAPL would basically be pre-emptive strike law.

The opposition to the SAPL continually asserted that the proposed law was none other than an attempted revival of the feared and hated notorious prewar Peace Preservation Law of 1925 in a seemingly democratic disguise; the government and its supporters with equal vehemence asserted that it was a necessary law to maintain public welfare and security within the "democratic" context of postwar Japan and with all necessary bureaucratic and democratic controls to prevent abuses that had occurred under the *ancien regime* which, though hobbled temporarily by forced Occupation measures, was still alive and kicking. Since 1868, Japan had enacted a series of internal security laws inter-related and inter-locking in thought and objectives, the most famous of which was the PPL. In light of the waves of attacks on public offices, fires, political robberies and assassinations, arson in 1951–1952, the conservative government believed a clearly stated internal security law was absolutely necessary to counter this seemingly direct Communist threat and challenge to the stability of the Japanese state and society. By emphasizing these attacks, linking them as a threat to the Japanese nation state with foreign connections they effectively appealed to the almost inborn Japanese fear and distaste for the "foreign Communist ideology". There was an unreality about attempting to "control" (up to and including disbandment of an organization for conducting destructive activities "as actions of that organization") at present or may conduct in the future. How were past actions to be judged by whom and how, by what standards, would these actions be deemed to be carried out in the future. Clearly constitutional issues and challenges were inherent in this philosophical approach and were so challenged in Committee Hearings. It was believed that in contrast to the prewar PPL amorphous philosophy of merely entertaining such dangerous thoughts which seemingly questioned the Emperor system and sanctity of private property were criminal, postwar judgments and actions against organizations committing "destructive activities" would be so clear cut, obvious and transparent. They felt vulnerable with no available counter measures—even though they had stated earlier that this threat was manageable. Nevertheless, they wanted an internal security law as part of the array of laws, like the government had before 1945 and like other sovereign nations with similar laws. The government had unrealistically hoped to secure the enactment of the SAPL so that it would become effective when the Peace Treaty became effective, thereby preventing the feared gap or vacuum from occurring—but that did not happen. While the SAPL was not a revival *per se* of the prewar Japanese internal security laws since it is radically different in legal structure, objectives and philosophy, it cannot be denied that it was part of the prewar-postwar continuum—especially since the SAPL emanated by force of circumstances from the prewar governmental personnel and institutional arrangements surviving inevitably and understandably into the postwar era.

The "dragnet" approach reflected in Phase I of the drafting process would not have passed through the bureaucratic vetting process and was already under fire from the opposition to any internal security law. Even Seki the drafter later regarded his own early drafts as a potentially dangerous law. If it had actually survived and had been submitted to the Diet, it may have passed the House of Representatives by cracking the whip of party discipline but passage through the House of Councillors would probably not have occurred. It was a "stroke of genius", so to speak, by Seki to include selected articles of the existing CC into the SAPL by reference and, in this process, strengthening and broadening those articles to apply to "violent destructive organizations". This very act of broadening and strengthening selected articles of the existing CC in the SAPL gave the opposition, based on its own prewar experiences, personal and otherwise, additional reason to oppose the SAPL. One of the major criticisms of the prewar application of the PPL was the gradual expanded interpretation of the applicability of the PPL to liberals (those who disagreed with the government), radical religionists, Christians, Buddhists and extreme Shintoists and others. While the referenced inclusion of articles from the CC with expanded attributes seemingly made the SAPL more palatable to moderates, it was the very act of strengthening and broadening the referenced articles of the CC in the SAPL that raised the alarm bells and deepened yet another notch the distrust and suspicions held by the political opposition to the SAPL about the motives behind the creation of the SAPL itself. Those suspecting these motives, maintained that the CC was being revised through the back door, through the SAPL; this was staunchly denied by the government. It should be remembered that the CC was one of the prewar laws that survived more or less intact from U.S. Occupation scrutiny, including criminal philosophy and importantly the style of language used in the CC. According to drafter Seki, the "claws" of the CC had been extended through the SAPL and the new SAPL itself created a *dantai keihō*, a criminal law for [violent destructive] organizations.[1]

If there was one phrase, one term over which both argued, verbally battled over, to the very end, it was the word *sendō,* incitement. It was included in the earliest draft and survived all subsequent drafts and became the one word which AG Kimura Tokutarō vowed would not be deleted from the SAPL so long as he was the Attorney General

---

[1] The claw idea is quoted in *Himitsu no Fuairu* [The Secret Files] by Haruna Mikio. Kyōdō Tsūshinsha. 2000. 2v. p. I:400.

defending the enactment of the SAPL; it was said he was weak politically as the AG, it was his Directors-General who insisted with the unspoken threat of resignation that *sendō* must be supported and included in the SAPL under any circumstances. AG Kimura insisted throughout all the confrontations at committee hearings that *sendō* was indeed the essence, core, the central issue (*kosshi*) of the SAPL, the essence which must never be compromised. From the government's point of view, Inclusion of *sendō* was a given; the attempt to delete it by the LM was a sad comic sideshow. To the opposition, it symbolized the revival of the old police system. This disagreement about the inclusion of *sendō* was yet another symbol of the distrust and suspicions that pervaded the parliamentary sparring. As described earlier, use of the word, *sendō*, in the SAPL was not something new that would arouse suspicions and distrust for it had been included in many postwar laws which had survived parliamentary scrutiny without much ado. But it was a word that when included in such a law as the SAPL immediately conjured up—fairly or not is another issue—a host of fears and distrust and suspicions from the days of the PPL. It was the adamancy of the government on insisting that *sendō* must be included in the SAPL that aroused such sustained and determined opposition and fear of a hidden agenda behind the meaning of this word and the potential impact of the bureaucratic interpretation of this word would have when the SAPL was implemented. It should be recalled that in the 1940 proposed revision of the CC (but not enacted), *sendō* would become a criminal offense and more importantly in the 1942–43 special wartime criminal law, *kyōsa sendō* were criminal offenses. Thus, there is a direct lineage—spiritually, philosophically, and from the point of view of legal thought and structure—from wartime exigencies to the postwar commitment to continue *sendō kyōsa* as criminal offenses. In order to avoid or mitigate a frontal confrontation with the labor movement, the Labor Minister in the Yoshida Cabinet did suggest the deletion of this controversial word, *sendō,* from the draft SAPL but was chided by his Cabinet colleagues for this suggestion; I can well imagine that AG Kimura as a *kendō* devotee and master brought himself to a *kendō* stance while sitting in his cabinet chair and admonishing him for his weak-kneed idea. Both sides fought persistently, determinedly, doggedly to have *sendō* deleted and with equal vigor to keep it in. The government conditionally won this skirmish.

If there is another word that energized the opposition, it would be "implementation" in light of historical precedent and personal experiences. There was an understandable and legitimate obsession in pursuing the government about the potential for "expanded interpretation" (*kakudai kaishaku*) in a similar fashion to that which occurred in pre-1945 years in the implementation of the PPL and how this must be prevented. Because of the real precedents, phrases, rather strong phrases, were added in more than one place in the SAPL emphasizing in the strongest possible way—the strong Japanese term "*iyashikumo*" was used—not in an admonishing manner but intended as a legal limitation and constraint, telling the security agencies that the SAPL must be interpreted and implemented in the narrowest possible manner.

The rationales used to justify the need for both the prewar PPL and the postwar SAPL, slightly more than a quarter century apart, were indeed quite uncomfortably similar: the need for and the essence of the prewar law, the inadequacy of the CC to handle these destructive activities, the international connections of the target activities, vagueness of terms and the need for heavier penalties. These almost identical rationales and justification gave added cogency to the opposition's concern about the fundamental need for the SAPL.

Senior members of the Liberal Party, the Social Democratic Party, the Sohyo Labor Federation and the group of expert witnesses of professors, media and industry representatives each played various roles in supporting and opposing the enactment of the SAPL. While their roles have been described in earlier chapters, let us summarize their overall impact. While senior civil servants, the expert bureaucrats such as Seki, the SAPL drafter, played a critical role as an expert in drafting legislation, they were influenced and instructed by specialized Liberal Party committees which took a special interest in the SAPL legislation to make sure certain important changes were made in the drafts; Seki and AG Kimura had to repeatedly return and report to these committees for additional guidance and approval. Some members of these Liberal Party committees could assert effectively a stronger voice in "instructing Seki and the AG" to make certain changes because of their previous bureaucratic positions; some were de-purgees who had established themselves in senior positions in the Liberal Party. Although this period is known for the overwhelming influence of the senior career civil service in legislation and management of the national government, the drafting of the SAPL was influenced substantially by these party committees and its selected members. Probably these party committees had a greater substantive impact in the drafting process than GHQ had had.

Opposition party leaders and Sohyo had basically little or no impact on drafting the SAPL; the government tried to pacify labor leaders by making rather technical and meaningless word and phrase changes, revisions and additions to the draft SAPL—but, of course, these tactics were rather transparent and not taken seriously by labor. On the other hand, Sōhyō labor leaders many of whom had survived the battles of prewar suppression of the labor union movement and leftwing political organizations, had to adopt a strong and determined stance with vigor, a do or die stance, not just opposing the SAPL but insistently demand its withdrawal, impractical as that may be from the political point of view. They had to take this drastic stance as a matter of self-respect since the proponents of the SAPL came from the very same prewar institutions which had suppressed them. In addition, their strong opposition to the SAPL was inextricably interwoven with political internal labor power struggles for leadership of Sohyo, the major labor federation. They had to take a strong anti-SAPL, anti-*kai'aku* of the labor laws to maintain their leadership positions and legitimacy. Their direct influence on revisions to the SAPL in Diet considerations was probably close to nil but they were a most important part of the incessant, loud and boisterous chorus of the opposition. The expert witnesses, a high proportion of whom opposed the SAPL were politely listened to in the HoR committee hearings and seemingly ignored. In the House of Councillors committee hearings more attention was paid for obvious political reasons; they were more seriously recognized but their impact is difficult to gauge. One thing for certain was that they were part of the more sedate but persistent intellectual opposition chorus. The parrying Q&A between government witnesses and Diet member droned on for weeks, for many hours each day; the hearings were unavoidably repetitious. It is not possible to point to any specific Q&A duel in Committee Hearings which led to a particular revision; nevertheless, the cumulative impact of the hearings in both sets of Committee did buildup "virtual" precedents when the enacted SAPL would be implemented; in this amorphous sense, probably the hearings did harbor some overall notion of success.

While PM Yoshida did indeed assign AG Kimura to be the lead Minister to create an acceptable SAPL draft bill for Cabinet approval, that did not guarantee his authority to carry out this mission. There was the task of defining "the police powers" of SAPL staff investigators to inspect, search, and seize materials, i.e. their compulsory investigative authority (*kyōsei sōsaken*). In early drafts, Seki, being a member of the Ministry of Justice naturally gave the SAPL this authority but was strenuously opposed by traditional police agencies as an invasion of their original and basic police authorities. In the bureaucratic tug-of-war over this turf issue among the security agencies, the Ministry of Justice was out-stared by the senior traditional police representatives at the negotiating table and indicative of the lack of political determination and will to effectively demand such authority for SAPL personnel by the AG himself and ultimately lack of support from the PM. There was also the concern that giving that authority to SAPL personnel would be/may be regarded by many as giving that critical authority to yet another agency, this time to an agency with an image associated with re-creating the prewar political thought prosecutors (*shisō kenji*). This was not a new turf issue between the two groups but one that was a controllably simmering issue. The legal authority of the PSIA was lessened, compromised not by pressure from the opposition, not by the Occupation, but through a resolution of the turf issue among the internal security bureaucracies concerned in the SAPL drafting process. The government argued with itself as to who would be given basic police authorities using what institutional arrangements in the government.

If there was one decisive event that decided whether the SAPL would or would not become law, it was the 1952 May Day. Prior to these presumably Communist led riots, turmoil, disturbances, destruction creating scenes of such conflict and mayhem in the Imperial/People's Plaza in the center of Tokyo, there was the parliamentary possibility in the HofC that the opposition could reasonably conjure up the idea that the SAPL could be stalled off the Diet calendar, or so watered down that the government would abandon the bill. But after these riots whose photographs in the print and voice media gave the impression of impending chaos, passage of an SAPL bill in some form was pushed successfully with greater determination in the House of Representatives; even in the HofC it was clear some sort of SAPL bill would be passed, the issue then became merely to what extent would it be revised and weakened or strengthened.

Since the Liberal Party had a comfortable majority in the House of Representatives, the outcome was known; the role of the opposition was to pursue the government witnesses as energetically as possible as to how the SAPL might be implemented and enforced under various scenarios, establish a legislative record loud and clear as to the probable meaning of controversial words and phrases for use in possible future legislation and court cases. Because the Liberal Party did not have a controlling majority in the House of Councillors, it had to court, listen to and accept many rather important demands of the Ryokufūkai in revising the draft to more narrowly interpret the meaning of the problem terms; these restricting changes probably had a major influence on the implementation of the SAPL. This is an example where, because of the political lineup, the Diet was able to have a major impact on the legislative outcome—"after the 1955 merger [of the two conservative parties], the Diet seldom performed its main function of deliberating bills, as it had done when it drastically modified the Subversive Activities Prevention Law in 1952".[2]

The initial drafts included everything, everything except the kitchen sink as the colloquial saying goes and even that may have been included. During the phase I drafting, a whittling down process began on this overly broad coverage of the SAPL, initiating a one-by-one retreating process to narrow the application of this law. This retreat seemingly continued during phase II in connection with the authority of PSEC, the denial of compulsory investigative authority to the PSIA and others described elsewhere; but the referenced articles from the CC included in the draft bill submitted to the Cabinet were uncomfortably supplemented, strengthened and broadened in coverage of individual criminal acts. Understandably no substantive revisions were made by the House of Representatives. The House of Councillors instructed the PSIA and PSEC that the SAPL shall be implemented within the "narrowest possible limits necessary", "must never deviate from the authorized limits of authority by unlawful limitations on the rights and freedom of the people under the Japanese Constitution" and the Agency was reminded that these were not hortatory words of admonition. The HofC more narrowly defined the controversial terms, *sendō* and *kyōsa*, gave the PSEC broader independent powers, and increased the prison sentence for abuse of authority by security officials. These revisions acted importantly as negative safeguards in implementing the SAPL. The HofC did not change the veto authority of the PM concerning an appeal to the courts over a PSEC decision; this veto authority hanging over an appeal to the courts made one of the potentially proactive principal safeguards basically meaningless. The conservative

[2] Misawa Shigeo. An Outline of the Policy-making process in Japan, in *Japanese Politics: An Inside View*. Hiroshi Itoh. Cornell University Press. 1973. 248 p., p. 32.

government under PM Yoshida had no alternative but to accept these various stiffer restrictions, additions, revisions. Despite the strong nationwide opposition to the SAPL by labor unions, intellectuals, academicians, political parties, eventually the SAPL was indeed passed and promulgated as the legal centerpiece in the post-treaty internal security structure. Thus, a potential legal route to ban the JCP under the organizational provisions of the SAPL had been created—IF the government could marshal the necessary evidence, overcome potential constitutional challenges and muster the necessary political will power. Since the SAPL did not specify the Communists as the target in the law, only violent destructive organizations and despite the limitations and restrictions, exhortations and admonitions that the law shall be interpreted in the narrowest sense and conversely shall not be broadened in implementation, an utterly ruthless Minister of Justice or Procurator General given a certain political climate could try to apply this controversial law to pursue "the presumed enemies of the state"—a law in waiting.

CHAPTER SEVEN

EPILOGUE

A. *Implementation of the SAPL and Court Cases*

As I had originally planned in 1955–56, the description and analysis of the complicated story about how the SAPL was created in 1951–52 has been accomplished. However, since over 50 years have elapsed since this law was promulgated in July 1952, inclusion of a summary would be useful and appropriate on how this law was implemented, what cases based on this law were brought to the Japanese Supreme Court, what revisions to the SAPL were considered, how the Aum Shinrikyō sarin gas attack of 1995 affected the SAPL, the PSIA and the enactment of a new law on indiscriminate killing of people, and other issues. This summary is not intended to be a legal exegesis of the several Supreme Court decisions, nor to provide an analysis of the on-going almost constant turf battles among the security agencies. It is intended to provide only an overview to lay the basis for a detailed future analysis of the implementation of the SAPL since 1952 by a researcher other than myself.

With the promulgation of the new Hakai Katsudō Bōshihō/Subversive Activities Prevention Law came cautious, anticipated, pious statements by the DG of the PSIA, the Minister of Justice Kimura Tokutarō that the implementation of the SAPL would not—repeat would not—be a repetition of the PPL of prewar notoriety, that it would be cautiously, carefully enforced in accordance with a strict interpretation and spirit of the law. At an August 7, 1952 national conference of senior prosecutors in Tokyo, the implementation of the SAPL was a natural topic but the first item raised in the Minister of Justice's comments on internal security did not center on the Japanese Communists and their activities but the criminal activities of some part of the North Korean residents in Japan and those affiliated with the JCP and its support groups, a threat to Japanese internal security which, it was thought, could not be ignored. (*Asahi* 8/7/1952, *Tokyo Shimbun* 7/22/1952)

A newspaper commentary on the future implementation of the SAPL opined that the targets of investigation and possible prosecution would be extreme leftwing non-public/secret/covert activities (*hi-kōzen katsudō*) using, for example, the new criminal categories of preparing and planning for (*yobi imbō*) instigating and inciting destructive activities, or the printing, distribution and display of materials advocating internal insurrection (*nairan*). The latter could now be prosecuted under the SAPL whereas they had been awkwardly prosecuted under local laws on traffic (*dōro kōtsū torishimari-hō*) and the minor criminal offenses law (*kei-hanzai-hō*). Prosecutions against individuals was not a new adventure; these could follow normal criminal procedures. But actions against organizations was a new paradigm. It was presciently surmised that application of the SAPL to organizations may occur sometime in the future, not in the near term, because of the need for additional more careful and detailed investigation, the establishment of detailed rules, regulations and standards, and the creation of adequate staff in the PSIA and the PSEC for these purposes. (*Asahi* 7/4/1952) Normally Japanese Ministries promulgate general implementation procedures (*shikō kisoku*) concerning a particular law and, in addition, issue detailed implementation procedures (*shikō saisoku*) specifying in fair detail how and in what way a law would be implemented. During Committee Hearings considerable concern was expressed by opposition Diet members about how the SAPL would be implemented, especially in light of how the PPL was implemented in the prewar years. The government was pressed to provide some assurances about how such abuses could be avoided in the future. The government promised it would issue two additional sets of regulations for this purpose: *kansatsu seido* (a supervisory system), *chōsakan no kantoku to sekinin seido* (supervision of investigators and a system of responsibility). The latter two were clearly intended to respond to the anxieties about future abuses of authority in the implementation of the SAPL, especially by lower ranking personnel. General implementation procedures (*habōhō shikō kisoku*) were issued on 7/21/1952. However apparently, not expecting to invoke the SAPL against "violent destructive organizations" in the near term, additional detailed implementation procedures (*shikō saisoku*) were not prepared nor issued—over the 50+ years as late as 2005, a copy of these promised procedures had not been found. Apparently, lack of these detailed procedures created belatedly an administrative problem for the PSIA when it was suddenly necessary for it to prepare a case against the Aum Shinrikyō for presentation to the PSEC; the PSIA had not prepared detailed administrative guidance to itself for preparing a thorough and effective case against a "violent destructive organization" recommending its dissolution.

Court Cases against Individuals. Over fifty plus years, the following eight cases were prosecuted under the SAPL against individuals.

1. Kushiro Jiken, 9/20/1952
2. Tsu Jiken, 9/13/1952
3. "Kyoto no Hata" Jiken, 9/6/1952, 9/9/1952, 9/10/1952
4. Gifu Jiken, late July through late October, 1952
5. Sammu (San'yū?) Jiken, early September through early December 1961
6. Sekigun-ha Daibosatsu Tōge Jiken, late October through early November 1969
7. Okinawa Dakkan Tōsō (Honda Habōhō Jiken), 4/15–24/1969
8. Okinawa Henkan Kyōtei Hijun Soshi Tōsō (Matsuo Habōhō Jiken), 10/21/1971 and 11/10/1971

A total of 34 persons were prosecuted, 12 declared guilty, 17 not guilty, four died during the proceedings, and one escaped. Those found guilty were often given suspended sentences. In all cases, articles 38, 39 and 40 were declared constitutional in an attempt to differentiate between criminal "actions" (*kōdō*) under the SAPL and the freedom of thought, philosophy under the Constitution; the courts maintained that freedom of expression itself contained a built-in limitation (*naizai-teki seiyaku*). Under certain circumstances, freedom of speech and expression, etc, will be subordinated to the maintenance of public welfare and security with unavoidable limitations. Basic freedoms as specified in the Constitution cannot compromise the maintenance of public security and welfare. The first four cases involved JCP members, the last three involved senior leaders of radical leftwing movements normally associated with the JCP. For good measure and balance, the fifth case was an anti-communist planned action against the government. The last three cases, involved leaders of the radical student movements in their 40s and 50s, e.g. chairman of the Central Executive Committee of the Chūkakuha of the Zengakuren, leader of the Red Army. These cases can be grouped conveniently into four cases involving SAPL article 38.2.b in 1952 and those involving SAPL articles 39 and 40 in 1961, 1969 and 1971. The fifth case involved the distribution of materials, planning (*imbō*) and preparations (*yobi*) to conduct crimes specified in Articles 38 and 39. Cases 7 and 8 involved the crime of incitement under article 39 and 40.[1]

i. *The Four Cases involving Article 38*

Three were for actions committed in September 1952 and one in July through October 1952, only a few months after the SAPL was promulgated. In light of the challenges in Diet hearings, there must have been a strong felt need in the PSIA for it to submit some cases to the courts to prove the SAPL's validity as an instrument of internal security control and to secure directly the Supreme Court's stamp of constitutionality which, as usual, came some years later. These cases involved violations of the following SAPL Article 38.2.b:

> **Article 38. Instigations to Insurrection and Crimes Involving the External Security of the State, etc.** 1) Any person who has instigated a crime under Article 77, Article 81 or Article 82 of the Penal Code and any person who has incited a crime with the object of performing such a crime will be sentenced to not more than seven years imprisonment with or without hard labor.
>
> 2) Any person, as indicated below, will be sentenced to not more than five years imprisonment with or without hard labor:
>
> b. Any person with the object of performing a crime under Articles 77, 81 or 82 of the Penal Code who publicly posts, distributes or prints any document or drawing which has proclaimed the propriety or the necessity of the performance of such crime.

- the defendants were accused of violating article 38.2.b
- but all were acquitted as not guilty.
- the defendants were Communist Party members or sympathizers, each case involving 2–6 persons for distributing printed matter entitled "Appealing to the Japanese people in this election, a Free Japan broadcast", "We must begin preparations and actions to arm

[1] In contrast to my neutral grouping by date and SAPL article, Professor Watanabe Osamu of Hitotsubashi University in Tokyo divided the application of the SAPL into four historical periods with a distinctly anti-government slant: 1) 1952–1960, failure to apply the SAPL against the JCP as an organization, instead party members were prosecuted, 2) 1961–67, another attempt to apply the SAPL in a changed political milieu, 3) 1967–90, where the government aimed to apply the SAPL against organizations but ended with three prosecutions against individuals, and 4) 1991–1996, the crisis of the need for the SAPL and its revival. Habōhō wa naze dekitaka, ikani tsukaware yō toshita ka, *Hōritsu Jihō* 68:9(8/1996):9–15.

ourselves", *Kyoto no Hata* (Flag of Kyoto) issue #2, "Directions for Mountain Travels".

- that the defendants were JCP members would strongly imply but not prove, that the real target of the SAPL was indeed the JCP and its supporters.[2]

ii. *The Four Cases involving Articles 39 and 40*

The second group of cases involved articles 39 and 40.1.a and 40.1.c:

> **Article 39. Preparation for the Crime of Arson for Political Purposes, etc.** Any person who, in order to promote, support or oppose any political doctrine or policy, plots, prepares for or instigates the crimes mentioned in Articles 108, 109 (paragraph 1), 117 (first part of paragraph 1), 126 (paragraphs 1 or 2), 199 or 236 (paragraph 1) of the Penal Code or any person who has incited a crime which has as its object the performance of the crimes listed above will be sentenced to not more than five years' imprisonment with or without hard labor.
>
> **Article 40. Preparations for Riot for Political Purposes, etc.** Any person who in order to promote, support or oppose any political doctrine or policy instigates, plots or prepares the crimes indicated below or any person who has incited a crime which has as its object the performance of these crimes will be sentenced to not more than three years' imprisonment with or without hard labor.
>
> a. Crimes in Article 106 of the Penal Code
> b. Crimes in Article 125 of the Penal Code
> c. Crimes as referred to in Article 95 of the Penal Code by carrying any deadly weapon or poison and acting collectively against any person engaged in procuratorial or police duties, any assistant to such officials, any person who guards or escorts persons detained by law or any person engaged in investigations under this law.

- the defendants were accused of violating articles 39, 40.1.b and 40.1.c for actions committed in September 1961, April and October–November 1969 and in October 1971.
- in each of the four cases, the defendants were accused of plotting, planning, attacks on government buildings (Diet, the PM's residence), attacks on the U.S. Embassy, calling on the Japanese armed forces for support, calling for the assassinations of senior

[2] The court decision for Case #4 was one of those selected for inclusion in *The Constitutional Case Law of Japan: selected Supreme Court Decisions, 1961–70.* Hiroshi Itoh & Lawrence W. Beer. University of Washington Press as "Case 30. Japan v. Kanemoto et al. (1964). The Kanemoto Pamphlet case", pp. 342–344.

government officials, planning the assemblage of stocks of military weapons, providing military training, calling for the destruction of police and military equipment and inciting people assembled at meetings to take these actions as part of opposition to government policies concerning the U.S.-Japan Security Treaty, the return of Okinawa to Japanese jurisdiction, removal of U.S. Forces from military bases. They attempted to incite people through these actions to create political chaos, riots.

- in one decision, the accused's actions would come under the category of plotting (*imbō*) for the assassination of people and creating riots *for political purposes* but had not reached the point of preparing (*yobi*) for these action and thus not guilty; but in another decision the accused was found guilty because his actions had reached the stage of preparing for such actions—indeed, a fine line of judicial judgment. In two other cases, the accused was found guilty of inciting riots, possessing dangerous weapons and obstruction of official duties for political purposes. In the so-called anti-Communist example, the Sammu case, the defendants were calling for the establishment of a society of three No's: Forever no Taxes, Forever No Unemployment, Forever No war. As part of the incitement, they planned to make a pilgrimage to Meiji Shrine in Tokyo to pray for and seek approval and support of this incitement for political purposes.

It should be emphasized that only articles 38, 39 and 40 of the SAPL had been declared constitutional by the courts but the conviction rate was imperfect and spotty; the constitutionality of those SAPL articles applying to restrictions on the activities of violent destructive organizations and disbandment of these organizations had yet to be decided since no successful case had been brought against an organization in over 50 years to the PSEC in the first instance and, therefore, no Supreme Court pronouncement on constitutionality.

B. *Sarin Gas Attacks in the Mid-1990s and the SAPL*

The Sarin Gas Attacks and Responses. First in Matsumoto city in mountainous Nagano prefecture on June 27, 1994 with seven dead and about 600 injured—a major prefectural city but not Tokyo or Osaka, then on 20 March 1995 in the subway in downtown Tokyo, the capital city with greater deadly results, 12 dead and 1000s injured from sarin gas. Only ten days later on March 30, 1995, the Commissioner of the Metropolitan Police was attacked by an unknown assassin and again a sarin gas attack in the Yokohama railway station with no deaths and no injuries. There was an immediate demand for quick and direct action against the Aum Shinrikyō, a Buddhist religious organization but also a stronger and decidedly go-slow advocates, especially when it came to any idea to increase police powers; there were those who thought this was the opportunity to reconsider and abolish the SAPL, let alone trying to revise the law so it could more effectively handle such disastrous situations. *The Washington Post* (4/29/1995) carried an interesting article by T.R. Reid on Japanese and American reactions to such terroristic acts. Whereas new sweeping laws were speedily introduced into the U.S. Congress in response to the Oklahoma City bombing of federal buildings, the Japanese government declared forcefully that it had no immediate plans for new security laws. There was grave concern in Japan that hastily reacting in the quest for security might undermine cherished national values. The Japanese have fewer police per capita than the United States and many other Western countries. "There is a lingering collective memory, particularly among those over 50 of the fascist police who ruled with an iron hand" in prewar years. The Aum Shinrikyō were the presumed culprits; nevertheless, "...the fear and rumor-mongering have not translated into political pressure for tough new laws or enhanced police powers." Such was the power of the "lingering collective memory". Nevertheless, after investigations several different actions were taken.

Applying the Religious Organizations Law (Shōkyō Hōjin Dantai-hō). Three months later on June 30, 1995, the Tokyo District Prosecutors Bureau and the Governor of Tokyo requested the Tokyo District Court to issue an order disbanding the Aum Shinrikyō in accordance with article 81.1.1 and 81.1.2. of the Religious Organizations Law; it was so ordered on October 30, 1995. This action was deemed constitutional by the Supreme Court. Later, this law was revised to adjust to the changed situation surrounding religious organizations and another law enacted to provide compensation to the victims of the sarin gas attacks.[3]

[3] Since an analysis of this law is not central to this study, see Yasuhiro Okudaira. Current Controversies on on the Control of Religious Organizations in Japan, in *Columbia Journal of Asian Law* 10:1(Spring 1996):127–156.

Applying the SAPL. Many months later on December 14, 1995, the government decided, after receiving a report on the gas attack from the PSIA, that the latter would initiate action against the Aum Shinrikyō, i.e. the PSIA would make a request to the PSEC to order the disbandment of this religious organization. This was a high risk political decision to take. Under the circumstances, this was the first seemingly real opportunity to apply the controversial organizational control and penalty aspects of the SAPL against not a "political" but a "religious" organization. Seemingly these dastardly sarin gas attacks would be an open and shut case against the Aum Shinrikyō; these were violent destructive acts committed with a political purpose. Although the SAPL was drafted in a neutral manner, the legislative history implied it was intended to apply to the Communists, the JCP and their supporters who presumably were the organization behind the numerous "destructive violent activities"; the initial cases, for example, were all taken against Communist party members. Application of the SAPL to religious organizations was not mentioned nor contemplated in drafting the SAPL nor was the potential application of the SAPL to religious organizations discussed in Diet Committee hearings. Successful application of the SAPL would have legally validated an "expanded" interpretation of the SAPL to a totally new and highly emotionally charged area, religious organizations; it would have validated a fundamental criticism of the SAPL voiced repeatedly in Committee hearings that the government would "expand" its interpretation of the SAPL as it did for the PPL and violate its own promise to the Diet and the people, yet again. Such an application and changing the Religious Organization Law would be highly sensitive for the Kōmeitō (the political arm of the Sōka Gakkai, a politically active Buddhist organization), then a member of the Cabinet. It took such a long time to reach a decision for a number of probable reasons: there were conflicting demands within and without the government for speedy direct action or a more cautious approach under the SAPL, the PSIA had to prepare belatedly a report on the Aum Shimrikyō and establish the procedures to be followed if it was decided action against the Aum Shinrikyō would be recommended by the PSIA to the PSEC, and lingering anxiety in the government about the constitutionality of such action. This decision was accepted with relish by some newspaper editorials, with considerable anxiety, and others with reluctance. Commentators suggested that the proposed application of the SAPL was a necessary evil (Sassa Atsuyuki, formerly chief of the of the Cabinet's Office of Security Maintenance,

Asahi 10/10/1995), abolition of the SAPL was the role the Legislature should carry out at this time (Okudaira Yasuhiro, *Asahi* 10/10/1995, a long time critic of the SAPL and retired professor of Tokyo University), do not apply the SAPL, create a new law (Atsumi Tōyō, professor of criminal law at Chūō University, *Asahi* 10/10/1995).[4]

After completing the detailed procedures specified in the law, the PSIA on July 11, 1996 requested the PSEC to order the disbanding of the Aum Shinrikyō religious organization. In contrast to the period when the SAPL was enacted, there were no demonstrations against this proposed application of the SAPL but there were pro and con editorials, numerous magazines articles, supporting and denouncing this action. Those opposing this action as unconstitutional were more numerous and organized.[5] After completing its hearings, the PSEC issued its decision on January 31, 1997 (*Kampō Gōgai* 2/4/1997. 20 p.). It agreed that the gas attacks were conducted as "organizational activities" of the Aum Shinrikyō as defined in the SAPL and that it had

[4] *Asahi* (12/15/1995) raised doubts about the application of the SAPL to a religious organization such as Aum Shinrikyō; *Yomiuri* (12/15/1995) and *Mainichi* (12/15/1995) urged that application of the SAPL proceed with great care; *Nikkei* (12/15/1995) recognized that in light of the emergency situation, the need for action, the unsatisfactory nature of an alternative possibility, and with little material available, the decision to request the PSEC to disband the Aum Shinrikyō could not be avoided but must not be regarded as a precedent for an enlarged interpretation of the SAPL.

[5] As might be expected, opposition to this decision was voiced by a number of different kinds of organizations, e.g. the Japan Lawyers Federation (Nihon Bengoshi Rengōkai), the Jiyū Hōsōdan, another lawyer association, the Japan Pen Club, Japan Journalist Conference (Nihon Jānarisuto Kaigi), and legal scholars. A first statement of opposition to the application of the SAPL to Aum Shinrikyō was issued initially by 62 legal scholars, eventually by 11/5/1995, 383 scholars from 86 universities had joined this opposition. A two-day symposium was held on 3/17/1996 and 4/27/1996. After the second symposium a second statement of opposition was issued on 4/27/1996(?). They challenged the very legitimacy of the SAPL, probable expanded interpretation of the SAPL as exemplified by this action against the Aum Shinrikyō, the probable unconstitutionality of the procedures followed by the PSIA in investigating this organization, to pursue the Aum Shinrikyō as an organization whose actions were committed with "a political motive" in mind would be a violation of the Constitution's guarantee of freedom of speech, thought and assembly, disbandment should not be ordered by a quasi-judicial agency, such as the PSEC, but by a court, restrictions on a publication would be censorship banned by the Constitution. These comments were derived from a series of four articles under the overall title of "Tekiyō sarenakatta Habōhō" as follows: Kawasaki Hideaki, Habōhō Mondai ga nokoshita mono, *Hōgaku Seminā* 42:9(9/97):27–30; Murai Yoshikuni, Habōhō no Sonzai Igi to Tōchō Hōan, *Hōgaku Seminā* 42:10(10/1997):26–30; Yamauchi Toshihirō, Habōhō Ikensei no Saikenshō, *Hōgaku Seminā* 42:11(11/1997):8–12; Serizawa Hitoshi, Habōhō Benmei Tetsuzuki ni tachi atte, *Hōgaku Seminā* 42:12(12/1997):14–18.

"a political objective" in conducting these actions. But the PSEC did not agree that there was a clear and present danger that these actions would be repeated again in the future because the Aum Shinrikyō group was now a bankrupt organization through actions taken under the Religious Organizations Law described above, thus, it was no longer a threat to society; PSEC evaluated that there was no evidence that the Aum Shinrikyō as reconstituted had the desire, inclination, human, financial and material resources to further its political aims through violent destructive activities. Since the accused organization had re-created itself into a religious organization spread throughout society and enormously changed from its days when it conducted gas attacks, there is not sufficient reason to believe that this organization would likely continue or repeat such activities in the future. It did not comment on the constitutionality issue thereby postponing this critical constitutional decision to another date. While this was a major blow to the government, especially to the PSIA, inevitably raising questions as to the need for and viability of the PSIA and even the SAPL itself. But, on the other hand, since the constitutional issue remained moot, it provided the legal and political leeway for the PSIA, the SAPL to continue to survive and its role to be somewhat re-defined as described below.

The PSEC, however, made some rather interesting, fascinating and important comments in the concluding section of its decision (6. Some concluding observations, pp. 16–17): 1) the standard for the moment and time for the PSEC to make a decision was not the moment when PSIA submitted its request but when the PSEC makes its judgment taking into consideration developments surrounding the Aum Shinrikyō that occurred after that submission. However, this approach does exclude the concept of double jeopardy. It would be, of course, acceptable for the PSIA to re-submit their request for disbandment if the Aum Shinrikyō conducts activities again which would come under the purview of the SAPL, a position well understood by the accused organization. 2) It would be acceptable and reasonable for the police and PSIA to pursue the serious criminal responsibilities of conduct using dangerous weapons, and the PSEC decision would have no impact whatsoever on the indemnity actions, bankruptcy proceedings etc now going forward, and any appropriate actions by the police and PSIA to monitor the Aum Shinrikyō. 3) There is considerable meaning concerning the large impact that the procedures taken by the PSIA in investigating this case had in precipitating important changes taken by the accused organization in order to avoid legally imposed disbandment, such as submitting regular reports to the PSIA, cooperating with bankruptcy proceedings, withdrawing peacefully from its various facilities, submission of names and statements of members, past and present to the PSEC, choosing a new top leader, etc, actions which, under the previous leadership would have been unthinkable. 4) The importance of fostering the return to society by Aum Shinrikyō members through various measures taken by the government, by volunteer organizations to change the closed nature of the Aum Shinrikyō to an open religious organization. This would seem, on the surface because all historical circumstances are different, to hark back to the prewar protective observation (*hogo kansatsu*) approach and encouragement for radical elements to recant and rejoin society, the large nation family—instead of taking strong punitive actions, perhaps a typically Japanese solution to a potentially explosive situation.

C. *The Viability of the SAPL*

The two sarin gas attacks of 1994 and 1995 forcibly brought the issue of the future of the PSIA, the need to revise or even abolish the SAPL to the forefront of political decision; it could no longer be ignored. Even when the SAPL was being considered in 1951–52, there were seemingly unending discussions about the governmental internal security structure (*chian kikō*), how PSIA/PSEC would fit into that structure and what authorities to give to these agencies and how reliable was PSIA as an investigating agency; even then the issue of the SAPL as a permanent law or a temporary law responding to a given seeming crisis at the time (1950–1952) was fleetingly raised. Each time a violent incident occurred, or might occur, this issue was regurgitated and each time a ministerial/cabinet level committee on internal security would be created, various alternative organizational solutions put forward, usually, however, there was no settled decision and the matter was postponed in good bureaucratic fashion to a later date.

When Japan-Soviet negotiations began in 1956 about restoring diplomatic relations, Japanese allergy about the potential infiltration of Communist ideology and tactics quickly led to creating a Cabinet-level consultative group and a similar corresponding committee in the LDP; this response was reminiscent of the Japanese response and anxiety in the 1920s under similar circumstances. When a more non-violent policy approach was pronounced for the JCP at the then Soviet Union's Communist Party Congress held in February 1956, the Japanese internal security machinery would start grinding, bureaucratic rivalries would surface as to how to confront the implications of these "unnerving" JCP policy changes from violence to something else. Waiting until after the 1956 HofC elections, the government decided it would like to strengthen "the political police" (*gaiji keisatsu*) by strengthening the capabilities of the police, the PSIA and the cabinet research/intelligence office—within the framework of existing budgets—along similar lines that now exist in some European countries, India, and the U.S. to keep track of potentially subversive foreign elements. There was also a growing concern that there would be an increasing number of people from Asian countries "visiting" Japan because of Chinese Communist Party influences. The decision was to expand and strengthen (*kakujū kyōka*) the PSIA so that the Japanese people could be educated about the Communist threat and challenge based on official findings. In order to appear somewhat even handed, the PSIA also "investigated" rightwing organizations such as the Kyūkoku Kokumin Sōrengō and declared its willingness to take action against them if the facts merit such action. Allegedly such an organization had conducted training to assassinate PM Hatoyama and AG Minister Kōno because of their dissatisfaction over negotiating with the Soviets. Diet members from the defunct prewar Ministry of Home Affairs pushed for a unified security structure (*chian kikō tōitsu*), implying a resurrection of this Ministry as the best solution but that idea aroused the anxiety of others in the government as giving the impression of re-creating the prewar police system and resisted by the existing security bureaucracies. An attempt was made under the guise of the administrative reform mandate under PM Hatoyama to create a unified Ministry of Internal Affairs (Naiseishō) but that also was anathema to the existing agencies. In an attempt to make the PSIA seemingly less political, it was suggested it be transferred to the PM's Office (Sōrifu) but that too was unwelcome by the Minister of Justice. Thus, notwithstanding the strongly held anxieties about the implications stemming from Soviet-Japan negotiations about restoring diplomatic relations, a unified position could not be found and again the restructuring effort concerning internal security was abandoned in summer 1956. Periodically over the years this exercise arose and subsided without a final resolution.

As described earlier in this chapter, individuals have been charged with violations of the SAPL and the Supreme Court has declared articles 38, 39, 40 to be constitutional. But the challenge still remained for the PSIA to recommend to the PSEC that it take punitive action (restricting an organization's activities and disbandment) against "an organization which had undertaken violent destructive activities for political purposes". Cases where the SAPL might be applied against organizations would seemingly be relatively obvious through actions taken by that organization and widely publicized in the media; just to put an organization on a "watch list"—more than just merely keeping track of them—would be a political decision, more than a mere administrative action. Such actions would be normally quietly held by a security agency and difficult for the public to discern. In reviewing the *Asahi Nenkan* and *Yomiuri Nenkan*, and other sources, there are a few instances where selected violent actions received prominent publicity and the PSIA would be forced to make a public decision as to whether the SAPL should be invoked.

There were political demonstrations and violent incidents over these decades: the 1960 assassination of Asanuma Inejirō, Secretary General of the Japan Socialist Party, against the 1960 renewal of the U.S.-Japan security treaty which were bigger than those against the SAPL and resulted in the cancellation of President Eisenhower's visit to Japan that year, against the construction of the Narita airport in 1968, against the visit to Sasebo naval base in 1968 by the U.S. warship, Enterprise, anti-war demonstrations in Okinawa on April 28, 1969, and again demonstrations in 1971 against the ratification of the agreement for the reversion of Okinawa to Japan, attempts to prevent the visits of the Japanese Prime Minister to South Vietnam in October 1967—by that time the "Vietnam War" had begun—and to the U.S. in December 1967, the three factions of the radical student movement, Sampa Zengakuren, clashed with the police, an attack on the home of the president of the magazine, *Chūō Kōron*, by a rightwing attacker. The latter two incidents prompted the PSIA to begin an investigation as to whether the SAPL provisions concerning "violent destructive organizations" should be applied to these organizations. The government proposed, however, yet another law for the prevention of politically violent acts which was not enacted; the government must not have been too serious. On April 11, 1968, the inter-agency consultative committee consisting of representatives from the PSIA, Ministry of Justice and the Police (Keisatsuchō) decided against invoking the SAPL because there would be little effect if the SAPL was applied to the three factional alliance, such action would give this alliance yet another objective and target as a new rallying point (*Asahi Nenkan* 1969:329). Nevertheless, there were also the serious university student disturbances in 1969, and, much later, several incidents leading to potential violence at the coronation of Emperor Akihito in 1990.

The construction of the Narita International Airport, east of Tokyo in Chiba prefecture, had been opposed by the local farmers from the beginning; their opposition was hi-jacked so to speak by the radical leftwing student movement into a violent confrontation with the government. Opposition to the airport had by now dragged on inconclusively without an amicable settlement with all local groups involved for about 12 years. On March 26, 1978, about 2000 protesters from the combined radical Zengakuren student movement, described as guerillas by the media, broke through the security cordon at Narita and got into the control tower and trashed the electronic equipment for air control purposes. These destructive activities were sufficient to wreak temporary havoc with the airport opening scheduled for March 30 but not with the actual final construction of the new airport which progressed inch-by-inch (*jiri-oshi ni*). The police regarded these activities as having "a political purpose", to disrupt, destroy a legitimately authorized government project stemming from a Cabinet decision, thus coming under the purview of the SAPL; this would mean charging individuals and an organization(s) for violating the SAPL. But these prosecutions would be after the fact indictments in contrast to earlier cases where individuals had been investigated before the incident occurred, were arrested and charged in the April 28, 1969 demonstrations concerning the struggle about the return of Okinawa and the October 21, 1971 anti-war day demonstrations. This had not been done prior to the attacks on the Narita control tower. Nevertheless, the government seriously considered submitting a draft bill to counter the guerilla tactics used against the Narita construction project. The political opposition parties opposed such new internal security legislation fearing that it would be used improperly, i.e., abusively against democratic movements critical of the government; and such special ad hoc legislation may create a dangerous precedent; they urged the government to use more effectively existing internal security laws, e.g. the SAPL which was envisioned to be used to control such violent destructive activities. With the complications of prosecuting such a legal case under the SAPL, the political opposition to ad hoc legislation, decisive action just disappeared into a hazy political netherworld.

The enthronement ceremonies for Emperor Akihito were scheduled for November 12, 1990. Those opposing the Imperial system bombed police barracks with fatalities. The chairman of the National Public Security Commission (Kokka Kōan Iinkai) called upon the cabinet to "take resolute action" against the organizations sponsoring these attacks. Resolute police measures were taken and the enthronement ceremonies took place without incident. The National Police Agency suggested that action be taken against these organizations but the PSIA, after investigating these activities, recommended against actions requesting the PSEC to order the disbandment of these violent organizations. Even though the Emperor's person might have been involved, no resolute action under the SAPL was taken and the issue was remanded to the future—in stark contrast to what did and would have happened in prewar years under the PPL and CC.

Despite all these periodic and sometimes violent disturbances, the Cabinet and the PSIA could not muster the political will to invoke the organization control measures of the SAPL. One can only surmise why this inaction occurred: sufficient evidence could not be mustered, fear of igniting the confrontation and passions of the 1950s over the SAPL, the possibility of radicalizing still further those elements in society, bureaucratic rivalry (the pro-active police and cautious PSIA), all the issues including constitutionality about such potential actions under the SAPL that surfaced during the Committee Hearings induced extreme caution, perhaps paralysis, in the PSIA and the Cabinet.

Amending, Re-structuring the SAPL and Administrative Reform. The need for possible revisions, even re-structuring, of the SAPL had been somewhat nonchalantly considered many years before the sarin gas attacks by the Aum Shinrikyō. These attacks, now compounded by the PSEC's rejection of the government's recommendation for disbandment, suddenly, forcefully and inevitably brought to the fore the future of the SAPL; the need for a political decision on this matter could no longer be postponed and equivocated. The Minister of Justice, Nakamura Shōzaburō, commented in September 1998 that the SAPL had been drafted and enacted in 1951–1952 under rather special circumstances, e.g., at the end of the U.S. Occupation and turmoil created by bombings, assassinations, attacks on governmental offices, should now be re-evaluated under new international and domestic circumstances.

Despite the seeming clarity that was asserted and accepted in 1952, by the 1990s, this position was now questioned: there are just too many ambiguous stipulations in the SAPL as was asserted by the opposition in 1952 committee hearings; the contemplation of taking steps against an "organization"—even a "violent destructive organization"—always triggered concerns about the constitutionality of such actions in relation to freedom of religion, property rights (*zaisanken*), etc. Was an action against such an organization based on "speculation, reasonable judgment, deduction, forward looking assessment" that this organization would probably repeat or undertake for the first time specific destructive violent actions, reliably constitutional? The SAPL was created in response to a given set of circumstances, the SAPL posture must be updated to 21st century needs. Miyazawa Hiroshi, member HofC and Minister of Justice when the Cabinet decided in December 1995 to initiate action against the Aum Shinrikyō, had been calling for a re-assessment, not abolition of the SAPL. Kajiyama Seiroku, Cabinet secretary general when the PSEC rejected PSIA's recommendation on January 31, 1997, had earlier left some "home work" with the PSIA when he resigned as Minister of Justice in December 1990—five years before the sarin gas attacks: study how the SAPL could be updated, modernized, revised, restructured appropriately.[6] Apparently in response to this "homework" legacy—even without this "homework" assignment, the need for some change in the SAPL was recognized by the PSIA—a revised draft was prepared loosening the conditions when the SAPL might be invoked and simplifying those procedures when taking action against an organization. Yet another draft revision was prepared in 1994 suggesting criminal management (*un'yō*) be given to the police but another opportunity for a political decision was postponed.[7]

Nevertheless, the pressure for political action on this issue continued unabated. The constitutionality of actions that must be taken against

[6] Part 2 of the above mentioned 3-part series in the *Asahi Shimbun*. Presciently, this account suggested that the PSIA could clarify (*meikaku-ka*) the nature of actual crimes that were delineated in the SAPL, loosen (*kanwa*) the conditions for applying the SAPL and the simplification of procedures against a potential defendant, and lastly re-create itself into an intelligence agency.

[7] Ibid. References to such early draft revisions were mentioned in this article but I have been unable to persuade the PSIA to share a copy with me even though they are unclassified.

an organization and its members constantly loomed in the background of this discussion. Various ideas were put forward to revise and restructure the SAPL: create a system of protection and observation (*hogo kansatsu*) of an organization where an organization would be observed to see whether it showed tendencies to commit dangerous activities, if so, then steps would be taken expeditiously to disband this organization; this would be an organizational version of the "protect and observe" (*hogo kansatsu*) concept which had prewar overtones and had been normally applied only to individuals; limit the defense of the organization under investigation to 100 days where there was no limit in the past under the existing SAPL (*Asahi* 9/25/1998); delete "for political purposes" as a condition of conducting violent activities when invoking the SAPL and broaden the definition of a "terroristic organization" and give the right of entry to governmental authorities to enter these premises. The latter idea stemmed from local criticism and those of affected prefectural governors that the national government was unwilling or unable to protect ordinary citizens from the various conflicts arising from the proximity of Aum Shinrikyō facilities (*Yomiuri* 5/23/99).

In the major re-shuffling, re-organizing, abolishing of agencies, in the 1990s–2000s in the administrative reform exercise, the PSIA would inevitably be one of many government agencies that came under somewhat closer scrutiny in light of the circumstances described above. After all since 1971, for almost 25 years (1971–1995), no criminal charges against individuals under the SAPL had been brought to the courts, and, more importantly, no successful recommendation made by the PSIA to the PSEC to take action against a "violent destructive organization". Since this approach had been a central tenet in the justification for the SAPL in 1951–52, it was highly significant bureaucratically, legally, politically that this aspect of the law had not been successfully invoked and its constitutionality tested; in all probability, although repeatedly assured that all aspects of the SAPL were constitutional, there were lingering suspicions and doubts over the years that it might not pass that test. Thus this central question of constitutionality remained moot for over 50 years. With the collapse of the Berlin Wall in 1989 signaling the gradual collapse of the Soviet Union, the Communist "threat" slowly receded, the changed nature of Communist tactics and the evolving role of the JCP in Japanese politics by declaring its acceptance of democratic practices, inevitably brought into focus the basic *raison d'etre* of the SAPL, the need for such a law especially in light of the legal record. It had become trapped by conditions beyond its control.

Whether fairly or not, the PSIA was caught seemingly flatfooted and off guard when the sarin gas attacks occurred in 1994 in Nagano city and then more spectacularly in 1995 in the Toranomon Tokyo subway station just under government avenue. While these attacks were indeed violent and destructive acts they were planned and executed by a "Buddhist" religious organization not, as expected under the SAPL, a violent and destructive communist organization. Critics of the PSIA/PSEC arrangement, raised the issue of the relevance, competence, governmental need for such a security apparatus. In any serious effort for administrative reform, the PSIA was an "outer bureau", not one of the long-standing existing Bureaus in the Justice Ministry as in any other ministry. The traditional mainstream and outer Bureaus in a Ministry were each headed by a Director-General: however, the DGs of a mainstream bureau were appointed by the Prime Minister with the attestation of the Emperor; the DG of an outer bureau was appointed by the relevant Minister. Thus the former were appointed by an officer one step higher (in order to differentiate from the prewar system of *chokuninkan*, an Imperial appointee, the equivalent post in the postwar period was called a *ninshōkan*). Outer bureaus are just outside the Ministerial mainstream, over there so to speak; they performed important functions in their heyday. In the case of the PSIA (and PSEC), it had always been a controversial organization, often involved in the tug-of-war in wrangling over the bureaucratic structure for maintaining public security.

The nature of PSIA as a permanent government organization vs one as a temporary organization responding to a special exigency of communist attacks, assassinations, and perhaps an attempt to create a climate for insurrection in the 1950s was always just below the surface. This topic of permanence vs temporariness or impermanence was not new; it was discussed in the Legal Affairs Committees of both Houses and mentioned in the eloquent summary comments by Nakayama Fukuzō in the final session of the House of Councillors. In light of the changed socio-political situation in Japan, 1950s to the 1990s, the spotty record of convictions under the SAPL, and the untested constitutionality of the punitive organizational aspects of the SAPL, perhaps indeed the SAPL was not needed and its objectives and its authorities could be achieved under the existing agencies with some modifications. Thus, the PSIA/PSEC were bureaucratically vulnerable and the sarin gas attacks brought this critical issue to a head. It initially survived this organizational threat of extinction but with a somewhat revised mandate.

Unfortunately for the PSIA, their problems stemming from the sarin gas attacks by the Aum Shinrikyō coincided more or less with a serious effort by the Hashimoto Ryūtarō Cabinet to push for administrative reform, i.e., streamlining, rationalizing, decreasing, simplifying the national governmental structure and number of "bureaucrats" to serve the people. Suddenly, various concerns about the PSIA/PSEC structure and how to handle the potential un-constitutionality of certain articles/clauses in the SAPL on the rationale for the disbandment of an organization—had to be re-visited and another decision made, all seemingly settled issues in the past. At the October 1, 1997 Administrative Reform Conference meeting chaired by PM Hashimoto it was agreed that, "for the defense of the Constitution" (*kempō yōgo no tame hitsuyō*) as advocated by Professor Satō Kōji of Kyoto University, the PSIA/PSEC would be maintained, but it would be "slimmed down" (decrease staff size) and its staff more efficiently used (*Sankei* 10/2/1997). Thus, the SAPL (the PSIA/PSEC structure) just barely survived in great measure due to the felt security needs stemming from the sarin gas attacks. Undoubtedly because of the factors outlined above, an important revised mission for the PSIA was outlined in the final report of December 3, 1997 on administrative reform. The basic philosophical approach underlying this administrative reform and its fundamental objective was to redirect central government agencies to a new administrative system appropriate to 21st Century needs from "the postwar administrative system which was showing signs of systemic fatigue". From that point of view, the posture of the PSIA had to be reviewed (*sono arikata no minaoshi*). While the necessity for the PSIA to maintain its functional capability to control organizations in order to maintain constitutional order (*kempō chitsujo iji*) was recognized, it must respond to the changing domestic and international circumstances by "slimming" down (*surimu-ka* in katakana)—note the identical words used by the government and the independent Administrative Reform Conference report—its organization, decrease personnel levels, assign more personnel to strengthen the collection of domestic and foreign information/intelligence, and appropriately assign personnel to strengthen the Cabinet's information and intelligence function. (*Naikaku ni okeru jōhō kinō no jūjitsu ni ateru*).

In this process, the functions of the PSIA to maintain effectively its existing function to control organizations and the government will conduct an assessment in specific detail on how this will be accomplished. The evolving character of the PSIA was "officially" revealed in the rather mundane English translated title of the Agency from the Public Security *Investigation* Agency to Public Security *Intelligence* Agency with no official change in the Japanese title, Kōan Chōsachō; I understand this change was made about 1997–1998 seemingly coinciding with the "administrative guidance".[8] This sleight of hand with the SAPL, reminds one of the strained interpretation of Article 9 of the 1947 Japanese Constitution in order to create ultimately one of the larger armed forces with a correspondingly larger military budget in the world and, additionally, to "re-interpret" many times over the 1960 U.S.-Japan Security Treaty through periodic defense guidelines to accommodate the evolving strategic equation. A new internal security law, or a revision of the existing SAPL would be politically unfeasible—just as revising or updating the Constitution had been totally unfeasible up to now, similarly with the U.S.-Japanese security treaty. As a result, the PSIA under the SAPL has become chameleon-like an intelligence agency without changing one word in the law, the Subversive Activities Prevention Law of 1952.[9]

While the continued existence of the SAPL had been positively decided, there remained what final action must be taken or not taken to strengthen, expand, or otherwise improve its capabilities and enhance its role in contributing to maintaining internal security. Because of the rising need to reach a political decision, stemming from the mounting

---

[8] 1. In preparing these paragraphs on administrative reform the *Asahi, Mainichi, Tokyo, Sankei, Yomiuri* newspapers, the *Asahi Nenkan, Yomiuri Nenkan*, 1952–2004, were reviewed.

2. The ideas about administrative reform were derived from *Saishū Hōkoku* (Final report, 12/3/1997, by the Gyōsei Kaikaku Kaigi), especially the section on the PSIA.

3. Just a few days after the PSEC judgment was announced on 1/31/1997, *Asahi Shimbun* ran a 3-part series (2/2–4/1997), *Habōhō Kikyaku* (Rejection of the SAPL). In part 2 it was reported that the PSIA itself was aiming to re-create its present functional responsibilities from management of the SAPL (*habōhō no un'yō kikan*) to an information/intelligence agency (*jōhō kikan*), implying that the "administrative reform guidance" apparently emanated from the PSIA.

[9] In response to The Final Conference Report of December 1997 which called for the strengthening of the functions of the Cabinet, the Cabinet on October 27, 1998 decided to create a "Cabinet Intelligence Council (Naikaku Jōhō Kaigi) chaired by the Cabinet Secretary General and consisting of MOFA and SDF Vice Ministers, DG of the National Police and the PSIA.; this Council became operational on 1/11/1999.

criticism from prefectural governors for action, conflict on the local level where the local government bodies were refusing to register Aum Shinrikyō members as residents, the ever crowded legislative schedule, the probability of another potential confrontation in the Diet over any proposed SAPL revisions reminiscent of 1951–1952, probable opposition from the political/religious party Kōmeitō if the government attempted to revise the SAPL which it feared would be expanded to include religious organizations, the government decided on 9/8/1999, slightly over five years after the first sarin gas attack in June 1994 in Nagano, to abandon any revisions of the SAPL at this time, another milestone in the tortuous bureaucratic and political process in Japan and instead submit a new draft bill to the upcoming special session of the Diet to control such organizations as the Aum Shinrikyō. A revision of the SAPL would have been too politically painful, too legally controversial and too legislatively complicated.

D. *The Final Response: Enactment of a New Law*

The government draft bill to control organizations which have committed indiscriminate mass murder was submitted to the Diet on 11/5/1999, enacted on 12/3/1999 barely a month later, promulgated on 12/7/1999. On that same day, the PSIA requested the PSEC to place the Aum Shinrikyō under surveillance in accordance with the new law; this request was approved by the PSEC on 1/31/2000 for three years and renewed again on 1/31/2003 for another three years based on the judgment that there was a danger that the Aum Shinrikyō may in the future carry out such attacks—this judgment would seem not to be consistent with PSEC's earlier decision on the Aum Shinrikyō. At the same time, the law to seize and use Aum Shinrikyō assets to contribute to helping victims of the gas attacks was enacted; immediately thereafter on 2/4/2000 the PSIA entered Aum Shinrikyō premises and facilities as part of its surveillance actions. The Aum Shinrikyō, of course, appealed the decision to the Tokyo District Court but its appeal was turned down. The principal points in this new law are as follows:

1. The new law was aimed specifically at controlling to the greatest extent possible, in an assuredly constitutionally acceptable manner, such organizations as the Aum Shinrikyō, which have committed "violent destructive activities"and may do so in the future. This

stems from the growing concerns, doubts over the years, that the application of the SAPL to organizations might be declared unconstitutional by the courts and led to the creation of the "surveillance system" described below. This is an attempt to avoid a conflict with or infringement upon the basic constitutional freedoms of expression, assembly, beliefs and property rights.

2. The central point of this new law was the creation of a system of surveillance (*kansatsu seido*) of an organization which had, within the past ten years, committed acts of indiscriminate mass murder and which might repeat such actions in the future. Even sarin gas was mentioned in the new law as an example of the method used. The PSIA with the approval of the PSEC, would be able to impose various surveillance requirements on such an organization for not more than three years in order to bring to light the nature of its activities and thereby prevent recurrences of such destructive activities. This surveillance may be imposed on an organization if that organization meets any one of five conditions and it is believed that it was necessary for that organization's activities to be made public: a principal leader (*shubōsha*) of the indiscriminate mass murders has influence over the activities of the involved organization, all or some of the members who took part in these murders are officials or members of that organization, all or some of the members who were officials of the concerned organization and participated in the decision-making process leading to the murders and are now members of the organization concerned, the organization concerned has a platform that approves murder whether directly/clearly or suggestively, or when there are sufficient facts which would lead one to believe that there is a danger this organization might carry out such activities.

   Once an organization is put under surveillance by the PSIA, it will be required to provide numerous reports to the PSIA within ninety days, the names and addresses of all officers and members, list and addresses of all properties, buildings and facilities owned by that organization, their size and purpose of use, list of all assets, credits and liabilities and any other information believed by PSIA to be necessary for this purpose. The PSEC may also renew this surveillance order if so requested by the PSIA.

3. If these reports are not made by the organization under surveillance or are incorrect, untruthful, or the organization obstructs PSIA's attempts to enter its premises, to obtain information, etc, etc it may

impose a variety of prohibitions on the activities of the organization itself and on its officers and members. (Articles 8 and 9) It provided for an incremental approach to the control of such organizations. But those restrictions do not include ordering the disbanding of such organizations in contrast to the SAPL. As in the SAPL, the penal penalties under the new law are inevitably concentrated on punishing people. (Articles 38–41) This studied approach to the control of such organizations was to avoid constitutional challenges. This kind of thinking and approach is similar to the SAPL; both would take precautionary security actions (*hoan shobun*).

4. In article 4.1 the term "indiscriminate mass murder" is defined as "violent destructive activity" as mentioned in SAPL article 4.1.B.vi (the *4-jō dai-ikkō dai-ni-gō he* clause in Japanese) which includes those who carry out indiscriminate mass murder or those who have started to carry out such acts but did not complete the act, thereby joining the two Acts at the hip, so to speak. It should be noted that article 4.1.B begins with "The performance of any act...which has as its objective the promotion or support of or opposition to a political doctrine or policy" and article 4.1.B.vi itself refers to article 99 on murder in the Criminal Code, thus the new law is tied in through a couple of layers to the basic CC.
5. The responsibility for the administration of this law was given to the PSIA and PSEC but with a diminishing budget and declining staff levels over the years.[10]
6. Because of the continuing anxieties about the abuse of this kind of law by security officials, the strong Japanese term, *iyashikumo*, was again used three times in articles 2 and 3.1 and 3.2 instructing security officials in the strongest terms, i.e. to apply this law to the necessary minimum extent, and in no way, shape or form expand its interpretation, and must not, again in no way, shape

[10] In 1953, the PSIA had an authorized personnel level of 1,702, climbing to the highest level of 2,019 in 1972–1980, then after the afore-mentioned administrative reform decisions personnel gradually declined to 1,487 in 2004. Similarly, the PSIA budget had been steadily increasing from ¥655,834,000 in 1953, peaking in 1997 at ¥18,101,851,000, then decreasing to ¥15,487,822,000 in 2004, a drop of 13% without taking inflation into account, as against a somewhat increasing Ministry of Justice budget, ¥607,256,473,000 in 2004. These figures were derived from the *Shokuin-roku* (1952–60), the *Gyōsei Kikan Soshikizu* (1961–2003, compiled by the Jinji-in Jimu Sōkyoku for authorized personnel numbers), and *Kuni no Yosan* and *Ippan Kaikei Yosan* for PSIA and Ministry of Justice budgets.

or form, deviate from the authorities given them, in conducting the minimum necessary investigation required under the law and shall not abuse these authorities. In addition, there were two similar but different collateral resolutions (*futai ketsugi*) by the HofR Legal Affairs Committees on 11/17/1999 with six paragraphs and the same committee in the HofC on 12/2/1999 with eight paragraphs re-emphasizing, among other matters, that there shall be no abuse, no expanded interpretation, no deviation from given authorities, no violations of the freedoms guaranteed in the Constitution, that the PSIA shall report to PSEC about visits to and entering the premises/facilities of targeted organizations, that counseling shall be provided to anyone who chooses to leave a targeted organization. This is in contrast to the Patriot Act hurriedly enacted by the U.S. Congress within a few months after the 9/11/2001 attacks on the New York World Trade Center and the Pentagon in the Washington, DC, area.

7. In order to attempt to assure that PSIA and the National Police Agency (NPA) will work together, the new law specifies in several places that when the DG/PSIA seeks to impose restrictions on an organization it must obtain the opinion of the DG/NPA, when the DG/NPA believes it is necessary for prefectural police to conduct certain investigations, it must first consult (*kyōgi*) the DG/PSIA, and the DG/NPA must provide in written form (*bunsho de*) the contents of the reports from the prefectural police to DG/PSIA. This is a new relatively clear cut instruction, not in the 1952 SAPL, to the constantly competing security agencies. As an additional safeguard, article 14.7 specifies that when prefectural police enter a premise for investigative purposes (*tachi iri chōsa*) that investigative authority shall not be interpreted to be regarded as a criminal investigation.
8. PSEC hearings must be held in public, and when deemed absolutely necessary and for the protection of certain personal secrets (*kojin no himitsu no hogo*) such information may not be made public—another constitutional safeguard consideration. (Article 16)
9. Unlike the SAPL, the new law must be reviewed every five years, and based on this review appropriate action will be taken including the alternatives of renewal and abolition of the law. (Supplemental clause #2)

As shown above, the new law to control organizations that have carried out "indiscriminate mass murder" is based on the assumption that by keeping selected organizations under detailed surveillance and making public the reports from this surveillance, such violent activities can be controlled and avoided WITHOUT the threat of disbandment, a passive approach rather than the more aggressive approach of ordering disbandment. It has gone to substantial lengths—almost obsessive lengths—in contrast to my understanding of how the U.S. Patriot Act of 2001 paid little heed to or concern for this fundamental issue to safeguard individual freedoms, has instructed personnel of security agencies in the strongest possible terms not to abuse their authorities under penalty of imprisonment, has attempted to force inter-agency cooperation, and made the law only semi-permanent by requiring a review of the law every five years.

Based on the record to date and contrary to sincere and deep-seated anxieties based on the record to 1945, implementation of the SAPL did not result in censorship, suppression, repression and restrictions on various human and civil rights guaranteed in the 1947 Japanese Constitution. There was no censorship, restrictions and suppression of legitimate labor union activities and of artists. While the postwar SAPL was part of the continuum from prewar internal security laws, the implementation of the SAPL was considered, judicious and careful and not expansive in comparison with the prewar PPL. The original SAPL was not directly and substantively revised to date although various revisions were contemplated and each time abandoned. As a result of the infamous sarin gas attack in the Japanese Tokyo subway in 1995, a new law on the control of organizations which had committed indiscriminate mass murder was enacted in 1999 instead of attempting to revise the SAPL.

This seeming inactive and sporadic use of the SAPL in part probably stemmed from strong, insistent and inevitably penetrating and continuous drumbeat of attacks and stringent criticism of the SAPL by the political opposition parties in Diet committee hearings, the barrage of attacks on this draft law by academia and the boisterous labor union demonstrations against the proposed law in 1951–52 and importantly the revisions in the HofC to more strictly define controversial terms and the much stronger "instructions"—much stronger than mere admonitions—to implement the SAPL within the narrowest limits and not to expand on the interpretation of the scope of the SAPL. In light of this drumbeat and in the political context of Japanese postwar politics and society, any government would have had to proceed with great caution. The SAPL by legislative history was aimed unmistakably at violent destructive activities being carried out by the JCP and supporting organizations. The attempted application of the SAPL, though seemingly a prima facie case—an open and shut case on the surface—was in reality a "re-interpretation" enlarged interpretation of the SAPL to include religious organizations. That attempt was uncomfortably reminiscent of how the prewar PPL was implemented, in a way underscoring the anxieties oft repeated in 1951–52 in the media and in Diet committee hearings by the political opposition. The scale, nature and character of political opposition apparently changed after the SAPL was enacted, there were no more May Day Riots, no more significant random violent attacks on government offices, no political assassinations except for the Asanuma assassination; even the widespread and massive labor union and student demonstrations against the security treaty revisions in 1960 did not result in major application of the SAPL against individuals, nor disbandment of organizations permitted under the SAPL but there were a fair number of manageable disturbances as enumerated above. A neat solution, the *dantai keihō* (organizational criminal code) had been created but the political pretext to use this authority did not arise or the political will and passion to apply the full force of the SAPL had been sapped in the legislative deliberative process. Nevertheless, so long as the SAPL remains on the books, it is a sleeping law that could spring to life under a ruthless government under difficult internal security circumstances.

BIBLIOGRAPHY

In preparation for this study, I first gathered materials directly related to the enactment of the SAPL when I was in Japan in 1955–56 under a Ford Foundation Grant. Later, as the years progressed, I collected other articles and books (post enactment) on the SAPL, and more recently I collected materials on the implementation of the SAPL and the several court cases involving the SAPL, and other materials on the general subject of Japanese politics of direct interest to the legislative process. I also looked for books and articles on the legislative and policy-making processes in Japan, especially case studies which would throw light on the early postwar period, 1945–1952. I found numerous case studies but only a few on the 1945–52 period. Rather than follow the conventional bibliographical form of listing books and articles by author in alphabetical order, I have arranged this bibliography in three topical parts. The first part is concerned with documents, books, proceedings, articles and newspaper reports leading to the enactment of the SAPL. The second part is on the implementation period of the SAPL, 1952+ involving court decision and commentaries. The third part is more like a conventional bibliography but even here the main emphasis was on finding case studies in English and Japanese involving Japanese issues. This list was assembled, in the first instance, not for my study, but as a reference work for future scholars on the evolution of the Japanese decision-making process and related case studies. A summary outline of the bibliography is given below.

I. Enactment of the SAPL
  A. Documents
    1. SAPL Drafts
    2. Diet Proceedings
    3. Material submitted to the Diet by SIB in connection of the SAPL
    4. Materials prepared by SIB and others in drafting SAPL
      i. Miscellaneous Papers
      ii. SIB Chōsa Shiryō
    5. SCAP Documents
  B. Books in Japanese
  C. Articles in Japanese
  D. Newspapers in Japanese
  E. Newspaper Clippings in Japanese
II. Implementation: Court Cases, Decisions, and Commentaries
  A. Japanese court decisions
  B. Indexes
  C. Legal Commentaries
III. Selected Books and Articles on Japanese government
  A. Internal Security Laws
    1. Prewar Internal Security laws
    2. Postwar Internal Security after Enactment of the SAPL
  B. General
    1. In Japanese
    2. In English
  C. Studies in Japanese Policymaking
    1. General
    2. Selected Case Studies
      i. In English
      ii. In Japanese

I. *Enactment of the SAPL*

The items in "I. Enactment of the SAPL" consist of a variety of materials on the drafting of the SAPL, Diet deliberations, newspaper and journal articles reporting on the draft bill and other issues. They were assembled in 1955–56 in Japan and were arranged in the following manner and exist to this day in eight bound volumes and in nine acco binders as follows, a total of 17: Hakai Katsudō Bōshi-hō I–II Diet Proceedings, Plenary and Committee Sessions, 1952; III–VIII the various drafts prepared by the government; IX–X about 100 magazine articles mostly published in 1951–52 on the +pros and cons of the draft SAPL and other aspects of internal security; XI–XIII 19 items submitted to the Diet by the government about Communist activities; XIV–XV, materials submitted to the Diet by the government in support of the SAPL; XVI drafts of various SAPL related items; XVII prewar-postwar security laws by Sohyo and the legislative process of the SAPL, prepared by Misawa Shigeo of NDL in February 1956 for Cecil H. Uyehara. There were, in addition to these materials which I garnered, many other items which were not purchased but which have been included in this bibliography.

A. *Documents*

1. *SAPL Drafts.* Collected in six volumes from the first government drafts of the bill to that submitted as a bill to the Diet, May 1951–May 1952.

2. *Diet Proceedings.* Complete set of proceedings of the two Houses of the 13th Diet and the committees which considered the SAPL:
   i. House of Representatives: Plenary and Committee hearings, April–July 1952
   ii. House of Councillors: Plenary and Committee hearings, April–July 1952

3. *Materials submitted to the Diet by SIB in connection with the SAPL*

- *Busō tōsō ni kansuru "Naigai Hyōron" no rombunshū*
- *Busō tōsō ni kansuru "heiwa to dokuritsu" no rombunshū*
- *Yon-zen-kyō no ketsugi ni okeru Gunji Hōshin*
- *Nijū Chūi ni okeru soshiki to senjutsu no mondai*
- *Go-zen-kyō ni okeru Gunji Hōshinsho*
- *Chūkaku Jieitai no soshiki to senjutsu oyobi ketsugō*
- *"Heiwa to Dokuritsu" oyobi "Naigai Hyōron" ni arawareta fuhō kiji*
- *Chian Kikan ni taisuru chōsa, kakushu kōsaku ni kansuru shirei oyobi hōkokushū*
- *Chian Kikan narabini Kōkyō Kikan ni taisuru Hakai Katsudō no Gaiyō*
- *Chian Kikan ni Taisuru tero Jihan ichiranhyō*
- *Go-zen-kyō ikō no busō kōryō jitsugen ni kansuru shirei, hōkoku, tsūtatsu*
- *Kikanshi ni kansuru rombun, shirei, tsūtatsushū*
- *Sakura-gai*
- *Eiyō Bunsekihyō*
- *Chūkaku Jieitai Ichiranhyō*
- *Jiyū Rōso kankei no Shokugyō Anteisho sonota no Kanchō tō ni taisuru Bōkō Kōmu Shikkō Bōgai Jiken Shirabe*
- *Bōryoku-shugi-teki Hakai Katsudō o senden sendō-suru bunsho no uchi shuyō na mono*
- *Zai-Nichi Chōsenjin Fuhō Jiken Nendo tsuki-betsu hassei kensūhyō*

4. *Materials prepared by SIB and others in drafting the SAPL (30 items assembled in two binders)*

i. *Miscellaneous Papers*

- Amerika Kyōsantō kambu jūichi-mei ni taisuru Sumisu [Smith]-*hō ihan jiken ni taisuru Amerika Saikō Saibansho hanketsu* (prepared by SIB)
- *Saikin no waga kuni ni okeru bōryoku shugi-teki hakai katsudō no jittai no gaikyō* (SIB)
- *Chian Iji-hō jōbun* (SIB)
- *Chian Ijihō ni yoru sendō-zai no jirei* (SIB)
- *Hakai Katsudō Bōshi-hō ni kansuru shiryō (by Nihon Shimbun Kyōkai)*
- *Jizen Ken'etsu seido, jigo ken'etsu seido, sōkō ken'etsu-sugi, todoke'ide-shugi* (from *Hōrei Yōgo Jiten*, p. 160)
- *Seiji Shikin Kisei-hō no chikujō kaisetsu* (by Kōri Yūichi)—one page missing
- *Kyōsa no misui no shobatsu-rei narabini misui no kyōsa to kyōsa no misui* (from Kimura Kameji, *Keihō no Kihon Gainen*)
- *Kakkoku sankō hō kitei no kōgai* (SIB)
- *Soren keihō hangyakuzai* (SIB)
- *Chūka Jimmin Kyōwakoku Chōchi Han-Kakumei Jōrei* (SIB)
- Yobi Imbō (from *Iwanami's Hōritsu-gaku Jiten IV.2550)*
- "Chian Iji-hō yori" Jikkō no Sendō *(Nihon Hyōronsha)*
- Sendō hanzai no kyōsa (*Iwanami's Hōritsu-gaku Jiten III-1843)*
- *Kageki Shakai Undō Torishimari hōan* (submitted by the Government 2/18/1922)
- Bōryoku kōi tō shobatsu ni kansuru hōritsu (from *Iwanami's Hōritsu-gaku Jiten* IV.2503 Ikeda Katsu)
- *1930-nen 3-gatsu 25-nichi no Kyōwakoku hogohō*
- *Seiji-teki kyōbo kōi ni taisuru 1932-nen 8-gatsu kokonoka no Daitōryōrei*
- *Doitsu kokumin ni taisuru uragiri oyobi taigyaku nairan-zai no himitsu undō ni taisuru 1933-nen 2-gatsu 28-nichi no kuni daitōryōrei*
- *Doitsukoku oyobi Doitsu kokumin o hogo-suru tame no 1933-nen 2-gatsu 28-nichi no daitōryōrei*
- *Sendō no yōgo-rei*
- *Habōhō kōjutsu-nin kōhosha*
- *Kakkoku sankō rippō kōgai* (SIB)
- Hakai Katsudō Bōshi Hōan ni taisuru Kenkyū Ketsuron (by Kainō Michitaka, Tanaka Kazuo, Endō Shigemitsu, Miyazawa Toshiyoshi, Yamane Shinjirō and Rōyama Masamichi
- *Hakai Katsudō Bōshi Hōan Chikujō Kaisetsu*
- *Chian Keisatsu-hō oyobi Chian Ijihō seitei tōji no shakai jōsei*
- *Chian Iji-hō hanrei tekiroku*
- *Nachisu Doitsu ni okeru Hakai Katsudō Bōshihō naishi Chian Iji ni kansuru rippōrei (sono 2)*
- *Nachisu Doitsu no seiji kessha kinshi narabini Kokka oyobi Tō e no imbō-teki kōgeki no kinshi no rippō-rei*
- *Chian Iji-hō seitei tōji no genronkai no iken*

ii. *Tokubetsu Shinsakyoku (SIB) Chōsa Shiryō*
The SIB also prepared *Chōsa Shiryō* a series of pamphlets for internal use and study. I am acquainted with only three items:

- *Gaikoku no Hankyō Rippō*. 8/1/1951, 115 p. (Same as *Gaikoku no Sankō Rippō*, 115 p.)
- *Amerika Gasshūkoku Sumisu-hō*. 10/1/1951, 44 p.
- *Amerika no 1950-nen Kokunai Anzen Hoshō-hō no Seitei Keika narabini sono Kitei no Gaiyō*, 4/1952. 91 p.

5. *SCAP Documents*: In order to discover, if possible, what may have been GHQ/SCAP's reaction and relationship to the Japanese Attorney-General's office, especially between Seki Itaru, the principal drafter of the SAPL, and the SCAP officer who had the main responsibility for providing Hqs "guidance" on such a sensitive legislative proposal, I visited the U.S. National Archives, first at the Suitland Documentation Center, Suitland, MD, and then at Archives II in College Park, MD, many times from 1978–2000 to study selected SCAP documents. About 300 pages of documents were copied from the following boxes in these Archives: 1447, 2187, 2188, 2189, 2194, 2225, 2226. These have been assembled into one binder.

B. *Books*

Numerous books were published during and immediately after the debate concerning the draft bill and enactment of the SAPL, particularly several by Seki Itaru, the drafter of the SAPL, on the background and philosophy underlying the creation and interpretation of the SAPL, and reasons for opposing the SAPL.

Aoyama, Haruki. *Chikujō Kaisetsu Hakai Katsudō Bōshi-hō*. Keisatsu. Jihōsha. 1968.

Hakai Katsudō Bōshi-hō: Chikujō Kaisetsu to Sō-Hihan. Hōritsu Jihō Bessatsu. Nihon Hyōron Shinsha. 1952, 238 p.

Hani, Gorō. *Hakai Katsudō Bōshi-hō to ikani Tatakau ka*. Mikasa Shobō. 1952. ? p.

Habōhō no Rippō Katei. Mimeographed. 32 p. [Prepared by Mikasa Shigeo, then with the National Diet Library]

Hayashi, Nobuo. *Hakai Katsudō Bōshi-hō*. Hyōronsha. 1952.

Hōrei Fukyūkai, comp. *Hakai Katsudō Bōshi-hō Chikujō Kaisetsu*. Insatsuchō. 1952.

Hyōronsha Hōgaku Henshūbu, comp. *Hakai Katsudō Bōshi-hō*. Hyōronsha. 1952. Hōgaku Benran:1.

Inomata, Kōzō. *Teikō no Keifu*. Tokyo. Sakai Shoten. 1964. 402 p.

Itō, Osamu. *Habōhō ni naze hantai shita ka*. Nihon Shakaitō Shuppanbu. 1952. 53 p.

Itō, Osamu. *Hakai Katsudō Bōshi-hō Kaisetsu to Shingiroku*. Hōritsu Keizai Kenkyūjo. 1952. 200 p.

Jikyoku Mondai Chōsakai, comp. *Buryoku Kakumei to Habōhō*. Jikyoku Mondai Chōsakai. 1952. 297 p.

Kamiyama, Kinji. *Chikujō Hakai Katsudō Bōshi-hō Kaisetsu*. Tachibana Shobō. 1952. 230 p.

Kitano, Hirohisa and Ichinose Kei'ichirō. *Narita Chianhō: Ima Kempō ga abunai*. Shakai Hyōronsha. 1992.

Kōan Chōsachō, comp. *Habōhō no hayawakari Montō*. Kōan Chōsachō. 1952.

Kokkai Toshokan. Chōsa Rippō Kōsakyoku. *Amerika no 1950-nen Kokunai Anzen Hoshō-hō no Seitei Keika narabini sono Kitei no Gaiyō*. 1952. 91 p.

Nakamura, Masao. *Rōdō Kumiai to Habōhō*. Shin-Nihon Hōki Shuppan KK. 1952. 566, 12 p.

Nihon Shakaitō Hombu Shuppanbu, comp. *Habōhō o tsuku*. Nihon Shakaitō Hombu Shuppanbu. 1952. 60 p.

Nihon Rōdō Kumiai Sōhyō Gikai. *Dan'atsu Kōan Sampō o tsuku*. Nihon Rōdō Kumiai Sōhyō Gikai. 1952. 112 p. Sō-hyō Shirīzu #4.

Nihon Rōdō Kumiai Sōhyō Gikai. *Senzen Sengo no Chian Rippō*. Sōhyō. 1956. 86 p. Sōhyō Hōtai Shiryō;18(7/1/56).

Nihon Shakaitō (Left). Chūō Shikkō Iinkai. *Dai-10-kai Teiki Zenkoku Taikai Hōhokusho*. 1953. pp. 54, 58–59 on Haboho.

Ono, Yoshio. *Hakai Katsudō Bōshi-hō to Kokkai no Shingi*. Keibunkaku. 1952. 66 p.

Sanada, Hideo. Hakai Katsudō Bōshi-hō no Kaisetsu. Jiji Tsūshinsha. 1952. 230 p.

Satō, Isaya. *Tōron Chikujō Hakai Katsudō Bōshi-hō no Kaishaku*. Gakuyō Shobō. 1952.

Seiji Suto wa naze sakenebanaranai ka: Habōhō hantai suto ni taisuru Nishio Suehiro no kenkai. Jikyoku Kenkyūkai. 1952. 20 p. Pamfuretto "Warera no Kenkei" #1.
Seki, Itaru. *Hakai Katsudō Bōshi-hō Kaisetsu.* 1952. Shin-Keisatsusha. 146 p.
Seki, Itaru and Isao Satō. *Hakai Katsudō Bōshi-hō no Kaisetsu.* Gakuyō Shobō 1952. 221 p.
Seki, Itaru. *Hakai Katsudō Bōshi-hō no Kaisetsu.* Bunka Kenkysha. 1952. 296 p.
Seki, Itaru. *Hakai Katsudō Bōshi-hō to sono Un'yō.* Shin-Nihon Keizaisha. 1952. 257 p.
Seki, Itaru. *Shisō Genron no Jiyū to sono Genkai.* Hakua Shobō. 1952. 194 p.
Shakai Taimususha, comp. *Habōhō wa kōtsukawareru.* Shakai Taimususha. 1952.
Tokunaga, Masatsugu. *Nihon Kyōsantō to Habōhō.* Hakurin Shobō. 1952. 266 p.
Yoshihashi. Toshio. *Dantai-tō Kisei-rei Kaisetsu.* Tokyo. Minori Shobō. 1951. 200 p.

C. *Articles*

The following list of articles on the draft SAPL consist of two groups: 1) those for which complete bibliographic data is available, 2) those for which the last page number of the article is not known because I did not purchase this article or could not actually find it. Of those listed below I personally have copies of about 100 articles. This list is based on research done in 1955–56 and augmented in the late 1990s–2001. It was already difficult in 1956, only four years after the enactment of the SAPL, to assemble these articles; it would be even more difficult now, in many cases well nigh impossible some 50+ years later. Many of the magazines have, in the meantime I am sure, gone out of existence. Although the following is quite an extensive list of articles, I know there are others that I was unable to locate. This extensive list of articles is provided here in an attempt to show the scope of interest, both pro and con, mostly con, in the draft SAPL that took place in a relatively short space of time of about one year.

We should take note not just merely of the number of articles on this subject but the range of journals that participated in this great controversy. The magazines that published articles on the draft SAPL, it's meaning and implications are: *Bijutsu Hyōron, Buraku, Chūō Kōron, Chūō Rōdō Jihō, Fujin Kōron, Gekkan Rōdō, Hanrei Sokuhō, Hōgaku Geppō, Hōgaku Shirin, Horitsu Jihō, Hōritsu no Hiroba, Hōsō Jihō, Jichi Jihō, Jikei, Jikyō Kenkyūkai, Jitsugyō no Nihon, Jitsugyō no Sekai, Jiyō to Seigi, Jurisuto, Kaihō, Kaizō, Kansai Keikyō, Keieisha, Keisatsu Jihō, Keisatsu Yobitai Shiryōshū, Keisatsugaku Rombumshū, Keisatsu Rombunshū, Keizai-jin, Keizai Ōrai, Keizai Tembō, Kikan Hōritsugaku, Koe, Kokkai, Kokutai Bunka, Kyōiku, Kyōiku no Hiroba, Meiji Gakuin Ronsō, New Age (Nyū Eiji), Nichirōken, Rōdō Hōritsu Jumpō, Rōdō Jihō, Rōdō Keizai Jumpō, Rōdō Shōhō, Rōdō-hō, Seiji Keizai, Seiji Ōrai, Sekai, Sekai Hyōron, Sekai Keizai Jumpō, Shakai Shisō Kenkyū, Shakai-shugi, Shimbun Gekkan, Shimbun Kenkyū, Shin-Bummei, Shin-Nihon Bungaku, Shin-Keisatsu, Shiro to Kuro, Shōsetsu, Shōsetsu Shirin, Shūbō, Shūkan Asahi, Shukan Nichirōken Shiryō, Shūkan Sankei, Shuppan Nyūsu, Tekkō Rōmu Tsūshin, Tenri Daigaku Gakuhō, Toki no Hōrei, Tōyō Keizai Shimpō, Ushio, Yuibutsu Ronja, Zen-Ginren Chōsa Jihō.*

Aikawa, Shigeyoshi. Chian Rippō no Genkai—Hakai Katsudō Bōshi-hō no Ritsuan o tsūjite, *Shakai Shisō Kenkyū* 4:4 (5/1952):4–6.
Akiyama, Shinji. Habōhō o meguru rōdō kōsei, *Sekai* 79(7/1952):179–184.
Aoki, Eigoro. Meihaku katsu Genzai no Kiken no Hōsoku—Habōhō ni kanrenshite, *Jiyu to Seigi* 3:10(10/1952):2–12.
Aoki, Kin'ichi. Chian Taisaku, *Tōyō Keizai Shimpō* 2524(5/17/1952):13.
Aoki, Kin'ichi. Chian Taisaku to Keisatsu Seido, *Keieisha* 6:8(8/1952):1–5.
Aoki, Suekichi. Nihon no Bunka Kiki ni suite—Habōhō to Rōdō Kaikyū Interigencha, *Rōdō Keizai Jumpō* 6:163(7/-1952):3–6.

Aono, Suekichi. Nihon no Bunka Kiki ni suite—Habōhō to rōdō kaikyū, interigencha, *Rōdō Keizai Jumpō* 6:163(7/-1952):3–6.
Aoyagi, Morio. Hakai Katsudō Bōshihō no funsai no tame ni, *Rōdō Hōritsu Jumpō* 98/99(7/1952):2–6.
Aoyama, Haruki. Hakai Katsudō Bōshi-hō ni tsuite, *Keisatsu Kenkyū* 23:8(8/1952): 61–78.
Aoyama, Haruki. Hakai Katsudō Bōshihō no Kaisetsu, *Shūkan Nichiroken shiryō* 186:5:31(8/6/1952):3–13.
Arai, Tatsuo. Habōhō, sono go ni kuru mono, *Fujin Kōron* 38:9(9/1952): 68–71.
Asai, Kiyonobu. Kokkai ni okeru Habōhō Dangi, *Rōdō Hōitsu Jumpō* 100 (8/1952): 39–42.
Asai, Kiyonobu, (Zadankai). Hakai Katsudō Bōshihō wa Kyōfu Seiji o umu—Dai-12kai Gakujutsu Kaigi ni okeru Hakai Katsudō Bōshi Hōan ni suite no seimeian o megutte, *Chūō Kōron* 67:7(6/1952):68–79.
Asao, Shinpo. Saikin no Sōjō jiken o megette, *Keieisha* 6:8(8/1952):6–7.
Chian Kankei Hōan Sakusei no Uchimaku, *Chūō Kōron* 66:13:82–96.
Chian Rippō no Kakujū iyoiyo kyū—Shūdan Jii Torishimari Keisatsuhō Ichibu Kaisei Hōan no Zenbun, *Rōdō Shōhō* 15:594(5/1952):22–24.
Chian Rippō o Utagau, *Jurisuto* 2:1/15/52:31–38.
Chian Rippō Seitei no Sui'i, *Hōritsu Jihō* 24:1(1/1952):40–49.
Chiba, Masashi. Keisatsukan no Jinken Jūrin ni suite—sono hō-shakaigaku-teki ichi kōsatsu, *Kōhō Kenkyū 9(10/1953)*
Danki-tō Kisei Hōan o Shingi-suru, *Jurisuto* 15:8/1/52:16–17.
Dantai tō Kisei Hōan to Jinken Yōgo, *Jurisuto* 1(1/1952):16–17.
Dantai tō Kisei-hō wa Kumiai Katsudō o dō Sokubaku-suruka, *Zen Ginren Chōsa Jihō* 1) 18(1/1952):14–16, 2), 19(2/1952):20–21.
Endo, Gōsuke. Habōhō no dekiru made, *Sekai* 80(8/1952):162–167.
Fujibayashi, Keizō. Chian Rippō to Rōdō Undō, *Jitsugyō no Nihon* 55:11(6/1952): 56–59.
Fujii, Hideo. Demo Torishimari Hōan to Kumiai Undō, *Rōdō Hōritsu Jumpō 95* (6/1952):17–20.
Fujiwara, Ichirō. Nikkyō no Paruchizan (Partisan) Sempō to Sangyō Bōei, *Keieisha* 8/1952:26–30.
Fukuhara, Tadao. Habōhō Ihan Dai-ichi gō Jiken, *Shūbō* 7:11(11/1952):14–18.
Funahashi, Michio. Seirei dai 325-gō ihan no menso hanketsu wa tadashii ka, *Hōritsu no Hiroba* 5:9(8/52):18–22.
Gon, Itten. Kankoku no Genjō ga oshieru mono—kokunai chian to no kanren ni oite, *Shin-Keisatsu* 7:7(8/1952):16–20.
Gotō, Ichiroku. Chihō—Kinō to Hito, *Kōmuin* 8:11(11/1952):68–81.
Habōhō ga Kessenjō Rōdō Taishū no Atsuryoku de Seiji Suto e, *Shiro to Kuro* 6/ 1952:25–.
Habōhō ni tsuite—Ankēto, *Bijutsu Hihyō* 6(6/1952):4–8.
Habōhō no dekiru made, *Keizai Ōrai* 4:5(5/1952):205–209.
Habōhō no Ronseki, Shūgiin Hōmu Iinkai no Gijiroku kara, *Rōdō Shūhō* 1) 15:593(5/1952):15–26, 2) 15:594(5/1952):25–28.
Habōhō no Seiritsu, *Tōyō Keizai Shimpō 2533*(7/19/1952):23–25.
Habōhō no Seiritsu—Genron no Jiyū wa dōka, *Keizai Tembō* 24:8(8/1952):16.
Habōhō Seiritsu to Seifu no Sekinin, *Tōyō Keizai Shimpō* 2533(7/19/1952):10–11.
Habōhō Shu-Mokuhyō wa Nikkyō no fūsa no ito-suru mono, *Shūkan Asahi* 7/20/ 1952:14–.
Habōhō Tanjōki, *Asahi Taimusu* 3:7(8/1952):7–23.
Habōhō to Rōdō Kumiai Undō, *Rōdō Hōritsu Jumpō 98/99* (7/1952):7–13.
Habōhō Unyō no Mondaiten, *Tōyō Keizai Shimpō* 2533(7/19/1952):26–28.
Habōhō wa naze seitei-sareta ka. *Rōdō Bunka*, 10/1952:34–.

Haga, Hisayuki. Habōhō to Shakai Undō, *Shūbō* 7:8(8/1952):14–18.
Hakai Katsudō Bōshi-hō, *Rōdō Keizai Hanrei Sokuhō* 68(7/1952):14–20.
Hakai Katsudō Bōshi-hō (Ketsugi Zembun), *Sekai* 81(9/1952):70–78, 117–.
Hakai Katsudō Bōshi-hō o meguru Seifu to Rōtō to no ugoki, *Tōyō Keizai Shimpō* 2521(4/26/1952):17–18. Also published by the Japanese Government Printing Office (Insatsuchō) in 1952.
Hakai Katsudō Bōshi-hō Chikujō Kaisetsu, *Toki no Hōrei* 67(7/1952):1–95.
Hakai Katsudō Bōshi-hō Kaishaku, *Keizai Jidai* 17:9(10:1952):59–60, 17:11(12/1952):96–99.
Hakai Katsudō Bōshi Hōan, *Keizai Ōrai* 4:5(5/1952):198–204.
Hakai Katsudō Bōshi Hōan, *Rōdō Keizai Hanrei Sokuhō* 58(4/1952):10–16.
Hakai Katsudō Bōshi Hōan, *Chūō Rōdō Jihō* 204(5/10/1952):28–33, *46*. Chūō Rōdō Iinkai, comp.
Hakai Katsudō Bōshi Hōan, *Rōsei Jihō* 1185(4/1952):27–37.
Hakai Katsudō Bōshi Hōan Jōbun no Shōseiten, *Rōsei Jihō* 1186(5/1952):37–38.
Hakai Katsudō Bōshi Hōan Kokkai e—Kōeki Jigyō Sōgi wa Kokka Hakai ni gaitō-suru ka, *Rōdō Shūhō* 15:588(4/-1952):15–19.
Hakai Katsudō Bōshi Hōan Jōtei e no settoku kōsaku naru ka, *Rōdō Shūhō* 15:589(4/1952):20–24.
Hakai Katsudō Bōshi Hōan ni taisuru Iken, *Rōdō Hōritsu Jumpō* 90(4/1952):18–21.
Hakai Katsudō Bōshi Hōan oyobi Yōkō, *Shūkan Nichirō-ken Shiryō* 169:5:14(4/9/1952):16–21.
Hakai Katsudō Bōshi Hōan Shūgiin Shūseiten, *Hōritsu no Hiroba* 5:7(7/52):40–41.
Hakai Katsudō Bōshi-hō Jisshi Ichinen o kaerimite, *Kaihō* 2:1(4/54):1–8.
Haran no 'Dokuritsu Kokkai' saikai—Habōhō de gekitotsu, *Shimbun Gekkan* 5/1952:49–.
Hasegawa, Masayasu. Habōhō Dai-38-jō to Kempō no Sho-mondai, *Hōritsu Jihō* 25–11(11/1953)
Hasegawa, Masayasu. Habōhō o meguru Kempō Mondai, *Hōgaku Geppō 6/52.*
Hasegawa, Masayasu. Kōan Jōrei o otte, *Hōritsu Jihō* 21:7(7/1949).
Hayashi, Tōnosuke. Habōhō no Yōten, *Gekkan Rōdō* 42/43(7/1952:27–28).
Hayashi, Shūzō. Rippō no Dōki oyobi kore ni kanren-suru jakkan no Mondai ni tsuite, *Jurisuto* 35(6/1/1953):6–10.
Hirano, Ryūichi. Habōhō to Sendō, *Hōritsu no Hiroba* 5:10(10/1952):23–24.
Hirano, Yoshitarō. Kihon-teki Jinken to Chian Iji-hō, *Hōritsu Jihō* 24:1(1/1952): 3–17.
Hirose, Gorō. Minshushugi o jūrin-suru akuhō—Hakai Katsudō Bōshi-hō to Keiji Tokubetsu-hō no Honshitsu, *Yuibutsu Ronja* 2:5(5/1952):10–13.
Hōmufu. Tokubetsu Shinsakyoku. Hakai Katsudō Bōshi-hō: Chikujō kaisetsu, *Toki no Hōrei* 67(7/1952):95p.
Hōmūfu. Hakai Katsudō Bōshi Hōan no Gaiyō, *Rōdō Keizai Hanrei Sokuhō* 58(4/1952):17–22; also in *Shin-Keisatsu Gaiyō* 7:4(4/1952):34–41.
Hōmufu. Kōan Chōsachō. Habōhō Jōshiki Mondō, *Shin-Keisatsu* 7:4(10/1952): 36–41.
Honda, Masayoshi. Shūdan Hanzai no Shimpan, *Hōritsu no Hiroba* 5:9(9/1952): 13–15.
Honda, Takeo. Dantai-tō Kiseirei to Keisatsu, *Keisatsugaku Ronshū* 7(7/1946).
Hori, Hajime. Hakai Katsudō Bōshi-hō to sono go no mondai o kaibō-suru, *Shūbō* 7:8(8/52):10–14.
Horie, Kenji. Akai Chigai Hōken, *Shōsetsu Asahi Hanashi no Techō* 1:1(8/1952): 64–73.
Hōritsu wa dare ga tsukuru, *Hōritsu Jihō* 25:1(1/1953):24–37.
Inoue, Isaburō. Habōhō wa Zanmaken ka Satsujinken ka, *Seiji Keizai* 5:8(8/1952):4–7.
Ishida, Toko'o. Habōhō no Kaji tori, *Hōritsu no Hiroba* 5:11(11/1952:35–.

Ishii, Teruhisa. Iwayuru Seiji Suto no Gōhōsei, *Jurisuto* 13:7/1/1952:11–13.
Isoda, Susumu. Hakai Katsudō Bōshi Hōan no Shikumi to Rōdō Undō e no Eikyō, *Rōdō Hōritsu Jumpō* 93/94(5/1952:-2–8.
Itami, Yoshio. Habōhō o megutte, *Koe* 896(7/1952):26–28 and 897(8/1952):58–59.
Itō, Osamu. Habōhō ni naze Hantai shita ka, *Hōritsu no Hiroba* 5:10(10/1952): 25–28.
Itō, Osamu. Hakai Katsudō Bōshi Hōan ni naze hantai shita ka, *Kokkai* 5:8(8/1952): 16–22.
Iwayuru Seiji Suto to Kumiai no Sekinin, *Rōdō Hōritsu Jumpō* 93/94(5/1952):15–20.
Kaga, Shigeyuki. Konran o okoshita "Habōhō" no keika, *Seiji Keizai* 5:7(7/1952): 30–31.
Kainō, Michitaka and Hasebe Gisuke (Taidan). Chian Iji-hō no Fukkatsu, *Shakai-shugi* 7:12:1951:8–16.
Kainō, Michitaka. Chian Rippō no Ito o tsuku, *Rōdō Keizai Jumpō* 5–138(10/1951).
Kainō, Michitaka. Chian Rippō to Jiyū, *Kaizō* 33:1(1/1952):53–59.
Kainō, Michitaka. Gōhō to Hi-Gōhō no Genkai, *Kaizō* 33–13(9/1952):42–44.
Kainō, Michitaka and Kido Mataichi.Habōhō-ka no Gōhō to Hi-Gōhō, *Kaizō Rinji Zōkangō* 9/1952:36–.
Kainō, Michitaka. Habōhō to Jinken no Yōgo, *Sekai* 81(9/1952):65–69.
Kainō, Michitaka. Ushinareru Kihon-teki Jinken—Hakai Katsudō Bōshi Hōan. *Keizai Ōrai* 4:5(5/1952):179–197.
Kaisetsu 'Habōhō' an o meguru sho-mondai,*Shiro to Kuro* 6/1952:46.
Kakkoku no Chian Rippo wa dō natte iru ka, *Rōdō Shūhō* 15:594(5/1952):9.
Kamiya, Masao. Kōan Jōrei ni kansuru Jakkan no Mondai, *Keisatsu Kenkyū* 21:3(3:1952).
Kamiyama, Kinji. Hakai Katsudō Bōshi-hō to sono mondai, *Shūbō* (The Police Journal) 7:5(5/1952):10–15.
Kamiyama, Kinji. Shūdan Ji'i Undō to no Chitsujo Hoji ni kansuru Hōritsu-an ni tsuite, *Hōritsu no Hiroba* 5:8(8/1952): 11–15.
Kanemasa, Yonekichi. Chian to Rōdō Kumiai, *Kansai Keikyō* 6:11(11:1952):12.
Kashiwamura, Nobuo. Bōryoku Shugi-teki Hakai Katsudō no Jittai to Hakai Katsudō Bōshi-hō no Un'yō Hōshin, *Rōdō Jihō* 5:9(10:1952):2–7.
Kawara, Shun'ichirō, Chian Rippō to Genron no Jiyū, *Shimbun Kenkyū* 18:3/1952): 1–3.
Kido, Mataichi. Habōhō wa 'Genron no Jiyū' ni tekitai-suru, *Kaizō* 33:13(9/1952): 42–44.
Kimura, Kameji. Habōhō to Nihon Bunka no Kiki—Atarashiki Fuashizumu no Tōjō, *Kaizō* 33:11(8/1952):110–114.
Kinrōsha no Danketsu oyobi Dantai Kōdōken to Hakai Katsudō Bōshi Hōan ni tsuite no Hōmu Sōsai Danwa, *Rōdō Keizai Hanrei Sokuhō* 58(4/1952):16–17.
Kitamura, Tokutarō. Minshu Seiji no Gensoku ni Rikkyaku shite, *Keieisha* 6:8(8/1952):10–11.
Kōan Chōsa-chō. Habōhō Jōshiki Mondō, *Shin-Keisatsu* 7:4(10/1952):36–41.
Kōan Jōrei wa iken, *Rōdō Hōritsu Jumpō* 73–74(11/1951):7–12.
Kobayashi, Yoshinobu. Sengo ni okeru Waga Chian Rippō no Hatten, *Tenri Daigaku Gakuhō 9(12/1952, 10(3/1952).*
Kokkai ni okeru Habōhō Shingi no Shōten, *Sekai* 80(8/1982):168–185.
Kokkai Tembō: Habōhō no Shingi, *Shimbun Gekkan* 6/1952:27–.
Kondō, Hidezō. Habōhō no Seisanchi, *Kaizō Rinji Zōkangō* 9/1952:32–.
Kudō, Tomochiya. Chian Mondai are kore, *Keizai-jin* 6:3(3/1952):48–56.
Kumakura, Takeshi. Chian Rippō no Kōsō to sono Igi, *Hōgaku Shirin* 49:3(2/1952): 57–73.
Kumakura, Takeshi. Kōan Jōrei—sono imi-suru mono to Haigo in arumono, *Sekai Hyōron* 4:8(8/1952).

Kuno, Osamu. Chian Iji-hō no Kyōkun, *Sekai* 79(7/1952):169–178.
Kuribayashi, Toshio. Tokkō Keisatsu no Fukkatsu o tsuku—Hakai Katsudō Bōshi Hōan no Botai, *Kaizō* 33:7(5/1952):158–164.
Maeda, Taneo. Rōdō Sampō, Habōhō no Ronten, *Shūkan Nichirō-ken Shiryō* 182:5:27(7/9/1952):11–18.
Makino, Eiichi. Hakai Katsudō Bōshihō ni tsuite, *Keisatsu Kenkyū* 23:7(7/1952): 1–16.
Makino, Eiichi. Hakai Katsudō Bōshihō no Seiritsu, *Keisatsu Kenkyū* 23:9(9/1952): 1–15.
Makino, Eiichi. Hakai Katsudō Bōshihō no Shakai-teki Igi, *Keisatsugaku Ronshū 5:9(9/1952):1–13.*
Masaki, Hiroshi. Jinken jūrin no Shosō, *Sekai* 78(6/1952):103–110.
Masuda, Masanori. Kokunai Chian Iji ni Kiwamete Jūyō no Zai-Nichi Chōsenjin Mondai ni suite, *Keisatsu Jihō 7:4*(4/1952):35–38.
Matsumoto, Yoneharu. Kyoto Kōan Jōrei to Kempō, *Keisatsugaku Ronshū 5:3(3/1952).*
Matsumura, Hisateru. Habōhō no Genkai, *Chūō Kōron* 67:10(9/1952):88–94.
Matsuoka, Saburō. Chian Rippō to Rōdōsha to Hō-gakusha, *Rōdō Keizai Jumpō 138:5(10/1951).*
Matsuoka, Saburō. Hakai Katsudō Bōshi Hōan to Rōdō Kumiai, *Rōdō Keizai Jumpō* 6:153(4/1952):8–9.
Matsuoka, Yukio. Seirei 325–gō no Kōryoku, *Hōritsu no Hiroba* 5:10(10/1952): 44–47.
Mēdē Sōjō Jiken no Shinsō, *Tōyō Keizai Shimpō* 2524(5/17/1952):20–25.
Minami Chōsen no 'Habōhō'—Fuashizumu to Senso e no michi, *Sekai Jōsei Jumpō* Rinjigō 5/1952:1–14.
Minshu-shugi Kagakusha Kyōkai. Habōhō Jisshi ni saishie Kagakusha ni uttaeru, *Rekishi Hyōron* 38(9/1952):1–4.
Mitamura, Chian Mondai to Keibi Keisatsu, *Shin-Keisatsu* 7:6(7/1952):8–11.
Mitamura, Takeo. Chian Taisaku to Keisatsu Seido, *Shin-Keisatsu* 7:5(6/1952):8–11.
Miyake, Masao. Minshu-teki na Todokeide-sei: Shūdan Ji'i Undō tō no totokeide ni kansuru Hōritsuan Hihan, *Rōdō Hōritsu Jumpō* 73–74(11/1952):2–6.
Miyauchi, Yutaka. Habōhō wa Buraku Kaihō o sobamu, *Buraku* 34(7/1952):5–8.
Miyauchi, Yutaka. Sengo Chian Rippō no Saihen no Kihon-teki Seikaku, *Kikan Hōritsugaku* 12(52:15):29–54.
Mizuno, Tōtaro. Kokunai Chian ni arata ni Hōritsu wa hitsuyō ka, *Jiyū to Seigi* 3:2(2/1952):35–36.
Mizushima, Shin'ichi. Handō-teki Kokka Kenryoku no Saihen—Chian Rippō Rōdō Hōki Kaisei Mondai o megutte, *Rōdō Keizai Jumpō* 6:158(6/1952):14–19.
Mizutani, Chōsaburō. Shakai Minshushugi Sensen Tōitsu ni igi, *Keieisha* 6:8(8/1952):12–13.
Morinaga, Eisaburō. Habōhō to Rōdōsha no Kokoro-game, *Shakai-shugi* 15(8/1952): 5–9.
Morinaga, Eisaburō. Hakai Katsudō Bōshi Hōan to Rōdōsha, *Rōdō Hōritsu Jumpō* 87/88(3–4/1952):31–38.
Murai Jun. Chian Mondai no Kaiko to Tembō, *Jichi Jihō 5*:10(10/1952):1–7.
Nabeyama, Sadachika. Ryūketsu Mēdē to Rōdō Kumiai Shuryū, *Keieisha* 6:6(6/1952): 8–10.
Nagano, Kunisuke. Hakai Katsudō Bōshi-hō ni taisuru iken, *Hōritsu no Hiroba* 5:7(7/1952):12.
Nakamura, Satoshi. Dantai tō Kisei Hōan to Jinken, *Rōdō Hōritsu Jumpō* 70(10/1952).
Nakamura, Satoshi. Seiji Keisatsu to Kakumei no Bōryoku, *Kaizō* 33–4(3/1952): 41–45.

Nawauchi, Reisaku. Chian Taisaku no yukisugi o fusegu ni wa, *Chūō Kōron* 67:9(8/1952):58–67.

Nihon Shimbun Kyōkai. Fatatabi Kokumin no Kenri no tame ni, *Sekai* 78(6/1952):114–115.

Nihon Shimbun Kyōkai. Kokumin no Kenri no tame ni: Shimbun Hōsei Kenkyūkai no Kenkyū Ketsuron, *Sekai* 75(3/-1952):115–117.

Nishimura, Hisayuki. Chian Mondai no Shōten to sono Taisaku, *Keieisha* 6:8(8/1952):8–9.

Nishio, Suehiro. 'Warera no Kenkai' Seiji Suto wa naze sakereba naran ka, *Jikyō Kenkyūkai.* 1952.

Numata, Inejirō. Hakai Katsudō Bōshi Hōan Hihan—sono Rikai to tatakau tame ni, *Rōdō Keizai Jumpō* 6:62(7/1952)*:* 3–20.

Numata, Inejirō. Mēdē Jiken no Rekishi-teki Imi, *Kaizō* 33–16(11/1952)*:108–113.*

Obase, Takuzō. Zen-Kokumin no Teikō, *Kaizō* 33:11(8/1952):78–82.

Oda, Hisashi. Habōhō to Kokumin Kanjō, *Jikei* 34:9(9/1952):60–64.

Oka, Eishi. Habōhō Hantai Undō sono go no Tembō, *Chūō Kōron* 67:11(10/1952):64–68.

Okada, Masata. Hakai Katsudō Bōshi-hō no egaku hamon, *Jitsugyō no Nihon* 55:9(5/1952):62–65.

Ouchi, Hyōe. Habōhō ni tsuite, *Sekai* 81(9/1952):60–64.

Ōyama, Yasuki. Habōhō to Rōdō Undō, *Shūbō* 7:8(8/1952):18–20.

Potsdam Meirei yo doko e yuku, *Jurisuto* 15:8/1/52:46–54.

Rekishi no Kumon, Habōhō, *Shūkan Sankei* 6/1/1952:3–

Rōdōshō, Rōseikyoku. Hakai Katsudō Bōshi Hōan ni tsuite, *Rōdō Jihō* 5:5(5/1952):14–19.

Rōtō Suto Habōhō no Hihan—Shōgyō Shimbun Shasetsu kara Riron o saguru, *Rōdō Shūhō* 15:591(4/1952):12–15.

Rōyama, Masamichi. Atsuryoku Dantai no Igi to Genkai, *Hōritsu Jihō* 25:1(1/1953):3–8.

Sadagasaki, Shungo. Chian Modai to Rōdō Undō, *Keieisha* 6:8(8/1952):16–17.

Saito, Noboru. Yuragu Chian o dō-suru, *Seiji Ōrai* 18:10(10/1952):50–63.

Sajin, Ujin. Habōhō no Hakai Katsudō-sei—Genron Hyōgen no Jiyū to Kiki, *Shuppan Nyūsu* 204(7/1952):8.

Sanada, Hideo. Hakai Katsudō Bōshi Hōan Kaisetsu, *Toki no Hōrei* 59(5/1952):1–9.

Sanada, Hideo. Habōhō ni yoru kisei shobun to Keiji Shobun, *Hōritsu no Hiroba* 5:10(10/1952):20–23.

Sangi-in Hōmu Iinkai no Tōron, *Rōdō Keizai Jumpō* 6:162:20–26.

Sata, Ineko. Mēdē Jiken to Habōhō, *Shin-Nihon Bungaku* 7:7(7/1952):65.

Satō, Tatsuo. Hōritsu ga umareru made, *Hōritsu Jihō* 25:1(1/1953):45–50.

Satō, Tatsuo. Hōseikyoku, are kore. *Hōritsu no Hiroba* 5:11(11/1952):19–22.

Satō, Tatsuo. Pikari, Chian Rippō, *Meisō* 2:12(4/1952):12–15.

Satomi, Kishio. Bōdō Chin'atsu-hō o Seitei seyo, *Kokutai Bunka* 357(2/9/1952):1–5.

Seki, Itaru. Hakai Katsudō Bōshi-hō ni suite, *Jikei* 34:9(9/1952):31–46.

Seki, Itaru. Hakai Katsudō Bōshi-hō no shuyō Ronten ni suite, *Hōsō Jihō* 4:10(10;1952):9–23.

Seki, Itaru. Hakai Katsudō Bōshi-hō no Yōshi, *Keisatsugaku Ronshū* 5:7(7/1952):1–11.

Seki, Itaru. Hakai Katsudō Bōshi-hō wa donna Hōritsu ka, *Hōritsu no Hiroba* 5:9(9/52):8–12.

Senō, Ken. Dantai tō Kisei Hōan to Jinken Yōgo, *Jiyū to Seigi* 3:l(1/1952):22–27.

Shigemitsu, Takenori. Hakai Katsudō Bōshi-hō to Kihon Jinken, *Keisatsu Jihō* 7:11(11/1952):31–34.

Shimamura, Kōzō. Habōhō Shingi no Uchimaku, *Keizai Orai*, 4:7(7/1952):157–161.

Shimizu, Ikutarō. Nihonjin no Jiyū—Habōhō no Jisshi ni yosu, *Kaizō* 33:12(9/1952: 2–11.
Shimizu, Shin. Habōhō kara PR e, *Shin-Bummei* 2:8(8/1952):22–25.
Shiomi, Toshitaka. Jiyū to Jinken wa kiki ni hinsu—Saikin no Chian Rippō no ugoki,*Ushio* 2(8/1952):37–41.
Shisetsu Hōritsu Ikenkyoku. Dantai tō Kisei Hōan o shingi-suru, *Jurisuto* 13(7/1/1952):16–17.
Shisetsu Hōritsu Ikenkyoku. Shūdan Ji'i Torishimari Hōan, *Jurisuto* 14(7/15/1952): 28–33.
Shūdan Ji'i Undō to no Chitsujo Hoji ni kansuru Hōritsuan, *Hōritsu Jihō* 24:6(6/1952):84–85, and *Rōdō Hōritsu Jumpō* 95(6/1952):21–23.
Sōshitsu shita Habōhō kaisetsusho, *Hōritsu no Hiroba* 5:11(11/1952):23.
Suehiro, Itsutarō. Sōhyō Kambu Taiho Jiken—Genron no Jiyū to Keisatsu no Mondai, *Hōritsu Jihō* 23:6(6/1951).
Suekawa, Hiroshi & Kainō Michitaka. Jiji Dansō—Habō Hōan, Rōdō Kaisei nado, *Rōdōhō 4(6/1952):54–61.*
Suekawa, Hiroshi. Riron tai Riron no Hoshō—chian rippō ni kanren-shite, *Jurisuto* 15:8/1/52:7–9.
Sugimoto, Moriyoshi. Tokkō Keisatsu ni jijihi naru mono, *Keisatsu Kenkyū* 21:6(6/1950).
Sugimoto, Moriyoshi. Tokkō Keisatsu no soshiki to Un'yō, *Jurisuto* Pt I:14:7/15/52: 19–25; II:15:8/1/52:38–43 & 33.
Sumiyoshi, Kenzō. Habōhō no koto, *Shin-Nihon Bungaku* 7:9(9/1952:78–81.
Sunada, Shūzō. Chian Mondai no Tembō, *Keieisha* 6:6(6/1952):4–7.
Sunada, Shūzō. Kōjō o Mokuhyō tosuru Hakai Katsudō ni tsuiste, *Tekkō Rōmu Tsūshin* 3:7(8/1952):2–3.
Suzuki, Yoshio. Minshuka ni Gyakkō-suru Chian Rippō *Sekai 72(12/*1952):46–55.
Tagami, Jōji. Kōan Jōrei no Kōryoku, *Keisatsu Rombushū 5:4(4/1952).*
Takada, Akira. Kempō dai-28-jō kara mita Seiji Sutoraiki, *Meiji Gakuin Ronsō* 30(10/53).
Takagi, Yumon. Hakai Katsudō Bōshi-hō Hihan, *Sekai* 78(6/1952):111–113.
Takatsuji, Masami. Rippō ni okeru Ritsuan no katei, *Jurisuto* 35(6/1/1953):11–15.
Takaya, Kakuzo. Jūdai Tenkan-suru Nikkyō no Būsō Tōsō, *Keieisha* 6:8(8/1952): 21–25.
Takayangi, Kenzō. Minshu-teki Hō Chitsujo no Kihon-teki Seikaku—Chian Rippō Mondai o Chūshin toshite, *Keizai Ōrai* 4:6(6/1952):6–15.
Takikawa, Kōshin. Genron Shisō, Gakumon no Jiyū, *Sekai* 78(6/1952):87–94.
Takikawa, Kōshin. Hendōki ni okeru Chian to Keihō, *Hōritsu Jihō* 24:11(11/1952): 3–7.
Takikawa, Mikio. Hakai Katsudō Bōshi-hō Bassoku ni tsuite, *Sōsa Kenkyū* 9(8/1952).
Takikawa, Mikio. Hakai Katsudō Bōshi-hō Kaisetsu, *Kenshū* 2 (9/1952).
Takikawa, Mikio. Kōan Chitsujo Hoji no tame ni seitei-sareta Bōryoku Kō tō Shobatsu-hō ni tsuite, *Keisatsu Jihō* 7:11(11/1952):26–30.
Takikawa, Mikio. Kōan Jiken ni suite no Mondai, *Keisatsu Jihō* 7:12(12/1952):45–48.
Takikawa, Mikio. Shūkai to Tashū Undō, *Sōsa Kenkyū* 16–18(3–5/1953). Three parts.
Takiuchi, Reiksaku. Chian Taisaku no Yukisugi o fusegu niwa, *Chūō Kōron* 67:9(8/1952):58–67.
Takiuchi, Reisaku. Kempō no Yōgo to Saibansho no Jitsujo, *Hōritsu Jihō* 24:1(1/1952):18–19.
Tanaka, Kei'ichi. Hakai Katsudō Bōshi-hō wa naze hitsuyō dearuka, *Kokkai* 5:8(8/1952):10–15.
Tanaka, Masasumi. Kōan Jōrei Iken-sei, *Hōritsu Shimpō 760(1/1952).*

Tanizuka, Susumu. Habōhō to Nōmin Undō, *Shūbō* 7:8(8/52):22–24.
Tominaga, Sōichi. Habōhō e no ke'nen—Bijutsika no Tachiba kara, *Bijutsu Hyōron* 6(6/1952):22–26.
Tokyo Bengoshi-kai. Chian Rippō ni taisuru mittsu no ikensho, *Sekai* 75(3/1952):118–121.
Tokyo Bengoshi-kai. Dantai-tō Kisei-rei ni taisuru ikensho, *Hōritsu Jihō* 24:1(1/1952):84.
Tokyo Bengo Shikai. Sampō ni Hantai, *Rōdō Hōritsu Jumpō* 73/74(11/1951):27–35.
Tsuchiya, Shōzō. Habōhō Rongi, *Keisatsu Kenkyū,* 23:8(8/1952):20–40.
Tsuji, Kiyoaki. Habōhō no San'in Tsūka, *Kyōiku* 2:8(8/1952):12–14.
Ukai, Nobushige. Chian Rippō ni tsuite, *Nichirōken* 156:5:1(½/1952):32.
Ukai, Nobushige. Chian Rippō no Mondai-ten, *Kyōiku* 3(1/1952):3–5.
Ukai, Nobushige. Habōhō no kyūmei, *Jurisuto* 10(5/1952):17–29.
Umeda, Hiroshi. Shin-Kadai ni men-suru Chian Mondai, *Seiji Keizai* 5 :1(1/1952): 15–17.
Umeda, Hiroshi. Tokubetsu Kōanhō no Kaisetsu to Hihan, *Seiji Keizai* 5:4(4/1952): 32–34.
Unno, Shinkichi. Danki Hōan wa Sekai no me ni ikani eijiru ka—Kōwa go no Nihon ni Minshu-shugi o kakuritsu-suru tame ni, *Sekai* 73(1/1952):164–166.
Unno, Shinkichi. Hakai Katsudō Bōshi-hō no mezasu mono, *Sekai* 78(6/1952): 95–102.
Unno, Shinkichi. Kokka to Jiyū, *Nyūeiji (Newe Age)* 4:11(11/1952):16–27.
Unno, Shinkichi. Risō o Tsuikyū-suru Chian Hōki, *Nyūeiji (New Age)* 4:10(10/1952):13.
Wada, Shōjirō. Hō o meguru tōsō no sho-yōsō to hō no seisei, *Jurisuto,* 13:7/1/52: 2–6.
Warera no Kenkai—Seiji Suto wa naze sakenebanaranuka, Habōhō Hantai ni taisuru Nishio Suehiro no Kenkai, *Jikyoku Kenkyūkai* 1952.
Watanabe, Mie. Keisatsuken to Jinken Jūrin , *Shūbō* 7:1(1/1952).
Watanabe, Tsuneo. Nairan wa dokokara kuru ka, *Kyōiku no Hiroba* 1:4(9/1952): 41–44.
Yabe, Teiji. Atarashii Nihon ni okeru Chian Kikō no Chii, *Keisatsu Yobitai Shiryōshū* 1:2–9.
Yagami, Shichirō. Habōhō to Seinen Gakusei Undō, *Shūbō* 7:8(8/1952):20–22.
Yamagata, Shōtarō. Habōhō no Jisshi to sono go ni kuru mono, *Jitsugyō no Nihon* 55:16(8/1952):53–55.
Yamakawa, Hitoshi. Bōatsuhō no Omoide—Chian Iji-hō to Hakai Katsudō Bōshi-hō, *Shakai-shugi* 12(5/1952):38–43.
Yamakawa, Hitoshi. Habōhō to no Tatakai, *Shakai-shugi* 15(8/1952):2–4.
Yamakawa, Hitoshi. Jinken to Jiyū—5.1 Bōdō to Habōhō, *Kaizō 33:8(6/1952):10–16.*
Yamanaka, Yasuo. Habōhō kara Keisatsu-hō Kaisei made, *Kaizō* 34:6(5/1952):50–55.
Yamane, Shinjirō. Shimbun Torishimari no Kaiko to Tembō—Habōhō o megutte, *Shimbun Kenkyū* 20(8/1952):19–24.
Yamazaki, Masao. Kenryoku Tōsō ni karamu Gunshū Hanzai—Kamata Jiken no Kentō, *Sōsa Kenkyū* 6(5/1952).
Yoshida, Saburō. Chian Taisaku wa Kampeki ka, *Keisatsu Jihō* 7:11(11/1952):40–42.
Yoshida, Shigeru. Hakai Katsudō Bōshi-hō no Seitei, *Kaisō Jū'nen* v. 2. 290–292.
Yoshihashi, Toshio. Dantai-tō Kiseirei ni tsuite, *Hōritsu Jihō* 22:10(10/1950):52–56.
Yoshihashi, Toshio. Saikin ni okeru Hakai Katsudō no Jittai, *Keizai Ōrai* 4:6(6/1952):144–149.
Yoshino, Keizō. Habōhō to Kokumin to Seifu, *Jitsugyō no Sekai* 49:8(8/1952):14–15.
Yuasa, Yūichi. Chian Rippō to Shakai Hoshō, *Keizaijin* 6:3(3/1952):10–12.
Zushiki Habōhō to Kaisetsu, *Shūbō* 7:8(8/1952):24.

D. *Newspapers*

The *shukusatsu* edition of the *Asahi Shimbun*, January–June 1972, during the debate of the SAPL.

E. *Newspaper clippings*

Two volumes of clippings from various Japanese newspapers on the SAPL, and one volume each from *Sōhyō* and *Nikkeiren Taimusu*.

II. *Implementation: Court Cases, Decisions and Commentaries*

Decisions by the Supreme Court of Japan concerning the SAPL can be found in several places: a special two volume collection compiled by the PSIA, compilation of Supreme Court decisions by the Court itself, an index of court decisions in several volumes covering the postwar period, and such magazines as the *Hanrei Jihō* and *Hanrei Taimusu* which summarize such decisions. The Supreme Court's compilation of its decisions also includes rather conveniently a list of articles appearing in various legal journals about a particular decision. The eight cases which reached the Japanese Supreme Court occurred on the following dates:

1. Kushiro Jiken, 9/20/1952
2. Tsu Jiken, 9/13/1952
3. "Kyoto no Hata" Jiken, 9/6/1952, 9/9/1952, 9/10/1952
4. Gifu Jiken, late July through late October, 1952
5. San'yū Jiken, early September through early December 1961
6. Sekigun-ha Daibosatsu Tōge Jiken, late October through early November 1969
7. Okinawa Dakkan Tōsō (Honda Habōhō Jiken), 4/15–24/1969
8. Okinawa Henkan Kyōtei Hijun Soshi Tōsō (Matsuo Habōhō Jiken), 10/21/1971 and 11/10/1971

A. *Compilations of Court Decisions*

Kōan Chōsachō. *Hakai Katsuodō Bōshi-hō Ihan Jiken Hanketsushū.* 2 v. Volume 1 was published in May 1980 (789 p.) covering the above first five court cases and volume 2 (388 p.) in March 1993 covering the remaining three cases. The first part of Volume two is an analysis of the various court cases, the constitutionality of articles 39 and 40 of the Habōhō as seen in the aforementioned Okinawa cases and the characteristics of the danger of the *sendō-zai* (crime of instigation).

Kōan Chōsachō. *Habō-hō Ihan Hikoku Jiken Dai-Isshin Hanshū.* Kōan Chōsa Shiryō (Shin). 6/10/1959. 333 p.

Saikō Saibansho. *Saikō Saibansho Saiban-shū* or *Saikō Saibansho Keiji Hanrei-shū* also contain the various decisions of the Supreme Court.

B. *Indexes*

The Administrative Directorate (Jimu Sōkyoku) of the Supreme Court has also compiled an overall index to its decisions. This compilation is arranged initially by laws, under each law by the article of that law involved in a particular court decision, under each article of a law there is a listing of the various levels of courts involved, and finally after each article of the law, it provides a list of articles, authors and name of journal where these essays were published. These compilations over the postwar period are divided as follows: 1947–1976, 1977–1985, 1986–92, 1993+. Under each of these periods, we will list the articles which comment on the Supreme Court decisions. Copies of these articles were made from resources in the Library of Congress; unfortunately, LC did not always have the cited journals so sometimes the bibliographic data is lacking a minor completeness, e.g. the beginning page is known but the ending page is not. Sometimes court decisions pass judgment on violations of more than one SAPL article; then the commentary also covers more than one article. In the indexes, the relevant commentaries are cited under each article, that would mean that one commentary could be cited one or more times for each SAPL article considered by the court. The articles cited in these indexes will be arranged into two groups: SAPL and the Dandai-tō Kisei-rei. The SAPL part would be divided by the three periods covered by the indexes. Those commentaries cited from *Saikō Saibansho Hanrei Kaisetsu: Shohō* (Explanations of Supreme Court cases: miscellaneous laws) compiled by the Saikō Saibansho Chōsakan-shitsu will be cited as from *Kaisetsu* giving dates. The three indexes used are:

Saikō Saibansho, Jimu Sō-Kyoku. *Keiji Saibanrei Sō-Sakuin: shohō tsuiho I and II.* Three volumes for 1947–1976, 1977–1985, 1986–92. The volume for 1993+ *Keiji Saibanrei Sō-sakuin: keihō tsuiho* was published in 1996 but contained no cases on the SAPL.

1947–1976. P. 354–358 affecting SAPL articles 1, 2, 27, 38, 39 & 40, 45
1977–1985. P. 348–349 no Supreme Court decision but lower court decisions affecting SAPL articles 39, 40
1986–1992. P. 199–201 affecting SAPL articles 39, 40

C. *Legal Commentaries*

Dantai-tō Kisei-rei (Organizations Control Ordinance)

Hashimoto, Kinmoto. Dantai tō Kisei-rei no ikensei, *Hōritsu Jihō* 34:2(2/1962): 60–63.
Kurita, Tadashi. Dantai tō Kisei-rei Ihan Jiken, *Jurisuto* 244(2/15/1962):42–50.
Kurita, Tadashi. Datai-tō Kisei-rei ihan hikoku jiken ni tsuki menso no iiwatashi o nasubeki ba'ai, *Kaisetsu* 1961:319–328.
Mitsui, Akira. Dantai-tō Kisei-rei Dai 2-jō dai 7-gō, Dai 3-jō wa ikenka. *Kaisetsu* 1961:328–331 and in *Hōsō Jihō* 14:2: 123–126.
S.H.E. Kyū-Dantai tō Kisei-rei ni motozuku Chōsaken to Kempō to no kankei, *Toki-no-Horei.* 416:42–, 417:40–48.
Sotoma, Hiroshi. Gyōsei Chōsaken ni motozuku Shuttō Yōkyū, *Jurisuto Rinji Zōkangō* 6/1963 (Kempō Hanrei Hyaku-sen): 89–90.
Tamiya, Yutaka. Dantai-tō Kisei-rei ihan to menso no iiwatashi, *Keisatsu Kenkyū* 49:3(3/1978):55–60.
Tejima, Takashi. Gyō Chōsaken ni motozuku Shuttō Yōkyū, *Bessatsu Jurisuto* 21(12/1968):96–97 and 44(6/1974):132–133.

SAPL, 1947–1976

Chikuma, Masayasu. Hakai Katsudō Bōshi-hō 39-jō oyobi 40-jō wa hanzai no Kōsei Yōken ga Fu-Meikaku ka, *Hōgaku Kenkyū* 46:5 (1–6/1973):103–106.
Fujio, Akira. Bunsho Hampu-zai no "Nairan o Jikkō saseru Mokuteki", *Bessatsu Jurisuto* 333(6/1971):138–139.
Fukuda, Taira. Hakai Katsudō Bōshi-hō 39-jō oyobi 40-jō wa Kōsei Yōken ga Fu-meikaku ka, *Bessatsu Jurisuto:* 33(6/1971):136–137(Zuku Keihō Hanrei Hyakusen).
Mitsui, Osamu. *Sōsa Kenkyū* 45:39–.

Miyauchi, Yutaka. Habōhō to Hyōgen no Jiyū, *Horitsu Jihō* 32(1/60):58–64.
Miyauchi, Yutaka. Kyōto Habōhō Jiken Hanketsu no Igi, *Hōritsu Jihō* 29:7(7/57):88–93.
Sakamoto, Takeshi. Hakai Katsudō Bōshi-hō 39–jō oyobi 40–jō wa hanzai no Kōsei yōken ga Fu-meikaku ka, *Kaisetsu* 1970:136–144. Also published in *Hōsō Jihō* 22:11(11/1970):159–164.
Shimizu, Mutsumi. Hakai Katsudō Bōshihō 38–jō 2–kō 2–gō ihan jiken: so Gōken-sei (Kempō 21–jō o chōshin to shite), *Hōgaku Shimpō* 66:7 (7/1959):53–59.
Tomita, Yasutsugu. *Sosa Kenkyū* 154:27–
Wakita, Tadashi. Taiho Kankin Kōi no ihō-sei no umu ni tsuki Hakai Katsudō Bōshi-hō no Gōken-sei tō no handan o yōshinai to shita jirei. *Kaisetsu* 1961:222–25. Also published in *Hōsō Jihō* 13:11(141–143).
Yoshikawa, Tsuneo. *Keisatsu Kenkyū* 51:7:73–.

SAPL, 1977–1985

Gendai Keisatsu Hanrei Kenkyū Gurūpu. *Kikan Gendai Keisatsu* 39:110.
Kagawa, Tatsuo. Hakai Katsudō Bōshi-hō 40-jō no Sendō-zai no Gōken-sei, *Hanrei Hyōron* 318(8/1/1985):223–227 included as part of *Hanrei Jihō* 1154(8/1/1985):223–227.

SAPL, 1986–1992

Hirakawa, Munenobu. Hakai Katsudō Bōshi-hō 39-jō oyobi 40-jō no Sendō o shobatsu-suru Kitei to Kempō 21-jō ikkō, *Keisatsu Kenkyū* 63:5:42–48. *Keiji Hanrei Kenkyū* 511.
Kimizuka, Masaomi, Sendō-zai to Habōhō—Iwayuru Shibuya Bōdō Jiken Saikōsai Hanketsu, *Handai Hōgaku (Osaka Law Review)* 41:4(#162):3/1992:501–518.
Mitsui, Yukio. Habōhō 39, 40-jō no Sendō-zai no Gōken-sei, *Hōgaku Seminā* 408(6/91):126.
Mōri, Harumitsu. Sendō-zai no Gōken-sei ni tsuite, *Hōritsu no Hiroba* 44:2(2/1991):56–62.
Nakanome, Yoshinori. Hakai Katsud ō Bōshi-hō 39-jō oyobi 40-jō no Sendō o Shobatsu-suru Kitei ga Kempō 21-jō 1-kō ni Han-suru ka inaka ga Awasoreta Jirei, *Hōgaku* Shimpō (The Chuo Law Review) 99:5/6(2/1993):339–355.
Sakai, Yasuyuki. Habōhō 39-jō, 40-jō no Sendō-zai Kitei no Gōken-sei, *Hanrei Taimuzu* 44:7(804)(3/1/93):40–46.
Sone, Takehiko. Hakai Katsudō Bōshi-hō no Sendō-zai Shobatsu Kitei no Gōken-sei, *Hanrei Hyōron* #391(9/1/91):218–222 in *Hanrei Jihō* 1388(9/1/91):218–222.
Utsunomiya, Jun'ichi. Hakai Katsudō Bōshi-hō 39-jō oyobi 40-jō no Sendō o Shobatsu-suru Kitei to Kempō 21-jō 1-kō, *Hōgaku* (Tōhoku Daigaku) 56:6(2/93):65–69.
Uzaki, Masahiro. Hakai Katsudō Bōshi-hō Sendō Kitei no Gōken-sei, *Jurisuto Renji Zōkan: Heisei 2-endo Jūyō Hanrei Kaisetsu* 90:6/1:22–23.
Yamashita, Takeshi. Hakai Katsudō Bōshi-hō 39, 40-jō no Gōken-sei, *Hōgaku Kyōshitsu* 126:12 (*Hanrei Serukuto '90* 126/Bessatsu Tokushū:12.
Yoshimoto, Tetsuya. Hakai Katsudō Bōshihō 39-jō oyobi 40-jō no Sendō o Shobatsu-suru Kitei to Kempō 21-jō 1-kō, *Hōsō Jihō* 44:7(7/1/1993):265–293. Also published in *Kaisetsu* 1990:132–.

III. *Selected Books and Articles on Japanese Government*

In preparing this bibliography, I looked for books and articles that would bear upon the Haboho. I found that in most cases if there was any mention of the Habōhō it was a short reference, once in a while a slightly longer reference; I found only one essay in English devoted entirely to the Habōhō and that was written in 1953 less than a year after the law was enacted and remains the only article in English.

Maki, John M. Japan's Subversive Activities Prevention Law, *The Western Political Quarterly* 6:3(9/53):489–511.

Furthermore, in a collection of Constitutional law cases of Japan, only the volume on the 1961–70 period contained a translation of a Supreme Court decision on the Habōhō: the other volumes covering 1948–1960 and 1971—did not include any decisions on the Habōhō:

Itoh, Hiroshi, Lawrence Beer, comp/tr. *The Constitutional Case Law of Japan: selected Supreme Court decisions, 1961–70.* Seattle, WA. University of Washington Press. 1978. 283 p. [The case was called Japan v. Kanemoto et al (1964). The Kanemoto Pamphlet Case, pp. 242–244.]

A. *Internal Security Laws*

1. *Prewar Internal Security Laws*

Only some books and articles in Japanese and English published since 1945 on the prewar internal security laws are listed below. Those who wish to study materials published on this subject before 1945 are referred to the following books in which bibliographies list a wide range of books, journals and articles. Since the subject of this book is the postwar SAPL it was felt that there was no need to replicate a voluminous listing of prewar publications in the following books:

Matsumura, Janice. More than a Momentary Nightmare: the Yokohama Incident and Wartime Japan. Ithaca, NY. East Asian Program. Cornell University. 1998. 172 p.
Mitchell, Richard. *Censorship in Imperial Japan.* Princeton, NJ, Princeton University Press. 1983. 424 p.
Mitchell, Richard. *Janus-Faced Justice.* Honolulu. University of Hawaii Press. 1992. 235 p.
Mitchell, Richard. *Thought Control in Prewar Japan.* Ithaca NY, Cornell University Press. 1976. 226 p.
Tipton, Elise K. *Japanese Police State: Tokkō in Interwar Japan.* Honolulu. University of Hawaii Press. 1990. 209 p.
Tipton, Elise K., ed. *Society and the State in Interwar Japan*, London/New York. Routledge. 1997. 242 p.
Uyehara, Cecil H. *Leftwing Social Movements in Japan: An Annotated Bibliography.* Tokyo. The Charles E. Tuttle Co. 1959. 444 p. (pp. 370–400).

Chian Iji-hō (tokushū), *Jurisuto* Pt I:13:7/1/52:26–46; II:14:7/15/52:2–18.
Chian Iji-hō, *Gendaishi Shiryō:45.* Misuzu Shobō 1973. 600, p. Commentary by Okudaira Yasuhirō.
Chian Iji-hō Giseisha Kokka Baishō Yōkyū Dōmei Chūō Hombu. *Ima mo ikiteiru Chian Iji-hō* Seijisha. 1980. 97 p.
Hisano, Osamu. Chian Iji-hō no Kyōkun, *Sekai* 79(7/52):169–178.
Kobayashi, Eizō. *Rekishi no Shinjitsu ni tatte: Chian Iji-hō Supai Chōhatsu tō no Tōsō.* Shin-Nihon Shuppansha. 1976. Shin-Nihon Shinsho:224.
Kobayashi, Yukio. Nisso Kihon Jōyaku Dai-5 Jō to Chian Iji-hō, *Jimbun Gakuhō* 10(1959):133–164.
Matsuo, Takayoshi. Kageki Shakai Undō Torishimari Hōan ni tsuite: 1922-nen dai-45 Gikai ni okeru shingi., *Jimbun Gakuhō* 20(1964):247–267.
Matsuo, Hiroshi. *Chian Iji-hō: Dan'atsu to Teikō no Rekishi.* Shin-Nihon Shuppansha. 1971. 234 p. Shin-Nihon Shinsho:41.
Matsuo, Hiroshi. *Chian Iji-hō to Tokkō Keisatsu.* Kyōikusha. 1979. 231 p.
Miyauchi, Yutaka. *Sengo Chian Rippō no Kihon Seikaku.* Yūshindō. 1960. 444 p.

Mori, Tadashi. *Chian Iji-hō Saiban to Bengoshi.* Nihon Hyōronsha. 1985. 346 p.
Nakajima, Makoto. *Tenkōron Josetsu.* Minerva Shobō. 1980. 265 p.
Okudaira, Yasuhiro. *Chian Iji-hō Shōshi.* Chikuma Shobō. 272 p.
Okudaira, Yasuhiro. Some Preparatory notes for the study of the Peace Preservation Law in Pre-war Japan, *Annals of the Institute of Social Science* 14(73):49–69.
Ono, Sada and Kiga Sumiko. *Yokohama Jiken: Tsuma to Imōto no Shuki.* Kōbunkan. 1987. 219 p.
Shibata, Yoshihiko. *Shisō Torishimari Kankei Hōrei Hanrei Gakusetsu Sōran.* Ganshōdō. 1932. 552 p. Shisō no Kagaku Kenkyūkai, comp *Kyōdō Kenkyū*: Tenkō. Heibonsha. 1959. 3 v.
Shiomi, Toshitaka. *Chian Iji-hō.*Iwanami Shoten. 1977. Iwanami Shinsho(ki):22.
Shisō no Kagaku Kenkyūkai. *Tenkō.* Heibonsha. 1959. 3 v.
Sugimoto, Moriyoshi. Tokkō Keisatsu no Soshiki to Un'yō, *Jurisuto* 1:14(7/15/52):19–25; II:15(8/1/52):38–43. Tokushū: Chian Ijihō: I:Chian Ijihō Seiritsu no Kei'i, *Jurisuto* 13(7/1/52):26–46; II:Chian Ijihō wa dō Un'ei saretaka, *Jurisuto* 14(7/15/52):2–18.
Steinhoff, Patricia G. *Tenkō* New York. Garland. 1991. 220 p.
Suda, Frances. *Peace Preservation Law.* Harvard University PhD dissertation.
Tipton, Elise Kurashige. *The Civil Police in the Suppression of the Prewar Japanese Left.* 1977. 377 p. Un-published PhD dissertation at Indiana University.
Ueda, Seikichi. *Aru Naimu Kanryō no Kiseki.* Ōtsuki Shoten. 1980.
Ueda, Seikichi. *Chian Rippō to Saiban.* Shin-Nihon Shuppansha. 1990. 230 p. Shin-Nihon Shinsho:397.
Ueda, Seikichi. *Showa Saiban Shiron—Chian Iji-hō to Hōritsuka-tachi.* Ōtsuki Shoten. 1983. 270 p.
Winant, Thomas T. *The Home Ministry and the Special Higher Police.* 1974. 19 p. Unpublished paper given at the 1974 AAS Convention.

2. *Postwar Internal Security after the Enactment of the SAPL*

When the SAPL was implemented and court cases began to be prosecuted by the Ministry of Justice, opposition groups supporting the defendants came into being. These were leftwing or communist supported organizations and they produced publications and journals defending the actions of the defendants and denouncing the SAPL as unconstitutional. I am aware of only two such journals devoted to the Habōhō and their purposes were to oppose the government's legal cases involving this law. They were obviously supported by leftwing sources but the actual source of this funding was not entirely clear.

Habōhō Kenkyū (Habōhō Studies). 73 issues, 1969–March 1992.
Habōhō Saiban Nyūsu (Habōhō News), about 1970+.

There are, of course, many other articles and essays on the Habōhō which are not polemical and are also to be distinguished from those articles commenting on the court decisions relating to the SAPL In preparing this list, I consulted several sources as follows:

Hōritsu Hanrei Bunken Jōhō. Dai-ichi Hōki KK. 1982–2005. It is on a CD in the Library of Congress Law Library. 180 citations were listed under "Habōhō"; most of these have been included in this section.
Ōya Sōichi Bunko. *Zasshi Kiji Sakuin Sō-mokuroku.* 1987–1995. These bound volumes are available in the Library of Congress, Asia Division. Entries from this collection were included but since 1995 it has used the online method and a CD, and LC does not have the either of them (2006).
Saikō Saibansho Toshokan. *Hōbun Hōritsu Zasshi Kiji Sakuin.* Numerous citations under "Habōhō, "Chian Rippō, Keiji Tobubetsu-hō, etc were included in this list.

I do not feel that the list below is exhaustive but is nevertheless quite representative. Except for selected articles, those in the above mentioned *Habōhō Kenkyū* are not included in the following list.

Adachi, Masakatsu. Hakai Katsudō Bōshi-hō no Ronri to Kōzō, *Nihon no Kagakusha* 31-7(7/1996):28–32.

Asada, Mitsuteru. "Bengodan Gasshuku Funsō" no Keika: Oitsumerareta Kaku-maru no Honne, *Gendai no Me* 11/1974–:230+.

Asada, Mitsuteru. *Chian Saiban to Habōhō: Zoku Habōhō Saiban Bōchōki.* Shinsensha. 1978.

Asada, Mitsuteru. Gendai Kokka no Kōzō to Shiyō Shiza: Hō o koeru Kokka, *Gendai no Me* 6/1973:100+.

Asada, Mitsuteru. *Habōhō o Sabaku: Okinawa Tōsō Habōhō Saiban 20-nen no Kiroku.* Tokyo. Ochanomizu Shobō. 1993. 488 p.

Asada, Mitsuteru. *Habōhō Saiban Bōchōki.* Renga Shobō. 1974. 396 p.

Asada, Mitsuteru. Shisō Hyōgen e no Chōsen—Saikōsai no Habōhō Sendō-zai Hanketsu (Tokushū: Chūtō hahei to Habōhō), *Habōhō Kenkyū* 70(3/1991):33–40.

Asano, Ken'ichi. *Ōmu Habōhō to Masu medea: Zoku, hanzai hōdō no saihan.* Daisan Shobō. 1997.

Asato, Zenshō. Hakai Katsudō Bōsho-hō no Kōsatsu, *Yamanashi Gakuin Daigaku Hōgaku Ronshū* 36 (12/1996):1–102.

Aso, Kazuko et al. Okinawa Habōhō Saiban-Saikōsai Kōhan o bōchō shite, *Habōhō Kenkyū* 69(9/1990):93–97.

Atsumi, Tōyō. "Habōhō" no tekiyō o dō kangaeru ka, *Ushio* 445(3/1996): 104–113.

Atsumi, Tōyō. Hō Tekiyō o sake, *Asahi Shimbun* 10/10/1995.

Azabu, Ki. Dokyumento: Ōmu ni Habōhō o tekiyō seyo, *Bungei Shunju* 9/1995:168–174.

Azabu, Ki. Habōhō Tekiyō mo Tōzen, *Bungei Shunju* 11/1995:148–155.

Chian to Jinken: Tokushū, *Hōritsu Jihō* 42–8(6/1970):5–494.

Chian Rippō Kankei Bunken, *Jurisuto* 235(10/1961):25.

Chiyomaru, Kenji. *Habōhō ni taikō-suru hon—tatakau shimin no jinken roppō,* Gendai Jimbunsha. 1996. 64 p.

Chiyomaru, Kenji. *Habōhō to tatakau hō.* San'ichi Shobō. 1996.343 p.

Ebashi, Takashi, Seiji-teki Kōi to "Hyōgen no Jiyū" no taiyō, *Habōhō Kenkyū* 64(2/1989):18–27.

Eda, Satsuki. ōmu to Habōhō—Kokumin no Fuan Jokyo e tekiyō o, *Mainichi Shimbun* 10/23/1995.

Enoyama, Gentarō. Konshū no Kotoba:Habōhō: Ōmu Shinrikyō ni Tekiyō-shite Kaisan ni oikomu-beki, *Hanako* 11/2/1995:85.

Fujii, Haruo. Hahei wa kanarazu kaiken ni yukitsuku, *Habōhō Kenkyū* 70 (3/1991):4–13.

Fujii, Toshio. Hakai Katsudō Bōshi-hō 40jō no Gōkensei, *Hanrei Serekuto* '87 (Gekkan hōgaku kyōshitsu 89 bessatsu furoku). Yūhikaku. 2/1988:10.

Fujimoto, Shigeo. Kusakute Kikoenai Hanashi:Kokkai Shingi (Habō hōan Shingi) Toki no Chinji, *Bungei Shunju* 7/1966:88+.

Fukuda, Masaaki & Kawakami Kazuo. Habōhō tetsuzuki—bemmei no "shōko" ni kachi nashi, *Mainichi Shimbun* 2/11/1996.

Fuōkasu Repōto: Murayama Naikaku wa oyobi koshi Ōmu ni Habōhō nara kōnaru, *FOCUS* 10/18/1995:62–65.

Furuta, Noriko. Sokui no Rei to Habōhō dantai tekiyō, *Shūkan Hōritsu Shimbun* 990(11/9/1990):2.

Gendai Hōsei Kenkyūkai. Ōmu Shinrikyō ni taisuru Habōhō no tekiyō, *Keisatsu Jihō* 51:3(3/1996):128–131.

Habōhō de pakuru: Kōan Kambu ga Gekihaku, *Shūkan Taishū* 10/2/1995:24–26.

Habōhō Kenkyūkai. comp. *Habōhō ga yatte kita*. Seiunsha. 1996. 191 p.

Habōhō Kenkyūkai, comp. *Habōhō Kōhan Bōchōki*. Ochanomizu Shobō. 1993. Vol. 5.

Habōhō Kenkyūkai, comp. Habōhō o Dangai-suru: Dai-ichiji, Dai-sanji Habōhō Saiban ni okeru Shōgen. 1984.2 v. *Habōhō Kenkyūkai Bessatsu*.

Habōhō ni Shōkyoku-teki no Keishichō: Jiyūtō Takaha to Kōan Chōsachō wa yakki, *Zaikai* 4/15/1968:19+.

Habōhō o meguru sho-mondai, *Hōritsu Jihō* 68:9(8/1996):6–27.

Habōhō Saiban Tōsō o Sasaeru-kai. *Habōhō to ikani Tatakau ka*. 1971.

Hakai Katsudō Bōshi-hō ni tsuite 40-jō (Sendō-zai) no Gōkensei, *Keisatsu Jihō* 42:8(8/1987):113–129.

Handa, Yūichirō. Yōkai-suru Kōan Chōsachō: Habōhō kaitei no jittai, Gendai Shokan. 1999. 270 p.

Hani, Gorō. *Akuhō to Kokumin no Teikō: Habōhō to ikani tatakau ka*. Hyōronsha. 1970. Ningen no Kenri Sōsho: 5.

Harano, Aki. Kōan Chōsachō ni yoru Hōrei no Kaishaku Kijun no Kōhyō ni tsuite, *Okayama Daigaku Hōgaku Zasshi* 46:1(9/1996):1–15.

Hasebe, Yukio. *Hakai Katsudō Bōshi-hō 40-jō no Gōkensei*, Yūhikaku. 1988. 288 p.

Hasegawa, Masayasu. Habōhō Dai-ichi gō, *Chūō Kōron Rinji Zōkangō*. 3/1953. P. 62+.

Hayama, Takeo. Dantai Kisei Hōan ni Hantai, *Shūkan Hōritsu Shimbun* 11/19/1999:2.

Hayama, Takeo. Habōhō "kaisei" ni Hantai: sensō e no chian dan'atsu hōi ni, *Shūkan Hōritsu Shimbun 6/25/*-1992:2.

Hayashi, Naomichi. Gakumon shisō no Jiyū no tameni, *Keizai* 90(3/2003):71–83.

Hirayama, Munenobu. Hakai Katsudō Bōshi-hō 39-jō oyobi 40-jō no Sendō o shobatsu-suru Kitei to Kempō, *Keisatsu Kenkyū* 63:5(5/19992):42–48.

Hōmu Tōkyoku mo Konwaku, Dare mo wakaranai tsukai kata, *Shūkan Asahi* 10/20/199:28–31.

Hoshino, Yasusaburō. Habōhō Tōjō to Hidaika-suru Chian, *Gendai no Me* 1/1968: 116+.

Hoshino, Yasusaburō. Sengo Chian Rippō no Seitei Katei, *Rinji Zōkan. Hōritsu Jihō* 30/13(12/1958):55–64.

Igarashi, Yoshio. Iki-shi o tou Shisō no Fukken: Habōhō Bengodan Shōgeki Jiken no sono go, *Gendai no Me* 7/1974:238+.

Ichido Kieta Habōhō Tekiyō o fukkatsu-saseta Kōan Chōsachō no Otoko [Kawachi Yūki Jichō], *Shūkan Asahi* 12/29/1995:138–139.

Ichikawa, Masato. Kessha no Jiyū: Tekisei tetsuzuki no hoshō to Hakai Katsudō Bōshi-hō, *Gekkan Hōgaku Kyōshitsu* 189(6/1996):19–23.

Inoue, Masaharu. Habōhō wa han-kakumei rippō ka. *Habōhō Kenkyū* 19(5/73):4–12.

Inoue, Masaharu. Hakai Katsudō Bōshi-hō no Kōzō, *Habōhō Kenkyū* 22(4/75): 20–32.

Inoue, Masaharu. Sabakareru gawa no Ronri: Sengo Minshu-sugi to Habōhō, *Ryūdō* 4/1974:70+.

Imuro, Katsuhiko. Medeia [media] e no Shinrai Kaifuku kakaru posuto [post] Habōhō Hōdō, *Shimbun Ken-kyū* 549(4/1997):20–23.

Ise, Satoshi. Jieitai Hahei to narabu mō hitotsu no Kempō Mondai: Himitsu-ri ni susumu Habōhō Dantai tekiyō e no ugoki, *Sō* 12/1990:140–145.

Ishihara, Tsutomu. Habōhō tekiyō o meguru kakutō no Shiwaku: Hō Chitsujo ka Sayoku Dan'atsu ka, *Toki* 5/1968:74+.

Kagawa, Tatsuo. Hakai Katsudō Bōshi-hō 40-jō no Sendō-zai no Gōkensei, *Hanrei Hyōron* 318(8/1985):61–65.

Kageki-ha Mondai Kenkyūkai. Habōhō tekiyō mondai to Kageki-ha, *Gekkan Chian Fuo-ramu* 2:5(5/1996): 37–46.

Kai, Michitarō. Nihonkoku Kempō no Kiki: Habōhō Saikōsai Hanketsu o hihan-suru. *Habōhō Kenkyū* 70(3/-1991):61–62.

Kaito, Yūichi. Nichi Benren Sōkai de Habōhō Tekiyō Hantai Ketsugi saitaku-sareru. *Kikan Keiji Bengo* 7(7/1996):179.

Kamei, Hiroto. Kyū-fujō-suru Habōhō Kaiseiron, *Habōhō Kenkyū* 70(3/1991):23–32.

Kamijō, Yoshiaki. Ōmu Jiken to Shūkyū Hōjin-hō Kaisei, *Kaikakusha* 425(12/1995): 12–16.

Kaneko, Jinyō. Media Watching: Watakushi no Shimbun Hihyō, Asahi Shimbun ga kakaeru "Ōmu Habōhō Rongi" no Mujun, *Shūkan Gendai* 10/28/1995:70.

Kano, Michitaka. Habōhō to Jinken no Yōgo, *Sekai* 81(9/52):65–69.

Kantō Gakuin Daigaku Hōgakubu Keijihō 4 semi [seminar], Kageki ni Habōhō?, *Masu Komi Shimin* (1) 338 (1/1997):29–35, (2) 339(2/1997):56–71, (3) 340(3/1997):34–39, (4) 341(4/1997):65–70, (5) 342(5/1995): 88–94, (6) 344(7/1997):85–91.

Kawakami, Kazuo. Hakai Katsudō Bōsho-hō Ikenron Hihan, *Keisatsu Kōron* 51:5 (5/1996):24–30.

Kawakami, Kazuo. Shūkyō Hōjin no Kaisan to Hakai Katsudō Bōshi-hō, *Gekkan Keisatsu* 13:9(9/1995):44–45.

Kawasaki, Hideaki. Habōhō ga nokoshita mono, *Hōgaku Seminā* 42:9(9/1997):27–30.

Kimura, Isamu. Shinsetsu-sareru Bassoku Kitei o megutte Habōhō Katsudō e no shi'iteki Bōatsu, *Gendai no Me* 8/1974:114+.

Kinoshita, Satoshi. *Hakai Katsudō Bōshi-hō no Sendō-zai to Hyōgen no Jiyū*. Yūhikaku. 2000. 244 p.

Kitahara, Tokihiko and Tabata Yutaka. *Habōhō Nihon o yurugashita 400-nichi*. Jiji Tsūshinsha. 1997. 261 p. Kōan Chō sachō. *Dai-13-kai Kokkai Hakai Katsudō Bōshi-hō Kankei Kaigiroku*. 69 p. (bessatsu), Dai-ichibu Kōan Chōsachō Shiryō (Shin). 1959. 432 p.

Kōan Chōsachō. *Habōhō Ihan Hikoku Jiken Dai-Isshin Hanketsu-shū*. Kōan Chōsa Shiryō (Shin). 1959. 333 p.

Koga, Kō. Ōmu e no Habōhō Tekiyō, *Mainichi Shimbun* 11/11995.

Koizumi, Keita. Saikōsai Habōhō Sendōzai de Gōken Hanketsu, *Shimbun Kenkyū* 473(12/1990):90–92.

Kojima, Naoki. *Yoru no Kao*. Shikisha. 1957. 250 p.

Kondo, Yasutarō. Habōhō o Tekiyō Ōmu wa kieru ka, *AERA* 12/25/1995:20.

Kongo no Gimon: Ōmu ga nokoshita itsutsu no Dai-Gimon: Konkai mo kara-furi hisshi!? Kōan ga koshitsu shitsuzukeru Habōhō Tekiyō no Narai, *DENiM* 8/1995:102.

Kumakura, Takeshi. Habōhō Saiban no Riron to sono Tekiyo Jōkyō, *Hōritsu Jihō* 6/1970: 184–191. Special issue on Chian to Jinken.

Maeda, Rō. Habōhō wa Jinken o assatsu-suru, *Masukomi Shimin* 334(9/1996):67–70.

Maeda, Rō. Narita Kūkō Mondai to Habōhō, *Hō to Minshushugi* 247(5/1990):72–73.

Maeno, Ikuzō. Habōhō to Kempō, *Kikan Kagaku to Shisō* 74(10/1989):97–122.

Matsuda, Kota. Ōmu de Hitsuyō ni Yoron Yūdō o nerau, *Uwasa no Shinsō* 12/1995: 46–51.

Matsui, Yukio. Habōhō 39, 40-jō no Sendō-zai no Gōken-sei: Shibuya bōdō jiken jōkokushin hanketsu, *Hōgaku Seminā* 36:6(6/1991):126.

Miyaoka, Yū. *Kōan Chōsachō no Bōsō*. Gendai Shokan. 1996. 236 p.

Miyauchi, Yutaka. Habōhō Saiban no Ronri, *Hōritsū Jihō* 38–5(4/1966):47–56.

Miyauchi, Yutaka. Iki o fukikaeshita Habōhō, *Sekai* 171(3/1960):74–78.

Miyauchi, Yutaka. Kyoto Habōhō Jiken no Igi, *Hōritsu Jihō* 29–7(7/1957): 88–93.

Miyauchi, Yutaka. Sengo Chian Rippō no Hatten to Tokuhitsu, *Hōritsu Jihō* Rinji Zōkan 30–13(12/1958):29–54.

Miyauchi, Yutaka. Sengo Chian Rippō-shi, *Aichi Daigaku Hōkei Ronshū* 21/22(3/1958):107–158; 23/24(11/1958):69–131.

Miyauchi, Yutaka. Terorizumu to Habōhō, *Hōritsu Jihō* 11(8/1961):46–49.

Mizushima, Chōho. Ōmu Mondai e no ichi shiten, *Hōgaku Seminā* 41:2(2/1996): 6–10.

Mōri, Harumitsu. Sendō-zai no Gōken-sei ni tsuite, *Hōritsu no Hiroba* 44:3(3/1991): 56–62.

Mori, Hideki. Habōhō 40-jō no Sendō-zai no Gōken-sei: Okinawa Dē Habōhō Jiken jōkokushin Hanketsu, *Hōgaku Seminā* 6:3(3/1991):112.

Murai, Toshio. Habōhō Dantai Kaisan Shobun Seikyū Kikyaku o megutte, *Hōritsu Jihō* 69:6(5/1997):2–6.

Murai, Toshio. Jinken kara Habōhō o kangaeru, *Hōritsu Jihō* 68:9(8/1996):6–8.

Murai, Toshio. Habōhō Mondai no Sonzai Igi to Tōchō Hōan, *Hogaku Seminā* 42:10(10/1997):26–30.

Murakami, Hiroshi. Shūkyō Dantai Arefu Kansatsu Shobun Torikeshi Seikyū Jiken Hanketsu, *Hōrei Kaisetsu Shiryō Sōran* 239(12/2001):108–109.

Murakami, Nobuo. Habōhō Kaisei wa Kokumin-teki Rongi kara, *Asahi Shimbun* 10/25/1998.

Nagaoka, Yoshiyuki. Habōhō de Toshokan no Jushusei wa dōnaru ka, *Hōgaku Seminā* 41:9(9/1996):10–13.

Nakamura, Ken'ichi. *Gendai Shakai to Chianhō*. Iwanami Shoten. 1970. Iwanami Shinsho(Ao):766.

Nakanishi, Akio. Kodomo wa kurubekarazu, *Gendai* 12/1995:23–25.

Nakayama Ken'ichi. Chian Rippō (Tokushū: Sengo hō-seido no 20-nen), *Jurisuto* 361(1/1967):226–238.

Natsume, Fumio. Chian Keihō no Kenkyū: Sengo chian rippō no kihon-teki kōzō, *Aichi Daigaku Hōkei Ronshū* 8 parts:#31–35, 39–41.

Naze, Ima Habōhō ka, *Habōhō Kenkyū,* 73[last issue](3/1992):6–69.

Naze, Ima Habōhō ka, *Hōgaku Seminā* 41:3(3/1996):4–15.

News File: "Ōmu o riyū ni" wa doko made yurusareru beki na no ka, *Shūkan Playboy* 10/17/1995:56–57.

News Interface: Nuka ka Denka no Hōtō Habōhō Tekiyō ni yureru, *Asahi Jānaru* 11/9/1990:100.

News Scramble: Abunai ze, Habōhō no ranyō!, *Shūkan Playboy* 11/20/1990:52–53.

Nihon Bengoshi Rengōkai. *Ōmu Shinrikyō ni taisuru Habōhō Kikyaku Kettei no Kentō Hōkokusho*. 1996. 64 p.

Nihon Bengoshi Rengōkai Kaichō Seimei/Danwa: Tokushū, Nichi-Ben-Ren no hatsugen 1996–1997, *Jiyū To Seigi* 48:8(8/1997)67–152.

Nihon Kyōsantō Chūō Iinkai. Shuppankyoku. *Habōhō to Kōan Chōsachō no Hanzai*. Tokyo. 1989. 157 p.

Nishio, Kanji. Doitsu no Kessha-hō to Nihon no Habōhō, *Gekkan Chian Fuo-ramu* 4:4(4/1998):59–68.

Nishioka, Masao. Hakai Katsudō Bōshi-hō no Katsu: Hō no shushi, kisei, shobatsu taishō kako no jirei tō, *Keisatsu Jihō* 27–5(5/1972)~27–7(7/1972).

Numata, Inajirō. Meidei [May Day] Jiken no Rekishi-teki Imi, *Kaizō* 33–16(1952–11):108–113.

Oda, Susumu. Sabaibaru [Survival] *Shinrigaku*: Dai-ni no Ōmu o manukanu tame ni Habōhō Tekiyō wa Zettai Fukaketsu, *DECIDE* 10/1995:70–71.

Oda, Susumu. Shūkyō-teki terorizumu no Kiki to Ōmu Shinrikyō: Habōhō tekiyō hantairon no haikei to sono hihan, *Gekkan Chian Fuo-ramu* 3:1(1/1997):24–32.

Odanaka, Satoki. Habōhō e no puroro-gu[prologue]: Ōmu bemmei tetsuzuki kaishi ni itaru purosesu [process] no kansatsu, *Keihō no Shosō, Nakayama Ken'ichi Sensei Koki Shukuga Rombunshū:4.*Seibundō. 1972. pp. 245–272.

Odanaka, Satoki. Habōhō no Shikumi to Mondaiten, *Hōritsu Jihō* 68:9(8/1996): 21–24.

Odanaka, Satoki. Habōhō to yū Muhō, *Sekai* 616(12/1995):225–231.

Odanaka, Satoki. Habōhō wa hatsudōsareru ka, *Sekai* 626(9/1996):193–198.

Odanaka, Satoki. Risei to Rentai o hakai-suru Habōhō, *Masukomi Shimin* 338(1/1997):21–28.

Ogasawara, Tadahiko. Habōhō tekiyō to Ōmu Shinja, *Hōritsu Jihō* 68:9(8/1996): 25–27.
Okudaira, Yasuhiro. Genkō-hō Haishi koso Rippōfu no Yakuwari, *Asahi Shimbun* 10/10/1995.
Okudaira, Yasuhiro. *Habōhō de nani ga warui?: Jiyū o mamoru tame no Takaku-teki Shiten*. 1996.
Okudaira, Yasuhiro. Habōhō Mondai o meggutte, *Jurisuto* 1087(4/1/1996):96–103.
Okudaira, Yasuhiro. *Kore ga Habōhō*. Kadensha. 1996. 218 p.
Ōmu Habōhō Bengodan, comp. *Ōmu Habōhō Jiken no Kiroku: Kaisan Seikyū kara Kikyaku made*. Shakai Shiso-sha. 1998. 425 p.
Ōmu no Habōhō no suimen-ka, *Sandé Mainichi* 10/15/1995:26–30.
Ōmu Shinrikyō ni taisuru Habōhō Kikyaku Kettei no Kentō Hōkokusho, *Jiyū to Seigi* 51:8(8/2000):71.
Osui Kokkai e nagaru komu Habō hōan ni tsunagaru? Edogawa Rantō Jiken, *Shūkan Yomiuri*. 6/29/1953:14.
Saragi Tokuji. *Ware kaku tatakaeri: Habōhō tōsō 32-nen*. Jōkyō Shuppan. 2001. 398 p.
Sasaki, Masataka. Ōmu Shinrikyō ni taisuru Habōhō tekiyō Mondai, *Gekkan Chian Fuo-ramu* 3:5(5/1997): 76–84.
Sassa, Atsuyuki. Genkōhō no Tekiyō wa "hitsuyō aku", *Asahi Shimbun* 10/10/1995.
Satō, Michio. Ōmu ni Habōhō no Tekiyō wa muri, *Shūkan Asahi* 11/10/1995:59.
Satō, Michio. Habōhō Tekiyō: Zen-Kenjichō wa kō kataru, *Shokun* 12/1995:50–59.
Satō, Tachio. Ōmu Kyōdan ni taisuru Hakai Katsudō Bōsho-hō tekiyō no Mondaiten: Kempō 20-jō no gen-ten ni sakanobotta rongi o, *Kokkai Geppō* 42:564(12/1995): 28–32.
Satō, Toshiaki. Habōhō Hantai Tōsō no zengo, *Jiyū Sekai* 9/1966:102+
Serizawa, Hitoshi. Habōhō Bemmei Tetsuzuki ni tachiatte, *Hōgaku Seminā* 42:12(12/1997):14–18.
Serizawa, Hitoshi. Ōmu e no Habōhō Dantai Tekiyō Kikyaku, *Gekkan Hōgaku Kyōshitsu* 203(8/1997):26–31.
Shijō Hajime. Tsui ni kessai-sareta Ōmu ni Habōhō, *Shūkan Bunshun* 10/5/1995: 30–32.
Shimbun Kurippa: Ōmu no Saihatsu Bōshi ni Seifu wa nani o shita ka, *Ushio* 12/1995: 258–259.
Shimizu, Mutsu. Hakai Katsudō Bōshi-hō 40-jō no Sendō-zai no Gōken-sei, *Shōwa 60-nendo Jūyō Hanrei Kaisetsu Jurisuto Rinji Zōkan* 862(6/1986):20–21.
Shimizu, Mutsu. "Meihaku ni shite Genzai no Kiken" Gensoku no tekiyō o meguru Mondai, *Kōhō Kenkyū* 22(8/1960):137–146.
Shinsō Kairyū: Ōmu Shinrikyō e no Habōhō Tekiyō Mondai de Chūmoku sareru Kōan Chōsachō Jinji, *Zaikai Tembō* 10/1995:46–47.
Shinsō Kairyū: Ōmu Shinrikyō e no Habōhō Tekiyō de Risutora [restructuring] saketai Kōan Chōsachō, *Zaikai Tembō* 12/1995:48.
Shiroto, Makoto. Habōhō to Daijōsai, *Sekai* 547(11/1990):15–18.
Shōten: Zen-Gakuren no Habōhō, *Gekkan Jiji* 5/1968:147+.
Soboku na Gimon Q&A: Habōhō Tekiyō de Ōmu wa dōnaru?, *FLASH* 10/17/1995: 20–21.
Sudō, Haruo. Watakushi no Terebi Hihyō: Habōhō, Kōan Chōsachō o sambi-suru Bamgumi no Fukenshiki *Shūkan Gendai* 11/4/1995:77.
Sugimura, Toshimasa, et al. *Sengo Himitsu Keisatsu no Jittai*. San-ichi Shobō. 1960. 496 p.
Sugita, Akira. *Habōhō to Chian Iji-hō: Gendai ni okeru Kokka to Kakumei*. Zenshinsha. 1987. 405 p.
Shūkyō Hōjin vs Habōhō no Anyaku, *Shūkan Bunshun* 10/19/1995:30–33.
Takada, Kiyoshi, comp. *Kokusai Kankei Fukkatsu: Habōhō*. SSB Shuppankai. 1992. Shimbun Shūsei Showa-shi no Shōgen:27(1952). Series compiled by Miyazaki Yoshimasa, et al.

Takano, Minoru. 1952-nen Habōhō funsai no Tatakai, *Habōhō Kenkyū* 19(5/75): 13–21.
Takeda, Masahiro. Habōhō no Dantai Kisei wa kanō ka: Ōmu Shinrikyō e no tetsuzuki o kenshō-suru, *Hō-gaku Seminā* 41:11(11/1996):12–16.
Takimoto, Tarō. *Habōhō to Ōmu Shinrikyō*. Iwanami Shoten. 1996. 60 p. Iwanami Pamphlet:398.
Tanaka, Jirō, et al comp. *Sengo Seiji Saiban Shiroku*. Daiichi Hōki Shuppan. 1970. 5 v.
Tanaka, Masaaki. Kyokusa Tero Shūdan ni Habōhō o Tekiyō seyo. *Sembō* 1/1991: 14–17.
Tawaratani, Toshiyuki. Habōhō to Shūkyō Dantai, *Hōrei* Nyūsu 30:9(9/1995):14–15.
Tawaratani, Toshiyuki. Kaisan Seikyū no Kikyaku, *Hōrei Nyūsu* 32:4(4/1997):16–17.
Tawaratani, Toshiyuki. Sendō-zai no Hanketsu to Dantai no Kisei, *Hōrei Nyūsu* 25:12(12/1990):30–31.
TEMPO Robī: Koshi kudake ka, Shūkyō Hōjin-hō Kaisei to Habōhō Tekiyō, *Shūkan Shinchō* 10/26/1995:22–23.
This Week:Tāgetto wa Chūkakuha, *Shūkan Bunshun 10/11/1990:* Wagatsuma, Sakae. *Nihon Seiji Saiban Shiroku. Dai*-ichi Hōki Shuppan. 1968. 5 v.
Torii, Kiyokazu. Hakai Katsudō Bōshi-hō ni miru Dantai Kisei to Kessha no Jiyū, *Ritsumeikan Hōgaku* 243/244(3/1996):121–146.
Torii, Kiyokazu. Ugokidashita Habōhō, sono Kiken-sei: kenshō, shimin shakai no anzen to hō, *Hōgaku Seminā* 241–242 (2/1996):38–43.
Tsubouchi, Toshihiko. Habōhō 40-jō no Sendō-zai no Kiki toshite no Seishitsu, *Keisatsugaku Ronbunshū* 40:10(10/1987):226–237.
Tsuchimoto, Takeshi. Dantai Kisei Shobun ni tsuite no ichi kōsatsu: Ōmu Shinkrikyō jiken ni kanren shite, *Hōritsu no Hiroba* 50:6(6/1997):37–45.
Tsuchimoto, Takeshi. Ōmu Shinrikyō Jiken o meguru Hōteki Sho-mondai, *Kenshū* 576(6/1996):3–20.
Ueda Seikichi. *Chian Rippō to Saiban*. Shin-Nihon Shuppansha. 1990. 230 p. Shin-Nihon Shinsho:397.
Uemaura, Takuya. Habōhō Ōmu Shinrikyō ni tekiyō-sarezu, *Keisatsu Jihō* 52:5(5/1997):94–98.
Ugoki dashita Habōhō: Tokushū, *Hōritsu Jihō* 41–13(11/1969):4–63.
Uzaki, Masahiro. Amerika ni okeru Chian Rippō no Keisei to Tenkai: Habōhō no rekishi-teki haikei, *Habōhō Kenkyū* 62(7/1988):4–19.
Uzaki, Masahiro. Habōhō Dantai Kisei Tekiyō e no Gimon, *Hōritsu Jihō* 68:3(3/1996): 2–5.
Uzaki, Masahiro. Hakai Katsudō Bōshi-hō Dantai Kisei no Iken-sei, *Hōritsu Jihō* 68:9(8/1996):16–20.
Uzaki, Masahiro. Hakai Katsudō Bōshi-hō Sendō Kitei no Gōken-sei, *Heisei 2-nendo Jūyō Hanrei Kaisetsu (Jurisuto Rinji Zōkan* 980(6/1991):22–23.
Wakasa, Masaru. Hakai Katsudō Bōshi-hō no Sendō to Hyōgen no Jiyū, *Kenshū* 596(2/1998):57–58.
Watanabe, Osamu. Habōhō wa naze dekitaka, ikani tsukaware yō toshita ka, *Hōritsu Jihō* 68:9(8/1996):9–15.
Yaguchi, Toshiaki. Tokubetsu Saibansho, *Kempō Hanrei Hyakusen* (2) *Bessatsu Jurisuto* 131(10/1994):380–381.
Yamaguchi-gumi ga osoreru Ōmu no "Ano koto": Murai Kambu shisatsu Kōhan no yamikata, *Shūkan Taishū* 10/2/-1995:40–43.
Yamanaka, Yukio. Ōmu e no Habōhō, sono kakusareta ito, *Shūkan Kinyōbi* 9/29/1995:18–19.
Yamashita, Susumu. Shūkyō Hōjin-hō to Hakai Katsudō Bōshi-hō, *THE21* 12/1995: 74–75.

Yamauchi, Toshihiro. Habōhō no Iken-sei no Sai-kentō, *Hōgaku Seminā* 42:11(11/1997):8–12.
Yanagisawa, Akio. Habōhō o ikikaireraseru Jidai Sakugo, *Zen'ei* 667(12/1995): 126–137.
Yasaki, Yasuhisa. Iitai koto o itte shimau Taikyū Tsūshin 'Akurei' o yomikaeshite wakatta koto, *So* 12/1995:132–135.
Yokota, Morihiro. Shūkyō Dantai Arefu Kansatsu Shobun Torikeshi Shobun Seikyū Jiken Hanketsu, *Hōgaku Seminā* 47:1(1/2002):107.

B. *General*

1. *In Japanese*

Araki, Yoshinobu. *Senryōki ni okeru Kyōsan-sugi Undō*. Ashi Shobō. 1993. 241 p. RFP Sōsho:3.
Hiwatari, Nobuhiro. *Sengo Nihon no Shijō to Seiji*. Tokyo Daigaku Shuppankai. 1991. 279 p.
Hōritsu wa dare ga tsukuru [Zadankai], *Hōritsu Jihō* 25:1(1/52):24–37.
Hosoya, Chihirō and Watanabe Jōji, eds. *Taigai Seisaku Kettei no Nichi-Bei Hikaku* (A comparison of Japan and the U.S. in foreign policy decisionmaking).University of Tokyo Press. 1977. 484 p.
Ikeda, Masaaki. Rippō Katei no Mondaiten, *Gendai no Rippō*. Iwanami Shoten. 1967. pp. 272–283.
Inomata, Kōzō. Teikō no Keifu. Tokyo. 1964. Sakai Shoten. 402 p.
Ishida, Takeshi. *Gendai Soshiki-ron*. Tokyo. Tokyo Daigaku Shuppankai. 1968. 378 p.
Iwai, Tomoaki. *Rippō Katei*. Tokyo Daigaku Shuppankai. 1988. 244 p. Gendai Seijigaku Sōsho:12.
Kaneko, Jin'yō. *Kanryō Shihai*. Kōdansha. 1994. 372 p.
Kawaguchi, Hiroyuki. *Kanryō Shihai no Kōzō*. Kōdansha. 1987. 271 p.
Kawanaka, Nikō. Gendai no Kanryōsei. Chūō Daigaku Shuppanbu. 1972. 235 p.
Kindai Nihon Kenkyūkai. *Kanryōsei no Keisei to Tenkai*. Yamakawa Shuppansha. 1986. 327 p.
Kosaka, Masataka. *Saishō Yoshida Shigeru*. Chūō Kōronsha. 1968. 260 p.
Masuda, Hiroshi. *Kōshoku Tsuihō: sandai seiji pāji [purge] no Kenkyū*. Tokyo Daigaku Shuppankai. 1996. 309 p.
Masuda, Hiroshi. *Kōshoku Tsuihōron*. Iwanami Shoten. 1998. 343 p.
Masumi, Junnosuke. *Nihon Seijishi*. Tokyo Daigaku Shuppankai. 1988. 4 v.
Misawa, Shigeo. Seisaku Kettei Katei no Gaikan, *Nempō Seijigaku: Gendai Nihon no Seitō to Kanryō*. Iwanami Shoten. 1967. pp. 14–18.
Miyake, Ichirō. Nihon Naikaku no Seiji Shakai-teki Kōsei: Itō Naikaku yori Kishi Naikaku made, *Jimbun Gakuhō* 20(1964):213–232.
Morito, Tatsuo. *Shisō no Henreki. Tokyo*. Shunjusha. 1972. 2 v.
Murakawa, Ichirō. *Seisaku Kettei Katei*. Kyōikusha. 1979. 237 p. Kyōikusha Shinsho:121.
Muramatsu, Michio. *Sengo Nihon no Kanryōsei*. Tōyō Keizai Shimpōsha. Tokyo. 1981. 343 p.
Muramatsu, Michio, Itō Mitsutoshi, Tsujinaka Yutaka. *Sengo Nihon no Atsuryoku Dantai*. Tōyō Keizai Shimpō. 1986. 283 p.
Naisei Mondai Kenkyūkai. *Kanryō no Keifu: Kenryoku no Za ni iru Hitotachi*. Kōbunsha. 1955. 223 p.
Nakamura, Akio. *Nihon Seiji no Seisaku Katei*. Aishi Shobō. 1996. 229 p. RFP Sōsho:4.
Nakamura, Akira. *Kanryō-sei to Nihon no Seiji*.Hokuju Shuppansha. 1997. 242 p.

Nakamura, Akira. *Nihon no Seisaku Katei [1965–1981]*. Hokuju Shuppansha. 1989. 289 p.
Nakamura, Mutsuo. *Gi'in Rippō no Kenkyū*. Shinzansha. 1993. 614 p.
Nakano, Minoru. *Nihongata Seisaku Kettei no Hen'yō*. Tōyō Keizai Shimpōsha. 1988. 319 p.
Nihon Keizai Shimbunsha, comp. *Jimintō Seichōkai*. Nihon Keizai Shimbunsha. 1983. 234 p.
Nihon Kyōsantō Chūō Iinkai Shuppanbu. *Kyōsantō* to Kōan Chōsachō no Hanzai. 1989. 157 p.
Nihon no Naikaku. Shin-Hyōron. 1981. 3 v.
Nihon Seiji Gakkai, comp. *Sengo Nihon no Seiji Katei*. Iwanami Shoten. 1953. 244 p.
Nihon Seiji Gakkai. *Nihon no Atsuryoku Dantai*. Iwanami Shoten. 1960 Annual Report. 266 p.
Nihon Shimbun Kyōkai. Nihon Shimbun Kyōkai Jū'nen-shi. 1956. 924 p.
Nihon Shimbun Kyōkai. *Shimbun no Jiyū*. Nihon Shimbun Kyōkai. 1952. 217 p.
Nojima, Teiichirō. *Ryokufūkai Jūhachi-nen shi*. Ryokufūkai-shi Hensan Iinkai.1971. 535 p.
Oka Yoshitake. *Gendai Nihon no Seiji Katei*. Iwanami Shoten. 1958. 517, 106 p.
Rekishigaku Kenkyūkai. *Sengo Nihonshi* [1945–1960]. Tokyo. Aoki Shoten. 1961. 5 v.
Rippo, *Hō Shakaigaku*: 6 (Sociology of Law). Nihon Hō Shakaigaku. 1955. pp. 81–144.
Sakamoto, Yoshikage, et al., comp. *Nihon Senryō Bunken Mokuroku*. Nihon Gakujutsu Shinkōkai. 1972. 373 p. Sakamoto, Yoshikazu and Robert E. Ward, eds. *Nihon Senryō no Kenkyū*. Tokyo Daigaku Shuppankai. 1987.
Satō, Tatsuo. Hōritsu ga umareru made, *Hōritsu Jihō* 25:1(1/52):45–50.
Shinobu, Seizaburō. *Sengo Nihon Seiji-shi*, 1945–52. 1967. 4 v.
Shisetsu Hōsei Ikenkyoku. Shūdan Ji'i torishimari han, *Jurisuto* 15(8/1/52):28–33.
Shūdan Ji'i Undō-tō no Chitsujo Hoji ni kansuru Hōritsuan, *Hōritsu Jihō* 24:6(265)(6/52):84–85.
Shūdan Ji'i Undō-tō no Chitsujo Hoji ni kansuru Horitsuan, *Rōdō Hōritsu Jumpō* 95(6/15/52):21–23.
Sōhyō. Hōki Taisakubu. *Senzen Sengo no Chian Rippō*. Sōhyō. 1956. 86 p. Sōhyō Hōtai Shiryō:18 (7/1/56).
Sone, Eki. *Watakushi no memoāru* (My memoirs). Nikkan Kōgyō Shimbunsha. 1975.
Sugimoto, Toshio. *Senryō Hiroku*. Mainichi Shimbunsha. 2 v.
Takano, Minoru. *Nihon no Rōdō Undō*. Tokyo. Iwanami Shoten. 1958. 234 p.
Takeda, Jun. Nihon no Gaikō Seisaku Kettei ni okeru Kanchō-kan Chōsei, *Kokusai Mondai*. 12/76:17.
Takemae, Eiji. *Amerika Tai-Nichi Rōdō Seisaku no Kenkyū*. 1970.
Takemae, Eiji. *Sengo Rōdō Kaikaku: GHQ Rōdō Seisakushi*. Tokyo. Tokyo Daigaku Shuppankai. 1982. 452 p.
Takemae, Eiji. *Senryō Sengo-shi*. Iwanami Shoten.1990. 432 p.
Takemae, Eiji. *Shōgen Nihon Senryōshi: GHQ Rōdōka no Gunzō*. Tokyo. Iwanami Shoten. 351 p.
Tsuchiya, Masazō. Iinkai Seido:Shingi no Semmonkai Kōritsuka. Kyōiku Shuppan. 1969. 398 p.
Uchida, Mitsuru, ed. *Seiji Katei*. Sanrei Shobō. 1986. 298 p.
Wada, Shōjirō 'Hō' o meguru tōsō no sho-yōsō to 'Hō no Seiritsu', *Jurisito* 13(7/1/52): 2–6.
Yomiuri Shimbunsha Seijibu. *Sōri Daijin*. Yomiuri Shimbunsha. 1971. 333 p.
Yoshida Naikaku Kankōkai. *Yoshida Naikaku*. Yoshida Naikaku Kankōkai. 1954. 686 p.
Yoshida, Shigeru. *Kaisō Jū'nen*. Shinchōsha. 1957–58. 4 v.

2. *In English*

Allinson, Gary D. and Frank Upham. *Bargaining, Not Dominance: How Politics are Negotiated in Japan*. Paper presented at Woodrow Wilson Center. Washington, DC. 1990. 9 p.

Allinson, Gary D. *Japan's Postwar History*. Ithaca, NY. Cornell University Press. 1997. 207 p.

Allinson, Gary D., and Yasunori Sone, eds. *Political Dynamics in Contemporary Japan*. Ithaca, NY. Cornell University Press. 1993. 311 p.

Angel, Robert C. *Japan's Prime Minister: The Individual and the Office*. Unpublished paper given at the Southern Political Science Association. Nov. 1987.

Angel, Robert C. *Supra-Ministerial Policy Coordination in Japan*. Unpublished paper given at the American Political Science Association Convention, 1987.

Apter, David E. and Nagayo Sawa. *Against the State: Political and Social Protest in Japan*. Cambridge. Harvard University Press. 1984. 271 p.

Baerwald, Hans H. Committees in the Japanese Diet [in 1960s], Committees in Legislatures, A comparative Analysis. Durham. NC. Duke University Press. 1979.

Baerwald, Hans H. *Japan's Parliament: an introduction*. New York. Cambridge University Press. 1974. 155 p.

Baerwald, Hans H. *Purge of Japanese Leaders under the Occupation*. Berkeley, CA. University of California Press. 1959. 111 p.

Bailey, Stephen Kemp. *Congress makes a Law: The story behind the Employment Act of 1946*. New York. Columbia University Press. 1950. 282 p.

Battistini, Lawrence Henry. *The Postwar Student Struggle in Japan*. Tokyo & Rutland VT. Charles E. Tuttle Co. 1956. 167 p.

Beer, Lawrence Ward. *Freedom of Expression in Japan: A study in comparative law, politics, and society*. Kodansha International. 1984. 415 p.

Cohen, Theodore. *Remaking Japan: the American Occupation as New Deal*. Ed by Herbert Passin. New York. Free Press. 1987. 533 p.

Dower, John W. *Embracing Defeat*. New York. W.W. Norton & Co. 1999. 676 p.

Dower, John W. *Empire and Aftermath*. Cambridge, MA, Harvard University, Council on East Asian Studies. 1979. 618 p.

Dower, John W. *Japan in War and Peace*. New York. New Press. 1993. 368 p.

Dower, John W. Occupied Japan as History and Occupation History as Politics, *AAS Journal* 43:2(2/75):485–504.

Duke, Benjamin. *Japan's Militant Teachers*. Honolulu. University Press of Hawaii. 1973. 236 p.

Eisenstadt, S.N. and Eyal Ben-Ari, eds. *Japanese Models of Conflict Resolution*. London. Kegan Paul International. 1990. 238 p.

Elving, Ronald D. *Conflict and Compromise: how Congress makes the law* [Family and Medical Leave Act of 1993]. New York. Simon & Shuster. 1995. 320 p.

Finn, Richard B. *Winner in Peace: MacArthur, Yoshida, and Postwar Japan*. Berkeley. University of California Press. 1992. 413 p.

Flanagan, Scott C. *Pathologies of Decision-Making in Prewar Japan*. 1973. 119 p. [Unpublished paper given to Japan Studies Seminar at Georgetown University, 4/28/73].

Frost, Peter. *General MacArthur and the Concept of "Reverse Course" in the Allied Occupation of Japan*. 1985. 38 p. [Unpublished paper given at the Washington & Southeast Regional Seminar on Japan, 2/16/85].

Goodman, Grant K. comp. *The American Occupation of Japan: a retrospective view*. Lawrence, KN. Center for East Asian Studies. University of Kansas. c1968. 41 p. International Studies, East Asian Series. Research Publication #2.

Gordon, Andrew. *Postwar Japan as History*. Berkeley, CA. University of California Press. 1993. 496 p.

Gross, Betram M. *The Legislative Struggle: A study in social combat.* New York. McGraw-Hill Book Co. 1953. 472 p.
Hirose, Michisada. Pressure Groups in Japanese Politics, *Japan Echo* 11:4(84):61–67.
Hosoya, Chihiro. Characteristics of the Foreign Policy Decisionmaking system in Japan, *World Politics* 26:3(4/1973):353–369.
Ishida, Takeshi, ed., et al. *Democracy in Japan.* Pittburgh, PA. University of Pittsburgh Press. 1989. 354 p.
Itoh, Hiroshi, Lawrence Beer, comp/tr. *The Constitutional Case Law of Japan: selected Supreme Court decisions, 1961–1970.* Seattle, WA. University of Washington Press. 1978. 283 p. [Contains one case on Habōhō]
Kim, Paul S. Japan's Civil Service System: Its structure, personnel and politics. New York. Greenwood Press. 1988. 193 p.
Koh, B.C. *Japan's Administrative Elite.* Berkeley. University of California Press. 1991. 312 p.
Kōsaka, Masataka. *100 Million Japanese: The Postwar Experience.* Tokyo. Kodansha. 1972. 282 p.
Krauss, Ellis G. ed, et al. *Conflict in Japan.* Honolulu. University of Hawaii Press. 1984. 417 p.
Krauss, Ellis S. *Hakuchū Kokkai: Toward the Institutionalization of Conflict Management in the Japanese Diet.* 1979. 71, 13 p. [Unpublished paper given at the 2nd workshop on "Conflict in Japan", Hawaii, 3/24–25/79].
Kyōgoku, Jun'ichi. *The Political Dynamics of Japan.* University of Tokyo Press. 1987(?). 250 p.
Langer, Paul F. *The Japanese Communists and their Struggle for Power.* The Rand Corporation. 1962. 39 p.
Leavell, James Berry III. *The Development of the Modern Japanese Police System: transition from Tokugawa to Meiji.* 1975 PhD dissertation at Duke University.
Levine, Solomon Bernard. *Industrial Relations in Postwar Japan.* Urbana, IL. University of Illinois Press. 1958. 200 p.
Lewis, Michael Lawrence. *Rioters and Citizens: Mass Protest in Imperial Japan.* Berkeley, CA. University of Californix Press. 1990. 314 p.
Luney, Percy R., ed. *Japanese Constitutional Law.* Tokyo. University of Tokyo Press. 1993. 340 p.
Maki, John M. Japan's Subversive Activities Prevention Law, The Western Political Quarterly 6:3(9/53):489–511.
Matsumura, Janice. *More than a Momentary Nightmare: the Yokohama Incident and Wartime Japan.* Ithaca. Cornell University Press. 1998. 172 p.
Moore, Joe. *Japanese Workers and the Struggle for Power, 1945–47.* Madison. University of Wisconsin Press. 1983. 305 p.
*Occupation of Japan—the impact of the Korean War.*The General Douglas MacArthur Foundation. 1990. 189 p. The Proceedings of the 7th Symposium, 1986.
Oppler, Alfred C. *Legal Reform in Occupied Japan: A Participant Looks Back.* Princeton. Princeton University Press. 1976. 345 p.
Park, Yung H. *Bureaucrats and Ministers in Contemporary Japanese Government.* Berkeley. University of California. Institute of East Asian Studies. Center for Japanese Studies. 1986. 192 p. Japan Research Monograph:8.
Scalapino, Robert A. *The Japanese Communist Movement, 1920–66.* Berkeley. University of California Press. 1967. 412 p.
Smith, Dennis B. *Japan since 1945: the rise of an economic superpower.* New York. St. Martin's Press. 1995. 180p.
Tsukahira, George. *Postwar Evolution of Communistry Strategy in Japan.* Center for International Studies. Massachusetts Institute of Technology. 1954.
Ward, Robert E. and Frank Joseph Shulman, eds. *The Allied Occupation of Japan, 1945–1952: An Annotated Bibliography of Western Language Materials.* Chicago. American Library Association. 1974. 887 p.

Ward, Robert E. and Yoshikazu Sakamoto, eds. *Democratizing Japan: The Allied Occupation.* 1987. Honolulu. University of Hawaii Press. 1987. 496 p. The Japanese version of this book is *Nihon Senryō no Kenkyū,* Tōdai Shuppankai. 1987.

Ward, Robert E., ed. *Political Development in Modern Japan.* Princeton. Princeton Princeton University Press. 1968. 637 p.

Williams, Justin. *Japan's Political Revolution under MacArthur: A Participant's Account.* Athens, GA. University of Georgia Press. 1979. 305 p.

Wolfe, Robert. *Americans as Proconsuls: United States Military Government in Germany and Japan, 1944–52.* Carbondale, IL. Southern Illinois University Press. 1984. 563 p.

C. *Studies on Japanese Policy-making*

In preparing this section, I surveyed the *Far Eastern Quarterly, Journal of Asian Studies, Journal of Japanese Studies, AAS Bibliographies* (the published volumes to 1991), and the *Newsletter on Japanese Political Research, Rebaesan* (Leviathan) #1, 4–24, Nempō Seijigaku (1950–1999) annual reports—all in LC. My objective in making this survey was to try to find specific studies on the decisionmaking process in the GOJ and the legislative process in the Diet for 1945–52 as a basis for comparing their findings with my study. Unfortunately, I found essentially nothing for this period except for *Shakai Kagaku Kiyō 1953* in Japanese. This study published seminar findings on the legislative process on how five laws were created. While this was probably not a "decisionmaking policy process study" like those of the 1970s+ it is an example that Japanese scholars were interested in this approach in the mid-1950s. I also found the following useful reviews in English:

Fukui, Haruhiro. Economic Planning in Postwar Japan: A case study in policy making [1945–70], *Asian Survey* 12:4(4/72):327–348.

Tokyo Daigaku, Kyōyō Gakubu, Shakai Kagaku-ka, comp. Sengo Jūyō Rippō no Rippō Katei Kenkyū, *Shakai Kagaku Kiyō,* 1953.Tokyo Daigaku Shuppan-kai. pp. 1–230. [case studies on anti-monopoly law, labor law, electricity development law, agricultural land, and family relations law]

I did find a substantial number of case studies in English and Japanese on various aspects of the Japanese government's operational processes from about the 1960s onwards. I decided to list my findings under "2. Selected Case Studies" below to show the range of these studies and because I have not found, in this search, an integrated list of case studies. I did find the following review articles on the study of the policymaking process in Japan in English:

Fukui, Haruhiro. Studies in Policy Making: A Review of the Literature, *Policy Making in Contemporary Japan.* T.J. Pempel, ed. Cornell University Press. 1977. pp. 22–59.

Goodwin, Crauford D. Public Policy Research in Japan: A coming golden age?, CGP Newsletter 23(Autumn 1999). pp. 3–5.

Hayao, Kenji. Literature on Policy Making in Japan. *The Japanese Prime Minister.* University of Pittsburgh Press. 1993. Pp. 6–14.

Richardson, Bradley M. Policymaking in Japan: An Organizing Perspective, *Policymaking in Contemporary Japan.* T.J. Pempel, ed. Cornell University Press. 1977. pp. 239–268.

and two review essays in Japanese:

Iwai, Tomoaki. Gendai Nihon ni okeru Seisaku Kateiron Moderu [model], *Leviathan* Rinji Zōkan:(1992 Sum): 170–192.

Sone, Yasunori. Kawaru Seiji Kawaru Seijigaku: Nihon Seijigaku no saikin no Henka, *Leviathan*:1(1987 Fall):161–173.

Hikaku, Hyōka, Kadai, [concluding chapter in] *Chūō Shōchō no seisaku keisei katei: Nihon kanryō-sei no kaibō.* Chūō Daigaku Shuppanbu. 1999. pp. 310–337.

Case studies in English seem to begin with T.J. Pempel's studies in the mid-1970s. Japanese studies of the decisionmaking, policymaking processes in Japan start appearing in numbers about a decade later with the publication of

Ōtake Hideo's studies, *Gendai Nihon no Seiji Kenryoku Keizei Kenryoku* in 1979 and *Nihon Seiji no Sōten:Jirei Kenkyū ni yoru seiji taisei no bunseki* in 1984 and

Nakano Minoru's study, *Nihon-gata Seisaku Kettei no Hen'yō* in 1986.

1. *General (in English and Japanese)*

Angel, Robert C. *Japan's Premiership and Cabinet: A study in democratic institutions and processes.* Paper presented to the Washington and Southeast Regions Japan Seminar. 1995. 15 p.

Campbell, John Creighton, The Politics of Governmental Decisonmaking, *Japan in the 1980s, V*, pp. 49–61. The Southern Center for International Studies, Atlanta, GA. Eds Cedric L. Suzman, Peter C. White. 1986. 95 p.

Chūō Shōchō no Seisaku Keisei Katei: Nihon Kanryōsei no Kaibō, Nihon Keikaku Gyōsei Gakkai. 1999. 365 p. Keikaku Gyōsei Sōsho-9.

Curtis, Gerald L. Ed., Policymaking in Japan: Defining the role of politicians. Tokyo. New York. Japan Center for international Exchange. 2002. 147 p.

Etō, Shinkichi. Foreign Policy Formation in Japan, *The Silent Power: Japan's Identity and World Role.* Japan Center for International Exchange. The Simul Press. 1976. 25l p., pp. 117–139.

Farnsworth, Lee W. *Changing Roles in Policymaking Patterns in Japan and their Effects on International Issues.* Paper presented at annual meeting of the American Political Science Association, New Orleans. 1985.

Farnsworth, Lee W. Clan Politics and Japan's Changing Policymaking structure, *World Economics* 12:2 (6/1989):163–174.

Farnsworth, Lee W. *Policymaking Patterns in Japanese Politics: Impact of Changing Regimes.* Paper given at the 16th World Congress of the International Political Science Association. Berlin.

Flanagan, Scott C. *Pathologies of Decisionmaking in Prewar Japan.* 1973. 119 p. Unpublished paper given to Japan Studies Seminar at Georgetown University. Published with same title by The Diplomatic Press. Spring 1975.

Fukui, Haruhiro. *Jiyū Minshutō to Seisaku Kettei.*

Fukui, Haruhiro. *Party in Power: The Japanese Liberal Democrats and Policymaking.* Berkeley. University of California Press. 1970. 301 p.

Fukui, Haruhiro. The Policy Research Council of Japan's Liberal Democratic Party: Policymaking role and practice, *Asian Thought and Society.* 3/1987.

Fukushima, M. The Rise of the Liberal Democratic Party in the Policymaking Process in Japan, *Teikyō Hōgaku* 15(1.2):(1985:12).

Glazer, Herbert. Understanding Japanese Decisionmaking, *Toward Better U.S.-Japan Relations.* Washington, DC, Foreign Service Institute. 1986. Pp. 39–42.

Hosoya, Chihiro. Characteristics of the Foreign Policy Decisionmaking System in Japan, *World Politics* 26:3(4/1973):353–369.

Iwai, Tomoaki. *Rippō Katei.* Tokyo Daigaku Shuppankai. 1988. 244 p. Gendai Seijigaku Sōsho:12.

Kataoka, Hiromitsu. Cabinet Decisionmaking in Japan, *Waseda Political Studies.* 18(1986):31–49.

Katsui, Kōji. Seisaku Katei Bunseki Shiron, *Waseda Seijikai Hō-Kenkyū*: 12 (1983:12).

Kernell, Samuel. *Parallel Politics: economic policymaking in the United States and Japan*. Brookings Institution. 1991. 390 p.

Krauss, Ellis S. Japan: Divided Bureaucracy in a Unified Regime, *Bureaucracy in the Modern State*. Jon Pierre, ed, London. Edward Elgar Publishers, Ltd.

Krauss, Ellis S. Politics and the Policymaking Process, *Democracy in Japan*. Pittsburgh. University of Pittsburgh Press. 1989. 354 p.

Langdon, Frank C. Japan's Foreign Policy-Making Processes, *Foreign and Defense Policies of Japan*. ed., Young C. Kim. Washington, DC. The Institute for Asian Affairs. Pan Asia Press. 1972.

Malik, Ahmad Rashid. Understanding the Pre and Postwar decisionmaking process in Japan, *Asia Profile* 16:4(8/1988):333–342.

Minor, Michael. Decision Models and Japanese Foreign Policymaking, *Asian Survey* 25:12(12/1985):1229–1241.

Misawa, Shigeo. An Outline of the Policymaking Process in Japan, *Japanese Politics: An Inside View*. Ed. Hiroshi Itoh, Ithaca, NY. Cornell University Press. 1973. Pp. 12–48. [Translation of the next item by Misawa]

Misawa, Shigeo. Seisaku Kettei Katei no Gaikan, *Nempō Seijigaku*:1967. Iwanami Shoten. 1968. Pp. 5–33.

Murakawa, Ichirō. *Nihon no Seisaku Kettei Katei*. Gyōsei. 1985. 260 p.

Muramatsu, Michio and Ellis S. Krauss. Bureaucrats and Politicians in Policymaking: the case of Japan, *American Political Science Review* 78:1(1984):126–146.

Muramatsu, Michio, Itō Mitsutoshi, Tsujinaka Yutaka. *Sengo Nihon no Atsuryoku Dantai*. Tōyō Keizai Shimpōsha. 1986. 283 p.

Nakamura, Akio. *Nihon Seiji no Seisaku Katei*. Ashi Shobō. 1996. 296 p.

Nakamura, Akira. *Kanryō-sei to Nihon no Seiji*. Hokuju Shuppan. 1997. 242 p.

Nakamura, Mutsuo. *Gi'in Rippō no Kenkyū*. Shinzansha. 1993. 614 p.

Nakamura, Mutsuo and Maeda Hideaki. *Rippō Katei no Kenkyū: Rippō ni okeru seifu no yakuwari*. Shinzansha. 1997. 526 p.

Nakano, Minoru. *Gendai Nihon no Seisaku Katei*. Tokyo Daigaku Shuppankai. 1992. 301 p.

Nakano, Minoru. *Nihon no Seiji Rikigaku: dare ga seisaku o kimeru no ka*. Nihon Hōsō Shuppan Kyōkai. 1993. 222 p.

Nakano, Minoru, ed. *Nihon-gata Seisaku Kettei no Hen'yō*. Tōyō Keizai Shimpōsha. 1986. 319 p.

Nakano, Minoru. *The Policymaking Process in Contemporary Japan*. New York. St. Martin's Press. 1997. 257 p.

Oka, Yoshitake. *Gendai Nihon no Seiji Katei*. 1958. 517 p.

Ōtake, Hideo. *Kōdo Seichōki no Seijigaku*. Tokyo Daigaku Shuppankai. 1999. 198 p.

Ōtake, Hideo. *Nihon Seiji no Sōten: jirei Kenkyū ni yoru seiji taisei no bunseki*. Tokyo. San'ichi Shobō. 1984. 296 p.

Ōtake, Hideo. *Seisaku Katei*.Tokyo Daigaku Shuppan. 1990. 253 p. Gendai Seijigaku Sōsho:11.

Pempel, T.J. Bureaucratization of Policymaking in Postwar Japan, *American Journal Political Science* 18:4(11/1974):647–664. Given as a paper at Columbia University Seminar on Modern East Asia: Japan. 11/1972.

Pempel, T.J., ed. *Policymaking in Contemporary Japan*. Ithaca. Cornell University Press. 1987. 345 p.

Shinoda, Tomohito. *Struggle to lead: The Japanese Prime Minister's Power and his Conduct of Economic Policy*. PhD dissertation. The Johns Hopkins University. 1994. 295 p.

Sone, Yasunori and Iwai Tomoaki. Seisaku Katei ni okeru Gikai no Yakuwari, *Nempō Seijigaku: 1987. Iwa*nami Shoten. 1988. pp. 149–174.

Tani, Katsuhiro. *Gendai Nihon no Rippō Katei: Ittō yūi-sei Gikai no Jisshō Kenkyū*. Shinzansha. 1995. 330 p.
Thayer, Nathaniel B. Formulating Policy, *How the Conservatives Rule Japan*. Princeton, NJ. Prince University Press. 1969. 340 p. pp. 207–236.
Tsuji, Kiyoaki. Decisionmaking in the Japanese Government: A study of Ringisei. *Political Development in Modern Japan*. Robert E. Ward, ed. Princeton. Princeton University Press. 1968. pp. 457–475.
U.S. House of Representatives, Committee on Foreign Affairs. *Government Decisionmaking in Japan: Implications for the United States*. U.S. Government Printing Office. 1982. 147 p.
Vogel, Ezra, ed. *Modern Japanese Organization and Decision-making*. Berkeley, CA. University of California Press. 1975. 340 p.
Watanabe, Hisamaru. *Gendai Nihon no Rippō Katei*. Hōritsu Bunkasha. 1980. 232 p.
Woodall, Brian. Bureaucratic Decisionmaking in Japan: The wellsprings of stability and flexibility, *Institute of Governmental Studies Working Paper*. Berkeley. University of California.
Yachi, Shōtarō. The Role of the Treaties Bureau of the Ministry of Foreign Affairs in Japan's Foreign Policy Decision Making Process, *Japanese Annual International Law* 1(1988):82–93.
Yamakawa, Katsumi. Seisaku Katei Kenkyū no Furonteia [Frontier], *Kōza Seijigaku III: Seiji Katei*. Uchida Mitsuru, comp. 1986. Sanrei Shobō. pp. 263–28932.
Yamamoto, Yoshinori. Seiji Kettei-ron no Keifu, *Seisaku Kettei no Riron*. Tōkai Daigaku Shuppankai. 1990.

2. *Selected Case Studies* (Jirei Kenkyū)

i. *In English*

Ahn, Choon-sik. Inter-ministry coordination in Japan's Foreign Policy making, *Pacific Affairs* 71:1 (Spring 1998):41–60.
Akaha, Tsuneo. *The 12-Mile Territorial Sea and the the 200-mile Fishery Zone of Japan: A cybernetic analysis of governmental decisionmaking*. PhD dissertation University of Southern California. 1981.
Akaha, Tsuneo. *Japan in Global Ocean Politics*. Honolulu. University of Hawaii Press. 1985. 224 p.
Akhavan-Majid, Roya. *Telecommunications Policymaking in Japan, 1970–1987: A case study in Japanese policymaking making structures and process*. PhD dissertation. University of Minnesota. 1988. 198 p.
Aldrich, Daniel P. The Limits of Flexible and Adaptive Institutions: The Japanese Government's Role in Nuclear Power Plan Siting over the Post War Period, *Managing Conflict in Facility Siting: an international comparison*. S. Hayden Lesbirel & Daigee Shaw, eds, Edward Elgar Publishing. 2005.
Allison, Gary D. *Public Servants and Public Interests in Contemporary Japan*. 1980. 36 p. Unpublished paper given to the Washington & Southeast Regional Seminar on Japan, 2/16/80.
Angel, Robert C. Explaining Economic Policy Failure: Japan in the 1969–71 International Monetary Crisis. Columbia University Press. 1991. 333 p.
Angel, Robert C. *U.S.-Japan Economic Relations: Lessons from the 1971 Yen revaluation crisis*. 1978. 38 p. Unpublished paper given to Columbia University Seminar on Modern Japan, April 14, 1978.
Apter, David Ernest. *Against the State: politics and social protest in Japan*. Cambridge, MA. Harvard University Press. 1984. 271 p.
Baerwald, Hans H. Nikkan Kokkai: The Japan-Korea Treaty Diet, *Cases in Contemporary Politics: Asia*. Ed:Lucian W. Pye. Little Brown. Boston. 1970. pp. 19–57.

Blaker, Michael. Foreign Policymaking in the Middle Taisho Period: an institutional case study of the Gaikō Chōsakai, *Japanese Negotiating Style*. Columbia University Press. 1977. Vol. 7 pp. 149–177. Andrew W. Cordier, ed.

Blaker, Michael. Probe, Push and Panic: The Japanese tactical style in international negotiations, in *The Foreign Policy of Modern Japan*. University of California Press. Robert A. Scalapino, ed. 1977. 3–35.

Blaker, Michael, ed. *The Politics of Trade: U.S. and Japanese policymaking for the GATT negotiations*. New York. Columbia University Press. 1978. 184 p.

Broadbent, Jeffrey P. *Environmental Politics in Japan: networks of power and protest*. Cambridge, UK. Cambridge University Press. 1998. 418 p.

Broadbent, Jeffrey P. *State and Citizen in Japan: Social structure and policymaking in the development of a "new Industrial city"*, 1960 to 1980. PhD dissertation. Harvard University. 1982. 542 p.

Campbell, John Creighton and Naoki Ikegami. *The Art of Balance in Health Policy: maintaining Japan's low-cost, egalitarian system*. Cambridge University Press. 1998. 227 p.

Campbell, John Creighton. Compensation for Repatriates: A case study of Interest-Group Politics and Party-Government Negotiations in Japan, *Policymaking in Contemporary Japan*. T.J. Pempel, ed. pp. 103–142.

Campbell, John Creighton. *Contemporary Japanese Budget Politics*. Berkeley. University of California Press. 1987. 308 p.

Campbell, John Creighton. *Entrepreneurial Bureaucrats and Programs for Old People in Japan*. 1978. Paper delivered at the 1978 Annual Meeting of the American Political Science Association.

Campbell, John Creighton. *How Policies Change: The Japanese government and the aging society*. Princeton. Princeton University Press. 1992. 418 p.

Campbell, John Creighton. *How Powerful is the Ministry of Finance*. 1971. 20 p. [Unpublished paper given to Columbia University Seminar on Japan, 12/10/91].

Campbell, John Creighton. Japan Budget Baransu [Balance], *Modern Japanese Organization and Decision-making*. University California Press. 1975. Ezra F. Vogel, ed. 1975. pp. 71–100.

Campbell, John Creighton. The Old People Boom and Japanese Policymaking, *Journal of Japanese Studies* 5:2(Summer 79):321–357.

Campbell, John Creighton. *Old People Problem: The career of an issue*. 1980. 38 p. Unpublished paper given to the Columbia University Seminar on Modern Japan, 2/13/80].

Campbell, John Creighton. *Progressive Local Government, Policy Innovation, and the Diffusion of Programs for the Agenda in Japan*. 1981. 14 p. Unpublished paper for the Washington & Southeast Regional Seminar on Japan, 4/18/1981.

Carlberg, Eileen. *The Legislative Process Surrounding Women's Labor Legislation in Japan* [1972 Working Women's Welfare Law]. Phd Dissertation.

Cho, Paul Bylung-chan. *Japan's Ratification of the Nuclear Non-Proliferation Treaty: A study of the Diffusion of Policymaking Power and Consensus Politics in Japanese Foreign Policy making*. PhD dissertation, West Virginia Univ, 1981. 455 p.

Clapp, Pricilla. Okinawa Reversion: Interaction in Washingtion, 1966–69. Okinawa Henkan Kōshō no Seiji Katei. Nihon Kokusai Seiji Gakkai. Kokusai 52 (1974). pp. 6–41.

Cohen, Bernard. *The Political Process and Foreign Policy: The Making of the Japanese Peace Settlement*. Princeton. Princeton University Press. 1957. 293 p.

Cooper, C.L. *U.S. and Japan Decisionmaking in Energy and the Environment—a comparative study*.

Cowhey, Peter F. and Matthew D. McCubbins, eds. *Structure and Policy in Japan and the United States*. Cambridge. Cambridge University Press. 1995. 292 p.

Curtis, Gerald C. The Tyumen Oil Development Project and Japanese Foreign Policy Decisionmaking, *The Foreign Policy of Modern Japan.* Berkeley. University of California Press. 1977. Pp. 147–173.

Destler, I.M. Country Expertise and U.S. Foreign Policymaking: The Case of Japan, in Morton A. Kaplan and Kinhide Mushakoji, eds. *Japan, America and the Future World Order.* New York. Free Press. 1976. 369 p.

Destler, I.M. & Hideo Sato, Priscilla Clapp, Haruhiko Fukui. *Managing An Alliance: the Politics of U.S.-Japanese Relations.* Washington, DC. The Brookings Institution. 1976. 209 p.

Donelly, Michael W. Setting the Price of Rice: A study in political decisionmaking, *Policy Making in Contemporary Japan.* T.J. Pempel, ed. pp. 143–200.

Etō, Shinkichi. Foreign Policy Formulation in Japan, *The Silent Power: Japan's Identity and World Role.* Japan Center for International Exchange, ed. Simul Press. 1976. pp. 119–139.

Fukami, Hiroaki. *Current Environmental (and Energy) Policymaking Process in Japan.* 1992. 51 p.

Fukui, Haruhiro. Compensating Former Landowners [1960s], *Party [LDP] in Power: The Japanese Liberal-Democrats and Policymaking.* Australian National University Press. Canberra. Pp. 173–197.

Fukui, Haruhiro. Constitutional Revision [1946–1963], same book as above, pp. 198–226.

Fukui, Haruhiro. Relations with the People's Republic of China [1949–1967], same book as above, pp. 227–262.

Fukui, Haruhiro. Economic Planning Postwar Japan: A case study in policymaking, *Asian Survey* 12:4(4/1972):327–348.

Fukui, Haruhiro. *Foreign Policy Making in Japan: Case studies for empirical theory.* 1974. 99 p. Unpublished paper given at 1974 AAS convention.

Fukui, Haruhiro. The GATT Tokyo Round: The Bureaucratic politics of Multilateral Diplomacy. Paper prepared for "U.S.-Japanese Relations in Multilateral Diplomacy". Project of the East Asia Institute. Columbia University. 1977.

Fukui, Haruhiro. The Japanese Farmer and Politics, *The Japanese Economy in International Perspective.* Isaiah Frank, ed. Baltimore. Johns Hopkins University Press. 1975. pp. 134–167.

Fukui, Haruhiro. *Party in Power: The Japanese Liberal Democrats and Policymaking.* Berkeley. University of California Press. 1970. 301 p.

Fukui, Harihiro. Policy-making in the Japanese Foreign Ministry, *The Foreign Policy of Modern Japan.* Robert A. Scalapino, ed. Berkeley. University of California Press. 1977. pp. 3–35.

Fukui, Haruhiro. Tanaka goes to Peking: A case study in foreign policymaking, *Policymaking in Contemporary Japan.* T.J. Pempel, ed. Pp. 60–102.

Fukui, Haruhiro. *The Textile Wrangle: conflict in Japanese-American Relations, 1969–71.* Ithaca. NY. Cornell University Press. 1979. 394 p.

Gale, Roger W. *The Failure of the U.S. Environmental Decisionmaking Process: Will a better way emerge?* 21 p.

Goodman, Roger, eds et al. *Case Studies on Human Rights in Japan.* Richmond, Surry. Japan Library. 1996. 309 p.

Harari, Ehud. Japanese Politics of Advice in Comparative Perspective: A Framework for Analysis and a Case Study, *Public Policy* 22:4 (Fall 74):537–77.

Harari, Ehud. *The Politics of Labor Legislation in Japan.* Berkeley. University of California Press. 1973. 221 p.

Hayao, Kenji. *The Japanese Prime Minister and Public Policy.* Pittsburgh. University of Pittsburgh Press. 1993. 334 p.

Hellmann, Donald C. *Japanese Domestic Politics and Foreign Policy: The Peace Agreement with the Soviet Union.* Berkeley. University of California Press. 1969. 202 p.

Higashi, Chikara. *U.S.-Japanese Trade Policy Formulation and Frictions in Trade Relations: 1978–79.* George Washing University. 1982. 594 p.

Hitchcock, David I. Joint Development of Siberia: Decisionmaking in Japanese-Soviet Relations, Asian Survey 11:3(3/1971):279–300.

Hosoya, Chihiro. *Case Study of Japanese Foreign Policymaking Process: Japan's Response to Germany-Soviet War, 1941.* Unpublished paper presented to Columbia University Seminar System: Modern Japan. 5/11/-1963.

Huff, Rodney Louis. *Political* Decisionmaking in the Japanese Civilian Atomic Energy Program. The George Washington University PhD dissertation. 1973. 474 p.

Ide, Yoshinori. Structure and Function of Decisionmaking pro con in Japanese Urban Development Planning, *The Second International Symposium on Regional Development.* Tokyo. 1968. pp. 119–128.

Igarashi, Takeshi. Peace-making and Party Politics: The Formation of the Domestic Foreign-Policy System in Postwar Japan, *Journal of Japanese Studies* 11:2(Sum 85):323–356 pp.

Ijiri, Hidenori. *The Politics of Japan's Decision to Normalize Relations with China, 1969–72.* PhD dissertation. University of California. 1987. 387 p.

Ikegami, Naoki and John Creighton Campbell, eds. *Containing Health Care Costs in Japan.* Ann Arbor, MI. University of Michigan Press. 1996. 311 p.

Itoh, Hiroshi, ed. *Japan's Foreign Policymaking.* Buffalo, NY. State University of New York. 1979. 80 p.

Itoh, Hiroshi, comp. *Japanese Politics: an inside view.* Ithaca. Cornell University Press. 1973. 248 p.

Iwai, T. *Rippō Katei. Tokyo. Tokyo Daigaku Shuppankai.* 1988. 244 p. Gendai Seijigaku Sōsho:12.

Johnson, Chalmers. MITI and Japanese International Economic Policy, The Foreign Policy of Modern Japan. Robert A. Scalapino, ed. Berkeley. University of California Press. 1977. pp. 227–279.

Johnson, Chalmers. Japan: Who governs? An Essay on Official Bureaucracy, *Journal of Japanese Studies* 2:1(Autumn 1975):1–28.

Kato, Junko. *The Problem of Bureaucratic Rationality: Tax politics in Japan.* Princeton. Princeton University Press. 1994.327 p. Dissertation title was *Tax Reform in Japan: The Influence and strategy of fiscal bureaucrats in policy-making.* 1992. 372 p.

Kawabata, Eiji. *Bureaucracy, politics and business in Japan: The Ministry of Posts and Telecommunications and contemporary economic policymaking.* University of Pittsburgh PhD dissertation. 1996. 185 p.

Kim, Hosup. *Policymaking of Japanese Official Development Assistance to the Republic of Korea, 1965–1983.* PhD dissertation. University of Michigan. 1986. 226 p.

Kobayashi, Naoki. Interest Groups in the Legislative Process, *Japanese Politics: An Inside View.* Ithaca, NY. Cornell University Press. 1973. pp. 68–87.

Kobayashi, Naoki. The Small and Medium-sized Enterprises Organization Law, Japanese Politics: An Inside View. Hiroshi Itoh, ed. Ithaca, NY. Cornell University Press. 1973. pp. 49–67.

Lee, Eugene. *Political Bureaucrats and Policymaking in Japan: The case of telecommunications reform.* PhD dissertation. University of Toronto (Canada). 1991. 264 p.

Lesbirel, S. Hayden. *NIMBY politics in Japan: energy siting and the management of environmental conflict.* Ithaca. Cornell University Press. 1998. 187 p.

Lewis, J.R. *Japanese Policymaking for International Big Science Projects.* Sheffield University (UK). 1997 PhD dissertation.

Lincoln, Edward J. *The Japanese National Railways: Interaction with the Government.* 1979. 28 p. Unpublished paper given to Washington & Southeast Regional Seminar on Japan, 4/28/79].

Lo, Shiu-hing. The Kim Dae Jung issue: a case study in Japanese Foreign Policymaking, *Japan Northeast Asia Studies.* 7:4(Winter 1988):52–67.

Marcot, Neal Abel. *The Japanese Foreign Policymaking Process: A Case Study, Okinawa Reversion.* PhD dissertation. Georgetown University. 1981. 396 p.
McKean, Margaret A. *Energy Conservation Policy in Japan Through Two Crises.* 1982. 20 p. Unpublished paper given to the Washington & Southeast Regional Seminar on Japan, 2/82.
McKean, Margaret A. Pollution and Policymaking, *Policymaking in Contemporary Japan.* T.J. Pempel, ed. Ithaca, NY. Cornell University Press. 1987. pp. 201–238.
Meyerson, Christopher. Designing and Testing a Model of Japanese Trade Policymaking: Japan's role in the GATT Uruguay Round Agricultural Negotiations, *Association of Japanese Business Studies Best Papers Proceedings,* Terrence W. Moore, eds et al. Cincinnati, OH, University of Cincinnati Center for the Enhancement of International Com-Competitiveness. 1997, pp. 1–13.
Milly, Deborah J. *Poverty, Equality, and Growth: The Politics of Economic Need in Postwar Japan.* Cambridge, MA. Harvard University Asia Center. 1999. 412 p.
Miyaoka, Isao. *Legitimacy in International Society: Japan's reaction to Global Wildlife Preservation.* New York. Palgrave. 2004. 214 p.
Miyashita, Akitoshi. *Beyond Passivism: Gaiatsu, interests and Japan's foreign aid diplomacy.* Columbia University PhD dissertation. 1997. 240 p.
Mochizuki, Mike Masato. *Managing and Influencing the Japanese Legislative Process: The role of parties and the National Diet.* Cambridge. Harvard University. 1982. 555 p. PhD dissertation.
Nakamura, Akira. Environmentalism and the Growth Machine: The System of Political Economy and "Kōgai"Control in Japan, Governance: An International Journal of Policy and Administration 5:2(4/1992):181–196.
Nakamura, Akira. The LDP and Policymaking in Japan, *The Japanese Party System.* Ronald J. Hrebenar, ed. Westview Press. 1992. pp. 270–281.
Nakamura, Minoru. The Electoral and Policymaking processes, *Policymaking Profess in Contemporary Japan,* Nakamura Minoru. St. Martin's Press. 1997. pp. 103–158.
Nakamura, Minoru. Local Politics and Policy Decisions, *Policymaking Process in Contemporary Japan.* St. Martin's Press. 1997. pp. 159–205.
Nakamura, Minoru. The political Process of Welfare Policy Formation: the 1985 Public Pensions System Reform, Policymaking Process in Contemporary Japan, Nakamura Minoru. St. Martin's Press. 1997. pp. 13–63.
Nakamura, Minoru. Technocracy and Political Friction in the Big City: The Tokyo Metropolitan Government Relocation Decisionmaking, *Policymaking Process in Contemporary Japan.* Nakamura Minoru. St. Martin's Press.1997. pp. 206–234.
Ojimi, Yoshihisa. A Government Ministry: the Ministry of International Trade and Industry, *Modern Japanese Organization and Decision-making.* Ezra F. Vogel, ed. University of California Press. 1975. Pp. 101–112.
Paarlberg, Robert L. *U.S. Environmental Policymaking: Institutions and Processes which prevent Consensus.* Paper given at Harvard Center for International Affairs. 1992. 43 p.
Packard, George R. *Protest in Tokyo: The Security Treaty: Crisis of 1960.* Princeton. Princeton University Press. 1966. 423 p.
Park, Yung H. The Central Council for Education, Organized Business and the Politics of Educational Policymaking in Japan, *Comparative Education Review* 19:2(6/75):296–311.
Park, Yung H. *Education Policy-making in Contemporary Japan: A study of the Liberal-Democratic Party and the Ministry of Education.* Paper presented at the Association for Asian Studies (Pacific Coast), University of Oregon. 6/1977.
Park, Yung H. The Politics of Japan's China Decision, *Orbis* 19:2(Sum 1975):562–590.

Park, Yung H. The Tanaka Government and the Mechanics of the China Decision, *China and Japan: A Search for Balance since World War I.* Hilary Conroy and Alvin D. Cox., eds. ABC-Clio Books. Santa Barbara, CA. 1978. pp. 387–397.

Passin, Herbert. The Sources of Protest in Japan, *American Political Science Review*: (6/62):…

Pekkanen, Robert. Japan's New Politics: The case of the NPO [Non-Profit Organization] Law, *The Journal of Japanese Studies* 26:1(Winter 2000):111–143.

Pempel, T.J. *Patterns of Japanese Policymaking: Experiences from Higher Education.* Boulder, CO. Westview Press. 1978. 248 p. Published version of *The Politics of Higher Education in Postwar Japan.*

Pempel, T.J. Patterns of Policymaking: Higher Education, *Policymaking in Contemporary Japan.* T.J. Pempel ed. pp. 269–307.

Pempel, T.J. *The Politics of Higher Education in Postwar Japan.* Columbia University PhD dissertation. 1975. 330 p.

Pempel, T.J. *Policy and Politics in Japan: Creative Conservatism.* Philadelphia. Temple University Press. 1982. 330 p.

Pempel, T.J. *The Tar Baby Target: "Reform" of the Japanese Bureaucracy under the American Occupation.* Paper for Allied Occupation of Japan Conference, Hawaii. 1978. 65 p.

Pollard, Vincent Kelly. *Executive Power in Foreign Policymaking:Stretched organizational pluralism and social process in the Philippines and Japan.* PhD dissertation, University of Hawaii. 1998. 304 p.

Redman, Eric. *The Dance of Legislation.* New York. Simon & Schuster. 1973. 319 p.

Reed, Steven R. *Japanese Prefectures and Policymaking.* Pittsburgh. University of Pittsburgh Press. 1986. 197 p.

Reid, T.R. Saga of a Senate Bill: Battle Lines Drawn over Waterway Fees, *Washington Post.* 3/30/1997, 4/10/1977, 4/20/1977, 5/2/1977, 5/3/1977, 5/22/1977, 5/29/1977, 6/1/1977, 6/22/1977, 6/23/1977, 7/6/ 1977, 7/20/1977, 7/26/1977, 8/13/1978, 9/4/1977, 9/10/1977, 9/22/1977, 10/8/1977, 10/14/1977, 10/20–10/20/1977, 12/19/ 1977, 3/3/1978, 5/2/1978, 5/3/1977, 5/4/1978, 6/21/1978, 10/11/1978, 10/14/1978.

Rix, Alan G. *Foreign Aid and Policymaking in Japan.* PhD Dissertation. Australian National University. EDC 77.

Rose, Caroline. *Interpreting History in Sino-Japanese Relations: a case study in political decision-making* in the history textbook issue. London. Routledge.1998. 253 p.

Sagara, Masako. *The Japanese Prime Minister between Foreign Policy and Domestic Politics.* PhD dissertation. George University. 1998. 279 p.

Saito, Motohide. *The "Highly Crucial" Decisionmaking Model for Postwar Japan and Prime Minister Hatoyama's Policy toward the U.S.S.R.* New York. Columbia University. 1986. 346 p. PhD dissertation.

Samuels, Richard J. Leadership and Political Change in Japan: The Case of the Second Rinchō, *Journal Japanese Studies* 29:1(2003):1–31.

Scalapino, Robert A. *Foreign Policymaking of Modern Japan.* Berkeley, CA. University of California Press. 1977. 426 p.

Schoppa, Leonard. *The Limits of Change in Japanese Policymaking: the case of education reform, 1967–1987.* PhD dissertation. Pembroke College. 1988.

Schoppa, Leonard J. *Zoku* Power and LDP Power: A case study of the *Zoku* role in education policy, *Journal of Japanese Studies* 17:1(Winter 91):79–106.

Sebata, Takao. *Japan's Military Expansion: An analysis of bureaucratic politics and change of the defense policy and the decisionmaking process.* PhD dissertation. University of Denver. 1992. 439 p.

Shiels, Frederick L. *The American Experience in Okinawa: A Case Study in Foreign Policymaking Theory.* PhD dissertation. Ithaca, NY. Cornell University. EDC 1976.

Shin, Hee Suks. Foreign Policy Making in Prewar and postwar Japan: an analytical framework, *Current Politics and Economics of Japan.* New York. 1:2(1991):155–167.

Shingikai no Kiso Kenkyū: Kinō Taiyō ni suite no Bunseki. Keio Gijuku Daigaku. 1985. 118 p. Report by Professor Sone Yasunori's Seminar at Keio University.
Shinoda, Tomohito. Japan's decisionmaking under the coalition governments, *Asian Survey* 38:7(7/98):703–723.
Shinda, Tomohito. Japan's Top-Down Policy Process to Dispatch the SDF to Iraq, *Japanese Journal of Political Science* 7(1):71–91.
Silberman, Bernard S. Bureaucratic Development and the Structure of Decision-making in the Meiji Period: The case of the Genro, *Journal of Asian Studies* 27:1(11/67):81–94.
Smith, Sheila. *Local Voices, National National Issues: Local Initiative in Japanese Policymaking*. Ann Arbor, MI. University of Michigan Press. 2000. 136 p.
Sohma, Katsumi. *The Process of Foreign Policymaking in Japan: The case of its relations with China*. Ph.D. dissertation Boston University. 1999. 259 p.
Steslicke, William E. *National Health Insurance: The Japanese experience*. 1974. 20 p. Unpublished paper given at 1974 AAS Convention.
Steslicke, William E. *Doctors in Politics: The Political Life of the Japan Medical Association*. New York. Praeger. 1973. 302 p.
Sugimoto, Yoshio. *Equalization and Turbulence: the Case of the American Occupation of Japan*. PhD dissertation. University of Pittsburgh. 1973. 314 p. Order #74–9452.
Suttmeier, R.P. *Policy Making for Science in China and Japan*. Paper delivered at Society for the Social Studies of Science.
Suzuki, Takaaki. *Japan's Budget Politics:Balancing Domestic and International Interests*. Lynne Rienner. 2000. 28 p. Thies, Michael Frederick. *Majority party decision-making and policy change: The Liberal Democratic Party and Japanese fiscal policy*. University of California (San Diego) PhD dissertation. 1994. 195 p.
Thurston, Donald R. *Teachers and Politics in Japan*. Princeton. Princeton University Press. 1973. 337 p.
Totten, George O. Ocean Policy of Japan: Rationalization of the Japanese Shipbuilding Industry. Public Policy Decision of 1978. Monograph. EDC: 12/80.
Tsurutani, Taketsugu. The Cause of Paralysis, *Foreign Policy* 14(Spring 1974):126–141.
Uriu, Robert M. *Troubled Industries: confronting economic change in Japan*. Ithaca, NY. Cornell University Press. 1996. 285 p.
Usui, Mikoto. *The Private Sector in Environmental Policymaking in Japan*. Paper presented at the US-Japan Study Group on Energy and Environment, Seattle Workshop. 1992. 62 p.
Watanabe, Akio. Government Departments and the making of a Policy [re Okinawa], *The Okinawa Problem: a chapter in Japan-U.S. relations*. Carlton, Australia. Melbourne University Press. 1970. 220 p.
Wilkening, Kenneth E. *The Role of Scientists and Scientific Knowledge in Policymaking on the Acid Deposition Issue in Europe, North America and East Asia*. University of Wisconsin(Madison). 1996 PhD dissertation. 651 p.
Witham, Wallace Fernald, Jr. *A Study of Meiji Japan's Foreign Policy Decision-making Structure: Japanese Attitudes Pertaining to the Expansion of the U.S. into the Pacific, 1888–1898*. PhD Dissertation. University of Minnesota. 1974. 337 p.
Wright. Maurice. *Japan's Fiscal Crisis: the Ministry of Finance and the Politics of Public Spending, 1975–2000*. 2002. 648 p.
Yoshida, Fumihiko. *Testing Models of Foreign Policy Decisionmaking in Japan, using the Iranian hostage crisis Moscow Olympics boycott, and history textbook issue*. PhD dissertation. University of Hawaii. 1987. 575 p.
Zhao, Quansheng. *Japanese Policymaking: the politics behind politics: informal mechanisms and the making of China policy*. New York/Hongkong. Oxford University Press. 1995. 230 p.
Zhao, John Quansheng. The Making of Public Policy in Japan: Protectionism in raw silk importation, *Asian Survey* 28:9(9/1988).

ii. *In Japanese*

Fukui, Haruhiro. Okinawa Henkan kōshō—Nihon Seifu ni okeru kettei katei, *Okinawa Henkan Kōshō no Seiji Katei*. Tokyo. Nihon Kokusai Seiji Gakkai, comp. 1974 ed. Yūhikaku. 1974.

Gendai Nihon ni okeru Seiji Katei e no apurōchi, *Handai Hōgaku* 136 (9/1985).

Hashimoto, Nobuyuki. Sengo no Nōgyō Seisaku to sono Keisei Katei, *Nempo Seijigaku: 1983: Seisaku Kagaku to Seijigaku*. Iwanami Shoten. 1984. pp. 247–264.

Hosoya, Chihiro and Watanuki Jōji, eds. *Taigai Seisaku Kettei no Nichi-Bei Hikaku*. Tokyo Daigaku Shuppankyoku. 1977. 484 p.

Ichioka, Yōichirō. Zaisei Kin'yū Seisaku Kettei no Katei to Kōzō, *Hōgaku Seminā Zōkan: Naikaku to Kanryō Sōgō Tokushū Shirīzu*:9 (1979):88–94.

Igarashi, Hitoshi. Gendai Nihon no Seisaku Katei to Jimintō, *Kenkyū Shiryō Geppō* 319(6/1985).

Ine, Masaki. Kyōiku Kaikaku kanren Rippō to Shingikai Tōshin, *Rippōo Katei no Kenkyū*, Nakamura Mutsuo, ed. 1997. 1997. pp. 197–217.

Iokibe, Makoto. *Beikoku no Nihon Senryō Seisaku: Sengo Nihon no sekkeizu*. Chūō Kōronsha. 1985. 2 v.

Iyama, Hideo. Kokutetsu Kaikaku Kanren Hōan o rei-toshite, *Rippō Katei no Kenkyū*. Nakamura Mutsu, ed. 1997. pp. 255–281.

Kato, Junko. Seisaku chishiki to Sei-Kan Kankei:80 nendai no Kōteki Nenkin Seido Kaikaku, *Iryō Hoken Seido* Kaikaku, *Nempō Seijigaku:1995*. Iwanami Shoten. 1996. Pp. 107–134.

Kiyama, Hideaki, ed. *Chūō Shōchō no Seisaku Keisei Katei*. Chūō Daigaku Shuppanbu. 1999.

Kobayashi, Naoki. Chūshō Kigyō Dantai Soshikihō no Rippō Katei, *Tōkyō Daigaku Kyōyōgaku Kiyō*: 7 (1978):34–55.

Kobayashi, Naoki. Sengo Jūyō Rippō no Rippō Katei Kenkyū, *Shakai Kagaku Kiyō: 1953*. Tokyo Daigaku Shuppankai. Tokyo Daigaku Kyōyō Gakubu. 1954. Shakaika Gakka-hen, comp. pp. 1–229.

Matsumoto, Susumu. Chūshō Kigyō Bun'ya-hō Kaisei ni kansuru Rippō Katei ni suite, *Rippō Katei no Kenkyū*. Nakamura Mutsuo, ed. 1997. Pp. 395–422.

Mikuriya, Takashi. *Tochō no Shikumi*. Toshi Shuppan. 1995. 362 p. Shirīzu Tokyo o Kangaeru:3.

Nakagawa, Hiroaki. Heisei Roku Nendo Chihō Jichihō Ichibu Kaisei no Rippō Katei ni suite, *Rippō Katei no Kenkyū*. Nakamura, Mutsuo, ed. 1997. Pp. 423–449.

Nakamura, Akio. Den-Den Kōsha no Min'eika Rinchō Tōshin. *Nihon Seiji Seisaku Katei*. Nakamura Akio. 1996. pp. 93–116.

Nakamura, Akio. Gyō-Zaisei Kaikaku to Kenkō Hokenhō Kaisei, *Nihon Seiji Seisaku Katei*. Nakamura Akio. 1996. pp. 117–146.

Nakamura, Akio. Kōshoku Senkyohō Kaisei no Seisaku Katei, *Nihon Seiji Seisaku Katei*. Nakamura Akio. 1996. pp. 147–176.

Nakamura, Akio. Nichi-Bei Bōeki Masatsu ni okeru Nihon no Taiō, *Nihon Seiji Seisaku Katei*. Nakamura Akio. 1996. pp. 177–202.

Nakamura, Akio. Uriagezei Hai'an to Senkyo, *Nihon Seiji Seisaku Katei*. Nakamura Akio. 1996. Pp. 65–92.

Nakamura, Akira. Keizai Kaihatsu to Kankyō Gyōsei, *Kanryō-sei to Nihon no Seiji*, Hokuju Shuppan. pp. 154–186.

Nakano, Minoru. Chihō Seiji to Seisaku Kettei: chihō rieki no hyōhitsu baikai to kōkyō-teki ishi kettei, *Gendai Nihon no Seisaku Katei*. Nakano Minoru. Tokyo Daigaku Shuppankai. 1992. pp. 207–260.

Nakano, Minoru. Chihō Seiji to Seisaku Kettei: Tokyo Tochō Iten no kettei katei, *Gendai Nihon no Seisaku Katei*. Nakano Nakano Minoru. Tokyo Daigaku Shuppankai. 1992. pp. 261–296.

Nakano, Minoru. Fukushi Seisaku Keisei no Seiji Katei, *Nempō Seijigaku-1988*. Nihon Seiji Gakkai.

Narita, Norihiko. Seiji Kaikaku Hōan no Seiritsu Katei, *Rippō Katei no Kenkyū*. Nakamura Mutsuo, ed. 1997. Pp. 304–394.

Nemoto, Toshio. Fukushi Seisaku no Seiji Katei, *Nihon no Seisaku Katei*. Nakamura Akira and Takshita Yuzuru, eds. Azusa Shuppan. 1984. Pp. 156–199.

Nemoto, Toshio. Jidō Teate Seido Keisei no Seiji Gyōsei Katei, *Kanryō-sei to Nihon no Seiji*. Hokuju Shuppan. 1997. pp. 187–206.

Ōmori, Wataru. Nihon Kanryōsei no Jian Kettei Tetsuzuki, *Nempō Seijigaku* 1985:87–116. Iwanami Shoten. 1986.

Ōtake, Hideo. *Gendai Nihon no Bōei to Kokunai Seiji detanto kara gunkaku e*. San'ichi Shobō. 411 p.

Ōtake, Hideo. *Gendai Nihon no Seiji Kenryoku Keizai Kenkyū* [defective autos and US-Japan textile negotiations]. 1979. 239 p.

Ōtake, Hideo, ed. *Nihon Seiji no Sōten: Jirei Kenkyū no yoru seiji taisei no bunseki*. San'ichi Shobō. 1984. 296 p. [police law revision, education, economic crisis management, environment, defense].

Oyama, Kōsuke. Gyosei Kikō ni okeru Senryō Kaikaku Sai-Kaikaku no Seika Seisaku Katei, *Sengo Kokka no Keisei to Keizai Hatten—Senryō Ikō*. Nempō Seijigaku 1991. Iwanami Shoten. 1992. pp. 97–114.

Oyama, Kōsuke. *Gyōsei Shidō no Seiji-Keizaigaku: Sangyō Seisaku no Keisei to Jisshi*. Yūhikaku. 1996. 284 p.

Satō, Atsushi. Gyōsei Jiken Soshō Tokurei-hō no Rippō Katei, *Gyōsei Tetsuzuki no Kenkyū*. Ukai Nobushige, ed. Tokyo. Yōshindō. pp. 239–266.

Shingikai no Kiso Kenkyū: Kinō Taiyō ni tsuite no Bunseki. Keio Gijuku Daigaku. 1985. 118 p.

Shiroyama, Hideaki, et al, eds. *Chūō Shōchō no Seisaku Keisei Katei: Nihon kanryōsei no kaibō*. Chūō Daigaku Shuppanbu. 1999. 365 p.

Tokyo Daigaku, Kyōyō Gakubu, Shakai Kagaku-ka, comp. Sengo Jūyō Rippō no Rippō Katei Kenkyū, *Shakai Kagaku Kiyō*, 1953.Tokyo Daigaku Shuppan-kai. pp. 1–230. [case studies on anti-monopoly law, labor law, electricity development law, agricultural land, and family relations law]

Watanabe, Hisamaru. Shiritsu Gakkō Shinkō Josei-hō no Rippō Katei to Mondai-ten, *Gendai Nihon no Rippō Katei*. Tokyo. Hōritsu Bunkasha. 1980. pp. 71–108.

Watanabe, Takeshi. Iwayuru Joshi Sabetsu Teppei Jōyaku Hijun no Giron o tegakari toshite, *Rippō Katei no Kenkyū*. Nakamura Mutsuo, ed. 1997. 132–169.

Yamada, Masashi. Sengo no Toshi Chi'iki Kaihatsu Seisaku no Tenkai, *Nihon no Seisaku Katei*. Nakamura Akira, Takeshita Yuzuru, eds. 1984. 94–155.

Yoshida, Hidenori. Bōryoku Dan'in ni yoru Futō no Kōi ni kansuru Hōritsu no Rippō Katei. *Rippō Katei no Kenkyū*. Nakamura Mutsuo, ed. 1997. 450–519.

VITAE

Cecil H. Uyehara, retired from the U.S. Department of State, has authored several books and articles on Japanese political issues: *The U.S.-Japan Science and Technology Agreement: a drama in five acts.* (Ashgate Publishing Ltd. Hampshire, UK, 2001); "The Nuclear Test Ban Treaty and Scientific Advice" in *Knowledge and Power*, The Free Press, 1966); *Socialist Parties in Postwar Japan*, co-authored with Allan B. Cole and George O. Totten (Yale University Press, 1966); *Leftwing Social Movements in Japan, An Annotated Bibliography* (Charles E. Tuttle Co., 1959). He has also written books and articles on Japanese calligraphy and philately. He has a BA from Keio University (1948), MA from the University Minnesota, and at Harvard University Littauer Center (now Kennedy School of Government) as National Institute of Public Administration Fellow. (1963–64).

INDEX

BRILL'S JAPANESE STUDIES LIBRARY

ISSN 0925-6512

1. Plutschow, H.E., *Chaos and Cosmos.* Ritual in Early and Medieval Japanese Literature. 1990. ISBN 90 04 08628 5
2. Leims, Th.F. *Die Entstehung des Kabuki.* Transkulturation Europa-Japan im 16. und 17. Jahrhundert. 1990. ISBN 90 04 08988 8
3. Seeley, Chr. *A History of Writing in Japan.* 1991. ISBN 90 04 09081 9
4. Vovin, A. *A Reconstruction of Proto-Ainu.* 1993. ISBN 90 04 09905 0
5. Yoda, Y. *The Foundations of Japan's Modernization.* A Comparison with China's Path Towards Modernization. Transl. by K.W. Radtke. 1996. ISBN 90 04 09999 9
6. Hardacre, H. and A.L. Kern (eds.) *New Directions in the Study of Meiji Japan.* 1997. ISBN 90 04 10735 5
7. Tucker, J.A. *Ito Jinsai's* Gomō Jigi *and the Philosophical Definition of Early Modern Japan.* 1998. ISBN 90 04 10992 7
8. Hardacre, H. (ed.) *The Postwar Development of Japanese Studies in the United States.* 1998. ISBN 90 04 10981 1
9. Hanashiro, R.S. *Thomas William Kinder and the Japanese Imperial Mint, 1868-1875.* 1999. ISBN 90 04 11345 2
10. Teitler, G. and K.W. Radtke (eds.) *A Dutch Spy in China.* Reports on the First Phase of the Sino-Japanese War (1937 – 1939). 1999. ISBN 90 04 11487 4
11. Mortimer, M. *Meeting the Sensei.* The Role of the Master in Shirakaba Writers. 2000. ISBN 90 04 11655 9
12. Scholz-Cionca, S. and S.L. Leiter (eds.) *Japanese Theatre and the International Stage.* 2000. ISBN 90 04 12011 4
13. Saltzman-Li, K. *Creating Kabuki Plays.* Context for *Kezairoku,* "Valuable Notes on Playwriting". 2003. ISBN 90 04 12115 3
14. Ozaki, M. *Individuum, Society, Humankind.* The Triadic Logic of Species According to Hajime Tanabe. 2001. ISBN 90 04 12118 8
15. Bentley, J.R. *A Descriptive Grammar of Early Old Japanese Prose.* 2001. ISBN 90 04 12308 3
16. Higashibaba, I. *Christianity in Early Modern Japan.* Kirishitan Belief and Practice. 2001. ISBN 90 04 12290 7
17. Schmidt, P. *Capital Punishment in Japan.* 2001. ISBN 90 04 12421 7
18. Foljanty-Jost, G. *Juvenile Delinquency in Japan.* Reconsidering the "Crisis". 2003. ISBN 90 04 13253 8
19. Tomida, H. *Hiratsuka Raichō and Early Japanese Feminism.* 2004. ISBN 90 04 13298 8
20. Ueda, M. *Dew on the Grass.* The Life and Poetry of Kobayashi Issa. 2004. ISBN 90 04 13723 8
21. Beckwith, C.I. *Koguryo: The Language of Japan's Continental Relatives.* 2004. ISBN 90 04 13949 4

22. Parker, H.S.E. *Progressive Traditions.* An Illustrated Study of Plot Repetition in Traditional Japanese Theatre. 2005. ISBN 90 04 14534 6
23. Eckersall, P. *Theorizing the Angura Space.* Avant-garde Performance and Politics in Japan, 1960-2000. 2006. ISBN-10 90 04 15199 0, ISBN-13 978 90 04 15199 4
24. Gramlich-Oka, B. *Thinking Like a Man.* Tadano Makuzu (1763-1825). 2006. ISBN-10 90 04 15208 3, ISBN-13 978 90 04 15208 3
25. Bentley, J.R. *The Authenticity of* Sendai Kuji Hongi. A New Examination of Texts, with a Translation and Commentary. 2006. ISBN-10 90 04 15225 3, ISBN-13 978 90 04 15225 0
26. Orbaugh, S. *Japanese Fiction of the Allied Occupation.* Vision, Embodiment, Identity. 2007. ISBN-10 90 04 15546 5, ISBN-13 978 90 04 15546 6
27. Crowley, C.A. *Haikai Poet Yosa Buson and the Bashō Revival.* 2007. ISBN-10 90 04 15709 3, ISBN-13 978 90 04 15709 5
28. Mase-Hasegawa, E. *Christ in Japanese Culture.* Theological Themes in Shusaku Endo's Literary Works. 2008. ISBN 978 90 04 16596 0
29. Van Goethem, E. *Nagaoka.* Japan's Forgotten Capital. 2008. ISBN 978 90 04 16600 4
30. Iles, T. *The Crisis of Identity in Contemporary Japanese Film.* Personal, Cultural, National. 2008. ISBN 978 90 04 17138 1
31. Commons, A. *Hitomaro.* Poet as God. 2009. ISBN 978 90 04 17461 0
32. Townsend, S.C. *Miki Kiyoshi 1897-1945.* Japan's Itinerant Philosopher. 2009. ISBN 978 90 04 17582 2
33. Uyehara, C.H. *The Subversive Activities Prevention Law of Japan.* It's Creation, 1951-52. 2010. ISBN 978 90 04 18092 5